AF832535

Gender Perspectives in Law

Volume 7

Series Editors

Dragica Vujadinović, Faculty of Law, University of Belgrade, Belgrade, Serbia
Ivana Krstić, Faculty of Law, University of Belgrade, Belgrade, Serbia

The series 'Gender Perspectives in Law' discusses all-encompassing gender-competent legal questions. Having a gender-competent approach is required when considering the highest values and normative standards of modern international, European, and national law. Raising awareness about gender equality issues means investing in the creation, interpretation, and implementation of legislation that is more fair, just, and equitable and will also contribute to a comprehensive understanding of social reality, as well as to gender-competent political, legal and economic decision-making and public policies.

The series accepts monographs focusing on a specific topic, as well as edited collections of articles covering a specific theme or collections of articles.

Susanne Baer · Ivana Jelić · Ivana Krstić
Editors

The Gender and the Judiciary

Springer

Editors
Susanne Baer
Faculty of Law
Humboldt-Universität zu Berlin
Berlin, Germany

Ivana Jelić
European Court of Human Rights
Strasbourg, France

Ivana Krstić
Department of International Law
and International Relations
University of Belgrade Faculty of Law
Belgrade, Serbia

ISSN 2731-8346 ISSN 2731-8354 (electronic)
Gender Perspectives in Law
ISBN 978-3-032-06884-2 ISBN 978-3-032-06885-9 (eBook)
https://doi.org/10.1007/978-3-032-06885-9

© The Editor(s) (if applicable) and The Author(s), under exclusive license to Springer Nature Switzerland AG 2025

This work is subject to copyright. All rights are solely and exclusively licensed by the Publisher, whether the whole or part of the material is concerned, specifically the rights of translation, reprinting, reuse of illustrations, recitation, broadcasting, reproduction on microfilms or in any other physical way, and transmission or information storage and retrieval, electronic adaptation, computer software, or by similar or dissimilar methodology now known or hereafter developed.
The use of general descriptive names, registered names, trademarks, service marks, etc. in this publication does not imply, even in the absence of a specific statement, that such names are exempt from the relevant protective laws and regulations and therefore free for general use.
The publisher, the authors and the editors are safe to assume that the advice and information in this book are believed to be true and accurate at the date of publication. Neither the publisher nor the authors or the editors give a warranty, expressed or implied, with respect to the material contained herein or for any errors or omissions that may have been made. The publisher remains neutral with regard to jurisdictional claims in published maps and institutional affiliations.

This Springer imprint is published by the registered company Springer Nature Switzerland AG.
The registered company address is: Gewerbestrasse 11, 6330 Cham, Switzerland

If disposing of this product, please recycle the paper.

Contents

Introduction: The Importance of Gender Perspective in the Judiciary ... 1
Susanne Baer, Ivana Jelić, and Ivana Krstić

Part I Courts ... 15

First Ladies on the Bench. A European Perspective on Gender and the Judiciary in the Interbellum Years ... 17
Marion Röwekamp

Gender Diversity in the Judiciary: A Matter of Law? An Approach Under the European Court of Human Rights ... 41
Saadet Yüksel

Gender Equality in Serbian Judiciary—An Examination of the State of Play ... 59
Ana Knežević Bojović and Monika Milošević

Part II Lawyers, Notaries ... 85

The Position of Female Attorneys in Montenegro in Comparison to Other Legal Professions: Between a Minority and a Majority ... 87
Matija Stojanović

Access to Justice Through Public Notary Service in the Republic of Serbia: How Can the Gender Perspective Move Things Forward? ... 109
Nenad Tešić and Ljubinka Kovačević

Part III Judicial Decisions ... 141

Can Gender Shape the Course of Justice? Some Insights from the European Court of Human Rights ... 143
Marko Bošnjak and Alice Leconte

Gender and Judiciary System in Spain From a Labor Perspective 167
Eva Bermúdez Figueroa and Raquel Pastor-Yuste

Gender Representation in the Brazilian Judiciary: Reflections Upon a Case Study of the Right to Abortion 193
Luana Mathias Souto and Jessica Holl

Overcoming Gender Bias in the Justice System's Response to Violence: A Call for Enhanced Academic and Professional Training 211
Oana Băluță

Part IV Doctrine 235

Gender Competent Legal Education of Criminal Justice Professionals—Case of Intimate Partner Violence 237
Natalija Lukić

Reframing Evidentiary Reasoning through a Gender Perspective 263
Marianela Delgado Nieves

A Feminist Critique of Traditional Patriarchal Professional Stereotypes: The Example of the Czech Custody Justice System 285
Kateřina Šimáčková

Abortion in the U.S. After Dobbs v. Jackson Women's Health Organization. A Comparative Perspective 305
Rosalba Potenzano and Guido Smorto

Part V Conflicts of Rights 337

Discrimination of Women Under Sharia Law and the *Molla Sali* Judgment of the ECHR 339
Ioannis Ktistakis

Part VI Histories 351

Roman Woman on Trial: Limited Access to Justice 353
Mirjana Miškić

Gender and the Judiciary in Medieval Serbia 367
Nina Kršljanin

Introduction: The Importance of Gender Perspective in the Judiciary

Susanne Baer, Ivana Jelić, and Ivana Krstić

The judiciary serves as a cornerstone of democratic societies, upholding principles of fairness, equality, and justice for all. Yet, the effectiveness of the judiciary can be compromised when it fails to reflect and respond to the diverse experiences and needs of those it serves. A gender perspective within the judiciary addresses this challenge by recognizing that laws and judicial decisions impact individuals differently based on gender, and by working to counteract systemic biases that may disadvantage certain groups. The integration of a gender perspective in the judiciary is essential to fostering an equitable, inclusive, and representative justice system. While judicial institutions uphold the principles of fairness and impartiality, they also operate within broader societal frameworks where gender dynamics and biases play significant roles. Across national jurisdictions and international judicial bodies, gender representation in the judiciary remains imbalanced, with women often underrepresented, particularly in higher courts and leadership roles. This disparity reflects and reinforces traditional power structures, limiting the judiciary's capacity to address the unique experiences and legal needs of all members of society. By incorporating a gender perspective, judicial systems worldwide can better respond to gender-based inequalities and ensure that their practices, policies, and decisions reflect the diverse realities of those they serve.

The inclusion of women in the judiciary brings invaluable perspectives that contribute to a more balanced and empathetic approach to legal interpretation and decision-making. Women judges and legal professionals often draw from their unique life experiences, which can offer insights into issues like discrimination, violence, and other gender-sensitive cases. When judicial bodies lack adequate female representation, they risk overlooking or misunderstanding the complexities

S. Baer · I. Jelić · I. Krstić (✉)
Department of International Law and International Relations,
University of Belgrade Faculty of Law, Belgrade, Serbia
e-mail: ikrstic@ius.bg.ac.rs

© The Author(s), under exclusive license to Springer Nature Switzerland AG 2025

S. Baer et al. (eds.), *The Gender and the Judiciary*, Gender Perspectives in Law 7,
https://doi.org/10.1007/978-3-032-06885-9_1

of gendered experiences. Promoting women's advancement within the judiciary, from entry-level positions to senior leadership, thus enhances the system's legitimacy and strengthens public confidence in judicial institutions as fair and representative. Efforts to increase female representation also address the glass ceilings women face in judicial careers, particularly in systems where promotions and leadership positions remain male-dominated. A judiciary that prioritizes career advancement for women ensures a pipeline of diverse legal professionals equipped to shape more inclusive legal standards.

At the international level, gender perspective is equally vital for organizations such as the European Court of Human Rights (ECtHR), the International Criminal Court, and other global judicial and quasi judicial bodies. These institutions play a critical role in setting human rights standards, which often involve gendered dimensions, from issues of equality and non-discrimination to rights in cases of violence and abuse. When women are well-represented on international benches, it signals a commitment to gender equality that resonates globally, influencing national systems to adopt similar standards. Moreover, a judiciary with balanced gender representation is better equipped to interpret and uphold international conventions that protect women's rights, advancing gender justice worldwide. On quasi-judicial bodies and administrative tribunals, gender-sensitive policies can similarly enhance workplace equality, enabling female professionals to pursue meaningful career paths and make impactful contributions within their roles.

For gender perspective to take root in the judiciary, it must extend beyond representation alone. Gender-sensitive policies, training, and awareness initiatives are needed to create judicial environments where women can advance professionally and where gender-based issues are comprehensively understood and addressed. Addressing both conscious and unconscious biases within the judiciary helps foster an environment where all judicial professionals are better equipped to handle cases with fairness and empathy. Gender-sensitive judicial training equips judges with tools to navigate the complex issues related to gender, whether they involve family law, criminal justice, or human rights, and helps prevent judgments that perpetuate harmful stereotypes. Through a commitment to gender-sensitive policies and practices, judicial institutions can promote a more balanced and just society, where laws and judicial outcomes reflect the true diversity of the populations they serve.

In sum, incorporating a gender perspective within the judiciary supports a more equitable legal system that honors the experiences and rights of all individuals. By improving women's representation at all levels, facilitating career advancement, and promoting gender-sensitive practices, judicial institutions can better fulfill their mandate of delivering impartial and fair justice. In both national and international contexts, a judiciary that values gender diversity and awareness is better positioned to address the nuances of gender in the law and to uphold the principles of justice in a way that truly reflects and serves society as a whole.

The collection of papers presented here underscores the importance of integrating a gender perspective into judicial systems worldwide, revealing how gender sensitivity enhances the legitimacy, equity, and efficacy of the judicial process.

Across diverse national contexts—from Europe and the United States to Brazil and Serbia—these papers collectively argue that a gender-sensitive judiciary not only promotes equality but also better represents the societies it serves. For instance, Saadet Yüksel's analysis of the ECtHR highlights how gender diversity among judges contributes to balanced and empathetic decision-making, particularly in cases involving gender-sensitive issues like human rights and discrimination. Similarly, Marko Bošnjak and Alice Leconte emphasize that female judges bring unique perspectives to the ECtHR, broadening the court's understanding of gendered experiences and enhancing its capacity to address gender-specific legal matters. This alignment of gender diversity with judicial fairness is further underscored by studies such as Luana Mathias Souto and Jessica Holl's examination of reproductive rights cases in Brazil, where increased female representation is linked to judicial outcomes that respect and uphold women's autonomy.

The historical context provided in several papers reveals that the lack of gender perspective within the judiciary is not a recent issue. Marion Röwekamp's exploration of women's entry into the judiciary in interwar Europe and Mirjana Miškić's analysis of gender exclusion in ancient Rome illustrate how patriarchal norms have long shaped legal systems, often sidelining women's voices and reinforcing discriminatory practices. These studies highlight the enduring impact of historical biases and the importance of dismantling traditional stereotypes that have restricted women's participation and influence in the judiciary. Moreover, as shown in Nina Kršljanin's research on medieval Serbia, women's limited but notable involvement in the judiciary has historically been contingent upon their social status rather than a recognition of their equal legal standing. These historical insights underline the necessity of adopting a gender perspective to correct longstanding structural inequalities and ensure that the judiciary does not perpetuate outdated gender norms.

In addition to historical and representational concerns, a gender perspective in the judiciary addresses the specific legal needs and rights of marginalized women. Several authors, such as Ana Knežević Bojović and Monika Milošević in their study on Serbia's judiciary, emphasize the need for targeted reforms to remove barriers that prevent women from reaching leadership roles in judicial systems. Similarly, Matija Stojanović's work on female attorneys in Montenegro sheds light on how patriarchal biases continue to limit women's professional advancement in law, suggesting that gender-sensitive policies are essential to achieving equitable representation. This issue extends beyond representation; Nenad Tešić and Ljubinka Kovačević, in their paper on Serbia's public notary system, argue that a gender perspective in legal services can improve access to justice for women, particularly those from marginalized backgrounds. These examples illustrate that gender sensitivity within the judiciary is critical for both protecting individual rights and fostering a legal environment that reflects and serves all members of society.

The significance of a gender perspective in the judiciary also lies in its ability to address biases and assumptions that affect judicial reasoning.

Marianela Delgado's exploration of evidence reasoning, for example, argues that a gender-sensitive approach can reduce judicial biases in cases involving testimony from women, particularly in instances of gender-based violence. Oana Băluță further supports this by advocating for gender-competent training for legal professionals, asserting that a judiciary trained in gender sensitivity is better equipped to handle cases of violence and discrimination. Together, these papers make a compelling case for the integration of gender-sensitive education and policies within the judiciary to mitigate bias, enhance empathy, and ultimately improve legal outcomes.

1 "First Ladies on the Bench: A European Perspective on Gender and the Judiciary in the Interbellum Years" by Marion Röwekamp

Marion Röwekamp's paper takes a historical look at the integration of women into the judiciary in Europe during the interwar period, focusing on the barriers and milestones that marked their journey. This period saw European women gain suffrage rights, but their entry into legal professions was met with considerable resistance, rooted in cultural and social biases. Röwekamp examines the German model of "Einheitsjuristen" (uniform legal training), which created a path for women to enter various legal professions, including the judiciary. She contrasts this with countries that imposed restrictive qualifications, limiting women's participation in legal fields. The paper highlights how many opponents of female judges argued that women lacked the authority and impartiality required for judicial roles, viewing them instead as emotionally vulnerable. However, Röwekamp underscores that these early female judges played a critical role in advocating for more compassionate interpretations of the law, which often introduced a greater focus on social justice in legal proceedings.

Röwekamp also highlights the broader societal shifts that enabled these developments, as well as the challenges that female judges continued to face even after formally entering the profession. She argues that women's inclusion in the judiciary did not only mark a victory for gender equality but also contributed to the evolution of the legal system itself by broadening the scope of judicial perspectives. This shift was particularly evident in family and social welfare cases, where women judges often advocated for outcomes that balanced legal principles with social considerations. By documenting the experiences of these pioneering women, Röwekamp sheds light on how their presence gradually changed perceptions about women's suitability for positions of authority. Her work emphasizes that these early advancements laid a foundation for future generations of women in law, helping to erode gendered stereotypes and open doors for a more inclusive judiciary across Europe.

2 "Gender Diversity in the Judiciary: A Matter of Law? An Approach Under the European Court of Human Rights" by Saadet Yüksel

Saadet Yüksel examines the importance of gender diversity within the judiciary, focusing on the ECtHR as a case study to illustrate the broader implications of gender representation in judicial systems. Yüksel argues that a judiciary with balanced gender representation is crucial for fair and legitimate legal proceedings, especially in cases that involve gender-sensitive issues such as discrimination and human rights. Through a review of ECtHR rulings and Council of Europe policies, she advocates for gender diversity to be enshrined in legal mandates, rather than left to fluctuating political priorities. Yüksel discusses the limitations of "token" diversity, where female representation is more symbolic than substantive, and emphasizes that meaningful participation is essential for creating an equitable judicial environment. She posits that a diverse judiciary is better equipped to interpret the law in ways that reflect a broader range of social values and experiences.

The paper goes on to recommend specific legal frameworks that could reinforce gender diversity in the judiciary, underscoring the ECtHR's potential role as a leader in setting binding standards. Yüksel suggests that without enforceable mandates, gender representation within judicial systems is likely to remain inconsistent, leaving women underrepresented and limiting the judiciary's ability to address gender-specific legal issues effectively. By advocating for structural changes that support gender diversity, Yüksel calls for the ECtHR to actively champion inclusivity in judicial appointments, which could set a precedent for other courts across Europe. Her analysis underscores the idea that gender diversity in the judiciary is not simply a matter of representation but a vital component of a functioning democracy that upholds justice for all citizens.

3 "Gender Equality in Serbian Judiciary—An Examination of the State of Play" by Ana Knežević Bojović and Monika Milošević

This paper by Ana Knežević Bojović and Monika Milošević provides a thorough examination of gender representation within the Serbian judiciary, highlighting progress but also pointing out significant areas needing improvement. They discuss the strong presence of women among Serbian judges while emphasizing the notable absence of women in leadership and senior decision-making roles. The authors examine existing formal frameworks supporting gender equality in Serbia, identifying gaps in implementation that prevent meaningful progress. Despite policies aimed at promoting gender equality, the Serbian judiciary still operates within structures that inherently favor male career advancement, largely due to workplace cultures that do not adequately support work-life balance. This discrepancy is compounded by the lack of mentorship programs and targeted leadership development for women, leaving many talented female judges without pathways to higher positions.

Knežević Bojović and Milošević suggest comprehensive reforms to address these structural issues, including policies that promote flexible work arrangements, gender-sensitive training, and mentorship initiatives that actively support women's advancement. They also recommend Serbia's alignment with European Union standards on gender equality to create a more inclusive judiciary that represents a diverse society. By strengthening both policy enforcement and workplace culture, the authors argue that Serbia can create a judiciary that not only achieves gender balance in numbers but also in influence and leadership. Their work highlights that true gender equality requires more than policies on paper—it requires institutional support systems that enable women to fully participate in shaping the judiciary.

4 The Position of Female Attorneys in Montenegro in Comparison to Other Legal Professions: Between a Minority and a Majority" by Matija Stojanović

Matija Stojanović's paper examines the unique challenges female attorneys face in Montenegro, comparing their experiences to those in other legal professions where women have achieved greater representation. He attributes the relatively low number of female attorneys to entrenched patriarchal norms and societal biases that discourage women from pursuing careers in advocacy, an area traditionally dominated by men. Through qualitative research, including interviews with female attorneys, Stojanović reveals the structural and societal challenges that limit women's participation and advancement in the field. For instance, clients often prefer male attorneys, perceiving them as more competent in court, which restricts women's client base and limits their professional growth.

Stojanović advocates for policy changes and public awareness campaigns to combat these stereotypes and support female attorneys' professional development. He suggests that creating mentorship programs, offering leadership training, and fostering supportive networks could provide women in legal advocacy with the resources they need to overcome existing biases. The paper argues that without a shift in both policy and public perception, female attorneys will continue to face limitations in their careers. By addressing these issues, Montenegro's legal system could become more inclusive, enabling women to pursue advocacy careers on equal footing with their male counterparts and ensuring that gender biases do not hinder access to justice.

5 "Access to Justice Through Public Notary Service in the Republic of Serbia: How Can the Gender Perspective Move Things Forward?" by Nenad Tešić and Ljubinka Kovačević

In this paper, Tešić and Kovačević examine how public notaries in Serbia can better serve women by adopting a gender-sensitive approach, particularly in handling cases related to family law and property rights. They argue that public notaries play a pivotal role in access to justice, especially for marginalized women who may lack resources or legal knowledge to navigate complex legal systems. The authors identify various barriers women face, such as limited access to property ownership and societal norms that undervalue women's rights in family disputes. Tešić and Kovačević propose gender-sensitive training for notaries to help them understand and address these issues more effectively.

Additionally, the paper calls for reforms to notarial procedures to ensure that they are more inclusive and supportive of women's legal needs. By fostering a gender-sensitive approach, public notaries could become key allies in promoting gender equality within the justice system. The authors suggest that such changes would empower women, particularly those in rural or economically disadvantaged positions, by making legal services more accessible and attuned to their specific challenges. Overall, the paper advocates for a more inclusive notarial service that aligns with broader efforts to improve gender equality and social justice in Serbia.

6 "Can Gender Shape the Course of Justice? Some Insights from the European Court of Human Rights" by Marko Bošnjak and Alice Leconte

Bošnjak and Leconte explore the impact of gender on judicial decisions, particularly within the ECtHR, by analyzing cases where gender-sensitive perspectives have influenced outcomes. They argue that the presence of female judges in the ECtHR brings valuable insights to cases involving gender discrimination, family law, and human rights issues, thereby enriching the court's decision-making process. The paper suggests that female judges may be more attuned to the nuances of gender-based cases, which enhances the court's ability to deliver fair and balanced judgments. By providing a range of case studies, Bošnjak and Leconte highlight the positive impact of gender diversity on the interpretation of rights and justice.

The authors advocate for increased gender representation within the ECtHR as a way to further strengthen its commitment to human rights. They argue that a diverse judiciary not only reflects the demographic composition of society but also ensures that judicial outcomes are more comprehensive and representative of diverse lived experiences. Bošnjak and Leconte suggest that the ECtHR has a responsibility to champion gender inclusivity as a model for other courts across Europe, setting a standard for judicial systems that aim to promote equality and human rights. Their paper underscores the idea that gender diversity is integral to a judiciary that seeks to uphold justice for all, recognizing that diverse perspectives are essential for fair legal interpretations.

7 "Gender and Judiciary System in Spain from a Labor Perspective" by Eva Bermúdez Figueroa and Raquel Pastor Yuste

Eva Bermúdez Figueroa and Raquel Pastor Yuste explore the gender dynamics within Spain's judiciary, focusing on labor issues that create barriers for women in this field. They examine occupational segregation and the persistence of the gender pay gap, arguing that traditional gender roles and societal expectations limit career progression for female judicial professionals. The authors analyze how inflexible work arrangements and inadequate family support policies contribute to a work environment that is less accommodating to women, particularly those with caregiving responsibilities. This, they argue, not only impacts women's career advancement but also perpetuates a gender imbalance in the judiciary.

To address these disparities, Bermúdez Figueroa and Pastor Yuste propose a range of policy reforms, including equitable parental leave policies, flexible work schedules, and wage equity initiatives. They argue that achieving gender equality within the judiciary requires changes not only in policy but also in workplace culture and public attitudes toward gender roles. Their paper emphasizes that without addressing these broader societal norms, gender equality within the judiciary will remain elusive. The authors call for a more comprehensive approach to workforce equality that includes both structural adjustments and cultural shifts, fostering an inclusive judicial environment where both men and women can equally thrive.

8 "Gender Representation in the Brazilian Judiciary: Reflections upon a Case Study of the Right to Abortion" by Luana Mathias Souto and Jessica Holl

Luana Mathias Souto and Jessica Holl investigate the representation of women in the Brazilian judiciary, focusing on its implications for sensitive legal issues such as abortion rights. Through a case study, they illustrate how male-dominated judicial perspectives often perpetuate gender biases, leading to rulings that can undermine women's rights to bodily autonomy. The authors argue that the inclusion of female judges can bring about more balanced and empathetic interpretations of such cases, ensuring that the judiciary reflects the diversity of society and addresses issues that disproportionately affect women.

The paper advocates for policies that would promote gender diversity within Brazil's judiciary, positing that such representation is essential for fair adjudication in gender-sensitive cases. Souto and Holl argue that increased female representation is not simply a matter of equality but also critical for achieving judicial outcomes that align with public sentiment on gender justice. By presenting this case study, the authors make a compelling case for judicial reform that prioritizes gender representation as a means of improving trust and fairness in legal interpretations, particularly on matters central to women's rights.

9 "Overcoming Gender Bias in the Justice System's Response to Violence: A Call for Enhanced Academic and Professional Training" by Oana Băluță

In her paper, Oana Băluță addresses the challenges posed by gender bias within the justice system, particularly in cases involving violence against women. She argues that many legal professionals lack the gender sensitivity required to handle such cases effectively, often leading to judgments that do not adequately protect victims. Băluță highlights the need for enhanced training programs that integrate gender competence into the education of legal professionals, from law school to continued professional development. Without this training, she suggests, the justice system risks reinforcing harmful stereotypes that undermine the experiences and rights of female victims.

Băluță calls for a systematic overhaul of legal education to include gender-sensitive curricula that address the social and psychological aspects of gender-based violence. She contends that by equipping legal professionals with the skills to recognize and address gender bias, the justice system can more effectively protect victims and uphold principles of equality. Her paper emphasizes that achieving justice for victims of gender-based violence requires a fundamental shift in how the legal community approaches such cases, promoting a judicial response that is both empathetic and informed by gender perspectives.

10 "Gender Competent Legal Education of Criminal Justice Professionals—Case of Intimate Partner Violence" by Natalija Lukić

Natalija Lukić critiques the current state of legal education regarding intimate partner violence, asserting that traditional training does not sufficiently prepare criminal justice professionals to handle these cases with the necessary gender sensitivity. She discusses how conventional legal curricula often overlook the complexities of gender-based violence, which can result in judgments that fail to offer adequate support and protection to victims. Lukić argues for curriculum reforms that would incorporate gender-sensitive modules, allowing future legal professionals to better understand the dynamics of intimate partner violence.

The paper advocates for a shift toward legal education that recognizes the unique challenges posed by intimate partner violence and the importance of a gendered approach in these cases. By incorporating gender competence into the training of criminal justice professionals, Lukić believes that the judiciary can deliver more just and effective outcomes for victims of domestic violence. Her work highlights that a comprehensive approach to legal education is essential for ensuring that the judiciary can address intimate partner violence with both empathy and an informed understanding of its societal implications.

11 "Reframing Evidentiary Reasoning through a Gender Perspective" by Marianela Delgado Nieves

Marianela Delgado's paper discusses how incorporating a gender perspective can significantly impact the reasoning and evaluation of evidence in legal cases. She argues that traditional evidence assessment methods often overlook gendered dimensions of testimony, which can lead to biased interpretations that unfairly disadvantage women. Delgado explores how a gender-sensitive approach can improve judicial reasoning by accounting for the unique experiences women bring to legal proceedings, especially in cases involving gender-based violence or discrimination.

Delgado advocates for methodological changes in how evidence is assessed, emphasizing that gender-sensitive reasoning can contribute to fairer legal outcomes. She suggests that by acknowledging the societal and psychological factors influencing women's testimony, the judiciary can deliver more balanced and inclusive judgments. Delgado's work underscores the importance of revising conventional legal practices to foster a more inclusive judicial process that recognizes and addresses the nuances of gender within evidence evaluation.

12 "A Feminist Critique of Traditional Patriarchal Professional Stereotypes: The Example of the Czech Custody Justice System" by Kateřina Šimáčková

Kateřina Šimáčková critiques the influence of patriarchal stereotypes within the Czech custody justice system, where traditional gender roles often dictate custody outcomes. She argues that societal expectations about motherhood and fatherhood create biases in favor of mothers as primary caregivers, while fathers are often marginalized. Through a feminist lens, Šimáčková examines how these stereotypes limit judicial decision-making, leading to outcomes that may not always prioritize the best interests of the child.

Šimáčková calls for a re-evaluation of custody cases that considers both parents equally, advocating for a judicial approach that moves beyond gendered expectations. She proposes reforms aimed at fostering equality in family law and promoting shared responsibility between parents. Her paper highlights the importance of challenging deep-seated cultural assumptions within the judiciary to create a more equitable system that genuinely reflects the diverse realities of modern family life.

13 "Abortion in the U.S. After Dobbs v. Jackson Women's Health Organization: A Comparative Perspective" by Rosalba Potenzano and Guido Smorto

Potenzano and Smorto examine the impact of the U.S. Supreme Court's decision in Dobbs v. Jackson Women's Health Organization on abortion rights, offering a comparative analysis with international standards. They discuss how the ruling, which overturned *Roe v. Wade*, marks a significant shift in reproductive rights in the U.S., contrasting sharply with the trend toward liberalization in many other countries. The authors argue that this decision has serious implications for women's autonomy, setting a precedent that could influence other conservative movements worldwide.

The paper highlights how the Dobbs decision diverges from international human rights norms, which increasingly recognize reproductive freedom as a fundamental right. Potenzano and Smorto call for a reassessment of abortion laws that aligns with global standards on women's rights and autonomy. By drawing on international examples, they advocate for a judicial approach that respects individual freedoms and upholds reproductive rights as essential to gender equality.

14 "Discrimination of Women Under Sharia Law and the Molla Sali Judgment of the ECHR" by Ioannis Ktistakis

Ioannis Ktistakis examines the landmark *Molla Sali v. Greece* case at the ECtHR, which addressed the application of Sharia law to civil disputes among Muslims in Greece. The judgment highlighted the gender discrimination inherent in Sharia-based legal frameworks, particularly concerning inheritance rights. Ktistakis argues that the decision sets an important precedent for balancing religious freedom with the protection of women's rights within minority communities.

The paper calls for stronger safeguards against discriminatory practices allowed under religious laws, emphasizing the importance of upholding gender equality in multicultural societies. Ktistakis contends that while respecting religious traditions is important, they should not override fundamental human rights. His analysis underscores the need for judicial systems to protect vulnerable individuals within religious minorities from practices that undermine gender equality and personal autonomy.

15 "Roman Woman on Trial: Limited Access to Justice" by Mirjana Miškić

Mirjana Miškić's paper delves into the historical limitations placed on Roman women in legal proceedings, exploring how societal biases prevented them from accessing justice. She examines the cultural norms that framed women as unreliable witnesses and restricted their ability to represent themselves or others in court. Miškić provides examples of how these limitations reflected broader societal views that confined women to domestic roles, excluding them from public life and decision-making.

Despite these restrictions, Miškić highlights cases where women in Rome managed to navigate the legal system and achieve limited successes. These instances underscore both the resilience of Roman women and the profound challenges they faced under a patriarchal legal structure. Miškić argues that the historical exclusion of women from the judiciary laid a foundation for enduring gender biases, with implications that continue to shape legal systems today.

16 "Gender and the Judiciary in Medieval Serbia" by Nina Kršljanin

Nina Kršljanin's paper explores the role and status of women in the judicial system of medieval Serbia, examining historical records to understand how societal norms influenced women's legal rights and participation in legal matters. Kršljanin provides insight into the patriarchal framework of medieval Serbian society, which generally restricted women's involvement in the judiciary and broader public life. However, she uncovers instances where noblewomen or women of influence exerted some level of judicial power or impacted legal proceedings, especially in family or inheritance disputes. These cases highlight that, while limited, women's participation in the judicial system was not entirely absent and depended on their social status and family connections.

Kršljanin argues that these instances illustrate both the adaptability of certain legal norms and the influence of societal structures on women's access to justice.

She notes that although the formal judiciary was largely closed to women, they still found ways to exert influence, whether through informal networks or their roles within family dynamics. By examining these historical contexts, Kršljanin reveals the deep-seated roots of gender inequality in Serbian legal history, highlighting how patriarchal norms in the medieval period set precedents that continued to affect women's legal rights in later centuries. Her research underscores the importance of understanding these historical underpinnings to address and challenge the gender biases that persist in modern judicial systems.

* * *

In conclusion, the papers in this collection collectively demonstrate that integrating a gender perspective within the judiciary is essential for achieving a fair, inclusive, and effective legal system. A judiciary that incorporates gender diversity, addresses historical biases, meets the needs of marginalized groups, and applies gender-sensitive reasoning is better positioned to uphold justice in a way that truly serves society as a whole. The arguments and examples presented here advocate for a comprehensive approach to judicial reform, one that prioritizes gender sensitivity at every level—from education and policy-making to representation and decision-making. By doing so, the judiciary can fulfill its role as a defender of democratic values and a promoter of equality and justice for all.

Part I
Courts

First Ladies on the Bench. A European Perspective on Gender and the Judiciary in the Interbellum Years

Marion Röwekamp

Abstract The European story of the first women lawyers is so far told as a story of the "firsts" attorneys which stand for all female lawyers. The narrative stands and falls with the narrative of the supposed progressive countries that had early women lawyers like France, Italy or Belgium and the supposed successors such like Germany and the new nations in Central and Southeastern Europe. But if one looks at the whole professional context and includes women's access to all legal professions, the narrative changes, because many of the supposed latecomers simultaneously admitted women to all legal professions, and thus were in fact the first countries in Europe to have women judges. The article follows the known argument of a close connection between suffrage and access to the bench, yet combines it with the observation that countries which followed the German legal education to form "Einheitsjuristen" (uniform lawyers) were the ones granting women access in the interwar time. Thus, it was not necessarily suffrage that automatically granted access, as we can see in Great Britain where women gained suffrage but not the right to judge. Rather, there is a relevant combination of suffrage, attempts to give women full citizenship rights as well as legal education qualifying for the whole range of legal professions, including the bench.

M. Röwekamp (✉)
Independent researcher, Berlin, Germany
e-mail: roewekampmarion@gmail.com

© The Author(s), under exclusive license to Springer Nature Switzerland AG 2025
S. Baer et al. (eds.), *The Gender and the Judiciary*, Gender Perspectives in Law 7,
https://doi.org/10.1007/978-3-032-06885-9_2

1 Introduction

"Female lawyers and judges tend to play the leading role among the first spectres of our opponents," wrote the Swiss feminist and historian Meta von Salis in 1884.[1] However, the spectres are more likely to be female judges than female lawyers, as the different histories of the two professions show.

The story of the first women lawyers is often told as a story of the "firsts" whom we rightly celebrate as our pioneers who paved the way for us to enter the legal professions. However, these narratives are not fully accurate. Just as women in almost all countries gained the right to vote in stages, i.e. women in England gained full suffrage in 1928, and in the U.S. in 1965 when Black women could vote, the story of the early women lawyers is also in need of revision. As a rule, reference is made to the first female attorneys who stand pars pro toto for all female lawyers. With them stands and falls the narrative of the supposed progressive countries that had early women lawyers like France, Italy or Belgium, and of the supposed successors like Germany and the later new nations in Central and Southeastern Europe as well as Spain. Yet if one includes women's access to all legal professions, the narrative turns, because many of the supposed latecomers were so late because they simultaneously admitted women to all legal professions. As such, they were the first countries in Europe to have women judges.

First, the focus on the difference between women's access to the bar and the bench shows that the countries which admitted women early to be attorneys were countries with separate legal education for different legal professions. The ones that admitted women later were countries with one common legal education for all professions. There, women gained access to the judiciary with their access to the bar. This is the German legal tradition of educating an *Einheitsjurist* (uniform jurist), meaning when a person studied law, the person was prepared to work in all legal professions. There, the state took full care of legal education though located in the law faculties of autonomous, yet public universities. The idea was never and is still not to educate independent lawyers, but the idea was and is to educate civil servants, including lawyers as "organs of the justice system" (Organe der Rechtspflege). This type of legal education was used, besides Germany and Austria, to a certain extent in all former crown lands of Austria, as well as in the later Baltic Republics. Most of these countries changed their political systems after World War I, gave women suffrage rights and guaranteed basic equality rights for women in their constitutions.[2] They became democracies which included an attempt to give female citizens a different set of equality rights than the older European democracies, like France and Great Britain, in the interwar times. In most of these countries the willingness for change came with independence, as in Czechoslovakia, Poland and the Baltic Republics; while in Germany, Austria and Spain, it

[1] Salis-Marschlins (1884), p.5.

[2] Forthcoming: Röwekamp (2026).

was the revolutionary potential that accompanied the change from monarchy to democracy. These changes provided new opportunities and spaces for women to move in, also within the professions, for example as judges.

The second argument regarding the obstacles of women gaining access to the legal profession is already known. It has been exposed by James Albisetti's pioneering article on the first female lawyers in Europe.[3] According to the argument, women's late admission to the legal professions in general was related to their missing political rights, e.g., suffrage. Amazingly enough, his lead on comparing access within Europe has not been followed. Thus, research has basically remained focused on national access or anthologies with chapters on single nations, that offer a European comparison only in introductions.[4] Yet Albisetti's approach also focused but on women's access to the bar. In this sense, he provides a perspective that does not consider the full picture of women's access to all legal professions. In fact, the suffrage argument was used around women's admission to the bar but primarily to prevent women claiming suffrage rights and access to state functions. The real obstacle was access to the profession of a judge and higher state administration. Opponents of women's access to the bar were basically afraid that this could be a first steppingstone to get full citizenship and voting rights. Sara Kimble and I have made this argument for France and Germany, and we also intended to draw a bigger picture in a study on female lawyers in Central Europe in the interwar time.[5]

Here, the focus is, for the first time, on the professional group of women judges throughout Europe. It is based on contemporary articles of the women's movement of the interwar time and on secondary literature from the respective countries. The first part of the article will contextualize the story of the first female judges historically, socially and in terms of cultural ideas. The second part will provide brief histories of the "first" ones in their respective countries. Certainly, the "first" ones as a categorization is prone to mistakes, and there is more to women's history than focusing on the "firsts" and on biographies in general. In fact, it often leads to a kind of mystification which does not serve the larger cause of women because it tells the story of the exception and not the norm, and thus tends to ignore changes of the norm that allow for such exceptions. But still, the experience of the "firsts" and their voices need to be heard. We still seem to have broad research lagunas here, and their collective experiences add to more comprehensive analysis. Luckily, women's movements in many countries have been documenting some of these first figures. But more often than they did, they did not because these women were already the second generation of feminists. They were welcome in the sense that they had fought for their opportunities to work as lawyers and hoped that these exceptions would become the norm over time, but they were also not welcome because these professional women laid claim on being stronger or more

[3] Albisetti (2000).

[4] Kimble, Röwekamp (2017), Schandevyl (2014).

[5] Kimble, Röwekamp (2018).

competent in legal questions than the first generation. The stories of women's history in Germany at least stopped with the self-description of the first generation. It may have left the professional women outside of this narrative on purpose, to it can be partly discovered by other means than the paper trail of the women's movement. This is the attempt here, to find the first female judges. It shall also enquire whether they treated the law differently from their male colleagues, since research on gender discrimination in the judiciary demonstrates how ingrained biases eventually shape the way that courts are seen, function, and are set up.

2 A Right to Plea but No Right to Judge

In Europe, a first phase in the equal rights movement aimed at justice and the law and focused on access to the bar and juries as well juvenile courts. Only in a second step and often later, after these rights were partly granted, feminist lawyers demanded also, as Sara L. Kimble has phrased it, the "right to judge."[6] They found allies in reformers of juvenile law, where they claimed the necessity of female professionals with a "maternal and natural caring function" in everything involving the protection of minors. These early pleas for access to one branch of the judiciary that was just in the process of being established in most countries were however met with resistance: The argument was that women could not pass a sentence because of their legal and political incapacity. Thus, there is a strong historical relationship between political rights for women and their access to the judiciary. Male lawyers and other opponents to women's access to the bar even went back to Roman law to argue their case. In France, the reason to deny Jeanne Chauvin's request to be admitted to the bar association rosters was that women were not allowed to practice law in Roman, Justinian, or French law, hence she was not qualified to take the required lawyers' oath. Her opponent maintained that because of Gaia Afriania's claimed "shrewish," "impudent," and "litigious" behavior, ancient Roman law already regarded the legal profession as "virile" and barred women from serving as court counsel.[7] In the case of Afriana's colleague Ancesia Sentia, the Roman senate consulted the oracle after one of her speeches at court. It asked how a woman could be equipped with so much sense, reason, education and a gift to talk.[8] Yet the offense by the behavior of Afriana was so big that Ulpian said that the pretor forbit women to appear in court because they could not mix *contra pudicitiam sexus* in the matters of others, and especially in male institutions. The Justinian Code thus forbade women from holding any public or civil office, from pleading, from sitting as judges, from intervening in court on behalf of another person, and from serving as procurators. It further cemented this

[6] Kimble (2008).

[7] Frank (1889); Kimble (2008).

[8] Pierantoni (1896).

exclusion by the fifth century.[9] And it did not end there. In Germany, the medieval law code of the *Schwabenspiegel* also contained this rule in par 245, II 63, par 1, as did French medieval law.

As the Roman law could not forgive Gaia Afriana, the Catholic church could not forgive Eva. Both public and canon law would stress the idea of women's role in the home and for the family while the public sphere and politics were reserved for men. As women were always excluded, they lacked, in the opinion of opponents, the worldly experience to work as lawyers. This would be held until the nineteenth and twentieth century: that women could not be attorneys and they could only exceptionally speak for themselves.[10]

When Lydia Poët in Italy wanted to be admitted to the bar in 1883, the appellate court confirmed the "known fact" that women could not work as attorneys. It argued that the profession of an attorney was a semi-public profession because attorneys could not refuse to represent a client when he was called as a defender by the state. As such, the Italian law considered the bar a subsidiary branch of the judiciary and thus a kind of office. One indicator was that members of the bar could also be later appointed as members of the judiciary. Thus, if women were admitted as attorneys, they also needed to be able to work as judges. For their admission, the appellate court thus deemed it necessary to change the law that women explicitly could be admitted. And note that Poët had written her PhD thesis on the legal situation of the Italian women, especially in terms of suffrage rights.[11]

The same arguments were also used in Belgium against Popelin and in France against Chauvin, where the general procurator mentioned in addition that it was always clear that women belonged to the family, and that their position in private law was so limited that they could not yet enter the public domain. The legal profession, as mentioned above, was still a "virile" one. Therefore, the Cour de Cassation rejected Chauvin's claim in 1897. It argued that women had no suffrage rights and thus were not allowed to serve in an office. And when the deputy René Viviani brought draft legislation to have women admitted to the bar he could only win his colleagues support by promising not to include women's access to the judiciary or gain voting rights.

In Switzerland, Emilie Kempin, a graduate of Zurich law school, appeared in court to plea for her absent husband. She was advised that she could not defend him because she was not an "active citizen", meaning she could not vote. But her case was the reason that Zurich formulated a new law which was passed in 1898. It stated in para. 5 explicitly, and exceptionally for Europe at the time, that female citizens are treated equally to male citizens when practicing as an attorney.[12] And note again that Kempin like Chauvin, Popelin and Poët, was

[9] Frank (1889); Mackenroth (1898); Feldner (2000).

[10] Ostrogorski (1893), p. 140; Mackenroth (1898).

[11] Poët (1881); Santoni de Sio (1884); Olgiati (2003).

[12] BGE 13, 1887; Ringwald (1931/32; 1933).

publishing and fighting for women's equal rights beyond access to the legal professions.[13]

Supporters of women argued that the legislator never assumed that it would be only men exercising the profession, but that the focus should be that every person with the abilities of a lawyer should be admitted. In fact, none of the laws mentioned that only men could access this position, but it was a customary interpretation. Only the Danish Royal ordinance of 1875 decreed, in Art. 3, that university examinations and academic degrees were not to give women access to administrative posts. Also, when Prussia opened its doors for women studying law, it laid down that they were not eligible to be admitted to the legal professions afterwards. Overall, women were only admitted to the bar in countries with a separate legal education for attorneys and judges and civil servants.

In fact, women had held offices for many centuries when there was no clear separation between public and private law, and where women held offices in the name of men and/or based on their property. But when modern law ended this confusion of private and public law, and when public offices were not anymore inherited but governed by the state, women had to leave. However, women were sometimes admitted to positions like teachers, with a clear understanding that education and, in some countries, some "minor" offices were open for female applicants as well.

Realizing early that equality arguments would not bear any fruit, civic maternalism became a political strategy. Women established institutions to empower women as mothers, and they pushed for nations to prioritize human welfare for the betterment of society and the nation. Many demands for welfare of children and minors came from the women's rights movement, and was driven by initiatives of women. Maternalism was a framework for action in which educated and usually well-off women were drawing equally on their faith in women's moral superiority, on motherly capacities, and on long experience in social and political work. They sought to represent women and children presumed to be more vulnerable, as defined by Susan Pedersen. Here, the idea of motherhood allowed them to become involved in public matters, including the area of law. Then, the entrance to legal professions came twofold, with the fight for access to juries as well as for judges in the newly established juvenile courts.[14]

2.1 Women in Juries

In terms of women's access to the jury, this also required first the right to vote. Only one European country, England, had an explicit statutory provision as to the sex of jurors. The Juries Act of 1870 declared that the word juror shall mean male

[13] Kempin (1895); Delfosse (1994); Kimble (2008), Olgiati (2003), Schandevyl (2017).

[14] Bock (2000); Offen (2000), p. 239; Pedersen (2001), p. 165.

persons only. It was based on William Blackstone's commentaries where he defined a jury as consisting out of twelve "liberos et legales homines." And he had added that "Under the word homo also, though a name common to both sexes, the female is however excluded, propter defectum sexus."[15]

Besides England, the movement for women in juries was also especially strong in France. There, since 1885, feminists strongly demanded a mixed-gender jury. The *jury féminin* commented in the *Journal de femmes* over five years the problems of cases with a male jury only. Also in Russia, the women's progressive party decided to present a Bill to the Duma for the admission of women to juries in 1913. At the Duma's request, the Bill was drafted by the St. Petersburg Society of Female Lawyers, but it did not succeed. In December 1917, the League of Women's Rights protested the Provisional Government's decree excluding women from juries. "They will not, and cannot, consent to such unjust measures, which prevent women accomplishing their civic duties."[16]

Regarding juries, the overarching argument for including women was that every person should be tried by a jury of peers. Without women jurors, female defendants never had the same chance and where thus treated differently from male defendants. Female jurors seemed especially needed in cases of women as defendants, based on the assumption that men could not claim to understand women. Yet again, opponents stressed women's duty at home, as well as the lack of ability to judge due to lack of education, and a motherly and womanly nature which could not take the strain of jury service. However, women picked this up and turned it around: Exactly due to the motherly and womanly nature, women were needed to complete society and the state. Yet in most countries, access was not granted until women got suffrage rights.

In Germany, the movement was therefore twofold: while the feminist movement fought for women jurors, they also argued for women in the legal profession. After suffrage was gained in 1918, both claims were won in 1922, with two laws passed within but months. After access of women to juries was won, arguments of keeping women out of the legal professions were difficult to maintain.[17]

Interestingly, the first female jurors seem to have had a strong impact on criminal convictions. When England's Sex Disqualification (Removal) Act of 1919 was passed and women were admitted as jurors, this was followed by significant changes in some conviction rates, specifically for sex offenses and violent crimes against women. They increased by 16% while the general conviction for other crimes decreased. Here, women seemed to view the impact of punishment on the victim from a different perspective than their male counterparts.[18]

Also, a study by Norwegian lawyers had found in 1910 that women's confidence in the legal system had increased significantly as a result of women's

---

[15] Blackstone (1809), pp. 351, 362.

[16] Sheepshansks (1918).

[17] Cornett (1997); Logan (2013); Kimble (2019); Pastocic (2016); Röwekamp (2011).

[18] Anwar et al. (2019); Logan (2006).

participation in juries and that women's interest in public life generally had grown with their inclusion. Norwegian feminist Fredritke Mórek reported on her own experience as a juror: "For me, the most interesting thing every time I acted as a juror was to gain an insight into the lives of these people, of which many of us women have not the slightest idea. I particularly noticed that these people have a completely different, I would say childlike, view of life, which is quite alien to us adults who are on the light side of life. It was only when I came into contact with these people that my eyes were opened to how difficult it is to be on the dark side of life. My judgment of people has become milder and, I hope, fairer. The most detailed descriptions in the newspapers do not give the same impression of the individual case as if I had attended the hearings myself; my confidence in the work of our courts has grown considerably since then; it is my conviction that the women here have great tasks to fulfil."[19]

2.2 *Juvenile Courts*

Another entrance door to the judiciary was access the newly established juvenile courts. Juvenile justice was a new area of the judiciary, and women claimed they were necessary as the "mothers of all children and minors", even if they were not literally mothers. They asserted that their presence was especially important for children in trouble with the law. And one way of doing that was to establish juvenile courts with women because they were more experienced with children than men. In England, Secretary of the NCW Public Service and Magistrate committee Amelia Scott claimed that "The value of women as magistrates in Children's Courts is so obvious, and is so often quoted as a unassailable argument in favor of the appointment of women as justices that, as so often happens, there is a danger that public opinion being narrowed down to one point, namely that women should be appointed as magistrates in children's court only."[20] In Great Britain, juvenile courts were established in the wake of the Children Act 1908. The suggestion to appoint female magistrates was made around the time of the report of the Royal Commission on Justices of the Peace in 1910. Yet the Juvenile Courts (Metropolis) Act 1920 reorganized London's children's courts by introducing a team of two lay justices, one man and one woman, to sit alongside a stipendiary magistrate on minor's cases, and the Children and Young Person's Act 1933 then prompted a wave of appointments of women. Numbers raised in 1927 in London to over 100 female JPs in juvenile courts.[21]

In France, juvenile courts were introduced in 1912. Feminists argued that they were a great opportunity to have women included as a first step to other

[19] Mórek and von Welczeck (1910).
[20] Logan (2017), p. 277.
[21] Logan (2005).

jurisdictions. Very similar was the case in Germany in debates in 1913. But despite the high numbers of qualified female lawyers already involved in social work and juvenile welfare, the first World War hindered such progress in both countries. Eventually however, many of the first judges like Wanda Grabińska in Poland, Mathilde Huici and Luz le Boucher Villén in Spain studied to be judges especially in the juvenile courts.

In fact, in most countries which allowed women early as attorneys, like France, Belgium and Italy, the interbellum debate, when the new democracies in Central Europe opened the judiciary for women, was stalled with the missing voting rights argument. In the Netherlands, the Minister was asked, in the discussion of the Budget of the Department of Justice, whether women could be appointed judges, and he said that it was a controversial question, the subject then not pressed.[22] At a conference of the French National Association of Lawyers, attorney Maria Vérone was acknowledged to be qualified and well-suited to be a judge, but the association collectively opposed women's admission to the judiciary because they had no suffrage. While there were around 220 female attorneys working as such for over 25 years in Paris by the end of the 1920s alone, women were still barred from being judges. "No Women Judges in France Yet", titled Equal Rights in 1930. And although French women had hoped that the amendment to the judiciary reorganization bill admitting women to magistrates' position would be successful, it was defeated with 378 to 200 votes in the Chamber of Deputies. Also, a separate bill to open the position for women in the judiciary, failed. Minister of Justice, Raoul Péret, pointed out that the question of women to the bench was intimately connected with the right to vote, which French women were still denied. And in both parliament and senate, all attempts to grant voting rights for women were defeated.[23]

In countries were women received suffrage rights and principally had the same rights and duties in the constitution, opponents had a harder time. They had to prove why women, due to their nature, could not serve in the judiciary. Scholars wrote lengthy opinions repeating cultural prejudices about women's nature not fit to serve in positions of authority, of their limited brain functions, their inability to serve while menstruating, nursing or being pregnant, and of their nature as women not being sangfroid, objective and impartial enough. Besides the supposed physical and emotional nature of women, opponents relied on the role of the woman in the family and the state. They feared the end of the family and in a higher order, the end of the state, if women entered the virile profession of the judiciary. Female lawyers and the women's movement again turned this around. They based their attempts to enter the legal professions onto the supposed motherly nature of women as well, now as an advantage. The legal professions, often not enjoying the best reputation, were meant to become more human, and the state and society complete if women and men equally participated in public life. For example, when Suzanne

[22] Sheepshansks (1918), p. 185.

[23] Anonymous (1930a); Kimble (2008).

Grinberg in 1909 made her first public declaration in France that she wanted to become a judge, she described the existing political and judicial systems as full of injustice, contradiction, and hypocrisy, all of which she believed women's presence could help to improve.[24]

Yet in France, the Netherlands, Belgium, Great Britain, Portugal, Italy, Yugoslavia, Bulgaria, Romania and Greece, women argued in vain for access to the judiciary in the interwar years. Here, women would only gain access when they gained suffrage rights after 1945.

There is another trend which characterizes the history of first female lawyers and judges. With suffrage or without, all the way from the beginning, women defended the rights of others. Indeed, activist female lawyers pinned down elements of law and legislation to show the ways in which it caused harm, and proposed means to alleviate the inequality that such legal structures engendered. Also, feminist lawyers envisioned and sought to secure the incorporation of women into all areas of society on equal terms—whether in education, employment, the family, politics or legal institutions. It was lawyers that provided the women's movement with arguments and knowledge, when drafting reform laws not only on access to the judiciary, but also for family law reform, criminal law and others, as well as by legal analyses or documenting that equal pay between women and men was not a reality in the labour market. They also did so on the national and international level, as with the founding of the first European legal sorority association, the FIFCJ.[25] Therefore, the movement for women on juries as well as for women in juvenile courts shows how broadly women participated in shaping the welfare state and modern democracies.

3 The First European Ladies on the Bench

3.1 Nordic Countries

As far as equal rights of women were concerned, the Nordic countries were the earliest within Europe. On the one hand, this might have been related to their position on the periphery of Europe, resulting in more rights for women outside the center, a phenomenon we can also observe in the U.S. and Oceania. On the other hand, the bigger sympathy for women's rights were due to the structure of Nordic societies, based on agriculture and thus more heavily relying on equal work of women, at least more so than in industrialized Europe. Besides, the Nordic countries had a strong women's movement that operated transnationally and especially trans-Nordic. Namely Finland was influenced by the ideas of Russian Revolutionary movement which included, to a certain extent, women's equal

---

[24] Boigeol (1996); Kimble (2008, 2019).

[25] Kimble (2023); Kimble and Röwekamp (2017, 2018).

rights.[26] In Sweden, women could vote on the communal and municipal level since 1862 (on the national level since 1921); in Iceland, women gained a partial communal right in 1882, Finland introduced suffrage for women in 1906, Norway in 1913 and Denmark in 1915. On the other hand, Finland, Iceland, and Norway had a strong nationalistic movement as they were occupied states where men and women fought together for independence. Thus, the success of women's suffrage was connected to the independence movements in these countries and the participation of women within this struggle.

Norway seemed the pioneering nation among the Nordic ones as far as women's rights were concerned. There, women could work in several official functions that usually required political rights before women officially gained suffrage in 1913. In the election period of 1908–1910, there were 140 to 200 women who participated in local councils, which is however less than 2%. They worked in chambers of commerce, councils for the poor, school boards, orphan's councils and as factory inspectors. Also, women could work as attorneys from 1904 onwards, with Elise Sem as the first female attorney.[27] However, and not coincidentally, the first woman judge in Norway was appointed at the same time when women gained suffrage, in 1913. The Superior Magistrate of Finmarken called Ruth Sörensen of Hammerfest, so far an attorney, into temporary office as a town judge during a leave of the absence of the male official. Sörensen was the daughter of the clergymean F.C. Sörensen, born in 1877 in Röken. She entered university in 1895 and passed her juridical exam in 1900. In 1907, she was admitted to the bar and opened an office on Kristiania in Oslo, then moved to Hammerfest, the northernmost town of the world, it said at the time.[28] She was a member of the legal commission of the National Women's Organization and of the Norwegian Federation of University Women. In late 1925, she was appointed a judge at the local court of Trontheim for civil law.[29] Later, she was involved in the reform of the Norwegian citizenship law and other activities to fight for equal rights of women in Norway. One year later, Anna Holmen was nominated as a sworn attorney of the judge of a district court of Holt, Nedenes. She had just passed her juridical exam at the university and did not exactly fill a position of a judge, but assisted the district judges who had to travel the circuits and more work than they could handle. Sworn attorneys took care of some of their work, and performed official duties at the proceeding in the courts of law.[30]

In Sweden, Elsa Eschelsson was the first woman to pass law studies at the University of Upsala in 1897. She was admitted as a tutor in civil law at that University in 1897, while her application as a professor was rejected in 1908.

[26] Martin (2000), pp. 123–33.

[27] Støren (1984).

[28] Anonymous (1923); Høg (1914), pp. 137–38; Quam (1913); Sørensen (1913).

[29] Anonymous (1925).

[30] Quam (1914).

Utterly distressed by this decision she took her life.[31] In November 1898 a bill was passed that allowed women the access to the bar, but it took more than a decade until the first female attorneys were admitted: since 1914, Eva Andén worked for a male lawyer, then with her own office since 1915 which the second female attorney, Mathilda Staël von Holstein, joined in 1919 as a partner. As far as civil service went, paragraph 28 of the Constitution made the male sex a precondition to enter state service, by explicitly refereeing to a Swedish man. As a result, women could not work as teachers in public schools nor as nurses, clerks, telegraph-, post- and bank officials in state service. And they certainly could not become a judge. In 1919, women suffrage was passed. Academic women, led by teachers, demanded a removal of paragraph 28 so women could access all professions. A committee formed by the Justice Department set out to free women of their husband's guardianship first, so they would be able to work; Staël von Holstein was a member. It's work resulted in a new marriage law as well as, in 1923, the *Behörighetslagen* or Qualifications Act to be enforced in 1925. When Minister of Justice Lofgren brought the bill into the council, he argued that it was to the State's undoubted advantage that requirements of merit and capacity and not the sex should be the grounds for admission to state service. As girls had the same education as boys, it would be a great injustice to prevent them from entering state service.[32]

In Sweden then, the first woman judge was appointed in 1926, Birgit Spångberg. Born in 1900 in Stockholm, she was the daughter of an editor and an actress. In 1925 she graduated from the law school of the University of Stockholm and worked as a notary. The Qualifications Act from 1923 made it possible for women to serve as district notaries, and Spångberg was one of the first ones, in Askim. In February 1926, she was accepted as an extraordinary notary at the Göta Court of Appeal, the second one ever. That same year, rules had been introduced to allow a female notary who had served at least six months in the Court of Appeal to be appointed to chair the district court, depending on approval. Spångberg was approved, and on August 31, 1926, she delivered her first judgment in about ten cases at the district court in Askim. "We hear that she acquitted herself with skill and showed considerable professional knowledge,"[33] the international women's news reported. From 1928 onwards, Spångberg served at the Ministry of Social Affairs; on several occasions, she held appointments as chancellery secretary and chancellor council. In 1936, she served at the International Labour Organization in Geneva. But on the way home to Stockholm, she contracted pneumonia and died in Copenhagen on September 11, 1937, aged 37.[34] Others came after her. In 1928, Marguerite Traugott was appointed judge, before she was working as a barrister in high courts.[35]

---

[31] Anonymous (1898); Sheepshansks (1918); Svensson (2011).

[32] Anonymous (1920).

[33] Anonymous (1926a).

[34] Trolle Önnerfor (2018).

[35] Anonymous (1928a).

In Denmark, women could study law from early on. Nanna Berg, later Kristensen-Randers, received her law diploma as early as 1887 and worked for a male lawyer who gave her permission to present in court. However, she could only work in lower courts and only as a representative of a male lawyer. In 1905, Henny Magnussen graduated from the University of Copenhagen. She managed to get support from members of parliament to change the law in 1906 which allowed female law graduates the same privileges as males. She joined a legal firm but was not allowed to work in higher courts. In 1909, she again rallied for support in parliament for women's access to the higher courts and was successful. She practiced as a high court barrister, headed the Copenhagen branch of the Danish Women's National Council and the Women's Suffrage Association.[36] In 1915, women got suffrage in Denmark, after 15 petitions had been voted down by the Conservatives in the County Council. In 1909, Elise Ussing, daughter of a judge, was temporarily appointed at the criminal section of the court of Copenhagen and was placed as a temporary judge at the Østre Landsret, the Hight Court of Denmark, in 1933, then officially appointed in 1939. She became a candidate for the Conservative People's Party in elections and was a member of the Danish Women's Conservative Association from 1918–1921, later also a member of the Danish Women's Society.[37]

The first officially mentioned female judge in Denmark seems to have been Ragnhild Fabricius Gjellerup, who was appointed in 1934. Born in 1896 in Copenhagen as the daughter of a lieutenant, she married a merchant in 1922, and became secretary at the municipal court in Copenhagen in 1923. In 1927, she was appointed secretary of the probate court until she became a judge in 1934. From 1946 to 1950, she headed the arbitral tribunal on housing, also covering business protection, and was one of the most active members of the Danish Women's Society.[38]

In 1939, the second woman judge, Karen Johnsen, became a substitute judge at the City Court of Justice in Copenhagen, after three years practice there, and King Christian X appointed her as a judge at Civil Courts at the beginning of 1939. The age limits for a judgeship at the time were 38 and 70, so that she acted as a Registrar in the Court of Justice until that age. In 1926 she was awarded the King's Gold Medal in recognition of her work on the position of married women and their property under Scandinavian law.[39] In 1949, she became a high court judge, also serving on the board of the Danish Women's Society, the Danish branch of the International University Women. In 1952, she represented Denmark at the UNESCO conference in Paris.

In Finland, the first woman to graduate from law was Agnes Lundell, in 1906. When women got the right to hold office and to be employed in Government

---

[36] Dübeck (2007).

[37] Anonymous (1933); Johannsen (2023).

[38] Holm (2015), p. 13.

[39] Anonymous (1939).

service on the same terms as men in 1926, the government gave with one hand but took with the other, because the the ordinance contained a number of exceptions. It needed another law in 1927 to give women the right to be judges and to enter diplomatic and consular service. Then, the first woman to enter the judiciary in Finland was Katri Hakkila in the 1930s.[40]

3.2 Central Europe and German Legal Education

Estonian women could study law from the beginning of the twentieth century and obtain a law degree since the foundation of the Republic of Estonia in 1918. Before 1939, 143 women worked as attorneys. In the 1920s, Auguste Susi-Tannebaum and Ollo Olesk, both graduates from the University of Tartu and members of the Estonian Bar association, applied for a career as judges unsuccessfully, and they appealed to the Supreme Court. This is ever more surprising because few European constitutions gave human rights to individuals, with constitution clauses for equality seen as guidelines, not claims. But Estonia had a Supreme Court to claim rights.

Context matters. Different than most other European countries, Estonia did not institute a special judicial education. In fact, in 1918, the government called on all people with a legal education to apply for judge positions because the new country did not have any. Any legal education from a faculty of law in Estonia or Russia was good. But the pay was low, the prestige not high, and most had almost no legal education at all, with only 2,4% studied law in 1921. Also, judges were no state officials but considered freelancers, highly unusual in Europe. Still, they needed to be appointed by the President of the National Court of Appeal. He held that job for the entire interwar time and decided just not to appoint women. In 1924, Susi-Tannebaum applied for a position of a judge, and was rejected the following day on the ground that Judicial Authorities prohibited women from being admitted. She appealed to the National Court of Appeals who affirmed that this decision was entirely to the presidents of the court and fully within their discretion. Susi-Tannebaum then went to the Supreme Court, and won. It decided that the decision need to be annulled and repealed according to the rules of the law. It held that "the law in force in the Republic of Estonia does not prohibit female persons who have citizenship of the Republic of Estonia and who have graduated from the Faculty of Law of the University of Tartu and where some of these special obstacles of a personal nature provided for in para. 201 of the Judicial Authorities Act do not prohibit entering the judicial service, are to be accepted as candidates for the judicial office." Still, Susi-Tannebaum was not appointed. And the same happened to Olga Olesk who applied in 1929. Again, the Supreme Court took a theoretical stand for women's equal rights but left the appointment to the President of the National Court of Appeal. After the occupation of Estonia, the Soviets appointed

[40] Anonymous (1928b); Anonymous (1930b); Korpiola (2018); Silius (2003).

six women as the first female judges, among them, in 1940, Leida Puusepp. She had graduated the same year from the University of Tartu, and in 1941 Miralda Tooma. The next four female judges were political appointments, most of them without a full legal education.[41]

Latvia and Lithuania had female judges in the interwar time. In Latvia, Rosalia Purgale was appointed the first judge in 1933. She had graduated in law in 1923 and since 1930 a candidate for the Latgale Regional Court. In 1933, she worked as Vice Prosecutor of the Latgale Regional Court and was appointed a judge, serving until the occupation of Latvia in 1940. Lithuania had her first female judge in 1923, Elena Jackevičaitė. She had worked as a court clerk in Kaunas since 1922 and was appointed as a judge in 1923. She was also a board member of the Lithuanian Women's National Council, participated in the Lithuanian Society of Abolitionist to prohibit prostitution, and fought for equal rights of married women. After World War II, she lived in exile in the United States.[42]

In Poland, women could study the law since 1915. The first female attorney, Helena Kononowicz-Wiewiórska, was admitted to the bar in Warsaw in 1925. By the end of the 1920s, the number of female law students increased considerably. However, out of the total number of 4656 barristers in 1932, there were only 40 women, 30 of whom practicing in Warsaw and 10 in country districts, thus a striking disproportion between the number of girl law-students and practicing lawyers. An article speculated in 1932 that there may be a the lack of confidence in female lawyers in general and difficulties in the way of women applying for official posts. It said that "This is the principal reason why many trained women lawyers are compelled to work in other fields, for instance in administration, banking, ministries, etc., where they sometimes attain high positions. In recent years a growth of confidence in women lawyers can be noticed, and their working number is continually augmenting."[43] In fact, a Polish decree of 1919 on judicial apprenticeship prevented women from entering the professions of prosecutor, judge and notary, expressly stating that only male Polish citizens could take judicial apprenticeships. This changed with the Act on the System of Common Courts, which came into force in 1929. That year, former attorney Wanda Grabińska-Wójtowicz was appointed the first woman judge in a children's court. In 1927, she had already applied for the position on the basis of the Polish constitution's equal rights guarantee for women and men in all public positions. Starting in 1930, she was the government's delegate to the Social Affairs Commission of the League of Nations as well as to the International Labour Organization, primarily working on the Set of Rules for Juvenile Courts, educational institutions and auxiliary bodies. In 1932 she resigned as a judge by decree of the President of the Republic of Poland to become, at the Ministry of Social Welfare, the head of the law section. In 1939, she escaped Poland with the help

[41] All citations and information from Ristikivi et al. (2022).

[42] Karčiauskaitė (2007).

[43] Trusiewicz (1932).

of the international women's movements networks first to Switzerland and then to London joining other Poles to fight the Nazis, and working with the Polish Government in exile in the department of Foreign Affairs as a social expert.

In 1932, several women judges worked in Poland or had applied for judgeship. Among them Janina Csáky Brzozowska (1929), Wanda Kamińska (1930), Maria Hasińska, Helena Lepiarzowa (1930 in Warsaw, 1932 transferred to Lviv), and Irena Wojnikonis (1930), Maria Podolszyńska (1931), Bogumiła Piekarska (1931), Izabella Szumanówna (1932), Irena Sierakowska (1932). There were perhaps seventeen female judges working in Poland before World War II.[44]

Czech women were not allowed to study at the university until the Austrian government opened the philosophic faculty in 1897 and medicine in 1900. The faculty of law remained closed to women until after the foundation of the Czechoslovak Republic in 1918. The number of female students was low at the beginning, between 5–7%. In 1923, Andela Kozáková-Jírová became the first woman to receive a law degree; she worked as a notary. In 1929, Matylda Mocová-Wíchová was the first woman admitted to the bar. In the academic year of 1913–14, there were 2154 students enrolled, while in 1930–31 there were 4495 studying law, 10% of them female. Legal education was based on two or three state exams, plus Czech citizenship, as in Austria and Germany. The 1920 Czechoslovak Constitution, under the new President Tomáš Garrigue Masaryk, guaranteed equal rights of women and men, including in employment and access to all public professions. Nonetheless, women were admitted to juries in 1920, but the judiciary remained closed to women even though they could work as attorneys. The Czech Association of University Women published a booklet, "The female lawyer", that described their situation and hinted at the fact that the civil service was closed to women because of a ministerial decree of September 1921 reacting to a woman applying in vain to the ministry of finance, which was a clear breach of the democratic constitution. Senator Františka Plaminková, president of the Czech National Council of Women, who was later executed by the Nazis, asked the Senate in 1927 and in 1928 why women could still not get access to state offices despite the constitution granting equal rights, especially in professions and state service: "How much superior was the belief of the learned Czech exile of the sixteenth century, Jean Amos Coménius, who saw no reason for excluding women from the study of languages and the sciences, including medicine and law, judging them capable of understanding everything and worthy of knowing everything! Three centuries later, we are still victims of prejudice in the country of Coménius, where the Minister of Education himself dares to go to the extent of attacking the constitution by refusing to women the rights it assures them."[45] In 1928 the Minister of Justice responded that access would need to be agreed with by the entire government, but that he planned to seek it. However, the Ministry of the

[44] Anonymous (1929a); Bachman L (1948); Dadej (2017, 2019); M.F. (1931); Kimble and Röwekamp (2018); Trusiewicz (1932).

[45] Anonymous (1927).

Interior argued that women did not have the capacity to understand the matters discussed, and the Ministry of Justice considered them only suitable in matters of guardianship and curatorial jurisdiction and non-contentious matters. In 1929, President Masaryk himself pointed to this problem in his jubilee speech, and that the judiciary could not find enough candidates to fill all necessary positions of judges. Still, the ministries refrained from employing women. The judiciary however opened its doors. In 1930, the Minister of Justice authorized women to qualify for the judgeships. There were special training courses for women, and four women were named as prospective judges, among them Ruth Beer (Mährisch-Ostrau) and Hertha Tiedge from Prague. The first woman finally appointed was Zdeňka Patschová. And immediately, Czech female judge received a special order as to what to wear in court: "A special gown is prescribed, as worn by the male judges. In addition, the female judges must wear white blouses that are closed up to the neck, a plain white collar and a black tie made of a shiny silk fabric. (That's worse than the papal audience!)"[46] The Czech Republic featured 86 women judges by 1937, 4% of the total number, and sixty women lawyers. Helene Bernadová was the first lawyer to by employed by the Foreign Ministry for diplomatic service.[47]

"German men resent feminine authority", former judge Marie Munk said in 1937, in a talk on sex inequality in the U.S.[48] She must have known because she was one of the first female judges in what is now called the Republic of Weimar. In Germany, women could study law because German states opened universities to women between 1900 and 1911. In Prussia, this happened only when the Ministries agreed that women could study law but not pass the required state exams to enter the legal professions. Only after women's suffrage in 1918, and with the new constitution from 1919 providing for equal rights for women in Art. 109, namely for civil service in Art. 128, a new law was passed on the admission of women to the offices and professions of justice, in 1922. It was a success of the German Female Lawyers Organization, established in 1914 to fight for access to the legal professions and also for equal rights of women and children. The organizations of attorneys and judges met to vote on the question whether women should be admitted to the bar and especially the judges were strongly opposed, as were lawyers within the justice administration. But the reference to women's rights in the new constitution were stronger. To help the women lawyers, the first 37 female members of parliament joined beyond party lines to push for the law admitting women to the legal professions. Eventually, Maria Otto became the first attorney in 1922, and the first woman to be appointed a judge was Maria Hagemeyer in 1928 in Prussia, followed by less than 10 women who became lifetime judges, before the Nazi regime, in 1933, first dismissed Jewish women, and two years later all women who were not yet admitted to the bar or lifetime judgeships. Many of them were

---

[46] Anonymous (1932).

[47] Anonymous (1930c); Anonymous (1929b); Anonymous (1929c); Mikulová (1936); Plamínková (1920); Rauchberg (1929); Zenska Rada (1928). Kimble and Röwekamp (2018).

[48] Anonymous (1937).

family law reformers, with Munk drafting a new family law proposal in the interwar time, and Hagemeyer drafting the new family law for West Germany after World War II.[49]

Austia was an exception in every regard. Women had gained suffrage in 1922, and access to German style legal education. Yet women were not admitted to the judiciary. To enter the "*Konzeptsdienst*" according to Article 3 of the "*Staatsgrundgesetz*" from 1878, candidates needed to pass exams, but that did not guarantee appointment. Article 18 stated the principal freedom to choose one's profession, but this proved to be weaker than Article 3. Thus, the government refused to appoint women until after World War II. Feminist Ernestine von Fürth asserted that Austria had no female judges due to a lack of understanding of gender equality in the Austrian elite, especially in the government, which was compounded by the weakness of the Austrian women's movement.[50]

3.3 Exception Spain: The Roman Law Countries

Spain was another exception to the European rule. It was exceptionally in the sense that it was the only country with a Roman law tradition in Europe that admitted women to the judiciary in the interwar time. It was also one of the last countries in which women began to organize to improve their status.[51] Compared to other Western European countries, Spain was dominantly rural and Catholic, yet also a federal state with very diverse regions united by an old and faltering monarchy and, in the 1920s, by military dictatorship under General Miguel Primo de Rivera. The triumph of the Second Republic in 1931 implied significant changes related to the transition into a democracy and a willingness to solve the deep social problems the country was suffering from. Regarding sex equality, women gained suffrage in May 1931 and in 1932 a new marriage law was passed giving women equal rights in the family.

Female attorneys worked in Spain since 1921, with famous ones like Victoria Kent and Clara Campoamor. In 1934, Teresa Argemí Meliá, attorney from Barcelona, turned to the Ministry of Justice claiming that according to articles 25, 36, 40 and others of the Constitution, women should be allowed to work as judges and in the judicial administration. She argued that the guarantees of equality of the sexes as well as the fact that women were allowed to work as notaries and in other public offices in the municipalities were strong precedent for opening the judiciary for women. But Minister of Justice Rafael Aizpún Santafé was absolutely opposed; he decreed on 16th of November 1934 that women were not allowed to work as regular or fiscal judges; to him, the condition was "that the candidate

[49] Röwekamp (2011).

[50] Anonymous (1928c); Beth (1931); Fürth (1929); Kimble and Röwekamp (2018).

[51] Röwekamp (2017); Vázquez Osuna (2009).

would be a man." Furthermore he argued "that among the functions exercised by Judges and Clerks, although there is none that by its nature cannot be performed by women, [...] they require conditions that education, especially in Spain, and nature together give to men as much as they deny it to women, apart from the possibility of other complications such as motherhood, which make the exercise of these professions totally unsuitable for women."[52]

The Civil War changed this: On December 2, 1936, Maria Lluïsa Algarra Coma was appointed by the Justice Department of the Catalonian Generalitat to be a judge of first instance in the city of Granollers. Born in Barcelona, she went to local schools and then studied at the Autonomous University of Catalonia. Yet with another change of government, Algarra was replaced by a male judge in February 1937, to then serve as an administrative helper in the Tribunal of Espionage, Defeatism and High Treason. But other women like Marta Dutrem, María de Tabassa, Ana Valls, Carmen Torres, María del Carmen Soler, Rosario Cuscó and Teresa Argemí were also judges of Catalonia tribunals.

At the borders of Europe, there were also changes. In Turkey, the Angora Government under Kemal Pascha appointed the first time two women as judges, Nizahet Hanum and Beghan Hanum.[53] In revolutionary Russia, women were admitted to law schools in 1906, but had an exceptionally difficult time in university and could not practice until 1917. When one woman came up as a defendant in a criminal case, the Chief Justice left the room in protest; later, women were entirely excluded from the Corporation of Lawyers. In May 1917, the government passed an act on the reorganization of the judicial system in Russia. It stated that "The office was to be elective, and fully qualified men and women to be eligible on equal terms."[54] Praskovya Danilova-Plotnikova was appointed the first female judge. During the Soviet period, involvement of women in the judiciary became a political topic, and reportedly, in 1924, women made up 13,7% of judges in the country, and 18,8% in 1926.

4 Conclusion

The story of the first female judges sheds light on the close relationship between suffrage and access to the judiciary. The latter was granted in countries where women had gained suffrage, as in the Nordic countries, Central Europe and Spain. In the Nordic countries we find female judges in the interwar period, but only in Norway did women gain suffrage and were immediately allowed to work as judges as early as 1913. In the other Nordic states, it took not only more time to gain

[52] Order of the Minister of Justice, 16.11.1934. Gaceta de Madrid, Nr. 324, 20.11.1934, pp. 1412–13.

[53] Anonymous (1926b), p. 250.

[54] Anonymous (1917); Sak and Krokos (1911); Sheepshansks (1918).

suffrage, but women were also not necessarily allowed to work in the judiciary even then. Prejudices against women sitting over men, and even sentencing, was unimaginable even in comparatively progressive societies, as in the Nordic countries. In fact, prejudices against women did not only prevent women's access to the bench, but impacted on the areas in which they were placed, namely juvenile and family law, even when they were admitted.

Next to the Nordic countries, the newly formed states and democracies in Central Europe are also interesting. They were either results of revolutions and/or established as new countries based on the contract of Versailles. Here, we find a mix between newly formed states and democracies willing to change and underline their tender attempts to democracy by integrating women as citizens. Part of this was access to the judiciary and other positions in civil service. But such negotiations were only made possible when women finally gained suffrage between 1918 and 1920, and when eight countries granted equal rights in the constitution. Suffrage only was not enough, as we can see in Great Britain where women gained partial suffrage in 1918 and full suffrage in 1928, but did not get access to the bench. To a lesser degree, this also exists in the Nordic countries where it often took decades after suffrage until women could access the judiciary.

The other ingredient in the recipe of success is the type of legal education. It greatly differs within Europe. Where countries allowed women access to the bench, they followed the idea of the German legal system with university studies qualifying for all legal professions. In this regard, the new democracies in the heart of Europe are a great example of an early attempt to include women into public life and grant more complete citizenship than women got in older democracies in Europe, such as France and Great Britain. Countries in Central Europe were a laboratory for new ideas about democracy and participation, and contributed to the emerging welfare states in which women in the interwar time were closely involved. Studies of women's citizenship beyond access to the legal professions show that they had hoped for more,[55] but they nonetheless got far more room and possibilities than women ever had before. Still, the missing citizenship rights as well as the link between democracy and women's lack of citizenship rights as well as its consequences for left or right totalitarianism remain a kind of riddle after this promising start into democracies and understudied.

The findings hint in the direction that the first female European judges are similar in their work for the feminist movement and equal rights for women, just like first female attorneys had done. These women were not only spearheading women's fight for equal rights in general but they also seem to have changed the law and the legal system by the way they worked. In addition to their awareness of and support for causes like juvenile protection and women's/human rights, women appear to be more likely to advance substantive justice. They seem to have preferred a more interdisciplinary approach rather than imposing strict adherence to dogmatic doctrine and universal principles. The atmosphere in the courtroom

[55] Feinberg (2006); Kimble and Röwekamp (2017, 2018); Röwekamp (2011, 2023, 2026).

mattered to them; they believed it should be more humane, and they often took more time to talk and deliberate.[56]

However, the study of obstacles to entering the judiciary uncovers long-standing prejudice towards women in these positions. Considering this, it is amazing how fast they changed. In all countries in Europe, it took less than 50 years, and thus less than the time the women's movement fought for equal rights in the family, to see more women in the judiciary than men. While women in the interwar time were more likely to work as attorneys because they could be married and have families, and access to the judiciary was much more restricted, the role models of today have changed to such an extent that we hardly find women in top law firms. Now, the judiciary tends to become a woman's domain, and not the world of lawyers.

Either way, the inclusion or exclusion of women from one or the other legal professions is an indicator of equal rights. Success like the early access of women to advocacy in France and Belgium also indicates a long-time exclusion from the judiciary. What can be seen as a success, like high numbers of women in the judiciary, can also be seen as an indicator that men do not attach the same prestige to these positions anymore, which then indicates another form of exclusion. What is important to see is that there are still strong but changing mechanisms of inclusion and exclusion for women in the legal professions. And this has a direct impact on the quality of our democracy and society.

References

Albisetti JC (2000) Portia Ante Portas: Women and the Legal Profession in Europe, ca. 1870–1925. J Soc Hist 33:825–857

Anonymous (1898) Vermischtes. Schweden. DJZ 3(1):15

Anonymous (1917) Women Judges. Int Women's News 10(11):154

Anonymous (1920) Sweden. Women's Admission to the Civil Service. Government Bill. Int Women's News 8(14):131

Anonymous (1923) Norsk Statsborgerret. Nylaende Tidsskrift for Kvindernes Sak 37(10):146–150

Anonymous (1925) Frauen als Richter. Die Frau 33(3):180

Anonymous (1926a) Sweden has quickly followed in the footsteps of Norway. Int Woman Suffr News 21(2):28

Anonymous (1926b) Woman Judge in Turkey. Equal Rights 13(31):250

Anonymous (1927) Mme. Plaminkova Pleads for Women. Equal Rights 12(14):91

Anonymous (1928a) Sweden. Woman of Today, 1.1.1928, 155

Anonymous (1928b) Finland. Women of Today, 1.1.1928, 123–124

Anonymous (1928c) Zur Lage der Juristinnen in Österreich. Die Frau 36: 502–503

Anonymous (1929a) Poland's Woman Judge. Equal Rights 15(27):37

Anonymous (1929b) Juristinnen im staatlichen Konzeptsdienst. Prager Tagblatt, 4.5.1929, 3–4

Anonymous (1929c) Frauen im juristischen Konzeptionsdienst, Behörden ablehnend. Prager Tagblatt 4.5.1929, 3

Anonymous (1930a) No Women Judges in France Yet. Equal Rights, June 7, 1930, 143

[56] Röwekamp (2013).

Anonymous (1930b) Finland's Swedish Women's Alliance, Landmarks of Finnish Women's Road to Equal Rights. Equal Rights 15, 52:414–415
Anonymous (1930c) Feminist Notes: Training Women to be Judges. Equal Rights 13(16):104
Anonymous (1932) Die tschechischen Richterinnen erhalten ein eigenes Kostüm. Salzburger Wacht 252:3
Anonymous (1933) Denmark Appoint Woman Judge. Equal Rights 16.9.1933, 262
Anonymous (1937) German Woman Judge Here: Dr. Marie Munk Says Countrymen Resent Feminine Authority. Los Angel. Times, 15.10.1937, 12
Anonymous (1939) Denmark Appoints Second Woman Judge. Christ Monit, 8.2.1939, 6
Anwar S, Bayer P, Hjalmarsson R (2019) A Jury of Her Peers: The Impact of the First Female Jurors on Criminal Convictions. Econ J 129:603–650
Bachman L (1948) Women in Poland. WLJ 34:17–36
Beth M (1931) Die Eignung der Frau zum Richterberuf. Die Österreicherin 1:3–4
BGE (1887) 13, I: 1–6, Staatsrechtliche Entscheidungen, Urtheil vom 29. Januar 1887, https://www.servat.unibe.ch/dfr/pdf/c1013001.pdf. Accessed 29 Oct 2025
Blackstone W (1809) Commentaries on the Laws of England. Book the Third. T. Cadell & W. Davies, London
Bock G (2000) Frauen in der europäischen Geschichte: Vom Mittelalter bis zur Gegenwart. Beck, München
Boigeol A (1996) Les femmes et les cours: la difficile mise en oeuvre de l'égalité des sexes dans l'accès à la magistrature. Genèses 22:107–129
Cornett JM (1997). Hoodwink'd by Custom: The Exclusion of Women from Juries in Eighteenth-Century English Law and Literature. Wm Mary J Women L. 4, 1:1–89
Dadej I (2017) "The Napoleonic Civil Code is to Blame for my Decision to Study Law": Female Law Students and Lawyers in the Second Polish Republic (1918–1939). In: Kimble S K, Röwekamp M (eds) New Perspectives on European Women's Legal History. Routledge, New York, pp 217–246
Dadej I (2019) Beruf und Berufung Transnational. Deutsche und polnische Akademikerinnen in der Zwischenkriegszeit. Trafo, Osnabrück
Delfosse M (1994) Emilie Kempin Spyri (1853–1901). Das Wirken der ersten Schweizer Juristin. Schulthess, Zurich
Dübeck I (2007) Reflexionen über Frauen als Rechtswissenschaftler. In: Eckert J, Letto-Vanamo P, Modéer KÅ (eds) Juristen im Ostseeraum. Dritter Rechtshistorikertag im Ostseeraum 20.–22. Mai 2004. Peter Lang, Frankfurt am Main, pp 19–29
Feinberg M (2006) Elusive Equality. Gender, Citizenship, and the Limits of Democracy in Czechoslovakia, 1918–1950. University of Pittsburg Press, Pittsburg
Feldner B (2000) Der Ausschluss der Frau vom römischen *officium*. Revue Internationale Des Droits de l'Antiquité (RIDA):381–396
Frank L (1889) The Woman Lawyer: In View of Mlle. Popelin. Chic Law Times 3:80–81
Führt E (1929) Was wird aus unseren Juristinnen? Die Österreicherin 2(4):3
Høg M (1914) Norske Kvinder. Berg & Hugh, Kristiania
Holm G (2015) Håndbog for feminister (og deres modstandere). Lindhardt og Ringhof, Kopenhagen
Johannsen W (2023) Elisa Ussing i Dansk Kvindebiografisk Leksikon på lex.dk. https://kvindebiografiskleksikon.lex.dk/Elisa_Ussing Accessed 29 Dec 2023
Karčiauskaitė I (2007) Katalikiškoji moterų judėjimų srovė Lietuvoje (1907–1940). VDU Lietuvos istorijos institutas, PhD Kaunas
Kempin E (1895) Die Rechtsstellung der Frau. Richard Taendler, Berlin
Kimble SL (2008) "No right to judge": Feminism and the Judiciary in Third Republic France. Fr Hist Stud 31:609–641
Kimble SL (2019) Of "Masculine Tyranny" and the "Women's Jury": The Gender Politics of Jury Service in Third Republic France. Law Hist Rev 27:867–902

Kimble SL (2023) Political Engagement by "apolitical" Female European Lawyers: The International Federation of Women Judges and Lawyers, 1928–1956. Clio@Themis 25: 342–366
Kimble SL, Röwekamp M (2017) New Perspectives on European Women's Legal History. Routledge, New York
Kimble SL, Röwekamp M (2018) Exclusion and Inclusion in the Legal Professions: Negotiating Gender in Central Europe, 1887–1945. Acta Poloniae Historica 117:52–93
Korpiola M (2018) Attempting to Advocate: Women Entering the Legal Profession in Finland, 1885–1915. In: Kimble SL, Röwekamp M (eds) New Perspectives on European Women's Legal History. Routledge, New York, pp 292–318
Logan A (2005) "A Suitable Person for Suitable Cases": The Gendering of Juvenile Courts in England, c.1910–39. Twent Century Br Hist 16:129–145
Logan A (2006) Professionalism and the Impact of England's First Women Justices, 1920–1950. Hist J 49:833–850
Logan A (2013) "Building a New and Better Order"? Women and Jury Service in England and Wales, c 1920–70. Women's Hist Rev 22:701–716
Logan A (2017) Feminism and Criminology in Britain, 1910–1950. In: Kimble SK, Röwekamp M (eds) New Perspectives on European Women's Legal History. Routledge, New York, pp 272–291
Mackenroth A (1898) Die weibliche Advokatur. Kosmodike Zeitung für den Internationalen Rechtsverkehr 7:145–151
Martin M (2000) The Almanac of Women and Minorities in World Politics. Westview Press, Boulder, Colorado
M.F. (1931) Une femme juge: Wanda Grabinska, in: Le movement féministe: organe official des publications de l'alliance nationale des sociétés féminines suisses 19(354):1
Mikulová M (1936) Žena v právním řádě československém: avec un résumé français. Nákladem vlastním, Praha
Mórek F, von Welczeck A (1910) Norwegische Frauen als Kommunalbeamte und Geschworene. Die Frauenbewegung 16(14):110
Offen K (2000) European Feminisms, 1700–1950. A Political History. Stanford University Press, Stanford
Olgiati V (2003) The Case of the First (Failed) Woman Lawyer in Modern Italy. In: Schultz U, Shaw G (eds) Women in the World's Legal Professions. Hart, Oxford, pp 419–436
Ostrogorski M (1893) The Rights of Women. A Comparative Study in History and Legislation. Swan Sonnenschein & Co, London
Pastović D (2016) "Defect of Sex": Exclusion of Women from Jury Service in Istria 1873–1918. JEHL 7:155–171
Pedersen S (2001) The Maternalist Movement in British Colonial Policy: The Controversy over "Child Slavery" in Hong Kong 1917–1941. Past Present 171:161–202
Pierantoni A (1896) Gli avvocati nell'antica Roma: Studio storico dell'avvocato. Tipografia elzeviriana, Roma
Plamínková F (1920) The Political Rights of Women in the Czechoslovak Republic. Gazette de Prague, Prague
Poët L (1881) Studio sulla condizione della donna rispetto al diritto costituzionale e al diritto amministrativo nelle elezioni. Chiantore & Mascarelli, Pinerolo
Quam (1913) Norway. The First Woman Judge. Jus Sufragii 8(1):7
Quam (1914) Norway: The First Woman Nominated Sworn Attorney of the Judge of a District in Norway. Jus Sufragii 8(10):125
Rauchberg H (1929) Juristinnen im Staatsdienst. Prager Tagblatt 7.5.1929:1
Ringwald E (1931/32) Swiss Women at the Bar. Women Lawyer's J 19:10–13
Ringwald E (1932/33) Die Juristin in der Schweiz. Die Frau 40:44–47.
Ristikivi M, Luts-Sootak M, Räis H (2022) Women's Access to the Profession of Judiciary in Estonia in 1922–1940s: Rules and Reality. Leg Gen Stud 19:85–109

Röwekamp M (2011) Die ersten deutschen Juristinnen: Eine Geschichte ihrer Professionalisierung und Emanzipation (1900–1945). Böhlau, Cologne

Röwekamp M (2013) First Female Judges in the Weimar Republic in Germany: Reflections on Difference. In: Schultz U, Shaw G (eds) Gender and Judging. Hart, Oxford, Portland, pp 103–121

Röwekamp M (2017) Profession und Exil: Spanisch-republikanische Juristinnen im Exil. Ariadne 72:35–43

Röwekamp, M. (2022). Challenging Patriarchism in the Family: Law Reform and Female Protest in European Modern History. In: Vujadinović D, Krstić I (eds), Gender Perspective in Law. Springer, Heidelberg, pp 109–122

Röwekamp M (2026, forthcoming) "The Constitution is only a Meaningless Piece of Paper." Citizenship, Constitution and the Limits of Equality for Women in Central Europe (1918–1933). In: Goldmann M, Menéndez A J (eds) Weimar Moments, Oxford University Press, Oxford

Sak N, Krokos A (1911) Russia. Int Women's News 3(6):29–30

Salis M von (1884) Unter neuen Fahnen. Weibliche Studenten. Thurgauer Zeitung 122, 24.5.1884, 5

Santoni de Sio F (1884) La Donna e l'Avvocatura. Studio giuridico-sociale. La questione giuridica. Tipografia della Nueva Roma, Rome

Schandevyl E (2014) Women in Law and Lawmaking in Nineteenth and Twentieth-Century Europe. Ashgate Publishing House, Farnham

Schandevyl E (2017) Women and the Courts in Twentieth-Century Belgium: an Historical Perspective. In: Kimble S K, Röwekamp M (eds) New Perspectives on European Women's Legal History. Routledge, New York, pp 152–173

Sheepshanks M (1918) Equal Eligibility of Women with Men for all Public Offices and Employments. Int Woman Suffr News 12:150–151

Silius H (2003) Women Jurists in Finland at the Turn of the Century: Breakthrough or Intermezzo? In: Schultz U, Shaw G (eds) Women in the World's Legal Professions. Hart, Oxford, Portland, pp 287–400

Sørensen R (1913) Nylaende Tidsskrift for Kvindernes Sak 27(15):272

Støren T (1984) Justitias døtre: de første kvinnelige jurister i Norge. Universitets-forlage, Oslo

Svensson E (2011) Forskaren Elsa Eschelsson — en modern civilist i tiden. Kvinnliga akademikers förening, Stockholm

Trolle Önnerfor E (2018) Birgit Spångberg. Svenskt kvinnobiografiskt lexikon. http://www.skbl.se/sv/artikel/BirgitSpangberg. Accessed 15 Dec 2023

Trusiewicz A (1932) Women in Polish National Culture. Int Women's News 26:140

Vázquez Osuna F (2009) Las primeras mujeres juezas y fiscales españolas (1931–1939). Arenal - Revista de historia de las mujeres 16:133–150

Zenska R (1928) Tchechoslovaquie. Int Woman Suffr News 7(22):114–115

Marion Röwekamp is a historian and a full-fledged lawyer. She was the owner of the Wilhelm and Alexander von Humboldt Chair of the DAAD at the Colegio de México in Mexico City. Previously, she worked several times in the USA (2000/2001 Columbia University, New York City, 2007 Five Women College Studies and Research Center, South Hadley/MA, 2009/2010 John F. Kennedy Fellow at the Center for European Studies, Harvard), in Mexico (Colegio de México, Instituto de Investigaciones Históricas of UNAM in Mexico City) and the Latin American Institute of the Free University of Berlin.

Gender Diversity in the Judiciary: A Matter of Law? An Approach Under the European Court of Human Rights

Saadet Yüksel

Abstract International discourse surrounding 'gender balance' or 'gender diversity' in public decision-making has tended to focus on political roles or institutions, rather than their judicial counterparts. However, there has been substantial progress towards considering the lack of gender diversity in the composition of the judiciary, but little consideration of distinctly legal approaches, thus gender diversity in the judiciary *as a matter of law*. The chapter will commence by outlining some of the wider issues surrounding gender diversity and the judiciary. Ultimately, it seeks to mainly analyse the jurisprudence of the European Court of Human Rights, together with the standards set out by the Council of Europe. It is widely acknowledged that positive measures for compositional diversity constitute an important means of removing, to varying extents depending on the measure, gender diversity in the judiciary from the mercy of political whim. However, misunderstandings regarding the nature and role of gender diversity within the judiciary, in relation to the broader pursuit of gender equality, can lead to positive measures going no further than achieving "token" diversity—that is to say, a merely symbolic and fragile form. Therefore, while the prospects of a supportive approach by the European Court of Human Rights remain open, the realisation of its emancipatory potential may likely turn on the Court's characterisation of the nature and role of gender diversity in the judiciary.

I sincerely thank my legal assistant at the Court, Ms Xhulia Tepshi, for her invaluable assistance during the research and drafting process.

For further discussion on token diversity please see Kenney (2013).

S. Yüksel (✉)
European Court of Human Rights, Strasbourg, France
e-mail: Saadet.Yuksel@echr.coe.int

© The Author(s), under exclusive license to Springer Nature Switzerland AG 2025

S. Baer et al. (eds.), *The Gender and the Judiciary*, Gender Perspectives in Law 7,
https://doi.org/10.1007/978-3-032-06885-9_3

1 Introduction

The late Lady Justice Ruth Bader Ginsburg once hauntingly recounted *"When I'm sometimes asked when will there be enough [female judges on the US Supreme Court bench] and I say, 'When there are nine,' people are shocked. But there'd been nine men, and nobody's ever raised a question about that."*

Ginsburg's sentiment reflects a very real issue which permeates contemporary debates on and measures for the promotion of gender diversity in the judiciary. The term "gender diversity" is described in relation to the respective hetero- or homogeneity of a given group from the aspect of its members' gender.[1] One speaks of a gender-diverse group where the gender identities of its members are characterized by a high level of heterogeneity. Inversely, a lack of gender diversity denotes a group made up of members with widely homogenous gender identities.[2] The judicial profession has historically been marked by the latter, with a high level of gender homogeneity amongst its members, having been invariably dominated by the male gender.

To name but a few, the predecessor of the International Court of Justice (ICJ), the Permanent Court of International Justice (PCIJ), existed from 1922 to 1946 and saw 31 judges and 8 deputy judges come and go during its lifetime. Amongst these legal professionals, none were women. Despite having been established as early as 1945, it was only in 1995 that member states elected the late Baroness Rosalyn C. Higgins as the first female judge to the ICJ.[3] Similarly, the European Court of Human Rights (ECtHR) only saw its first female judge with the appointment of Helga Pedersen in 1971, more than 22 years after the Court's inception in January 1959.[4] And this trend amongst the international judiciary is also reflected in its domestic counterparts. Similar figures can be reported for the U.S. Supreme Court where of the 116 judges who have served in the court only 6 have been women.[5]

While women have gained more seats in the judiciary in the past decades, their occupation of high judicial offices is still a relative rarity. In the 2021 edition of its yearly report "Government at a Glance", the OECD detailed that, as of 2018, women made up an average of 61% of the judiciary in OECD-EU countries.[6] This is, however, only superficially encouraging. The average share of female judges in

[1] Lehmann Nielsen and Madsen (2017), p. 79.

[2] Lehmann Nielsen and Madsen (2017), p. 79.

[3] United Nations, "International Court of Justice names its first female president" *UN News* (6 February 2006), https://news.un.org/en/story/2006/02/168,322.

[4] Keller et al. (2020), p. 187.

[5] Andrea Kmak, "Fast facts about our female U.S. Supreme Court justices" *Illinois State Bar Association* (December 2018), https://www.isba.org/committees/women/newsletter/2018/12/fastfactsaboutourfemaleussupremecou.

[6] OECD, Government at a Glance, 2021 Report, https://www.oecd-ilibrary.org/sites/2f520410-en/index.html?itemId=/content/component/2f520410-en.

first instance courts across OECD-EU countries in 2018 amounted to around 63%, and their share in second instance courts to circa 54%.[7] But numbers reported by OECD-EU countries differ starkly when it comes to high and supreme courts; the share of female judges in the supreme courts of OECD-EU countries in 2018 recorded a value of merely 36%.[8]

Gender diversity, apart from being a noble end in itself, is widely regarded as crucial also in ensuring the legitimacy and effectiveness of a given legal system and its judiciary. As such, it is argued in contemporary scholarship, as discussed below, that a gender-diverse composition of the judiciary is pivotal for that institution to be truly reflective and representative of the societies it adjudicates on, and in turn, it is this representation which garners widespread trust in and identification with the judiciary and guarantees that its rulings are accepted and complied with. Scholars furthermore emphasize the innovation potential that can be brought about by a higher level of gender diversity amongst a judiciary's members. In this sense, commentators have highlighted how female judges can enrich a judiciary with their understanding of roles and responsibilities within their communities and bring gendered sensibility in decision-making processes.[9] This way, as will be discussed further, a higher share of female judges in judiciaries is conducive to abandoning the historically androcentric nature of law and adopting a gender-sensitive approach in the development of the law. In light of these benefits, the current number of appointments of female judges may seem far from fulfilling the promises of a truly gender-diverse judiciary.

This chapter aims to shed light on the current state of female representation in the judiciary. It seeks to specifically showcase how prevalent attitudes and measures adopted in the spirit of strengthening gender diversity amongst members of the judiciary may result in a numerical or symbolic form of diversity. To this end, this chapter will show how the absence of female judges in high domestic and international courts may hinder many of the promises of a gender-diverse judiciary from coming to fruition. The same may be shown to be true for the situation in which women, while represented on the bench, still find themselves greatly outnumbered by their male colleagues. Within this context, this chapter will start with a discussion of positive diversity measures *à la* female quotas from a long-term perspective. Ultimately, the argument will be that the key to a truly and substantively gender-diverse judiciary may lie in a culture change that affects the conceptualization of the nature and role of gender diversity in the judiciary. To this end, this chapter will explore international human rights law in general, and especially the jurisprudence of the European Court of Human Rights, together with the standards set out by the Council of Europe, with a view to discerning supportive anchors for gender diversity in the judiciary which go beyond the support of mere token diversity but generate

---

[7] OECD (2021).

[8] OECD (2021).

[9] Hunter (2015), p. 124.

a real change of mentality. Only then the late Lady Justice Ginsburg's declaration, that there will only be enough women on the US Supreme Court when there are nine, may not be so shocking.

2 The Basis of Gender Diversity in International Human Rights Law—CEDAW

The modern imperative of gender diversity seems to be grounded firmly in international human rights law. Before embarking on an analysis of gender diversity in the judiciary and the measures necessary to achieve it, one must first shed some light on this underlying legal basis.

As also acknowledged by the Organization for Security and Co-operation in Europe (OSCE), "all international human rights and non-discrimination conventions are applicable to all spheres of private and public life, including the judiciary."[10] The instrument which could be considered the prime international convention on gender—and sex-based discrimination is the Convention on the Elimination of All Forms of Discrimination Against Women (CEDAW).[11] The provisions of CEDAW, *inter alia*, condemn unequivocally any form of discrimination against women (see Article 2 CEDAW), oblige State Parties to take measures to ensure the full development and advancement of women, in particular in the political, social, economic and cultural fields (see Article 3 CEDAW), and demand that State Parties take all appropriate measures to modify men's and women's social and cultural patterns of conduct to achieve the elimination of ideas and practices based on female inferiority. Article 7 CEDAW furthermore compels State Parties to take all appropriate measures to eliminate discrimination against women in the political and public life of the country, and this includes in particular the right to hold public office (Article 7(b) CEDAW). In addition, Article 4(1) CEDAW states that special measures temporarily adopted by State Parties with a view to accelerating *de facto* equality between men and women do not constitute discrimination for the purposes of the Convention.

What then do these provisions tell us about gender diversity in the judiciary? It is clear that CEDAW prohibits the discriminatory exclusion of women from judicial office. Apart from curtailing actual discrimination, however, State Parties are also explicitly called upon to actively promote gender equality and women's inclusion in the public and political life of their countries. This includes holding public offices

---

[10] OSCE Mission to Skopje, Gender and Diversity in the Judiciary, December 2021, https://www.osce.org/files/f/documents/1/7/531194.PDF.

[11] UN General Assembly, Convention on the Elimination of All Forms of Discrimination Against Women, (18 December 1979), United Nations, Treaty Series, vol. 1249, https://www.refworld.org/docid/3ae6b3970.html.

which encompasses judicial posts. To achieve gender diversity in these spheres, the Convention allows for the adoption of specifically targeted measures.

In CEDAW General Recommendation No. 33,[12] the CEDAW Committee specifically addressed women's access to justice. Apart from stressing a number of structural impediments and obstacles faced by women trying to realize their right to equal access to justice,[13] the Committee also emphasised the importance of women's participation as professionals in all bodies and on all levels of judicial systems.[14] To remove barriers to women's equal representation within the judiciary and other law implementing institutions, the Committee *inter alia* recommended that State Parties introduce temporary special measures.[15]

In General Recommendation No. 25,[16] the CEDAW Committee comments on the nature and effectivity of temporary special measures. There, the Committee made sure to emphasize that a purely formal legal approach cannot suffice to achieve equality between men and women, and to ensure gender diversity in public institutions.[17] Instead, these goals could only be realized by an effective strategy which actually aims to overcome the underrepresentation of women in public life and redistribute resources and power between men and women.[18]

International human rights law on gender equality as reflected in CEDAW could therefore be interpreted to encompass and offer a concrete legal basis for the realization of gender diversity in the judiciary. To this end, CEDAW legally sanctions and could, in fact, be said to encourage the implementation of positive special measures such as gender quotas.

3 Positive Measures and the Question of "Token" Diversity

It is not only CEDAW which is formally preoccupied with positive measures as a means to achieve gender diversity in the judiciary. Accordingly, such measures have indeed often been applied in practice to ensure increased female representation in other public or private decision-making bodies, including national parliaments and corporate boards respectively. Continuously, however, the application of positive measures for the purposes of achieving gender diversity has been associated with mere "tokenism".

[12] Committee on the Elimination of Discrimination Against Women (CEDAW), CEDAW General Recommendation No. 33: Women's access to justice, (2015).

[13] CEDAW General Recommendation No. 33: Women's access to justice, (2015), para. 3.

[14] CEDAW General Recommendation No. 33: Women's access to justice, (2015), para. 15(f).

[15] CEDAW General Recommendation No. 33: Women's access to justice, (2015), para. 15(f).

[16] Committee on the Elimination of Discrimination Against Women (CEDAW), CEDAW General Recommendation No. 25: Temporary special measures, (2004).

[17] CEDAW General Recommendation No. 25: Temporary special measures, paras. 7–8.

[18] CEDAW General Recommendation No. 25: Temporary special measures, para. 8.

The concept of tokenism denotes "the practice or policy of admitting an extremely small number of members of racial [...], ethnic [...], or gender [...] groups [...] to give the impression of being inclusive, when in actuality these groups are not welcomed".[19] A crucial characteristic of tokenism is that the respective institutions' attempts to fulfil their obligations with regard to an established target (such as the appointment of a set number of women within a court) are implemented in ways which do not actually challenge men-dominated power and/or institutional arrangements.[20] In the field of gender diversity (but also other kinds of diversity), the measures that could be considered most closely associated with tokenism are quotas. As such, gender quotas are positive measures which establish "a defined proportion (percentage) or number of places or seats to be filled by, or allocated to, women and/or men".[21]

In the literature, positive measures such as gender quotas are discussed in close affiliation with tokenism and indeed explained to partially contribute to this phenomenon. When it comes to gender diversity specifically, a particular form of tokenism prevalent in this context has come to be known as the "Smurfette" or "Snow White" principle.[22] Inspired by the comic books surrounding the *Smurfs* amongst which lives only one female, the *Smurfette*, or alternatively, the tale of Snow White who lives as the only woman amongst seven dwarfs, this principle "refers to the (visual) role of a single woman amidst a group of men".[23] Where gender quotas only manage to import a relatively small number of women into a judicial bench, it is observed that this positive measure ends up not serving the fulfilment of the benefits expected from increased gender diversity within the judiciary.[24] Indeed, it has been argued how gender quotas may actually affirm the maleness of the (high) judicial office and sensationalize female judges as odd exceptions otherwise confirming the rule.[25] Conversely, when a certain threshold of representation is met, studies show that substantive change can come about.[26] But what are the benefits hoped to be reaped from a gender-diverse judiciary? Why is the existence of female judges said to be not only important but actually necessary for the life of the judiciary?

As already briefly touched upon in the introduction, it is considered that the presence of female judges increases the democratic legitimacy of a given judiciary as a bench including female judges becomes more representative of the society it

[19] Ruby (2021), 675, referencing Riccucci (2008), p. 132.

[20] European Institute for Gender Equality, "tokenism", https://eige.europa.eu/publications-resources/thesaurus/terms/1261?language_content_entity=en.

[21] European Institute for Gender Equality, "gender quotas", https://eige.europa.eu/publications-resources/thesaurus/terms/1304?language_content_entity=en.

[22] See in general Lijnzaad (2020).

[23] Lijnzaad (2020), p. 30.

[24] See discussion in Hunter (2015).

[25] Lijnzaad (2020), p. 31.

[26] Collins et al. (2010) p. 264.

serves and adjudicates on.[27] This representation is said to then contribute positively to raising public confidence in the judiciary and its development of the legal system.[28] Therefore, gender diversity in a given judiciary is considered to serve to reduce the sense of courts being isolated from the society they serve and ultimately enhance legitimacy.[29]

Apart from increasing the judiciary's and legal system's democratic legitimacy and public support, the inclusion of female judges on benches is also seen as a way to raise gender-awareness in the courts. Feminist legal scholars have written extensively on the law's role in constructing gender and vice-versa.[30] To quote Rosemary Hunter et al. "law does not simply operate on pre-existing gendered realities but contributes to the construction of those realities".[31] It is argued that the law, having been historically dominated by men and still constructed from a male perspective, necessarily centers men in a way which renders the law an instrument of male supremacy. Whether or not one subscribes to the idea that law has been purposefully designed to disadvantage and dominate women, what is said to remain true is that policies by men and for men "have fit badly with women's lives".[32] Therefore, increasing gender diversity in the judiciary by including, for a start, women in the profession might make a difference in the future development of the law by eliminating the persisting effects of "conventional legal doctrines, developed by men in a society dominated by men, [that] have a fundamental male bias even when they are ostensibly gender-neutral".[33] Indeed, commentators claim that the elimination of gender bias in the corpus of law is one of the principal tasks of the judiciary in contemporary democracies.[34] The unveiling and eradication of the law's male bias is explained to possibly entail "uncovering how law was moulded by male life experiences and values and aiming to change it by writing women's life experiences and values into such legal principles as justice and freedom".[35]

Assuming that these are indeed the expected and desired outcomes of heightened gender diversity amongst the members of the judiciary, one must now ask whether positive measures *à la* quotas, as provided for and encouraged by CEDAW, actually serve that goal. One question is, then, whether quotas empower female judges to make a real impact on the reception of the judiciary and its delivery of justice. One aspect to consider is the aforementioned "Smurfette

[27] See Lady Hale of Richmond (2017), p. 184, as referenced in Kessedjian (2022), pp. 196–197.

[28] Lijnzaad (2020), p. 31; see also Ruiz (2019).

[29] See Lady Hale of Richmond (2017), p. 184, as referenced in Kessedjian (2022), pp. 196–197. See also Caielli (2018), pp. 160–161 highlighting the increased call for representative judiciaries and the role of diversity in the debate.

[30] Caielli (2018), p. 167. For further references see also D. Vujadinović et al. (eds.) (2023) Gender-Competent Legal Education.

[31] Caielli (2018), p. 167, referencing Hunter et al. (2010).

[32] Baer (2011), p. 307.

[33] Baer (2011), p. 306.

[34] Caielli (2018), pp. 167–168.

[35] Dahl (1987), p. 55, as referenced in Caelli (2018), p. 168.

principle" which is said to occur where a gender quota imports a relatively small number of women into male-dominated institutions and fails to bring about substantive gender equality beyond mere token gender diversity. In addition, it is argued that empirical studies have shown that where the Smurfette principle manifests within the judiciary, female judges may even distance themselves from appearances of difference.[36]

However, it is acknowledged in the literature that there is hardly any tangible difference in decision-making between male and female judges, for which there are many and perhaps simultaneous reasons. But one pertinent explanation relates directly to female judges continuing to be outnumbered by their male colleagues.[37] As set forth by Baroness Helena Kennedy, a sentiment that persists amongst female judges (and perhaps, unfortunately, even the wider public) is that women have been "let in" to the judiciary on the condition that they conform to the prevailing masculine ethos at the bench.[38] This is described as female judges "selling" their own voices to be allowed to enter the courtroom.[39]

Indeed, several studies conducted on female judges in several different jurisdiction, including those of England and Wales and Germany, have empirically confirmed the unwillingness of women and other non-traditional judges to step out of line and their need to eliminate any perception of difference between themselves and their colleagues so as to establish their judicial authority and be respected by their peers and the judicial hierarchy.[40] Such performances of neutrality are explained to not only be rooted in subjective anxieties; they are in fact objectively enforced by the structure of the judicial hierarchy. Accordingly, the knowledge that there are more male judges in the higher courts who would be the ones to hear their cases' appeals may already be taken to push female judges towards stifling their own opinions and following the lines of their male colleagues and higher-ups.[41] Given the statistics that show that female judges are overwhelmingly represented in lower courts, while still a clear minority of high court benchers, such structural pressures into neutrality seem particularly understandable and acute. Some scholars have even pointed out how gender quotas in and of themselves reinforce the imaginary of the (high) judiciary as an inherently masculine institution. Accordingly, the introduction of singular "Smurfettes" to the judicial bench is argued to affirm the relevant female judges as constituting mere exceptions to the general rule of the quintessentially male judiciary.[42]

But what follows from these observations? Are gender quotas best abandoned in the pursuit of a gender-diverse judiciary? Scholarship on gender diversity in the

---

[36] See Hunter (2015), p. 127.

[37] Hunter (2015), pp. 126–127.

[38] Helena Kennedy (1978), as referenced in Hunter (2015), p. 127.

[39] Rackley (2013), as also referenced in Hunter (2015), p. 127.

[40] See Hunter (2015), p. 127, see also in general Sommerlad (2013), or Schultz (2003).

[41] Sommerlad (2013), p. 367.

[42] Lijnzaad (2020), p. 31.

judiciary accepts it as known fact that where gender quotas achieve the appointment of women in cohorts to form a significant share of judges on the bench, that may overcome the Smurfette syndrome and its negative impact on the ability of female judges to speak their minds and fulfil the promises of a gender-diverse judiciary.[43] If executed correctly, thus moving beyond a performance of mere symbolic female inclusion, gender quotas might contribute to achieving substantive gender diversity and equality within the judiciary without falling victim to tokenism.

Numbers matter, but they are thus not all that counts. It could therefore be concluded that for positive measures to have the desired effect, it may also be necessary to bring about a culture change on the perception of the role and nature of gender diversity within the judiciary. To this end, gender diversity would have to cease to be regarded as a "women's only interest" and indeed come to be widely accepted as indispensable to any judiciary operating in a modern democracy.

4 Gender Diversity and the Judiciary Under the Council of Europe and the ECtHR

Law carries a prescriptive as well as normative quality. As such, it is particularly well-equipped to not only reflect but also trigger changes in formerly prevalent societal beliefs and attitudes. Accordingly, law may be able to increase support for the achievement of substantive gender diversity amongst members of the judiciary and the effective employment of positive measures such as gender quotas. Given its cross-border jurisdiction and its authority on anti-discrimination and general human rights matters, the ECtHR has a special potential, and responsibility, to legally define the relationship between gender diversity and the judiciary and strengthen the value placed on a gender-diverse judiciary.

Article 14 of the European Convention on Human Rights (ECHR) prohibits discrimination in the enjoyment of the rights and freedoms enshrined in the Convention on any ground, including sex, and Protocol No. 12 to the ECHR expanded the provisions of Article 14 of the Convention. As such, Protocol No. 12 provides a general non-discrimination clause, affording protection beyond the enjoyment of the specific rights and freedoms outlined in the Convention.

A document which, while not constituting binding law, may nevertheless guide the Court's decision-making is the "Council of Europe Plan of Action on Strengthening Judicial Independence and Impartiality".[44] Addressing the judiciary specifically, the Action Plan stresses that, in the composition of tribunals and the judiciary, states must adequately take into account society as a whole so as to

[43] Kessedjian (2022), pp. 207–208.

[44] Council of Europe, Council of Europe Plan of Action on Strengthening Judicial Independence and Impartiality, 2016, https://rm.coe.int/1680700285.

increase public confidence in judicial institutions.[45] To this end, the Action Plan highlights that states should consider adopting policies aimed at ensuring gender diversity and representation of society as a whole in the judiciary.[46]

The ECtHR thus has at its disposal legal provisions and a soft law guideline to firmly anchor the need for a gender-diverse judiciary in its case-law. Until recently, the Court has not heard a case directly concerning gender discrimination in the context of appointment to judicial office or similar. That being said, the Court has developed a strong body of case-law endorsing some general approaches to gender diversity in the context of other instances of gender discrimination.[47]

In its first gender discrimination case of *Abdulaziz Cabales and Balkandali v. the United Kingdom*,[48] the Court declared that "the advancement of the equality of sexes is today a major goal in the member States of the Council of Europe",[49] and that "very weighty reasons would have to be advanced before a difference of treatment on the ground of sex could be regarded as compatible with the Convention".[50] This proactive language shows the Court's readiness to take measures to advance gender equality and therefore gender diversity within the judiciary. However, *Abdulaziz, Cabales, and Balkandali v. the United Kingdom* marks the Court's adoption of the 'sameness approach' to sex equality, intended as a strict level of scrutiny where persons experience differential treatment on the basis of their gender.

However, this approach of sameness has not always been applied rigidly, with the Court showing a certain level of flexibility in this matter. In this sense, depending on the facts, the Court has been more than ready to grant respondent states in gender discrimination cases a wider or narrower margin of appreciation. Previous commentators have attempted to classify this jurisprudence so as to identify facts or themes on which the Court adopts a more lenient or strict application of the sameness approach.[51] The cases in which the Court granted only little leeway to justify persons' differential treatment due to their sex concerned three thematic areas: (i) cases in which (stereotype-based) differences between men and women were advanced as justification for their different treatment; (ii) cases of alleged indirect discrimination; and (iii) challenges to discriminatory policies on family surnames.

---

[45] Council of Europe, Council of Europe Plan of Action on Strengthening Judicial Independence and Impartiality, 2016, p. 11, para. G.

[46] Council of Europe, Council of Europe Plan of Action on Strengthening Judicial Independence and Impartiality, 2016, p. 11, para. G.

[47] For a discussion of the role of a gendered human rights approach in the field of new technologies please see: Yüksel (2022), p. 281.

[48] *Abdulaziz Cabales and Balkandali v. the United Kingdom* (No. 9214/80; 9473/81; 9474/81, 24 April 1985).

[49] *Abdulaziz Cabales and Balkandali v. the United Kingdom*, para. 78.

[50] *Abdulaziz Cabales and Balkandali v. the United Kingdom*, para. 78.

[51] See for example mapping made by Radacic (2009).

Examples of this first category of cases are *Abdulaziz, Cabales, and Balkandali v. the United Kingdom*, *Schuler-Zgraggen v. Switzerland*,[52] and *Karlheinz Schmidt v. Germany*.[53] What they have in common is that the respective governments attempted to justify differentiated treatment of men and women in various spheres of public law on the basis of women's allegedly different working patterns and biological factors. In *Abdulaziz v. the United Kingdom*, the Court was faced with an Article 14 complaint concerning UK immigration rules which made it harder for female immigrants than male immigrants to obtain permission for their non-national partners to enter or remain in the UK. To justify this discrepancy, the government sought to argue that immigrant husbands had a different effect on the domestic labour market because men of working age were assumed to be more likely to seek employment than women.[54] The Court refused leniency, holding that even if there were indeed such differences between men and women with regard to their working patterns and its impact on the labour market, that did not justify this differential treatment between men and women.[55] Similar arguments pertaining to women's allegedly differing working patterns were advanced in *Schuler-Zgraggen v. Switzerland*. The applicant complained of having been denied an invalidity pension. It was argued that the domestic authorities had justified this denial on the basis that women with young children did not work.[56] The Court applied strict scrutiny and declared that, regardless of the question of whether or not the government's assumptions held truth, the reasons were not weighty enough to justify the denial of invalidity pension to women with young children, such as the applicant.[57] In *Karlheinz Schmidt v. Germany*, the applicant challenged German law that required only men to pay a fire service levy as amounting to discrimination under Article 14 of the Convention. The government attempted to justify this differential treatment of men and women on the grounds that women could not be asked to serve as firemen or pay a levy given biological differences between the sexes, and a need to protect women in light of their "physical and mental characteristics".[58] The Court rejected the argument because of the essentially financial nature of the disputed duty and its doubts as to whether there might still exist any differences between men and women which would justify different treatment as regards service in the fire brigade.[59] Thus, it can be said that when confronted with justifications based on stereotypes about women's working patterns and biological characteristics, the Court has repeatedly rejected them as insufficient for the purposes of Article 14 of the Convention. And this might carry great significance

[52] *Schuler-Zgraggen v. Switzerland* (No. 14518/89, 24 June 1993).
[53] *Karlheinz Schmidt v. Germany* (No. 13580/88, 18 July 1994).
[54] *Abdulaziz Cabales and Balkandali v. the United Kingdom*, para. 75.
[55] *Abdulaziz Cabales and Balkandali v. the United Kingdom*, para. 79.
[56] *Schuler-Zgraggen v. Switzerland*, para. 64.
[57] *Schuler-Zgraggen v. Switzerland*, para. 67.
[58] *Karlheinz Schmidt v. Germany*, para. 27.
[59] *Karlheinz Schmidt v. Germany*, para. 28.

when it comes to the emancipatory potential of the Convention and the Court regarding gender diversity in the judiciary. In this sense, the Court's refusal to accept stereotypes about women's working patterns in *Abdulaziz* and *Schuler-Zgraggen* might be taken to show a readiness to further combat gender-stereotypes which harm women's career prospects in general.[60]

However, it is highly unlikely that the unequal gender distribution of judicial seats would be justified on account of the judicial candidates' gender directly. Therefore, the Court's case-law on instances of alleged indirect discrimination might also send a hopeful signal for gender equality endeavours in the judiciary. In this sense, the case of *Zarb Adami v. Malta*[61] might indicate the Court's readiness to let numbers speak for themselves, and infer gendered discrimination from numerically unequal representation. There, a male applicant complained that the respondent state was discriminating against men due to the negligible percentage of women called to jury service. While the government tried to argue that men were only overrepresented in jury service due to the adoption of certain policies in the selection of jurors,[62] the Court reiterated that "if a policy or general measure ha[d] disproportionate prejudicial effects on a group of people, the possibility of its being considered discriminatory [could] not be ruled out even if it [was] not specifically aimed or directed at that group".[63] In light of the numbers submitted, the Court found that the domestic policies on jury member selection had a disproportionate effect on men.[64] And while *Zarb Adami* concerned a situation quite flipped from cases concerning a gender-diverse judiciary, in that in *Adami* men were fighting not to be jurors as opposed to women seeking to become judges, the judgment might nevertheless show that the Court might be ready to draw inferences from statistical data showing an overwhelming lack of gender diversity in, for example, the judiciary.

Another such case is *Opuz v. Turkey*.[65] There, the applicant and her mother had been continuously assaulted and threatened by the applicant's ex-husband over many years, which eventually culminated in the mother's death. The domestic authorities responded to the women's respective complaints with either complete inaction or lenient punishment of the ex-husband. The applicant complained to the Court based on Articles 2, 3, and 14 of the Convention. Specifically, she argued (i) that the domestic authorities had violated her mother's right to life as she was killed by the applicant's ex-husband despite the fact that the domestic authorities were repeatedly alerted about his abuse and violence; (ii) that there had been a violation of Article 3 of the Convention on account of the authorities' failure to protect the applicant against her ex-husband; and (iii) that, read in conjunction with Articles 2

[60] For another case challenging gender roles see also *Beeler v. Switzerland* (No. 78630/12, 11 October 2022).

[61] *Zarb Adami v. Malta* (No. 17209/02, 20 June 2006).

[62] *Zarb Adami v. Malta*, paras. 53–55.

[63] *Zarb Adami v. Malta*, para. 80.

[64] *Zarb Adami v. Malta*, paras. 77–78.

[65] *Opuz v. Turkey* (No. 33401/02, 9 June 2009).

and 3, there had been a violation of the Article 14 right to non-discrimination given that the violence suffered by the applicant and her mother was gender-based. The novelty and significance of *Opuz* lies in the fact that this judgment marks the first time the Court considered and applied Article 14 of the Convention in the context of domestic violence. In finding a violation of Article 14, the Court accepted domestic abuse to be gendered by disproportionately affecting women.[66]

In linking domestic violence and gender discrimination for the purposes of Article 14 of the Convention, the Court also referenced international human rights law and relied principally on the system surrounding CEDAW. It noted the CEDAW Committee's repeated findings that "gender-based violence is a form of discrimination that seriously inhibits women's ability to enjoy rights and freedoms on a basis of equality with men".[67] In this context, gender-based violence has been interpreted by the Committee to mean "violence that is directed against a woman because she is a woman or that affects women disproportionately".[68] In light of this interpretation of gendered violence, the Court concluded that the case's facts and circumstances amounted to a violation of Article 14 of the Convention.[69] It noted that domestic violence mainly and disproportionally affected women, and that the authorities' general and discriminatory passivity further promoted such abuse.[70] While the context of domestic violence is of course markedly different from the question of gender-diversity in the judiciary, *Opuz* might nevertheless prove valuable for the promotion of a more gender-diverse judiciary through the Court's jurisprudence. In this sense, *Opuz* might be taken to demonstrate a willingness to infer the existence of gender discrimination even where the discriminatory nature of a situation is not overt, but where facts and figures show the disproportionate suffering and affectedness of women.[71] In particular, the Court's acknowledgment that discrimination may be found, *inter alia*, in the domestic authorities' passivity to improve the situation complained of may indicate that similar findings might be made in the context of judicial gender-diversity, should it be demonstrated that the underrepresentation of female judges is systematic and upheld by the authorities' unresponsiveness to issues raised.

---

[66] *Opuz v. Turkey*, paras. 184–187.

[67] *Opuz v. Turkey*, para. 74, referencing Committee on the Elimination of Discrimination Against Women (CEDAW), CEDAW General Recommendation No. 19: Violence against women, (1992), para. 1.

[68] *Opuz v. Turkey*, para. 75, referencing Committee on the Elimination of Discrimination Against Women (CEDAW), CEDAW General Recommendation No. 19: Violence against women, (1992), para. 6.

[69] *Opuz v. Turkey*, para. 202.

[70] *Opuz v. Turkey*, paras. 197–198.

[71] For further cases concerning domestic abuse and public authorities' passivity see, *inter alia*, *Talpis v. Italy* (No. 41237/14, 2 March 2017), *M.S.v. Italy* (No. 32715/19, 7 July 2022), and *A.E. v. Bulgaria* (No. 53891/20, 23 August 2023).

Moving on, there is the case-law on family surnames. There, one of the most famous cases is *Ünal Tekeli v. Turkey*.[72] A female applicant complained that the prohibition on women using their surnames as the family name, while allowing it for men, amounted to unlawful discrimination in violation of the Convention. The respondent authorities tried to justify the differential treatment of men and women in this sphere by invoking the need to reflect family unity through the adoption of the husband's name. The Court rejected these arguments, adopting a strict approach of sameness, and interpreting Article 14 of the Convention as prohibiting discrimination on the grounds of gender in the sphere of family names. Similarly in *Burghartz v. Switzerland*,[73] the applicant complained that Swiss domestic law did not provide husbands who had taken their wives' surnames as their family name with the option to add to it their own names. Taking arguments surrounding the family unity and tradition into account, the Court however stated that this discrepancy amounted to discrimination under the Convention.[74]

Yet there are also cases where the Court uses an apparently lenient interpretation of the non-discrimination clause, regarding eligibility for welfare benefits. In *Runkee and White v. the United Kingdom*,[75] the Court heard a challenge to a denial of a widow's pension to men in a situation where it would have been available to women. It was noted that the different treatment of men and women for the purposes of widow's pension was justified given that, historically, older widows faced particular financial hardship and inequality due to married women's traditional confinement to domestic labour.[76] The Court recognized these long-standing economic differences between men and women and accepted that the measure was aiming to address that.[77] This might demonstrate a willingness to accept socioeconomic positive measures adopted by states in pursuit of gender equality in the judiciary and other segments of society. In particular, the Court seems potentially open to positive measures and consider them as justified in seeking to eradicate historical disadvantages faced by women in the judicial profession. This might render relevant measures more widely acceptable. It may eventually even lead to a change of culture and mentality needed for the achievement of substantive instead of symbolic token equality.

The importance of gender equality in public offices for the culture of modern democracies has been discussed in *Staatkundig Gereformeerde Partij v. the Netherlands*.[78] There, a political party lodged a complaint after domestic courts had ordered it to open its lists of candidates for representative bodies to women. In ruling the complaint inadmissible as manifestly ill-founded, the Court reiterated

---

[72] *Ünal Tekeli v. Turkey* (No. 29865/96, 16 November 2004).

[73] *Burghartz v. Switzerland* (No. 16213/90, 22 February 1994).

[74] *Burghartz v. Switzerland*, para. 28–30.

[75] *Runkee and White v. the United Kingdom* (Nos. 42949/98 and 53134/99, 10 May 2007).

[76] *Runkee and White v. the United Kingdom*, para. 37.

[77] *Runkee and White v. the United Kingdom*, para. 40.

[78] *Staatkundig Gereformeerde Partij v. the Netherlands* ((dec.), no. 58369/10, 10 July 2012).

that "democracy is the only political model contemplated in the Convention and the only one compatible with it"[79] and that "the advancement of the equality of the sexes in the member States of the Council of Europe prevents the State from lending its support to views of the man's role as primordial and the woman's as secondary".[80] Apart from demonstrating the Court's commitment to upholding the equality of the sexes when it comes to access to public offices (which could also include the judiciary), this decision could be particularly remarkable due to its emphasis on democracy. As such, the Court's judgment could be taken to reveal the conviction that gender equality and diversity in public offices are a fundamental corollary of any democratic system. Rooting gender diversity in the very foundations of modern political life could promote a change of mentality in which the inclusion of women in public offices (such as and including the judiciary) is no longer viewed as a concession to the female sex but indeed a political necessity. This may contribute to achieving substantive gender diversity in the judiciary through law.

What might be particularly noteworthy about the Court's decision-making in gender-related complaints is perhaps its interplay with international human rights law instruments. As mentioned, CEDAW is often regarded as the prime instrument giving the quest for gender-equality a legal basis. As could be seen in *Opuz*, the Court has relied on CEDAW to inform its interpretation of what acts and omissions may constitute gendered discrimination and give rise to a violation of Article 14 of the Convention. The Court's approach may however not necessarily be identical to that put forward under CEDAW. Its imperative is seemingly premised on pursuing equal treatment of men and women. But as was shown in this survey of the case-law, the Court has been prepared to accept unequal treatment where it served to rectify vulnerabilities and disadvantages that are particular to the social standing of women. In the case of *Stec and Others v. the United Kingdom*,[81] the Court held expressly that "in certain circumstances a failure to attempt to correct inequality through different treatment may in itself give rise to a breach of Article 14".[82] The Court's decisions have favoured remedies of (historical) gendered disadvantages, therefore indeed implementing the aspirations of CEDAW. In any case, a divergence between approaches to gender equality adopted by CEDAW and the Court may exist only *prima facie*. In Article 3, CEDAW calls on states to take measures to ensure the full development and advancement of women. Fittingly, Article 4(1) CEDAW permits State Parties to adopt (temporary) special measures to accelerate the *de facto* equality between men and women. In doing so, Article 4 (1) specifically states that gendered distinctions made pursuant to such measures will not amount to discrimination. Insofar as

[79] *Staatkundig Gereformeerde Partij v. the Netherlands*, para. 70.

[80] *Staatkundig Gereformeerde Partij v. the Netherlands*, para. 73.

[81] *Stec and Others v. the United Kingdom* (Nos. 65731/01 and 65900/01, 12 April 2006).

[82] *Stec and Others v. the United Kingdom*, para. 51.

the ECHR and its Court come to the same conclusion, they seem to be embedded in and conducive to international human rights law's broader efforts towards more gender equality. And then, there might be a well-founded hope that the principles and approaches developed in these efforts might translate into a substantive and sustainable diversification of the (high) judicial profession's gender.

5 Conclusion

A gender-diverse judiciary is desirable due to a number of reasons, ranging from concerns of democratic legitimacy to the eradication of law's androcentric nature. The fulfilment of the promises of a gender-diverse judiciary are, however, contingent upon the achievement of substantive as opposed to a mere token diversity. The literature seems to conclude that substantive gender diversity cannot be achieved by implementing low-threshold positive measures alone. Instead, what is called for is the import of a critical mass of women into the judiciary. This is argued to rethink gender diversity and its relation to the judiciary as a modern necessity and not just an issue which can be addressed through mere symbolic gestures. The ECtHR's past case-law might be taken to demonstrate its readiness to combat the sort of gender-stereotypes which have harmed women's careers and endorse policy measures which, while differentiating between men and women, actually further gender equality by rectifying women's historic disadvantages and vulnerabilities. Then, the ECtHR's practice and international human rights law more broadly appear to be in a symbiotic relationship in the quest for more gender equality and, potentially, a more gender-diverse judiciary. Interestingly enough, the Court was recently given the opportunity to adjudicate on alleged gender discrimination in the judicial appointments process in the case of *Alonso Suara v. Spain.*[83] This case concerned the applicant's allegations that the domestic authorities did not give adequate reasons for choosing another candidate for the post of President of the High Court and that their decisions were arbitrary and discriminated against her on the basis of her gender and was considered solely under Article 6 of the Convention. Thus, the emancipatory potential of the Court's case-law with regards to gender diversity in the judiciary remains to be seen.

[83] *Alonso Saura v. Spain* (No. 18326/19, 8 June 2023).

References

Literature

Baer J (2011) Feminist theory and the law. In: Goodin R (ed) The Oxford handbook of political science, Oxford University Press, Oxford

Caielli M (2018) Why do women in the judiciary matter? The struggle for gender diversity in European courts. Federalisimi 5:157–172

Collins P M, Manning K L, Carp R A (2010) Gender, critical mass, and judicial decision making. Law Policy 32(2):260–281

Committee on the elimination of discrimination against women (CEDAW), CEDAW General Recommendation No. 19: Violence against women, (1992)

Committee on the elimination of discrimination against women (CEDAW), CEDAW General Recommendation No 33: Women's access to justice, (2015)

Committee on the elimination of discrimination against women (CEDAW), CEDAW General Recommendation No 25: Temporary special measures, (2004)

Dahl T (1987) Women's law: an introduction to feminist jurisprudence. Norwegian University Press, Oslo

European institute for gender equality, "gender quotas" https://eige.europa.eu/publications-resources/thesaurus/terms/1304?language_content_entity=en

European institute for gender equality, "tokensim" https://eige.europa.eu/publications-resources/thesaurus/terms/1261?language_content_entity=en

Hunter R (2015) More than just a different face? Judicial diversity and decision-making. Curr Leg Probl 68(1):119–141

Hunter R, McGlynn C, Rackley E (2010) Feminist judgements: an introduction. In: Hunter R, McGlynn C, Rackley E (ed) Feminist judgements: from theory to practice, Hart Publishing, Oxford

Keller H, Heri C, Christ M (2020) Fifty years of women at the European court of human rights: successes and failures of the council of Europe's gender agenda. In: Baetens F (ed) Identity and diversity on the international bench: who is the judge, Oxford University Press, Oxford

Kennedy H (1978) Women at the bar. In: Hazell R (ed) The bar on trial, Quartet Books, London

Kenney, S J (2013) Gender & Justice: Why women in the judiciary really matter, Routledge

Kessedjian C (2022) Gender equality in the judiciary—with an emphasis on international judiciary. In: Gender equality in the mirror: reflecting on power, participation and global justice, Brill, Leiden

Kmak A (2018) Fast facts about our female U.S. supreme court justices. Illinois State Bar Association (December 2018) https://www.isba.org/committees/women/newsletter/2018/12/fastfactsaboutourfemaleussupremecou

Lady Hale of Richmond (2017) How diverse are judges. In: Cooper J (ed) Being a judge in the modern world, Oxford University Press, Oxford

Lijnzaad L (2020) The smurfette principle: reflections about gender and the nomination of women to the international bench. In: Baetens F (ed) Identity and diversity on the international bench: Who is the judge, Oxford University Press, Oxford

Nielsen VL, Bo Madsen M (2017) Does gender diversity in the workplace affect job satisfaction and turnover intentions? Int. Public Manag. Rev. 18(1):77–115

OECD, Government at a glance, 2021 Report https://www.oecd-ilibrary.org/sites/2f520410-en/index.html?itemId=/content/component/2f520410-en

Rackley E (2013) Women, judging and the judiciary: from difference to diversity. Routledge, Oxford

Radacic I (2009) Critical review of jurisprudence: an occasional series gender equality jurisprudence of the european court of human rights. Eur J Int Law 19(4):841–857

Riccucci N. M (2008) Tokenism. In: J. Hartwell Moore (ed), Encyclopedia of race and racism, Macmillan Reference, New York City
Ruby M (2021) Tokenism. In: Casey Z (ed) Encyclopedia of critical whiteness studies in education, Brill, Leiden
Ruiz V (2019) Le Rôle des Femmes Juges et d'une Prise en Compte des Questions de Genre pour Assurer l'Indépendance et l'Intégrité du Système Judiciaire. ONUDC https://www.unodc.org/dohadeclaration/fr/news/2019/01/the-role-of-women-judges-and-a-gender-perspective-in-ensuring-judicial-independence-and-integrity.html
Schultz U (2003) women lawyers in Germany: perception and construction of femininity. In: Schultz U, Shaw G (eds) Women in the world's legal professions, Hart Publishing, Oxford
Sommerlad H (2013) Let history judge? gender, race, class and performative identity: a study of women judges in England and Wales. In: Schultz U, Shaw G (eds) Gender and judging, Hart Publishing, Oxford
UN general assembly, convention on the elimination of all forms of discrimination against women, (18 December 1979), United Nations, Treaty Ser., vol 1249, p. 13
United Nations, "International Court of Justice names its first female president" UN News (6 February 2006) https://news.un.org/en/story/2006/02/168322
Vujadinović D et al (eds) (2023) Gender-competent legal education, Springer
Yüksel, S (2022). New technologies through a human rights lens: Reflecting on personal autonomy and non-discrimination. Ceza Hukuku Ve Kriminoloji Dergisi, 10(2), 281–305

Case Law

ECtHR, *A.E. v. Bulgaria* (No. 53891/20, (23 August 2023)
ECtHR, *Abdulaziz Cabales and Balkandali v. the United Kingdom* (No. 9214/80; 9473/81; 9474/81, 24 April 1985)
ECtHR, *Beeler v. Switzerland* (No. 78630/12, 11 October 2022)
ECtHR, *Burghartz v. Switzerland* (No. 16213/90, 22 February 1994)
ECtHR, *Karlheinz Schmidt v. Germany* (No. 13580/88, 18 July 1994)
ECtHR, *M.S.v. Italy* (No. 32715/19, 7 July 2022)
ECtHR, *Opuz v. Turkey* (No. 33401/02, 9 June 2009)
ECtHR, *Runkee and White v. the United Kingdom* (Nos. 42949/98 and 53134/99, 10 May 2007)
ECtHR, *Schuler-Zgraggen v. Switzerland* (No. 14518/89, 24 June 1993)
ECtHR, *Staatkundig Gereformeerde Partij v. the Netherlands* ((dec.), no. 58369/10, 10 July 2012)
ECtHR, *Stec and Others v. the United Kingdom* (Nos. 65731/01 and 65900/01, 12 April 2006)
ECtHR, *Talpis v. Italy* (No. 41237/14, 2 March 2017)
ECtHR, *Ünal Tekeli v. Turkey* (No. 29865/96, 16 November 2004)
ECtHR, *Zarb Adami v. Malta* (No. 17209/02, 20 June 2006)

Saadet Yüksel is currently a Judge of the European Court of Human Rights, elected in respect of Türkiye in 2019. Judge Yüksel holds a Master's Degree from Harvard Law School and obtained her Doctorate Degree (PhD) in Law from the Istanbul Law School. She worked as a visiting scholar at Georgetown Law School and at the International Law Institute, Washington, DC. As a constitutional lawyer focusing on constitutional reform and design, she conducted and presented research on a variety of legal issues, including research on the constitutional arrangements of Türkiye, right to privacy in electronic communications and free exercise of religion. She worked as a visiting researcher at Harvard Law School before she was appointed as associate professor at Istanbul Law School. From 2017 to 2019 she was Chair of the Constitutional Law Department at the University of Istanbul where she also served as Member of the Board of Directors.

Gender Equality in Serbian Judiciary—An Examination of the State of Play

Ana Knežević Bojović and Monika Milošević

Abstract Gender equality in the judiciary has been historically uneven and still varies considerably among countries, where women often remain underrepresented in high-ranking positions. Since its 2010–2012 evaluation cycle, the European Commission for Efficiency of Justice (CEPEJ) recognized the need for a better understanding of gender issues in the judiciary, tracking progress and changes in female representation in the judiciary. CEPEJ reports show that Serbia consistently boasts a figure of over 60% of female judges overall, including a comparatively high percentage of female court presidents. However, it remains questionable whether this track record can be attributable to clear policy and legislative measures fostering improved access of women to judicial careers. A closer look at the regulatory framework on the status, appointment and promotion of judges in Serbia shows that there are no sector-specific rules aimed at furthering such an approach. The paper provides a systemic overview of position of women in the Serbian judiciary from a legal perspective. This is done through a qualitative and quantitative analysis of data on the percentage of women judges at courts of all instances, including specialized courts, female court presidents and the High Judicial Council. The paper also sheds lights on tendencies in judicial appointments and promotions

This work is a result of research within the project "Adapting the Legal Framework to Social and Technological Changes with a Special Focus on Artificial Intelligence," carried out in 2025 by the Institute of Comparative Law with financial support from the Ministry of Science, Technological Development and Innovation (contract number 451-03-136/2025-03/200049).

A. Knežević Bojović (✉)
Institute of Comparative Law, Belgrade, Serbia
e-mail: a.bojovic@iup.rs

M. Milošević
Belgrade, Serbia
e-mail: monikaninkovic@yahoo.com

© The Author(s), under exclusive license to Springer Nature Switzerland AG 2025

S. Baer et al. (eds.), *The Gender and the Judiciary*, Gender Perspectives in Law 7,
https://doi.org/10.1007/978-3-032-06885-9_4

in recent years. Employing normative, comparative and exegetic methods, the authors analyse the current relevant regulatory framework in Serbia, identify and pinpoint indirect disincentives for women, assessing the state of play in Serbia against neighbouring countries and global trends.

1 Introductory Remarks

Rule of law is the key element of democratic societies[1] and independent judiciary stands at the very heart of the rule of law. The rule of law is an inherently inclusive concept, as it calls, inter alia, for non-discrimination and equality before the law.[2] At the same time, it is said that societies in which women are excluded from public life and decision-making cannot be described as democratic, as democracy can have a true effect only if political decisions are made by men and women, taking into account and paying attention to interests of both women and men.[3] There is increased recognition that the composition of the judiciary should reflect the composition of society, which also relates to ensuring that women have full and equal participation in the judiciary.[4] A gender-sensitive judicial system is thus seen as a *conditio sine qua non* for achievement of gender equality on the ground.[5]

Since the 1970s, the number of women in the judicial profession has started to rise, particularly in Europe; globally the numbers have increased since the 1990s.[6] The sociology of legal professions also notes that in countries of European-continental legal tradition, women are more represented in the profession of judges (and prosecutors) than in the profession of lawyers.[7] The phenomenon, also known as the feminization of judiciary, is becoming increasingly visible in Europe, where since 2010, on average over 40% of the judicial corps is comprised of women, and the figures have been on the rise.[8] Serbia is one of the eight countries that are

[1] Tamanaha (2012), p. 235. Admittedly, Tamanaha also has some reservations towards this approach, pointing out that human rights and democracy should not be a part of the definition of the rule of law.

[2] Act4Rule of Law https://www.act4ruleoflaw.org/en/news/gender; European Commission for Democracy through Law (Venice Commission) Report on the Rule of Law CDL-AD(2011)003rev, para.41.

[3] UN Committee on the Elimination of Discrimination Against Women (CEDAW) General Recommendation No. 23: Political and Public Life, A/52/38, para. 14.

[4] International Commission of Jurists (2013).

[5] Special Rapporteur on the Independence of Judges and Lawyers (2011), para. 18.

[6] Schultz and Shaw (2013) p.14.

[7] Hammerslev (2013).

[8] CEPEJ (2022) 69. Nevertheless, there still seems to be a difference between common law and civil law countries, where the former have judiciaries that are still dominated by men (Schultz and Shaw (2013), make a clear distinction between the two systems and provide supporting evidence). Additionally, the average number of female judges in courts is strongly affected by Azerbaijan with 88% of judges being men, Armenia with 75%, Scotland with 74%, Morocco with 73%, England with 66%, Ireland with 65%, and Iceland with 62% of judges being male. See: Deljkić et al. (2023), p. 283.

currently leading in Europe in terms of the percentage of female judges—over two-thirds are women. The figures are particularly important it viewed in the light of the fact that pre-World War I, women with law doctorates in Serbia were neither allowed to teach at law faculties nor to be appointed judges.[9]

This paper will firstly provide a birds-eye view on the relevant international standards related to the gender equality in the judiciary. Secondly, it presents the current state of play with regards to legislative norms and the statistical data on the feminization of Serbian judiciary, look at statistical evidence with regards to the existence of a glass-ceiling in the Serbian judiciary and point to the lack of systemic efforts geared towards promoting a feminized judiciary in Serbia.

2 International Legal Basis of Gender Equality in the Judiciary

As indicated above, in the international fora there is a multitude of hard- and soft-law instruments aimed at ensuring equality between men and women in general, and specifically, at ensuring and promoting the equal participation of women in all public institutions, including the judiciary. The efforts of various supranational organisations in this respect are continuous and ongoing. Therefore, it would be very difficult to collect and present a definitive corpus of legal documents that are relevant on both global and European level. Nevertheless, it is worth recalling that the idea of a gender-balanced judiciary can be found in documents that address the need to achieve and sustain gender equality in general and is reaffirmed in documents targeting balanced participation of women in public life and judicial decision-making.

2.1 Gender Equality in Judiciary—Universal Sources

Equal rights of men and women are embedded in the Preamble to the Charter of the United Nations (hereinafter: the Charter) and affirmed in its Article 1.[10] The Preamble to the Universal Declaration of Human Rights reaffirms the equal rights of men and women as one of its key guiding principles.[11] The International Covenant on Economic, Social and Cultural Rights[12] and the International

[9] Mršević (2003) p. 144.

[10] Charter of the United Nations.

[11] Universal Declaration of Human Rights.

[12] Article 2, paragraph 2 of the International Covenant on Economic, Social and Cultural Rights, Adopted and opened for signature, ratification and accession by General Assembly resolution 2200A (XXI) of 16 December 1966.

Covenant on Civil and Political Rights,[13] which in fact implement the principles of the Declaration in a legally binding form, emphasize that the rights guaranteed by them apply to all persons without distinction and further, that distinction based on gender is impermissible. Both pacts expressly oblige the states that accede to it or ratify them to ensure that women and men have the equal right to enjoy all the rights they establish.

Further, in the context of international legal documents with global reach, the Commission on the Status of Women (hereinafter: CSW) is of particular relevance. Its work has resulted in a series of important declarations and conventions that protect and promote the human rights of women.[14] In the context of the present paper, the Convention on the Political Rights of Women, adopted by the General Assembly on 20 December 1952[15] is relevant, as it affirms that women are entitled to hold public offices and exercise all public functions without discrimination.[16]

The Convention on the Elimination of All Forms of Discrimination (hereinafter: the CEDAW),[17] often described as an international bill on women's rights, defines what constitutes discrimination against women and sets the agenda for national action to end such discrimination.[18] In the context of feminization of the judiciary, its particular importance is in providing the basis for achieving equality between women and men by ensuring equal access and opportunities for women in political and public life. CEDAW General recommendation No. 23 on political and public life, in Article 7 places special emphasis on ensuring the equality of women and men in political and public life. This is a broad term which includes the exercise of political power, especially the exercise of legislative, judicial, executive and administrative powers.[19] It additionally mandates for a wide range of measures to be implemented by contracting state enabling women for appointment to public positions such as the judiciary.[20] Further to that, CEDAW General recommendation

[13] Article 2, Paragraph 1 of the International Covenant on Civil and Political Rights Adopted and opened for signature, ratification and accession by General Assembly resolution 2200A (XXI) of 16 December 1966.

[14] In 1946, the Commission was originally established as a sub-commission of the Commission on Human Rights. However, it soon obtained the status of a full commission. Its work was focused on the preparation of recommendations related to urgent problems that required immediate attention in the field of women's rights, as well as drafting proposals for the implementation of these recommendations. It also developed the Declaration on the Elimination of Discrimination against Women, A/RES/22/2263.

[15] Convention on the Political Rights of Women, adopted by the General Assembly on 20 December 1952, A/RES/640.

[16] Article 3 of the Convention on the Political Rights of Women.

[17] Convention on the Elimination of All Forms of Discrimination against Women Adopted and opened for signature, ratification and accession by General Assembly resolution 34/180 of 18 December 1979.

[18] Article 1 of the Convention on the Elimination of All Forms of Discrimination against Women.

[19] CEDAW General recommendation 23, para. 5.

[20] CEDAW General recommendation 23, para. 15.

No. 33 on women's access to justice[21] is of particular importance for the judicial sector as it for the first time explicitly calls for gender equality in the judiciary. It asserts the need for improving the gender responsiveness of the justice system and women's unhindered access to justice systems, thereby empowering them to achieve de jure and de facto equality. In terms of women's careers in the judiciary, this recommendation calls for removing barriers to women's participation as professionals within all bodies and levels of judicial and quasi-judicial systems and providers of justice-related services.[22] The recommendation further proclaims the need for women to be equally represented in the judiciary and other law implementation mechanisms, including as magistrates and judges.[23]

These hard-law instruments are complemented by a plethora of soft-law instruments adopted at the UN level. For instance, the 1995 Beijing Declaration and Platform for Action[24] prompts the Member States to commit themselves to establishing the goal of gender balance in governmental bodies and committees, as well as in public administrative entities, and in the judiciary".[25] In the context of the judiciary, it specifically emphasizes that the States should ensure that women have the same right as men to be judges, advocates or other officers of the court.[26]

The 2030 Agenda for Sustainable Development,[27] recognizes and highlights the importance of ensuring „women's full and effective participation and equal opportunities for leadership at all levels of decision-making in political, economic and public life".[28]

The Declaration of the High level Meeting of the General Assembly on the Rule of Law at the National and International Levels[29] adopted by the General Assembly of the United Nations acknowledges importance of ensuring that women, on the basis of the equality of men and women, fully enjoy the benefits of the rule of law, and commit to using law to uphold their equal rights and ensure their full and equal

[21] UN Committee on the Elimination of Discrimination Against Women (CEDAW) General Recommendation No. 33 Convention on women's access to justice CEDAW/C/GC/33.

[22] UN Committee on the Elimination of Discrimination Against Women (CEDAW) General Recommendation No. 33 Convention on women's access to justice CEDAW/C/GC/33, para. 1.

[23] UN Committee on the Elimination of Discrimination Against Women (CEDAW) General Recommendation No. 33 Convention on women's access to justice CEDAW/C/GC/33, para. 15.

[24] Beijing Declaration and Platform for Action of 1995, https://www.un.org/womenwatch/daw/beijing/pdf/BDPfA%20E.pdf.

[25] The Beijing Declaration and Platform for Action, para. 19.

[26] The Beijing Declaration and Platform for Action, para. 232.

[27] Resolution adopted by the General Assembly on 25 September 2015 Transforming our world: the 2030 Agenda for Sustainable Development A/RES/70/1, Goal 5 (Achieve gender equality and empower all women and girls)

[28] 2030 Agenda for Sustainable Development, p. 20.

[29] Declaration of the High-level Meeting of the General Assembly on the Rule of Law at the National and International Levels A/67/L.1.

participation, including in institutions of governance and the judicial system."[30] In a similar vein, the Special Rapporteur on the Independence of Judges and Lawyers has called for not only the promotion of equality policies but concrete measures aimed to ensure equal access to the higher courts, as well as guarantees of work-life balance in the judiciary.[31] The UN Working Group on discrimination against women and girls emphasized that it is the duty of states to promote women's equality and empower women in public and political life. In order to achieve this goal, they must take legal measures at the constitutional, legislative and judicial levels.[32]

Another very important legal basis of gender equality in decision-making in public life is the 2015 Organisation for Economic Co-operation and Development (OECD) Recommendation of the Council on Gender Equality in Public Life.[33] *Inter alia*, this document aims at encouraging women to participate in politics and abolishing both implicit and explicit barriers to gender equality. OECD recommends consideration of comprehensive regulatory or voluntary measures to enable women equal access to opportunities in senior public service and judicial appointments.

2.2 Gender Equality in Judiciary—European Sources

The Council of Europe also affirms that the main condition for justice and democracy is the balanced participation of women and men in political and public decision-making.[34] In 2003, the Council of Ministers adopted the Recommendation on the Balanced participation of women and men in political and public decision-making,[35] according to which the representation of either women or men in any decision-making body in political or public life should not fall below 40%. Similarly, the European Union Gender Equality Strategy 2020–2025[36] recognizes the promotion of equality between women and men as "a task for the Union, in all

[30] Declaration of the High-level Meeting of the General Assembly on the Rule of Law at the National and International Levels, para. 16.

[31] Special Rapporteur on the independence of judges and lawyers (2021), paras. 89 and 90.

[32] Working group on Discrimination Against Women and Girls (2013) Report of the Working Group on the issue of discrimination against women in law and practice, A/HRC/23/50, para. 77.

[33] OECD (2016).

[34] For an overview of relevant documents, see: https://www.coe.int/en/web/genderequality/balanced-participation.

[35] Balanced participation of women and men in political and public decision-making Recommendation Rec (2003) 3 adopted by the Committee of Ministers of the Council of Europe on 12 March 2003.

[36] Communication from the Commission to the European Parliament, the Council, the European Economic and Social Committee and the Committee of the Regions A union of equality: Gender equality strategy 2020–2025, COM/2020/152 final.

its activities" and foresees a dual approach, combining targeted measures with effective gender mainstreaming. European Union's commitment to promoting gender equality also extends to its external actions. The EU Gender Plan[37] identifies six priority areas of action, one of which is advancing equal participation and leadership. While it does not address gender issues in the judiciary, it does state that European Union action should contribute to enhancing equal legal capacity and access for women to justice through support to grassroots efforts and to legal and justice systems reforms.

3 Gender Equality in Serbian Judiciary

Gender equality is a generally recognised principle of Serbian legislation, as promulgated in the Constitution, legislation (including signed and ratified international treaties), and streamlined through sectorial public policy documents.[38] Article 15 of the Serbian Constitution[39] thus proclaims equality and equal opportunities for women and men, while its Article 21 prescribes the prohibition of both direct and indirect discrimination on any grounds, including the one based on sex. Serbia has a Law on Gender Equality[40] which is complemented by the Law on Prohibition of Discrimination.[41] The Law on Gender Equality provides the definitions of gender equality and discrimination. In its Article 3, this Law asserts that gender equality means, *inter alia*, equal participation and balanced representation of women and men in all spheres of public life.

[37] Joint communication to the European Parliament and the Council EU Gender Action Plan (GAP) iii—An Ambitious Agenda for Gender Equality and Women's Empowerment in EU External Action, SWD(2020) 284 final.

[38] In Serbia, signed and ratified international treaties are a part of the internal legal order (Article 194 of the Constitution). Serbia has signed and ratified a number of international documents concerning human rights in general and gender equality in particular, including the UN Convention on the Political Rights of Women, the International Covenant on Civil and Political Rights; the International Covenant on Economic, Social and Cultural Rights, the Convention on Elimination of All form of Discrimination Against Women and the Council of Europe Convention on preventing and combating violence against women and domestic violence (Istanbul Convention); it has also committed to the Beijing Declaration and Platform for Action (Equality, Development and Peace). See: Ferigra Stefanović (2021), p. 9.

[39] Constitution of the Republic of Serbia, RS Official Gazette No. 98/2006-3, 115/2021-3 (Amendments I–XXIX), 16/2022-3, https://www.pravno-informacioni-sistem.rs/SlGlasnikPortal/eli/rep/sgrs/skupstina/ustav/2006/98/1/reg.

[40] Law on Gender Equality, RS Official Gazette No. 51/2021 https://www.pravno-informacioni-sistem.rs/SlGlasnikPortal/eli/rep/sgrs/skupstina/zakon/2021/52/3/reg?fbclid=IwAR1tvje9ljSS7Y3zupNXGEX0yat4Zs7vBHQICDDR60HDiWQ557iSO9rhfXA.

[41] Law on Prohibition of Discrimination, RS Official Gazette No. 22/2009 and 52/2021, https://www.pravno-informacioni-sistem.rs/SlGlasnikPortal/eli/rep/sgrs/skupstina/zakon/2009/22/1/reg/.

The Strategy for Gender Equality for the 2021–2030 period[42] includes a comprehensive set of measures, one of which also concerns equal access to justice and ensuring gender equality. However, the measure is geared towards improving the gender-sensitivity of relevant judicial institutions mostly through training. In the Strategy, the gender structure of the Serbian judiciary is described as imbalanced in favour of women. The Judicial Development Strategy for the 2020–2025 period[43] remains silent on the matter of the gender structure in Serbian judiciary. Similarly, the Revised Action Plan for Chapter 23[44] does not address the issue of the gender structure in the judiciary but does include activities aimed at further improving the gender equality regulatory framework.[45]

Despite a seemingly robust legal framework, *de facto* gender equality in Serbian society is yet to be achieved.[46]

The Gender Equality Index,[47] a composite indicator used in EU and candidate countries to measure gender equality and track progress in reducing gender gaps, for Serbia, based on 2018 data is 58.0 points (out of 100) and reportedly shows a continued, although slow progress in gender equality (compared to 2014, it increased by 5.6 points).[48] It is estimated that if progress were to continue in the same tempo, it would take Serbia 58 years to achieve a high level of gender equality.[49] The biggest progress made since 2014 was in the area of power, which can be largely attributed to the statutes prescribing a mandatory quota of women in legislative bodies at all governmental levels.[50] At the same time, the results declined in the economic power sub-domain. In the domain of work, Serbia recorded 69.4 points, where it also shows a relatively small gap compared to the EU.[51] Serbia also

[42] Strategy for Gender Equality for the 2021–2030 period, RS Official Gazette No. 103/2021, https://www.pravno-informacioni-sistem.rs/SlGlasnikPortal/eli/rep/sgrs/vlada/strategija/2021/103/1.

[43] Judicial Development Strategy for the 2020–2025 period, RS Official Gazette Nos 101/202, 18/2022, https://pravno-informacioni-sistem.rs/SlGlasnikPortal/eli/rep/sgrs/vlada/strategija/2020/101/1/reg.

[44] Revised Action Plan for Chapter 23, https://www.mpravde.gov.rs/tekst/30402/revidirani-akcioni-plan-za-poglavlje-23-i-strategija-razvoja-pravosudja-za-period-2020-2025-22072020.php.

[45] Activities related to interim benchmark 3.4.2. in the Revised Action Plan for Chapter 23 include the adoption of the new gender equality strategy and amendments to the Law on Gender Equality.

[46] Dokmanović (2018), Ferigra Stefanović (2021).

[47] Gender Equality Index is a composite indicator used to measure gender equality and progress made in reducing gender gaps. It consists of six core domains: work, money, knowledge, time, power, health and two satellite domains: intersecting inequalities and violence. The methodology, developed by the European Institute for Gender Equality (http://eige.europa.eu/) for the European Union and its Member States has been used in Serbia, an EU candidate country, since 2016 to track Serbia's progress in reducing gender gaps and achieving gender equality. The highest score that can be achieved is 100, denoting full gender equality.

[48] Babović and Petrović (2021), p. 10.

[49] Babović and Petrović (2021), p. 11.

[50] Babović and Petrović (2021), p. 20.

[51] Babović and Petrović (2021), p. 20.

shows a considerable gap compared to the EU in domains of money, (21,9) time (16.2) and knowledge (6.8).[52]

It is not easy to ascertain how these general tendencies reflect on the Serbian judiciary. The key corpus of legislation pertaining to the status and career of judges include the Law on Judges,[53] the Law on High Judicial Council,[54] and the Law on Organisation of Courts.[55] A comprehensive constitutional and legislative reform aimed at securing judicial independence, implemented under strong EU conditionality,[56] has been carried out in 2022[57] and 2023.[58] The process of adoption of the secondary legislation supporting the implementation of the new set of judicial laws is still ongoing. This means that the new laws have a limited impact on the appointments and promotion of judges in Serbia in the period under observation in this paper. However, it is worth noting that, unlike the case is in some neighbouring countries such as Montenegro and North Macedonia,[59] where the regulations mandate for gender equality to be considered in judicial appointments despite high percentage of feminization of their judiciaries, neither the "old" nor the new set of Serbian judicial laws include such provisions.

Additionally, there is no systemic gender-sensitive statistics in the Serbian judiciary[60] apart from the information collected under the CEPEJ reporting exercises,[61] nor is such statistics commonly communicated in annual statistical reports on the performance of the Serbian judiciary.[62] The information used in the present article is a combination of information processed by CEPEJ, information obtained from the Serbian High Judicial Council through a request for free access to information related to a specific dataset and desk research.

---

[52] Babović and Petrović (2021), p. 20.

[53] Law on Judges, RS Official Gazette No. 10/2023, https://www.pravno-informacioni-sistem.rs/SlGlasnikPortal/eli/rep/sgrs/skupstina/zakon/2023/10/6/reg.

[54] Law on High Judicial Council, RS Official Gazette No. 10/2023, https://www.pravno-informacioni-sistem.rs/SlGlasnikPortal/eli/rep/sgrs/skupstina/zakon/2023/10/11/reg/.

[55] Law on Organisation of Courts, RS Official Gazette No. 10/2023, https://www.pravno-informacioni-sistem.rs/SlGlasnikPortal/eli/rep/sgrs/skupstina/zakon/2023/10/7/reg.

[56] For more on challenges of EU conditionality in the field of rule of law and judiciary see: Knežević Bojović A and Ćorić (2023) and Knežević Bojović, Ćorić (2022). As to the specific aspects of judicial reforms in Serbia and their specific challenges see, inter alia: Rakić-Vodinelić et al. (2012); Milošević and Knežević Bojović (2017). Early efforts aimed at streamlining the harmonization of national law with EU *acquis* through a scientific approach can be found in a series of eight monographs published by the Institute of Comparative Law in early 2000s e.g. Ninković et al. (2004).

[57] Amendments to the Serbian Constitution were promulgated in 2022, following a national referendum held in late 2021.

[58] A set of three laws concerning the judiciary and two concerning the prosecutorial service were all adopted in early 2023.

[59] CEPEJ (2022), p. 72.

[60] Vujadinović (2013), p. 39.

[61] CEPEJ (2022), p. 72.

[62] See annual reports on the work of courts in Serbia at https://www.vk.sud.rs/sr-lat/publikacija-izve%C5%A1taj-o-radu-sudova.

For a better understanding of the information provided, some general information about the Serbian judicial system needs to be made. The court system in Serbia consists of courts of general jurisdiction and courts of special jurisdiction. Courts of general jurisdiction include 66 basic courts, 25 higher courts 4 courts of appeal and the Supreme Court. Courts of special jurisdiction include 44 misdemeanour courts, 16 commercial courts, Commercial court of appeal, Misdemeanour court of appeal and the Administrative court.[63]

In addition, a specialised department of the Higher Court in Belgrade processes war crime cases,[64] four specialised departments of the higher courts in Novi Sad, Belgrade, Niš and Kraljevo process corruption cases, while special departments of the Higher Court in Belgrade and the Appellate Court in Belgrade process organised crime and terrorism cases in first and second instance, respectively.[65]

Judges are appointed, promoted and dismissed by the High Judicial Council (hereinafter: HJC) a judicial self-governance body with additional powers in the disciplinary, ethical, educational and budgetary dimensions of judicial self-governance.[66] Requirements for judicial appointments, promotions and dismissals, including the appointments of court presidents are prescribed in the Law on Judges, but are regulated in more detail in secondary legislation promulgated by the HJC.

3.1 Overall Gender Balance in the Serbian Judiciary

In terms of general gender balance in the judiciary, over the past fourteen years, Serbia boasts a high percentage of female judges overall.[67] Data from December 2022, as recorded by the Serbian HJC is very persuasive (see Figs. 1 and 2).

---

[63] Law on Organisation of Courts, Articles 14–17. In 2023, the promulgated changes to the Constitution and the law governing the organisation of courts included the alignment of the name of the highest court in the country with its role. Namely, in the 2008–2023 period, the highest court was called the Supreme Court of Cassation, even though it did not have a purely cassation function. On the issue of finality of judicial decisions see Milošević (2016).

[64] Law on Organisation and Competences of State Bodies in War Crime Proceedings, RS Official Gazette No. 67/2003, 135/2004, 61/2005, 101/2007, 104/2009, 101/2011—other law, 6/2015 and 10/2023, https://www.pravno-informacioni-sistem.rs/SlGlasnikPortal/eli/rep/sgrs/skupstina/zakon/2003/67/4/reg.

[65] Law on Organisation and Competences of State Bodies in Combating Organised Crime, Terrorism and Corruption, RS Official Gazette No. 94/2016, 87/2018—other law and 10/2023, https://www.pravno-informacioni-sistem.rs/SlGlasnikPortal/eli/rep/sgrs/skupstina/zakon/2016/94/3/reg.

[66] For an elaboration of various dimensions of judicial self-governance see: Šipulova et al. (2023). For a recent exploration of the educational dimension in Serbian judiciary see: Knežević Bojović, Ćorić (2024).

[67] As reported to the European Commission for the Efficiency of Justice (CEPEJ) under its regular process for evaluating judicial systems of the Council of Europe's member states. Since 2010, the Serbian judicial system has consistently reported to include at least 69% of women in its judicial corps overall. The historical data can be explored at https://public.tableau.com/app/profile/cepej/viz/GenderEqualityEN/GenderEquality.

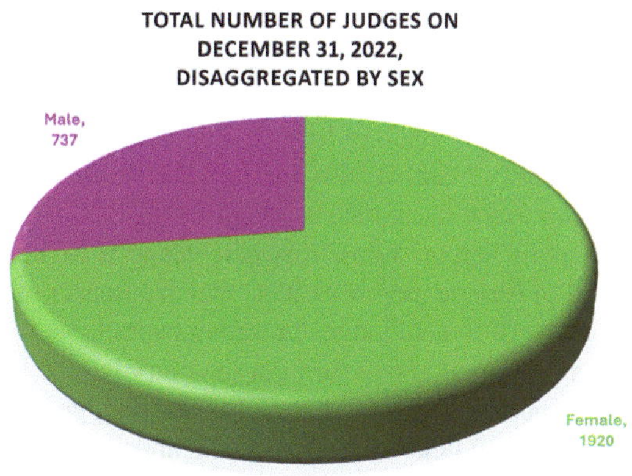

Fig. 1 Total number of judges

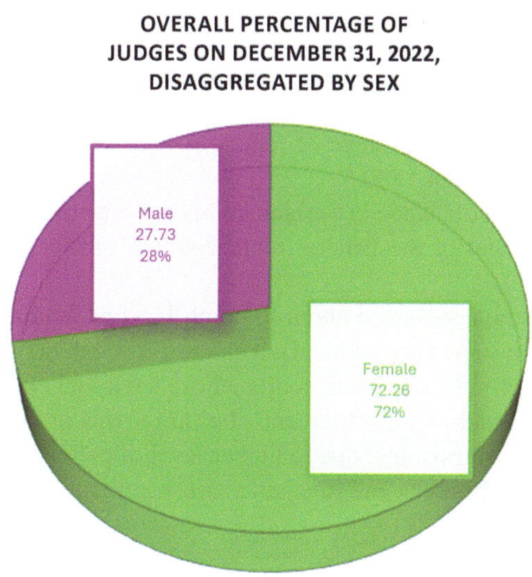

Fig. 2 Overall percentage of judges. *Source* High Judicial Council official records

Such a high percentage is consistent with the data presented by CEPEJ, where the reported percentage of female judges in Serbia in 2012 was 69%, and as high as 72% in 2020.[68] The high percentage of appointed female judges is not uncommon in former Socialist Federative Republic of Yugoslavia (SFRY) countries—out of the eight countries reported by European Commission for the Efficiency of Justice

[68] https://rm.coe.int/country-profile-serbia-en/1680a9673b.

(CEPEJ) to have the highest percentage of women in the judiciary, three are former Yugoslav republics (Croatia, Serbia and Slovenia).[69] Although Montenegro demonstrates a somewhat lower figure (57.2% of judges are women), it is still, even though slightly, above the median in Council of Europe member states amounting to 55% of female judges in all courts[70] Serbia also has a rather high percentage of female prosecutors—according to the latest data reported by CEPEJ, women accounted for 57% of all prosecutors in Serbia. While this percentage is higher than the median percentage in Council of Europe member states, which amounts to 52%, it is still not as high as the percentage of female judges in Serbia overall.[71]

Based on the data presented above Serbian judiciary can be assessed as feminized. The reasons for such a high percentage of women judges can be found in the general perception of the judicial office as a fair and stable public sector work environment.[72] The perception of a judicial office as a secure, family-friendly but a relatively low-paying job in Serbia, was additionally underlined during the 1990s, when, according to prominent Serbian judges, men left their judicial positions to pursue better paid careers in the private sector, mostly as attorneys-at-law, while women kept their secure jobs.[73]

The trend of increased feminization of Serbian judiciary has been identified in the 1980s, when an 25% increase of female judges was identified in then lowest, municipal courts in Serbia, going from only 6% in 1948 to 30% in 1980. The same research showed that the percentage of female judges in Serbia overall increased from 5% in 1948 to 27% in 1980.[74]

Currently, the gender balance in Serbian courts per type of court largely follows a pattern similar to that of the general representation of men and women in the judiciary (see Fig. 3).

To test whether the conclusion about the high level of feminization in Serbian judiciary comes with some geographical caveates, it is worth taking a closer look at the gender balance of judges in basic courts whose territorial competence includes mainly smaller rural and urban settlements, but not towns or cities (see Table 1). Starting from the hypothesis that, due to higher level of patriarchal values found to be more present in rural areas and in smaller urban settlements in Serbia,[75] fewer

[69] CEPEJ (2022), p. 69.

[70] CEPEJ (2022), p. 69.

[71] CEPEJ (2022) p. 116.

[72] See: OSCE (2019), p. 15. In-depth studies conducted in Montenegro (Janashia and Elezović 2022) and North Macedonia (Beker and Chalovska Dimovska 2022), two countries that share societal and legal history with Serbia, confirm this perception.

[73] Andrić (2023).

[74] Zvekić (1985).

[75] One socio-demographic research shows that in Serbia, the place of residence—urban vs. rural is a relevant predictor of both public and private patriarchy See: Petrović, I... and Radoman. M. (2019) Another research demonstrates that in Serbia, the size of the place of residence affects the adoption and replication of patriarchal values, where villages show the highest results on the patriarchy scale, followed by small and medium-sized urban residences, cities and the capitol city.

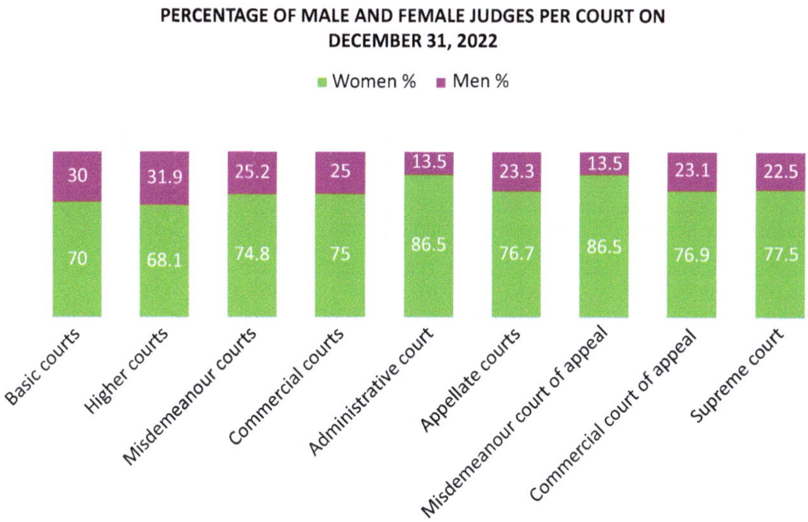

Fig. 3 Percentage of male and female judges per Court in 2022. *Source* High Judicial Council official records

women could be appointed as judges in courts in such areas, the authors had a look at the gender representation of women in courts of first instance whose territorial competence includes mostly rural areas or smaller towns.[76] The occurence seems to be relatively rare and has been identified in several courts accross three Serbian regions.[77] The most striking outlier in this regard is the Basic Court in Sjenica, where only one out of six judges is a woman. Similarly, in the basic court in Dimitrovgrad, two out of six judges are women, and in Bečej, two out of eight judges are female. However, other basic courts having territorial jurisdicition over territories of similar characteristics show a different pattern. The basic courts in

See: Pešić (2016). Relevant Serbian legislation (Law on the Territoral Organisation of the Republic of Serba, RS Official Gazette Nos. 129/07, 8/16, 47/18, 9/20) differentiates between municipalities (having at least 10.000 inhabitants) and cities, having at least 100.000 inhabitants. The Law on Seats and Territories of Courts and Public Prosecutors Offices, RS Official Gazette No. 101/2013 defines the seats and territories of courts. The authors took into account the names of judges of basic courts territories do not include towns as per the relevant legislation on territorial organisation, as available on the webpage of the Serbian High Judicial Council https://vss.sud.rs/sr-lat/spisak-sudija.

[76] As a rule, the territorial jurisdiction of second-instance courts includes towns, meaning that second-instance courts do not lend themselves for exploring the rural/urban predictor of patriarchy in terms of potential gender disparities.

[77] As classified by the Ordinance on the Nomenclature of Statistical Territorial Units, FRY Official Gazette 109/2009 and 46/2010. According to this law, the regions include: the Belgrade region, the Vojvodina region, Šumadija and Western Serbia region, South and Eastern Serbia region, Kosovo and Metohija region.

Table 1 Number and percentage of male and female judges in selected basic courts in Serbia

Region	Basic court	Number of female judges in the court/ total number of judges	Percentage of female judges in the court (%)	Difference in percentage points compared to percentage of women in all basic courts (%)
Šumadija and Western Serbia	Ub	2/5	40	–30
Šumadija and Western Serbia	Sjenica	1/6	16.7	–53.3
Šumadija and Western Serbia	Priboj	5/6	83.3	+3.3
Šumadija and Western Serbia	Brus	7/7	100	+30
South and East Serbia	Bujanovac	3/10	30	–40
South and East Serbia	Dimitrovgrad	2/6	33.33	–37.66
South and East Serbia	Surdulica	10/13	76.9	–0.1
Vojvodina	Bečej	2/8	25	–45
Vojvodina	Kikinda	11/11	100	+30

Brus and Kikinda are comprised of female judges only. Given that the judicial appointment process in Serbia is centralised, the instances of predominantly male courts can not be attributed to the gender bias within the appointment bodies, but could perhaps be accounted for by a somewhat to a stronger patriarchial culture within the local community itself, which may discourage women from pursuing certain professions. Neverthless, due to the existence of two all-female basic courts in similar, geographically very close communities, it is clear that deeper sociolegal research is needed to gain more insight into the root causes of the said occurences.

Currently, the Administrative court and the Misdemeanour Administrative Courts are major outliers in the Serbian legal system when it comes to the gender structure of the judicial corps, with over 85% of female judges.

The lowest percentage of women in Serbian courts can be found in higher courts—these are also the courts which have specialized departments for adjudicating in cases of organized crime, terrorism and corruption. Overall, 68,1% of judges of higher courts are women, compared to 70% of women in basic courts, almost 75% (74.8%) in misdemeanour courts or 75% in commercial courts. Even this, lowest percentage of women in Serbian courts is well over the COE median, which is 62%.[78] It is also a considerable leap forward compared to 1980 data for Serbia, when women comprised only 14% of judges in second-instance courts

[78] CEPEJ (2022).

(county courts).[79] A more elaborate analysis of the issue is quite difficult, if not completely impossible. The information on the number of judges appointed to specific judicial offices recorded by the High Judicial Council in general is not disaggregated by sex. Data, of the January 1, 2019—December 31, 2022 obtained from the High Judicial Council, sheds some light on the percentage of women and men appointed to the highest judicial offices—namely, to the courts of appeal and the Supreme Court (see Table 2). The available data suggests that, in the given period there was no considerable presence of gender bias, with the percentage of women appointed to appellate courts of general and special jurisdiction and the Supreme Court largely coinciding with the general gender balance within the Serbian judiciary. One notable exception can be seen in 2021, when out of the ten judges appointed to appellate courts of general jurisdicition, 50% were men and 50% were women. This can also be seen as a testament to the current lack of a prominent glass ceiling for female judges in Serbia.[80] This is, again, in considerable contrast to the observations made in 1980s, when the judicial profession was still assessed, from the socio-legal perspective, as a predominantly male profession which lacks gender democracy.[81]

For instance, in the observed four-year period, out of the eleven judges appointed to the Commercial Court of Appeal in the observed period, nine were female, while only two were male. When it comes to the Misdemeanour Court of Appeal, out of the eight judges appointed in the observed period, six were female and two males. Out of the total of 75 judges appointed to Appellate courts, 54 (72%) were female while 21 (28%) were male. Finally, out of the total number of judges appointed to the highest, Supreme Court, 21 were female and only 3 were male.

Table 2 Number of men and women appointed to highest court instances in Serbia in 2019–2022 period

Year/ Court	Commercial Court of Appeal		Misdemeanour Court of Appeal		Administrative Court		Appellate Courts		Supreme Court	
	M	F	M	F	M	F	M	F	M	F
2019		6				2	9	26	2	10
2020	1	2	1	4		3	5	11		
2021			1	2		3	5	5	1	6
2022	1	1					2	12		5

Source High Judicial Council official records

[79] Zvekić (1985).

[80] For regional comparison, for instance, see: Keller (2013) and Janashia and Elezović 2022.

[81] Zvekić (1985).

The above data shows that nowadays female judges in Serbia are not overlooked in appointments to high judicial offices.

It is worth noting, however, that the perceptions of female judges towards the gender issue in the judiciary seem to have evolved over time. For instance, in early 2000s, when interviewed on gender issues in the judiciary, some judges even refused to be "interviewed as women", underlining that gender is an irrelevant category within the profession.[82] However, in 2016, an Association of Female Judges in Serbia was formed, aiming to advocate for gender equality and judicial independence.[83] This is an indicator of a shift in the attitudes of women judges towards challenges they face in trying to achieve work-life balance and a level playing field in career promotion.

3.2 Gender Balance of Court Presidents in Serbia

Another very prominent judicial post in Serbian judiciary is that of the court president. Court presidents, while in principle being considered as *primus inter pares* in fact have considerable powers vis-à-vis everyday work of the court, as they are responsible for adopting the annual workplan of the court, which includes the assignment of subject-matter of cases for judges (annual work schedule) and appointments to positions such as court vice-presidents, court department heads, deciding on recusals and complaints, etc.[84] The data on December 31, 2022, in terms of gender structure of court presidents in Serbia, shows discrepancies compared to the general gender structure of the Serbian judiciary (see Fig. 4).

More specifically, out of 159 court presidents and acting court presidents, 90 (56.6%) are women, while 60 (43.4%) are men. The percentage of female court presidents is therefore 11.5% lower than the lowest percentage of female judges in courts. At the same time, the percentage of male court presidents is 15.6% higher than the average percentage of male judges in courts, and 11.4% higher than the highest percentage of male judges in a certain type of courts. What can be seen, however, is a change compared to 2013, when second-instance Serbian courts were mostly presided by men.[85]

It is worth noting that the president of the Supreme Court of Serbia is a women, as are the presidents of the Administrative Court and the Commercial Court of Appeal. Conversely, currently only one Court of Appeal has a woman as

[82] Mrševic (2003), p. 146.

[83] Paragraflex (2016).

[84] The powers and duties of the court president are elaborated in Article 53 of the Law on Organisation of Courts.

[85] http://www.mdtfjss.org.rs/sjfr/sr/analiza-unutrasnjeg-ucinka/4-3h-rodna-ravnopravnost-u-zaposljavanju-u-pravosudju-u-srbiji.

Fig. 4 Percentage of male and female court presidents. *Source* High Judicial Council official records

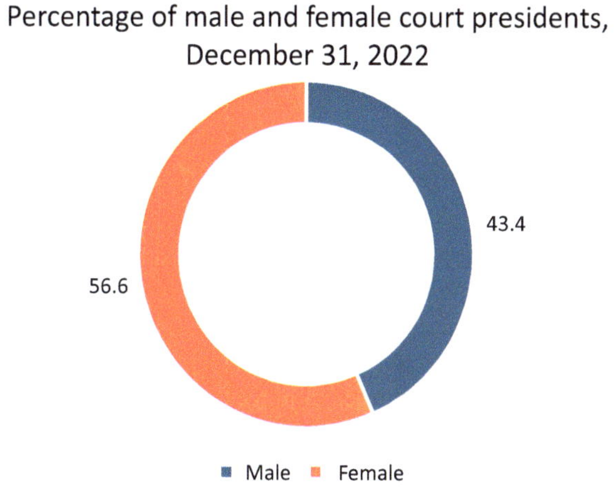

the president.[86] When it comes to second-instance courts of general jurisdiction (higher courts), out of the 25 higher courts, men are court presidents or acting court presidents in 11 courts (44%), while women are court presidents or acting court presidents in 14 courts (56%). It is also worth noting that, among these 25 court presidents, four are appellate court judges,[87] which also somewhat affects the overall ratios of male and female judges compared to male and female court presidents in the same types of courts. Compared to the percentage of female heads of prosecution offices in Serbia, the courts still have a higher percentage of court presidents. Namely, according to the publicly available data on the High Prosecutorial Council webpage,[88] 49% of all public prosecutor's offices in Serbia are headed by women, while 51% are headed by men.[89]

We cannot say with certainty whether the smaller percentage of female court presidents compared to overall percentage of women judges in Serbia can be attributed to men generally being more likely to apply for managerial posts in the judiciary, men being more likely to apply to such posts in smaller urban and

[86] https://vss.sud.rs/en/list-judges.

[87] The Serbian legal system allows for a judge of a higher instance court to be appointed as a president of a lower instance court. In this case, the judge is obligated to exercise the judicial office both in the court to which he or she is appointed and, in the court, where he or she is a court president (Article 76 of the Law on Judges of 2022). This provision ensures that the court president can adjudicate in cases where court presidents are by law vested with exclusive or primary powers to make decisions (e.g. in cases related to protection of the right to a trial within a reasonable time, in cases when recusal of judge is requested etc.).

[88] https://vst.jt.rs/spisak-nosilaca-javnih-tuzilackih-funkcija/.

[89] Notably, at present, the Supreme Public Prosecutor and two heads of Appellate Public Prosecutors' Offices (in Niš and Novi Sad) are women.

rural communities, which are also somewhat more patriarchal[90] or to a slight gender preference on the part of the bodies which appoint court presidents.[91]

3.3 Gender Balance of Judges in the High Judicial Council

It is also interesting to look at the gender structure of the HJC, the key judicial self-governance body in the Serbian legal system. The HJC has a wide set of competences, including those related to: judicial appointments and dismissals of judges and court presidents, judicial transfers, deciding on disciplinary issues, prescribing and monitoring the rules of judges' professional conduct (judicial ethics), initial and in-service training of judges, court budgeting, setting the number of judges, and more.[92] The HJC is comprised of six judges, who are elected by their peers, the Supreme court president, who is a member of the HJC *ex officio*, and four renowned lawyers elected by the National Assembly, following a public call.[93] The elections for HJC members coming from the ranks of judges took place in December 2020.[94] Out of six elected judges, five are female (83.3%), and only one is male (16.7%). This is a percentage that is almost on par with that in the courts with the highest percentage of female judges. What is more interesting, the female candidate for HJC members from the ranks of the highest courts (Supreme Court, Administrative Court, Commercial Court of Appeal) won against her single male opponent. Similarly, the female candidate from the ranks of judges of courts in autonomous provinces won over her one male candidate. Two judges elected from the ranks of basic and misdemeanour courts and the Misdemeanour court of Appeal, one male and one female, were elected among 15 candidates, 7 of whom were male, and 8 female. In other words, the gender balance among candidates did not reflect the composition of the Serbian judiciary, as the percentage of male candidates was higher than their gender representation in the judicial corps. However, female candidates have dominated this particular election and dominate the gender

[90] Petrović and Radoman (2019); Pešić (2016).

[91] Until the judicial reform of 2022 and 2023, this body was the Serbian National Assembly, but as of May 2023 and the constitution of the new High Judicial Council, it is the High Judicial Council that is responsible for all judicial appointments, including the appointment of court presidents.

[92] A non-exhaustive list of HJC competences can be found in Article 17 of the Law on HJC of 2022; additional competences are prescribed in the Law on Judges, the Law on Organization of Courts and the Law on Judicial Academy. A comprehensive view of the judicial self-governance in Serbia, including the delimitation of competences between the HJC and the line ministry is provided in Knežević Bojović, Ćorić (2024a).

[93] This composition of the HJC is prescribed in the amended Serbian Constitution and the Law on HJC of 2022 (Article 151 of the Serbian Constitution and Article 7 of the Law on HJC). Previously, the composition of the HJC differed with regards to its non-judicial members, but the number and structure of its judicial members have not been changed. For more details, see: Stanić (2022).

[94] High Judicial Council (2020).

structure of HJC members from among judges. In 2021, elections were organised for one HJC member from among appellate court judges. There were only two candidates, who were both female, and one of them was elected.[95]

3.4 Gender and Judicial Appointments and Promotion?

The above discussion seems to show that women in general do not have major issues in advancing through the judicial career, as the percentage of female judges is fairly constant throughout the judicial hierarchy, with the two major discrepancies being a high percentage of male court presidents, on the one hand, and a high percentage of female judges in the High Judicial Council.

However, some caveats need to be made before a conclusion going in favour of affirmative female gender representation in the Serbian judiciary is made. This is because the norms of relevant laws and bylaws governing judicial appointments and performance appraisal, which is closely linked to appointment requirements, in fact do not include any systemic mechanisms that would be beneficial for female judges or even mandate gender equality considerations.

When it comes to judicial appointments in Serbia there is no single-entry point to the judicial system. Judges are appointed based on a public call issued by the High Judicial Council, and anyone meeting the relevant requirements can apply. The requirements for judicial appointments in the law include Serbian citizenship, a given number of years of professional experience,[96] which gets progressively longer as the judicial ranks go higher, and having passed the Bar exam. This is complemented by the requirement of qualification, competence and worthiness, the criteria and indicators for which are prescribed by the High Judicial Council.

Firstly, it is important to note that the prerequisite years of professional experience needed for judicial appointment need not be acquired by exercising the judicial office only; quite to the contrary, judicial vacancies can also be filled with lawyers having a very general "professional experience record in the legal profession", which traditionally includes judicial assistants, whose majority is also female.[97] This means that the pool of candidates for judicial offices is very wide and includes all those with a law degree and a Bar exam. Additionally, this means that access to higher judicial offices is not restricted to acting judges only. Consequently, the percentage of female judges in these courts does not necessarily imply an upward career trajectory for women in the judiciary.

[95] https://vss.sud.rs/sites/default/files/document_category/Коначна%20листа%20кандидата%20за%20изборног%20члана%20из%20реда%20судија%20апелационих%20судова_1.pdf.

[96] But not too high—for instance, the appointment to Supreme Court presupposes at least twelve years of professional experience record, as prescribed in Article 49 of the Law on Judges.

[97] MDTF (2021) states that over 70% of case-related judicial staff in Serbia are women.

Secondly, the judicial appointment requirement of qualification and competence for judges that already exercise judicial office is, in fact, their performance appraisal for the past three years.[98] According to the former Law on Judges[99] (hereinafter: LoJ 2008) the performance appraisal criteria and indicators are prescribed by the High Judicial Council[100]; the current Law on Judges sets out eight general criteria which are then elaborated in more detail by the HJC.[101] Currently, the relevant Rulebook governing performance appraisal[102] is aligned with the LoJ 2008; the only criteria are quantity and quality of judge's work.[103] The criteria rely exclusively on quantitative, statistical data on the judge's performance in a three-year period. However, the Rulebook is completely silent on how to address prolonged absences from work, such as pregnancy or maternity leave. This is a particularly poignant issue, since the Serbian labour legislation recognises statutory maternity leave of at least three months (starting at least 28 days before the due date), which can be extended with a parental leave, making for up to 365 days in total.[104] If interpreted strictly, the Rulebook would in fact result in female judges who were on such leaves to be assessed as "unsatisfactory" or not to be assessed at all, given that there would be no statistical data to be used in their performance appraisal. Consequently, they are disqualified from promotion. This has been identified as problematic by Serbian judges.[105]

While the lack of regulation is equally problematic for judges who find themselves on long-term sick leaves, given that the majority of judges in Serbia are female, it is rather surprising that the relevant Rulebook completely ignores

[98] Article 4, paragraph 3 of the Rulebook on the Criteria and Indicators for Assessing Competence, Expertise, Capacity and Worthiness for Appointing Judges to Permanent Judicial Offices in Other or Higher Court and on Criteria for Nominating Court Presidents, RS Official Gazette No. 94/2016 and 48/2023, https://www.pravno-informacioni-sistem.rs/SlGlasnikPortal/eli/rep/sgrs/pravosudje/pravilnik/2016/94/2/reg.

[99] Law on Judges RS Official Gazette Nos. 116/2008-11, 58/2009-11 (CC), 104/2009-3, 101/2010-4, 8/2012-147 (CC), 121/2012-7, 124/2012-277 (CC), 101/2013-12, 111/2014-51 (Cc), 117/2014-3, 40/2015-6, 63/2015-301 (CC), 106/2015-61, 63/2016-28 (CC), 47/2017-3, 76/2021-3, https://www.pravno-informacioni-sistem.rs/SlGlasnikPortal/eli/rep/sgrs/skupstina/zakon/2008/116/2/reg.

[100] Article 32.

[101] Article 36.

[102] Rulebook on the criteria, indicators, procedure and bodies for assessing the performance of judges and court presidents, RS Official Gazette No. 81/2014, 142/2014, 41/2015, 7/2016, https://www.pravno-informacioni-sistem.rs/SlGlasnikPortal/eli/rep/sgrs/pravosudje/pravilnik/2014/81/1/reg.

[103] The quality of work is viewed through the percentage of quashed decisions made by the judge and the time in which the decisions were drafted. The quantity of work is viewed through the percentage in which the expected workload ("the norm") is achieved by a judge.

[104] Article 94 of the Labour Law, RS Official Gazette 24/2005-3, 61/2005-69, 54/2009-26, 32/2013-13, 75/2014-3, 13/2017-64 (CC), 113/2017-273, 95/2018-441, https://www.pravno-informacioni-sistem.rs/SlGlasnikPortal/eli/rep/sgrs/skupstina/zakon/2005/24/1/reg. On the legal gaps in the labour status and rights of Serbian judges see Knežević Bojović (Bojović A and Ćorić 2022).

[105] Andrić (2023).

issues such as pregnancy and maternity leaves. In some European countries, this issue is addressed through an assumption that, during the absence, the judge would have performed similarly as in the period before the leave or through the extension of the periods used for performance evaluation.[106] On the contrary, in Serbia, female judges of reproductive age are to an extent penalised for having babies in as much as they cannot be promoted. This indirect obstacle for the career advancement of female judges should also be viewed in the fact that Serbia has an aging judiciary[107] with over 500 judges retiring by the end of 2026, meaning that an influx of both young men and women in the judicial corps should be expected. In April 2024 the HJC has promulgated a new Rulebook on evaluation of the work of judges and court presidents,[108] which is aligned with the new Law on Judges. In addition to relying on a wider set of mostly qualitative and some quantitative indicators, this Rulebook expressly states that, in case of judges' absences for any reason prescribed by law (which covers pregnancy, maternity and parental leave but also sick leaves etc.), the performance appraisal period (once every five years), will be extended for the duration of the leave.[109] This is a step forward, as it will allow for the work of female judges who use pregnancy/or maternity and parental leave to be evaluated rather than overlooked. The new Rulebook will apply as of January 1, 2026, meaning that its full effects will be evident in three to four years. Whether this will be enough of a motivation for young women to opt for pursuing a career in the judiciary, remains to be seen. Namely, one recent research conducted in Serbia among law students shows that, despite the feminization within the judicial profession, both male and female law students are almost equally unmotivated to pursue careers in the judiciary—as only one in ten students wants to become a judge.[110] Additionally, the same research showed that the opportunities for future career advancement i.e. promotion is the most important factor that law students take into account when choosing their future profession. The students view the judiciary profession as unpromising, highly structured and inflexible.[111] Coupled with the perception that

[106] For the first option, see Portuguese Novo Regulamento de Inspeções do Conselho Superior da Magistratura No. 852/2021, https://diariodarepublica.pt/dr/detalhe/regulamento-extrato/852-2021-171207690, Article 12, paragraph 6. For the second option, see Italian Circolare n. 20691 dell'8 ottobre 2007 "Nuovi criteri per la valutazione di professionalità dei magistrati, con le modifiche apportate dall'Assemblea plenaria nelle sedute del 25 luglio 2012, 6 marzo 2014, 13 marzo 2014, 14 maggio 2014, 23 luglio 2014, 24 luglio 2014, 10 settembre 2014, 26 marzo 2015, 12 aprile 2017, 25 ottobre 2017 e 21 febbraio 2018". Capo XIII, 1 bis.

[107] Strategy for Human Resources in the Judiciary for the 2022–2026 period.

[108] RS Official Gazette No. 34/2024.

[109] Article 6, paragraph 3.

[110] Đorđević (2022) underlines that, while somewhat more women than men wish to become judges, the difference is not statistically significant.

[111] Đorđević (2022), p. 698.

the appointment to judicial positions in Serbia is uncertain and slow[112] it seems that Serbian judiciary will need to put in considerable efforts to replace its ageing judicial corps with both male and female judges.

4 Concluding Remarks

Serbia has a highly feminized judiciary, with over two thirds of the overall judicial corps being comprised of women. The glass ceiling in the Serbian judiciary is not particularly prominent when it comes to appointments to higher court instances. While improvements have been recorded over the past ten years, the percentage of male court presidents in Serbia remains notably higher than the percentage of men judges in courts overall.

Given the high figures of women in judicial offices, it is perhaps unsurprising that there are no systemic mechanisms aimed at facilitating women's access to judicial appointments and promotions, particularly given that as a rule, gender equality rules in Serbia are introduced and implemented precisely in order to increase women's participation.

While the present analysis has shown that the Serbian legal system currently suffers from deficiencies that may adversely affect the career advancement of female judges, this issue will be somewhat mitigated once the new set of rules on performance assessment starts to apply. While. Before considering the introduction of a mechanism that would mandate for gender to be taken into account in the judicial appointment process, a more profound sociolegal analysis would need to be conducted. That being said, Serbia seems to be facing a more systemic problem relating to the judiciary—one of depleting interest of law students to pursue a career in the judiciary. To address this challenge, key actors will need to take steps so as to render the judicial profession equally attractive to men and women.

References

Andrić G (2023) Kako je biti sutkinja u Srbiji. https://www.bbc.com/serbian/lat/srbija-64903129. Accessed 12 Nov 2023

Babović M, Petrović M (2021) Indeks rodne ravnopravnosti u Republici Srbiji. Tim za socijalno uključivanje i smanjenje siromaštva Vlade Republike Srbije.

Bajović V, Knežević Bojović A, Kostić J (2019) Analysis of the position of judicial assistants in the Republic of Serbia with recommendations for its improvement, Beograd, Beogradska konferencija pravnika. https://bekop.rs/wp-content/uploads/2019/06/BEKOP-Analysis-of-Position-of-Judicial-Assistants-in-the-Republic-of-Serbia-with-recommendations-for-improvements.pdf.

[112] Bajović, Knežević Bojović, Kostić (2019), p. 11.

Beijing Declaration and Platform for Action of 1995, https://www.un.org/womenwatch/daw/beijing/pdf/BDPfA%20E.pdf
Beker K, Dimovska C (2022) Gender and diversity in the judiciary North Macedonia, OSCE, Skopje
CEPEJ, European judicial systems CEPEJ Evaluation Report 2022 Evaluation cycle (2020 data), 5 October 2022, https://www.coe.int/en/web/cepej/special-file-report-european-judicial-systems-cepej-evaluation-report-2022-evaluation-cycle-2020-data
Circolare n. 20691 dell'8 ottobre 2007 "Nuovi criteri per la valutazione di professionalità dei magistrati, con le modifiche apportate dall'Assemblea plenaria nelle sedute del 25 luglio 2012, 6 marzo 2014, 13 marzo 2014, 14 maggio 2014, 23 luglio 2014, 24 luglio 2014, 10 settembre 2014, 26 marzo 2015, 12 aprile 2017, 25 ottobre 2017 e 21 febbraio 2018"
Committee of Ministers of the Council of Europe (2003) Balanced participation of women and men in political and public decision-making Recommendation Rec (2003) 3 adopted by the on 12 March 2003Communication from the Commission to the European Parliament, the Council, the European Economic and Social Committee and the Committee of the Regions A union of equality: Gender equality strategy 2020-2025, COM/2020/152 final
Constitution of the Republic of Serbia, RS Official Gazette No. 98/2006-3, 115/2021-3 (Amendments I-XXIX), 16/2022-3, https://www.pravno-informacioni-sistem.rs/SlGlasnikPortal/eli/rep/sgrs/skupstina/ustav/2006/98/1/reg.Declaration of the High-level Meeting of the General Assembly on the Rule of Law at the National and International Levels A /67/L.1
Deljkić I, Mališ-Sazdovska M, Spasić D (2023) Gender balance in the criminal justice system: Bosnia and Herzegovina, North Macedonia, and Serbia. In: Stojanoska A, Dimovski D, Maksimova E (eds) The handbook on female criminality in the former yugoslav countries. Springer
Dokmanović M (2018) Ka evropskom društvu - ograničenja i perspective. Institut društvenih nauka
Đorđević M (2022) Between the judiciary and advocacy: professional preferences of law students in Serbia. Sociol Pregled 56:680–708
European Commission for Democracy through Law (Venice Commission) Report on the Rule of Law CDL-AD(2011)003rev
Ferigra Stefanović A (2021) EU country gender profile for Serbia, https://www.rodnaravnopravnost.gov.rs/sites/default/files/2021-11/EU%20Gender%20Country%20Profile%20for%20Serbia.pdf
Hammerslev O (2013) Studies of the legal profession. In: Banakar R, Travers M (eds) Introduction to law and social theory, hart publishing, pp 325–339
High Judicial Council (2020). Voting results and detailed statistics for the election of High Judicial Council Members in 2020, https://vss.sud.rs/sites/default/files/document_category/Statistika%20i%20%20rezultati%20izbora%202020.pdf.
International Commission of Jurists (2013) Women and the Judiciary, Geneva Forum Series No.1, Materials relating to the 2013 Geneva Forum of Judges and Lawyers convened by the International Commission of Jurists. https://www.icj.org/wp-content/uploads/2014/10/Universal-Women-and-Judiciary-Gva-For-1-Publications-Conference-Report-2014-ENG.pdf
Janashia N, Elezovic S (2022) Gender equality in the judiciary in Montenegro. Council of Europe
Joint communication to the European Parliament and the Council EU Gender Action Plan (GAP) iii – An Ambitious Agenda for Gender Equality and Women's Empowerment in EU External Action (2020) SWD 284final
Keller L (2013) Feminizacija i stakleni strop u sudačkoj i odvjetničkoj profesiji u Hrvatskoj. Zagrebacka Pravna Revija 2(1):41–60
Knežević Bojović A (2022) Analiza radnopravnog položaja sudija, sudijskih saradnika i zaposlenih u pravosuđu u pravnom sistemu Srbije. Visoki Savet Sudstva http://ricl.iup.rs/id/eprint/1398

Knežević Bojović A, Ćorić V (2022) Vladavina prava – načelni izazovi i presek stanja u Srbiji na odabranim primerima iz oblasti pravosuđa. In: J ĆP, V Đ, Višekruna A (eds) 65 years since the rome treaties: European union and perspectives of Serbia's European integration, Institut za uporedno parvo pp 51–72

Knežević Bojović A, Ćorić V (2023) Challenges of rule of law conditionality in EU accession. Brat Law Rev 7(1):41–62

Knežević Bojović A, Ćorić V (2024) Educational dimension of judicial self-governance in the exercise of the judicial independence principle: the case of Serbia in the European integration process. Sociol Pregled 58(1):191–205

Knežević Bojović A, Ćorić V (2024a) Judicial self-governance in Serbia: challenges to and results of a quantitative approach. Pravn Zapis 25(2):352–393

Law L, RS Official Gazette 24/2005-3, 61/2005-69, 54/2009-26, 32/2013-13, 75/2014-3, 13/2017-64 (CC), 113/2017-273, 95/2018-441, https://www.pravno-informacioni-sistem.rs/SlGlasnikPortal/eli/rep/sgrs/skupstina/zakon/2005/24/1/reg

Law on High Judicial Council, RS Official Gazette No. 10/2023, https://www.pravno-informacioni-sistem.rs/SlGlasnikPortal/eli/rep/sgrs/skupstina/zakon/2023/10/11/reg/

Law on Judges, RS Official Gazette No. 10/2023, https://www.pravno-informacioni-sistem.rs/SlGlasnikPortal/eli/rep/sgrs/skupstina/zakon/2023/10/6/reg

Law on Judges RS Official Gazette Nos. 116/2008-11, 58/2009-11 (CC), 104/2009-3, 101/2010-4, 8/2012-147 (CC), 121/2012-7, 124/2012-277 (CC), 101/2013-12, 111/2014-51 (Cc), 117/2014-3, 40/2015-6, 63/2015-301 (CC), 106/2015-61, 63/2016-28 (CC), 47/2017-3, 76/2021-3, https://www.pravno-informacioni-sistem.rs/SlGlasnikPortal/eli/rep/sgrs/skupstina/zakon/2008/116/2/reg

Law on Judicial Academy, RS Official Gazette No. 4/2009, 32/2014 (CC), https://pravno-informacioni-sistem.rs/SlGlasnikPortal/eli/rep/sgrs/skupstina/zakon/2009/104/6

Law on Organisation and Competences of State Bodies in Combating Organised Crime, Terrorism and Corruption, RS Official Gazette No. 94/2016, 87/2018 – other law and 10/2023, https://www.pravno-informacioni-sistem.rs/SlGlasnikPortal/eli/rep/sgrs/skupstina/zakon/2016/94/3/reg

Law on Organisation and Competences of State Bodies in War Crime Proceedings, RS Official Gazette No. 67/2003, 135/2004, 61/2005, 101/2007, 104/2009, 101/2011 – other law, 6/2015 and 10/2023, https://www.pravno-informacioni-sistem.rs/SlGlasnikPortal/eli/rep/sgrs/skupstina/zakon/2003/67/4/reg

Law on Organisation of Courts, RS Official Gazette No. 10/2023, https://www.pravno-informacioni-sistem.rs/SlGlasnikPortal/eli/rep/sgrs/skupstina/zakon/2023/10/7/reg

Law on Prohibition of Discrimination, RS Official Gazette No. 22/2009 and 52/2021, https://www.pravno-informacioni-sistem.rs/SlGlasnikPortal/eli/rep/sgrs/skupstina/zakon/2009/22/1/reg/

Law on the Territorial Organization of the Republic of Serba, RS Official Gazette Nos. 129/07, 8/16, 47/18, 9/20, https://pravno-informacioni-sistem.rs/eli/rep/sgrs/skupstina/zakon/2007/129/1/reg

Milošević M (2016) Pravnosnažnost kao ustanova konfirmacije pravosudne delatnosti. In: Varady T, Mitrović D, Hiber D, Pavić V, Đorđević M, Jovanović M (eds) Liber amicorum: gašo Knežević. Pravni fakultet Univerziteta u Beogradu. Beograd, pp 516–535

Milošević M, Knežević Bojović A (2017) Trial Within Reasonable Time in Eu Acquis and Serbian Law. EU Comp Law Issues Chall Ser (ECLIC) 1:447–470

Mršević Z (2003) Žene u pravnim profesijama, Genero: časopis za feminističku teoriju istudije kulture 02-03

Multidonatorski poverenički fond za podršku sektoru pravosuđa u Srbiji (2021) Serbia Judicial Functional Review, http://www.mdtfjss.org.rs/en/mdtf_activities/2022/2021-serbian-judicial-functional-review-final-report

Ninković M, Damnjanović K, Cvijan V (2004) Građansko pravo; Intelektualna svojina: harmonizacija domaćeg zakonodavstva sa pravom Evropske unije. Institut za uporedno pravo, Beograd
Novo Regulamento de Inspeções do Conselho Superior da Magistratura No. 852/2021, https://diariodarepublica.pt/dr/detalhe/regulamento-extrato/852-2021-171207690
OECD (2016) 2015 OECD Recommendation of the Council on Gender Equality in Public Life. Paris, OECD Publishing https://doi.org/10.1787/9789264252820-en
Ordinance on the Nomenclature of Statistical Territorial Units, FRY Official Gazette 109/2009 and 46/2010
OSCE (2019) Gender, diversity and justice Overview and Recommendations. https://www.osce.org/files/f/documents/3/4/419840_0.pdf
Paragraflex (2016) Osnovana Asocijacija žena sudija Srbije: asocijacija se zalaže za rodnu ravnopravnost, efikasniji rad pravosuđa i zaštitu nezavisnosti sudstva. U članstvo prima i muškarce sudije koji se zalažu za ciljeve udruženja. https://paragraflex.rs/dnevne-vesti/050516/050516-vest1.html
Pešić J (2016) Value orientations in Postsocialist Societies of Serbia and Croatia, Doctoral dissertation, University of Belgrade Faculty of Philosophy
Petrović I, Radoman M (2019) Patrijarhalnost, autoritarnost i nacionalizam u Srbiji – promene vrednosnih orijentacija. In: M L, S C (eds) Stratifikacijske promene u periodu konsolidacije kapitalizma u Srbiji, Univerzitet u Beogradu – filozofski fakultet Institut za sociološka istraživanja, pp 215–246
Rakić-Vodinelić V, Knežević Bojović A, Reljanović M (2012) Judicial reform in Serbia 2008-2012. Centar za unapređivanje pravnih studija. Beograd
Report of the Special Rapporteur on the independence of judges and lawyers, Diego García-Sayán, Participation of Women in the Administration of Justice A/76/142
Resolution adopted by the General Assembly on 25 September 2015 Transforming our world: the 2030 Agenda for Sustainable Development A/RES/70/1
Rulebook on Evaluation of the Work of Judges and Court Presidents, RS Official Gazette 34/2024, https://pravno-informacioni-sistem.rs/eli/rep/sgrs/pravosudje/pravilnik/2024/34/4/reg
Rulebook on the Criteria and Indicators for Assessing Competence, Expertise, Capacity and Worthiness for Appointing Judges to Permanent Judicial Offices in Other or Higher Court and on Criteria for Nominating Court Presidents, RS Official Gazette No. 94/2016 and 48/2023
Rulebook on the Criteria and Indicators for Assessing Competence, Expertise, Capacity and Worthiness for Appointing Judges to Permanent Judicial Offices in Other or Higher Court and on Criteria for Nominating Court Presidents, RS Official Gazette No. 94/2016 and 48/2023
Rulebook on the Criteria, Indicators, Procedure And Bodies For Assessing The Performance of Judges and Court Presidents, RS Official Gazette No 81/2014, 142/2014, 41/2015, 7/2016, https://www.pravno-informacioni-sistem.rs/SlGlasnikPortal/eli/rep/sgrs/pravosudje/pravilnik/2014/81/1/reg
Rulebook On The Criteria, Indicators, Procedure And Bodies For Assessing The Performance Of Judges And Court Presidents, RS Official Gazette No 81/2014, 142/2014, 41/2015, 7/2016, https://www.pravno-informacioni-sistem.rs/SlGlasnikPortal/eli/rep/sgrs/pravosudje/pravilnik/2014/81/1/reg
Schultz U, Shaw G (2013) Introduction: gender and judging: overview and synthesis. In: Schultz U, Shaw G (eds) Gender and judging. Hart Publishing, Oxford/Oregon, pp 1–47
Šipulova K, et al (2023) Judicial Self-Governance Index: towards better understanding of the role of judges in governing the judiciary. Regul Gov 17:22–42
Special Rapporteur on the Independence of Judges And Lawyers (2011) Report of the Special Rapporteur on the Independence of Judges and Lawyers, Gabriela Knaul, A/HRC/17/30
Stanić M (2022) Sudski saveti: sastav i nadležnosti širom Evrope, Institut za uporedno parvo.

Strategy for Gender Equality for the 2021-2030 period, RS Official Gazette No. 103/2021, https://www.pravno-informacioni-sistem.rs/SlGlasnikPortal/eli/rep/sgrs/vlada/strategija/2021/103/1
Tamanaha B (2012) The history and elements of the rule of law, Singap J Leg Stud: 232–247
UN Committee on the Elimination of Discrimination Against Women (CEDAW) General Recommendation No. 23: Political and Public Life, A/52/38
UN Committee on the Elimination of Discrimination Against Women (CEDAW) General Recommendation No. 33 on women's access to justice CEDAW/C/GC/33
United Nation, Convention on the Elimination of All Forms of Discrimination against Women (CEDAW) Adopted and opened for signature, ratification and accession by General Assembly resolution 34/180 of 18 December 1979
United Nations, Convention on the Political Rights of Women, adopted by the General Assembly on 20 December 1952, A/RES/640
United Nations, Declaration on the Elimination of Discrimination against Women, A/RES/22/2263
United Nations, International Covenant on Civil and Political Rights, adopted and opened for signature, ratification and accession by General Assembly resolution 2200A (XXI) of 16 December 196. https://www.ohchr.org/en/instruments-mechanisms/instruments/international-covenant-civil-and-political-rights
United Nations, International Covenant on Economic, Social and Cultural Rights, adopted and opened for signature, ratification and accession by General Assembly resolution 2200A (XXI) of 16 December 1966. https://www.ohchr.org/en/instruments-mechanisms/instruments/international-covenant-economic-social-and-cultural-rights
United Nations, Charter of the United Nations, 24 October 1945, 1 UNTS XVI
Universal Declaration of Human Rights Adopted and proclaimed by General Assembly resolution 217 A (III) of 10 December 1948
Vujadinović D (2013) Rod i pravna regulativa. In: Lilić S (ed) Perspektive implementacije evropskih standarda u pravni sistem Srbije (knjiga 3). Pravni fakultet Univerziteta u Beogradu pp 60–80
Working group on Discrimination Against Women and Girls (2013) Report of the Working Group on the issue of discrimination against women in law and practice, A/HRC/23/50
Zvekić U (1985) Profesija sudija: sociološka analiza, Institut za kriminološka i sociološka istraživanja.

Ana Knežević Bojović is a Senior Research Associate at the Institute of Comparative Law in Belgrade, with over 20 years of research experience in the field of comparative law, EU law, judiciary and judicial reform. Her work includes a comprehensive corpus of research dedicated to judiciary and judicial reform issues. Most notably, she co-authored the monographs "Evropski sud pravde" and "Judicial Reform in Serbia 2008–2012". Recently, her work focuses on judicial ethics and the disciplinary liability of judges. She represents the Institute of Comparative Law in the Members Consultative Committee for the development of ELI-Mount Scopus European Standards of Judicial Independence.

Monika Milošević is a legal scholar with over 25 years of research and teaching experience. Her academic work focuses on civil procedure, environmental law and alternative dispute resolution. Ms Milošević has authored or co-authored monographs and articles in prestigious national journals and participated in a number of international conferences, relying mostly on dogmatic, normative, comparative and exegetic methods. Her teaching methods are universally recognized to foster a participative approach, continuously engaging students and ensuring their thorough understanding of complex legal issues. Currently, Ms Milošević is committed to developing her family business while she continues to explore current legal issues as an independent researcher.

Part II
Lawyers, Notaries

The Position of Female Attorneys in Montenegro in Comparison to Other Legal Professions: Between a Minority and a Majority

Matija Stojanović

Abstract This paper presents a critical study of the evolution, development, and current status of female attorneys in Montenegro, a country whose society was historically deeply influenced by patriarchal societal patterns and outlooks. Although the Bar Association of Montenegro had been founded in 1909, the first female to practice law in Montenegro registered in 1959. As of 2023, the share of women in the total number of registered attorneys of Montenegro is 33%. Although this number is significantly higher than the percentage of women who practiced law during the mid-nineties (1996) when the total number of women registered in the Bar Association was roughly 14.55%, it corresponds neither to the percentage of women in the judiciary, where they make up for the majority of judges (57%) nor to the percentage of women in Public Prosecution Offices, where they make up for the majority of prosecutors (62.14%), nor to the percentage of women in Notary Public—where they also present a majority (64%). In this article, the author will conduct an analysis aimed at defining the sociological determinants which contribute to such an uneven percentage of women among attorneys compared to other legal professions in Montenegro. The method the author will use will be that of qualitative empirical research, consisting of interviews with female attorneys from Montenegro.

M. Stojanović (✉)
Faculty of Law, University of Montenegro, Podgorica, Montenegro
e-mail: matija.s@ucg.ac.me

© The Author(s), under exclusive license to Springer Nature Switzerland AG 2025

S. Baer et al. (eds.), *The Gender and the Judiciary*, Gender Perspectives in Law 7,
https://doi.org/10.1007/978-3-032-06885-9_5

1 Introduction

1.1 Patriarchy in Montenegro—Historical Perspective

The patriarchal social structure of Montenegro is attributed to the specific historical and cultural background of this society. Prior to the mid-nineteenth century, no centralized state institutions or monopoly of force existed in most of modern-day Montenegro. Its inhabitants enjoyed *de facto* independence from any form of rule and legal order.[1] Instead of employing state order, its inhabitants were organized in tribes and other forms of collectives based on the principle of kinship. Lacking state institutions, distribution of justice was left to individuals and their kinsmen, earning Montenegro the unflattering title of "lawless land" plagued by blood feuds and other ills of a stateless society.[2] Such a stateless, tribal society was in a permanent state of conflict, nurturing a particularly male centered warrior culture in which it was understood that the primary role of every man is that of a warrior.[3]

In such a constellation, women were understood to employ the role of a housekeeper.[4] The subordination of women to wider collectives (tribe, kin) was more emphasized than that of men, this being reflected in the existence of arranged marriages, abductions for marriage,[5] and overall preference of male offspring.[6] Women were virtually absent from public life in Montenegro. They lacked the right to both attend and vote on the tribal assemblies.[7] In general, women were rarely seen in public with their husbands. In case they would show up together, the husband would always walk ahead of his wife, with her following him.[8] Gradual installment of state institutions and state-sanctioned law in the nineteenth century brought with it gradual but slow disintegration of tribal structures. Attempts of state authority to emancipate the position of the women in society were present, but the disintegration of patriarchal cultural patterns, especially in private matters, was of limited success as women remained generally subordinated to their husbands and their family.[9] Moreover, even after the installment of state parliamentary system in Montenegro, women didn't gain the right to elect or be elected, nor did they employ visible positions in state hierarchy—with public life remaining almost exclusively male.[10]

---

[1] Стојановић (2020), pp. 82–89.
[2] Boem (1998), pp. 50–55.
[3] Temidzer (2017), p. 45.
[4] Tepavčević (2018), p. 242.
[5] Stojanovic (1974), pp. 213–222.
[6] Tepavčević (2018), pp. 239–240.
[7] Rakonjac (2020), p. 63.
[8] Filipović (2003), p. 57.
[9] Stojanovic (1974), pp. 237–239; Rakonjac (2020), pp. 188–190.
[10] Filipović (2003), p. 57.

The understanding that the primary role of every woman was that of a mother and a wife which should be focused on providing care for her household and family, was particularly undisputed until after the Second World War (WWII).[11] It was only after WWII and the socialist revolution, with the adoption of Constitution of the Federal People's Republic of Yugoslavia (FPRY) from 1946, that women were proclaimed nominally equal to men and granted rights to elect and be elected. It was then that women in Montenegro, which was at a time a federal republic of FPRY, gained the right to hold public offices.[12] However, the nominal equation of women with men didn't significantly affect the inherited patriarchal social patterns. Out of all Yugoslav Republics, feminization of public life had the least success in Montenegro. Comparing data from former Yugoslav Republics, it is evident that Montenegro continuously produced the lowest number of women in its representative organs.[13] In the period between 1946–1963, the number of female parliamentarians was constantly under 5%, with it being as low as 2.80% in 1946–1950. Other parliamentary periods witnessed quite low numbers as well, as women made up only 3.54% of parliamentarians in the period of 1969–1974. In the period of 1990–1992, this number was 4.8%, and in the period of 1998–2002 it was 5.12%.[14] Analyzing overall data from 1946–2002, the highest percentage of women in Montenegrin Parliament was recorded in 1958–1963, when 14.56% of overall parliamentarians were women.[15] It is argued that the feminization of public life which was introduced after WWII, despite being of limited success, had nevertheless "melted away" with the fall of communist regime, with repatriarchalisation occurring in Montenegro.[16] Much like elsewhere in post-socialistic countries, the process of repatriarchalisation implied women once again retreating from public life and labor market, focusing more on the private sphere and playing a more dominant role in the upbringing of children and family.[17]

Today, even though the equality of both genders has nominally been proclaimed, as well as having measures of affirmative action introduced by contemporary Montenegrin legislature,[18] which intensified the feminization of public life, patriarchal norms continue to influence both private sphere of Montenegrin society as well as the labor market in general. Studies suggest that the traditional understanding of

---

[11] Djurić (2023), pp. 179–188; Filipović (2003), pp. 57–58.

[12] Women are equal to men in all areas of state, commercial and socio-political life", Article 24, para. 1 of the Constitution of the People's Republic of Montenegro from 1946 (Устав Народне Републике Црне Горе од 1946, "Сл. лист НР ЦГ", бр. 2/1947), the same provision was present in the Federal Constitution, see Article 24 of the Constitution of the Federal People's Republic of Yugoslavia (Устав Федеративне Народне Републике Југославије од 1946, "Сл. лист ФНРЈ", бр. 10/1946").

[13] Filipović (2003), p, 48.

[14] Filipović (2003).

[15] Filipović (2003), p.58.

[16] Filipović (2003). p. 53, Djurić (2023), pp. 186–187.

[17] Babović (2021), p. 1, Blagojević (2007), pp. 178–179.

[18] Janashia N, Elezovic S (2022), pp. 10–12.

gender roles still produces a distinction between female and male professions, with men traditionally holding all positions of power, while women are more directed towards professions of providing services or caretaking.[19] Official statistics supplement this claim, as women are most dominantly present in professions related to the upbringing of children, such as education,[20] and caretaking services such as health and social work.[21]

1.2 Female Attorneys in Montenegro—Comparative Perspective

In Montenegro, much like in other former Yugoslav Republics: "the term 'lawyer' (pravnik in Serbian/Croatian/Bosnian) simply denotes someone who has completed a legal education, which qualifies the holder for various jobs, including administration, civil service, and management".[22] In opposition to the term "pravnik", the term "advokat" (for which we will use the English term "attorney") is more specific, referring to someone who practices advocacy, a free and independent profession which provides legal aid before courts of Montenegro and other institutions.[23] In order for a lawyer to become an attorney, he/she must enroll in the Bar Association of Montenegro (BAM). In order to enroll in BAM, one must pass the bar exam (*advokatski ispit*),[24] prior to which he must also pass the judiciary exam (*pravosudni ispit*), which presumes having spent three to five years in apprenticeship in relevant legal professions.[25] Most prominent such professions are: Judiciary (*sudstvo*), Public Prosecution (*javno tužilaštvo)* and Public Notary (*notarijat*). In addition to these, apprenticeship can be carried out in commerce or state institutions.[26]

As was previously pointed out, women in Montenegro started entering public life only after WWII. Because of this, despite being founded in 1909, the Bar Association of Montenegro (BAM) had no women enroll in it for half a century. The first woman to enroll as an attorney in Montenegro was Antonija Bulat-Stojanović.[27] She joined BAM on 1st of October 1959,[28] and she had been, for a long time, the only female attorney in Montenegro. The next female attorney

[19] Uljarević, et al. (2013), p. 21.

[20] Statistical Office of Montenegro (2022), pp. 34–48.

[21] Statistical Office of Montenegro (2022), p. 64.

[22] Vuković D, Dabetić V, Forić S. (2020), p. 353.

[23] Constitution of Montenegro (2007, rev. 2013), article 21.

[24] Zakon o advokaturi (2017), article 5, line 1 point 3.

[25] Zakon o pripranvicima u sudovima i državnom tužilaštvu i pravosudnom ispitu (2016), article 29.

[26] Zakon o pripranvicima u sudovima i državnom tužilaštvu i pravosudnom ispitu (2016), article 29.

[27] Marinović (2009), p. 443.

[28] Marinović (1997), p. 270.

joined BAM in 1968.[29] However, despite such numbers, Bulat-Stojanović was elected president of the BAM for the term of 1984–1985.[30] At the time of her term as the president of BAM, only four female attorneys, including her, existed in Montenegro.[31] Although the number of men which were attorneys at the time is hard to determine precisely, it can be approximated as around 70.[32] Higher influx of women in advocacy occurred only after the end of Bulat-Stojanović's term, during the second half of the 1980's and during early 1990's, which coincides with the fall of socialism and the introduction of market-oriented economy.

Five female attorney joined BAM in 1990, and 14 more in 1993. Based on the list of members of BAM from 1996, the share of women within the total number of attorneys enlisted in BAM by 1996 was approximately 14.55%.[33] This percentage gradually increased, as by 2003, women made up 18.87% of attorneys in Montenegro.[34] In 2003, the percentage of female legal apprentices training to become attorneys was as high as 30.55% of overall apprentices, testifying to the rise of interest towards advocacy in the eyes of the younger female population. However, according to data from 2003, at this time women made up 18.87% of overall attorneys, but up to 40.95% of overall judges, 69.23% of prosecutors in basic prosecutors' offices and 60.86% of prosecutors in higher prosecutors' offices.[35] This points to the existence of a phenomenon that attracts the central

---

[29] Marinović (1997), p. 288.

[30] Marinović (2009), p. 443.

[31] Marinović, (1997), pp. 270, 288, 307, 314; Although the records state that one of these attorneys, Kosa Medenica, quit her practice in 1976, this information seems to be a typo since it is also stated that she had started her practice in 1979. So, it is most likely that she started her practice in 1979, having ended it in 1986 or sometime later. This assumption is supported by the list of attorneys published by the same author in 2009, in which Kosa Medenica is attorney no. 186, categorized listed as having started her practice *after* 1972, *see:* Marinović (2009), p. 464.

[32] Marinović, (1997), pp. 257–330; The reason the number is approximate is because we do not possess exact data for the number of attorneys enlisted in BAM in the period of 1984–1985, which corresponds to Bulat-Stojanović's term as president of BAM. Rather, the number of approximately 70 attorneys is reconstructed by referring to the list of all attorneys enlisted in BAM by 1996 and taking into account only the male attorneys which have not ended their practice before 1984. (start of Bulat-Stojanović's term) as well as those who have started it during her term, i.e. before the end of 1985 (end of Bulat-Stojanović's term). Considering the information on the dates of retirement of some male attorneys is not stated, the number of male attorneys active in 1984–1985. could have been somewhat higher then 70.

[33] Marinović, (1997), pp. 257–488; The percentage was calculated by referring to the list of attorneys BAM had provided in 1996, which included a number of (male) attorneys who had stopped practicing law by 1996, because of which the estimate of 14.55% cannot be taken as reflecting the number for year 1996. per se, but rather the total number of attorneys enrolled in BAM by 1996. However, data from 2003. shows that the percentage of female attorneys does roughly correspond to this number.

[34] Filipović (2003), p. 68–69.

[35] Filipović (2003).

attention of this article: the fact that in comparison to other legal professions, in Montenegro, advocacy contains the strikingly lowest percentage of women.

Data from 2013 further proves the existence of this phenomenon. By 2013, the overall status of women in Montenegrin legal professions further improved in comparison to 2003. Women made up the majority of judges in Montenegro (56.03%), making up the majority of judges in the Supreme Court (55.56%) as well as the Commercial Court in Podgorica (68.75%). By then, a woman had been elected president of the Supreme Court of Montenegro. In 2013, women also made up significant majority of public prosecutors (60%).[36] The then newly-established profession of public notaries was also predominantly female, with women making up 56% of overall public notaries in Montenegro.[37] On the other hand, in comparison to these professions, the percentage of female attorneys, despite having increased, still remained strikingly lower, making up only 26.71% of overall attorneys.[38]

The situation remains relatively unchanged in 2023 as well. Data from 2023 shows that women still make up the majority of judges in Montenegro (57%),[39] as well as the majority of public prosecutors (62.14%),[40] and public notaries (64%).[41] In the mean-time, the share of women among attorneys amounts to 33% of overall attorneys in 2023, numbering 363 female attorneys out of total 1100 attorneys enlisted in BAM.[42] Despite having significantly increased in the last decade, the number of female attorneys remains comparatively lower when compared to other legal professions.

2 Research Hypothesis, Methodology and Sample

The uneven distribution of women within advocacy in comparison to other legal professions cannot be explained by historical reasons, as judiciary and public prosecution were also closed for women prior to the end of WWII. According to some reports, the first female judge in Montenegro assumed office in 1954, only five years before the first female attorney.[43] The question therefore arises: how to explain

[36] Statistical Office of Montenegro (2014), pp. 74–75.

[37] Advokatska komora (2013), data based on the list of public notaries presented in this publication.

[38] Advokatska komora (2013), pp. 197–2015; The percentage was calculated based on the official list of attorneys enlisted in BAM on 4.11.2013.

[39] Sudski savjet Crne Gore (2023), p. 18; This report utilized data from up to the end of 2022.

[40] Tužilački savjet Crne Gore (2023), p. 42; This report utilized data from 31.12.2021.

[41] Advokatska komora Crne Gore (2023), pp. 203–206. This percentage was calculated based on the official list of public notaries as of 7.10.2023.

[42] Advokatska komora Crne Gore (2023), pp. 165–199; This percentage was calculated based on the official list of attorneys enlisted in BAM on 1.11.2023.

[43] Parliament of Montenegro (2018), p. 26; This information was presented in a speech to the parliament by the then-president of parliament of Montenegro. No additional information regarding this could be found.

the relatively less successful feminization of advocacy in comparison to other legal professions? Filipović, who was the author of the first study of women in Montenegrin judiciary, tried to explain this discrepancy in following terms: "the profession of attorneys is a profession of defense and not many would want, regardless of whether they are a man or a woman, to be 'defended' by a woman. The second reason could be connected with the fact that the female 'nature' is quiet, not too loud, which gives the person being defended the impression that it is not being defended 'strongly' enough, and that the attorney is 'not trying enough'."[44]

The factor that Filipović believes to have contributed to the lower number of women within attorneys is the patriarchal perception of gender traits and roles, which supposedly produces a negative perception and reception of women in this profession, especially in the eyes of potential clients who'd much rather be represented by men. Such perception can therefore be understood as an external sociological barrier which is barring women from successfully practicing advocacy. Other than Filipović's study, no other attempts to address this phenomenon had been made in Montenegro.

However, results of research conducted in societies not much different from Montenegro, such as Republic of Serbia, provide additional hypotheses which could be explored in trying to explain the discrepancy between the share of women in advocacy in comparison to other legal professions. The lower number of women in advocacy in comparison to other legal professions could be explained by the inclination of woman towards establishing a family and balancing work with private family life.[45] Considering that in Montenegro women generally employ dominant role in the upbringing of children as well as in maintenance of household, often choosing to sacrifice work in favor of private obligations once they're employed, it can be assumed that it is the disposition of women towards family life, especially motherhood, which contributes to women willingly avoiding the profession of advocacy, which is perceived as particularly unsuitable in providing a good work-family balance.

In this article, we will test out both of these hypotheses. We will research whether patriarchal perception of female traits does influence, and if yes to what extent, the labor market in Montenegro and whether it makes advocacy particularly unwelcoming for female attorneys. We will also research whether and to what extent does the disposition of women to start a family and achieve motherhood influence the prospect of choosing advocacy as a potential choice of career. Ultimately, we will try to assess to which of these two factors, if any, can we attribute the uneven distribution of women within advocacy in comparison to other legal professions.

In order to achieve this, we utilized the method of qualitative research, conducting a total of thirteen semi-structured in-depth interviews with female attorneys practicing in Montenegro. The respondents were roughly aged 25–49, and

[44] Filipović (2003), pp. 69–70.

[45] Stanojević (2022), pp. 75–80; 86–88.

were selected using a method of deliberate sample and "snowball" technique. This technique implies that the author started with a small number of initial respondents who fit the research criteria. After having been interviewed, these respondents recommend other potential respondents that fit the research criteria who also might be willing to participate in the research. The new respondents, in turn, also recommend other potential participants, and so on.[46] Using this method, a total of thirteen interviews were conducted. The interviews were held in person, and in some rare cases online or by phone. The oral interviews were, when granted permission, recorded and transcribed. Although the interviews were semi-structured, each of the interviews revolved around a certain order of questions. Each interviewee was asked why and how she decided to become an attorney, as well as to describe the reaction of their immediate surroundings to their choice of profession. The interviewees were then asked to determine the main advantages and disadvantages advocacy carries with it, as well as to share their perception of whether gender equality is on a satisfactory level within advocacy. Afterwards, the interviewees were also asked whether women face additional (dis)advantages in this profession, as well as to describe how they balance their work and family obligations. They were also asked to share their opinion on whether it is same for a woman to practice criminal and civil law. Ultimately, the interviewed women were asked whether they'd recommend the profession of an attorney to younger women, specifically law students.

3 (Self)-Perception of Female Attorneys in Montenegro—Influences of Patriarchal Understanding of Gender Roles

Nine out of thirteen of the interviewed female attorneys (respondents) claimed women are generally disadvantaged in legal practice. Most of them described having a "sense" or rather a "feeling" of inequality, which they attributed to the patriarchal notions of Montenegrin society. One of the respondents explained:

> I think women are faced with additional obstacles when dealing with this profession because in our environment, in Montenegro, a man's word is simply valued more and it always has a specific gravity to it. I best felt that in some cases in which (other) attorneys were male.

> You simply feel it, that it exists in Montenegro, this primacy. We are a long way from equality.

Another respondent provided a very similar answer when describing her overall experience in advocacy: "I think this is a product of our patriarchal mentality, because of which even female judges see male attorneys as having bigger authority. Even if I cannot prove it, I simply have this feeling". Other respondents also

[46] Parker & Scott (2019), p. 3.

reported having an entrenched feeling of inequality: "No one from the court or from the colleagues will tell you this, but you can see it in their attitude, the way they communicate with you in comparison to the way they communicate with others, you see a difference. These are some things that you feel, but an external observer perhaps wouldn't notice". Others were much more concise in their answers, but still pointed in the same direction: "It is harder for a woman, she must fight more, even for a decision." Another attorney explained: "There is a prejudice in this society that a woman cannot be as successful of an attorney as a man, which influences the work of female attorneys".

However, outside of general statements claiming that women are disadvantaged in comparison to men, only a few respondents produced telling examples of discriminatory behavior. One of the respondents, a young female attorney, explained how she received threats from the opposing party in the courtroom. Despite her insisting, the judge, who was male, refused to insert the threats in the court record and sanction them. After having raised her voice and insisting that the judge inserts the threats into court records, the judge suggested to the respondent not to be hysterical, also asking her if she's married. After receiving a negative reply, the judge suggested that no one will marry her if she behaved like that, attributing her outburst to "female hysteria". This respondent commented: "I believe that in my relation to clients, especially in my relation to some judges who are older or have remained in office from some past times, that I am foremost seen as a woman and someone whose place is not in advocacy. My effort, the fact that I passed the Bar Exam, that I have fought for my position and gained experience, it's all secondary. I must fight for my position more than my colleagues."

Some of the respondents agreed that feminine characteristics do not enjoy preference neither in the eyes of the clients nor in the eyes of judges and other attorneys, while masculine traits are generally associated with success. One of the respondents said that when entering a courtroom a woman must "put on pants" and behave like a man: "You cannot have it any other way. If you display female characteristics, such as femininity, and kindness, they see it as a weakness. It happened to me a great load of times that my kindness had been interpreted as a weakness". Another respondent claimed that a woman must adopt male characteristics in order to be taken seriously in the court: "Clients knew to criticize me for not being aggressive enough. (…) I would get compliments whenever I'd show temper, react a bit more strongly. (…) They would tell me I am a good attorney and that they will always pick me from now on". She concluded that the more aggressive and masculine you are, the better attorney you're perceived to be.

Another respondent concurred, explaining how she realized that after practicing law for many years she "needed to change her character": "When one encounters all the temptations which advocacy carries with it, one must change their character, one must become tougher, more arrogant. That's the only way one will manage to succeed, clients are like that, they take advantage of softness and sensitivity." Some of the respondents, further, concluded that most of the successful female attorneys in Montenegro exhibit masculine traits, and that even judges who exhibit particularly feminine traits are not taken as seriously as those who do not. Another respondent admitted that it seems to her that male attorneys have more clients in general, and that it might have something to do with the "Montenegrin mentality".

However, outside of general impressions of unequal treatment and male-preference, the majority of respondents, when asked what was the reaction of their immediate surroundings to their decision to become attorneys, reported having received positive or natural feedback. However, it is telling that almost all respondents who reported having received negative feedback from their immediate surroundings, attributed such feedback to their gender. One of the respondents claimed that, despite being an attorney for six years, her father still suggests her to become a judge. She commented that: "That's one of the stereotypes a woman in advocacy is faced with. She's told to become a judge, that's a job for a woman, you have the state standing behind your back. What do you want to be an attorney for? That's a man's job!". Other respondents reported similar experiences. One of them, a married woman in her late 20's, claimed that advocacy is associated with being a dangerous and male job: "The first comment with which I was faced with, is that this is not a job for a woman. It was from my immediate surroundings, not only from my colleagues. When I told them I am interested in commercial crime, they asked me what do I need to deal with that sort of job for, that I should become a civil servant, to have it easy and not get in much trouble. A lot of professional and long-time attorneys told me that this is no job for a woman." Another respondent also explicitly identified her gender as the main reason behind the initial negative feedback: "There were reactions that there is no success in my decision to become an attorney. That it is something that won't be helpful for me, that it won't be of good quality, that there is no way for me to succeed and overcome all the obstacles. Most of them were based on the fact I'm a woman".

Similarly, when talking about the reaction of their professional colleagues, most of respondents reported not having experienced any form of particular reaction from their colleagues based on their gender at the time they started practicing law, positive or negative. However, the women who reported having received negative feedback from their immediate surroundings also reported having faced negative feedback from their colleagues. "When I started as an apprentice, whenever I met a (male) colleague, the first thing he told me was that this is not a job for a woman. That he would never let his woman become an attorney. I heard this from a lot of colleagues. That I as a woman should be interested in achieving a marriage and a family and not only a career. This all makes you think if a state job or something similar is a better option." Another attorney explained: "Nowadays not as much, but in the beginning a lot, especially when you're young. I am not talking only about myself, but also about other female attorneys. Especially if you are a woman who takes care of herself and looks good. There is this prejudice that a good-looking woman cannot be an expert and particularly smart. Because of that, I often came across an attitude with older men but also with judges who were, so to say, looking down on me.

You can feel it in their attitude, in the way a judge treats you in comparison to a man. It took me six years to be considered an equal".

However, while these statements prove the existence of certain patriarchal forms of perception and behavior towards women in advocacy, they fail to precisely establish whether they actually influence the practice of female attorneys in a manner that is significant, let alone in a manner which could explain the relatively low number of female attorneys in Montenegro. Despite testimonies claiming that women experience a feeling of inequality, it is hard to establish if and to what extent such occurrences repel women from joining advocacy, as almost none of the respondents reported them having significantly influenced their determination towards this profession, while none of them reported it having presented a lasting obstacle in their careers. Likewise, no respondent reported knowledge of anyone choosing to leave or not enter advocacy because of such interactions. However, contrary to that, the patriarchal understanding of gender traits does seem to have a recognizable influence on shaping client preferences within different branches of legal practice.

3.1 Female Traits as a Disadvantage—Criminal Law

Based on the responses gathered, it seems that the preference for male attorneys and masculine traits is specifically present when searching for a defender in criminal cases. This perception of women being disadvantaged in criminal law was shared by almost all respondents. Respondents provided two groups of reasons why they consider this to be the case. One group identified the clients as the cause behind this phenomenon, claiming that it is they who prefer male attorneys in criminal cases. The other group of explanations, however, placed greater emphasis on the fact that it is female attorneys themselves who are disinclined towards picking up criminal cases, because of the risk they entail.

Regarding the first group of explanations, one respondent claimed that clients in this branch of law often expect a "spectacle" in the courtroom: "They think that there will be some sort of a spectacle, that you (the attorney) must be yelling, that you must be arguing with the opposing party, that you must raise your tone to the judge, so they think that if you are a man, that everything will be more effective. A man is a man, at the end of the day". This respondent also claimed she was fired as an attorney by one foreign client solely because of her gender. She said that she had achieved great success defending him. Still, at one point, his translator who was from Montenegro suggested this client to hire a male attorney, explaining to him that having a male attorney would increase his probability of success. The translator notified the respondent of this interaction, and the client eventually did fire her and hire a male attorney.

Other respondents also pointed out that there is a clear preference in favor of male attorneys among clients in criminal cases. One of them commented that, despite her opinion that women can represent in criminal matters just the same:

"Clients who are deprived of their freedom ask for a male attorneys in ninety percent of the cases. It's undisputable (…) Clients themselves prefer men, they have greater confidence if they hire a man as their attorney (…) God forbid that a woman should defend me, there is this attitude." Similarly, another respondent noticed: "It sometimes happens that in the eyes of the clients you have this, I cannot say deficiency, but they do not look at you the same way they look at a man. In criminal cases, a very small number of women appears as attorneys. The clients think that it will be better dealt with by a man."

However, as was said, the second category of explanations attributed the cause of this phenomenon not primarily to the clients, but to the female attorneys themselves. Some of the interviewed attorneys admitted not feeling "comfortable" around criminals or when visiting prisons. They also suggested that women generally are not as ready to face the pressure that representation in criminal law brings with it: "there are clients in criminal cases which are ready to blackmail and threaten, so women are not ready to face and fight such a pressure", reported one of the respondents. Ultimately, when talking about their preferences, most of the interviewed women either didn't report nurturing specific preference towards criminal law or reported dealing with it only when they are granted a public defense.

3.2 Female Traits as an Advantage—Family Law

On the other hand, most of the respondents, regardless of their overall stance on gender equality in Montenegrin advocacy, reported family law as a branch of law in which female attorneys excel. However, what was interesting was the fact that it is reportedly not primarily female clients that insist on having female attorneys represent them, but rather male clients. Based on the responses gathered, it can be assessed that a significant number of men actually prefer having a female attorney in divorces and other family-related disputes.

"To tell you the truth, I am sometimes really surprised by the number of men who hire me being led by the wish to have a woman represent them", says one of the respondents. She explains this number in following terms: "When they see that a woman is representing them before a court, they think that it will surely enable them to express their opinions. Perhaps they will be able to challenge the picture their wife is presenting (…), and (they believe) that female attorneys, especially if the judge is a woman too, will be able to express their arguments".

Another respondent claimed that she even had a situation in which a man revoked power of authority previously given to a male attorney, in order to hire her, despite the fact that the previous attorney represented this client properly: "He simply thought that a man in such a sensitive family dispute will not be able to protect him in the manner a woman will. It's a form of a fake picture he wants to create before the court—that he's a protector of women, that he takes care of women". Another attorney provided a similar explanation, claiming that men resort to hiring a woman, among other things, to increase their probability of gaining custody over children: "When men come to me, they want to ask for a female attorney because they think it's an advantage, especially if the judge is a woman. (…) They ask for a woman to represent them as a sort of comparative advantage because law is not just representation, but also psychology, non-verbal communication, trust."

Others explained the inclination of men towards female attorneys in family disputes, primarily by the fact that women possess traits that are specifically sought after in such disputes: "In essence, all divorces which I was hired for, I was hired by men. I think they do it not because they lack a discriminatory stance, but for a different reason. Every divorce has a lot of dirty laundry and ugly things, and I think it's easier for them to share it with a woman, than with a man. (…) They're ashamed to share it (with men)." Another attorney admitted that family disputes are "something that's more for a woman". She explained that such disputes are "more peaceful", and they provide the client with the opportunity to "tell everything like it was": "For example, I had this case, where a policeman specifically hired me. Perhaps it was easier for him to tell me everything that happened to him during his civil partnership". Another respondent said that she believes female attorneys have an advantage in family law disputes in general, attributing it "perhaps to the maternal instinct and so" and their "family experience". When asked if it is female clients that hire her in family law cases, she answered: "I represent men more. (…) There are a lot of men who are getting divorced and are being represented by women". Although she couldn't explain the reason behind this, she suggested it could be because of the "feeling women possess".

Based on these responses, it can be concluded that the very same patriarchal mode of thinking that produces a preference for male attorneys in criminal law also produces a preference for female attorneys in cases concerning family law. Therefore, it can be concluded that contrary to the starting hypothesis, clients are not generally disinclined towards hiring female attorneys, nor are patriarchal informal norms such that they (only) generate an unwelcoming atmosphere for female attorneys. Based on these findings, it cannot be concluded that the comparatively lower number of women in advocacy can be explained by the supposedly negative influence gender preferences of clients have on the market and on the possibility of women achieving a successful career as an attorney.

4 Family Obligations—A Challenge for Female Attorneys

Almost all respondents reported that reconciling private (family) obligations with work is the main obstacle in their profession. In addition, although none of the respondents said that their decision to become an attorney had been directly influenced by their disposition of starting a family and/or achieving motherhood, many of them did report knowing women who avoid or had avoided this profession because of such disposition.

One respondent reported that two of her female colleagues who passed the Bar exam together with her, chose not to continue their careers as attorneys. One of them entered state administration, while the other entered a bank. Both explained their decisions by their wish to focus on their family, claiming that they would enter advocacy once their children grow up. Reportedly, one of them said: “I will enter advocacy after I turn fifty, when I will be able to commit more to my job, and less to the family”. Another respondent claimed that the lack of stable working hours as well as the intense dynamic of advocacy also contributed to one of her colleagues leaving advocacy after having passed the Bar exam. She concluded that uncertainty and lack of predictable working hours and leisure are: “one of the main things that repel women from working as attorneys. It is connected with the opinion that you might not be able to realize yourself as a mother in the future, since you won’t be able to balance all the obligations.“

Another respondent claimed that she knows “a lot of colleagues” who stopped working as attorneys once they got children: “They transferred into notaries and public enforcement offices. Regardless of how hard their job is, they have working hours. No one will come to them on a Saturday, because they know they do not work then, they won’t even try to call them”. Another respondent shared the reaction of a female judge who saw her enter the courtroom after two years of maternity leave. Commenting on the length of her leave, the judge told the attorney that: “it’s precisely because of that that she (the judge) is not hurrying to become an attorney. Let the kids grow first, and then (become an attorney)”.

The fact that women find it hard to reconcile the job of an attorney with their private obligations was generally confirmed by all of the respondents. The respondents who were mothers, additionally, pointed out how hard is it to sustain the job of an attorney without help from other family members:

“I personally think that women face difficulties, especially after getting married and having children, women in Montenegro are expected to be excellent housewives, excellent wives, excellent mothers, and of course to earn money, not to burden anyone. I belong to the category that has really big help, my mother raises my children. If I didn’t belong to this category, I surely wouldn’t be able to conduct business at this scope”. This respondent added: “For women, I personally think that in some way motherhood is a decisive moment, (…) I think the fact that you are not left with sufficient time—is an important factor.”

Another attorney explained: “I reconciled private and professional obligations (…) by decreasing the scope of business, in order to make it possible for me to achieve everything on my own. I do not have help, that was my choice. But my colleagues either have someone’s help because they are committed one hundred percent to the job or they balance—they write at home, after midnight, when they finish their family obligations. It’s a downside, that you take the job at home.”

Another attorney concurred: “I try to complete everything in due time. But when a woman starts her family, it’s harder. When it’s only you and the husband, that’s alright. But when the children come, then (it's hard), especially if you do not have someone, a mother, a mother-in-law, to take care of the kids."

Other respondents, despite not being mothers themselves, also concurred to the particular difficulties mothers in advocacy are faced with. They explained that everyday chores and family obligations present significant obstacle female attorneys are faced with: "A woman is expected to do some trivial things in everyday life, your child gets a fever in kindergarten, they call you to pick it up and treat it at home. As a judge, if you receive such a call, you just pack, the assistant says that the judge had an emergency and you postpone the trial. (…) I think that this is one of the main reasons why there are so many women in the judiciary and in the prosecutor's office, because they have that kind of comfort". This occurrence was noticed by another attorney: "I often see problems, stress, when I'm with female colleagues. When they have to stay someplace for some time without the possibility of leaving their work, they start receiving calls from the kindergarten, telling them that they have to go pick up the children, because of which their husband leaves work. She works, and he looks after children."

4.1 Maternity Leave

Maternity leave has also been recognized as another downside of advocacy.[47] Many of the respondents recognized the fact that realizing pregnancies is particularly hard for female attorneys. Although the Law on Advocacy recognizes the possibility for a pregnant attorney to name a "transferee" of her office who will take over her cases while she enters a paid maternity leave,[48] this solution has been

[47] The Labor Law of Montenegro (*Zakon o radu*) recognizes two forms of leave, pregnancy (*porodiljsko odsustvo*) and parental leave (*roditeljsko odsustvo*), as two separate forms of leave (Zakon o radu (2024), articles 126 and 127). However, considering advocacy is a "free profession" which does not imply a formal employment relationship (*radni odnos*), the provisions of Labor Law are not applicable to attorneys (truth be told, according to article 29, para. 4, point 4 and article 66, para. 1, point 10 of Law on Advocacy, it could be argued that an attorney could be formally employed in a law partnership firm, but such an arrangement, to the authors knowledge, does not exist in practice in Montenegro). Therefore, the Law on Advocacy recognizes "temporary suspension of attorney practice" (*privremeni prestanak bavljenja advokaturom*) because of "other justified reasons" (*drugi opravdani razlozi*) as a basis under which female attorneys realize both pregnancy and parental leave (Zakon o advokaturi (2017), article 63, para. 1, point 4). Because of this, attorneys colloqually use the term "maternity leave"(*porodiljsko odsustvo*) as an all-encompassing term which covers what would otherwise be pregnancy and parental leave according to Labor Law. This is also the term we will be using in this article.

[48] Zakon o advokaturi (2017), article 63, as is explained in the footnote above, recognizes the opportunity for temporary suspension of practice due to pregnancy and parental leave. The immediate basis according to which female attorneys realize allowance due to such "leave" is article 52 of the Law on Social and Child Care, with the rules according to which this allowance is calculated being contained in article 51 of the same Law (Zakon o socijalnoj i dječjoj zaštiti, 2025).

widely criticized, primarily because of two reasons. Firstly, the fact that having a transferee in reality does not absolve the female attorney of her professional obligations, as she often continues to perform them from home. It only absolves her of the obligation to physically attend court hearings. Secondly, many attorneys choose not to use maternity leave in its eternity or to not use it consecutively, in order to avoid losing clients as well as presence on the market.

Describing her experience with pregnancy and maternity leave, one of the attorneys explained: "I worked up to the very moment of birth, I attended hearings with my stomach up to my teeth". She also explained how: "I formally used maternity leave, I had colleagues step in for me. But it only meant that I didn't attend hearings, that some colleague did it instead of me. I distributed my cases, and four to five colleagues attended my cases. But this didn't imply (them) writing applications and pleas, I was at work after all. You work at home when the kid goes to sleep. I was independent then, when my oldest reached five months, I started working again". She also added: "In reality, I never went out. I followed the cases, they sent me court records every day, I insert them in the files, I write an application where that is needed, I precise my claims, I just had colleagues who physically attended hearings and read what I prepared for them". This attorney, mother of three, also explained how she planned pregnancies in order to avoid negative effects on her practice caused by the lack of her presence in court and on the market: "I made a big gap (between pregnancies). It is simply one of the bad sides of advocacy, because if you are not in business for three years, it will affect the business negatively. (…) In order to sustain the business, we had to make bigger pauses''.

Another attorney explained how she gave birth to her first child only two days after she stopped working. She also explained how she continued working only two days after she had left the hospital. "I didn't have a pause. Your clients want you to attend hearings. My transferee attended the hearings, but I did the meetings, the writing and everything. Generally, clients, since they hired you, want you to go".

It was generally recognized that the fact that attorneys are unable to effectively utilize maternity leave constitutes a great comparative disadvantage of advocacy in comparison to other professions, especially judiciary and state administration. One attorney claimed: "My general impression is that if a female attorney is pregnant or if she gives birth tomorrow, the majority of them do not use the maternity leave in order not to lose clients and so. On the other side, they come back from maternity leave even before the end of one one-year period the law provides them. I can say that is not the case with other professions and other women. Everyone (else) uses what the law provides them with, as they should". Other respondents shared the opinion that female attorneys do not have a proper possibility of maternity leave: "A lot of colleagues from judiciary who have been elected as judges, they have the salary which they have, they use maternity leave and they do it consecutively, they use them in the real sense of the word. Meaning that you are dedicated to your child non-stop. We in advocacy cannot do that. Sixty to seventy percent of us do not use maternity leave. We go, we finish what must be finished, a month, month and a half. Someone steps in for us until we recover and we go back." This was also corroborated by other responses: "In a state organ you say you're pregnant and you say goodbye! Here, they condition you with choosing an office transferee, the state conditions you as well, they discourage you. One (attorney) had to return to work after four months. She said that it was harder than anything for her to open a pregnancy leave once she decided to stop working as an attorney. You must report your transferee to the Bar, and so on …".

4.2 *Female Attorneys—Dilemma of Independent Attorneys Versus In-Office Attorneys*

While it was generally recognized that female attorneys have it particularly hard reconciling private and business obligations, a question arose regarding—what form of legal practice is better suited for a female attorney—independent practice or work in an office? The Law on Advocacy in Montenegro allows for attorneys to practice law either independently, or through a joint office or a partnership.[49] In case of independent practice, the attorney is exposed to the market and directly generates his/her own salary. In case he/she works in a joint office or a partnership, he/she most often receives a relatively fixed monthly salary.[50] Normally, working in an office or a partnership reduces the risk of market exposure and provides a certain level of stable income, often saving the attorney the trouble of searching for clients, while implying the obligation of having to attend the office 8 hours per working day. Respondents were, however, split in their assessment of what form of practice is better suited for a woman. Women working in law firms pointed out that working in a law firm provides stability, a certain salary, and professional support from the work collective as well as guaranteed clients. Because of this, they presented this form of practice as preferable for women. On the other hand, women who were practicing as independent attorneys reported that independent practice provides freedom, flexibility as well as a good opportunity to generate income.

Generally, all of the attorneys with an independent practice saw such practice as better suited for women, especially if they are mothers: "If you work in an office, it's even worse. I worked like that, I worked with one attorney for three years. You need to respect the working hours. As with any other employer. That's how it works. If you are independent, you organize your own time, eventually, you hire someone who will help you, and so on." This attorney later added: "I wouldn't trade places with women who work in offices. It was harder for me when I worked

---

[49] Zakon o advokaturi (2017), article 2.

[50] Despite being often in a *de facto* employment relationship, attorneys working in a joint office or a partnership are almost always, from the standpoint of law, "free entrepreneurs" outside of any employment relationship. For more details, see *supra,* footnote no. 47.

in an office. I had three years of such experience and one child. I completed my work by one, but I had to be at work until four o' clock."

The respondent, a mother of three, claimed that being an independent attorney grants her the possibility to arrange her own time and working days, making it easier for her to manage her family obligations: "I will finish my obligations by 10–11am tomorrow, after that I will go home. When I get home, I will prepare a meal for two days, clean the house, and complete some other chores. That would be impossible if I worked in an office. Who would give you a salary, for you to go home?"

Another respondent concurred that being independent enables her to fulfil her family obligations with greater success. This attorney, a mother of two, concluded: "I would never work in these big (law) offices. When you work there, you have to be there during the working hours after all. If I worked like that, I would have either to take a sick leave or make excuses. This way, I don't need to make excuses to anyone. If I don't have trials, I do what needs to be done over the phone, I have a laptop at home, I bring my cases at home (…) I spend a lot of time with my children (…). Even if it's more tiring for me afterwards, because I have to work after I take them to bed (…) it seems to me that I would never work in an office." This attorney also pointed out how independent practice makes it easier for her to adjust her work with her husband's work schedule, who is also self-employed, enabling them to look after the children. She explained how her husband and she take turns, with her remaining home when he's at the office and vice-versa: "Today I am at home (…) and tomorrow is my day to work at the office. If I were to work for someone now, I would have to be in the office today. (…) It's your job and you have to work, even if you can do it at home, someone who pays you, expects you to be at the office and to go to work. Therefore, there is much more flexibility in an independent practice".

Another respondent who was independent in her practice, even if she didn't have a family, was of the impression that it's easier to organize a family as an independent attorney: "What is important is the schedule of working hours. For example, I, as a woman, don't have a family yet. But even if I did have it now, it would be much easier for me, because I don't have the obligation to work from seven to three (o' clock), I can work in the evening when I want, late at night, early in the morning, I can organize my time how I want. Except when there is a time defined for a hearing, then I have to be there. But I think that it is easier to arrange myself and a family, I don't have to be active every day and full-time, and these are the advantages that I have already become accustomed to and it would be difficult for me to be in an office".

Contrary to this, interviewed attorneys who were working in a law office seemed to be oblivious of these advantages and much more focused on the potential disadvantages of independent practice. They were of the opinion that it's harder for a woman to work as an attorney in independent practice, highlighting as a comparative advantage the security working in a law office provides: "I think that it is more difficult for women with a family to practice law independently because it is difficult to coordinate and achieve everything due to the excessive obligations and responsibilities that this profession carries." Similarly, another respondent answered: "I believe that it is especially difficult for women to practice law independently, bearing in mind that in our society, families most often depend on women in the sense that absolutely every obligation is assigned to them: from running a household, taking care of children, and many other obligations that come on top work obligations. After all, when you practice advocacy independently it is much more difficult to find regular clients, and therefore income, there are also the costs of office space, equipment, and everything necessary for your work."

Furthermore, contrary to the attorneys who had their own independent practice, attorneys who were employed didn't name "independence" and "flexibility" as general advantages of their profession, but rather financial and stability as well as the possibility of relying on your colleagues. Unlike them, the attorneys who ran their own practice all described "being your own boss" as one of the main advantages this profession carries with it, expressed an opinion that they'd not work in an office given the opportunity: "The main advantage is that you're your own boss. You organize on yourself" said one of the respondents, with others commenting just the same: "You're independent and you have your own business, your own working hours, you decide with what you'll deal with, how many cases you'll take, you're pretty free to shape your own destiny"; "At the end of the day, after all the traps and hardships, this job really does have its advantages, even more than its bad sides. You are your own boss, you balance your time and your obligations how you find it fitting."

5 Conclusion

Based on the results of our research, the discrepancy existing in Montenegro between the number of women practicing advocacy and a number of women being employed in other legal professions such as the judiciary, public prosecution or notary can foremost be attributed to the inclination of women in Montenegro towards choosing a career which provides them with a better opportunity to establish a balance between work and private family life, specifically motherhood. Regardless of whether they were mothers, respondents seemed to agree on the fact that motherhood is a turning point for most women in the context of considering advocacy as their profession, as many of them witnessed women either leaving or choosing not to enter this profession specifically because of it. The influence that private family obligations, especially motherhood, seem to have over the careers of female attorneys is evident and indisputable. Respondents reported that their family obligations stand in direct correlation with the scope of work they can manage to accept. Particular significance has been attributed to maternity leave and the way pregnancy influences the work of an attorney. Most respondents claimed that other professions provide better opportunities for realizing pregnancy and maternity leave, which seems to influence women to choose such professions in opposition to advocacy. The same incentive is present in the fact that other professions provide for a more stable and predictable working schedule, allowing women to dedicate themselves more to private affairs. Additionally, the idea of being able to better sustain the balance between work and private life, especially family matters, seems to play a role in choosing whether to practice law independently or in an office. Independent attorneys were motivated to practice law in such a capacity because of the flexibility it provides for their private life, reportedly making it easier for them to organize and take care of their children. On the other hand, attorneys who worked in an office also seemed to base their preference for such a form of work based on the claim that it better supplements women's private obligations, giving however preference to financial stability and certainty over the flexibility of work schedule.

At the same time, the lower representation of women among attorneys raises concerns beyond numerical disparity. The absence of women in legal advocacy contributes to the lack of diverse perspectives within legal proceedings and undermines gender competence across the justice system.

Gender-sensitive approaches in legal professions are vital, not only for ensuring fairness in representation but also for countering the biases that affect judicial reasoning and court outcomes. Stereotypes about women being too emotional or too soft to succeed in litigation reinforce discriminatory expectations of how a "competent" legal professional should act. This not only shapes the perception of women by clients and colleagues but also affects how arguments are received in courtrooms, ultimately influencing legal outcomes.

Returning to the starting hypotheses, it is clear that the hypothesis that female preference towards a suitable work-family balance plays a much more noticeable role in the overall unattractiveness of this profession in the eyes of women. The specific work dynamic advocacy carries with it is a reason many women chose not to enter this profession, believing it will not provide them with a suitable possibility to realize their ambitions of achieving family life and motherhood.

Additionally, based on our findings, it is clear that a relatively strong patriarchal understanding of gender roles does exist in Montenegro and that it does influence the preferences of the clients. However, contrary to the starting hypothesis, the influence of this mentality on the practice of female attorneys cannot be described as monovalent and decisively negative, but rather as polyvalent, as it shapes the practice of female attorneys in different ways. As was attested, the very same structural understanding of gender roles and traits which disfavors women in some branches of law (criminal law), makes female attorneys favorable in other branches of law (family law). Because of this, the premise that clients in Montenegro have a negative preference towards women representing them before the court is only partially true, when referring to criminal law, while it is completely untrue when referring to family law. In other branches of law, the gender of the attorney seems to play no significant role in the eyes of the clients. Therefore, the hypothesis that it is the negative preference of clients towards female attorneys that explains the lower number of women within attorneys does not hold up. Furthermore, despite most female attorneys reporting having a general sense of inequality in comparison to male attorneys, this inequality doesn't seem to be of such intensity and manifestation that it impacts the capacity in which a female attorney can perform her practice, nor does it seem to significantly affect the resolution of women to became attorneys or to recommend this profession to young women. Rather, the manifestations and intensity of such experiences seem to be of anecdotal and ephemeral nature, and not of one constituting an atmosphere that makes advocacy inherently unwelcoming for women, especially not at the level which could explain the comparatively low number of female attorneys in comparison to other legal professions in Montenegro.

References

Advokatska komora Crne Gore (2013) Advokatski rokovnik za 2014. Podgorica
Advokatska komora Crne Gore (2023) Advokatski rokovnik za 2024. Podgorica
Babović M (2021) Rodna ravnopravnost u Srbiji. In: Spasojević D (ed) Podrivanje demokratije - procesi i institucije u Srbiji od 2010. do 2020. godine. CRTA, Beograd, pp 143–157
Blagojević M (2007) Rodni barometar u Crnoj Gori, društveni položaj i kvalitet života žena i muškaraca-2007. Kancelarija za rodnu ravnopravnost. Vlada Crne Gore
Boem K (1998) Krvna osveta – regulisanje i upravljanje sukoba u Crnoj Gori i drugim plemenskim društvima. CID, Podgorica
Устав Федеративне Народне Републике Југославије од 1946, ("Сл. лист ФНРЈ", бр. 10/1946)
Устав Народне Републике Црне Горе од 1946 ("Сл. лист НР ЦГ", бр. 2/1947)
Constitution of Montenegro - Ustav Crne Gore ("Sl. list CG", br. 1/2007 i 38/2013)
Djuric J (2023) Women's emancipation in Montenegro before Socialist Yugoslavia: the roots of retraditionalization in Montenegrin society. Montenegr J Soc Sci 7:163–191
Filipović M (2003) Društvena moć žena u Crnoj Gori. CID, Podgorica
Janashia N, Elezovic S (2022) Gender equality in the judiciary in Montenegro. Council of Europe, Strasbourg
Marinović S (2009) Crnogorska advokatura. Advokatska komora Crne Gore, Podgorica
Marinović S, Prelević R (1997) Istorija crnogorske advokature. Pokret, Podgorica
Parker C, Scott S, Geddes A (2019) Snowball Sampling. SAGE Research Methods Foundations. http://eprints.glos.ac.uk/6781/1/6781%20Parker%20and%20Scott%20%282019%29%20Snowball%20Sampling_Peer%20reviewed%20pre-copy%20edited%20version.pdf
Parliament of Montenegro (2018) Records from the sixth seating of the first regular session of spring parliament of 2018. https://zakoni.skupstina.me/zakoni/web/dokumenta/sjednice-skupstine/166/2282-.pdf
Rakonjac M (2020) Pod okriljem patrijarhata: društveni identitet žene u patrijarhalnoj kulturi crnogorskog društva. Sociološka Luca 14(1):58–70
Stanojević D (2022) Addressing the depopulation challenge from the family life perspective – is fertility rise possible? In: Vuković D (ed) Serbia National Human Development Report 2022. UNDP, New York
Стојановић М (2020) „О правном поретку Петра I Петровића Његоша". Весник Правне Историје/herald of Legal History 1(2): 62–91. https://doi.org/10.51204/HLH_20203A
Statistical office of Montenegro (2014) Women and men in Montenegro. Podgorica
Statistical office of Montenegro (2022) Women and men in Montenegro. Podgorica
Stojanović P (1974) Lični subjektivitet crnogorske žene u XVIII, XIX i u početku XX vijeka. Istorijski Zapisi 27:213–241

Sudski savjet Crne Gore (2023) Godišnji izvještaj o radu Sudskog savjeta i ukupnom stanju u sudstvu za 2022. Godinu, Podgorica. (https://sudovi.me/static//sdsv/doc/Izvjestaj_o_radu_2022(1).pdf

Temidzer A (2017) Warrior culture of Montenegro (1878-1912) In: Temizer A (ed) Glimpses of Balkans – cultural history, Gece Kitapligi, Ankara, pp 43–67

Tepavčević I (2018) Jedan pogled na položaj žena u Crnoj Gori u XIX i početkom XX vijeka. Linguistica et Litteraria 21:237–247

Tužilački savjet (2023) Izvještaj o radu tužilačkog savjeta i državnog tužilaštva za 2022. godinu, Podgorica. https://zakoni.skupstina.me/zakoni/web/dokumenta/zakoni-i-drugi-akti/732/3100-17953-00-72-23-9.pdf

Uljarević M et al (2013) Socio-ekonomski položaj žena u Crnoj Gori, Evropski pokret u Crnoj Gori. Podgorica. https://www.emim.org/images/publikacije/socio-ekonomski_polozaj_zena_u_crnoj_gori.pdf

Vuković D, Dabetić V, Forić S (2020) Serbia and Bosnia and Herzegovina: challenges of liberalisation and democratic consolidation. In: Richard A et al (eds) Lawyers in 21st century societies volume 1: national reports. Hart Publishing, Oxford, pp 353–377

Zakon o advokaturi ("Sl. list RCG", br. 079/06 od 26.12.2006, Sl. list CG", br. 073/10 od 10.12.2010, 022/17 od 03.04.2017)

Zakon o pripranvicima u sudovima i državnom tužilaštvu i pravosudnom ispitu ("Sl. list CG", br. 55/2016 i 57/2016)

Zakon o radu ("Sl. list CG", br. 074/19, 008/21, 059/21, 068/21, 145/21, 077/24, 084/24, 086/24)

Zakon o socijalnoj i dječjoj zaštiti ("Sl. list CG", br. 027/13, 001/15, 042/15, 047/15, 056/16, 066/16, 001/17, 031/17, 042/17, 050/17, 059/21, 145/21, 145/21, 003/23, 048/24, 084/24, 033/25)

Matija Stojanović is a Teaching Assistant at the University of Montenegro Faculty of Law. He is a PhD Student in Constitutional Law at the University of Belgrade Faculty of Law, from where he also obtained his LLM in Theory of Law (2021). His scientific research covers multiple fields such as Constitutional Law, Philosophy and General Theory of Law and State, Legal History as well as problems of Normative Pluralism. He worked as a trainee lawyer for the period of three years (2021-2024) and also participated in the implementation of numerous projects of national and international significance.

Access to Justice Through Public Notary Service in the Republic of Serbia: How Can the Gender Perspective Move Things Forward?

Nenad Tešić and Ljubinka Kovačević

Abstract In many European countries, public notaries are part of the judiciary system (judiciary in a functional sense) empowered by the state to issue authenticated documents and certify legal transactions. Bearing in mind the role of public notary service in ensuring effective access to justice and protecting the right to a trial within a reasonable time, comprehensive consideration of the gender perspective in the judiciary system must include gender equality issues related to the notary profession as well as notary services. In this regard, the paper will analyse the issue of equal opportunities for men and women to engage in the notary profession without discrimination based on sex/gender. Moreover, the authors will examine the data generated by empirical research on a sample of 100 legal professionals in the Republic of Serbia who used the notary public service, reviewing to what extent public notaries in practice contribute to the access to justice, legal certainty, and protection of the weaker party. Finally, special attention will be given to the legal position of married and cohabiting partners not registered as joint owners in real estate records. Exercising their advisory function, notaries are obliged to provide special protection to the weaker party. As a rule, women are the weaker party in the notary proceedings, which is why it is necessary to make notary services more gender responsive, particularly in the light of the sensitive position of those women, who are facing the risk of intersectional discrimination in real estate property transactions: there is no information in the public registers, either on their status as cohabiting partners or on their position as co-owners of a property.

N. Tešić · L. Kovačević (✉)
Faculty of Law, University of Belgrade, Belgrade, Serbia
e-mail: nenad.tesic@ius.bg.ac.rs
e-mail: ljubinka@ius.bg.ac.rs

© The Author(s), under exclusive license to Springer Nature Switzerland AG 2025

S. Baer et al. (eds.), *The Gender and the Judiciary*, Gender Perspectives in Law 7,
https://doi.org/10.1007/978-3-032-06885-9_6

1 Gender Perspective in Developing the Notarial Profession

The development of legal professions included a long period in which women had limited access to the field, and even after the integration of women into legal professions, there was a pattern of gender-based segregation, primarily because of stereotypes about male and female roles in society and difficulties in balancing work and family obligations. In some countries (e.g. France),it has long represented one of the last 'patriarchal bastions'.[1] In this regard, we should bear in mind that the notary profession is often seen as a 'privileged' and 'elite' legal profession, mostly due to professional prestige and income, which are among the highest among members of all liberal professions, as well as due to the high costs of taking the notary exam and setting up a notary office (especially in attractive locations).[2] Moreover, in patriarchal societies, it was believed that women were not suitable to work as notaries due to their 'fragility, passivity, and malleability'.[3] In other words, they lacked 'masculine' qualities required for notarial work, such as discretion (because notaries are 'guardians of family secrets'), reliability (since notaries take custody of documents, money, and securities), and 'inherent authority' (since the state entrusts notaries with the prerogative to give legal documents the power of evidence and to carry out certain procedural actions).[4] Finally, we should not lose sight of the fact that numerous rights were denied to women in some legal systems, creating a legal obstacle to entrusting them with the public prerogative to perform notarial work.[5]

In the second half of the twentieth century, gender-based differences started to gradually decrease in European countries, with just a small number of women working in the notary profession until the mid-1980s. This was especially pronounced in countries such as France, where access to the notary profession was restricted by the possibility of selling or bequeathing the notary's office, which is why the notaries-successors were almost exclusively male or sometimes female family members of the notaries-predecessors.[6] The last decade of the 20th and the first decade of the twenty-first century saw a large number of women entering this profession, with women making up more than 50% of notaries in Bulgaria, Croatia, Estonia, Greece, Hungary, Latvia, Lithuania, Malta, Poland, Portugal, Romania, and Slovakia in 2021.[7] Meanwhile, women made up 30–40% of all notaries in Belgium, France, Italy, and Spain.[8] Men predominate the notary profession in

[1] Delmas (2023), p. 1.

[2] Delmas (2019a), p. 127; Delmas (2022), pp. 17–19.

[3] Thaw (1998), p. 708.

[4] Delmas (2019a), p. 141; Delmas (2019), p. 11.

[5] Delmas (2019a), p. 141.

[6] Galligan et al. (2017), p. 24.

[7] European Commission for the Efficiency of Justice (2021), p. 6.

[8] European Commission for the Efficiency of Justice (2021), p. 6.

European common law countries (on average, 75% of the notaries are men).[9] This is clarified by looking at the general reasons for the feminisation of legal professions, which include the transparency of the appointment process and the development of notary work.[10] Moreover, we should not lose sight of the diversification of professional positions, since female lawyers perform notarial work both as self-employed persons and as employees (e.g. as trainees, assistants, and deputy notaries). The increase in the number of women in the notary profession is therefore accompanied by *gender segmentation*, as most women work as employees, while a significantly lower percentage work as partners in notary offices, or as self-employed persons.[11] This makes a big difference since employees are subordinated to their employers (notaries), who organize and manage their work, supervise and evaluate their performance, regulate their rights, obligations, and responsibilities, and can impose disciplinary sanctions. Moreover, employee salaries are much lower than the income of the self-employed, and women are oftentimes not employed long enough in a notary's office for their knowledge and contacts to become indispensable to the employer, which is why they may be the first whose employment is terminated in the event of reduced workload. Because of the above, we can assume that for the majority of employees in notary offices, subordinate work for the notary-employer is not their 'first choice', or that if it is, it is a 'lesser of two evils' type of choice, if the alternative to working as an employee is to look for another job.

The substantial share of women working as employees in the notary profession can be explained by the family duties they are saddled with, which often prevent them from being self-employed. Moreover, we should not lose sight of gender stereotypes, since it is assumed that women, precisely because of family duties and expected social behaviour, will agree to work as employees often for long periods, unlike men who will want to become partners as soon as possible or go independent.[12] In other words, this supports specific gender roles and the belief that men are more ambitious and career-focused, whereas women choose or accept arrangements where career interruptions due to family duties do not represent serious obstacles. Furthermore, there is a stereotype that women lack self-confidence and 'entrepreneurial spirit', which is often accompanied by differences in creditworthiness, real estate ownership, and

---

[9] Galligan et al. (2017), p. 68.

[10] Delmas (2019a), p. 141.

[11] For example, in France in 2014, women made up 34% of all self-employed notaries, while 65% of women were employed as clerks in notary offices. In just three years, the number of self-employed women rose to 41%, although we should bear in mind that in France, women make up 72.73% of members of the notary profession and 63.35% of lawyers who passed the notary exam. Acc. to: Bolton and Muzio (2007), p. 47;Ministère de la justice (2017), p. 38.

[12] Delmas (2019a), p. 137. There are different views on the difficulties of balancing work and family life. Certain authors believe that the self-employed have a better chance of achieving that balance than employees, since they enjoy greater flexibility in terms of organising their working hours, and if the job allows it—greater chances of working from home. This can further reduce the costs that self-employed parents have for hiring household help or using the services of childcare institutions. The European Institute for Gender Equality (2015), pp. 8–9.

access to financial resources.[13] In addition, there are differences in terms of access to informal social networks, since women have lower chances of accessing these networks due to family responsibilities, among other things, making it more difficult for them to advance in a career. Also, a significant number of women prefer working as employees because, in many legal systems, self-employed persons enjoy limited social security law protection, especially in the event of maternity.[14]

Finally, gender segmentation in the notary profession is reflected in the underrepresentation of women in bodies that make decisions related to the development of notary activity and the improvement of the position of notaries(chambers of notaries, regional and supreme councils of notaries, etc.), because the increase in the number of notaries had no effect on the structure of these bodies.[15] Although there is no reliable data that the greater participation of women in these organisations would contribute to solving gender-based problems, there is still a need to there to have the percentage of women on boards that would reflect their presentation in the profession. When it comes to the International Union of Notaries (*UINL*), which was founded in 1948, the first woman president of the Association (Cristina Noemi Armella) was elected in 2020.[16]

2 Should We Regard Public Notaries as Part of the Judiciary?

Latin notaries have traditionally contributed to legal certainty by notarising and certifying legal documents.[17] In modern times, there is a clear tendency to delegate judicial powers to notaries that enjoy *fides publica*, particularly in the field of non-litigation

[13] The European Institute for Gender Equality (2015), p. 8.

[14] The European Institute for Gender Equality (2015), p. 9. In this regard, interesting data has been collected from a survey conducted by the Council of the Notariats of the European Union (*CNUE*) in 22 states with a European-continental legal tradition, where the respondents were notary organizations. Tradition in the performance of notary activities, lack of work flexibility, especially inflexible working hours (since notary offices have a statutory obligation to work during prescribed working hours to meet the needs of the citizens), as well as gender stereotypes, were observed as the main factors promoting gender inequality in the notary profession. Galligan et al. (2017), pp. 79–80.

[15] In 2016, women were presidents of chambers of notaries in only four countries (Croatia, Lithuania, Romania, and Slovenia), but made 40% of vice presidents of chambers of notaries. Also, women made up the majority in the management boards of professional associations of notaries in four countries. Galligan et al. (2017), p. 69.

[16] At her suggestion, a working group under the name 'Women and Men Notaries of the twenty-first Century for the Development and Protection of Women's Rights' was established in 2022 with the task of devising ways to achieve *de facto* gender equality, as well as to improve the role of public notaries in this area. One of the ways to achieve this goal is to raise awareness of the achievements of women who were the first notaries in International Association of Notaries member states. Consequently, a book was published in honor of Aurora Teixeira de Castro, the first woman notary in Portugal. Ataíde (2022).

[17] Tešić (2014), p. 482.

procedures,[18] as types of civil proceedings aimed primarily at avoiding long-lasting litigations.[19] Accordingly, under Serbian law,[20] notaries are empowered to issue death certificates and to carry out the inventory and valuation of the deceased's property.[21]

In a situation where the distribution of inheritance is governed by the law of the Republic of Serbia, the probate court may entrust the notary to complete the probate proceedings.[22] Notaries are also engaged in other legal procedures, such as those relating to the acquisition of rights in immovable property. After the notarization of the contract, Serbian public notaries *ex officio* initiate the registration of the acquirer in public real estate records.[23] Additionally, notaries are involved in the creation of executive titles:[24] agreements on hypothec or unilateral hypothec statements that hypothec creditors may use for commencing enforcement proceedings. Such an extensive process of entrusting judicial power to professionals with public authority in the legal system of the Republic of Serbia raised numerous theoretical issues about the legal status of public notaries. In order to resolve these dilemmas, it is natural to look into how European courts approach the issue.

2.1 Notaries Are Not Judges

In some cases, the Court of Justice of the European Union (CJEU) distinguished sharply between notaries and judges.[25] In the *Pula Parking* case,[26] in the

[18] Dika (2009), pp. 1153–1777; Šago (2021), p. 173.

[19] Maganić (2022), p. 49.

[20] Notaries were introduced into the Serbian legal system in 2014, when the Law on Public Notaries began to be implemented. For the historical background of this legal profession in Serbia, see Trgovčević Prokić (2009), 283 *et seq*; Drakić (2014), 201 *et seq.*

[21] Law on Non-Litigation Procedure, *Official Gazette of the Socialist Republic of Serbia*, nos. 25/82 and 48/88, and *Official Gazette of the Republic of Serbia*, nos. 46/95, 18/05, 85/12, 45/13, 55/14, 6/15, 106/15, and 14/22—Law on Non-Litigation Procedure, Art. 92, para. 2 and Art. 96, para. 1.

[22] Law on Non-Litigation Procedure, Art. 110a, para. 1. In 2020, basic courts in the Republic of Serbia handed over 91,430 requests for the preparation of death certificates and 87,871 cases (out of a total of 136,534 'O' cases received) to public notaries, as entrusted tasks, for the purpose of probate proceedings. Annual report on the work of courts in the Republic of Serbia for 2020, https://www.vk.sud.rs/sites/default/files/attachments/pdf (accessed: 5.5.2024).

[23] Law on Registration Procedure in the Cadaster of Real Estate and Utilities. *Official Gazette of the Republic of Serbia*, nos. 41/18, 95/18, 31/19, and 15/20—Law on Registration in the Cadastre, Art. 22, para. 1 (2).

[24] Law on Public Notaries. *Official Gazette of the Republic of Serbia*, nos. 31/11, 85/12, 19/13, 55/14, 93/14, 121/14, 6/15, and 106/15—Law on Public Notaries, Art. 85, para. 1; Law on Hypothec. *Official Gazette of the Republic of Serbia*, nos. 115/05, 60/15, 63/15, and 83/15—Law on Hypothec, Art. 15; Tešić (2019), p. 490.

[25] Nourissat (2017), p. 33.

[26] Notaries who act within the framework of the powers conferred on them by national law in enforcement proceedings do not fall under the definition of 'court'. *Pula Parking d.o.o.* v *Sven Klaus Tederahn*. See also: *Ibrica Zulfikarpašić* v *Slaven Gajer*. For more details, see: Uzelac (2018), p. 641.

context of enforcement proceedings for the recovery of an unpaid public parking debt and judicial cooperation in civil matters, the Court held that writs issued by notaries acting in enforcement proceedings on the basis of an 'authentic document' were not given by a court within the meaning of Regulations No 805/2004[27] and No 1215/2012.[28] Furthermore, such a writ could not be classified as a 'judicial decision' in the light of Article 2(a) of the latter regulation and could not be circulated on the basis of that regulation without that situation constituting reverse discrimination.[29] 'Article 18 TFEU and Article 47 of the Charter of Fundamental Rights of the European Union must be interpreted as not precluding national legislation which gives notaries, acting within the framework of the powers conferred on them in enforcement proceedings based on an authentic document, the power to issue writs of execution which, as is clear from the judgment,[30] cannot be recognised and enforced in another Member State'.[31]

However, in the context of inheritance, this issue is approached differently in EU law. The term 'court' is taken to mean any judicial authority and all other authorities and legal professionals with competence in matters of succession which exercise judicial functions or act pursuant to a delegation of power by a judicial authority or under the supervision of judicial authority, provided that such other authorities and legal professionals offer guarantees with regard to impartiality and the right of all parties to be heard, and provided that their decisions under the law of the Member State in which they operate: (i) are subject to appeal to or review by a judicial authority; (ii) have a similar force and effect as a decision of a judicial authority on the same matter.[32]

---

[27] Regulation (EC) No 805/2004 of the European Parliament and of the Council of 21 April 2004 creating a European Enforcement Order for uncontested claims. *Official Journal L 143, 30.4.2004, pp. 15–39.*

[28] Regulation (EU) No 1215/2012 of the European Parliament and of the Council of 12 December 2012 on jurisdiction and the recognition and enforcement of judgments in civil and commercial matters (recast). *Official Journal L 351, 20.12.2012, pp. 1–32.*

[29] See: *EOS Matrix d.o.o.* v *Entazis d.o.o.*, and the case-law cited.

[30] *Pula Parking* v *Sven Klaus Tederahn*. According to Poretti, certain parts of the given interpretation are controversial. For example, the fact that the CJEU does not take a functional approach and does not recognize that, at the same time, the norm of Regulation 650/2012 on succession included a public notary within the notion of the 'court', with the explanation that the Brussels I bis Regulation does not contain a general provision with such an effect. Poretti (2019), p. 10. Such a position of the Court is inconceivable without additional reasoning. Schlürmann (2018), p. 952.

[31] Joined Cases *Parking d.o.o.*v *Sawal d.o.o.* and Interplastics *s.r.o.* v *Letifico d.o.o.*

[32] Regulation (EU) No 650/2012 of the European Parliament and of the Council of 4 July 2012 on jurisdiction, applicable law, recognition, and enforcement of decisions and acceptance and enforcement of authentic instruments in matters of succession and on the creation of a European Certificate of Succession. *Official Journal L 201, 27.7.2012, pp. 107–134,* Art. 3, para. 2.

2.2 *Notaries Are Bound by Similar Principles Like Judges*

The notion of 'tribunal' in European Court of Human Rights (ECtHR) jurisprudence has an autonomous meaning and does not necessarily require that the persons and bodies leading the proceedings formally belong to the judicial authority, but that they fulfil the guarantees prescribed in Article 6, para. 1 of the ECHR.[33] According to the ECtHR, an authority that is not classified as a state court may, in the sense of Art. 6, para. 1 of the Convention, be covered by the notion of tribunal in the material sense of the term. In one instance, the regional authority for real estate transactions was recognised as an authority with the status of a 'tribunal'.[34] The tribunal does not have to be part of the state judicial system.[35] The fact that it performs many functions (administrative, regulatory, judicial, advisory, and disciplinary) does not by itself disqualify it from being classified as a tribunal.[36]

For the purpose of applying Art. 6. para. 1 of the ECHR, it is irrelevant whether the procedure in which civil rights and obligations are determined takes place before a court or any other authority entrusted with public powers. When assessing whether the enforcement proceedings are completed within a reasonable time, it is necessary to consider the time spent on court proceedings, but also the time spent in proceedings before other state bodies or authorities performing certain acts in or in connection with the proceedings, and whose participation may affect its duration.[37] The ECtHR considers the proceedings as a whole, from its commencement to its finalisation.[38]

---

[33] *Benthem* v *Netherlands*, para. 43.

[34] Under local regulations, the contract could not take effect unless it was approved by the local Real Property Transactions Authority (*Grundverkehrsbehörde*). Under Austrian law, the Regional Authority is not classified as one of the courts of the respondent State. For the purposes of Art. 6 of the Convention, however, it comes within the concept of a 'tribunal' in the substantive sense of this expression. *Sramek* v *Austria*, para. 36. For more details see: Guide on Article 6 of the European Convention on Human Rights Right to a fair trial (civil limb) Updated to 31 August 2022, https://www.echr.coe.int/documents/d/echr/guide_art_6_eng (accessed: 5.5.2024), p. 47.

[35] For the purposes of Art. 6, para. 1 a 'tribunal' need not be a court of law integrated within the standard judicial machinery of the country concerned (*Xhoxhaj* v *Albania*, para. 284, concerning a body set up to re-evaluate the ability of judges and prosecutors to perform their functions; *Ali Rıza and Others* v *Turkey*, paras. 194–195, 202–204, and *Mutu and Pechstein* v *Switzerland*, para. 139, concerning arbitration).

[36] *H.* v *Belgium*, para. 50. Guide on Article 6 of the European Convention on Human Rights Right to a fair trial (civil limb). Updated to 31 August 2022, p. 47.

[37] See, among others, *Ringeisen* v *Austria*, para. 94.

[38] Such practice was also accepted by the Constitutional Court of the Republic of Serbia, Decision Už-315/2008, 13 November 2008, and Decision Už-7451/2016, 25 October 2018.

In *Ana Ionita* v *Romania*,[39] the Court notified that the rules governing their conduct clearly arose from their specific role as 'out-of-court magistrates', explicitly and completely reflecting their hybrid nature as independent professionals and public service.[40] In most European countries, notaries have the status of private professionals under the authority (control) of public authorities or public agents.[41] Although it is not feasible to equate notaries with courts or administrative judges, it remains true that this characterisation of notaries can give rise to the 'right to (complete) the notarial procedure within a reasonable time' under Article 6 of the ECHR, as well as a 'right of access to a notary'.[42]

According to contemporary legal literature, public notaries improve access to justice.[43] Although it is controversial to claim that notaries belong to the judiciary in the strict (normative) sense, it cannot be denied that this legal profession is part of the judicial system, which can be classified as the *judiciary in the substantive (functional) sense.*

Public notaries are subject to the same ethical principles as the judiciary. They must carry out their professional duties with independence[44] and impartiality,[45] avoiding any personal influence on their activities and any form of discrimination against parties.[46] The role of the notary is vital in protecting the weaker party, such as minors,[47] persons deprived of contractual capacity,[48] particularly disadvantaged parties in legal transactions, for instance, hypothec consumers,[49] etc.

---

[39] *Ana Ionita* v *Romania*, para. 47.

[40] Marguénaud, Dauchez, Dauchez (2018), p. 3.

[41] In only two countries they have the status of private professionals (without control from public authorities). European Commission for the Efficiency of Justice—Working Group on the evaluation of judicial systems (2021), Table 1—Status of notaries in 2018, pp. 4–5.

[42] Marguénaud, Dauchez, Dauchez, (2018), p. 7.

[43] Zendeli, Selmani (2017), p. 145; Notaries' Role in Access to Justice in BC, October 5, 2019, https://www.bcnotaryassociation.ca/resources/blog/?id=2.

[44] 'However, the independence of a notary does not mean that he is not subject to control and that he is not accountable for his work'. Bodul, Grbić (2014), p. 50.

[45] On impartiality of public notaries: Tešić (2015), p. 478.

[46] International Union of Notaries, Principles of notarial ethics, Approved by the General Meeting of Member Chambers of Notaries of the UINL, Mexico City, 17 October 2004, https://www.uinl.org/en_GB/principios-de-deontologia.

[47] For instance, in Serbian law, minors are entitled to stipulate the legal transactions from which they acquire only rights, without being legally supervised, and therefore, in our opinion, as a particularly vulnerable party, they deserve the highest level of care in advising by public notaries. Tešić (2013), pp. 411–416.

[48] Sokić (2012), pp. 43–47.

[49] Josipović (2018), p. 800. According to our suggestion, the enforceability clause in a loan agreement notarized by the notary public must be worded in such a way that a particularly vulnerable consumer is able to fully understand and foresee the consequences arising from such a contractual term, for their legal and economic position. Tešić (2022a), p. 287.

3 On the Gender Ratio in Serbian Judicial System

3.1 Differences in Gender Structure among the Judicial Professions

The former Socialist Federal Republic of Yugoslavia (with Serbia as one of its federal units) was among the first European countries, along with France and Norway, where the number of female law students exceeded 50% of the total number of students, while in most European countries that number ranged between 30 and 40%.[50] Law schools in Serbia continue to enrol more female than male students, with the difference in the sex structure of the student population being much greater in undergraduate studies (women make up around 60% of students), but also present among master's students and, to a lesser extent, among PhD students. Meanwhile, a higher percentage of girls complete their undergraduate law studies within the stipulated period (over 60%). More women completed master's studies, whereas more men completed doctoral studies which are comparable to the European average, in which 10–20% fewer women complete the highest level of law studies.[51] Particularly challenging for law school graduates is the period of transition from the world of education to the world of work. In Serbia, that period is quite long; one must go through additional training, as well as pass a state exam, to start practising law. Many law school graduates are unable to undergo training as employees but have to do so as unpaid trainees.[52] In some cases, a volunteering contract is used as a legal basis for their training. Although this is contrary to the noble goals of volunteering, the Law on the Organization of Courts and the Law on Advocacy enables internships and traineeships to be qualified as volunteering.[53] While these circumstances pose a serious challenge for both men and women, the challenge is even bigger for female lawyers who decide to become mothers in their transition to the world of work.

The influence of socialist ideology on achieving gender equality in Serbia is visible in the gradual increase in the number of female judges. In 1948, women made up only 5% of the total number of judges in the Federal People's Republic of Yugoslavia; that number rose to 27% in the Socialist Federal Republic of Yugoslavia in the 1980s.[54] The 1990s, however, saw drastic changes in the sex

---

[50] Menkel-Meadow (1996), p. 4.

[51] Galligan et al. (2017), p. 13. For the Faculty of Law of the University of Belgrade, the largest law school in Serbia and the Balkans, detailed data for each of these domains for the last 10 years is available in: Vujadinović et al. (2020), pp. 34–36.

[52] Kovačević (2022), p. 208 *et seq*; for a detailed analysis of the position of young lawyers training to work in law firms, see: Đorđević and Vlajić (2023), p. 126 *et seq*.

[53] Law on the Organisation of Courts. Official Gazette of the Republic of Serbia, no. 10/23, Art. 69; Law on Advocacy, Art. 62, para. 1; see: Ministry for Labour, Employment, Veterans and Social Policy of the Republic of Serbia (2020), p. 39.

[54] Dabetić (2023), p. 115.

structure of judges, since the wars and the war-generated inflation significantly lowered judges' salaries. Due to extremely low salaries (and the incompatibility of judgeship with other forms of paid work), judges could not provide for their families, causing many of them to leave the profession. Most of them were men who found new jobs, while vacant positions in the courts were filled by new judges, many of whom were women. Despite improvement in the material status of judges in the meantime,[55] in 2019, judges in general jurisdiction courts were 70% women and 30% men, with the highest number of female judges working in appellate courts (77%).[56] Women have the dominant majority as judges in specialised courts (77%), with the highest percentage of women judges in the Administrative Court (86%) and Misdemeanour Appellate Court (89%).[57] The most striking example of growing 'feminisation' is the Supreme Court of Serbia. In 2016, 59% of judges in this Court were women; 65.2% in 2019; and 80.5% in 2023.

When it comes to gender ratio in the Serbian judiciary in the functional sense, females are in the slight majority among notaries, but form a minority among bailiffs. According to the Ministry of justice archive, in 2023, 44% of total number of 197 public notaries are men and 56% are women. In the same year, 58% of public bailiffs are men, while 42% are women. Moreover, notary and bailiff professions are relatively new in Serbia: public bailiffs have existed since 2011, and notaries since 2015. Because there has been little change in the individuals first entrusted with public authority, it is not possible to observe trends in the gender structure with sufficient certainty. On the other hand, men predominate the attorney's profession in Serbia with 64%.

When attempting to identify the key socio-economic and cultural causes of gender disparity, we suggest that the following key indicators of choice be highlighted: earning potential, employment security, autonomy at work, and work-family balance.

In comparison to other judicial professions, judges and prosecutors have the lowest salaries and the least professional freedom. Given the permanent nature of these positions, their employment security is very high, as is the possibility of combining parenthood with work. These factors combined result in a significantly higher number of women than men in the judiciary in the strict sense.

In the case of notaries and bailiffs, there is less job security in comparison to the courts, but the earning potential is significantly higher and there is greater freedom in

[55] We should bear in mind that Serbia is a country with a high poverty rate and great inequalities, but also that judges' salaries are one of the guarantees of their independence. The average annual salary of judges at the beginning of their career is around 15,000 euros, which makes this income 2.42 times higher than the average annual salary in the Republic of Serbia. Judges' salaries increase throughout their careers, with the average annual salary of Supreme Court judges being 34,870 euros (European Commission for the Efficiency of Justice [2018], p. 123). Nevertheless, 87% of judges believe that they do not receive adequate salaries for their work, and only 11% of judges believe that the salaries they receive can be considered a 'guarantee' of their independence. Đorđević (2022), p. 683.

[56] The The Statistical Office of the Republic of Serbia (2020), p. 122.

[57] The The Statistical Office of the Republic of Serbia (2020), p. 122.

everyday practice. Independent legal professions, assigned with prerogatives of public power, can be reconciled with parenthood, but this is much more difficult than with a career in the public sector. The above characteristics of notaries and bailiffs allow us to describe the differences in the representation of women and men in these two professions as minor. In the case of attorney service, the earning potential is the highest, although there are large income differences within the profession.[58] Moreover, we should not lose sight of the reality that the attorney profession often ensures autonomy at work. Employment, on the other hand, is uncertain, and it is difficult to balance professional commitments with family life.[59] As a result, men dominate the profession.

3.2 The Persistence of Gender Stereotypes in Terms of Legal Services

While the gender stereotypes we have discussed so far are based on how members of the legal profession see themselves in relation to society's expectations (gender stereotype regarding the commitment to a particular legal occupation), the gender stereotypes we will discuss further concern how society sees members of the legal profession (gender stereotype regarding entrusting a particular legal assignment).

The results of the 2022 survey showed that 50% of the respondents preferred to use the services of female notaries when they needed to arrange a notarial deed, while 50% of the respondents used the services of both male and female notaries equally.[60] There were no respondents who stated that they primarily visited the

[58] Income will depend on specialisation, professional experience, and length of service (women are more likely to have career breaks due to family obligations), but also the size and location of law firms, especially if one takes into account the trend of 'informal corporatisation of the attorney profession'(women are more likely than men to work in smaller law firms or in lower positions in medium-sized or large firms). According to the results of a recent survey, the average annual income of lawyers in Serbia is 27,500 euros, which is almost twice the average annual income of judges and four times more than the average annual salary in the country. Vuković (2017), pp. 105–106.

[59] 'Women continue to confront the profession's lack of accommodation for family responsibilities, as well as negative career repercussions associated with motherhood'. Kay and Gorman (2008), p. 323.

[60] Tešić (2022b). In order to create a representative sample, the researcher interviewed 100 respondents using the 'expert sampling' method, where respondents are chosen for their specific profession and in-depth knowledge of the relevant field. Most of the respondents are legal experts who have passed the bar exam and have more than 10 years of professional experience in the field of law. The author was guided by the idea that the selected experts have diverse work experience in the sense of a proportional representation of judges, scholars, attorneys, authorised appraisers, lawyers employed in commercial banks and civil society organisations, but also lawyers from various state bodies and institutions, for example Ministry of Justice, Ministry of Finance, Agency for Business Registers, Republican Geodetic Institute, National Bank of Serbia, National Credit Insurance Agency, Deposit Insurance Agency, and Agency for Licensing of Bankruptcy Trustees (hereinafter: 2022 survey).

offices of male notaries.Although all public notaries have the same or very similar legal education and additional professional qualifications—bar exam and notary exam—the same minimum professional experience and technical equipment of the office and are subject to the supervision of the Ministry of Justice, *users of notary services in Serbia mostly chose women public notaries.*

On the other hand, the same research showed that in enforcement procedures, 68% of respondents chose male and female enforcement agents equally, while 29% of them suggested male bailiffs in the majority of cases. An insignificant number of respondents (3%) mostly nominated female bailiffs. Although all bailiffs have the same or similar legal education and additional professional qualifications—bar exam and bailiff exam—the same minimum work experience and technical equipment of the office and are subject to the supervision of the Ministry of Justice, *the users of enforcement services in Serbia mostly chose male bailiffs.*

If the number of male and female members in these legal professions is relatively equal, and if the expertise and technical equipment of their offices are objectively uniform according to the law, but the collected data on the selection of parties for the conduct of non-litigious and enforcement proceedings show a clear gender imbalance, it can be assumed that such a result is the outcome of subjective criteria, primarily prejudice about the gender division of judicial occupations.

In other words, conducted survey confirmed the persistence of gender stereotypes, about men's and women's occupations, according to which women are better suited for office work that requires patience, concentration, and accuracy (for instance, the profession of notary), while out-of-office work that requires strength and determination, involves greater risk, cooperation with the police and technical services such as fire-fighters, locksmiths, and transporters—'belongs' to men (for instance, the profession of bailiffs).

The above-mentioned stereotypes in Serbian society are still so strong that they not only determine users' choices in everyday tasks of minor importance (when selecting a fruit seller, butcher, or hairdresser) but also significantly influence their decisions when choosing the legal professionals: notaries and bailiffs to carry out their complicated, often life-changing legal procedures. It might be speculated that gender stereotype regarding entrusting a particular legal assignment recognised in the 2022 survey has significantly influenced the fact that 56% of the notary professionals in Serbia are woman, as opposed to 42% of female public bailiffs.

4 Public Notaries with Family Responsibilities—Is There a Need for Special Protection of Self-Employed Persons?

For the majority of women, paid work is not their only engagement, because they still perform most of the housework and take care of children and other family members who rely on others for care and support. Women in the notary profession also face these challenges, which can result in their later entry into this profession, since family duties limit the time and energy they invest in education, specialization, and training for work.[61] Moreover, women have more interruptions in their professional careers than men and work more as employees, since, unlike men, they encounter prejudices that, due to family obligations, they will not be able to devote themselves completely to the notary work, which is expected of the self-employed. In Serbia, 67.9% of women and only 11.5% of men perform daily household chores.[62] As for caring for the elderly children, and family members with disabilities, the gender gap is somewhat smaller, but still very pronounced, with 41.2% of women who have reached the age of 18 performing these activities daily and only 29.5% of men doing the same.[63] Hence, even in notary offices that allow part-time work, employees who adopt this form of flexible work are often seen as less dedicated workers.[64] This strongly demonstrates the need for notaries working in the Republic of Serbia to develop strategies to help their employees (both male and female) reconcile work and family responsibilities more easily. Furthermore, the capacity and quality of health and social care services must improve while maintaining reasonable prices. On the other hand, the needs of men with family responsibilities are also neglected since they often encounter the stereotype that caring for dependent family members is a 'female responsibility' and that men are not expected to take time off from work to care for a child or other dependent person.[65] Finally, we must keep in mind that in many legal systems, self-employed persons have limited access to social security rights in the event of pregnancy, childbirth, and childcare.[66]

Serbian legislation unjustifiably discriminates between the employees and the self-employed in terms of the duration of leave for childbirth and childcare, as well as the amount of accompanying social benefits. Although employees require special protection because they perform subordinated work, and the (economic and legal) independence enjoyed by the self-employed is, in principle, incompatible with the special protection provided to employees—these differences cannot justify the existence of different regimes for employees and the self-employed in terms of rights connected to childbirth and childcare.[67] The Serbian Law on

[61] Delmas (2019a), p. 143.

[62] Babović and Petrović (2021), p. 37.

[63] Babović and Petrović (2021), p. 37.

[64] Menkel-Meadow (1996), p. 7.

[65] Collier (2022), p. 159.

[66] Pedersini and Coletto (2010), pp. 58–59.

[67] That conclusion stems from, among other things, the practice of the supervisory bodies of the International Labour Organisation (*ILO*). Although the Maternity Protection Convention No. 183 applies to 'all employed women, including those in atypical forms of dependent work' (Art. 2, para. 1), the provisions of this ILO convention are interpreted broadly, with the obligation of the contracting states, including the Republic of Serbia, to extend maternity protection to all forms of work, which is especially important for self-employed women.

Financial Support for Families with Children[68] stipulates that, for childbirth and childcare, employed mothers have the right to compensation that cannot be less than the minimum wage, but minimum amount of compensation for self-employed mothers is not introduced. Moreover, when self-employed women are prevented from working due to complications related to pregnancy, they do not have the right to compensation, unlike employed women. Until 2023, there was a difference between self-employed and employed women in the notary profession in terms of the duration of leave due to pregnancy, childbirth, and childcare. Unlike employees, who must start using paid maternity leave before giving birth, self-employed workers are entitled to benefits only after the birth of the child. Employed mothers (and fathers) had the right to a two-year paid leave for the birth of their third and subsequent children, while self-employed mothers (but not fathers) had the right to a one-year paid leave, regardless of the number of children. This rule was abolished by the Decision of the Constitutional Court of Serbia[69] after the Law on Financial Support for Families with Children was passed to achieve a better balance between work and parenting, as well as to support parents to have as many children as they wish. The previous solution resulted not only in the unequal position of mothers who were in comparable situations (working before childbirth but prevented from working as a result of childbirth or childcare) but also in favouring employment relationship compared to other forms of work.

Reconciling work and parenthood are equally important for employed and self-employed women, and the right to receive compensation for the birth of the third and subsequent children represents a measure of population policy. Because of the extremely unfavourable demographic situation in Serbia (negative population growth and emigration trend), this measure should encourage working women to have more children, and thus there is no justification for it to depend on the type of work engagement. For the same reasons, there was no basis for discrimination against fathers, but the Serbian legislator did discriminate. A self-employed father could have exercised the right to compensation only if the mother had died, abandoned her child, or had been prevented from directly caring for the child for objective reasons, unlike employed fathers who had the right of leave for childcare without any additional conditions. Since the state did not support the parenthood of self-employed men in the same way as it did for employees, the aforementioned legal rule was repealed in 2023; however, there is still much room to improve the position of fathers. This is very important because men in Serbia face gender stereotypes related to childcare, especially since this type of care is still often understood as the responsibility of mothers.

[68] Law on Financial Support for Families with Children. Official Gazette of the Republic of Serbia, nos. 13/17, 50/18, 46/21, 51/21, 53/21, 66/21, 130/21, 43/23, and 62/23.

[69] *Decision of the Constitutional Court of Serbia, IUz-299/2018. Official Gazette of the Republic of Serbia, no.* 43/23.

The solutions presented attest to the importance of measures for the reconciliation of parenthood and work for the position of members of the notary profession, as disregarding this issue would have negative consequences for the development of this legal profession. They are primarily reflected in the stifling of self-employment,[70] which has a particularly negative impact on the advancement of women in the notary profession because being an employee is a better way for the majority of them to provide adequate care for dependent family members. Self-employed women notaries who are prevented, due to family obligations, from working longer than the time frame for which they are legally entitled to compensation, face numerous challenges, starting with having to find ways to balance childcare and work in order to provide salaries for their employees and cover the technical costs of work. They are almost certainly not able to attend training and coaching programs during that period. It seems that appointing a deputy to ensure the smooth performance of notarial activities does not eliminate these problems. The appointed deputy will most likely be a male for fear that the deputy may also take leave for pregnancy, childbirth, and childcare, which further deepens the segmentation within the notary profession. Finally, we must not lose sight of the fact that achieving gender equality in the notary profession is not possible without respecting the needs of men in relation to balancing parenthood and work, as well as the need to ensure greater involvement of men in child care in every way.

5 Notaries' Contribution to the Implementation of the EU's Fundamental Values

5.1 Is the Notarial Contribution to the Legal System Measurable?

The previously mentioned research, completed in 2022, confirmed the tested hypothesis that Serbian notaries contribute to the enactment of EU core legal values and principles: access to justice, legal certainty, and protection of the weaker party. The findings show that the majority of respondents believe that the contribution of public notaries to core legal values in Serbia is significant or moderate. Furthermore, a minimal number of respondents indicated that notaries' influence is exceptional, whereas a relatively small number of notarial service users responded that notaries' influence is insignificant (see Table 1 and Figs. 1, 2, and 3).

[70] Commissioner for Protection of Equality, Opinion on the Draft Law on Amendments to the Law on Financial Support for Families with Children, no. 011–00-4/2023-02, of 20 March 2023.

Table 1 Service users' perception of public notaries' contribution to core legal values in Serbia (2022)[71]

Perception of public notaries' contribution	Core legal values		
	Access to justice	Legal certainty	Protection of the weaker party
Outstanding contribution	7%	5%	4%
Significant contribution	30%	44%	34%
Moderate contribution	41%	37%	28
Insignificant contribution	12%	5%	14%

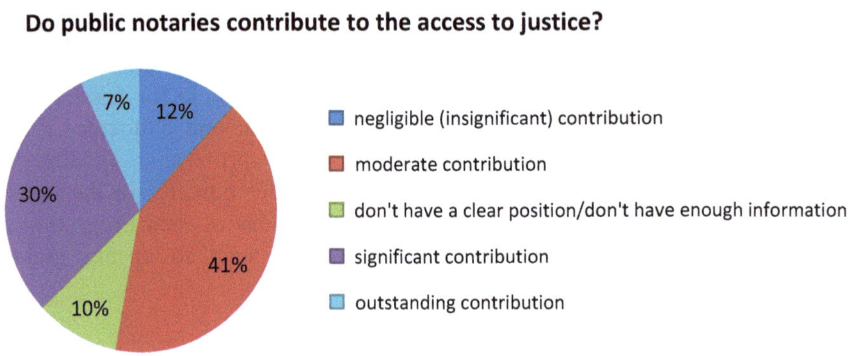

Fig. 1 Questionnaire results on notaries' contribution to the access to justice[72]

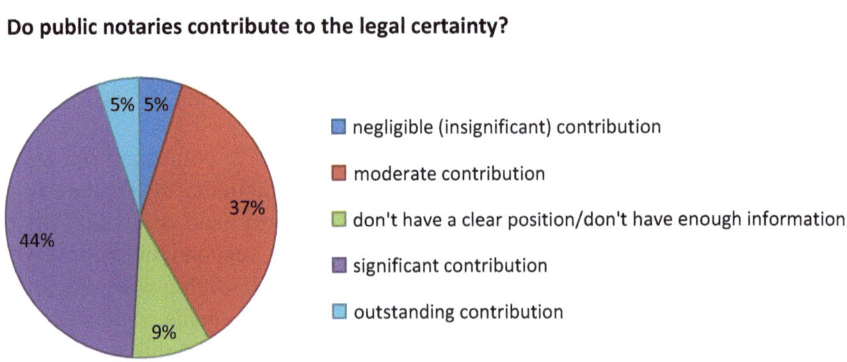

Fig. 2 Questionnaire results on notaries' contribution to legal certainty[73]

[71] Tešić (2022c).

[72] Out of 100 respondents, 84 answered this question. Tešić (2022c).

[73] Out of 100 respondents, 96 answered this question. Tešić (2022c).

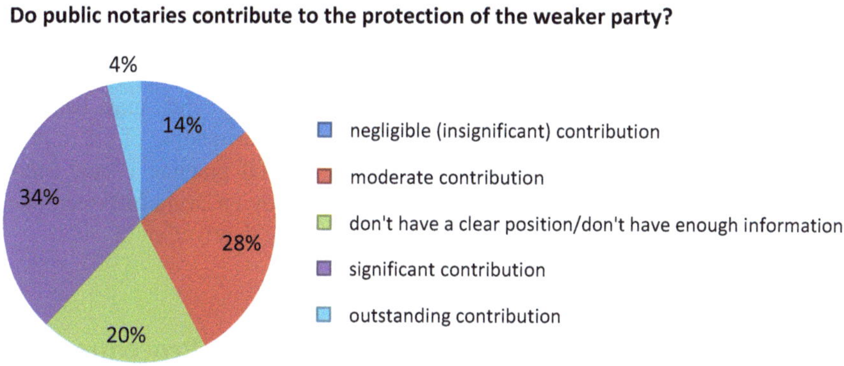

Fig. 3 Questionnaire results on notaries' contribution to the protection of the weaker party (often a female spouse)[74]

The evaluated data clearly demonstrate that this legal profession has enabled a significant step forward in the implementation of key legal principles. However, we must not overlook that there is considerable space for improvement in notarial services, particularly in the area of protecting the weaker party, which implies that notaries must play a gender responsive advisory and protection role, being able to improve gender equality.

5.2 *Making Notarial Advisory Function Gender–Responsive*

In general, the notary has an advisory function as a professional and impartial authority that is expected to look after the contracting parties' interests thus discouraging the conclusion of harmful contracts. For instance, when solemnizing the (pre)marital contract, between spouses or future spouses, the notary public must warn the contracting parties that such an agreement excludes the legal regime of joint property, which must be noted in the confirmation clause.[75] In this type of agreements, as well as in agreements on the division of marital property,[76] the notary is obliged by law to protect the weaker party,[77] bearing in mind that access to relevant information is a valuable tool for overcoming gender inequality and empowering individuals to understand and exercise their rights.

What we recognize as a need in Serbian law is a broader integration of gender competence into notarial procedure. A gender-competent notary should be able to

[74] Out of 100 respondents, 95 answered this question. Tešić (2022c).

[75] Law on Family, Art. 188, para. 2.

[76] Law on Family, Art. 179, para. 2.

[77] One of the important functions of solemnization is to prevent the recklessness of the contracting party. More about the considering function implied in notarial forms: Tešić (2014), p. 509.

detect situations where formal equality masks substantial inequality—particularly in the negotiation and execution of property-related contracts. Such competence entails the capacity to identify whether a weaker party, particulary a woman from a marginalized or socioeconomically disadvantaged background, may be under pressure to sign away property rights, or may lack full understanding of the implications of her consent. Therefore, gender-sensitive notarial practice is not simply procedural niceties; it directly affects justice outcomes by ensuring informed decision-making, enabling access to remedies and preventing deprivation of right.

6 Looking for a Gender-Responsive Notarial Procedure

6.1 *An Important Step Forward: Strengthening the Legal Position of the Hypothec Debtor's Spouse*

It is essential to emphasize that public notaries have significantly contributed to the empowerment of the hypothec debtor's spouse. Since the introduction of notaries in the Republic of Serbia, there have practically been no disputes in which spouses of hypothec debtors claim that the agreement on hypothec or the unilateral hypothec statement is null and void. In this context, public notaries have an important preventive role. If the security provider is married, they insist on the formal consent of the spouse, thus preventing numerous disputes when the hypothec debt comes due.[78] Despite the above-mentioned significant progress in terms of gender responsiveness in notarial practice, there are still many outstanding issues in the property relations of married/cohabiting partners with inherent gender vulnerability. In this sense, it is important to consider whether it is possible to achieve a substantial shift towards the establishment of a gender-neutral notarial procedure through the recognition of best notarial practice and eventual changes in material and procedural norms.

6.2 *Addressing Gender-Based Vulnerability in Terms of Property*

6.2.1 Vulnerability of Female Spouses in Acquiring a Real Estate Property

The Serbian Law on Registration in the Cadastre provides that if the entry in the real estate registry is made on the initiative of a public notary, the property will not be registered as joint property of the spouses: if there is no information about the

[78] 'Some legal transactions must be checked and approved by a certain public authority in order to avoid later disputes'. Seger (2000), p. 20.

marriage and the spouse in the attached documents, or if a spouses' statement is submitted to the Cadastre that in the particular case acquired real estate is the separate property of one spouse, or if, according to the legal title for registration, the spouses acquire co-ownership with defined shares.[79] Although the rule on rebuttable presumption regarding the acquisition of joint property by spouses is based on 'good legislator intention', it seems that it will not bring about a fundamental change in household practices until the dominant gender values in society have been corrected. If the real estate is acquired during the 'happiness time', the acquirer's wife may feel guilty or fear that her request in terms of joint property or co-ownership will be misunderstood. She may irrationally consider her subjective right as a potential trigger for suspicion and conflicts with her husband and his extended family which will consequently disturb the harmony of the marital relationship ('fear of marital mistrust'). It appears that the vast majority of female spouses, especially those living in rural areas and smaller communities, will act in accordance with the gender stereotype that she is 'his other half': spouse, housewife, and mother of joint children, with the important life task of supporting her husband in 'good and bad'. The 'average woman' is regularly driven by the simple thought that if she does not understand 'men's business', it is not appropriate for her to get involved in the making of business decisions. There is a high probability that fearing social condemnation and blame, a female spouse would give consent for registration the real estate acquired during the marriage as separate property of her husband, even though this is not the case ('fear of stigmatization'). Subsequently, in a period of marital disharmony—separation or divorce—her chances of proving that the property acquired during marriage was joint property will be completely lost or severely limited. Accordingly, the future legislation should be more balanced and gender-responsive in this regard, taking into account the existence of distinct periods in marriage: 'happiness time' and 'crisis time'. The legislator should consider the great differences in the level of emancipation of women living in the capital city compared to those living in small towns and rural areas where the 'fear of marital mistrust' and 'fear of stigmatization' are more pronounced and thus the freedom to decide on the status of immovable property acquired in marriage is significantly limited.

If the rule that consumers, as weaker parties, have the *right to withdraw* from the contract within a certain period is almost universally accepted, it is legitimate to ask whether it would have been possible for undisclosed joint owners to withdraw (without giving reasons) their consent to the registration of immovable property acquired during the marriage as the separate property of only one spouse. Such a legislative approach should not neglect the principle of legal certainty. The possibility of withdrawing the consent for the exclusive acquisition of one spouse should be made visible to third parties *ex officio* by notary through corresponding

[79] In addition, if the immovable property is already registered in the cadastre of one of the spouses, joint property will be subsequently registered in the cadastre based on the statement of both spouses that in the specific case it is joint property. Law on Registration in the Cadastre, Art. 7, para. 5.

entry in the public real estate records which would be expired after a certain period of time ('period of reflection'), for example, one year from the registration of the spouse's sole property. In our view, the above approach is more balanced and gender sensitive. It would reduce the pressure on the weaker spouse and allow her to make an informed final decision about property, after having rationalised certain personal concerns that are immanent when the decision to register one partner as the owner of the real estate is taken in a hurry and in the presence of another spouse.

6.2.2 Vulnerability of Female Partners in Acquiring a Real Estate Property

Young people's interest in marriage as a traditional form of partnership in the Republic of Serbia is steadily decreasing.[80] The new generation prefers informal unions where partners live together (cohabit) in an intimate relationship but are not married according to marital law. 'Often this will refer to couples who are married under custom or religious laws, where such marriages are not recognised or do not meet the requirements of formal law'.[81] If the informal partnership meets certain requirements, the law may grant specific rights, obligations, and protections to the partners. According to Serbian Family Law, an extramarital union is a lasting cohabitation of a woman and a man between whom there are no marital impediments.[82] In the same way, as it regulates the property relations of married couples, Serbian law introduces the legal fiction of joint property for cohabiting partners, according to which the registration in the real estate records in the name of one partner is considered to be the entry of the couples' common ownership.

This norm makes sense when it comes to the division of joint property. However, the position of the cohabiting partner as an invisible joint-owner in real estate transactions is much more complex. According to the Serbian Law on Registration in the Cadastre.[83] the 'undisclosed joint-owner' is protected only if he/she is married; on the contrary, if he/she is a cohabiting partner whose status cannot be determined by public records, his/her ownership rights are not adequately guaranteed. Given that the majority of unmarried partners whose joint property is not registered in public real estate records are women,[84] it is clear why it is particularly important to consider this issue from a gender equity perspective. The notarial duties concerning the conveyance of immovable property imply not only the determination of the status of the property but also the identification of the

---

[80] Devrnja (2014), p. 205.

[81] FAO (2018), p. 23.

[82] Law on Family, Art. 4, para. 1.

[83] Law on Registration in the Cadastre, Art. 7, para. 5.

[84] According to one research 'only 15 out of 52 reporting countries included sufficient provisions in their legal frameworks to protect women's rights to land'. The Sustainable Development Goals Report 2022, https://www.un.org/sustainabledevelopment/gender-equality/.

personal status of the parties involved in the transactions.[85] However, the scope of this rule is quite limited with regard to cohabitation. In practice, the notary does not investigate whether the transferor is in an informal union and consequently does not obtain the consent of his/her cohabitant to the disposal of the immovables. Similarly, when it comes to buying a property, the notary is not obliged to check whether the buyer is in an informal partnership. The other issue is whether such a duty can be derived from an interpretation of the constitutional norm that marriage and cohabitation are equal,[86] the provision of the Law that unmarried partners have the rights and obligations of spouses,[87] and the norm that the same rules apply *mutatis mutandis* to the property rights of spouses as to the property relations of unmarried partners.[88] However, despite the certainty of such an interpretation,[89] the application of the above-mentioned norms in real—life cases is not entirely straightforward. The public notary obtains information about the existence of the marriage from the public register, in other ways prescribed by law or from the documents submitted by the parties. On the other hand, although the Constitution and the Family Law give cohabitation the same legitimacy as marriage, these rules are often a 'dead letter'.[90] In the Serbian legal system, cohabitation between persons of different sexes is sufficient to establish a non-marital union, with no minimum duration requirement. While the marital status of the seller can be verified through the marriage certificate, there is no such guarantee for the seller who is in an informal union.[91] Given that there is no register of this kind of union in the Republic of Serbia, non-marital union may be suggested by the facts that two persons of different sexes have a child in common or residence at the same address, but these indications are not necessarily sufficient.[92]

In the absence of plain statutory conditions for establishing the non-marital union, the common property of cohabitants is also blurred and vague. In theory, cohabitants acquire joint property *ex lege,* but in practice, it is often not so easy to

---

[85] FAO and GIZ (2019), pp. 17–18.

[86] The Constitution of the Republic of Serbia. *Official Gazette of the Republic of Serbia*, nos. 98/06 and 115/21, Art. 62, para. 5.

[87] Law on Family, Art. 4, para. 2.

[88] Law on Family, Art. 191, para. 2.

[89] Some authors correctly conclude that the fiction on unregistered common property is still applied to the extramarital union. Dabić and Dolović Bojić (2019), p. 435.

[90] 'When it comes to identifying and protecting the property rights over the property acquired during cohabitation, informality of union creates challenges for notary and for the parties. Nevertheless, the notary must try to determine the existence of a legally recognised cohabitation.' FAO and GIZ (2019), p. 20.

[91] 'The basic problem when it comes to the legal protection of informal unions is to determine exactly what conditions extramarital cohabitation should meet in order to create a family status between partners and how to prove the fulfilment of those conditions in legal transactions.' Lucić, Duić and Muhvić (2020), p. 34.

[92] In determining whether an informal partnership enjoys the protection of 'family life' under Art. 8 of the ECHR, the ECtHR has held that several factors may be relevant, such as the period of cohabitation, joint upbringing of children, etc. *Van der Heijden* v *the Netherlands*, para. 50.

prove that two people were in an extramarital union at the time of the acquisition. For this reason, the notary must rely on the joint declaration of the cohabitants made in his/her office as regards the existence of the informal union. Even if the buyer informs the public notary that he/she is in a non-marital partnership, this cannot result in the registration of the common property of cohabitants, because the Law on the Registration in the Cadastre is *lex specialis* in relation to the Law on Family. In the case of married partners, there is a presumption in terms of acquiring the joint property, with three legal exceptions that must be explicitly stated in the registration documents. On the contrary, there is no such provision in the case of unmarried partners. Moreover, in accordance with the general rules on autonomy of will, unmarried partners may state in the purchase contract that they are buying the immovable property as co-owners. This disparity has led to indirect discrimination against individuals living in non-marital partnerships as compared to married couples.[93]

Although cohabitation is formally the equivalent of marriage in Serbia, an informal partner is not equal to a spouse as a party to a real estate transaction: neither when he/she would like to transfer ownership as an invisible joint seller, nor when he/she would like to purchase a property as an invisible joint buyer. If we take into account the fact that in the Republic of Serbia, every fourth woman is the owner or co-owner of real estate and that in rural areas every sixth woman is registered in the real estate Cadastre,[94] and examine it in conjunction with the data from the Serbian population census (2022) that 277,140 persons (4.87% of the population) live with a partner in a cohabitation,[95] it becomes plain to what extent the *'real estate ghosts'–the phenomenon of persons whose rights on real estate assets are not visible from public records–is widespread in Serbia.* As mentioned above, the largest proportion of undisclosed joint owners are women, and it appears that within this group, female cohabitants are particularly vulnerable.

This issue can be approached in two ways. According to one perspective, it would be necessary to change the legal framework by introducing a proper public register of non-marital unions, with simple and efficient registration rules. The digital transformation of society would potentially bring the possibility of registering extramarital unions through the e-government system.[96] Another perception of the same dilemma is that cohabitants deliberately refuse to be registered in any way. Informal unions should not be given the same legal significance as formal ones. Consequently, property issues in this kind of partnership should be resolved in accordance with general legal rules, which imply that non-marital partners have the freedom to contractually regulate their property relations within the limits of

[93] This seems to be one of those cases 'when rules, regulations or procedures appear to be neutral, but actually result in different treatment for certain groups of people'. OSCE (2019), p. 9.

[94] 'Only one in six women in rural areas is an owner of real estate', 31 May 2020, https://www.naled.rs/vest-nekretninu-poseduje-tek-svaka-sesta-zena-na-selu-3631.

[95] Statistical Office of the Republic of Serbia, Marital Status. Data by municipalities and cities, Belgrade, 2023, https://publikacije.stat.gov.rs/G2023/Pdf/G20234008.pdf.

[96] https://euprava.gov.rs/.

private autonomy. In the theory of notarial law, the prevailing attitude is that a public notary 'should exercise due diligence by uncovering the existence of any rights and interests in the property. The unregistered party (spouse) should be identified and included in the sale of the real estate property under joint ownership or co-ownership'.[97] However, even legal theory does not address the inclusion of an unmarried partner as an invisible joint owner whose legal position is extremely weak. In our view, in accordance with the principle of protection of a particularly vulnerable party, notaries should inquire the contracting parties about:[98] 1) whether the seller is in a non-marital union and, if so, to require the seller's cohabitant to agree to the sale; 2) whether the buyer is in a non-marital union and if so, to hold a preparatory meeting with the unmarried couple in order to inform and advise them that one of them will not be registered in the public real estate records, although by law they are or might be the joint owners. Subsequently, in accordance with the principle of private autonomy, cohabitants can avoid such an outcome by concluding an agreement to acquire real estate co-ownership.

If the seller deliberately conceals the existence of a non-marital union, the immovable property will be sold without the consent of the informal partner, but at least there will be a notarial record that the seller was asked on cohabiting status. If the buyer keeps silent about cohabitation status, he/she will be registered in the public real estate records as the sole owner, but at least there will be a clear declaration of this fact before the notary. By making a false statement, a *mala fide* informal partner would make it much more cumbersome to prove the existence of an extra-marital union in other situations when it would be in his or her interest to do so.

6.2.3 Vulnerability of Women Living with the Spouse/Partner in Unregistered Real Estate

The women who live married or cohabiting with partners in immovable properties that do not exist in the public record ('out-of-record ownership'), because they were built without building permission are highly disadvantaged.[99] It is a common practice for the male partner to be the one who submits the request for legalisation (special administrative procedure to verify whether the building meets the

[97] FAO and GIZ (2019), p. 19.

[98] If the search for citizens' data were more advanced, the notary public could easily determine whether the party concluding the real estate sales contract has a child and with whom, as well as whether there is another adult of a different gender who does not have the same last name as party residing at the party's address.

[99] The conclusion on number of real estate female ghosts in Serbia can be drawn from the fact that according to data obtained through satellite images, over 5,000,000 buildings on the territory of the Republic of Serbia are not registered in the public real estate records. See: *Every other real estate in Serbia is unregistered*, 29 June 2023, https://naled.rs/en/news-every-other-real-estate-in-serbia-is-unregistered-8182.

minimum urban requirements) in his own name, who is the property taxpayer, and in whose name the bills for electricity and other utilities are issued. Regardless of whether the woman actually participated in the acquisition of real estate, from a legal point of view she is a 'real estate ghost' that is invisible in public data.

6.2.4 Vulnerability of Women Living in a De Facto Union with a Partner Whose Marriage Has Not Been Officially Ended

From the aspect of property relations, the legal position of women living in a *de facto* union with a man whose marriage has not yet been formally terminated is particularly challenging. While a female non-marital partner whose immovable property is not registered in the public records can exercise the subjective right against her partner, as a sole owner, before the court, although with considerable difficulties, a woman in a *de facto* union with a person whose marriage has not been formally dissolved cannot enter into a legally recognised relationship with him,[100] due to the rule that an existing valid marriage is marital and cohabitation impediment. Consequently, the woman in such a *de facto* union does not acquire joint property with her informal partner, at all.[101]

6.3 Strengthening the Position of 'Real Estate Ghosts': The Next Step in Tackling the Gender Inequality

We believe that strengthening the legal position of informal partners whose personal status (cohabitation) or property status (joint ownership of the real estate) is not visible in public records, is a particularly important assignment of public notaries.[102] The notary must ensure that the rights of the informal partner in a legally recognised cohabitation are identified, respected, and protected.[103] During cohabitation, common property should be managed and disposed of jointly and by mutual consent of cohabitants. Therefore, if one partner, as the registered owner, would like to dispose of common real estate, the notary should obtain

[100] Persons of the same sex living in a *de facto* union are in a similar legal position. Due to the marital impediment, these persons cannot acquire joint property. The general principles of freedom of contract, unjust enrichment, etc. apply to their mutual property rights. This legal issue deserves a separate analysis of a similar scope, so we did not deal with it in detail in this paper.

[101] A man in this kind of union is privileged since all acquired assets become his separate property and not joint property nether with his *de facto* partner, nor with his ex-wife. Lucić, Duić and Muhvić (2020), p. 34.

[102] At this point, it is important to emphasize the need for continuous education of public notaries, through seminars organised by the Notaries' Chamber, where experienced legal experts could highlight the significance of the above-mentioned advisory approach.

[103] FAO and GIZ (2019), p. 20.

written consent to the transaction from his/her partner, even if he/she is not registered in the public record.[104] At the same time, special care must be taken to prevent the abuse of the legal fiction on the extramarital partners' joint property. A person pretending to be in the extramarital union should not be able to successfully claim the nullity of the agreement on sale or hypothec on the grounds that he/she did not consent to the disposal of joint property. There are two possible approaches to the acquisition of immovable property for persons in an extramarital union:

1) make joint registration of real estate compulsory for married and/or unmarried couples; or
2) encourage joint registration of real estate for married and/or unmarried couples through economic incentives.[105]

In our opinion, legal certainty will not be significantly improved, if the relevant law is amended to require the mandatory registration of co-ownership in the name of both spouses and/or informal partners in the public real estate records. Therefore, the registration of co-ownership should remain voluntary, followed by a strong state initiative to make this formal.[106] For example, it is possible to amend tax and fee regulations so that the registration of co-ownership of the married and/or unmarried partner is exempt from the payment of the public record registration fee, and/or the co-owners pay only half of the real estate tax value in the first year after the acquisition, and/or the co-owners receive a discount on the fee for the urbanisation of the construction plot, and so on. Through continuous promotion and economic encouragement, the legal situation regarding the joint property of married and unmarried partners in public real estate records could be gradually brought into line with the actual situation on the ground. We believe that the rules governing the non-litigious procedure before public notaries should be amended *de lege ferenda,* in a way *that* in case of alienation of real estate or establishing the hypothec, regardless of whether the parties are men or women, married or cohabiting, adequate protection is provided to the joint owners whose right is not visible from the public records. Moreover, introducing gender-competent notarial practice here means that notaries proactively engage with parties to assess whether there is a risk that the property rights of the vulnerable spouse or an informal partner in legal transactions are being diminished or overlooked—not through overt discrimination but through structural inequality or informational disadvantage. This role goes beyond neutrality and demands an active stance to ensure that both partners,

[104] Compare with: FAO and GIZ (2019), p. 19.

[105] FAO (2018), p. 22.

[106] In order to benefit from positive aid schemes in favour of working women in agriculture, 'they should be recognised as owners or co-owners, which would have a positive impact on their situation in the labor market, social entitlements and economic independence, thus ensuring their greater visibility (and recognition of their contribution to the economy and income) in rural areas and better access to land'. European Parliament resolution of 4 April 2017 on women and their roles in rural areas (2016/2204(INI)).

especially women, understand the long-term implications of legal actions before the notary. In this way, a gender competent notary becomes a safeguard against the erosion of women's property rights.

7 Final Remarks

In the sociology of professions, one of the characteristics of all contemporary professions is 'differentiation within'. It is connected to the development of a post-industrial society, characterised by the diversity and mobility of workers, in which citizens acquire higher levels of qualifications.[107] In such circumstances, women are not excluded from professions; in fact, professions (but not all positions within a certain profession) are more or less easily accessible to them. This is aided by the introduction of various legal bases for engaging in a certain profession, which, further, has the consequence that all members of one profession do not enjoy the same security of employment, nor the same security and level of income.[108] In this sense, we could conclude that today's professions are not immune to social and gender-based inequalities, which have an adverse effect on the broader labour market. This conclusion also applies to the legal professions, since the 'feminisation' process continues in the form of a steady increase in the number of female members of the profession. This process, however, is accompanied by gender-based segmentation, which manifests itself in the dominance of men in the highest positions within a certain profession, primarily because of stereotypes about male and female roles in society and difficulties in balancing work and family obligations.

As holders of public authority, notaries safeguard justice, which is a fundamental value in a state based on the rule of law. As such, they must enjoy public confidence in the same way as judges.[109] To achieve this goal in the context of gender equality, it is not enough to make frequent changes to the legislation. It is important to encourage values that enhance gender equality, especially those that contradict deeply rooted gender prejudices, particularly considering that 'formal and informal values-based education has an important role to play in promoting both the principles and the practice of equality and non-discrimination',[110] as well as equal access to justice, which is recognised as a human right and an integral part of the rule of law. Ultimately, specific measures to achieve gender parity in the judicial system should be part of a broader strategy to promote equality between women and men in all

[107] Bellini and Maestripieri (2018), p. 7.

[108] Bellini and Maestripieri (2018), p. 7.

[109] 'The special role in society of the judiciary which, as the guarantor of justice, a fundamental value in a state governed by the rule of law, must enjoy public confidence [...]'. *Morice* v *France*, para. 128.

[110] Insights Gender and the rule of law, http://act4ruleoflaw.org/en/news/gender.

social domains. A gender-balanced notarial practice will be impossible to achieve if other aspects of community life remain substantially unbalanced.[111]

In this regard, there are reasons to argue that the contribution of the notary profession to attaining gender equality rests on two main pillars. The first is the actual provision of equal opportunities for men and women to engage in the notary profession and to advance their professional careers without discrimination based on sex/gender (*gender neutral selection and promotion of public notaries*). The second is the contribution of notaries to the fight against gender inequality in their entire field of activity (*gender responsive notary services)*. All members of the notary profession are obliged to ensure impartial and thorough guidance to the parties, without difference, and provide them with valuable support in making important decisions.[112] This includes informing vulnerable and marginalised groups about the legal scope of transactions they undertake within a particular notarial form, which contributes to the equality and respect for human rights and fundamental freedoms, and shows that the notarial profession is characterised by 'power and knowledge, responsibility and expertise'.[113]

Notaries can contribute to the achievement of gender equality through their practice, especially when it comes to the protection of the weaker party. This especially applies to the duty of notaries to advise the parties enabling them to identify and eliminate the risk of seemingly neutral regulations affecting men and women differently, primarily due to deeply rooted societal gender stereotypes. The integration of gender competence in notarial duties ensures that inequality risks are recognized in time, and that interventions—such as additional clarification, or even delaying the important property decisions—can be made to protect women from entering into unjust legal transactions. Gender-sensitive notarial procedure helps bridge the gap between formal legal equality and actual equality of outcomes. This considerably reduces the risk of violating the principle of gender equality, as informing the parties about the rights and obligations stemming from the contract they are entering into prevent one party (usually a woman) from being harmed for lack of knowledge of the objective law and subjective rights and, therefore, from making decisions based on stereotypes. In exercising their advisory function, the notaries have to pay particular attention to the legal position of married and cohabiting partners not registered as joint owners in real estate records. As a rule, women are the weaker party in the notary proceedings, which is why it is necessary to make notary services more gender responsive, particularly in the light of the sensitive position of those women, who are facing the risk of intersectional discrimination in real estate property transactions due to the fact that there is no information in the public registers, either on their status as cohabiting partners or on their joint ownership. In this sense, notaries appear as agents of transformation,

---

[111] *Cf.* Gender Equality Commission, Balanced participation of women and men in decision-making, Analytical report—2016 data, p. 12.

[112] European Commission for the Efficiency of Justice (2021), p. 3.

[113] Delmas (2019), p. 11.

if we consider the need to achieve—in Hepple's words—transformative equality,[114] which rests on the renewal of the spirit of social solidarity and joint action.[115]

The law continues to play a significant role in modifying cultural patterns that affect the position of women in the notary and other legal professions. Therefore, we should persist in further improving the legal framework, as well as the corresponding strategic documents of importance for the empowerment of women in these professions.

A proper gender responsive policy in terms of public notary should focus on the implementation of the EU[116] and National equality strategy[117] objectives, which are mainly aimed at challenging gender stereotypes; closing gender gaps and achieving equal participation of man and women. Legislative solutions to integrate the gender perspective into the Serbian judicial system need to be in line with the Law on Gender Equality.[118] On the example of the Law on Public Notaries, this would mean the introduction of gender-sensitive mechanisms both in the notarial selection procedure and in the election of governing bodies in the Chamber of notaries. Furthermore, legal and strategic acts must not ignore the importance of men in achieving gender equality, which is why they should consider the problems they face in this area, especially with regard to the stereotypes related to the implementation of measures for the reconciliation of professional and family responsibilities, since these measures are often viewed as favouring women. This further means that, although vital, the role of legislation—as an instrument for achieving gender equality—is nevertheless limited. Therefore, achieving true equality of men and women in the notary profession as well as in the notary practice necessitates the participation of the entire society, in all of its segments.

References

Literature

Annual report on the work of the courts in the Republic of Serbia for (2020). https://www.vk.sud.rs/sites/default/files/attachments/pdf

Ataíde LM (2022) Aurora Teixeira de Castro. A primeira notária de Portugal. Edições Cosmos

Babović M, Petrović M (2021) Gender Equality Index for the Republic of Serbia 2021. Digitalization, future of work and gender equality. Social Inclusion and Poverty Reduction Unit of the Government of the Republic of Serbia, Belgrade

---

[114] Hepple (2014), p. 59.

[115] Hepple (2014), p. 59.

[116] European Commission, Communication from the Commission to the European Parliament, the Council, the European Economic and Social Committee and the Committee of the Regions—A Union of Equality: Gender Equality Strategy 2020–2025, Brussels, 5.3.2020 COM(2020) 152 final.

[117] The Gender Equality Strategy for the Period 2021–2030. *Official Gazetteof the Republic of Serbia*, no. 103/2021.

[118] Law on Gender Equality. Official Gazette *of the Republic of Serbia*, no. 52/2021.

Bellini A, Maestripieri L (2018) Professions within, between and beyond: varieties of professionalism in a globalizing world. Cambio 8(16):5–14
Bodul D, Grbić S (2014) O međusobnoj komplementarnosti pojmova „sud" i „javni bilježnik" u praksi Europskog suda za ljudska prava. Javni bilježnik 40:35–52
Bolton SC, Muzio D (2007) Can't live with 'em; Can't live without 'em: Gendered segmentation in the legal profession. Sociology 41(1):47–64
Collier R (2022) Men, masculinities and the legal professions: Asking the 'man question'. In: Abel RL, Sommerlad H, Hammerslev O, Schultz U (eds) Lawyers in 21st-century societies: comparisons and theories. Hart Publishing, Oxford, pp 151–172
Commissioner for Protection of Equality (2023) Opinion on the Draft Law on Amendments to the Law on Financial Support for Families with Children, no. 011-00-4/2023-02, of 20 March 2023
Conclusions of the 1st UINL International Forum on the Role of Women Notaries in the Twenty-First Century. https://www.notariesofeurope.eu/en/uinl-international-forum-on-the-role-of-women-notaries/
Council of Europe/European Court of Human Rights (2022) Guide on Article 6 of the European Convention on Human Rights Right to a fair trial (civil limb). https://www.echr.coe.int/documents/d/echr/guide_art_6_eng
Delmas C (2019) Les notaires en France: Des officiers de l'authentique entre héritage et modernité. Presses Universitaire de Rennes, Rennes
Delmas C (2019a) Les notaires, le genre d`une profession à patrimonie. Travail, genre et société 41:127–145
Dika M (2009) Izvanparnična i koncilijacijska funkcija javnih bilježnika – de lege lata i de lege ferenda. Zbornik Pravnog fakulteta u Zagrebu 59 (6):1153–1777
Đorđević M (2022) Between judiciary and advocacy: professional preferences of law students in Serbia. Sociološki pregled/Sociological Review 56(2):680–708
Dabetić V (2023) Izazovi konsolidacije sudstva kao nezavisne grane vlasti u Srbiji na početku 21. veka, PhD dissertation. University of Belgrade Faculty of Law, Belgrade
Dabić S, Dolović Bojić K (2019), Raspolaganje jednog (van)bračnog druga nepokretnošću u zajedničkoj svojini. Pravo i privreda 57(7-9):407–436
Delmas C (2022) La quête des apparences: l'habit fait-il le notaire? La mise en image d'un métier et d'un groupe professionnel. Images du travail, travail des images 13:1–31
Delmas C (2023) The feminisation of the notary profession in France: end of a patriarchal bastion or sedimentation of a gender stratification? International Journal of the Legal Profession. https://doi.org/10.1080/09695958.2023.2190898
Devrnja Z (2014) Vanbračne zajednice: Kanonskopravna perspektiva. Anali Pravnog fakulteta u Beogradu 62(1):205–222
Đorđević M, Vlajić M (2023) How much for a legal intern? Internship in law offices in Serbia. Pravni zapisi 1:126–147
Drakić G (2014) Normativno uređenje ustanove javnog beležništva u Kraljevini Srba, Hrvata i Slovenaca (Kraljevini Jugoslaviji). Zbornik radova Pravnog fakulteta u Novom Sadu 48 (4):201–215
European Commission for the Efficiency of Justice – Working Group on the evaluation of judicial systems (2021), Specific Study of the CEPEJ on the Legal Professions: Notaries – 2018 data. Contribution from the Notaries of Europe (CNUE). Strasbourg, CEPEJ-GT-EVAL(2021)14rev
FAO (2018) Realizing women's rights to land in the law. Rome. http://www.fao.org/3/I8785EN/i8785en.pdf. Accessed 20 Nov 2023
FAO and GIZ (2019) Guidelines on Strengthening Gender Equality in Notarial Practices – South-East Europe (prepared by Arsova Mitic K et al.), Rome
Gender Equality Commission, Balanced participation of women and men in decision-making, Analytical report - 2016 data
GIZ and FAO (2021) Notarial practices in Montenegro – strengthening gender equality in land ownership and control. Rome

Guide on Article 6 of the European Convention on Human Rights Right to a fair trial (civil limb). https://www.echr.coe.int/documents/d/echr/guide_art_6_eng. Updated to 31 Aug 2022
Galligan Y, Haupfleisch R, Irvine L, Korolkova K, Natter M, Schultz U, Wheeler S (2017) Mapping the representation of women and men in legal professions across the EU. European Parliament, Brussels
Hepple B (2014) The key to greater gender equality. The Equal Rights Review 12:59–61
International Union of Notaries (2004), Principles of notarial ethics, Approved by the General Meeting of Member Chambers of Notaries of the UINL. https://www.uinl.org/en_GB/principios-de-deontologia. Mexico City, 17th Oct 2004
Josipović T (2018) Zaštita potrošača od nepoštenih ugovornih odredbi – načela i standardi zaštite u odlukama suda Europske unije. Narodne novine, Zagreb
Kay F, Gorman E (2008) Women in the legal profession. Ann Rev Law Soc Sci 4:300–332
Kovačević L (2022) Legal framework for traineeships in the Republic of Serbia. Revue de droit comparé du travail et de la sécurité sociale 4:208–213
Lucić N, Dulć D, Muhvić D (2020) Izvanbračna zajednica: analiza međunarodnih i europskih normi u svrhu stvaranja nacionalnih standarda. Zbornik radova Pravnog fakulteta u Nišu 59(86):15–38
Maganić A (2022) Javni bilježnik u izvanparničnom postupku. Javni bilježnik 26(49):25–34
Marguénaud JP, Dauchez C, Dauchez B (2018) The notary, "out-of-court magistrate" with regard to the European judge of Human Rights. https://hal.science/hal-01878216/document
Menkel-Meadow C (1996) Feminization of the legal profession: the comparative sociology of women lawyers. In: Label R, Lewis P (eds), Lawyers in society. An overview. University of California Press, Berkeley - Los Angeles – Oxford, pp 221–280
Ministry for Labour, Employment, Veterans and Social Policy of the Republic of Serbia (2020) Ex-post analiza efekata Zakona o volontiranju. Belgrade
Ministère de la justice (2017) La féminisation des métiers du Ministère de la justice. Paris
Notaries' Role in Access to Justice in BC, October 52019. https://www.bcnotaryassociation.ca/resources/blog/?id=2
Nourissat C (2017) Le notaire n'est pas une juridiction au sens des règlements européens de coopération judiciaire civile. La Semaine Juridique Notariale et Immobilière 21
OHCHR. Gender stereotyping and women's human rights and gender equality (2023) https://www.ohchr.org/en/women/gender-stereotyping
OSCE (2019) Gender diversity and justice – overview and recommendations. https://www.osce.org/files/f/documents/3/4/419840_0.pdf
Pedersini R, Coletto D (2010) Self-employed workers: industrial relations and working conditions. European Foundation for the Improvement of Living and Working Conditions, Dublin
Poretti P (2019) Uloga javnih bilježnika u pravu EU-a s osvrtom na sudsku praksu. Javni bilježnik 23(46):7–24
Šago D (2021) Neki aspekti uloge javnog bilježnika kao povjerenika suda u sudskim postupcima u Republici Hrvatskoj. Zbornik radova Aktualnosti građanskog i trgovačkog zakonodavstva i pravne prakse 18:173–189
Schlürmann L (2018) Croatian public notaries under European Civil Procedure Law. A Commentary on the Judgment of the Court of Justice of the European Union (Second Chamber) March 9, 2017, Case C-551/15 – Pula Parking. Cuadernos de derecho transnacional 10(2):947–953
Seger C (2000) Lex est quod notamus – o uvođenju latinskog notarijata u tranzicijskim zemljama Istočne i Jugoistočne Evrope. Nova pravna revija 1–2:19–27
Sokić K (2012) Uloga javnih bilježnika u nekim gledištima imovinskopravne zaštite osoba lišenih poslovne sposobnosti. Javni bilježnik 36:43–47
Statistical Office of the Republic of Serbia (2017) Women and men in the Republic of Serbia. Belgrade
Statistical Office of the Republic of Serbia (2020) Women and men in the Republic of Serbia. Belgrade. https://publikacije.stat.gov.rs/G2021/Pdf/G20216001.pdf

Statistical Office of the Republic of Serbia (2023) Marital Status, Data by municipalities and cities. Belgrade. https://publikacije.stat.gov.rs/G2023/Pdf/G20234008.pdf
Supreme Court of Cassation of the Republic of Serbia (2021) Annual report on the work of the courts in the Republic of Serbia for 2020. Belgrade. https://www.vk.sud.rs/sites/default/files/attachments/Godi%C5%A1nji%20izve%C5%A1taja%20za%202020%20FINAL_0.pdf
Tešić N (2013) O pravnoposlovnom osamostaljivanju fizičkih lica. In: Radović V (ed) Usklađivanje poslovnog prava Srbije sa pravom Evropske unije. Pravni fakultet Univerziteta u Beogradu. Belgrade, pp 404–437
Tešić N (2014) O značaju forme za promet nepokretnosti – analiza sudske prakse pre uvođenja javnobeležničkog zapisa u srpsko pravo. In: Radović V (ed) Usklađivanje poslovnog prava Srbije sa pravom Evropske unije. Pravni fakultet Univerziteta u Beogradu. Belgrade, pp 482–513
Tešić N (2015) Ustavnopravni meč advokati protiv javnih beležnika okončan je službenim rezultatom 3:0 za fiskus Republike Srbije. In: Radović V (ed) Usklađivanje poslovnog prava Srbije sa pravom Evropske unije. Pravni fakultet Univerziteta u Beogradu, Belgrade, pp 470–496
Tešić N (2019) O izvršnosti založne izjave. Pravni život 68(10):489–518
Tešić N (2022a) Pravo zaštite hipotekarnih potrošača - Pravna trilogija, Knjiga prva: pojam hipotekarnog potrošača, Pravni fakultet Univerziteta u Beogradu, Belgrade
Tešić N (2022b) Assessment on the roles of public notaries and public bailiffs in the Republic of Serbia for achieving the values and objectives stated in the EU Negotiation Chapter 23, Annex II „Gender equality" (Unpublished)
Tešić N (2022c) Assessment on the roles of public notaries and public bailiffs in the Republic of Serbia for achieving the values and objectives stated in the EU Negotiation Chapter 23, 2022 (Unpublished)
Thaw DM (1998) The feminization of the office of the notary public: from *femme covert* to *notaire covert*. Marshall Law Review 31(3):703–734
The European Institute for Gender Equality (2015) Promoting women's economic independence and entrepreneurship: Good practices. Luxembourg
The Statistical Office of the Republic of Serbia (2020) Women and men in the Republic of Serbia. Belgrade
Trgovčević Prokić M (2009) Zakon Kraljevine Jugoslavije o javnim beležnicima. Pravna riječ 20:283–295
United Nations Human Rights Office of the High Commissioner, Gender stereotyping and the judiciary. https://www.ohchr.org/sites/default/files/OHCHR_JudicialStereotyping_Session3.pdf
Uzelac A (2018) Javnobilježnička ovrha i zaštita potrošača: novi izazovi europeizacije građanskog postupka. Zbornik Pravnog fakulteta u Zagrebu 68(5–6):637–660
Vujadinović D, Kovačević L, Marinković T, Krstić I, Davinić M (2020) Achieving gender equality at the University of Belgrade Faculty of Law: research and policy study. University of Belgrade Faculty of Law, Belgrade
Vuković D (2017) Advokatura u Srbiji: rezultati empirijskog istraživanja. Branič 1-4:103–113
Zendeli E, Selmani A (2017) The notary service - justice services. SEEU Review 12(1):135–147

Case Law

CJEU, Case C-551/15, Pula Parking d.o.o. v Sven Klaus Tederahn, Judgment of the Court (Second Chamber) of 9 March 2017, EU:C:2017:193. https://eur-lex.europa.eu/legal-content/EN/AUTO/?uri=ecli:ECLI%3AEU%3AC%3A2017%3A193&locale=en
CJEU, Case C-484/15, Ibrica Zulfikarpašić v Slaven Gajer, Judgment of the Court (Second Chamber) of 9 March 2017, EU:C:2017:199. https://eur-lex.europa.eu/legal-content/EN/AUTO/?uri=ecli:ECLI%3AEU%3AC%3A2017%3A193&locale=en

CJEU,C-234/19,*EOS* Matrix d.o.o. v Entazis d.o.o., Order of the Court (Sixth Chamber) of 6 November 2019, EU:C:2019:986. https://eur-lex.europa.eu/legal-content/EN/TXT/PDF/?uri=ecli:ECLI%3AEU%3AC%3A2019%3A986
CJEU, Joined Cases Parking d.o.o.v Sawal d.o.o. (C-267/19), and Interplastics s.r.o. v Letifico d.o.o. (C-323/19), Judgment of the Court (Sixth Chamber) of 7 May 2020, ECLI:EU:C:2020:351
CJEU, Case C-32/14, ERSTE Bank Hungary Zrt v Attila Sugár, Judgment of the Court (Third Chamber) of 1 October 2015, ECLI:EU:C:2015:637
CJEU, Case C-34/18, Ottília Lovasné Tóth v ERSTE Bank Hungary Zrt., Judgment of the Court (Third Chamber) of 19 September 2019, ECLI:EU:C:2019:764
Constitutional Court of the Republic of Serbia, Decision Už-315/2008, of 13 November 2008
Constitutional Court of the Republic of Serbia Decision Už-7451/2016, of 25 October 2018
Constitutional Court of the Republic of Serbia DecisionUž-6193/2018, of 19 July 2018
Constitutional Court of Serbia, Decision IUz-299/2018. Official Gazette of the Republic of Serbia, No 43/23
Constitutional Court of Montenegro, Decision Už-III no. 50/14 of 31 March 2017
ECtHR, Benthem v Netherlands, App. no 8848/80, A/97, (1986) 8 EHRR 1, IHRL 54 (ECHR 1985), 23rd October 1985
ECtHR, Sramek v Austria, App. no. 8790/79, 22 October 1984
ECtHR, Xhoxhaj v Albania,App. no. 15227/19, 9 February 2021
ECtHR, Ali Rıza and Others v Turkey, Applications nos. 30226/10 and 4 others,28 January 2020
ECtHR, Mutu and Pechstein v Switzerland, Applications nos. 40575/10 and 67474/10, 2 October 2018
ECtHR, H. v Belgium, App. no. 8950/80, 30 November 1987
ECtHR, Ringeisenv Austria,App. no. 2614/65, 16 July 1971
ECtHR, Ana Ionita v Romania, App. no. 81270/12, 10.01.2017
ECtHR, Morice v France, Application no. 29369/10, 23 April 2015
ECtHR, Van der Heijden v the Netherlands, App. no. 42857/05, 3 April 2012
Supreme Court of Montenegro, Judgment Rev. no. 1046/13 of 12 November 2013
Supreme Court of Cassation of Serbia, Rev 793/2019 of 26 September 2019

Nenad Tešić is an Associate Professor at the University of Belgrade Faculty of Law. He teaches Introduction to Private Law, Property Law and Secured Transactions. He spent the academic year 2004/2005 as a visiting scholar at Brooklyn Law School on the basis of the Junior Faculty Development Program. In 2007 and 2010, he was awarded a doctoral research fellowship at the Max Planck Institute for Comparative and International Private Law in Hamburg. He has published more than 50 scientific papers, mainly in the field of private law, the most important of which are three monographs: on the registered pledge (2007), on the true sale of receivables (2012) and on the notion of mortgage consumer (2022). More recently, his research has focused on consumer protection and digital property topics.

Ljubinka Kovačević is Full Professor at the University of Belgrade Faculty of Law. Prior to joining this Faculty in 2005, she was a researcher at the Institute of Comparative Law in Belgrade. Currently, she is teaching Labour Law, International Labour Law, and Social Security Law. She is the author of three monographs ("Legal Subordination in Employment Relationship and Its Limitations" /2013/, "Valid Grounds for Dismissal" /2016/ and "Entering into Employment Relationship" /2021/) and many papers on Serbian, international and comparative labour law.

Part III
Judicial Decisions

Can Gender Shape the Course of Justice? Some Insights from the European Court of Human Rights

Marko Bošnjak and Alice Leconte

Abstract This article relies on the commonly accepted postulate according to which personal characteristics of judges, including gender, could influence the interpretation and application of law, and by consequence, shape the jurisprudence. This assumption is of particular relevance in an international court like the European Court of Human Rights where judges from various cultural and professional backgrounds sit together and where around one third of judges are women. Comparing the findings of empirical studies with key principles such as collegiality and impartiality, the paper explores the existence of a potential "gender effect" in differentiating its expression on the bench from its concretization in judgments. Whereas multiple elements contribute to highlight the existence of "female voices" on the Strasbourg bench, its materialisation in judgments tends to be relative. Nonetheless, the participation of female judges on the bench is crucial in that it enriches deliberations and contributes to bring a gender-sensitive approach of the law of the Convention.

M. Bošnjak
European Court of Human Rights, Strasbourg, France
e-mail: Marko.Bosnjak@echr.coe.int

A. Leconte (✉)
University of Lille, Lille, France

© The Author(s), under exclusive license to Springer Nature Switzerland AG 2025

S. Baer et al. (eds.), *The Gender and the Judiciary*, Gender Perspectives in Law 7,
https://doi.org/10.1007/978-3-032-06885-9_7

1 Introduction

1.1 Gender Parity at the ECtHR: State of Play

In sixty-four years of existence the European Court of Human Rights (ECtHR) has experienced profound changes in various ways. Some changes have been discreet such as the reforms of the applications' processing.[1] Others have been more visible and commented such as the inscription of the principle of subsidiarity and the margin of appreciation in the Preamble of the European Convention on Human Rights.[2] Yet, some of the most profound transformations have concerned the composition of the Court itself.

In 1959, at the establishment of the Court, the judges were all men. It was not until 1971, that Helga Pedersen, the first female judge, sat at the ECtHR. From 1971 until 1998 only two other female judges joined Judge Pedersen, yet not simultaneously.[3] In November 1998 eight female judges sat on the bench of the new permanent Court.[4] Today, the proportion of female judges stagnates at around 30%.[5] This percentage puts the Court on the top four of the international courts in terms of gender representation, after the International Criminal Court (ICC) (61% of female judges), the African Court on Human and Peoples' Rights (ACtHPR) (45%) and the Inter-American Court of Human Rights (IACHR) (43%).[6] Moreover, symbolically, each of these courts counts or has once counted a female president.[7] Despite being the

---

[1] See for instance the introduction of committees by Protocol 11 entered into force in 1998 or the introduction of single judges by Protocol 14 entered into force in 2010. See also the introduction of a new admissibility condition brought by Protocol 14 and modified by Protocol 15 entered into force in 2021.

[2] Protocol 15 amending the Convention for the Protection of Human Rights and Fundamental Freedoms.

[3] Hennette Vauchez (2015), p. 200. Helga Pedersen was Judge in respect of Denmark between 1971 and 1980. Denise Bindschedler-Robert was Judge in respect of Switzerland from 1975 to 1991. Elisabeth Palm was Judge in respect of Sweden between 1988 and 2003.

[4] Were judges at the ECtHR in 1998: Françoise Tulkens (Belgium), Snejana Botoucharova (Bulgaria), Nina Vajić (Croatia), Wilhelmina Thomassen (Netherlands), Margarita Tsatsa-Nikolovska (North Macedonia), Hanne Sophie Greve (Norway), Viera Strážnická (Slovak Republic) and Elisabeth Palm (Sweden).

[5] See *infra* the figures in footnote 25.

[6] At the time of the writing of this article, in May 2024, the ICC counts 11 female judges out of 18 judges; the ACtHPR counts 5 female judges out of 11 judges; the IACHR counts 3 female judges out of 7 judges. These percentage are subject to change. See for instance: Pillai (2018).

[7] From 2008 to 2009, Cecilia Medina Quiroga (Chile) was President of the Inter-American Court of Human Rights. From 2012 to 2014, Justice Sophia A. B. Akuffo (Ghana) was President of the African Court on Human and Peoples' Rights. The second woman to hold this position is Imani Daud Aboud (Tanzania) elected President in 2023. At the International Criminal Court, the first woman elected President was Silvia Fernández de Gurmendi. She was the third president of this institution and held that position from 2015 to 2018.

oldest Court, the first female President of the ECtHR, Síofra O'Leary (Ireland), was only elected in 2022.[8]

Unsurprisingly, the common feature of these courts is the existence of a rule aiming at improving the gender parity on their respective bench. Article 12 paragraph 2 of the Protocol to the African Charter on Human and People's rights on the establishment of an African Court on Human and Peoples' Rights provides that "[d]ue consideration shall be given [by Member States] to adequate gender representation in the nomination process". Article 36 paragraph 8 of the Rome Statute sets forth that "[t]he States Parties shall, in the selection of judges, take into account the need, within the membership of the Court, for: [...] (iii) [a] fair representation of female and male judges". Regarding the European Court of Human Rights, the Resolution 1426 (2005) of the Parliamentary Assembly (PACE)—the organ in charge of electing the judges of the ECtHR on a list of three candidates submitted by Member States—modifying especially the Resolution 1366 (2004) states that "[t]he Assembly decides not to consider lists of candidates where: [...] 8. ii. the list does not include at least one candidate of each sex, except when the candidates belong to the sex which is under-represented in the Court, that is the sex to which under 40% of the total number of judges belong". The Resolution of the General Assembly of the Organization of American States (OAS) "encourage Member States to ensure that in the nomination and selection process of IACHR judges and commissioners to consolidate gender balance and regional geographical representation as well as an adequate balance of population groups, in particular those in situations of vulnerability, and legal systems of the Hemisphere".[9]

The study of these rules allows to understand the legal relevance of the gender criterion and the effectiveness of its implementation.

Firstly, it should be noted that they all relate to the same stage, *i.e.*, when the States nominate the candidates for a judge's position. The emphasis on the nomination stage is relevant for at least two reasons. On the one hand, it focuses on the crux of the problem. To sit on the bench, women must be selected as candidates. Given the increasing presence of women in the legal field, the paucity of female candidates could illustrate the existence of a glass ceiling and to that extent, constitute a point of vigilance.[10] On the other hand, it places the Member States as responsibility bearers,[11] underlying implicitly the subsidiary nature of this

[8] It should be noted that the 2020 election of Marialena Tsirli, the first female Registrar of the Court could indicate important steps towards gender parity have been done not only on the Court's bench but also in the Court's Registry.

[9] Translated from Spanish: Assembly General of the OAS, Resolution AG/CG/doc.10/22, Promotion and Protection of Human Rights, October 2022, Lima, p. 55.

[10] Keller, Heri, Christ (2020), pp. 193–196; Lijnzaad (2020), p. 31.

[11] See on the contrary Article 8 of the United Nations Charter. Badejogbin (2020), p. 133 quoting Rose (2016).

procedural criterion. Indeed, without a political will stemming from the Member States, it is impossible to achieve gender parity in international courts.[12]

Secondly, gender and gender parity are considered as one element among others determining the quality of the candidates. It appears clearly from the Rome Statute which mentions gender representation in article 36 after two other criteria, namely representation of diverse legal culture[13] and equitable geographical representation.[14] In the PACE Resolution,[15] gender is also cited along with the field of expertise, linguistical knowledge and the competence criteria provided for in Article 21 paragraph 1 of the Convention.[16] While the difficulty to bypass the gender representation criterion differs according to the organ concerned,[17] it can be deduced from such layout that gender is perceived as a central but not unique criterion ensuring diversity among the candidates and *in fine* on the bench.

Thirdly, the non-binding character[18] of these provisions does not prevent their effectiveness. Indeed, the introduction of a gender representation rule seems to be correlated to an increase in the percentage of female judges in a given court. Before the ECtHR, a major surge in the percentage of female candidates[19] and *in fine* female judges[20] is observed from 2004–2005. It coincides with the publication of two resolutions[21] from the PACE. Regarding the IACtHR, the elections of Nancy Hernández López, Verónica Gómez and Patricia Pérez Goldberg in November 2021 concur with the advocacy campaign promoting women on the IACtHR's bench.

---

[12] Fura (2010), p. 186; Tulkens (2015), p. 227: "In the field of international law, the states are the bastions that pose most resistance to various forms in which the concept of gender can be taken into account".

[13] Article 36(8)(a)(i) of Rome Statute of the International Criminal Court.

[14] Article 36(8)(a)(ii) of Rome Statute of the International Criminal Court.

[15] Resolution 1366 (2004) Candidates for the European Court of Human Rights.

[16] Article 21 para.1 of the European Convention on Human Rights states that "[t]he judges shall be of high moral character and must either possess the qualifications required for appointment to high judicial office or be jurisconsults of recognised competence".

[17] Gender representation is part of the "minimum voting requirements" of the voting procedure for judges at the International Criminal Court. A defined minimum number of each candidate per gender is provided. See: Procedure for the nomination and election of judges, the Prosecutor and Deputy Prosecutors of the International Criminal Court, (ICC-ASP/3/res.6), §§20(c)-21. Regarding the ECtHR, gender representation criterion can be disregarded if it impedes the fulfilment of the other selection criteria. See: ECtHR, Advisory opinion on certain legal questions concerning the lists of candidates submitted with a view to the election of judges to the European Court of Human Rights, 12 February 2008, para. 42 *sqq*.

[18] ECtHR, Advisory opinion on certain legal questions concerning the lists of candidates submitted with a view to the election of judges to the European Court of Human Rights, 12 February 2008, para. 34 and 50. The formulation of the provision in the Resolution of the General Assembly shows its non-binding nature.

[19] Hennette Vauchez (2015), p. 211.

[20] The percentage of female judges at the ECtHR rose from 25% in 2004 to 42.6% in 2011. Keller, Heri, Christ (2020), p. 184.

[21] PACE, Resolution 1366 (2004); PACE, Resolution 1426 (2005).

Nonetheless, the evolution of the percentage of female judges at the European Court of Human Rights case indicates that the gender representation criterion is not self-sufficient. In an extensive study on the identity of female judges at the ECtHR, Helen Keller, Corina Heri and Myriam Christ have shown that between 1998 and 2011, the number of women has increased from 20% to 42.6%.[22] In two resolutions issued in 2004 and 2005, the PACE decided it would no longer consider single-sex lists, unless the candidates belong to the under-represented sex. The threshold to determine the underrepresentation was set at 40%. This threshold presents the advantages of setting a precise benchmark for the Court and implicitly for the Member States, as this threshold is autonomous.[23] Despite this initial rise, the trend post 2011 can be analysed either as a decrease in the percentage of female judges[24] or at best as a stabilization at around 33%.[25] Yet, some States opposed this rule and failed to submit a list with at least one female candidate. In such circumstances, the Court was requested, in accordance with Article 47 of the Convention to issue its very first advisory opinion.[26] The Committee of Ministers asked the Court whether the PACE could refuse a list which complies with Article 21 of the Convention solely on the basis of the gender criterion. The Court dampened the absolute character of the 40% threshold and favoured the introduction of exceptions "where a Contracting Party has taken all the necessary and appropriate steps with a view to ensuring that the list contains a candidate of the under-represented sex, but without success, and especially where it has followed the Assembly's recommendations advocating an open and transparent procedure involving a call for candidatures".[27] By emphasising the Member States' margin of appreciation regarding procedural rules,[28] some authors commented that the Court contributed to "soften" the

[22] Keller, Heri, Christ (2020), pp. 184–185.

[23] Indeed, the percentages of female judges in domestic courts tend to be under this threshold. Keller, Heri, Christ (2020), p. 196.

[24] Keller, Heri, Christ (2020), p. 200.

[25] Keller, Heri and Christ's study is based on data collected up to 2018. In 2018 the percentage of female judges at the ECtHR was of 32%. We have therefore continued the study, although the method of calculation does not appear to be the same. We took the composition of the Court recorded in the annual reports from 2019 to 2023 and the composition of the Court as at 3 May 2024. We counted the number of women out of the total number of judges. The percentages obtained are as follows: 31,9% in 2019; 30,4% in 2020; 34% in 2021; 34% in 2022; 34,8% in 2023; 36,9% in 2024.

[26] To read a detailed chronology of the rule of gender parity on the ECtHR's bench, see: Hennette Vauchez (2015), pp. 200–211.

[27] ECtHR, Advisory opinion on certain legal questions concerning the lists of candidates submitted with a view to the election of judges to the European Court of Human Rights, 12 February 2008, para. 54.

[28] Mowbray (2008), p. 559.

gender criterion and was, to that extent, criticised.[29] Whereas the recent rejection of the Danish list shows that the gender criterion is not outdated, its effective implementation could be improved. Indeed, in view of some, its softness, the practical figures of female judges' percentage and the 40% threshold used by some States to justify, when achieved, the validity of an all-male list[30] all contribute to transform this quota into "a ceiling—not a floor".[31]

The introduction of a gender representation rule is coherent with the commitment of the Council of Europe towards the promotion of gender mainstreaming and gender equality at domestic level.[32] The Court is not only inspired by this framework but is also integral part of it.[33] The importance of gender equality was first underlined by the Court in 1985[34] and has been repeatedly stressed since.[35] In its 2008 advisory opinion, the Court insisted on the "far-reaching consensus as to the need to promote gender balance within the State and in the national and international public service, including

[29] Such criticism arose even before the Court issued its advisory opinion and came both from the institutional discourse—see for instance the 2007 opinion of PACE Committee on Equal Opportunities for Women and Men—as from academic literature. To that regard, Françoise Tulkens underlined the risk for female judges to be "token women". Indeed, accepting exceptions to the gender parity lists can lead to reinforce the perception that "men are seen as natural occupants of such positions … and that enough women have been appointed". Tulkens (2014), p. 590 quoting Kenney (2012a). Such argument overlaps with the *Smurfette* principle. Lijnzaad (2020), pp. 30–31.

Furthermore, Françoise Tulkens and Stéphanie Hennette Vauchez highlighted the absence of any nationality requirement. Hennette Vauchez (2015), p. 206; Tulkens (2015), p. 226. However, the Court replied to that argument in its 2008 advisory opinion by stating that "it would be incompatible with the Convention to require a State to nominate a candidate of a different nationality solely in order to achieve a gender balance". ECtHR, Advisory opinion on certain legal questions concerning the lists of candidates submitted with a view to the election of judges to the European Court of Human Rights, 12 February 2008, para. 52.

[30] This was one of the Belgian arguments in 2012. Hennette Vauchez (2015), p. 209.

[31] Hennette Vauchez (2015), p. 209.

[32] Argren et al. (2023), pp. 284–285. See especially the Gender Equality Strategy 2018–2023. This strategy is based on six principles among which gender mainstreaming, achieving a balanced participation of women and men in political and public decision-making. The agenda of the CoE is deemed to be one of the most ambitious ones for gender equality. Fife (2020), p. 57.

[33] Fife (2020), p. 284 quoting Giegerich, Jötten (2017). The jurisprudence of the Court is a source of inspiration for the establishment of the next Gender Equality Strategy 2024–2029. Speech by Síofra O'Leary on the exchange of views with the Gender Equality Commission (GEC) held in Strasbourg on 16th November 2023. https://www.echr.coe.int/documents/d/echr/speech-20231116-oleary-exchange-views-gender-equality-commission-eng.

[34] ECtHR, nos. 9214/80 et al., *Abdulaziz, Cabales and Balkandali v. The United Kingdom*, 28 May 1985, para. 78.

[35] Even if the Court's expressions to frame the concept have progressively evolved from "equality of the sexes" (*Abdulaziz, Cabales and Balkandali v. The United Kingdom*) to "gender equality" (ECtHR, GC, no. 30078/06, *Konstantin Markin v. Russia*, 22 March 2012, para. 127).

the judiciary".[36] Recently, the Court referred to "the right of gender equality" alluded by the institutions of the CoE.[37]

Beyond the many reasons that may motivate this concern for gender representation, both procedurally and substantively, this contribution aims at focusing on the potential effect of the changes in the Court's composition, especially the growing presence of female judges, on the Court's caselaw.

1.2 Can We Explain the ECtHR Jurisprudence by the Gender of Its Judges?

Despite the strong concern and struggle for gender parity on the Court's bench, gender remains one frame of reference to interpret changes in the Court's composition. Intertwining the gender variable with other variables such as the age, the background and the nationality of judges offers new perspectives and shows the determining effect of the accession of new Member States to the Council of Europe.[38] In this context, three motives can be advanced to underline the relevance of the choice of gender as an interpretative lens for ECtHR's decisions and judgments.

To begin with, it is theoretically conceivable to investigate for the influence of gender on the jurisprudence—*i.e.* to look for a "gender effect"[39] on the ECtHR caselaw. The neutrality of judges is linked to the need for a separation of powers as depicted by Montesquieu. Alongside emphasizing the limited role of the judge through the expression "*bouche de la loi*", Montesquieu described the judge as an inanimated being or "*être inanimé*".[40] However, this perception has been nuanced in two respects.[41] First, even Montesquieu admitted that this neutrality should be

[36] ECtHR, Advisory opinion on certain legal questions concerning the lists of candidates submitted with a view to the election of judges to the European Court of Human Rights, 12 February 2008, para. 49.

[37] ECtHR, déc., no. 54893/18, *Zevnik* et al. *V. Slovenia*, 12 November 2019, para. 34.

[38] Keller, Heri, Christ (2020), p. 189.

[39] Voeten (2020), p. 6. This theoretical movement studying the impact of gender in the judge's decision-making process seems to originate from the arrival of women on the bench raising such subject. See: Hunter (2015), p. 122 referring to Madam Justice Bertha Wilson (1990), Will Women Judges Really Make a Difference? Osgoode Hall LJ 28:507–522. From the 2010s, this topic has been increasingly discussed. See especially: Kenney (2012b); Schultz, Shaw (2013). Insofar as the question of the diversity of judges has mainly arisen with regard to national benches, some have questioned the transferability of diversity concerns to the European courts: Bobek (2015), pp. 19–20.

[40] Montesquieu (1748), Livre XI, Chapitre VI, p. 268.

[41] Regarding the conception of the judges' role and its evolution: Bošnjak, Zajac (2023), pp. 3–4.

counterbalanced with the humanity of judges towards parties.[42] The ECtHR also admitted that the mere expression of sentiments of courtesy or sympathy towards a civil party could not be seen in itself as a reflection of bias against the defendant but, on the contrary, could be said to show the 'human face' of the justice system.[43] Second, in the middle of the twentieth century, the studies of North-American legal realism's disciples questioned the political values and ideologies of the judges in the decision-making process.[44] Between legalism and realism, academics tried to model modern figures of judges and introduced a subjective aspect of judging.[45] It is now widely accepted that the art of legal interpretation combines legal norms, facts of the case and subjective social elements surrounding the case including personal elements.[46] According to some scholars, this subjective part is all the more significant when it relates to human rights, as "there are almost always extremely sensitive moral, social and political problems showing through".[47] Thus, human rights and the underlying values would contribute to render this field receptive to a "feminine perspective".[48] Nevertheless, the vast plurality of legal fields covered by the ECtHR's cases—from security issues to property rights by way of civil liberties—justifies a flexible gender effect depending on the area concerned.[49]

Further, it would be of theoretical interest to identify and measure such a feminine perspective. It would not only shed light on the "black box" of judging but would also allow judges themselves to depart from their own bias and reinforce their impartiality. Indeed, the notion of neutrality is not unequivocal. It has been suggested that neutrality could be dissociated from impartiality and independence to the extent that "[n]eutrality may refer to the absence of some kind of nearness, and an adjudicator may have that nearness or affinity or proximity without it necessarily compromising her impartiality".[50] The former ECtHR Judge

---

[42] Spector (2015), p. 89 analysing and quoting Montesquieu, *Discours sur l'équité qui doit régler les jugements et l'exécution des loix*, 1725: "Montesquieu insiste beaucoup sur la nécessité que le devoir de neutralité ne se convertisse pas en rigueur et en froideur. L'aptitude du juge à entendre les plaintes est jugée essentielle: 'Ainsi dans nos mœurs, il faut qu'un juge se conduise de manière envers ses parties, qu'il leur paraisse bien plutôt réservé que grave, et qu'il leur fasse voir la probité des Catons sans leur en montrer la rudesse er l'austérité'".

[43] ECtHR, no. 61344/16, *Karrar v. Belgium*, 31 August 2021, para. 35: "en tant que telle la manifestation de simples sentiments de courtoisie ou de compassion à l'égard d'une partie civile ne peut s'assimiler à l'expression d'un parti pris à l'égard de l'accusé, et qu'elle peut au contraire s'analyser comme l'expression d'une justice à visage humain".

[44] Jack, Knight (2015), pp. 591–592.

[45] Faget (2018), pp. 27–28.

[46] Tulkens (2014), p. 592; Dworkin (2003), p. 5.

[47] Tulkens (2014), p. 591; Dworkin (2003), pp. 6–7.

[48] Wilson (1990), p. 515.

[49] Some areas of law have been identified as slightly more submitted by female applicants such as property rights and alleged violations of the right to a fair trial: Voeten (2020), pp. 10–11. See also: Tulkens (2007). These patterns do not echo the gender effect of violations findings: Voeten (2020).

[50] Papayannis (2016), para. 36.

Françoise Tulkens reckoned that "[i]f the objective judge exists and must exist—even if the characteristic of the subjective argument is to hide behind the appearance of law—the neutral judge does not exist".[51] Yet, the ECtHR does not resort to the notion of neutrality. To that regard, neutrality, when argued by applicants, seems to be examined under impartiality, *in fine* overlapping this principle protected under Article 6 of the ECHR and defined as "the absence of prejudice or bias".[52] A lack of neutrality can thus amount to partiality, bearing in mind that the factors of neutrality differ, depending in particular on whether the court concerned is international or national.[53] The coexistence of the impossibility for a judge to be neutral—as portrayed before—and the impartiality principle makes it necessary for judges to be aware of their own conscious or unconscious biases during the decision-making process. Acknowledging the existence of bias due to the judge's gender contributes to their elimination.[54] Yet, the awareness on one's own neutrality is highly subjective.[55]

Finally, despite its interests, carrying out a study seeking for a gender effect is highly complex, as the scarce existing literature explains.[56] The hurdles are first and foremost methodological, but some theoretical underpinnings need also to be clarified. Whereas the consequences of the presence of female judges on the bench cannot be detected[57] or is an impression for some scholars,[58] the resort to a solid database can help discern the contours of a potential gender effect.[59] Additionally, in order to observe a gender effect, the gender variable should be isolated from other variables.[60] Nevertheless, some obstacles remain such as the fact that dissention between male and female can exist during deliberations—protected by confidentiality—but not reproduced in the judgments[61] or the fact that judges do not work in their native language.[62] A clear and precisely defined methodology can

[51] Tulkens (2014), p. 591.

[52] ECtHR, GC, no. 73797/10, *Kyprianou v. Cyprus*, 15 December 2005, para. 118. For cases in which the Court analyses the neutrality of judges under the aegis of impartiality, see ECtHR, no. 12748/06, *Panyik v. Hungary*, 12, July 2011, para. 29.

[53] Nußberger, Baetens (2020), p. 479.

[54] Faget (2018), p. 27.

[55] Wilson (1990), p. 510.

[56] On the ECtHR, see: Voeten (2020).

[57] See for instance: Crawford (2020), pp. 416–417.

[58] Keller, Heri, Christ (2020), p. 202.

[59] Such a database seems to find a definition *a contrario*. Indeed, it has been argued that this database should go beyond dissenting opinions. Keller, Heri, Christ (2020), p. 201.

[60] This has been made possible through the matching technic. Boyd, Epstein, Martin (2010), pp. 398–399; Voeten (2020), p. 12: "Matching allows us to construct reasonable counterfactuals by matching each female judge with the most comparable male judge on the same panel (if such a judge exists), eliminating judges from the respondent government. Matching makes inferences less model-dependent".

[61] Keller, Heri, Christ (2020), p. 201.

[62] Fura (2010), p. 187.

also help overcome the risk of essentialism,[63] by testing the validity of the four main theories regarding gender and judging: the attitudinal, representational, informational, and organizational theories.[64] According to the attitudinal theory, women and men have a different perception of the world, thus giving women a 'different voice' even on questions that do not concern women's rights. According to the representational theory, female judges represent women and to that extent, should express themselves in matters concerning women. According to the informational theory, women have different experiences than men, experiences from which women get unique information and expertise. According to the organizational theory, women and men underwent similar professional and training programs and such a standardization tends to eliminate gendered differences.

Bearing in mind these studies, we argue that the conditions are met at the ECtHR for the existence of a consequential link between the change in the Court's composition and its decision-making.[65] In order to investigate the extent of this "gender effect", this study should not limit itself to the violation assessments in the Court's judgment but start the analysis at the deliberations on the ECtHR's bench. This approach allows a sharpened scrutiny on a two-tier gender effect. While female judges do make a difference on the ECtHR's bench (2), the impact of the gender criterion on the judgments needs to be put into perspective (3).

2 Gender Effect on the Bench: A Component of Its Diversity

Following the distinction made between "individual effects", *i.e.* the particular individual position of a judge towards a case, and "panel effects", *i.e.* the influence of female judges in the decision-making process, we contend that there exist obvious female voices on the bench of the ECtHR (2.1). Nonetheless, this voice can be heard to the extent permitted by the collegiality principle (2.2).

2.1 The Existence of Female Voices on the ECtHR's Bench

Gender, as part of personal characteristic, can influence the way in which a judge will apprehend a case and render a decision. The roots of this phenomenon could be explained by two theoretical underpinnings introduced by Rosemary Hunter which intertwine the four aforementioned theoretical accounts.[66]

---

[63] Keller, Heri, Christ (2020), p. 201.

[64] For a more complete overview of the four theories and their implementation to benches' analysis, see: Voeten (2020), pp. 3–4; Boyd, Epstein, Martin (2010), pp. 390–392.

[65] Hunter (2015), pp. 140–141.

[66] Hunter (2015), pp. 124–125.

The first one is the impact of life experience of judges in their judgments. This first argument could be drawn closer to the informational theory in that it assumes that women and men undergo different experiences.[67] By way of comparison, judges who have previously worked in international judicial or quasi-judicial bodies tend to support cross-fertilization.[68] On another note, a category of Strasbourg judges has been identified as regrouping "individuals who not only have the grand vision and technical expertise but also have served governmental interests in various capacities and are thought to be sensible enough to infuse nascent human rights law with the necessary flexibility".[69] It has been underscored that, in drawing the three-candidates list, some Member States rely on this political and legal backgrounds in order to assess the degree of "activism" of the candidate,[70] illustrating a link between the personal characteristics of the person appointed and the substance expected of judgments. Like professional experiences and political opinions, gender could shape the approach of female judges. The relevance of a feminine perspective in human rights as regards life experiences is substantiated by the fact that women, through belonging to a "historically oppressed group"[71] are affected differently than men on many human rights issues.[72] Indeed, according to some scholars, a gender effect can be expected if the existing law is viewed as not neutral.[73] Furthermore, it could be argued that the mere introduction of a 40% threshold or a gender rule proves the acknowledgment of a feminine perspective in human rights issues examined on the ECtHR bench.[74]

The second line of reasoning is known as the theory of a "different voice" or the attitudinal theory.[75] It assumes "gender differences in moral reasoning", opposing a "feminine 'ethic of care'" to a "masculine 'ethic of justice'".[76] As indicated by Professor Hunter, despite being simplistic and essentialist, these two contentions might contain a part of the truth.[77]

These theories have been verified in a study dedicated to the ECtHR. Indeed, Voeten's study tends to corroborate the experiential and attitudinal accounts. If the gender of the applicant does not seem to influence the violation finding of female judges,[78] the gender of judges could have consequences on the violation

---

[67] Boyd, Epstein, Martin (2010), pp. 391–392.

[68] Ruiz Fabri, Paine (2022), pp. 63–65.

[69] Hennette Vauchez (2015), p. 217.

[70] Lemmens (2015), p. 112.

[71] Keller, Heri, Christ (2020), p. 201.

[72] See *mutatis mutandis* in the field of trade law: Hughes (2020), p. 354.

[73] Wilson (1990), pp. 511 and 515.

[74] ECtHR, GC, no. 21906/04, *Kafkaris v. Cyprus*, 12 February 2008, partly dissenting opinion of Judge Borrego Borrego, para.13. See *mutatis mutandis*: Hughes (2020), p. 351.

[75] Voeten (2020), p. 2.

[76] Hunter (2015), p. 125.

[77] Hunter (2015), p. 125.

[78] Voeten (2020), p. 14.

finding more globally. According to Voeten, "female judges are 8–9 percentage points more likely to favor the applicant than their male counterparts".[79] This is especially visible in two types of cases: the first brought by women on discrimination issues, the second related to physical integrity rights issues.[80] The first outcome chimes with the experiential theory, explaining such disposition towards discrimination issues raised by female applicants by the experiencing of a similar situation.[81] The second conclusion resonates with the attitudinal theory in that female judges would be in general more liberal and less punitive than male judges.[82] These findings put into question the attitudinal theory since they show a gender effect on fields that go beyond women's rights. They also question the organizational theory according to which female and male judges underwent standardized professional paths, limiting the gender effect.[83] The scholar acknowledges himself the limits of his study and explains that ultimately "[t]he proportion of female judges does not correlate significantly with a greater probability of a violation finding by the Court".[84]

More limits could be advanced regarding this study. Rejecting the essentialist underpinnings of the notion of "female voice", it may be argued that the reality tends to merge the two strands of different life experiences and "different voice"; justifying the difference of "voices" by the life experiences of female judges.[85] This finds a certain veracity in light of the Strasbourg female judges' profiles. Next to what Stéphanie Hennette Vauchez described as "*hommes comme les autres*",[86] *i.e.* female judges who tend to have legal and political resources or internationalized experiences similarly to male judges, some female judges tend to be younger and holders of mainly legal resources.[87] The gender variable is thus combined with age, background but also legal cultures.[88] It stems from such a setting that the novelty of women's

[79] Voeten (2020), p. 13.

[80] Voeten (2020), p. 15.

[81] Voeten (2020), p. 16.

[82] Voeten (2020), p. 16.

[83] Voeten (2020), p. 16.

[84] Voeten (2020), p. 15.

[85] This approach of the gender effect tends to depart from the essentialist vision of differences between male and female perceptions from looking at a broader picture. On the contrary, some scholars seem to admit different characteristics between female and male judges while departing from the "different voice" account. Tulkens (2014), pp. 588 and 593: "A different voice? No, rather a different place"; "[women] do [. . .] sometimes and even often, bring 'something different'. Simply because they occupy a very different position on account of their gender and other elements that form part of their own history".

[86] Hennette Vauchez (2015), p. 216.

[87] Hennette Vauchez (2015), p. 219; Keller, Heri, Christ (2020), pp. 190–191.

[88] On the importance of legal culture in the decision-making of judges: Nußberger, Baetens (2020), pp. 492–493.

profile seen as a whole confirms the different perspective brought by women on the ECtHR's bench.[89]

At the same time, this plurality of factors constituting a judge's profile temper the existence of a gender effect *per se*. While it can be argued that a female voice does exist, the latter is neither univocal—due to the multiple elements constituting the identity of an individual—nor unified—given the dissents among female judges. First, such a female voice is equivocal. As formulated by Rosemary Hunter, "gender difference disappears when other factors are controlled for, particularly judicial political affiliation".[90] A study reveals the overriding effect of ideology over *inter alia* gender.[91] Before the ECtHR, ideology determines the role of a judge and is materialized by a choice between individual justice or legal security.[92] Nevertheless, gender and ideology maintain mutual influence links.[93] Second, such a female voice is fragmented. The very existence of a gender effect in itself is contested among female judges.[94] In this regard, the case *S.H.* et al. *v. Austria* had been used as a topical illustration of such dissents between female judges.[95] This case concerned the prohibition on the use of ova and sperm from donors in the context of an in vitro fertilization.[96] The Grand Chamber composed of nine female and eight male judges concluded to the non-violation of Article 8 of the ECHR. Four female judges wrote a joint dissenting opinion condemning an unclear and minimalist reasoning. They also underlined the failure to consider the mother's health in accepting the Austrian restrictions given the fact that couples could go abroad to resort to an artificial procreation technique. Another case illustrating a dissent between female judges is the case *Mariya Alekhina and others v. Russia*.[97] It related to the conviction and prison term of a woman for performing political song in a cathedral. The Chamber concluded to the violations of Article 3, 5, 6 and 10 of the ECHR. Among the five female judges in the Chamber, Judge Elósegui, female Spanish Judge, issued a partly dissenting opinion, contesting the finding of violation of Article 10 of the ECHR. In an even more recent case, *A.M. v. Norway*,[98] concerning rights of an intended mother in respect of a child born by way of gestational surrogacy, the only two female judges on the panel

[89] For practical evidence of such conclusion, see Hunter (2015), p. 133 quoting Rehaag (2011) according to which "female refugee adjudicators with prior experience in women's rights had higher average grant rates overall, in cases involving female claimants; and in cases involving claims of gender-based persecution".

[90] Hunter (2015), p. 126.

[91] Harris, Sen (2019), p. 242.

[92] Nußberger, Baetens (2020), p. 491.

[93] Harris, Sen (2019), pp. 251–252.

[94] Fura (2010), pp. 186–187; Badejogbin (2020), p. 126.

[95] Keller, Heri, Christ (2020), p. 201.

[96] ECtHR, no. 57813/00, *S.H. and others v. Austria*, 3 November 2011.

[97] ECtHR, no. 38004/12, *Mariya Alekhina and others v. Russia*, 17 July 2018.

[98] ECtHR, no. 30254/18, *A.M. v. Norway*, 24 March 2022.

issued divergent separate opinions. Judge O'Leary wrote a concurring opinion, while in her dissenting opinion Judge Jelić disagreed with the findings of non-violation of Articles 8 and 14 of the ECHR.

From an individual perspective, many reasons, be they theoretical or practical, seem to lean more towards the existence of a feminine perspective and even of feminine perspectives rather than their absence. However, from a collective perspective, the transformative potential of these voices[99] needs favourable conditions to be heard, starting on the bench.

2.2 Collegiality and Its Correlations on the ECtHR's Bench

In order to assess the reality of gender effect in the ECtHR's decision-making process, it is necessary to confront it to the principle of collegiality. Indeed, gender representation gains ground within the judicial formations through Rule 25 paragraph 2 of the Rules of the Court providing that "[t]he composition of the Sections shall be geographically, and gender balanced and shall reflect the different legal systems among the Contracting Parties". Given the fact that Committees and Chambers' formations are based on the Sections' distribution, this rule requires implicitly gender representation for judicial formations. Around one third of the Grand Chamber composition seems to be indirectly subjected to a gender representation rule through Rule 14 providing for a balanced gender representation for the Presidency and the Bureau of the Court, namely the President, Vice-Presidents of the Court and Section Presidents. The remaining judges are chosen taking into account a "geographically balanced composition reflecting the different legal systems among the Contracting Parties" according to Rule 24 paragraph 2 point d. The introduction of these rules[100] does not affect the existing principles, and especially collegiality. In a context of collegiality, understood as a working method of the ECtHR, its members enjoy equality in their rights and duties.[101] This principle has two main contradictory consequences on the gender effect.

On the one hand, collegiality reinforces the gender effect in allowing each judge to participate in the decision-making process. As provided for in the Rules of the

---

[99] Hodson (2022).

[100] It should be noted that even the appointment of *ad hoc* judges should meet a gender representation rule according to Rule 29 paragraph 1 point a second indent.

[101] Flauss (2009), p. 119. It could be argued that collegiality would be jeopardized by the very large number of cases handled by single judges (30, 585 in 2022 compared to around 6000 issued by collegial formations). It should be remembered that these procedures are surrounded by guarantees such as a principle of motivation. In addition, they focus on obvious inadmissibility reasons, leaving the more sensitive substantive issues to collegial formations. The single judge may also forward the application to a Committee of a Chamber (Rule 52A paragraph 2 of the Rules of the Court).

Court, the bench should be diverse from a gender, but also a geographical and even legal cultural perspectives. This brings to the forefront the search for diversity. Among other reasons, it has been advanced that "[i]deally, a collegial decision is not simply the aggregate of individual preferences about a case's outcome. If judges engage in good faith deliberation, the resultant decision has the potential to reflect a collective wisdom that is greater than the sum of its constituent parts".[102] This mutual enrichment process in decision-making has been theorized as "panel effect".[103] The more diverse is a panel, the more enriched the discussion and *in fine* the judgment will be.[104] It appears that some cases would benefit more than others of a diversified panel such as those requiring "a full range of human experience and understanding"[105] or the ones echoing the life experience of a judge. In this last hypothesis, the presence and stance of female judges would be particularly beneficial for cases related to sex discrimination.[106] Indeed, some argue that male judges are more likely to find a violation in such cases in a gendered parity bench than an all-male bench.[107] Such effect is maybe not limited to sex discrimination cases or cases related to women's rights[108] but seems to spread to legal issues that go beyond what are perceived as cases of differential treatment of women and men. The case *Couderc and Hachette Filipacchi Associés v. France* is an illustration of a case in which female judges shared a common conclusion but faced male judges sharing an opposite point of view.[109] Before being referred to the Grand Chamber which would find unanimously a violation of Article 10 of the Convention,[110] this case was examined by a Chamber.[111] This case related to the revelations of the existence of the Monegasque monarch's secret child in an article. The Chamber was divided between a majority of four female and one male judge voting in favour of a violation of Article 10 and a minority of three male judges for whom, in the case at hand, respect for the Prince's private life took precedence over freedom of expression.

However, on the other hand, collegiality mitigates any individual effect in aid of a common consensus. Be it through the personal manoeuvres when facing

102 Dzehtsiarou, Schwartz (2020), p. 623.

103 Boyd, Epstein, Martin (2010), p. 402.

104 Dzehtsiarou, Schwartz (2020), p. 628: "panel diversity—in terms of ideology, gender, or ethnic/racial background—does improve decisions by counteracting biases and making judges more sensitive to alternative or minority perspectives".

105 Hunter (2015), p. 137.

106 Dzehtsiarou, Schwartz (2020), p. 628; Boyd, Epstein, Martin (2010), p. 406.

107 Boyd, Epstein, Martin (2010), p. 406.

108 See the input of female judges in international criminal law in the definition of rape: Nosworthy (2020), pp. 552–553.

109 Keller, Heri, Christ (2020), p. 202.

110 ECtHR, GC, no. 40454/07, *Couderc and Hachette Filipacchi Associés v. France*, 10 November 2015.

111 ECtHR, no. 40454/07, *Couderc and Hachette Filipacchi Associés v. France*, 12 June 2014.

a majority[112] or the "feeling of being all 'European judges'",[113] the principle of collegiality contributes to establishing "a unified court—in spite of its diversity".[114]

Between the two opposite effects, the truth might lie in the casuistic elements of a situation. As mentioned by Rosemary Hunter, conditions have to be met to allow a substantive effect of the bench's composition.[115] The conditions are based both on personal and opportunity factors.[116] That is why some female judges would, for instance, feel the need to exercise restraint because of judicial authority considerations[117] or because of the manifestation of an implicit distrust from their male counterparts.[118] It seems also that the influence of a judge in a given deliberation does not stem primarily from their gender but rather from their function—judges rapporteurs and national judges are perhaps more carefully listened to—or from their overall capacity to convince.[119]

To summarise, a gender effect on the Court's judgements needs conditions to exist. First, a gender perspective has to exist in order to be, second, listened to.[120] These conditions seem to be met at the ECtHR. There are reasonable theoretical and practical grounds to believe that female judges, due to their life experiences and as shown by their profiles, could share a different perspective on certain cases. Moreover, to the extent that their colleagues open up to their interpretation, their voice could be listened to on the bench and enrich the deliberations. However, a certain form of consensus, resulting from the collegiality principle, bring us to observe the concretization of such a perception in the judgments of the Court.

3 Gender Effect on the Judgements

Prima facie, a gender perspective in ECtHR's judgments, especially stemming from female judges, could be seen as favourably promoting women's rights and their effectiveness. Conversely, if a positive gender effect is accepted, why a negative gender effect, *i.e.* the existence of stereotypes and prejudices

[112] Flauss (2009), p. 122.

[113] Nußberger, Baetens (2020), p. 493.

[114] Nußberger, Baetens (2020), p. 493.

[115] Hunter (2015), p. 140.

[116] Hunter (2015), p. 129 *sqq*.

[117] Dzehtsiarou, Schwartz (2020), pp. 628 and 642; Hunter (2015), p. 127. On the place given to the judicial authority of ECtHR's judgments before national courts in the establishment of a gender rule, see: Keller, Heri, Christ (2020), pp. 198–199.

[118] Tulkens (2014), p. 594.

[119] Flauss (2009), p. 122.

[120] Hunter (2015), pp. 129 *sqq*.

in the judge's reasoning and ultimately in the judgment, should be excluded? These remarks must be confronted with the reality of judicial work at Strasbourg, which on the one hand limits the existence of feminist activist judgments (3.1) and on the other hand protects the judgments from possible gender stereotypes (3.2).

3.1 Feminism and the ECtHR Jurisprudence

Three main reasons appear to mitigate the existence of a gender effect finding its illustration in feminist judgments of the ECtHR.

Firstly, the identification of feminist judgments is not an easy task. There is no unique definition of feminism. Indeed, in international human rights law, feminism is a critique of human rights according to which "[human rights] are a product of a dominant male half of the world, framed in their language".[121] This critique is itself subdivided in many different currents such as liberal feminists, cultural feminists or radical feminists.[122] All these strands have in common a methodological ambition for international law, especially taking into account women' situations in their context.[123] The input of feminist theories for international law is significant. Yet, in view of this plurality of definitions, it seems clear that the identification of judgments as feminist judgments can differ depending on the perception of the reader. For instance, the case *Konstantin Markin*,[124] in which the Court acknowledged the necessity to extend the right to parental leave for military servicemen, is read by some authors as progressive when others admit that it reached inclusivity but regret the failure to promote a real transformation of the gender inequalities structures.[125]

Secondly, the diversity in feminist approaches render the identification of feminist judges also challenging. Judges do not necessarily identify themselves as feminists. Stéphanie Hennette Vauchez studied the CVs of female judges and revealed that, even if not stated explicitly, some clues indicate a feminist commitment from the judges concerned.[126] However, in line with the first point, not all judges agree on what can be deemed as a feminist approach. While some judges say "they [are] feminists but not feminist judges",[127] others

[121] Brems (1997), p. 137.

[122] See: Brems (1997), pp. 137–141; Tulkens (2007), pp. 1–7.

[123] Brems (1997), p. 141; Tulkens (2007), p. 7.

[124] ECtHR, GC, no. 30078/06, *Konstantin Markin v. Russia*, 22 March 2012, para. 127.

[125] Timmer (2012), p. 149.

[126] Hennette Vauchez (2015), pp. 214–215.

[127] Hunter (2015), p. 132.

acknowledge the constraints inherent to the judicial function to restrain them from following a total transformative approach.[128] In short, "feminist judging is not a singular programme"[129] and each judge has its own vision of the role and office of judges.[130]

Thirdly, the gender effect is based on the existence of a different perspective depending on the gender of the judges. Yet, a judge's gender does not prejudge his or her commitment to feminism. In other words, male judges can also be feminist. Some major progressive judgments have been issued by mainly male benches such as *Dudgeon v. The United Kingdom*[131] regarding the criminalisation of male homosexuality in which only one female judge sat on the bench. Indeed, the use of tools such as the living instrument doctrine or the promotion of the values defended by the Council of Europe—use and promotion which do not seem to be correlated to a specific gender—contribute to promote a feminist perspective advocating for the protection of women's rights.

In the absence of concrete and explicitly stated feminist approaches and thus judgments, the identification of a gender effect is far more nuanced and confined to the margins. In this framework, a focal point is the relevance of separate opinions in acknowledging a feminist approach. The constraints inherent to the judicial formations such as the search for consensus or a sense of judicial restraint can be overcome through separate opinions. In this regard, Fionnuala Ní Aoláin, the former ECtHR's Judge in respect of Ireland, noted the existence of a "gendered, if not feminist space"[132] through the dissenting opinions in *S.H.* et al. *v. Austria* previously mentioned. Another topical illustration is the case *S.A.S. v. France*[133] related to the ban on wearing religious face covering veil in public space in which the Court found no violation of Articles 8 and 9 of the ECHR. Two of the six female judges composing the Grand Chamber, namely Judges Nußberger and Jäderblom, dissented specifically on this conclusion affirming that "[i]n [their] view, the restrictive measure cannot be expected to have the desired effect of liberating women presumed to be oppressed, but will further exclude them from society and aggravate their situation". Concurring opinions can also convey feminist underpinnings and to that extent, offer the possibility to deepen the reasoning of the majority. This is for instance illustrated by the case *Bouton v. France*[134] related to a Femen activist's prison sentence for having performed topless in church protesting against Catholic church's position on abortion. The Chamber concluded unanimously to a violation of Article 10. The

---

[128] Hunter (2015), p. 139. For instance, "there is the necessity for juridical institutions, such as the ECtHR, of embracing legal positivism in order to achieve objectivity, predictability and impartiality in the adjudication of cases" explaining to some extent why the ECtHR cannot borrow the formulations of NGOs or institutions when "defining LGBT identities". Ammaturo (2019), p. 588.

[129] Hunter (2015), p. 139.

[130] Nußberger, Baetens (2020), p. 488.

[131] ECtHR, no. 7525/76, *Dudgeon v. The United Kingdom*, 22 January 1981.

[132] Ní Aoláin (2015), p. 235.

[133] ECtHR, GC, no. 43835/11, *S.A.S. v. France*, 1 July 2014.

[134] ECtHR, no. 22636/19, *Bouton v. France*, 13 October 2022.

female Judge Šimáčková, elected in respect of Czech Republic, wrote a concurring opinion in which she condemned the pressure put by State on the way women dress. Even if these opinions do not enjoy the same authority as Court's judgments, they take part in precedent-settings.[135]

While the identification of feminist judgments is complex, Judge Jelić seems to prefer the expression "gender-sensitive judgments".[136] This expression emphasizes rightly the existence of a sensitivity towards women's rights beyond the gender of the judge. It does not preclude the "room for improvement"[137] that the Court enjoys in the promotion of gender equality and women's rights. However, this gender sensitivity should not be assimilated to gender bias or stereotypes.

3.2 Eliminating Gender Stereotypes in ECtHR Judgments

As alluded to by Montesquieu,[138] the figure of the judge needs to remain "human". The former Judge Tulkens supports the room for emotions on the bench: "[a]ppealing to sentiments, to conviction, does not mean being irrational. It is, on the contrary, in my view, a way to achieve justice by understanding the real human dimension of the legal controversy".[139] This perception is aligned with the existence of judges' sensitivity towards specific questions and the absence of a neutral judge as recalled by Judge Borrego Borrego in its partly dissenting opinion in the case *Kafkaris v. Cyprus*.[140]

However, such emotions should not transform into actual gender bias or stereotypes. Gender stereotypes[141] are defined as "preconceived ideas whereby males and females are arbitrarily assigned characteristics and roles determined and limited by their sex".[142] The fight against such stereotypes is one objective of the Gender Equality Strategy 2024–2029 adopted by the Council of Europe. In 2012, the Court issued the landmark judgement in *Konstantin Markin v. Russia* in which it identified and explicitly condemned the gender stereotypes underlying the refusal of authorities to extend the right to parental leave to men.[143] Further, in 2021, the

135 Voeten (2020), p. 16.

136 Jelić (2023), p. 36.

137 Jelić (2023), p. 50.

138 *Cf.* point 2.

139 Tulkens (2014), p. 594.

140 ECtHR, GC, no. 21906/04, *Kafkaris v. Cyprus*, 12 February 2008, partly dissenting opinion of Judge Borrego Borrego, para. 13: "I object to the presentation of judges as sexually neutral individuals in a society made up of men and women".

141 The ECtHR does not seem to differentiate gender bias and gender stereotypes. It uses the term "gender stereotypes": ECtHR, GC, no. 30078/06, *Konstantin Markin v. Russia*, 22 March 2012, para. 143.

142 CoE, Gender Equality, Combating Gender Stereotypes and Sexism. Online, at: https://www.coe.int/en/web/genderequality/gender-stereotypes-and-sexism.

143 ECtHR, GC, no. 30078/06, *Konstantin Markin v. Russia*, 22 March 2012, para. 143.

Court specifically stressed the key role of the judicial authorities in combating sexist stereotypes, thereby strengthening victims' confidence in the justice system.[144] The struggle against gender bias is not confined to Member States. A 40% threshold has been introduced for the selection-process to the Sub-Committee on the Election of Judges to the European Court of Human Rights to "exclude possible gender bias in decision-making processes".[145] The Court is also directly concerned by the elimination of gender stereotypes.

Insofar as impartiality is defined by the Court as "the absence of prejudice or bias",[146] the fight against gender stereotypes can be analysed through the prism of impartiality. In this respect, two main guarantees exist to protect ECtHR's judgments from potential bias. The first one is embodied in the independence and impartiality principles according to Article 21 of the Convention. This requirement is recalled by a solemn oath taken before the plenary Court by judges.[147] Above all, these provisions impose a moral duty which could be likened to the duty of institutional loyalty expected from ECtHR's judges.[148] To complete the written guarantees, it is interesting to note the willingness to resort to concrete guarantees such as the presence of women on the bench. Indeed, impartiality and independence are parts of the grounds enunciated by the PACE for diversifying the bench: "[i]t is in the interest of impartiality and of the Court's effectiveness for the Committee of Ministers, the Assembly, and the high contracting parties to address the issue of the gender imbalance of the Court".[149] Following the principle of collegiality, the presence of female judges is said to counterbalance and extend the perspectives of their male counterparts, thus reinforcing judicial impartiality.[150]

Whether it is a matter of militant ideas or gender stereotypes, the personal and subjective undertones of these issues could be overcome through what Françoise Tulkens names the "right distance"[151] and which echoes the notion of "detachment",[152] an individual way of becoming aware of the factors underlying one's judgment and reacting according to one's vision of the role of judge.

[144] ECtHR, no. 5671/16, *J.L. v. Italy*, 27 May 2021, para. 141.

[145] Resolution 1366 (2004) Candidates for the European Court of Human Rights.

[146] See *inter alia*: ECtHR, GC, no. 17056/06, *Micallef v. Malta*, 15 October 2009, para. 93.

[147] Rule 3 paragraph 1, Rules of the Court.

[148] Keller (2023), p. 261.

[149] Resolution 1649 (2004).

[150] Wilson (1990), p. 515.

[151] Tulkens (2014), p. 591.

[152] Wilson (1990), p. 515.

4 Concluding Remarks

Gender, as a personal characteristic of a judge, could be deemed to influence the decision-making process when one accepts to exceed a legalist reading of the act of interpretation. However, the existence of an actual gender effect has to be relativized. Completing the practical research done on gender and judging, this article carries the principles of the ECtHR judging process, such as collegiality, independence and impartiality to ascertain the extent of such a gender effect. It highlights the visibility of a gender effect at the margins. The presence of female judges on the bench contributes to the enrichment of deliberations and to some extent, the development of a gender-sensitive lecture of the Convention. Nevertheless, this primary substantive aspect of women presence in the Court does not exclude other aspects.[153] In particular, the presence of female judges might convey a message to other women, encouraging their presence in legal professions.[154]

Pursuant these considerations, the representation of women on the bench needs to be improved. Neither does the average of 30% of female judges compared to the Court's beginning suffice to make the Court enter a "post-gender age"[155] nor does it manifest the disappearance of a gendered hierarchies or gender bias in Europe.[156] To achieve these goals, the input of academics is necessary to raise awareness on such biases. Yet, the theoretical writings are nurtured by and should be completed by a political willingness from Member States to increase the presence of women and to a larger extent, candidates from discriminated groups.

Alongside the arguments supporting multiple identities on a bench, the diversification of the ECtHR cannot be depicted as panacea for the protection of human rights in Europe. From a substantive approach, the actual key point in judicial reasoning resides in judges' sensitivity to "the perspectives and voices of different types of applicants".[157] Bearing this in mind, it is to be recalled that a gender-sensitive approach is of great relevance in adjudicating cases concerning human rights.

[153] Hunter (2015), p. 141. See regarding legitimacy concerns through the representativeness of the bench: von Bogdandy, Venzke (2014), p. 159. The social legitimacy is the most difficult to grasp: Ravarani (2019), p. 266.

[154] Hunter (2015), p. 123.

[155] Keller, Heri, Christ (2020), p. 205.

[156] Hennette Vauchez (2015), p. 221.

[157] Hessler (2020), p. 478.

References

Ammaturo FR (2019) The Council of Europe and the creation of LGBT identities through language and discourse: a critical analysis of case law and institutional practices. Int J Hum Rights 23:575–595

Argren R, Evola M, Giegerich T, Krstić I (2023) The Evolving Recognition of Gender in International and European Law. In: Vujadinović D, Fröhlich M, Giegerich T (eds) Gender-Competent Legal Education. Springer, Cham, pp 261–303

Badejogbin RE (2020) African Women's Paths to the International Bench: How to Overcome the Hurdles. In: Baetens F (ed) Identity and Diversity on the International Bench: who is the Judge? Oxford University Press, Oxford, pp 122–141

Bobek M (2015) Prologue: the Changing Nature of Selection Procedures to the European Courts. In: Bobek M (ed) Selecting Europe's judges: a critical review of the appointment procedures to the European Courts. Oxford University Press, Oxford, pp 1–23

Bošnjak M, Zajac K (2023) Judicial Activism and Judge-Made Law at the ECtHR. Hum Rights Law Rev 23:1–15

Boyd CL, Epstein L, Martin AD (2010) Untangling the Causal Effects of Sex on Judging. Am J Pol Sci 54:389–411

Brems E (1997) Enemies or Allies? Feminism and Cultural Relativism as Dissident Voices in Human Rights Discourse. Hum Rights Q 19:136–164

Crawford J (2020) Appearing Before and Sitting With Female Adjudicators. Reflections from Practice. In: Baetens F (ed) Identity and Diversity on the International Bench: who is the Judge? Oxford University Press, Oxford, pp 412–424

Dworkin R (2003) The Judge's New Role: should Personal Convictions Count? Int Crim Justice Rev 1:4–12

Dzehtsiarou K, Schwartz A (2020) Electing Team Strasbourg: professional Diversity on the European Court of Human Rights and Why it Matters. Ger Law J 21:621–643

Faget J (2018) L'acte de juger et ses biais. Délibérée 5:27–30

Fife RE (2020) Generating Incentives to Appoint Women to the International Bench: experiences with State practice. In: Baetens F (ed) Identity and Diversity on the International Bench: who is the Judge? Oxford University Press, Oxford, pp 50–61

Flauss J-F (2009) La collégialité à la Cour européenne des droits de l'homme. Revista do Instituto Brasileiro de Direitos Humanos 9:119–126

Fura E (2010) The 'Feminization' of the Court. In: The Conscience of Europe: 50 Years of the European Court of Human Rights. Third Millennium Publishing Limited, London, pp 186–189

Giegerich T, Jötten S (2017) Anti-discrimination policy. In: Schmahl S, Breuer M (eds) The council of europe. Its law and policies. Oxford University Press, Oxford, pp 589–616, para.26.63

Harris AP, Sen M (2019) Bias and Judging. Annu Rev Political Sci 22:241–259

Hennette Vauchez S (2015) More Women – but Which Women? The Rule and the Politics of Gender Balance at the European Court of Human Rights. Eur J Int Law 26:195–221

Hessler K (2020) The Significance of Religious Diversity in International Human Rights Adjudication. In: Baetens F (ed) Identity and Diversity on the International Bench: who is the Judge? Oxford University Press, Oxford, pp 462–478

Hodson L (2022) Gender and the international judge: towards a transformative equality approach. Leiden J Int Law 35:913–930

Hughes V (2020) Adjudicating International Trade Cases in the World Trade Organization: does Gender Make a Difference? In: Baetens F (ed) Identity and Diversity on the International Bench: Who is the Judge? Oxford University Press, Oxford, pp 330–354

Hunter R (2015) More than Just a Different Face? Judicial Diversity and Decision-making. Curr Leg Probl 68:119–141

Jack L, Knight E (2015) Les préférences des juges. Pour une approche réaliste. Les Cahiers de la Justice 4:589–612

Jelić I (2023) Feminist Justice and the European Court of Human Rights. In: Krstić I, Evola M, Ribes Moreno MI (eds) Legal Issues of International Law from a Gender Perspective. Springer, Nature Switzerland AG, Cham, pp 35–53

Keller H (2023) How to improve independence and impartiality of judges of the european court of human rights. European Conv Hum Rights Law Rev 4:259–266

Keller H, Heri C, Christ M (2020) Fifty Years of Women at the European Court of Human Rights: successes and Failures of the Council of Europe's Gender Agenda. In: Baetens F (ed) Identity and Diversity on the International Bench: who is the Judge? Oxford University Press, Oxford, pp 179–205

Kenney S J (2012a) Choosing judges: A bumpy road to women's equality and a long way to go. Mich St L Rev 1499–1528

Kenney S J (2012b) Gender and justice. Why women in the judiciary really matter. Routledge, New York, p 328

Lemmens K (2015) (S)electing Judges for Strasbourg: a (Dis)appointing Process? In: Bobek M (ed) Selecting Europe's judges: a critical review of the appointment procedures to the European Courts. Oxford University Press, Oxford, pp 95–119

Lijnzaad L (2020) The *Smurfette* Principle: reflections about Gender and the Nomination of Women to the International Bench. In: Baetens F (ed) Identity and Diversity on the International Bench: who is the Judge? Oxford University Press, Oxford, pp 29–49

Montesquieu (1748) De l'esprit des lois. Available online, at https://gallica.bnf.fr/ark:/12148/bpt6k62730454/f300.item#

Mowbray A (2008) The Consideration of Gender in the Process of Appointing Judges to the European Court of Human Rights. Hum Rights Law Rev 8:549–559

Ní Aoláin F (2015) More Women – but Which Women? A Reply to Stéphanie Hennette Vauchez. Ejil 26:229–236

Nosworthy JM (2020) Epilogue. Diversity, Inclusion, and Legitimacy in International Courts and Tribunals: insights from Within, Perspectives from the Periphery – an Island Girl Speaks. In: Baetens F (ed) Identity and Diversity on the International Bench: who is the Judge? Oxford University Press, Oxford, pp 538–555

Nußberger A, Baetens F (2020) Diversity on the Bench of the European Court of Human Rights. A Clash of Paradigms. In: Baetens F (ed) Identity and Diversity on the International Bench: Who is the Judge? Oxford University Press, Oxford, pp 479–493

Papayannis DM (2016) Independence, impartiality and neutrality in legal adjudication. Revus 28:33–52

Pillai P (2018) Women in International Law: a Vanishing Act? OpinioJuris. Online, at http://opiniojuris.org/2018/12/03/women-in-international-law-a-vanishing-act/

Ravarani G (2019) Quelques réflexions sur la légitimité du juge de Strasbourg. RTDH 118:261–296

Rehaag S (2011) Do women refugee judges really make a difference? An empirical analysis of gender and outcomes in canadian refugee determinations. Canadian J Women L, 23:627–660

Rose C (2016) Justifying arguments about selection procedures for judges at international courts and tribunals: A response to nienke grossman AJIL unbound 110:86–91

Ruiz Fabri H, Paine J (2022) The Procedural Cross-Fertilization Pull. In: Giorgetti C, Pollack M (eds) Beyond Fragmentation. cross-Fertilization, Cooperation and Competition among International Courts and Tribunals. Cambridge University Press, Cambridge, pp 39–86

Schultz U, Shaw G (2013) Gender and judging. Bloomsbury Publishing, London, p 640

Spector C (2015) La bouche de la loi ? Les figures du juge dans L'Esprit des lois. Montesquieu Law Review 3:87–102. https://hal.sorbonne-universite.fr/hal-02476028/document Online, at

Speech by Síofra O'Leary on the exchange of views with the Gender Equality Commission (GEC) held in Strasbourg on 16th Nov 2023. Online, at https://www.echr.coe.int/documents/d/echr/speech-20231116-oleary-exchange-views-gender-equality-commission-eng

Timmer A (2012) From inclusion to transformation: rewriting Konstantin Markin v. Russia. In: Brems E (ed) Diversity and European Human Rights. Cambridge University Press, Cambridge, pp 148–170

Tulkens F (2015) More Women – but Which Women? A Reply to Stéphanie Hennette Vauchez. Eur J Int Law 26:223–227
Tulkens F (2014) Parity on the bench: why? Why not. Eur Hum Rights Law Rev 6:587–595
Tulkens F (2007) Droits de l'homme, droits des femmes. Les requérantes devant la Cour européenne des droits de l'homme. Online, at https://rm.coe.int/1680597b22
Voeten E (2020) Gender and judging: evidence from the European Court of Human Rights. J Eur Public Policy 28:1–21
Von Bogdandy A, Venzke I (2014) In: Whose Name? A Public Law Theory of International Adjudication. Oxford University Press, Oxford, p 304
Wilson B (1990) Will Women Judges Really Make a Difference? Osgoode Hall Law J 28:507–522

Marko Bošnjak is the former President of the European Court of Human Rights (2024–2025). He held this position after serving as Vice-President of the Court (2022–2024) and President of Section (2022–2024). In June 2025 Marko Bošnjak was appointed as a Judge at the Court of Justice of the European Union. He holds a PhD (2002) on the Developments in modern biomedicine and criminal law from the University of Ljubljana and is Associate Professor of criminal law. Before joining the Court, in parallel with his academical missions, he was adviser to the Constitutional Court of Slovenia and attorney in criminal law. Apart from criminal law, his field of expertise extends to constitutional and international law.

Alice Leconte was legal trainee to Judge Bošnjak (Winter 2023–2024). She is a PhD student at the University of Lille and works on the applicants' litigation strategies before the European Court of Human Rights under the supervision of Prof. Larché. She holds a master's degree in human rights (University Grenoble Alpes) and an LL.M degree (Europa-Institut) in European and international human rights law.

Gender and Judiciary System in Spain From a Labor Perspective

Eva Bermúdez Figueroa and Raquel Pastor-Yuste

Abstract The aim of this paper is to provide a general overview of the position of women in the Spanish judicial system from a labour perspective. The theoretical framework taken as a starting point is the literature on gender and public administration and the conceptual development related to the supposed bureaucratic neutrality of organisations. The data analysed from official statistical sources, for the case of Spain and from a comparative perspective, show the occupational segregation suffered by women in the Administration of Justice despite the feminisation of legal studies.

1 Introduction

This chapter analyses the presence of women in Spanish Judiciary System from a work perspective. The approximate approach of this research is based on three main premises.

First, it is based on the evidence of the feminisation of legal studies in most democratic countries. This dominance of women in legal studies should have correlated with the corresponding professions and occupational categories so that women would be overrepresented in most areas and spaces of the legal-judicial system, as they are at the educational level.

Secondly, the Organic Spanish Law 3/2007 of 22 March 2007 on the effective equality of men and women established that all public bodies are obliged to provide statistical data disaggregated by sex. Disaggregated data became an

E. Bermúdez Figueroa (✉) R. Pastor-Yuste
University of Cadiz, Cadiz, Spain
e-mail: eva.bermudez@uca.es
e-mail: raquel.pastor@uca.es

© The Author(s), under exclusive license to Springer Nature Switzerland AG 2025
S. Baer et al. (eds.), *The Gender and the Judiciary*, Gender Perspectives in Law 7,
https://doi.org/10.1007/978-3-032-06885-9_8

excellent tool for providing indicators of the differential impact of different social phenomena on men and women.

Thirdly, there is extensive literature on gender and the law that focuses mainly on the influence of gender bias in judicial decisions or its impact on the treatment of victims, i.e., how the legal system is imbued with the practices of patriarchal society and how this phenomenon permeates the administration of justice.[1] However, this literature only marginally addresses the place of women as employees within the judicial system from a labour perspective. This paper attempts to fill this gap in the literature on women's employment in the judiciary in Spain by providing a descriptive analysis of the distribution of women and men in the judiciary, taking into account their location at the different levels of the judiciary and the job categories, positions, and occupations that men and women occupy in each of them.

This chapter has sought to answer critical questions such as: Where are women in the judiciary? Are women represented in all areas of the judiciary? What are their most ordinary occupations? What positions do they hold? To this end, quantitative data on the characteristics of women's employment in the Spanish judiciary have been analysed, based on publicly available data from the General Council of the Judiciary, the Public Employment Bulletin and the National Public Employment Statistics. The Spanish Organic Law 3/2007 of 22 March 2007 on the effective equality of men and women, has established that all public bodies are obliged to provide statistical data disaggregated by sex. Disaggregated data became an excellent tool for providing indicators of the differential impact of different social phenomena on men and women. Those data show that, despite the growing presence of women in the judicial organisation, there is still a clear occupational segregation between men and women, which places women in the lowest and least visible categories of the judicial career ladder.

After explaining our objectives and the methodology used for this descriptive analysis, the chapter is structured as follows: a summary explaining the organisation of the judicial system in Spain, together with the form of access to the judicial career. In order to analyse this from a gender perspective, we will frame some theoretical concepts within the sociology of organisations and work that explain inequalities. We will then provide specific data on the presence and distribution of women in the Spanish judicial system. To do so, we will refer to the feminisation of legal studies and contextualise the presence of women in European legal bodies before going on to detail where women are in the judiciary in the Spanish state.

[1] Feenan (2008), Gastaldi and Pezzano (2021), Grey et al. (2021).

2 Objectives, Data and Methodology

The general objective of this research is to make an exploratory approach to the position of women in the Spanish judicial system. To this end, we pose a series of questions to be answered: How are women represented, from a labor perspective, in the Spanish judicial system? Are women in the judicial system represented proportionally to the feminisation of legal studies? Are they in the majority in all areas? As secondary objectives, we will try to detect the gender gap related to vertical and horizontal segregation, providing some explanations from the field of sociology of work and previous studies of gender and administration in general, as well as from the specific literature explaining the position of women in public administration. Given the exploratory nature of this research, the methodology is mainly based on data analysis from secondary sources. It is necessary to contextualize the reality of women within the judicial system through statistical data, mainly related to the presence of women in the different judicial bodies and the roles played, to detect both horizontal and vertical segregation. The quantitative data used are extracted from official statistical sources and their databases. For the international case and the European comparison, we rely on: Women in the judiciary (OECD), European Judicial Systems Efficiency and quality of justice (CEPEJ) and European Institute for Gender Equality (EIGE) Gender Statistics Database. The data provided at the international level are only exhaustive for some European countries, but only some are discussed for length reasons.

At the national level, the data analyzed correspond to the following sources: National Statistics Institute (INE); Statistical Bulletin of Personnel in the Service of Public Administrations (BEPSAP) of the Ministry of Public Administrations; Ministry of Justice, and within it, the statistics provided by the Report on the demographic structure of the judiciary, from General Council of the Judiciary (CGPJ) and the II Judicial Career Equality Plan of the General Council of the Judiciary. The primary indicators we have used are related to professional promotion, access to the judicial career, and the reconciliation of work and family life.

Quantitative analysis provides us with a rigorous and faithful perspective of reality, but at the same time, it is a fixed and static image. Likewise, quantitative analysis loses a great wealth of nuances and a deepening of the subjective experience that women professionals have of their work experience and the daily barriers and obstacles they face in developing their working lives. It would be essential to provide a qualitative analysis showing how women interpret the limitations of balanced representation in the judicial system. However, for the sake of space, this is left for future work that will allow us to complete the quantitative analysis of the available data.

3 Some Notes on Spanish Territorial Judiciary Organization

In order to give the international reader a clear idea it is timely to give a very brief summary of the territorial organisation of the judicial system in Spain to better understand the differences in representation between men and women in the different courts, each with its sphere of competence.

The Spanish legal system is renowned for its intricate structure, encompassing numerous courts, each tailored to fulfil distinct roles. This complexity exceeds that of many other nations and is primarily shaped by the framework established in the 1978 Spanish Constitution.[2] Its territorial organization is central to the Spanish legal framework, divided into municipalities, districts, 50 provinces, and 17 Regional Governments (*Comunidad Autónoma*). While most courts operate within this framework, it is crucial to recognize that only the highest levels of the judiciary possess national jurisdiction.[3]

In this sense, Spanish Law establishes that the exercise of jurisdictional power is attributed to the following courts and tribunals: Courts of the Peace, Courts of First Instance and Instruction, Commercial Courts, Courts for Violence against Women, Criminal Courts, Administrative Courts, Social Courts, Juvenile Courts and Prison Supervision Courts, Provincial Courts, High Courts of Justice, National High Court and the Supreme Court.[4]

As for the unipersonal or collegiate nature of the bodies, they are all unipersonal except for the Supreme Court, the National High Court, the High Courts of Justice, and the Provincial Courts.

From a territorial point of view, Spain is organised, for judicial purposes, into Municipalities, Districts, Provinces and Regional Government.[5] The following Table 1 provides an overview of the Spanish judicial system, its territorial demarcation and specific structure, and the leading specific regulations and articles that govern it.

The *Juzgados de Paz* (Peace Courts or Magistrates' Courts) have administrative headquarters in the municipalities. These courts are located in those municipalities that do not have Courts of First Instance and Instruction. They are responsible for civil conciliations and conciliations in criminal matters, as

---

[2] Nieto (2007).

[3] Book I of Organic Law 6/1985 of 1 July 1985 on the Judiciary regulates the extension and limits of jurisdiction and the layout and organisation of the courts and tribunals. Law 38/1988, of 28 December 1988 on Judicial Demarcation and Judicial Plant develops the matter.

[4] Article 26, of the Organic Law 6/1985, of July 1, 1985, of the Judiciary.

[5] Article 30, of the Organic Law 6/1985, of July 1, 1985, of the Judiciary.

Table 1 Spanish Judicial System: Courts, Territorial Scope, Structure and Basic Legal Framework

Courts and tribunals	Territorial demarcation	Structure	LOPJ[6]
Magistrates' Courts	Municipal	Territorial bodies	Book I, Title IV, Chapter VI (Articles 99–103)
Courts of First Instance and Instruction, Commercial Courts, Courts for Violence against Women, Criminal Courts, Contentious-Administrative Courts, Social Courts, Prison Supervision Courts and Juvenile Courts.	Judicial Districts/ Province[7]	Territorial bodies	Chapter V of Title IV of Book I (Articles 84–98)
Provincial Courts	Provincial Capitals	Territorial bodies	Chapter IV of Title IV of Book I (Articles 80–83)
High Courts of Justice	Autonomous Community	Territorial bodies	Chapter III, Title IV, Book I (Articles 70–79)
Audiencia Nacional	National	Central Body	Chapter II of Title IV of Book I (Articles 62–69)
Supreme Court	National	Central Body	Chapter I of Title IV of Book I (Articles 53–61)

Source Compilation based on Organic Law 6/1985, of July 1, 1985, of the Judiciary, in Spain

well as some misdemeanour trials. They are headed by Justices of the Peace, appointed for four years and democratically elected by the Town Council.[8]

The Courts of First Instance and Instruction exercise their legal jurisdiction within the judicial district, resolve civil and commercial disputes, and, in short, judge in the first instance minor offences, mainly those that occur in the area of the family.[9]

The Commercial Courts have their jurisdiction in the capital of each province. These courts deal with commercial companies and cooperatives, transport, maritime and air law matters.[10]

The Courts of Violence against Women are established to combat gender-based violence, these specialised courts provide legal recourse and protection to victims across Spain's provinces, emphasising the nation's commitment to gender equality. There is minimum one in each judicial district, and also have their headquarters in the capital of each province.

[6] Spanish acronim for Organic Law of the Judiciary.

[7] Article 32 of the Organic Law of the Judiciary establishes that the judicial district (*Partido judicial*) which is the territorial unit comprised of one or more neighbouring municipalities in the same province.

[8] Articles 99 to 103, of the Organic Law 6/1985, of July 1, 1985, of the Judiciary.

[9] Articles 84 and 85 of the Organic Law 6/1985, of July 1, 1985, of the Judiciary.

[10] Article 86 of the Organic Law 6/1985, of July 1, 1985, of the Judiciary.

The Criminal Courts also have jurisdiction in each provincial capital and try less severe crimes and some serious crimes, i.e. those punishable by imprisonment of up to five years.[11]

The Contentious-Administrative Courts rule in the sole or first instance on appeals against local entities' acts or the Regional Governmemnt's administration. They are responsible for authorising entry into homes for the forced execution of acts of the public administration.[12]

The Social Courts are responsible for settling disputes between employees and employers or between employees and each other, provided that they originate in the employment contract and Social Security claims.[13]

The primary function of the Prison Supervision Courts, like all the previous ones, with a provincial location, is the execution of custodial sentences and security measures, the jurisdictional control of the disciplinary power of the prison authorities, and the protection of the rights and benefits of the inmates in the penitentiary establishments.[14]

Finally, and within the provincial territorial demarcation, there are the Juvenile Courts. They are responsible for judging misdemeanours and crimes committed by persons over 14 and under 18. Suppose the alleged perpetrator of a crime or misdemeanour is under 14. In that case, he or she is placed at the administrative institutions' disposal to protect minors, which depends on the Regional Government.

The highest judicial body at the provincial level in Spain is the Provincial Courts. Their seat is in the province's capital, exercising jurisdiction over the entire province.

The Provincial Courts (*Audiencia Provincial*) reflect Spain's diversity, as each autonomous community houses a provincial court responsible for administering justice within its province. These courts have jurisdiction over civil and criminal cases, serving as appellate bodies for lower court decisions. They are comprised of a president and two or more magistrates. They shall hear civil and criminal cases, and there may be sections with the same composition.[15]

On the other hand, the Autonomous Community constitutes the territorial scope of the High Courts of Justice. The High Courts of Justice *(Tribunales Superiores de Justicia)* consist of three chambers (civil and criminal, contentious-administrative and social).[16] They are made up of a president, who will also be the president of the civil and criminal chambers, the presidents of the chambers, and the judges, who are determined by law for each of their chambers.[17]

---

[11] Article 89 of the Organic Law 6/1985, of July 1, 1985, of the Judiciary.

[12] Articles 90 and 91 of the Organic Law 6/1985, of July 1, 1985, of the Judiciary.

[13] Articles 92 and 93 of the Organic Law 6/1985, of July 1, 1985, of the Judiciary.

[14] Articles 94 and 95 of the Organic Law 6/1985, of July 1, 1985, of the Judiciary.

[15] Articles 80 to 83 and 95 of the Organic Law 6/1985, of July 1, 1985, of the Judiciary.

[16] Articles 70 to 79 of the Organic Law 6/1985, of July 1, 1985, of the Judiciary.

[17] Cabanas Gancedo (1991).

The National Court (*Audiencia Nacional*) is a court with jurisdiction over the whole of Spain. The National Court comprises its president, the presidents of the chambers, and the judges determined by law for each of its chambers and sections (Appeals, Criminal, Contentious-Administrative, and Social).[18] Also headquartered in Madrid, the National Court holds jurisdiction over matters of national importance, such as terrorism and fraud. It adjudicates severe offenses against the state and manages extradition requests from foreign jurisdictions, bolstering Spain's national security.[19]

Finally, the Supreme Court (*Tribunal Supremo*), located in Madrid, stands as the apex judicial body in Spain, wielding national jurisdiction over all legal matters.[20] Comprising five specialized chambers, it adjudicates Civil, Criminal, Labour, Public Affairs, and Military law cases. Additionally, it serves as the appellate body for lower court decisions and handles cases involving government official issues. It comprises its president, the presidents of the chambers, and the judges determined by law for each of its chambers and sections. It has five chambers: Civil, Criminal, Contentious-Administrative, Social, and Military.

In the same vein, explaining the different ways of exercising the judiciary is necessary since it is formed by judges and magistrates responsible for administering justice. The essential difference lies in the fact that judges are professionals in the judicial system who generally hold positions in first-instance courts, investigating courts, and other primary courts. Their main function includes decision-making in more minor court cases, as well as the investigation of criminal cases. First-instance judges are responsible for resolving less complex civil and criminal disputes, such as divorces, contracts, and less severe criminal cases. On the other hand, investigating judges (*Juez de instrucción*) conduct preliminary investigations in criminal cases and make decisions based on precautionary measures and evidence.

However, Magistrates are senior judges who generally hold positions in second-instance courts, such as the High Courts of Justice or the Supreme Court. They are responsible for making decisions in more complex cases and, in many cases, act as appellate judges, reviewing decisions made by first-instance judges. Magistrates in the High Courts of Justice have jurisdiction over matters in a specific autonomous community and handle various civil and criminal cases of greater relevance and complexity.

For their part, the magistrates in the Supreme Court are the highest-ranking judges in Spain and play a crucial role in interpreting the Constitution and unifying jurisprudence throughout the country.[21]

---

[18] Articles 62 to 69 of the Organic Law 6/1985, of July 1, 1985, of the Judiciary.

[19] Asencio Mellado (2003).

[20] Articles 53 to 61 of the Organic Law 6/1985, of July 1, 1985, of the Judiciary.

[21] Casasola (2013).

In short, judges are the decision-makers in less complex court cases, while magistrates are senior judges who deal with more complex matters and often act as appellate judges.

Regarding the hierarchy of judicial bodies, the Supreme Court is the highest. It exercises its function as the interpreter of the Constitution and the unifier of jurisprudence throughout the national territory. It acts as a court of cassation and supervises the correct application of the law by the lower courts. Its decisions establish case law.

3.1 Accessing Judicial Career in Spain

Access to the Judicial Career in Spain is governed by Articles 301 and following of Organic Law 6/1985, of 1 July, of the Judiciary, based on the principles of merit and capability essential for the exercise of judicial functions. The entry into the Judicial Career as a Judge is achieved through the successful completion of an open competitive examination and a theoretical and practical selection course conducted at the Judicial School in Barcelona. Since 2001, this selection process has been conducted jointly with the entry into the Public Prosecutor's Career, allowing candidates who pass the selective phase to choose, based on their scores and the available positions, to undertake the theoretical-practical course at the Judicial School or the Centre for Legal Studies of the Ministry of Justice.

The Selection Committee, responsible for calling the examinations, is composed of several members: a member of the General Council of the Judiciary (where there are a 31% of women in 2024, none of them President or Secretary, as we will see later) and a Chief Prosecutor, who will preside alternately each year; a judge; a prosecutor; the Director of the Judicial School; the Director of the Centre for Legal Studies of the Administration of Justice; and a member of the technical bodies of the General Council of the Judiciary, as well as a civil servant from the Ministry of Justice with a minimum level of Deputy Director, both holding a law degree, who will alternate in the secretarial duties of the Committee.

The Tribunal that evaluates the entrance examinations for the Judicial and Prosecutorial Careers consists of: a Judge of the Supreme Court (a women out of eleven members, not president or secretary) or a Superior Court of Justice, or a Chief Prosecutor of the Supreme Court or a Prosecutor of a Superior Court of Justice, who will preside over the Tribunal; two judges; two prosecutors; a university professor in legal disciplines; a State Attorney; a lawyer with more than ten years of professional practice; and a senior legal officer from the Administration of Justice, who will act as the secretary member.

The procedure for entry into the category of Judge, which takes approximately three years, includes the following phases: the open competitive examination and a second phase at the Judicial School, divided into twelve months period for a theoretical-practical course at the Judicial School in Barcelona; a practical phase involving assistance and collaboration with the incumbents of the judicial bodies where the practical training takes place, who will act as mentors (six months); and a substitution and reinforcement phase in judicial bodies, performing duties with the same scope as the incumbents of those judicial bodies, for approximately five months. After all this period, which endures about ten years of preparation in practical terms in Spain since they finished their professional degree, they start their judicial career.

4 Bureaucratic Neutrality, Merit, and Ability, or Universal Masculinity?

Once the basis for the understanding of the Spanish judiciary is established and to frame theoretically the gender analysis of the data, we need to reflect on some concepts that mark and determine the normal processes in every organisation independently from its nature.

Bureaucratic neutrality and the emphasis on merit as a criterion for selection and promotion within organisations have long been regarded as pillars of fair and equitable management. This neutrality applies to any organisation, especially the business and labour environment, and primarily to public administration; more specifically for accessing judicial career, based on the principles of merit and capacity for exercising the judicial function,[22] as we will see later.

The supposed bureaucratic neutrality, which seeks to focus solely on individual capacity and performance, often overlooks the inequalities embedded in the organisational structure. In this sense, Joan Acker (2006) defines regimes of inequality, which operate at the core of organisations, are based on gender relations, and form an intrinsic part of how work is distributed, the goals that are set, and which mark interactions from everyday life, physically and symbolically producing and reproducing existing inequalities.[23]

On the other hand, as a purportedly neutral universal model, the male figure is challenged by various organisational theorists who agree in highlighting how the underlying pattern of processes, relationships and the very definition of occupations and their competencies are determined by male traditional models. Acker's analysis of the ideal of organisational leadership coincides with a fundamental aspect. Acker (2006) argues that leaders are perceived as endowed with strength, aggressiveness and competitiveness. These attributes define a leader within the context of business or trade unions and are shared by society. In line with this, the author argues that the work structure within organisations may vary significantly and tends to be configured to suit men's needs and traditional stereotypical characteristics (Acker, 2012). This configuration assumes that men can devote themselves entirely to work without requiring a balance between their work and

[22] Articles 301 and follows Organic Law 6/1985 of 1 July 1985 on the Judiciary.

[23] Acker (2006, 2012).

family responsibilities, as women are assumed to take care of the latter. This dynamic is reflected in an unequal distribution of work in organisations.

Otherwise, merit-based promotion, can be an insidious trap. While, in theory, it should recognize and reward those who demonstrate outstanding skills, the concept of merit itself can be skewed. Standards of "merit" are often shaped by culturally ingrained male standards. This disadvantages women, whose contributions may not be recognised or valued to the same extent as their male colleagues. Moreover, the emphasis on merit can lead to rigid adherence to qualities traditionally associated with men, to the exclusion of characteristics and competencies that women can bring to the table. Generally underrepresented on boards, women often face difficulties being heard and valued equally with their male colleagues. Brescoll (2016)[24] revealed that participants in her study believed that female leaders' decisions were influenced by emotions, resulting in a lower likelihood of hiring women for leadership roles. Similarly, in the field of psychology, Fischbach, Lichtenthaler, and Horstmann's (2015) research on the "Think Manager-Think Man" paradigm demonstrated that the emotions exhibited by successful managers align more with those stereotypical traits traditionally attributed to men rather than women.[25] This discussion highlights the prevailing stereotypes about women in managerial positions, which can also be translated into power and decision positions. We could take the social value of care, and the undervaluation—not only in terms of social assessment, but on salaries and reputation—of traditional women trades linked to professions (enfant and primary education, psychology, lower levels of health professions or positions, cleaning, nursing, and others) and check the corresponding gender gap, even in political representation. Social areas related to minors, migrants, family, social work, women, are usually occupied by women, but they lack the heavy specific weight, consideration and remuneration that some others associated with male traits such as finance management, engineering, business, and other male dominated sector.[26] In business organisations, trade unions, as well as in public institutions, and fundamentally in politics, the image of a successful leader is that of a white heterosexual man, fully committed to the organisation.[27] In the face of this reality, notable authors such as Raewyn Connell shed light on the concept of hegemonic masculinity, which is configured as a prevalent and prescriptive manifestation of masculinity that is embedded in the fabric of all institutions.[28] This type of masculinity does not necessarily have to be the most frequent in statistical terms. However, it is the way of being a man in the collective imagination of a patriarchal society, and consequently, it permeates

[24] Brescoll (2016), pp. 415–428.

[25] Fischbach, Lichtenthaler, and Horstmann's (2015).

[26] Bermúdez et al. (2023).

[27] Hunter (2002); Gastiazoro (2008); Gastiazoro and Moguillansky (2021) Zaikosky Biscay and Betsabé Policastro (2023).

[28] Connell (2006); Connell and Messerschmidt (2005).

all forms of organization. These papers address how this predominant conception of masculinity leads to excluding any alternative expression of masculinity that deviates from this standard. The net of power relations rooted in this notion of hegemonic masculinity produces and maintains the dominant position of men in comparison to women, or any variant of masculinity that comes close to stereotypes and roles considered feminine.[29]

From the field of politics and administration, many authors support these theses concerning the need to study formal and informal institutions, as well as the symbolic processes they perpetuate, despite all the institutional efforts to apply gender equality and gender mainstreaming policies without achieving the expected results. At the same time, there is resistance to implementing equality policies, as the lack of actual implementation of compulsory equality plans in public administration since 2008.[30] The long-awaited social change towards equality in organisations is still not taking off, and some research points to the coexistence of two types of norms: the formal, explicit and superior norms that promote and support gender equality, and the implicit patriarchal social norm, where power dynamics based on male domination prevail.[31] The coexistence of these two categories of norms in institutions results in a slow and gradual, yet internal, process of change that eventually leads to the generalisation of the new norm, which in this case is legally imperative.

5 Feminisation of Law Studies in Spain

At this point, and before delving in the representation of women in the judiciary, it is helpful to provide a general view of the feminisation of Law studies. Current statistics for Spain show the evolution in the number of people enrolled in public universities between 2015 and 2022, specifically in the branch of social and legal sciences knowledge according to gender.

The data in Table 2 show a clear feminisation in the branch of knowledge of social and legal sciences in the case of Spain in terms of students enrolled, since although the overall number of people enrolled in this branch of knowledge has fallen, from just over 502,000 people in the 2015–2016 academic year to 479,000 in the 2021–2022 academic year, there is a clear and constant trend towards feminisation in these studies, given that throughout the period analysed there are 20% more women than men enrolled in these studies. 479,000 in the academic year 2021–2022, a clear and constant trend of feminisation of these studies is

[29] Bermúdez and Roca (2022); Chappell (2010); Chappell and Waylen (2013); Verge Mestre (2021).

[30] At the university context, see Lombardo and Bustelo (2021); Alonso Álvarez and Diz Otero (2022); Castaño Collado and Vázquez-Cuperio (2023); at general administration level, see Gelambí (2015) and Bermúdez-Figueroa (2021).

[31] Alfama (2015).

Table 2 Evolution of enrolments in Spanish public universities by sex in the branch of knowledge of social and legal sciences (2015–2022)

Period under consideration	Total number of persons enrolled	Men	Women
2015–2016	502.468	39,9%	60,1%
2016–2017	500.093	40,0%	60,0%
2017–2018	496.985	40,0%	60,0%
2018–2019	493.009	39,8%	60,2%
2019–2020	488.710	39,4%	60,6%
2020–2021	494.832	39,2%	60,8%
2021–2022	479.864	38,8%	61,2%

Source Ministry of Universities. General Secretariat of Universities. Integrated University Information System (SIIU). https://www.universidades.gob.es/estadistica-de-estudiantes/

maintained, given that throughout the entire period analysed there are 20% more women than men enrolled in these disciplines, six out of every ten students are women while four out of every ten students are men.

In particular, if we focus on Law studies as a specific field of study within the branch of knowledge of social and legal sciences in Spanish public universities, the data in Table 3 also show the feminisation of Law studies since around 60% of the students enrolled are women. In contrast, only 4 out of 10 students are men, which has remained stable throughout the period.

Concerning the number of graduates, the data provided in Table 4 show a clear feminisation in terms of the number of people completing their Bachelor's Degree in Law at Spanish public universities, as it can be seen that 20% more women than men complete their studies over the entire period considered, a figure that remains constant between 2015 and 2022 (Table 4).

Table 3 Evolution of enrolments in Law in Spanish public universities by sex (2015–2022)

Period under consideration	Total number of persons enrolled in law	Men	Women
2015–2016	92.461	43,7%	56,3%
2016–2017	93.422	43,3%	56,7%
2017–2018	92.267	42,9%	57,1%
2018–2019	91.734	42,3%	57,7%
2019–2020	89.255	41,6%	58,4%
2020–2021	91.326	40,8%	59,2%
2021–2022	88.078	39,6%	60,4%

Source Ministry of Universities. General Secretariat of Universities. Integrated University Information System (SIIU). https://www.universidades.gob.es/estadistica-de-estudiantes/

Table 4 Evolution of graduates in Law in Spanish public universities by sex (2015–2022)

Period under consideration	Total number of law graduates	Men	Women
2015–2016	9.778	40,0%	60,0%
2016–2017	10.967	40,6%	59,4%
2017–2018	11.199	40,4%	59,6%
2018–2019	11.098	42,0%	58,0%
2019–2020	12.653	39,3%	60,7%
2020–2021	12.509	39,4%	60,6%
2021–2022	11.380	38,3%	61,7%

Source Ministry of Universities. General Secretariat of Universities. Integrated University Information System (SIIU). https://www.universidades.gob.es/estadistica-de-estudiantes/

The data show that for the period considered and in the case of Spain, there is a clear feminisation of law studies in terms of both the number of enrolments and the number of graduates. These data, though, are not correlated with the levels and distribution of female presence in the different judicial bodies, especially at the top of these bodies, as statistics on the judiciary analysed below clearly demonstrate.

6 The Presence of Women in the Administration of Justice: From European Context to National Spanish Data

Although the paper focuses on the situation of women in the administration of justice in Spain, it is important to contextualise it within the European context, given that this comparative reading allows us to have a picture of the features that define the presence of women in the different institutions linked to the administration of justice.

Looking at the presence of women in the judicial bodies of the European Union—see Table 5—it can be seen that the level of female presence has gone from a deficient level, as shown in the 1999 data, to 22% in the European Court of Justice,

Table 5 Evolution of the percentage presence of women in judicial bodies in the European Union

Entity/Year	1999	2009	2019	2022
CST: Civil Service Tribunal	–	28,6	-ND	-ND
ECHR: European Court of Human Rights	–	37	31,9	**31,9**
GC: General Court	13,3	22,2	23,9	**30,8**
CJEU: Court of Justice of European Union	7,7	19,7	21,9	27,8
ECJ: European Court of Justice	4,2	14,8	18,5	22,2

Source Authors' elaboration on *Data collection on women and men in decision-making* (WMID) European Institute for Gender Equality (EIGE)

27.8% in the Court of Justice of the European Union and almost 32% of women in the European Court of Human Rights.

In short, although the presence of women has been increasing, the data show that women continue to be very poorly represented at the international level in the judicial bodies of the European Union and have a clear disadvantage concerning their male colleagues.

When comparing the percentage of women currently members of the European Courts in their respective countries—graph 1—there is significant variability between them. Spain is one of the European countries with the fewest women in the Supreme Court, only surpassed by the United Kingdom, Turkey, Malta, Denmark, and the Czech Republic. On the other hand, Montenegro, Serbia, Romania, and Bulgaria are at the top regarding the presence of women judges in their high courts. This variability highlights the differential processes of access to the Supreme Court, making the presence of women difficult when the election depends less on merit than on political decisions of a different nature, which may be linked to the defining features of the processes through which discretionary appointments are made at the judiciary's top.

6.1 The Presence of Women in the Administration of Justice in Spain: Professional Promotion and Administrative Situation

As we can see, Fig. 1 presents an interesting overview of access to the Spanish judiciary from 2014 to 2021 and shows variability in the percentages of women entering the judiciary. These percentages offer global figures ranging from a minimum of 40% in 2019 to a maximum of 69.23% in 2021. Despite the oscillations, the overall average of women entering the judicial career during this period is 65.61%, which exceeds half of the total and indicates the feminisation of the judiciary. The increase in the percentage of women in years such as 2021 could be considered a step towards gender equality in access to the judiciary.

However, it is essential to analyse these percentages in light of the overall composition of the judicial career and the structure of opportunities available to women and men. Although the percentages indicate a more significant entry of women in specific years, examining how these women are distributed in terms of categories and hierarchical levels is essential. Mere presence in the initial stages of the judicial career does not guarantee equality in promotion and leadership, as discussed below.

The gender breakdown of male and female judges in collegiate bodies until 31 December 2022 reveals evident disparities in career advancement within the judiciary concerning gender. This data sheds light on the lack of equity in leadership and decision-making positions in the judiciary, reflecting deep-rooted patterns of inequality.

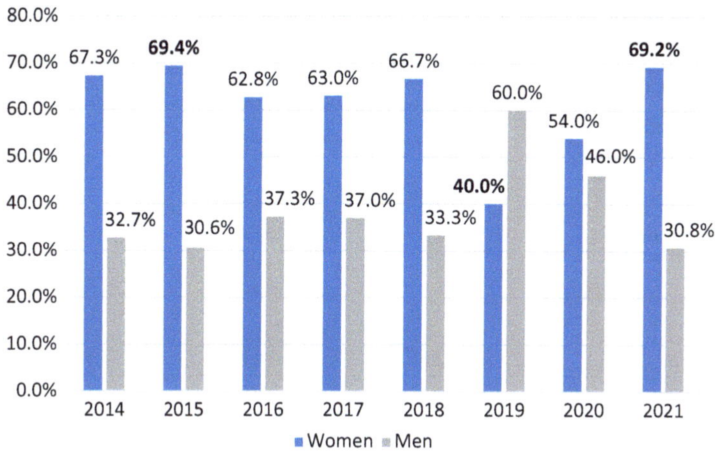

Fig. 1 Evolution of women's access to the judicial career (2014–2021). *Source* Authors' elaboration on data from General Council of the Judiciary (CGPJ) in 2022 in Spain

As seen in Table 6, and in the specific case of Spain, the judicial leadership of the courts, high courts of justice, and the Supreme Court are male. Specifically, there are no women in the presidency of the Supreme Court or the National High Court. At the same time, in the case of the jurisdictional bodies of the Regional Government (High Courts of Justice) and the provinces (Provincial Courts), their presence as presidents is symbolic or at least a tiny minority, as only 2 out of every ten presidents are women. As one moves up the jurisdictional ladder and in their positions, a clear gender bias in terms of female presence is evident.

There is also a specific variability in the levels of female presence in the different Chambers that make up the judicial bodies, as shown in Table 3. Thus, there is a gender balance in terms of presence in the Social Division of the Supreme Court or the High Courts of Justice, while the presence of women in the Civil Division or the Military Division of both judicial bodies is very much in the minority.

More specifically, it can be pointed out that in the Supreme Court, a marked asymmetry in gender representation in senior positions is revealed. The total absence of women in the Vice-Presidency and the exclusive occupation of men in the Chamber Presidencies indicate an institutional structure that perpetuates the marginalisation of women in leadership roles. Furthermore, in the specific chambers, the presence of women is notably reduced, as can be observed in the Civil, Criminal, Contentious-Administrative, and Military Chambers. These figures underline a gender gap in the distribution of power and decision-making. The Supreme Court, the pinnacle of the judicial hierarchy, shows an apparent male domination. The Presidencies of Chambers, the fundamental pillars of decision-making, exhibit male predominance to a remarkable degree. This inclination is manifested in a 100% male presence in the Vice-Presidency and 87.50% male

Table 6 The gender breakdown of male and female judges in collegiate bodies

	Men	Women	Total
SUPREME COURT			
Vice-presidency			
Presidence of chambers	100%	0%	4
Civil Chamber	87,50%	12,50%	8
Criminal Chamber	80%	20% (20,00%)	15
Contencious-Administrative Chamber	75%	25%	24
Social Room	55,56%	44,44%	9
Militar Room	80%	20%	5
Total	76,92%	23,08%	65
NATIONAL AUDIENCE			
Presidence	100%		1
Civil Chamber Presidencce		100%	1
Contencious-Administrative Presidence	100%		1
Social Room Presidence	100%		1
Rest of Magistrates	59,70%	40,30%	67
Total	60,56%	39,44%	71
HIGH COURTS OF JUSTICE			
Presidence	88,24%	11,76%	17
Civil Chamber Presidencce	80%	20%	20
Contencious-Administrative Presidence	66,67%	33,33%	18
Social Room Presidence	52,63%	47,37%	19
Rest of Magistrates	59,37%	40,63%	443
Total	60,20%	39,80%	500
PROVINCIAL HEARINGS/COURTS			
Presidencies	80,00%	20%	40
Rest of Magistrates	56,96%	43,04%	947
Total	57,89%	42,11%	995

Source Authors' Compilation based on information from the General Council of the Judiciary 2023

representation in the Civil Chamber. Despite some efforts to diversify, as illustrated by a 20% female presence in the Criminal Chamber, a marked imbalance prevails.

The National Court shows similar patterns, with a significant lack of female representation in positions of influence, such as the Presidency and the Presidencies of the Chambers. Although there is a notable female presence in the presidency of the Criminal Chamber and other instances, the general profile is that of a male majority. These results suggest the persistence of barriers that limit women's access to leadership roles at a critical institutional level.

As far as the High Courts of Justice are concerned, inequalities are still notorious. However, there is a more significant presence of women in some posts, such as the Administrative and Social Courts Presidencies—33,33 and 47,33%, respectively—and the general group of magistrates – 40,63%[32] The figures indicate that men occupy most of the Presidencies and remain the majority in the overall group of male and female judges. These findings highlight the existence of a hierarchical structure that perpetuates gender segregation and suggest, as previous research has pointed out, that women still face severe obstacles in their advancement to more influential roles.

The Provincial Courts also reflect gender imbalances in the Presidencies and the general group of male and female judges. Although there is a higher representation of women compared to higher instances, – 42,11% of the members are women— the majority presence of men in leadership positions and the unequal distribution in the general group is evidence of the persistence of discriminatory patterns.[33]

Overall, this analysis of gender ratios in the judiciary underlines the need to address gender inequality at all levels. The figures show that women are under-represented in positions of power and that the gender gap persists in the judiciary.

The data analysis thus reveals an intrinsic pattern of gender inequality in the upper echelons of the Spanish judiciary. In the hierarchy of the judicial system, the higher levels of responsibility, such as the presidencies and specialized chambers, show a marked asymmetry in gender distribution.

In short, the data underline the persistent gender inequality in career advancement within the Spanish judicial system. The under-representation of women in leadership roles and positions of responsibility reflects an institutional structure rooted in historical and cultural patterns. Despite initial efforts to address this disparity, persistent obstacles remain, and specific policies and measures are required to achieve equal representation and active participation of women at all levels of the judiciary.

Table 7 shows the results of elections to government chambers in various judicial jurisdictions and reveal a gender disparity in participation in administrative

[32] The High Courts of Justice, as indicated in the Organic Law of the Judiciary, consist of three chambers (civil and criminal, contentious-administrative and social). They are made up of a president, who will also be the president of the civil and criminal chambers, the presidents of the chambers, and the judges, who are determined by law for each of their chambers. At this point, it is explained why the presidency of the jurisdictional body and each of the chambers is held by a single person, who, as the data show, tends to be male, while the rest of the persons who comprise it have a more significant gender variability, facilitated by the number of members.

[33] The available data are not disaggregated by gender at the provincial level for each Provincial court, so it is impossible to analyse the differences in the level of female presence among them, not being able to state the trend of certain traditionally conservative areas.

Table 7 Participation in government posts appointed by the election of the remaining members of the judicial career. Elections to Chambers of Government

ELECTIONS 2019									
	Accepted Applications			Headlines			Subsites		
	Women	Men	Total	Women	Men	Total	Women	Men	Total
Supreme Court	3 (16,7%)	15 (83,3%)	18	1 (20%)	4 (80%)	5	2 (20%)	4 (80%)	5
National Court/ Audience	3 (50%)	3 (50%)	6	2 (67%)	1 (33%)	3	1 (33%)	2 (67%)	3
High courts of Justice (Regional courts)									
Andalucía	25 (42%)	35 (58%)	60	13 (44%)	17 (56%)	30	12 (40%)	18 (60%)	30
Aragón	8 (42%)	11 (58%)	19	4 (67%)	2 (33%)	6	1 (17%)	5 (83%)	6
Asturias	4 (50%)	4 (50%)	8	2 (50%)	2 (50%)	4	2 (50%)	2 (50%)	4
Baleares	7 (50%)	7 (50%)	14	2 (50%)	2 (50%)	4	2 (50%)	2 (50%)	4
Canarias	14 (47%)	16 (53%)	30	3 (43%)	4 (57%)	7	4 (57%)	3 (43%)	7
Cantabria	16 (73%)	6 (27%)	22	3 (75%)	1 (25%)	4	2 (50%)	2 (50%)	4
Castilla y León	23 (41%)	33 (59%)	56	6 (43%)	8 (57%)	14	8 (57%)	6 (43%)	14
Castilla la Mancha	8 (38%)	13 (62%)	21	3 (38%)	5 (62%)	8	3 (38%)	5 (62%)	8
Cataluña	30 (53%)	26 (47%)	56	5 (71%)	2 (29%)	7	2 (29%)	5 (71%)	7
Comunidad Valenciana	23 (66%)	12 (34%)	35	4 (67%)	2 (33%)	6	3 (50%)	3 (50%)	6
Extremadura	10 (50%)	10 (50%)	20	2 (40%)	3 (60%)	5	3 (60%)	2 (40%)	5
Galicia	21 (62%)	13 (38%)	34	4 (57%)	3 (43%)	7	5 (71%)	2 (29%)	7

(continued)

Table 7 (continued)

ELECTIONS 2019									
La Rioja	8 (57%)	6 (43%)	14	1 (14%)	6 (86%)	7	2 (29%)	5 (71%)	7
Madrid	12 (63%)	7 (37%)	19	3 (75%)	1 (25%)	4	2 (67%)	1 (33%)	3
Murcia	8 (50%)	8 (50%)	16	2 (50%)	2 (50%)	4	1 (25%)	3 (75%)	4
Navarra	7 (70%)	3 (30%)	10	3 (75%)	1 (25%)	4	3 (75%)	1 (25%)	4
País Vasco	13 (54%)	11 (46%)	24	2 (33%)	4 (67%)	6			0
Total	**243 (51%)**	**239 (49%)**	**482**	**65 (48%)**	**70 (52%)**	**135**	**57 (45%)**	**71 (55%)**	**128**

Source Compilation based on data on the demographic structure of the judicial career in statistical information from the Judiciary (Available at https://www.poderjudicial.es/cgpj/es/Temas/Estadistica-Judicial/Estudios-e-Informes/Estructura-demografica-de-la-Carrera-Judicial/)

positions. Although the number of successful applications appears to be gender-balanced, there is a notable pattern of under-representation of women in tenured positions. Gender differences are marked in the higher courts, i.e., the Supreme Court and the National High Court. The High Courts of Justice in some autonomous communities show, in the results of administrative elections, a greater gender parity. However, even though the number of admitted applications varies, the presence of women in the incumbent positions is not equal.

The data in the table above underline that, despite a relatively equal number of successful applications between genders, notable differences persist in the representation of women in administrative positions. These disparities, which may vary between different jurisdictions, point to a challenge regarding gender equity in the judicial career field.

Table 8 provides a comprehensive analysis of the distribution of judges and magistrates according to their administrative status in the years 2023 and 2006. From a critical gender perspective, this data sheds light on the dynamics of gender equity and inequality within the judicial system. One of the most significant figures in this table is the number of voluntary leaves of absence due to paternity or maternity, reflecting a very significant gender divide, as for 2006 represented 100% of women, and almost twenty years later, has decreased just a 3.36%, which means that man judges do not exert their right for paternity leaves in 95% during 2023.

The category "Seconded"[34] shows an increase in both total and representation of women in 2023 compared to 2006. This increase could suggest a growing recognition of women's capabilities in secondment roles. However, it is essential to examine the criteria for secondment in depth to ensure that women have equal opportunities and do not face systemic barriers. In contrast, the drastic decrease in the total number of judges and magistrates "On secondment" in 2023 is a cause for concern, particularly given the sharp decline in the presence of women in this category. This raises questions about the reasons behind this decline and whether there are factors that disproportionately affect women in terms of secondment.

The emergence of "In Court Dean"[35] judges is an encouraging development, with a notable increase in their number in 2023, including a representation of women. However, the fact that the overall number of women in this category remains low highlights the need to continue to advocate for equal opportunities and the removal of obstacles to the advancement of women in leadership positions.

[34] The territorial assignment judge is appointed to carry out judicial work in vacant positions as a reinforcement or substitution in response to the need to expedite justice. They are appointed by the president of the High Court of Justice (Article 347 bis of the Organic Law of the Judiciary).

[35] The Dean judge is a figure that appears in those localities where there is more than one single-person court. He or she is a primus inter pares who assumes the functions of organising the different courts in matters such as ensuring the proper functioning of the on-call service, convening the Judges' Meetings, overseeing the correct use of the judicial premises or the distribution of cases (Articles 166, 167 and 168 of the Organic Law of the Judiciary).

Table 8 Judges and magistrates by administrative situation

	2006		2023	
	Women	Total	Women	Total
Seconded (adscritos)	2 (25%)	8	11(57,89%)	19
On secondment (en Comisi6n de Servicios)	35 (28%)	121	-	-
In the Dean's Court (en Juzgado-Decano)	0	0	4 (36,36%)	11
With permanent position	1856 (45,89%)	4044	2930 (56,16%)	5217
Total Actives	**1936 (45,21%)**	**4282**	**3003 (56,20%)**	**5343**
On Voluntary Leave of Absence for private interests	0%	1	0	2
With Provisional Suspension	0%	2	-	-
In Special Services + S.E. 351	40 (30,53%)	131	57 (44,53%)	128
Family Care Leave	1 **(100%)**	1	0 (0,0%)	0
Voluntary Parental Leave	16 (**100%**)	**16**	17 **(94,44%)**	18
Total non actives	**57 (37,5%)**	**152**	**74 (49,33%)**	**150**

Source Compilation from The Instituto de la Mujer y para la Igualdad de Oportunidades based on data from the Ministry of Justice and the General Council of the Judiciary

Similarly, in the analysis of non-active status, there is an overall increase in the number of judges and magistrates on suspension and leave in 2023 compared to 2006. Women constitute the majority in these situations, indicating that they face unique challenges in reconciling work and family life, as pointed out in the literature analyzed.

Furthermore, the data show that in the administration of justice, it is also women who are the majority of those who request voluntary leave for childcare, reproducing traditional gender roles in this sphere as well, with the differential consequences that this can have for men and women in terms of their professional projection and careers.

In conclusion, these data underline the persistent gender inequality in the judiciary, with progress in some areas but challenges in the face of inequality in others.

7 Conclusions

The situation of women in employment within the judiciary in Spain has been the subject of analysis and debate in the context of gender equality and employment equity. Although significant progress has been made in recent decades, challenges and disparities affecting women's participation and progress persist.

In terms of access to employment in the judiciary, there has been an increase in the presence of women in judicial careers. However, a gender gap persists at the higher levels of the judiciary, where women are under-represented. This under-representation may be due to several factors, such as cultural barriers, entrenched gender stereotypes, difficulties in reconciling work and family life, as well as the existence of selection and promotion practices that may not be entirely gender-neutral.

The lack of gender balance in the judiciary is also reflected in governance and decision-making bodies. The general councils of the judiciary and collegiate bodies have an unequal representation, with a low presence of women in key positions of influence and decision-making. Regarding women's participation in the judiciary, the Spanish case data have shown a more significant presence in the lower levels of the judicial career, such as the courts of first instance and examining magistrates. However, as one moves up the judicial hierarchy, the presence of women decreases notably. For example, in higher bodies, such as the Supreme Court or the National High Court, the representation of women is significantly lower.

In terms of pay and linked to the lower positions for women we have analysed, women in the judiciary also face pay disparities. Although equal pay is a legally established principle, evidence indicates that women in judicial positions may receive lower salaries than their male counterparts, even considering factors such as experience and seniority, given the inequalities in the positions described in this chapter.

In response to these challenges, measures have been implemented to promote gender equality in the judiciary in Spain. These measures include training and awareness-raising programs, the promotion of gender quotas in the selection and promotion of male and female judges, and the adoption of measures to reconcile work and family life.

However, this paper also highlights the need to broaden the understanding of gender balance in the judiciary beyond employment and career advancement. Gender balance in the judiciary must not be understood solely in terms of numerical representation, but also in terms of its impact on the quality of justice. The absence of gender-sensitive workplace policies and cultures may negatively affect not only women's career paths but also judicial reasoning and outcomes. Therefore, promoting gender competence is essential not only for achieving equal career opportunities but also for enhancing the legitimacy and fairness of judicial decision-making.

It is essential to continue working to ensure equal opportunities for women in the judiciary, addressing remaining structural and cultural barriers, raising awareness and changing attitudes, and strengthening gender equality policies at all levels of the judiciary. Only through a comprehensive and continuous approach can full gender equality in employment within the judiciary in Spain be achieved.

Finally, from a research perspective, it is necessary to deepen qualitative studies that enrich the cold quantitative data, which do not reflect the motivations, interpretations, and analyses that the women themselves make of their professional and personal experience in the judiciary. Analyzing their perceptions surely could provide richer details and critical explanations of these disparities.

References

Acker J (2006) Inequality regimes: gender, class, and race in organizations. Gender Soc 20(4):441–464. https://doi.org/10.1177/0891243206289499

Acker, J. (2012). Gendered organizations and intersectionality: problems and possibilities. Equality, Diversity and Inclusion: An International Journal, 31(3):214–224. https://doi.org/10.1108/02610151211209072

Alfama E, Cruells M, De la Fuente M (2015) ¿Qué ha cambiado con esta crisis? El mainstreaming de género en la encrucijada. Investigaciones Feministas Universidad Complutense de Madrid (UCM) 5:69–95. 10.5209/rev_infe.2014.v5.47957Alonso

Alfama Guillén E (2015) Género, poder y Administraciones públicas: sobre la (im)posibilidad del cambio hacia una mayor igualdad. Una revisión de la literatura. Revista Española de Ciencia Política 39:263–287

Álvarez A, Diz Otero I (2022) ¿Nadando contra corriente? Resistencias a la promoción de la conciliación en las universidades españolas. Revista Internacional de Sociología 80(2):e208. https://doi.org/10.3989/ris.2022.80.2.21.01

Asencio M, José M (2003) La Audiencia Nacional: una visión crítica. Documentos de Trabajo, Laboratorio de Alternativas 1–50

Balaguer Callejón F (2000) Poder Judicial y Comunidades Autonómas. Revista de Derecho Político 47:53–67

Bermúdez Figueroa E, Dabetić V, Pastor R, Saeidzadeh Z (2023) Gender and structural inequalities from a socio-legal perspective. In Vujadinović D, Fröhlich M, Giegerich T (eds) Gender-competent legal education. Springer International Publishing, pp 95–142

Bermúdez-Figueroa E, Gallardo R (2021) ¿Dónde están las mujeres en la administración local?: lecciones de un estudio de caso. Editorial UCA

Bermúdez-Figueroa E, Roca B (2022) Gender labor inequalities in the public sector: the interplay between policy and micro-politics. Employee Relat 44(7):96–112

Brescoll V L (2016) Leading with their hearts? how gender stereotypes of emotion lead to biased evaluations of female leaders. Leadersh Q 27(3):415–428

Cabanas G, JM (1991) Las Audiencias Provinciales en la encrucijada, La Ley Revista Jurídica Española de Doctrina, Jurisprudencia Y Bibliografía 4: 1025–1030

Casasola D, José M (2013) La planta judicial española. Estructura y distribución competencial: ¿Hacia el final de una nueva era? ExToikos 12:11–15

Castaño Collado C, Vázquez-Cuperio S (2023) Resistance and counter-resistance to gender equality policies in Spanish universities. Papers 108(2):1–25. https://doi.org/10.5565/rev/papers.3105

Chappell L (2010) Comparative gender and institutions: directions for research. Perspect Politics 8(1):183–189. https://doi.org/10.1017/S1537592709992751
Chappell L, Waylen G (2013) Gender and the hidden life of institutions. Pub Admin 91(3):599–615. https://doi.org/10.1111/j.1467-9299.2012.02104.x
Connell RW, Messerschmidt JW (2005) HEGEMONIC MASCULINITY: rethinking the concept. Gender Soc 19(6):829–859. 10.1177/0891243205278639
Connell R (2006) The experience of gender change in public sector organizations. Gender Work Organ 13(5):435–452. 10.1111/j.1468-0432.2006.00316.x
Feenan (2008) Women judges: gendering judging, justifying diversity. J Law Soc 35(4): 490–519. https://doi.org/10.1111/j.1467-6478.2008.00448.x
Fischbach A, Lichtenthaler PW, Horstmann N (2015) Leadership and gender stereotyping of emotions. J Pers Psychol 14(3):153–162
Gastaldi P, Pezzano S (2021) Juzgar con perspectiva de género. Desigualdades por razón de género como propiedad relevante en la toma de decisiones judiciales. Revista Argumentos 12:36–48
Gastiazoro ME (2008) La concentración de las mujeres en la administración de justicia. Anuario XI del Centro de Investigaciones Jurídicas y Sociales, pp 705–721
Gastiazoro ME, Moguillansky MO (2021) Brechas de género en las designaciones del sistema judicial argentino: análisis de tendencias». Revista Electrónica Instituto de Investigaciones Ambrosio L Gioja 27:275–320. https://ri.conicet.gov.ar/handle/11336/152655 Disponible en
Gelambí Torrell M (2015) Gender mainstreaming in times of austerity. An analysis of the Catalan municipalities». Gestión Y Análisis de Políticas Públicas, Nueva Época 14
Grey R, McLoughlin K, Chappell L (2021) Gender and judging at the international criminal court: lessons from ´feminist judment projects´. Leiden J Int Law 34:247–264
Hunter R (2002) Talking up equality: women barristers and the denial of discrimination. Feminist Legal Stud 10:113–120
Lombardo E, Bustelo M (2021) Sexual and sexist harassment in Spanish Universities: policy implementation and resistance agains gender equality measures. J Gender Stud 31(1):8–22. https://doi.org/10.1080/09589236.2021.1924643
Lucas Murillo de la Cueva P (2000) El poder judicial en el Estado Autonómico, UNED. Teoría Y Realidad Constitucional 5:89–113
Lucas Murillo de la Cueva P (2022) Los Tribunales Superiores de Justicia. Balance de tres décadas. Revista D'estudis Autonòmics I Federals 35:91–113
Nieto A (2007) La Administración de Justicia y el Poder Judicial. Revista de Administración Pública 174:31–47
Pastor Yuste R, Bermúdez Figueroa E (2022) El género en los estudios jurídicos y actitudes hacia el género del profesorado. Del Mar M, et aled Innovación Docente e Investigación en Ciencias Sociales, Económicas y Jurídicas: nuevos Enfoques en la Metodología Docente, Dykinson. 755–768
Porras R, José M (2003) Unidad Jurisdiccional y Autonomía Política. La Política Constitucional de los Tribunales Superiores de Justicia. Revista Español de Derecho Constitucional 67:69–87
Saiz Garitaonandia A (2009) La Administración de Justicia en las Comunidades Autónomas. Situación actual y perspectivas de reforma. Tirant Lo Blanch, Valencia
Verge Mestre T (2008) Cuotas voluntarias y legales en España. La paridad a examen. Revista Española de Investigaciones Sociológicas 123:123–150. https://doi.org/10.2307/40184895
Verge Mestre T (2021) Resistencia a las políticas de igualdad y contra-resistencia feminista: un análisis discursivo del ámbito universitario. Discurso Y Sociedad 15(3):542–568
Zaikosky Biscay D, Betsabé Policastro M (eds) (2023) Desigualdades de género en el campo jurídico: trabajo, familias, cuidados y violencias. Prohistoria Ediciones

Eva Bermúdez-Figueroa is Ph.D. in Sociology, Master in Gender, Identity and Citizenship, lecturer at the University of Cadiz, member of the Board in Research Network RN14 for research on gender relations in the labour market and the welfare state of the European Sociology Association (ESA) and Member of the Board in Andalusian Sociological Association. She is member of the research group Transformations and Conflicts in Contemporary Societies (SEJ 657). Her research focuses on women and collective action, together with women's work and labour relations. She developed research stays at Queen Mary University of London, at the Research Centre of Equality and Diversity, and at the European Work and Employment Research Centre (EWERC), in university of Manchester. She has been Principal Researcher in the project "The participation of women in the trade union movement (1960–2017)" and "The under-representation of women in the Administration". She is author of scientific articles in journals such as International Migration, Employee Relations, Journal of International Womens' Studies, International Labour and Working-Class History, Labor History, and Spanish journals as Sociología del Trabajo and Cuadernos de Relaciones Laborales.

Raquel Pastor Yuste is Ph.D. in Sociology, lecturer at the University of Cadiz, member of the Research Group Labour, Politics and Gender (SEJ-545), of the Permanent Group Gender and Politics of the Spanish Association of Political Science and of the Andalusian Association of Sociology. Her line of research focuses on issues related to politics from a gender perspective. She stayed as reseacher at the Universitat Pompeu Fabra in Barcelona, the University of Valladolid, Birbeck College, London and the University of Ottawa, Canada. She has participated in research projects dedicated to the analysis of the gender dimension of sport; the style and symbolic impact of the political representation of women; the socio-legal and criminological dimension of paedophilia; the interdisciplinary analysis of homicides and murders committed and prosecuted in Spain; and the determinants of the life itineraries of unaccompanied migrant children. (Co)author of scientific articles in journals such as: Empiria Revista de Metodología de las Ciencias Sociales, Revista Española de Ciencia Política, Política y Sociedad, Journal of Women, Politics and Policy, Feminist Media Studies.

Gender Representation in the Brazilian Judiciary: Reflections Upon a Case Study of the Right to Abortion

Luana Mathias Souto and Jessica Holl

Abstract This study aims to debate gender issues in the Brazilian judiciary system through a case study of the controversial decision made by Judge Joana Ribeiro Zimmer in 2022. In her decision, she denied the right to abortion to an 11-year-old girl who had experienced rape. This decision, besides being contrary to Brazilian legislation which allows abortion for rape victims and contrary to international human rights norms to which the Brazilian state is bound, also exposes the socio-economic implications of no gender-sensitive decisions from the Brazilian judiciary. Moreover, the case led to major social repercussions, including demonstrations from religious groups aiming at the continuation of the pregnancy of the 11-year-old girl. Starting from this case study, we intend to demonstrate why having more women in decision-making places sometimes does not promote gender equality, even when gender parity is on the agenda for these places. The theories of intersectionality and representation, as well as analyses provided by scholars on the Brazilian socio-economic background will assist in the debate. The current political polarization in the country, as well as the rise of a religious right in the public debate, are key factors here, considering the patriarchal element in Brazilian politics of 'us and them'. Therefore, this study discusses how the decision cannot be considered an isolated case but has to be understood within the broader current Brazilian social-legal context.

L. Mathias Souto (✉)
Universitat Oberta de Catalunya, Barcelona, Spain
e-mail: luana.mathias.souto@gmail.com

J. Holl (✉)
Erfurt University, Erfurt, Germany
e-mail: jessica.holl@uni-erfurt.de

© The Author(s), under exclusive license to Springer Nature Switzerland AG 2025

S. Baer et al. (eds.), *The Gender and the Judiciary*, Gender Perspectives in Law 7,
https://doi.org/10.1007/978-3-032-06885-9_9

1 Introduction

Recently, the importance of women occupying public spaces and how representation constitutes an element of justice has been the focus of frequent debate.[1] However, representation is often not enough to overcome injustices, even those injustices based on gender issues. In this sense, the paper starts from the notion that representation—in the case discussed here, women's representation—is a necessary element to achieve justice, yet it is not enough. Not having any women, or too few, in the public space is a clearly unjust scenario. However, after, or while, having women in spaces like the judiciary and parliament, it is also necessary to discuss other social factors that may surround their decision-making.

In order to illustrate this argument, we present a case study related to the right to abortion in Brazil. It shows how interpretations of legal documents are frequently developed in disregard of women's rights,[2] even when a more gender-friendly interpretation of norms is available. Notably, this can happen even when there are women as judges and prosecutors. Nonetheless, it is important to locate such cases within a broader scenario, in which reproductive rights are being systematically contested, often in the context of an illiberal wave accompanied by conservative and religious arguments. In that sense, theories about intersectionality and representation will be applied to the case study to explain why women's representation alone is incapable of guaranteeing pro-gender-sensitive decisions in the following sense:

In 2022, Judge Joana Ribeiro Zimmer from the 1ª Civil District Court of Tijucas/Santa Catarina-Brazil denied the right to a humanitarian abortion for an eleven-year-old girl. The girl was systematically raped by her uncle. When the girl went to the hospital for an abortion procedure with 22nd week of pregnancy, the hospital refused to take on the procedure. Because of it, it was requested a judicial authorization which according Brazilian legislation should not be demanded. Therefore, even a female judge with descriptive representation decided against the right for a humanitarian abortion. Hence, based on the framework offered by the mentioned theories and the considerations on the right to abortion in the country, the paper argues that racial and socioeconomic inequalities are also central to the outcome of such claims in Brazil. Therefore, it argues for the importance of a more diverse judicial system in order to achieve decisions that promote gender rights.

After describing the legal grounds of the right to abortion in Brazil in Sect. 2, we will briefly contextualize the disputes around this topic in the 2020s. Based on this, we present the case involving Judge Joana Ribeiro Zimmer, an 11-years-old child and the right to abortion of rape victims in Sect. 4, with four focus points. These are the challenges in female representation in decision-making places and gender equality promotion; the intersectionality default of judicial representation in

[1] Fraser (2010) and Holl (2023). On representation, see Pitkin (1985) and Phillips (1998).

[2] Barak-Erez (2012), p. 85.

Brazil; the patriarchal element in Brazilian politics of 'us and them'; and the Brazilian illiberal agenda against reproductive rights. In Sect. 5, we then conclude with some considerations indicating why the reflections on such a case are relevant beyond the Brazilian context.

2 Right to Abortion in Brazil

In Brazil, there is no comprehensive right to abortion. Abortion is considered a crime under articles 124 to 126 of the Brazilian Criminal Code (CP). The only exceptions are when it is necessary to save the pregnant life, i.e. therapeutic abortion (article 128, I, CP); in case of rape, i.e. humanitarian abortion (article 128, II, CP), and in case of an anencephalous fetus, the last one based on the Brazilian Supreme Court (STF) decision on the Action Against Violating a Constitutional Fundamental Right n. 54 (ADPF 54). Therefore, abortion is only legally possible in Brazil in cases when the pregnancy presents a danger to the life of the mother, in cases of rape and when the fetus is anencephalic. However, it is important to highlight that in those situations, the mother has the right to an abortion, and this does not allow for discretionary decisions.

Moreover, it is important to highlight that any further restriction on the right to abortion in Brazil would violate the understanding of international human rights bodies, to which the country is bound through international conventions. Along these lines, the Inter-American Commission on Human Rights—to whose jurisdiction Brazil is bound—in its report *Violencia y discriminación contra mujeres, niñas y adolescentes,*[3] highlighted that sexual and reproductive rights include the right to equality and non-discrimination, life, personal integrity, health, dignity and access to information, among others. Based on these rights, the fundamental obligation of states includes guaranteeing prompt and adequate access to health services that only target the needs of women and girls, based on their gender and reproductive function, free from all forms of discrimination and violence, following existing international commitments concerning gender inequality. Therefore, the right to abortion in case of rape and when the life of the mother is threatened could also be understood under the umbrella of access to health services.

It should also be noted that the Inter-American Commission on Human Rights[4] reiterates the negative impact of laws that criminalize abortion on the rights to life, personal integrity, health, and the right of women to live free from violence and discrimination in cases of health risk and non-viability of the fetus and pregnancies resulting from sexual violence or incest. These provisions impose a disproportionate burden on the exercise of the rights of women and girls, creating an environment conducive to unsafe abortions. In this regard, the Commission

[3] CIDH—Comisión Interamericana de Derechos Humanos (2019).

[4] CIDH—Comisión Interamericana de Derechos Humanos (2019).

warns that the absolute criminalization of abortion (or the creation of barriers that prevent safe access to the procedure) imposes a disproportionate burden on the exercise of women's rights and is, therefore, contrary to the international obligations of States to respect, protect and guarantee women's rights to life, health, and integrity. Again, according to this understanding of the IACHR, the cases when abortion is legal in Brazil constitute the very minimum and could not be further restrained.

Moreover, the IACHR has received constant information about the direct consequences of the criminalization of abortion in all circumstances and its link to maternal morbidity and mortality figures. Given the absence of legal, safe, and timely options, many women subject themselves to dangerous and even deadly practices. They refrain or are discouraged from seeking medical services and experience obstetric emergencies without the necessary medical care. Finally, when they are forced to continue with the pregnancy, they are subjected to prolonged and excessive physical and psychological suffering. This trend shows, once more, the importance of assuring access to abortion in the three cases when it is legal in Brazil. Along these lines, not granting this access would be incompatible with the understanding of the Inter-American Court and would lead to more women and girls risking their lives while attempting abortion through other means.

Going beyond the regional human rights system, the Convention on the Elimination of All Forms of Discrimination against Women[5] also provides that state parties, in which Brazil is included, shall take all appropriate measures to eliminate discrimination against women in the sphere of health care to ensure, on an equal basis between men and women, access to medical services, including those relating to family planning (art. 12 para. 1).

In particular, states must ensure, based on equality between men and women, the same rights to decide freely and responsibly on the number and spacing of their children and to have access to information, education, and the means to enable them to exercise these rights, under art. 16 of the Convention. As stated before, the right to abortion in cases of rape can be understood as access to means that enable women and girls to decide on the number of children. Considering that if abortion is denied in this case, they would be forced into a pregnancy that was never planned. Once more, the right to abortion in cases when the life of the mother is threatened can be understood as access to health.

The Human Rights Committee's General Comment No. 36 (2018) on art. 6[6] of the International Covenant on Civil and Political Rights also deserves special attention. According to the Committee, state parties should provide safe access to abortion to protect the life and health of pregnant women. State parties should also provide such access in situations where carrying the pregnancy to term would cause severe pain or suffering to the woman, in particular, where the pregnancy is the result of rape or incest or the fetus has a serious abnormality. Furthermore, the

[5] CEDAW—Convention on the Elimination of All Forms of Discrimination against Women (1980).

[6] OHCHR—Office of the High Commissioner on Human Rights (2019).

Human Rights Committee also recognized that imposing a duty on doctors and other health officials to report cases of women who have undergone abortions does not respect the principle of non-discrimination. These provisions highlight, once more, now based on soft law mechanisms, that the cases in which abortion is legal in Brazil could not be restricted.

All those international norms (in the form of conventions and soft law) should also be considered when deciding upon the right to abortion in Brazil. Based on those norms, it is even possible to defend a more comprehensive right to abortion in the country than the one based strictly on the national criminal code and jurisprudence. However, it is highly difficult to justify, based on international norms, a restriction on the currently applicable standards according to Brazilian laws. That means that there is no legal argument capable of justifying, in Brazil, the denial of abortion in cases of rape and when the life of the mother is in danger because of the pregnancy. Furthermore, the cases in which abortion is legal in Brazil represent the very minimum in terms of protection of women's rights. So, any restrictions on them would lead to a violation of international obligations that bind Brazil. Therefore, attempts to restrict the right to abortion through the judiciary cannot be seen as a misinterpretation but must be understood as a clear choice to do so, violating a series of existing norms.

It is central to highlight that abortion is a practice that is pursued by Brazilian women regardless of such prohibitions, especially in very sensible cases when the woman is the victim of rape or when her life is threatened because of the pregnancy. Therefore, norms may just limit the access of more vulnerable women to safe abortion. According to The National Abortion Survey (PNA) 2021, "evidence shows that abortion remains a common event in women's lives and a large-scale public health issue in Brazil. A linear extrapolation from PNA 2021 data estimates that nearly one in every seven women (13%) has interrupted a pregnancy by the age of 40."[7] The data also indicates that criminalizing abortion in Brazil has socioeconomic and racialized impacts. "Among those who have had an abortion, more than ⅕ (21%) have had two or more abortions (67% had the last abortion between 20–39 years old; 74% among Black women (. . .)".[8]

Along those lines, socioeconomic and racial vulnerabilities also affect access to a safe abortion choice in Brazil, where middle- and high-income women have access to medical abortions and in-clinic abortion care, while on the other hand, black and poor women are part of a "sub-group of women who face heightened vulnerability in their reproductive lives and are likely exposed to increased negative health outcomes",[9] which sometimes can result in their death. This reflection is important for the following case study because there might also be a class cut-off regarding abortion cases that are judicialized, especially considering that higher classes would probably have access to in-clinic abortion care despite de discussion of

[7] Diniz et al. (2023), p.1605.

[8] Diniz et al. (2023), p. 1602.

[9] Diniz et al. (2023)., p. 1603.

whether it is legal or not. Moreover, guaranteeing the right to abortion also protects girls' childhood "since this population is especially vulnerable to the effects of criminalization on abortion needs"[10] and represents more than half (52%) of the women interviewed who had their first abortion between 19 and younger.

Having this panorama of the right to abortion in Brazil is also relevant to introduce the discussion on how such a right has been at the center of political disputes in the country. Along those lines, in the following section, the paper presents how, during Bolsonaro's government in Brazil, there were systematic attempts to restrict access to abortion, going against all international norms on the matter.

3 The Dispute on the Right to Abortion in Brazil

Before discussing the case involving Judge Zimmer and the 11-year-old child, it is important to contextualize the current dispute regarding the right to abortion in Brazil. The debate on refraining from the right to abortion gained special prominence during Bolsonaro's government 2019 until 2022. Especially, there were the actions of the by-then Minister of Women, Family, and Human Rights, Damares Alves, when another case of a child trying to have access to abortion was broadly publicized. This occurred in August 2020. Therefore, this part of the text aims to present a narrative of the context that surrounded the decision of Judge Zimmer (that will be presented and analyzed in the next topic).

It came to the news that a ten-year-old girl had been systematically had been raped by an uncle by an uncle for four years leading to a pregnancy. The pregnancy was discovered when the girl was taken to the hospital with stomach discomfort and abdominal pain. According to the doctors, the child had a swollen belly and, after tests, it was found that she was 22 weeks pregnant. After that, the abortion was authorized by the courts despite the third month of pregnancy, as it would be a risk to the life of the "mother".

Nonetheless, the information was disclosed, violating the rights of the child, and religious demonstrators protested outside the hospital where the procedure was to be carried out. The demonstration, organized by a group opposed to abortion, began after right-wing extremist Sara Giromini posted the name of the child and the hospital on social media. Eventually, the child could not have the abortion procedures in that hospital because it refused to carry it on, stating it did not have the necessary protocols for an abortion after the third month of pregnancy.[11]

After the denial of the hospital, the child had to go to another state to have her right to abortion assured. Moreover, with the repercussions of the case and after having their personal data exposed on the internet, the girl's family agreed to the

[10] Diniz et al. (2023), p. 1605.

[11] Estado de Minas (2020).

Support and Protection Program for Witnesses, Victims, and Families of Victims of Violence (Provita), offered by the state government to change their identity and address.[12]

What later came to public knowledge was how Minister Alves acted in trying to prevent the abortion. On her social media account, the Minister mentioned she would follow the case closely, yet did not disclose she would try to convince the 10-year-old girl to continue a pregnancy.[13] However, the Minister sent officials to the girl's city to try to convince the guardianship counselors to prevent the abortion and convince the girl to continue the pregnancy. They used religious arguments as there was no legal basis to prevent abortion. They also offered material benefits, such as a better infrastructure to work, to the guardianship counselors.

In that same month, the Ministry of Health issued Ordinance 2.282,[14] which introduced new and restrictive rules for performing legal abortion in the units of the Unified Health System (SUS). Notification to the police authority would be mandatory for the doctor, other health professionals, or those responsible for the health facility that received the patient in cases where there is evidence or confirmation of the crime of rape. Based on the mere assumption, the professionals must also preserve possible material evidence of the crime of rape to be immediately delivered to the police, such as fragments of embryo or foetus in order to perform genetic comparisons that may lead to the identification of the respective perpetrator of the crime, regardless of the woman's consent.

Thus, the Procedure of Justification and Authorization of Interruption of Pregnancy, necessary for the procedure of legal abortion, would consist of four stages, which would prolong the time needed to address the vulnerability of the woman. The demand was to first draw up a Term of Circumstantiated Report by health professionals (including place, day and approximate time of the fact, type and form of violence, description of the agents of the conduct and identification of witnesses); to then provide a detailed report by the attending physician after a detailed anamnesis, general physical examination, gynaecological examination, evaluation of the ultrasonography report and other complementary examinations; then a signature of a Term of Responsibility that would contain an express warning about the foreseen crimes of false identity (art. 299 CP) and abortion (art. 124 CP), in case the woman would not be a victim of rape; and finally the signature of the Free and Informed Consent Term that would need to contain the possible discomforts and risks to health, the procedures that would be adopted when the medical intervention is performed, the form of accompaniment and assistance, as well as the responsible professionals and the guarantee of secrecy that assures privacy regarding the confidential data involved—that could be shared in case of judicial request.

[12] Cultura UOL (2020).

[13] Vila-Nova (2020).

[14] Brazil. Ministério da Saúde (2020).

Furthermore, in the second step of this Procedure, the medical team would have to inform the pregnant woman about the possibility of visualizing the foetus or embryo through ultrasonography, and she would have expressly stated her agreement, to be documented as well.

Just for the record, the constitutionality of Ordinance 2.282 was questioned before the STF by ADI 6.552[15] and ADPF 737. However, in 2021, the lawsuits were extinguished without judgment of merit for procedural issues. In January 2023 (the first month of Lula's government), the Ordinance was revoked[16] as being contrary to the protection of the rights of women and girls.

Before going deeper into the case that this paper intends to discuss, it is important to mark that this Ordinance made it extremely bureaucratic and time-demanding to pursue an abortion—through official means—after an episode of rape. This procedure could discourage women from going to the SUS aiming to undergo abortion procedures, even when they had the right. This new procedure also made an appeal to a certain understanding of morality when it forced women to have information about the possibility of seeing the foetus or embryo. Finally, this procedure would also revictimize women and girls who were already in a very vulnerable situation. This conceptualization supports that the case study was encompassed in a broader socio-political dispute. A scenario of growing pressure against the three hypotheses in which abortion is legal in Brazil, which are consequently against the norms previously presented in part 2.

4 Case Study: A Controversial Judicial Decision Denying Humanitarian Abortion to an 11-Year-Old Girl in Brazil: From Gender Equality to the Illiberal Agenda

It is in this context that the case evolved that is discussed in this paper. It is the controversial decision by Judge Zimmer who denied the right for a humanitarian abortion to an 11-year-old child. Notwithstanding many decisions by male judges that are highly problematic,[17] this will be used to explain the complex participation of the Brazilian Judiciary in anti-democratic and non-gender-sensitive decisions that impact in country's gender equality achievements.

The case happened in the Brazilian state of Santa Catarina. There, the child, systematically raped by her uncle, was taken to a hospital by her mother to undergo an abortion. As the child was in the 22nd week of pregnancy, the hospital refused

[15] Guimarães et al. (2022).

[16] g1 (2023).

[17] As the decision on the case of the victim of the Brazilian Dictatorship Inês Etienne also illustrates, the lack of a gender mainstream perspective is a widespread problem within the Brazilian judiciary. For a deeper analysis on this case and the need of a gender mainstreamed perspeective, see Gonçalves and Holl (2019).

to perform the procedure, which, as exposed, should not demand judicial authorization. According to the medical reports, the pregnancy represented a risk to the life of the so-called "mother". As exposed, the case was then taken to court. There the behavior of Judge Zimmer, from the 1ª Civil District Court of Tijucas/Santa Catarina, caught public attention.

A few days after the mother and the girl tried to have access to the abortion procedures in the hospital, the public prosecutor, Mirela Dutra Alberton, filed an action asking for the girl to be placed in institutional care, where she should "remain until it is verified that she is no longer at risk [of sexual violence] and can return to her natural family".[18] The prosecutor also recognizes that the pregnancy is high-risk: "Obviously, a child at such a young age (10 years old) does not have a biological structure in a stage of formation suitable for pregnancy".[19] When authorizing the protective measure, the judge focused especially on the health of the fetus. According to her, "this situation must be assessed as a way not only to protect her [the girl] but also to protect the unborn baby if extrauterine life is viable".[20]

So, the child was taken to a shelter away from her family. This should have been a measure to assure the girl would no longer be the victim of sexual violence. However, keeping her in there was not to preserve her health and integrity. According to the Judge, "The fact is that, from now on, the risk is that the mother will carry out some procedure to cause the baby's death".[21] So, along the proceeding, the argument changed and even considering that the girl would be safe in her house, she was kept in the shelter in order to avoid any attempt to undergo an abortion procedure.

During the hearings, the situation got even more problematic. Judge Zimmer asked, "Can you bear to stay a little longer?",[22] referring to the child maintaining the pregnancy. The prosecutor Alberton went further: "We would keep your belly for another week or two because for it to have a chance of surviving longer, it needs to take the medication for the lungs to form completely". She continued arguing that the 22nd-week fetus was a baby "(. . .) he's already a child—instead of taking him out of your belly and watching him die in agony, that's what happens because Brazil doesn't agree with euthanasia, Brazil doesn't have it (. . .) He's going to be born crying, there's no [inaudible] medicine for him to die".[23]

The child also had to explain her expectations of the baby and whether she wanted to see the birth. Although the response was "no" to those questions, the Judge told the girl that she could choose the baby's name or deliver her/him for adoption. In the same sense, the Judge informed the girl that an abortion after the 22nd week of pregnancy would not be allowed, referring to the Ordinance n. 2.282/2020, mentioned above.

---

[18] This and all following quotes from Guimarães et al. (2022).

[19] Guimarães et al. (2022).

[20] Guimarães et al. (2022).

[21] Guimarães et al. (2022).

[22] Guimarães et al. (2022).

[23] Guimarães et al. (2022).

All this information came to the public's knowledge when an anonymous source leaked a video to the press.[24] In Brazil, a legal procedure involving infants is a closed proceeding. But in this case, it seemed that disclosure of the hearing was the only measure to protect the child and expose the institutional violence against her. As said, Brazilian legislation gives the right to abortion to rape victims. However, the judge denied her this right to a humanitarian abortion in a decision that must thus be deemed illegal.

It is also worth mentioning that, in 2022, Judge Zimmer was promoted, which allegedly had no connection with the above-mentioned case.[25] However, in 2023, the Brazilian National Council of Justice (CNJ) started an investigation of a disciplinary administrative process (PAD n. 0003770–59.2022.2.00.0000) against her for institutional violence.[26] According to article 15-A, §2° of Brazilian law against institutional violence (Law n. 13.869/2019), the re-victimization of victims of violent crimes is considered an aggravating circumstance.

As such, this controversial decision features important elements which can be used to analyze and debate gender issues and the judiciary in Brazil. Thus, this study will outline four focus points to understand this complex phenomenon.

4.1 Challenges of Female Representation in Decision-making Places and Gender Equality Promotion

According to Pitkin, there are four types of political representation: authorized, symbolic, descriptive, and substantive.[27] Even though Pitkin's work is based on political representation, fundamental analyses regarding descriptive and substantive representations are important to understand the challenges of female representation in decision-making places, such as the Brazilian Judiciary system.

From a feminist perspective, descriptive and substantive representation are important to understand why having more female representatives in decision-making sometimes does not mean gender equality, even when gender parity—the equal number of women and men—is important for these spaces. Namely, descriptive representation is based on the idea that the representative possesses the same characteristics and personal background as those they represent. Like a mirror, they are a reflection of who they represent. Based on such a notion, the feminist demand has been to have more women in public spaces. On the other hand, substantive representation is related to the representative´s efforts to advocate the preferences and interests of those they represent.[28] This is not what happened in the case.

[24] Guimarães et al. (2022).

[25] Powell and Mclaughlin (2022).

[26] Agencia Brasil (2023).

[27] Pitkin (1985).

[28] Pitkin (1985).

The eleven-year-old girl had her right to abortion illegally denied by a female Judge. The woman violated the girl´s rights during the hearing, and she was followed by a female prosecutor. Their actions demonstrated why descriptive representation in decision-making places is sometimes not enough to promote gender equality. The failure of descriptive representation as a feminist claim is well-known by feminist political experts. This is why they "gradually shifted from a focus on descriptive representation (counting the numbers of women present) to considerations of substantive representation".[29] Therefore, the claim for a substantive representation in the Brazilian judiciary is the key to effectively safeguarding female rights through pro-gender sensitive judicial decisions.

Also, they were responsible for revictimizing this little girl when they should have protected her by acting under the law, which guarantees humanitarian abortion. Instead, they decided to violate the legislation and the girl's fundamental rights based on their socioeconomic biases of who (or which woman) deserves to be legally protected. They did not see this girl as a reflection of them because, for them, she was not like 'them'.[30] Their socioeconomic biases demonstrated the importance of debating intersectionality[31] in the Brazilian judiciary system.

4.2 *The Intersectionality Default of Judicial Representation in Brazil*

In Brazil, to become a judge "in theory, [there is] no class or economic barriers bar the way to a judgeship".[32] Access to a Brazilian judicial career requires passing oral and written competitive public examinations that could be made a "(. . .) few years after graduating from law school (. . .) Thus, theoretically, a broad social and political spectrum with young men from all levels of society should be represented on the bench".[33]

However, the reality is far from the theoretical diversity spectrum of young (female) lawyers in Brazil. The Brazilian judiciary is, in fact, male-dominant. Women represent less than half of their members and the majority comes from Brazilian elites, thus is there are women, these are white women from well-established socioeconomic backgrounds.[34] Studying for competitive public examinations requires years of effort and commitment that cannot be afforded by the majority of the Brazilian population, even by those who had the privilege of achieving a law degree.

---

[29] Childs and Lovenduski (2013), p. 4.

[30] Stanley (2018).

[31] Crenshaw (1989) and Davis (2016).

[32] Scheman (1962), p. 1.

[33] Scheman (1962), p. 1.

[34] Bonelli and Oliveira (2023) p. 1359.

Unfortunately, non-diversity processes are perpetuated "throughout their career, they create hierarchies, shaped in terms of privileged versus undervalued duties, of distinctions and notions of excellence versus the common, the average.[35]" Throughout this context, the judiciary coexists with gender, racial, and socio-economic stereotypes that will affect court decisions and thus, people's achievement of their rights. As an example, they created "the 'panties quota' (Uliano n.d.), a derogatory way of referring to the discussion of measures which guarantee the inclusion of women on promotion lists, as well as their presence in other positions of professional power.[36]". Furthermore, racial discrimination processes are internalized by black female judge's "such as the idea that a woman judge's curly hair does not fit her rank and position.[37]" For this reason, an intersectional dimension of representation could not be enough to guarantee black female rights when whiteness ideologies shape their representatives.

Since the second feminist wave, intersectionality has been a key point of debate regarding political representation. "Which women are represented?"[38] is one of the main questions that assisted in the feminist shift to substantive representation. The struggle between gender and race was the first to be denounced during the suffragist movement in the USA,[39] and the question of Sojourner Truth, now, echoed in the eleven-year-old girl's claim: "Ain't I am a Woman?"

As stated above, the majority of women in Brazil who had a non-safe abortion are black and poor. They also are underrepresented in the judiciary: "Black female judges represented 4% of the total judges entering the career until 1999, and 5% of those who joined the bench after the implementation of affirmative action policy."[40] In addition, the intersectionality default of representation in the Brazilian judiciary is also framed by the country's socioeconomic inequality, also building a Brazilian judicial bias which eventually results in rights violations and a lack of people's trustworthiness of the Brazilian judiciary system. "Empirical evidence corroborates the thesis judges do not 'simply' interpret the law, as legalists would argue. Internal factors—such as one's ideology—and external factors—such as pressures from public opinion—strongly impact their decisions".[41]

In the case at hand, Judge Zimmer indeed made a socio-economically and racially biased decision, demonstrating her incapacity of providing an impartial judgment apart from her prejudices, as well as her religious ideologies, as further discussed in the sequence.[42] She was not able to see the little girl as equally worth of justice, and she "simply" interpreted the law of a humanitarian abortion decision

[35] Bonelli and Oliveira (2023) pp. 1371–1372.

[36] Bonelli and Oliveira (2023) p. 1372.

[37] Bonelli and Oliveira (2023) p. 1372.

[38] Childs and Lovenduski (2013), p. 6.

[39] Davis (2016).

[40] Bonelli and Oliveira (2023), p. 1359.

[41] Yeung (2019), p. 5.

[42] Agência Brasil (2023).

the way she did because she only saw the girl's poverty and her color of skin, wrongly assuming she could handle a little bit more of the suffering by bearing a child from abuse. This is a slavery/colonial idea that dehumanized Black and poor women for centuries, and it was naturalized in Brazilian culture. The judge´s biases in re-victimizing the girl who has already been raped further decreased people's trustworthiness of the Brazilian judiciary system to "simply" interpret the law. It exposed the need for intersectional judicial decisions to achieve the equal promotion of gender rights in Brazilian society.

4.3 The Patriarchal Element in Brazilian Politics of 'Us and Them'

Based on what has been called judicial populism theory, it is argued that "the Judicial Branch in Brazil is threatening democratic constitutionalism by ignoring the constitutional text and substituting constitutional rules with personal conceptions of moral and justice."[43] This phenomenon reaches beyond judicial activism practices, including lawfare, to undermine democracy in an erosion process in which the judicial system is included. "In judicial populist decisions, there is less concern about the legal reasoning and the respect for the Constitution and more references to the 'will of people'."[44]

Decisions about the right to abortion for young girls in Brazil led to major political and social repercussions, including demonstrations from religious groups aiming for the continuity of pregnancy. During Bolsonaro's presidency, this kind of anti-abortion campaign became more common, followed by a social-political division of "us" and "them"[45] to undermine gender, racial, and diversity claims. Most of these claims were debated by the judiciary throughout the years and statutes as fundamental rights, especially, as an element of its activist profile.

However, during Bolsonaro's term, they were severely attacked. To pursue his political endeavour to constrain gender, racial, and diversity rights achievement, he also nominee Minister Alves in an "autocratic genderwashing"[46] strategy to refrain, under executive orders, from any progressive agenda on this matter. The gender element in this context was largely used by the Executive power following the idea of the "myths of a patriarchal past"[47] based on "an extreme version of the patriarchal family"[48] in an oppositive discourse between "globalism, liberal

[43] Salgado and Gabardo (2021), p. 732.

[44] Salgado and Gabardo (2021), p. 740.

[45] Stanley (2018).

[46] Bjarnegård and Zetterberg (2022).

[47] This and all following quotes from Stanley (2018).

[48] Stanley (2018).

cosmopolitanism, and respect for 'universal values' such as equality"[49] and the desire to return to "a time of glory of the nation, with wars of conquest led by patriotic generals, its armies filled with its countrymen, non-disabled, loyal warriors whose wives were at home raising the next generation.[50]" In this regard, "any progress for a minority group stokes feelings of victimhood among the dominant population".[51] The dominant group—Brazilian elites—also stands for "law and order politics [with] mass appeal, casting 'us' as lawful citizens and 'them', by contrast, as lawless criminals whose behavior poses an existential threat to the manhood of the nation".[52] All those elements are designed to delegitimize gender and diversity claims, even at institutional levels.

Nonetheless, the central analysis brought to debate in this paper is how the Brazilian judiciary system has been acting "as elite actors that endanger the constitutional system, giving it the characteristics of unstable constitutionalism"[53] and violating fundamental rights. They embraced the "politics of 'us and them'" and the "myths of a patriarchal past" embodied during Bolsonaro's term into the Judiciary system where all the impartial principle that reigns in a judicial decision was replaced by "a sense of panic at the loss of hierarchal status, both for men and for the dominant group's ability to protect its purity (. . .)".[54] For this reason, Judge Zimmer was incapable of "simply" guaranteeing the humanitarian abortion. She is part of the dominant group that acknowledges any progressive gender rights achievement as a threat to their return to the glorious patriarchal past.

This case study highlights the possibility of the Brazilian judiciary becoming the new *locus* where "strategic behaviours evolving Brazilian elites would reinforce the politicization of justice without the need for a constitutionalization movement[55]". However, as broadly recognized, the politicization of justice regarding gender issues is not just a Brazilian problem, as discussed in the last section.

4.4 The Illiberal Agenda Against Reproductive Rights in Brazil

Illiberal political procedures to undermine democratic goals have been developed in countries such as Hungary and Poland, where their "attacks on reproductive rights fill the headlines, as do government-sponsored billboards promoting motherhood and condemning abortion".[56] On this matter, Petö discusses the rise of

[49] Stanley (2018).
[50] Stanley (2018).
[51] Stanley (2018).
[52] Stanley (2018).
[53] Meyer (2018), p. 727.
[54] Stanley (2018).
[55] Meyer (2018), p. 730.
[56] Pető (2022), p. 228.

illiberal tendencies even in liberal democracies considering how "traditional visions of gender relations are a defining feature of what (. . .) [she] sees as the new ideology of 'illiberalism'",[57] disseminated mainly by right-wing parties.

Bogaards and Petö also explain its transnational dimensions. E.g., U.S. anti-abortion activists are heavily investing in spreading their conservative agenda on reproductive rights worldwide as an ante-room for a transnational illiberal war on gender. The result is anti-abortion protests in front of abortion clinics worldwide, and anti-abortion debates in judiciaries where they have the know-how to constrain fundamental rights.[58] The recent overturn of *Roe v. Wade* is a major alert in these regards.[59] The conservative ideologies widespread by Donald Trump during his term remain in the judiciary due to the "nomination of Brett Kavanaugh as a Supreme Court Justice, who has conservative views about abortion and homosexual marriage.[60]" This stresses how powerful anti-gender ideas embodied by right-wing Executive power are. It also highlighted its dissemination into the Judiciary system.

Furthermore, in Brazil, the religious background may be considered a key element in the promotion of an illiberal agenda against reproductive rights[61] based on its capacity for unity and careful selection of "trusted participants based on strong personal connections, along shared values across different religions and continents[62]". The creation of a global network addressed to "the transformation of the language of human rights—from the universal language of freedom into a vocabulary of globalized traditionalism[63]" requires the recruitment of members of the Judiciary system because their decisions can give meaning to fundamental rights. So, the return to the glorious patriarchal past is a vital aspect of judicial participation in this illiberal project to change the meaning of the interpretation of progressive rights.

---

[57] Bogaards and Petö (2022), p. 2.

[58] Whittle (2023).

[59] On 24, June 2022 the US Supreme Court decided in Dobbs v. Jackson Women's Health Organization to overturn Roe v. Wade precedent that guarantees the constitutional right to an abortion in the country. Dobbs v. Jackson Women's Health Organization is a decision based on fetal life and the state's interest in legislating abortion. Jackson Women's Health Organization, an abortion clinic, challenged the Mississippi's Gestational Age Act "in Federal District Court, alleging that it violated this Court's precedents establishing a constitutional right to abortion, in particular Roe v. Wade, 410 U. S. 113, and Planned Parenthood of Southeastern Pa. v. Casey, 505 U. S. 833.

[60] Souto (2020), p. 171.

[61] Uitz (2022).

[62] Uitz (2022).

[63] Uitz (2022).

5 Conclusion

The paper demonstrated, through this case study, that assuming women will always attend to women's claims is an inaccurate common sense. Descriptive representation is a feminist dilemma well-explored in political representation theories that should also be incorporated into female representation in the Judiciary system.

In the Brazilian context, to achieve pro-gender-sensitive decisions, substantive representation must be aligned with intersectionality due to racial and socioeconomic country inequalities. However, based on the case study, the research demonstrated that promoting gender rights through the judiciary could be more complex than advocating for a substantive and intersectional judicial presence. The ongoing process of politicization of justice increased in the last decade because of the country's political polarization as a result of a conservative pathway to overturn gender rights achievements, as demonstrated by Judge Zimmer's decision. This harmful combination between courts and politics in drawing non-democratic and non-egalitarian decisions is, unfortunately, a worldwide phenomenon.

In conclusion, this paper critically explored the case study through a theoretical framework that allowed for a broader understanding of the relevant variables included in the decision-making process beyond solely the gender perspective. Additionally, it highlighted the transnational use of judicial discourses to naturalize the violation of rights worldwide. Along these lines, it demonstrated that reshaping the constitutional and legal meaning as well as juridical interpretations is a powerful resource to undermine gender rights. Finally, therefore, the paper supports the need for more research into these matters, aiming globally a more intersectional judiciaries, more careful of the role of ideologies, religious standards, and political affiliations.

References

Agência Brasil (2023) CNJ investigará juíza que tentou impedir aborto em menina de 11 anos. Agência Brasil June 21

Barak-Erez D (2012) Her-meneutics: feminism and Interpretation. In: Baines B, Barak-Erez D, Kahana T (eds) Feminist Constitutionalism: global Perspectives. Cambridge University Press, New York, pp 85–97

Bjarnegård E, Zetterberg P (2022) How Autocrats Weaponize Women's Rights. J Democracy 33(2):60–75

Bogaards M, Petö A (2022) Gendering De-Democratization: gender and Illiberalism in Post-Communist Europe. Politics Govern 10(4):1–5

Bonelli M, Oliveira F (2023) Changes in gender and race composition of the Brazilian Judiciary Oñati Socio-Legal Series 13(4):1351–1375

Brazil. Ministério da Saúde (2020) Portaria 2.282, de 27 de agosto de 2020

CEDAW. Convention on the Elimination of All Forms of Discrimination against Women (1980) https://www.ohchr.org/sites/default/files/Documents/ProfessionalInterest/cedaw.pdf

Childs, S, Lovenduski, J (2013) Political representation. In: Waylen, Georgina et al. (eds). The Oxford handbook of gender and politics. Oxford: Oxford University Press

CIDH - Comisión Interamericana de Derechos Humanos (2019) Violencia y discriminación contra mujeres, niñas y adolescentes: Buenas práticas y desafíos en América Latina y en el Caribe
Crenshaw K (1989) Demarginalizing the Intersection of Race and Sex: a Black Feminist Critique of Antidiscrimination Doctrine, Feminist Theory and Antiracist Politics. Univ Chicago Legal Forum 8(1):139–167
Cultura UOL (2020) Notícias. Em meio a protestos contra e a favor, menina de 10 anos que engravidou após estupro passa por aborto legal. Cultura UOL, August 17
Davis A (2016) Mulheres, raça e classe. Boitempo, São Paulo
Diniz D, Medeiros M, Madeiro A (2023) National Abortion Survey – brazil, 2021. Ciênc Saúde Coletiva 28(6):1601–1606
Estado de Minas (2020) Menina de 10 anos vai para outro estado após ter aborto negado no Espírito Santo. Estado de Minas, August 16
Fraser N (2010) Scales of Justice: reimagining Political Space in a Globalizing World. Columbia University Press, New York
g1 (2023) Ministério da Saúde revoga portaria sobre aborto e outras medidas contrárias às diretrizes do SUS. g1, January 16
Gonçalves RCP, Holl J (2019) Por que uma Crítica Feminista ao Direito? Reflexões a partir do caso Inês Etienne. In: Bertotti BM, et al. Gênero e resistência, vol 1. memórias do II encontro de pesquisa por/de/sobre mulheres. Editora Fi, Porto Alegre, pp 137–164
Guimarães P, Lara B, Dias T (2022) 'Suportaria ficar mais um pouquinho?' Intercept_Brasil. June 20, online source
Holl J (2023) Mulheres e Participação Política: Análise histórica e contexto atual no Brasil. Conhecimento Editora. Belo Horizonte
Meyer E (2018) Judges and Courts Destabilizing Constitutionalism: the Brazilian Judiciary Branch's Political and Authoritarian Character. German Law J 19(4):727–768
OHCHR - Office of the High Commissioner on Human Rights (2019) General Comment No. 36 on article 6: Right to life
Pető A (2022) Reproductive Rights as Battlefield in the New Cold War: a Historical Comparison of Illiberal Gender Politics Regarding Reproductive Rights in Hungary. In: Scheele A, Roth J, Winkel H (eds) Global Contestations of Gender Rights. Bielefeld University Press, Bielefeld, pp 227–244
Pitkin H (1985) El concepto de representación. Centro de Estudios Constitucionales, Madrid
Phillips A (1998) The Politics of Presence. Clarendon Press, Oxford
Powell M, Mclaughlin C (2022) Female judge who banned 11-year-old rape victim from having an abortion is PROMOTED by legal officials in Brazil. MailOnline, June 22
Salgado ED, Gabardo E (2021) The role of the Judicial Branch in Brazilian rule of law erosion. Revista de Investigações Constitucionais 8(3):731–769
Scheman LR (1962) The social and economic origin of the Brazilian judges. Inter-Am L Rev 4:45
Souto L M (2020) Life-narratives and human rights: Reflection about women's rights and state of exception. Anamorphosis: Revista Internacional de Direito e Literatura. Porto Alegre 6(1):151–175
Stanley J (2018) How fascism works: the politics of us and them. Random House, New York
Uitz R (2022) Illiberals of the World Unite in Budapest https://verfassungsblog.de/illiberals-of-the-world-unite-in-budapest-yet-again/
Vila-Nova C (2020) Ministra Damares Alves agiu para impedir aborto de criança de 10 anos. Folha de São Paulo, September 20
Whittle H (2023) German abortion clinics targeted by US-style protests. DW, April 3
Yeung L (2019) Bias, insecurity and the level of trust in the judiciary: the case of Brazil. J Inst Theor Econ 15(1):163–188 https://doi.org/10.1017/S1744137417000625

Luana Mathias Souto is a Postdoctoral Researcher at the Gender and ICT Research Group at Universitat Oberta de Catalunya (Spain). Principal Investigator of the project "Reproductive Health under Algorithm Surveillance (THELMA)," with a Marie Skłodowska-Curie (MSCA) Postdoctoral Fellowship by Horizon Europe. Doctoral and master's degrees in Law from Pontifícia Universidade Católica de Minas Gerais (Brazil). Formerly Guest Postdoctoral Researcher at the Max Planck Institute in Frankfurt (MPILHLT/2023) and in Hamburg (MPIPriv/2024), and Research Fellow at the Weizenbaum Institute in Berlin (2024). Develop theoretical research in the areas of Gender Studies, Legal Theory, Law and Literature, Human Rights, and Democracy.

Jessica Holl is the Coordinator of the Global Justice Clinic and a Research Fellow at the Assistant Professorship of Public International Law and International Administrative Law, Erfurt University (Germany). Ph.D. candidate in Law at Goethe-Universität Frankfurt am Main (Germany). LLM and Bachelor's Degree in Law from the Federal University of Minas Gerais (UFMG) (Brazil). Researcher at the Center Constituições: Constitutionalism and Comparativism from UFMG (Brazil).

Overcoming Gender Bias in the Justice System's Response to Violence: A Call for Enhanced Academic and Professional Training

Oana Băluță

Abstract The argument of the chapter is that decision making of justice professionals in cases of gender-based violence is shaped by multiple factors; while certain limitations may be inevitable, there are others that are needless and should be overturned to enhance the quality of decision-making. The issue extends beyond mere legislation and the politics of presence; it encompasses the construction of gender within a profession and by justice professionals. This chapter embraces a critical approach of essentialist arguments concerning the feminization of the judiciary and highlights that support for gender equality, and better justice outcomes for women occur under certain conditions. Gender knowledge embedded in the training and education of justice professionals represents an essential condition to deliver justice for victims of gender-based violence or other gender based offences. The chapter underscores that essentialist expectation from women justice professionals may not be the pathways towards delivering gender justice when one accounts for the role of the societal conservative gender regime and the confinements of the profession. The problem appears to be not so much the feminization of the profession, but rather women's inclusion in a domain that reproduces structural gender inequalities in terms of legal education and profession.

I would like to thank the anonymous reviewers for their insightful comments. This chapter would not be the same without their considerate and knowledgeable suggestions.

O. Băluță (✉)
National University of Political Studies and Public Administration, Bucharest, Romania
e-mail: oana.baluta@politice.ro

© The Author(s), under exclusive license to Springer Nature Switzerland AG 2025

S. Baer et al. (eds.), *The Gender and the Judiciary*, Gender Perspectives in Law 7,
https://doi.org/10.1007/978-3-032-06885-9_10

1 Introduction

The Romanian justice system constitutes both a curious and a challenging case due to its notable level of feminization among judges and prosecutors and the controversial decisions made in gender-based violence cases by domestic courts.[1] Research emphasizes improved outcomes for women issues in cases where female legal professionals are involved.[2] In particular, scholars note that "judges, prosecutors, attorneys, and court associates bring not just their academic education, professional experience, legal diligence, and good intentions to their work, but they also bring their values, beliefs, and opinions".[3] While gender equality of the justice system can be evaluated by the descriptive criteria of women's presence as professionals, it is not restricted to it. An analysis of gender equality in the justice system should include a substantive examination of legal decisions, particularly judgments in gender-based violence cases. This examination would aim to identify whether these judgments are influenced by stereotypical beliefs or other factors that could negatively impact gender justice (as I will discuss throughout this chapter).[4]

The argument of the chapter is that decision making of legal professionals in cases of gender-based violence is shaped by multiple factors; while certain limitations may be inevitable, there are others that are needless and should be overturned to enhance the quality of decision-making. The issue extends beyond mere legislation and descriptive representation. As this chapter will explore, it encompasses the construction of gender within a profession and by legal professionals, specifically among judges and prosecutors. By no means do I dispute the importance of descriptive representation. Critical reflections on essentialist expectations grounded in feminization of justice should not be considered a distinct line of reasoning and separate from

[1] The feminization of the justice system is a broader topic in Central and Eastern Europe, see Galligan et al. (2017).

[2] The Report Women Delivering Justice: Contributions, Barriers, and Pathways, 2018, International Development Law Organization, IDLO, 2018, pp. 13–19; Dawuni (2018), Hunter (2015), Halilović and Huhtanen (2014), Boyd et al. (2010) and others.

[3] Halilović and Huhtanen (2014), p. 1, also see Cusak (2014).

[4] Descriptive representation emphasizes the importance of political institutions reflecting the major social characteristics of society, including gender. Substantive representation, on the other hand, focuses on ensuring that the concerns, perspectives, interests, and needs of women are actively considered within political institutions. Feminists advocate for increased women's presence in politics based on several key arguments: achieving justice, fostering symbolic representation, enabling substantive representation, and potentially introducing a different style of political discourse. However, the relationship between descriptive and substantive representation is perhaps the most debated aspect (Childs 2004, 16–17). While the current study's descriptive analysis focuses on the gender composition of the judiciary (judges and prosecutors), a more substantive approach investigates the relationship between gender and the delivery of gender justice.

support for gender balance in the making of judiciary.[5] This chapter embraces a critical approach of essentialist arguments concerning the feminization of the judiciary and highlights that support for gender equality, and better justice outcomes for women occur under certain conditions. Gender knowledge embedded in the training and education of legal professionals represents an essential condition to deliver justice for victims of gender-based violence or other gender based offences. This chapter explores potential constraints faced by legal professionals (among judges and prosecutors) in their decisions concerning gender-based violence with a particular emphasis on gender knowledge and stereotypes. The exploratory research, focused on Romania, aims to enhance comprehension of barriers impeding gender justice in cases of gender-based violence. It also seeks to identify future theoretical and empirical approaches to understand the construction of gender in the judiciary, moving beyond essentialist expectations of women professionals delivering justice and the value-free construction of the profession. The case study draws on a wide range of literature, and it is carried out by both desk research (analysis of previous existing data and of legal education curricula, media articles, case law of domestic and international institutions etc.) and through field research entailing expert interviews. The question it seeks to address is: How do multiple factors influence the decision-making process of legal professionals in cases of gender-based violence, and what specific limitations do they face in their judgments? The chapter begins by presenting the national context of the research, and then it establishes the theoretical framework for the study. It examines the relationship between the feminization of the justice system and the concept of gender knowledge. This is followed by an exploration of how gender stereotypes can influence judicial bias. The chapter then shifts focus to the empirical analysis presenting data, methods, research ethics and the key findings gleaned from the interviews. The analysis concludes by reflecting on the significance of gender knowledge for legal professionals and by suggesting avenues for future research. Here, the focus is not on the feminization of the justice system itself as the problem, but rather on the potential for women's inclusion to occur within a system that perpetuates structural gender inequalities in legal education and practice.

2 Context of the Research

A brief overview of the national context is necessary. Data on tolerance towards gender-based violence and sexual aggression are crucial as they delineate important features of the societal gender regime. According to the 2016 special Eurobarometer on gender-based violence, Romania exhibits the highest tolerance of sexual aggression in the EU.[6] The 2022 Barometer on gender-based violence

[5] See, for example, the case of "Romania's failure to (substantially) respect the CoE's requirements to ensure gender balance in the selection of its ECtHR judge", Epure and Brodeală (2023), https://strasbourgobservers.com/2023/06/30/gender-imbalance-and-the-making-of-the-ecthr-bench-a-critical-discussion-of-romanias-selection-process-for-its-strasbourg-judge/.

[6] https://europa.eu/eurobarometer/surveys/detail/2115.

revealed that stereotypes influence police reactions, justice system processing, and judicial decisions.[7] Examining domestic violence judiciary practices in Romania, Nemeș and Crișan identified victim-blaming stereotypes and inconsistent application of protection orders by courts. Underlying beliefs suggest victims will reconcile or misuse the order.[8] When examining the descriptive representation of judges and prosecutors,[9] we notice a significant presence of women in both professions. Data indicate gender parity among prosecutors, with 51.4% being women and 48.6% men in January 2023.[10]

However, the judiciary exhibits a more pronounced female dominance, with women judges comprising 71.44% compared to 28.56% men in January 2023.[11] An examination of court rulings in gender-based violence cases offer crucial insights into the potential relationship between the feminization of these professions and the delivery of gender-based justice.

In 2019, media investigations[12] by two important media outlets in Romania[13] revealed that national courts often held that minor victims of sexual violence consented to engage in sexual relations leading to more lenient sanctions for the perpetrators. This was generally based on a lack of understanding of consent to sexual relations and attitudes blaming the victims to what had happened to them. This problem persisted despite that these patterns of judicial reasoning had already been sanctioned by European Court of Human Rights (ECtHR, the Court). In the 2016 case of *M.G.C. v. Romania*, the ECtHR ruled that "there has been a violation

---

[7] Băluță and Claudiu (2022), p. 48.

[8] Nemeș, Crișan (2017) pp. 6–7.

[9] While mapping the descriptive representation of judges and prosecutors is valuable, it provides only a limited picture of gender dynamics within the legal profession. This study does not explore the horizontal distribution across different positions within the justice system. For a more comprehensive analysis, see Galligan et al. (2017) who map the representation of women and men in legal professions across the European Union.

[10] The data were communicated by the Superior Council of Magistracy at the request of the author on the basis of Law No. 544/2001 regarding free access to public information, with subsequent amendments and completions. However, the formal request solicited more detailed data, such as the number of prosecutors, broken down by gender, who handle cases of sexual offenses. The institution does not have such evidence. https://www.csm1909.ro/Pages.aspx?PageId=276&PageTitle=Eviden%C5%A3%C4%83-nominal%C4%83.

[11] The data collected by the Superior Council of Magistracy is not sex segregated. The available data was downloaded and processed by the author to identify the proportion of women and men among the judges. https://www.csm1909.ro/Pages.aspx?PageId=276&PageTitle=Eviden%C5%A3%C4%83-nominal%C4%83.

[12] https://beta.dela0.ro/dreptate-stramba-3-din-4-cazuri-de-acte-sexuale-cu-victime-copii-sunt-judecate-in-instantele-romanesti-ca-fapte-consimtite/, https://www.libertatea.ro/stiri/cum-batjocoreste-justitia-fetele-de-10-ani-violate-2516773; https://adevarul.ro/news/societate/protest-8-martie-tribunalul-bucuresti-mai-multe-organizatii denunta-iresponsabilitatea-justitiei-cazurile-viol-1_5c824d84445219c57e03da92/index.html.

[13] Dela0 and Libertatea.

of the respondent State's positive obligations under both Articles 3 and 8 of the Convention".[14] The key facts are as follows. An 11-year-old girl was raped multiple times over a 7-month period by relatives of the children she was visiting to play with. The perpetrators were a 52-year old man and four minors. The girl became pregnant, had an abortion. She told the police that she did not make allegations after being raped first because she was ashamed and the 52-year old had threatened to beat her if she told anyone. The five men testified that the girl had always initiated the sex and was "always scantily dressed" when she went over to their house. The police noted that "even if the perpetrators' statements were to be accepted as truthful",[15] the girl's age precluded the existence of valid consent. The forensic psychiatric report concluded that the girl showed signs of post-traumatic stress, and "had difficulties in foreseeing the consequences of her actions and had insufficient discernment due to her age".[16] The adult man was convicted of sexual intercourse with a minor. He was not convicted of rape because no signs of violence had been detected on the girl's body, and the court credited the suspects' testimony that the girl acted provocatively and initiated the sex. The court did not discuss the forensic psychiatric report and dismissed the evaluation that the girl lacked capacity to consent. The ECtHR judgment also highlighted that during the criminal investigation and trial: "(. . .) the prosecutor held as proved the fact that the applicant had gone to the neighbours' house scantily dressed and had had a sexual relationship with J.V. The prosecutor therefore inferred that from the documents in the file it was not proved beyond doubt that the applicant had not given her consent to the sexual acts".[17] ECtHR concluded that "the domestic courts failed to demonstrate a child-sensitive approach in analyzing the facts of the case", and in regard to consent.[18] More similar cases were brought before the Court.[19] In all of these, the ECtHR held that Romanian authorities' failed to properly investigate rape allegation, therefore raising doubts about the prosecution and punishment of sexual offences against girls at the national level.

The judiciary's rulings documented by the journalists triggered public outrage and protests of women's rights and feminist activists.[20] They argued that these represented a failure to protect girls' rights and reinforced gender stereotypes. Concurrently, the feminization of the judiciary emerged as a topic in the public discourse, eliciting both surprise and apprehension regarding the decisions made by female justice professionals. In her article, Oncioiu identified several women judges that reinforced gender stereotypes regarding the behavior of gender-based

[14] Application no. 61495/11, https://hudoc.echr.coe.int/eng#{%22itemid%22:[%22001-161380%22]}.

[15] https://hudoc.echr.coe.int/eng#{%22itemid%22:[%22001-161380%22]}.

[16] https://hudoc.echr.coe.int/eng#{%22itemid%22:[%22001-161380%22]}.

[17] https://hudoc.echr.coe.int/eng#{%22itemid%22:[%22001-161380%22]}.

[18] https://hudoc.echr.coe.int/eng#{%22itemid%22:[%22001-161380%22]}.

[19] *E.B. v. Romania*, application no. 49089/10, *I.C. v. Romania*, Application no. 36934/08.

[20] www.libertatea.ro/stiri/protest-impotriva-magistratilor-care-iarta-violatorii-la-tribunalul-bucuresti-2568384.

violence victims. Just to illustrate, in the 2016 case of *M.G.C. v. Romania* one female judge refused to change the classification to rape because M.G.C. continued to go to the neighbor's yard after the first sexual contact, instead of avoiding encounters with the defendant, knowing he would be there. Additionally, the court judged that the victim did not say anything to her parents. "If the sexual intercourse had taken place through coercion or by taking advantage of her inability to defend herself or express her will, surely the civil party would not have continued the same previous habits".[21]

In response to extensive media investigations into judicial decisions, the Romanian Superior Council of Magistracy[22] exhibited varying reactions. Two days after the article was published on November 21, 2019, its President requested the Judicial Inspection to verify whether the facts exposed by Oncioiu's investigation compromised the independence[23] and impartiality of magistrates. The concepts of "independence" and "impartiality" are closely linked. "Impartiality" refers to a state of mind or attitude and denotes the absence of bias. "Independence" reflects the traditional constitutional value of impartiality, and defines the relationship of justice with other powers or institutions of the state, and with society in general. However, in 2020, the Superior Council of Magistracy shifted its stance. On May 25, it decided to notify the Judicial Inspection to conduct a "thematic control of courts and attorney's offices concerning the investigation and rulings of cases involving crimes against sexual life with minor victims (rape, sexual intercourse with a minor) from February 1, 2014, to the present".[24] One of the control's objectives[25] was to investigate how the courts assessed valid consent. The 2021 Judiciary Inspection Report highlighted more than 18,000 reports of sexual crimes involving minors, with less

[21] https://beta.dela0.ro/acte-sexuale-victime-copii-judecate-fapte-consimtite/.

[22] The Superior Council of the Magistracy (CSM) is a public institution that serves as the guarantor of judicial independence. The Council is the competent body for the recruitment, promotion, transfer, secondment, disciplinary investigation and dismissal of judges and prosecutors. The Council also has a decisive influence on the initial and continuous training of magistrates, by coordinating the activity of the National Institute of Magistracy (INM) and the National School of Clerks.

[23] The principles of independence and impartiality of magistrates are enshrined in Art. 124 para. 2 and 3 of the Constitution, Art. 2 para. 3 and 4 and Art. 3 para. 2 and 3 of Law no. 303/2022 on the status of judges and prosecutors, as well as Art. 3 of the Code of Ethics for Judges and Prosecutors, approved by Decision no. 328/2005 of the Plenary Session of the Superior Council of Magistracy.

[24] https://beta.dela0.ro/o-investigaie-dela0-ro-determina-consiliul-superior-al-magistraturii-sa-dispuna-verificari/?fbclid=IwAR3s5PaxnGnIFpKV5kVSJQ9Hz63Bed-dTFi92fKDSSMAkojEo-I5E4Amxjw.

[25] https://beta.dela0.ro/o-investigaie-dela0-ro-determina-consiliul-superior-al-magistraturii-sa-dispuna-verificari/?fbclid=IwAR3s5PaxnGnIFpKV5kVSJQ9Hz63Bed-dTFi92fKDSSMAkojEo-I5E4Amxjw. Also see, https://www.inspectiajudiciara.ro/sitewebservice/Resources/Rapoarte-de-control/RAPORT-privind-practica-instan%C8%9Belor-de-judecat%C4%83-%C8%99i-a-parchetelor-de-pe-l%C3%A2ng%C4%83-acestea-%C3%AEn-investigarea-%C8%99i-solu%C8%9Bionarea-cauzelor-privind-infrac%C8%9Biuni-la-via%C8%9Ba-sexual%C4%83-cu-victime.pdf, p. 7.

than 20% resulting in prosecution. Notably, it noted that there was no uniform practice regarding the concept of consent. Depending on the prosecutor's office or court handling the case of a victim under the age of 12, these crimes were prosecuted either as sexual activity with a minor or as rape.[26] As the Judiciary Inspection Report states "unlike the crimes of rape (Art. 218 of the Criminal Code) and sexual assault (Art. 219 of the Criminal Code), which are committed without the victim's consent (through coercion, incapacity to defend themselves or to express their will, or by taking advantage of such a state), sexual intercourse with a minor is regulated as an act committed with the minor's consent, which is considered by the legislator to be flawed due to the victim's young age".[27] Human and women's rights organizations in Romania noted that, the Judiciary Inspection Report reveals deeply ingrained gender and racial bias in prosecutor's and judge's arguments.[28] As stated by the Judiciary Inspection Report, "the criminal investigation bodies recognized the validity of the minor victims' consent, consequently deciding on procedural solutions to close the cases, considering criteria such as (. . .) the ethnicity or so-called tradition of the victim/perpetrator (the low age at which minors traditionally marry) (. . .)".[29]

Collective actions by women's rights groups led to legal change[30] in the age of consent, establishing 16 as the minimum age.[31] There is an exception clause; if the age difference between the adult and the minor does not exceed 5 years, the act is

[26] The Judicial Inspection Report—Mixed Theme No. 20–2770/20-2771 on the 'Practice of Courts and Prosecutors' Offices in the Investigation and Resolution of Cases Related to Sexual Offenses with Minor Victims', https://www.inspectiajudiciara.ro/sitewebservice/Resources/Rapoarte-de-control/RAPORT-privind-practica-instan%C8%9Belor-de-judecat%C4%83-%C8%99i-a-parchetelor-de-pe-l%C3%A2ng%C4%83-acestea-%C3%AEn-investigarea-%C8%99i-solu%C8%9Bionarea-cauzelor-privind-infrac%C8%9Biuni-la-via%C8%9Ba-sexual%C4%83-cu-victime.pdf.

[27] https://www.inspectiajudiciara.ro/sitewebservice/Resources/Rapoarte-de-control/RAPORT-privind-practica-instan%C8%9Belor-de-judecat%C4%83-%C8%99i-a-parchetelor-de-pe-l%C3%A2ng%C4%83-acestea-%C3%AEn-investigarea-%C8%99i-solu%C8%9Bionarea-cauzelor-privind-infrac%C8%9Biuni-la-via%C8%9Ba-sexual%C4%83-cu-victime.pdf, p. 15.

[28] https://centrulfilia.ro/reteaua-vif-lanseaza-petitia-pentru-justitie-transparenta-in-cazurile-de-violenta-sexuala/.

[29] https://www.inspectiajudiciara.ro/sitewebservice/Resources/Rapoarte-de-control/RAPORT-privind-practica-instan%C8%9Belor-de-judecat%C4%83-%C8%99i-a-parchetelor-de-pe-l%C3%A2ng%C4%83-acestea-%C3%AEn-investigarea-%C8%99i-solu%C8%9Bionarea-cauzelor-privind-infrac%C8%9Biuni-la-via%C8%9Ba-sexual%C4%83-cu-victime.pdf, p. 27.

[30] Analysis of legal provisions and decision-making by legal practitioners prior to the 2023 legislative changes highlights their complexity see the Judiciary Inspection Report https://www.inspectiajudiciara.ro/sitewebservice/Resources/Rapoarte-de-control/RAPORT-privind-practica-instan%C8%9Belor-de-judecat%C4%83-%C8%99i-a-parchetelor-de-pe-l%C3%A2ng%C4%83-acestea-%C3%AEn-investigarea-%C8%99i-solu%C8%9Bionarea-cauzelor-privind-infrac%C8%9Biuni-la-via%C8%9Ba-sexual%C4%83-cu-victime.pdf.

[31] https://violentaimpotrivafemeilor.ro/16-ani-varsta-minima-pentru-consimtamant-in-relatiile-sexuale-cu-minori/.

not considered a crime, provided there was no coercion, abuse of authority, or use of force.[32] Holzleithner (2018) reasonably highlights that"legal provisions do not implement themselves—they have to be effectuated".[33] Therefore, to ensure the tangible impact of these legislative changes, other civil society entities stress the importance of educating 'personnel within law enforcement, justice, and social assistance structures to overcome biases arising from diverse social practices and to implement the new legal framework.[34] It is essential to emphasize that the Council of Europe has also issued recommendations regarding the execution of judgments against Romania.[35]

An intricate divergence exists between normative expectations, feminist scholarship, legal goals, ECtHR judgments, and judicial decision-making in gender-based violence cases, which will be further explored in subsequent sections.

3 Feminization of the Justice System and Gender Knowledge

The topic of women's presence in the justice system has prompted scholars to consider the contributions of women legal professionals. Their participation, beyond being a moral imperative, can enhance justice outcomes and experiences. These contributions encompass enhanced legitimacy of justice institutions, advocacy for gender equality, improved justice outcomes in specific

[32] While this chapter focuses on the construction of gender within the legal profession, it is worth noting that the legal change was met with criticism from legal professionals and criminal law professors. These critics identified several errors in the legal act passed by Parliament, such as "uncorrelated penalty limits, the terminology used and the implications for interpretation, the legislative technique options chosen by the legislator, as well as the rather accelerated legislative process" (Ioan 2024, p. 215). After the publication of Law no. 217/2023 in the Official Gazette, the non-governmental organizations united in the Network for the Prevention and Combat of Violence against Women, communicated to the Ministry of Justice and the Parliament of Romania, through hearings, debates, meetings, and conferences, the message regarding the necessity of supplementing Law no. 217/2023 with two new hypotheses of incrimination: the hypothesis provided by art. 220 para. (3) of the Criminal Code, as well as sexual intercourse with penetration between minors who are not close in age and level of development. See, for example, https://www.juridice.ro/718,103/avertisment-privind-dezincriminarea-violului-asupra-adolescentilor-savarsit-prin-abuz-de-autoritate-sau-incredere-si-a-violului-savarsit-de-minori-asupra-copiilor-mai-mici-sau-mai-vulnerabili.html; https://www.bizlawyer.ro/mobile/stiri/interviuri-opinii/ciudatul-viol-de-la-televizor-cand-legiuitorul-adopta-reglementari-trasnite or https://www.bizlawyer.ro/mobile/stiri/interviuri-opinii/consimtamant-vs-discernamant-in-cazul-actului-sexual-cu-un-minor-problema-pragului-de-varsta. This component falls outside the scope of this chapter; however it needs further research.

[33] Holzleithner (2018), p. 136.

[34] Băluță (2020), http://www.romaniapozitiva.ro/administratie/instituirea-varstei-minime-pentru-consimtamant-la-16-ani-si-marirea-pedepselor-pentru-infractiunile-sexuale-impotriva-minorilor-un-pas-inainte-pentru-a-i-proteja-de-agresiune-si-exploatare-s/.

[35] These recommendations can be found here https://hudoc.exec.coe.int/fre?i=004-13219.

cases, and an enriched justice experience for women.[36] However, existing studies emphasize the need for more in-depth research to comprehensively understand the dynamics of gender representation.[37] The relationship between descriptive representation and substantive outcomes is both complex and complicated. Researchers are more cautious nowadays in arguing that descriptive representation necessarily brings more substantive representation. Empirical studies suggest that this may happen but will not inevitably occur. And it will only occur under certain conditions. According to Hunter those conditions are a combination of opportunity (in terms of both subject matter and legal space), personal commitment and/or external encouragement.[38] In light of this argument, I assert that access to gender knowledge through education is crucial for delivering justice in gender-based violence cases. Legal education and training for legal professionals are crucial areas to consider when analyzing disparities in gender justice outcomes. This chapter delves deeper into the role of gender knowledge by utilizing in-depth interviews with key respondents of different organizations, professions, expertise.

Gender knowledge encompasses "statements or representations concerning the differences between the sexes and the relations between them, the origins and normative significance of these, the rationale and evidence underpinning them and their form".[39] Understanding current judicial narratives on gender-based violence requires exploration of the judiciary beyond feminization, focusing on gender knowledge, stereotypes and bias. It provides the basis to understand that gender stereotypes create not only a normative framework, but judicial practices in which discrimination and violence against women and girls are normalized, perpetuated, hence reinforcing and reproducing gender hierarchy. In this chapter, gender knowledge is considered a requisite for professionalization.

4 Gender Stereotypes and Judicial Bias

This chapter follows feminist definitions of violence understood as a gendered phenomenon and a manifestation of gender inequality.[40] Gender-based violence is defined as "violence that is directed against a woman because she is a woman or

[36] The Report Women Delivering Justice: Contributions, Barriers, and Pathways, 2018, International Development Law Organization (2018), pp. 13–19; Dawuni (2018), Hunter (2015), Halilović and Huhtanen (2014), Boyd et al. (2010), and others.

[37] The Report Women Delivering Justice: Contributions, Barriers, and Pathways, 2018, International Development Law Organization, pp. 13 and 18.

[38] Hunter (2015), p. 140.

[39] Cavaghan (2013), p. 410.

[40] Montoya (2013), p. 16.

that affects women disproportionately".[41] The chapter aligns with Montoya's argument that "when violence is perpetrated against a woman, her behaviour might be questioned, framed in the context of traditional gender roles"; therefore, "traditional justifications of violence might include knowledge or suspicion of sexual promiscuity, infidelity, inadequacy as a housekeeper or mother, refusal to engage in sex, the questioning of male authority (by answering back or even nagging)".[42]

Gender stereotypes are a generalized view or preconception about attributes, characteristics that are or ought to be possessed by, or the roles that are or should be performed by women and men. Judicial stereotyping is researched by academics, international institutions, and nongovernmental organizations active in the field of gender justice. 'Judicial stereotyping' refers to "the practice of judges ascribing to an individual specific attributes, characteristics or roles by reason only of her or his membership in a particular social group (e.g. women)".[43] Cusack highlights that judicial stereotyping, especially concerning women victims and survivors of violence, is a prevalent and harmful obstacle to justice. Such stereotyping may lead judges to make decisions influenced by predetermined gender biases, jeopardizing the impartiality and integrity of the justice system "which can, in turn, lead to miscarriages of justice and the revictimization of complainants".[44] Peroni and Timmer identify gender stereotyping as a structural factor contributing to domestic violence and ineffective state responses.[45] This highlights the necessity of addressing gender stereotypes to effectively tackle gender-based violence. Scholars further emphasize the critical importance of naming these stereotypes and their negative effects on women. For the argument of this chapter, it is important to highlight that judicial stereotyping undermines justice for victims and survivors of gender-based violence. Studies and reports that include countries in Eastern Europe highlight that gender stereotypes are present in the judiciary.[46] Analysis of judiciary practice in domestic violence cases identified victim blaming stereotypical beliefs and unevenly practices of law courts and magistrates when issuing the restraining order in Romania.[47] Hence, the impact of judicial stereotyping is significant, to only select a few examples: it can lead judges to permit irrelevant or highly prejudicial evidence to be admitted to court and/or affect the weight judges' attach to certain evidence, cause judges to misinterpret or misapply laws, distort judges' perceptions of what occurred in a particular situation of violence or the issues to be determined at trial.[48]

---

[41] Council of Europe Convention on Preventing and Combating Violence against Women and Domestic Violence, art. 3, https://rm.coe.int/CoERMPublicCommonSearchServices/DisplayDCTMContent?documentId=090000168008482e.

[42] Montoya (2013), p. 16.

[43] Cusack (2014), p. 2.

[44] Cusack (2014) p. ii.

[45] Peroni and Timmer (2016), p. 46.

[46] Halilović, Huhtanen (2014), p. 1.

[47] Nemeş and Crişan (2017), p. 6–7.

[48] Cusack (2014), p. 20.

5 Data, Methods, and Ethics

With this theoretical framework and broad context in mind, I conducted 7 in-depth interviews with key respondents of different organizations, professions, expertise.

5.1 Description of Key Respondents

The first interviewee is a criminal prosecutor with 22 years of experience investigating violent crimes and crimes against life. He possesses extensive experience in gender-based violence, sexual violence against children, and training magistrates at the National Institute of Magistracy. The second interviewee is a judge, also experienced in training magistrates at the National Institute of Magistracy and supportive of collaboration with NGOs on women's rights. The third interviewee, Cristi Danileț,[49] a judge of criminal courts at the time of the interview, with expertise in gender-based violence and sexual offenses against children. He served on the Superior Council of Magistrates (2011–2017) and has experience promoting dialogue with NGOs on women's rights, as well as academic experience. The fourth interviewee is a lawyer with a Master's degree and professional experience in criminal law, specifically defending gender-based violence cases at the European Court of Human Rights (ECtHR). The fifth interviewee is a lawyer with a Master's degree in Human Rights and experience with ECtHR litigation cases against Romania, who also collaborates with NGOs on gender-based violence and sexual violence issues. The sixth interviewee is a feminist activist and member of a collective action group advocating for legislative changes regarding the age of consent and transparency in judicial reasoning for sexual violence cases. The seventh interviewee is a journalist with 15 years of experience in both mainstream and alternative media, covering social issues, including gender-based violence topics and domestic court decisions.

Prior to field research, I analyzed the academic standards and guidelines for law education set by The Romanian Agency for Quality Assurance in Higher Education and the curriculum of three Faculties of Law, following: fundamental and field disciplines, their proportion in the curriculum, gender sensitive disciplines etc. Due to the chapter's inherent length limitations, the presentation of these findings is not included.[50] Nevertheless the desk research played an important role in further

[49] The interviewee asked to **include his full name** when citing him in the text.

[50] I presented partial findings of the curriculum analysis at "Women's Human Rights in the Twenty-First Century: Developments and Challenges under International and European Law" Conference, European Court of Human Rights on 14 February 2020. Romania does not have gender legal studies. The faculties do not teach law and gender, there are no dedicated programs. The descriptive analysis explored academic standards and guidelines of law education set by The Romanian Agency for Quality Assurance in Higher Education (fundamental and field disciplines, their proportion in the curriculum, gender sensitive disciplines etc.) and the curriculum of three

exploring the topic of knowledge for legal professionals and curriculum content during subsequent interviews with participants. The area of action, knowledge, experience and expertise of interviewees is wide; therefore the participants provide substantial information covering 10 hours of interviewing. I also contacted another two potential key respondents besides the participants already secured, a university law professor and a criminal court judge. The first contact asked to respond through email, an option I declined due to methodological consistency while the second refused to be interviewed due to constraints imposed upon the profession, even if I communicated the aim of the study and the strong commitment to research ethics, including protection of their identity.

The selection of participants aligns with the interview's objectives, in addition to addressing common themes, each interview guide was specifically designed to encompass the research objectives and knowledge, experience and expertise of the respondent, and therefore it included tailored questions. The interviews took place from September 2020 to July 2023, 6 facilitated through Google Meet, and one conducted in person. Each session, lasting between one and a half to two hours, was recorded to ensure precise transcription of the discussions. The result of these steps generated substantial empirical material that has been explored by thematic analysis.[51] Qualitative data collection and the analysis were accompanied by reflection on ethical issues. Prior to beginning of an interview, I explained again the aim of the research and gained a verbally registered informed consent. I informed the participants that data analysis will be conducted without the disclosure of their identity. One interviewee asked that his identity be disclosed, and I respected his request (Interview 3, Judge Cristi Danileț). Data analysis raised an ethical dilemma when participants recounted conversations and work experiences to illustrate gender stereotypes and bias. Even if language reproduces gender prejudices, and is descriptive, I opted to incorporate verbatim quotes to illustrate the interpretation of data. The decision better serves the objectives and the argument of the study. The limitations associated with the number of interviews,

Faculties of Law. Just to illustrate, the curriculum of the Faculty of Law of Alexandru Ioan Cuza University, Iași, bachelor's level, includes disciplines such as: Judiciary Sociology covering violence against children, domestic violence, prejudices, Criminal Law encompassing violence and rape topics, Legal medicine, an optional discipline integrating topics such as rape, sexual intercourse with children. It is worth mentioning that The Faculty of Law from the University of Bucharest has included Domestic violence among the 2025–2026 optional disciplines, but during third year, the second semester. Nevertheless, such research should have an interdisciplinary approach, explore the qualitative content of disciplines from a juridical and gender studies approach and critically reflect on the status of disciplines within the overall educational architecture, as well. An optional discipline in the final semester has a secondary status in the logics of the curriculum; the students will be less interested to work on specific topics for their graduation exam etc. It is important to highlight that this is not only about including topics related to women in the curriculum, but also about teaching from a gender, feminist perspective. One could teach about the regulation of domestic violence for example and do it from a very conservative, family-focused perspective.

[51] Braun and Clarke (2013), p. 205.

contingent on the study's design,[52] should be acknowledged as a potential constraint in the research. However, the research suggests more comprehensive ways of assessing gender and justice particularly in light of the existing gap within domestic studies and it involves a nuanced consideration of the feminization phenomenon and a critical interrogation of gender knowledge in the delivering of justice. Therefore, these findings may be a significant benchmark for further research in this widely unexplored area.

6 Navigating Justice: Professionalization, Feminization Challenges and Gender Stereotypes in Legal Decision-Making

The interview analysis reveals key themes encompassing professionalization, knowledge, feminization of justice, gender stereotypes, judicial bias, and structural challenges within the justice system. These themes highlight systemic difficulties in addressing gender-based violence, extending beyond formal legislative changes. The intricate interconnection between professionalization, knowledge, and systemic issues emphasizes the complexity of the challenges in addressing gender-based violence.

6.1 Professionalization and the Quality of Justice

Professionalization is a cross-cutting theme of interviews and a dominant component of quality of justice (Interview 1, 7). Professionalization is not only perceived as multifaceted, encompassing inter and multi-disciplinary knowledge, but also an important component that allows legal professionals to understand the nature and seriousness of sexual crimes. It has a crucial role in understanding the psychology of victims, hence the professionalization process should include knowledge to enable legal professionals in comprehending societal dynamics related to victim blaming. Experienced professionals dealing with sexual offenses often liken them to crimes against humanity due to their profound impact on victims and the difficult process of recovering from trauma, particularly given inadequate systemic support (Interview 1, 2). At the same time, they also notice that gender-based violence, such as revenge porn or rape are approached as secondary crimes in comparison to cases that have an economic stake (Interview 1, 4): "Yes, from practice, I learned that if there is no case with economic stakes, if the prosecutor doesn't put a seizure on something, if there is no promotion involved … forgive me, maybe I'm wrong, but such cases, with female victims, with revenge porn, with the violation of

[52] Roulston (2018), p. 244.

privacy, with blackmail, they just stay neatly tucked away in a drawer and nothing happens" (Interview 4).

Interdisciplinary legal education also comprising gender-based violence was systematically correlated with professionalization. During the interviews, a recurring topic underscores the need for gender-based violence sensitive legal education and training, particularly on sexual violence. Furthermore, some participants highlighted the importance of interdisciplinary legal education as a benchmark to addressing abuse against both adults and children. Interviewees argued that when dealing with sexual crimes involving children, justice professionals, such as prosecutors and judges, should possess knowledge about the psychology of children and their defense and coping mechanisms since "investigating sexual assault cannot be approached in the same manner as investigating other crimes like robbery" (Interview 7).

The respondents underscored the responsibility of faculties of law and the National Institute of Magistracy in shaping the education of legal professionals. They emphasized the need for these institutions to revise their curricula, focusing on cultivating essential skills that enhance the ability of legal professionals to effectively handle cases related to gender-based violence (Interview 7). This also includes a comprehensive understanding of human rights issues, the European Convention on Human Rights (ECHR)[53] and its legal rationale, which can be compared and contrasted with the principles underpinning the Romanian legal system, as rooted in jurisprudence (Interview 5). Respondents (Interview 1, 5, 7) stressed that this type of knowledge should be acquired prior to magistrates commencing their training at the National Institute of Magistracy "to comprehend the broader context of abuse" (Interview 7). ECtHR made significant rulings over the years in gender-based violence cases against Romania, thus drawing attention to reinforcement of prejudices and the failure of national judiciary to protect girls and women's rights.[54] Studies that reflect on feminist justice and the role of ECtHR highlight that its case law contribute to "more complete protection of women's rights, effective gender equality, breaking down prejudices and barriers stemming from the mentality of historically patriarchal societies".[55] As Jelić further emphasizes "those judgments bridge the victims with justice where national judiciary failed to protect their rights and, thus, contributed to their violations".[56]

---

[53] Simultaneously, the respondent highlighted that unlike the European Union (EU), the ECtHR lacks infringement mechanisms to impose sanctions on states. Additionally, she noted the ongoing debates within the EU regarding adherence to the European Convention on Human Rights; the evolving dynamics will strengthen the outcomes of ECtHR decisions within member states.

[54] Nevertheless, the ECtHR is not that progressive when it comes to gender stereotypes in violence against women cases either. See in particular the book chapter "Gender Stereotyping in Domestic Violence Cases. An Analysis of the European Court of Human Rights' Jurisprudence" by Lourdes Peroni and Alexandra Timmer. The book is available here: https://backoffice.biblio.ugent.be/download/7,225,334/7,226,257.

[55] Jelić (2023), p. 36.

[56] Jelić (2023), p. 36.

The interviews revealed a significant degree of convergence among respondents serving as judges and prosecutors, particularly concerning the perceived secondary status of certain disciplines within the curriculum of law schools. Criminalistics, Legal Logics, Legal Sociology, and Legal Psychology were subject to scrutiny and questioning while also highlighting their role (Interview 1, Interview 3, Interview 4). The dialogue between academia and professionals is supported by formal mechanisms and procedures; for example each course syllabus includes a section that describes the alignment of the course content with the expectations of representatives from the epistemic community, professional associations, and relevant employers associated with the program's field. The argument I make is that the formal ecosystem for dialogue is not absent. Respondents have also criticized the "education content" that is no longer relevant, accurate and does not align with current standards or best practices, such as newly developed hearing methods (Interview 1, Interview 3). This critical reflection extends beyond juridical education and reveals a tension between two logics, of the academia and the professional field. However, respondents highlighted that faculties face significant challenges, and their role is considerably diminished unless gender stereotypes and prejudices are addressed earlier in school (Interview 3, 4, 5).

6.2 *Feminization of Justice: Unpacking Essentialism, Knowledge Nexus, and the Construction of the Profession*

Respondents highlighted contradictory perceptions on the topic, such as: potential gender expectations in ruling as an outcome of shared experiences of harassment, followed by irrelevance of beneficial outcomes of feminization for victims of gender-based violence when education does not provide means to acknowledge and deconstruct stereotypes and judicial bias. One participant stressed that decisions based on gender stereotypes: "(. . .) pinpoint exactly to what I was previously highlighting: education, training and bias. It is irrelevant that they are women. Both women and men underwent the same training; they have been educated by the same system. Their robotic behavior makes their gender unimportant. Irrespective of women and men, if this is the judicial practice, you follow it" (Interview 7). The interviews revealed widespread discrepancy between professional and gendered normative expectations and descriptive behavior and decision-making. Another respondent reflected on potential shared experiences of women and outcome on judicial ruling drawing from a domestic case covered in the media. Two female judges acquitted a man who touched a woman's buttocks without consent, claiming it wasn't sexual assault: "I wonder how two female judges can make such a decision? Have they never come home late at night in an apartment building? Have they never felt this fear? I mean, how can you say it has no sexual connotation and that it doesn't fit the criteria?" (Interview 5). The respondent advanced one potential explanation rooted in the demands of the criminal system, emphasizing strict adherence to rules and procedures. The participant noticed that this approach maintains decisions on a familiar trajectory, minimizing the risk of errors and potential repercussions stemming from ECtHR convictions.

Perceptions on the feminization of the field are not devoid of ambivalence, necessitating thoughtful reflections. The process of feminization takes place in a larger societal gender regime and within the boundaries and praxis of a profession. The qualitative data sheds light on the intersection between gender order and the occupational structures.[57] The construction of the profession emerged as a salient topic during the interviews, constituting a structural challenge within the domain of justice. Respondents highlighted the boundaries that enclose professionals, hinder dialogue with other interested parties and preclude reflexivity. After the fall of communism, the legal profession underwent transformations due to the lingering influence of the former regime. In the transition to democracy, the reconstruction of the field led to an occupational closure, particularly for judges, to shield them from interference. However, the concepts of independence and impartiality have come to be associated with decisions that are presumably free from value-oriented considerations, detached from stereotypes and prejudices, as the rule of law is deemed to be neutral and objective. This mechanism further contributed to increased enclosure, resulting in non-transparency (closure to new ideas) (Interview 1, 5); as pinpointed by one participant: "in my view, independence and impartiality are poorly understood, because independence and impartiality do not mean that you are not open to ideas and that you cannot accept them, hear them, and then try to integrate them" (Interview 5). Another participant stressed occupational closure resulting from high skills and competencies. This elevated expertise fosters reluctance among those with professional authority to engage in dialogue or contemplate potential criticism from either the media or non-governmental organizations (Interview 3). Notably interesting is the association of occupational closure with reactive interventions on dedicated professional forums, wherein legal professionals respond to criticism from their colleagues (Interview 1). Nevertheless, there are a few instances of openness and collaboration, exemplified by roundtables organized by The Superior Council of Magistracy involving non-governmental organizations, journalists, The Public Prosecutor's Office. One such instance focused on the topic of the temporary restraining order in cases of domestic violence (Interview 2).

In this context, the idea that "justice must not only be done but must also be seen to be done" is particularly challenging. Gender and justice scholarship has identified several strategies to enhance judicial capacity in addressing stereotyping. These include: conducting evidence-based research to underscore the harms of judicial stereotyping, advocating for legal and policy reforms that prohibit such practices, challenging judicial stereotyping through petitions and expert evidence, and showcasing examples of judges who exemplify good practices in countering stereotyping.[58]

---

[57] Boni-Le Goff et al. (2019), Le Goff and Le Feuvre (2017).

[58] Cusack (2014), p. 29.

It is important to emphasize that the Superior Council of Magistracy has made the decision not to publish court judgments in cases related to sensitive matters such as sexual acts with a minor, sexual aggression, sexual harassment, and rape.[59] While writing this chapter, 64 human and women's rights associations dedicated to combating gender-based violence, in collaboration with scholars, submitted a petition to the Superior Council of Magistracy. This petition urged for the anonymization and publication of all final court judgments related to sexual offenses. The proponents argue that "for a safer society for girls and women, it is essential for the public and the press to have access to this information" because "the anonymized publication of court judgments helps us monitor the long-term impact of legislative changes regarding the protection of victims of sexual offenses".[60]

Societies have culture(s) that reflect attitudes and beliefs about gender. Gender scholars have compellingly argued that throughout their lives, individuals learn and perceive the expectations, act, and react accordingly, thus contributing to the construction and maintenance of gender order. Our everyday gendered interactions "build gender into the family, the work process, and other institutions, which in turn reinforce gender expectations for individuals".[61] Critical knowledge of current institutional practices is one important component of education and training because "gender is a primary way of signifying relationships of power".[62] Therefore, the feminization of the field and its potential impact on gender equality offer one explanatory narrative, but it requires augmentation by a more complex theoretical and methodological framework.

6.3 Gender Stereotypes and Bias in Legal Decision-Making. Perceptions on Prejudice

Addressing gender stereotypes and biases given the substantiated evidence provided by empirical research might not be that unreasonable. It is rather unreasonable to consider that Romanian legal professionals are free from gender stereotypes and biases given opposite evidence drawn from their judgments and overall cultural bias in cases of sexual offences. All the respondents put an emphasis on explicitly manifested stereotypes and biases of legal professionals that they have encountered during their activity. The respondents training magistrates recounted conversations and behavior of prosecutors and judges that displayed gender stereotypes and prejudices. This phenomenon occurs because judges and prosecutors often operate under these biases without awareness. A respondent, who provides

[59] Superior Court of Magistracy, Judges Section, Decision no 998, March 17, 2022.

[60] https://centrulfilia.ro/reteaua-vif-lanseaza-petitia-pentru-justitie-transparenta-in-cazurile-de-violenta-sexuala/.

[61] Lorber (1994), p. 32.

[62] Scott (1986), p. 1069.

training for prosecutors at the National Institute of Magistrates, reflects on the entrenched nature of stereotypes and prejudices. He emphasizes that these biases, often overlooked, are learned at home and become deeply ingrained, shaping perceptions and decision-making. He provides a disconcerting example of a triple murder, underscoring the insensitivity and gender bias exhibited by some colleagues during discussions about the case: "Yeah, man, but she was a whore too .... Seriously ... we're talking about 3 people shot in front of a child, and you're telling me she was a whore ..?!" (Interview 1). Another respondent, who is also involved in training legal professionals at the National Institute of Magistrates, recounted instances of prejudicial behavior and beliefs related to both domestic violence and child rape. As several interview participants highlighted "(...) the mindset we carry from home is much stronger and better rooted in our minds than what someone teaches us. And we refuse to step out ... " (Interview 1).

Bias often stems from ignorance and misunderstanding. Respondents highlighted the societal and individual bias that need to be acknowledged and create context for such awareness.

One respondent heightened her awareness on the topic by engaging in work related to gender-based violence cases, reading interdisciplinary scientific literature, and collaborating with non-governmental organizations: "But slowly, you realize that it's actually society, it's the way you've been socialized" (Interview 5). Therefore, future magistrates should also be exposed to knowledge on gender equality and stereotypes and the role of gender bias in judicial decision-making (Interview 5). However, these prejudices need to be addressed at an earlier stage in the education system, as I have already highlighted when addressing professionalization (Interview 1, Interview 5).

There exists a pervasive societal bias that continues to significantly influence work and the evaluation of victims of gender-based violence, unless actively confronted and brought into visibility. Another respondent underscored the reinforcement of bias and prejudices within the judiciary, particularly among judges and prosecutors, especially when assessing sexual crimes through preconceived notions of the "ideal victim." A prevailing stereotype observed in the respondents' professional engagements was the perception of women's morality being utilized to rationalize instances of rape and sexual assault. In instances of revenge porn, a prosecutor cited the alleged 'exacerbated sexuality' of a young woman as part of the justification for closing the case, a decision subsequently endorsed by the judge: "It was disconcerting to discover that one of the cited reasons among the six motivations within a revenge porn case, closed by the prosecutor, was that the defendant's actions were deemed to possess a retaliatory and juvenile nature. Additionally, the victim was characterized as displaying an exaggerated level of sexuality. Consequently, the argument was posited that the state need not allocate its resources to pursue the case" (Interview 4). Respondents also noticed that gender stereotypes were also associated with children victims of sexual abuse, an observation consistent with the European Court of Human Rights' ruling in the *M.G.C.* case (Interview 7). However, it is crucial to understand that gender intersects with both ethnicity and class, multiplying obstacles for victims of gender-based violence (Interview 4, 6). When girls and women are both Roma and poor, they are treated differently by state authorities, such as police officers, prosecutors and justice. These findings are consistent with data on gender and racial bias reflected in the arguments of prosecutors and judges, as emphasized in the contextual section. Therefore, an intersectional approach of gender-based violence is highly important to support access to justice.[63]

One respondent provided a more normative response, acknowledging the existence of prejudices but emphasizing the crucial importance of recognizing and disengaging from these biases. This respondent argues that impartiality does not imply the absence of prejudices but rather the ability to acknowledge and address them (Interview 3). However, the assertion that legal professionals can simply distance themselves through the idea of impartiality is challenged by scholarly literature, empirical studies, and decision-making in domestic cases where prosecutors and judges demonstrated an inability to achieve impartiality, grounding their judgments in stereotypical perceptions of claimants, as highlighted by the ECtHR and reports from the Judicial Inspection. In this context, it is noteworthy that the respondents reiterated the overall role of education (Interview 1, Interview 3). In addition, international human rights treaties ratified by Romania highlight that states bear obligations to address stereotyping.[64] It is important to stress that "stereotyping has emerged as a human rights law topic".[65]

Respondents further engaged in critical reflections on various structural obstacles, including judges' age and experience, the operational logics of the courts, and the allocation of sexual crimes cases within the system, the failures in checks and balances (Interview 1, Interview 3). Workload and the insufficient number of justice professionals, such as police-officers and prosecutors, also emerged as a potential systemic challenge, warranting further investigation in research and evaluation in regards to gender justice (Interview 1, 2).

7 Conclusion

The chapter underscores that essentialist expectation from women legal professionals may not be the pathways towards delivering gender justice when one accounts for the role of the societal conservative gender regime and the confinements of the profession. At the same time, it weakens institutional accountability, including the responsibility of faculties of law and of the National Institute of

[63] Bragă (2020).

[64] See e.g. 2 (d) and (f) and 5 (a) of the Convention on the Elimination of All Forms of Discrimination against Women (CEDAW), adopted in 1979 and ratified by Romania in 1982. See also the following general recommendations of the Committee on the Elimination of Discrimination against Women: General Recommendation No. 33 on women's access to justice (2015), para. 26 and General Recommendation No. 35 (2017), para. 26 (c).

[65] Brems and Timmer (2016), p. 1.

Magistracy to provide education and training or of the Council of Magistracy to monitor and enact changes that create better conditions for professionals to deliver gender justice. This observation does not dispute the importance of descriptive representation. It offers an importance nuance to the process of gendering the justice system by stressing that the construction of gender within a profession and by legal professionals should not be neglected and that knowledge has an important contribution that further affects the process of delivering justice for gender-based violence victims.

The exploratory qualitative part of the study sheds light on the complexities involved in the gendering of justice system, highlighting the intersections between professionalization, structural challenges such as the construction of the profession, and the need to decode gender stereotypes. Respondents also make visible the complex paradigm inherent in addressing gender-based violence and emphasize the pivotal role of numerous professionals. The findings resonate with the widespread critique voiced by civil society professionals and scholars in Central and Eastern Europe, underscoring the challenges encountered in the implementation of legislative changes in the domain of gender-based violence. Neither transposition, nor additional amendments of legislation equate with successful implementation.

An important outcome of the research is the need to integrate different levels of analysis in addressing judicial decision-making in gender-based violence cases. Gender inequalities are the result of complex processes that show a combination of formal and informal mechanisms, construction of the profession that risk denying the mere existence of gender bias and judicial stereotyping due to intrinsic qualities of the professional authority, such as impartiality and independence. The dominant ethos of the professional practice should be considered alongside professionalization and training. The problem appears to be not so much the feminization of the profession, but rather women's inclusion in a domain that reproduces structural gender inequalities in terms of legal education and profession. The chapter draws attention to the important role of gender knowledge for justice professionals. Gender knowledge renders visible, challenges and (de)constructs power within society, politics, family, legal system, it can challenge stereotypes and enhance the reach of gender equality. By integrating gender knowledge, the profession may meet the desired and required standards of impartiality. At the same time, it may pave the way for an occupational gender regime that challenges the societal gender regime infused by stereotypes regarding gender-based violence. These results lay the groundwork for future analysis that should also address (wo)men legal professionals as potential change agents, and case law targeting gender stereotypes. Following Cusack who argues that "education and training is key to building capacity to address judicial stereotyping and ensuring decision-making is not adversely affected by harmful stereotypes",[66] legal professionals can challenge stereotyping. Therefore, it is important to strengthen the judicial capacity to address stereotyping. Equally important, stereotyping needs to be understood

---

[66] Cusack (2014), p. 42.

from an intersectional perspective, where gender intersects with ethnicity, class and creates multiple systems of oppression that impede access to justice.

My emphasis on legal education and training does not imply that I consider them a panacea for eliminating gender stereotyping and gender bias. The point I make is gender knowledge integrated in juridical education is more consistent with improving judicial capacity to address stereotyping than the essentialist expectations from justice professionals. Further research should include police officers as well because of their important place in the justice system. Equally important, research on the curriculum is necessary. Alongside faculties of law, the support materials of the National Institute of the Magistracy need also be interdisciplinary explored because they play an important role as highlighted by the respondents that were training future magistrates. The qualitative content and the learning materials need an in-depth analysis that undertakes an interdisciplinary approach, with input coming from both legal and gender scholars and professionals. While engaging in a challenging conversation within Romanian society, marked by conservative resistance, it is imperative to carefully consider and contemplate the broader educational system and the norms it imparts to students. Failing to do so may lead to unrealistic expectations regarding the role of educational institutions as a universal remedy for addressing gender stereotypes and prejudices. Education, as a domain, has persistently demonstrated resistance to more gender-sensitive and egalitarian norms. Furthermore, with the proliferation of anti-gender campaigns and their focus on education, the potential changes of the curricula and the training of teachers may face even more resistance. Likewise, criticism against the Istanbul Convention that reverberate anti-gender arguments and also come from legal professionals work as additional challenges to gender justice for victims of gender-based violence.

Strengthening accountability mechanisms, alongside gender education and cooperation with gender scholars and women's rights associations need to be further considered and explored. Scholars have argued that "an effective justice system is one of the hallmarks of a democratic and governed by the rule of law country".[67] Equally important, gender and feminist scholars have addressed different dimensions of democracy that have often been marginalized or overlooked before. Following the two lines of reasoning, judicial decision-making in gender-based violence cases can reveal the strength or weakness of a democratic system.

References

Băluță I, Claudiu T (2022) Barometer of gender-based violence 2022. Violence against women in Romania: representations, perceptions. The FILIA Center

Băluță O (2020) Stereotipurile de gen și violența asupra femeilor. Sunt practicienii din sistemul de justiție imuni? In: Nemeș C, Crișan G (eds) Violența domestică. Paradigme și practică judiciară. Universul Juridic, Bucharest, pp 21–31

[67] Reznik et al. (2020).

Bragă A (2020) Intersecţionalitate şi violenţă domestică. In: Nemeş C, Crişan G (eds) Violenţa domestică. Paradigme şi practică judiciară. Universul Juridic, Bucharest

Boni-Le Goff I, Le Feuvre N, Mallard G, Lépinard E, Morel S (2019) Do gender regimes matter? Converging and diverging career prospects among young French and Swiss lawyers. In: Choroszewicz M, Adams T (eds) Gender, age and inequality in the professions. Routledge, London

Boni-Le Goff I, Le Feuvre N (2017) Professions from a gendered perspective. Oxford Research Encyclopedia of Business and Management

Boyd CL, Epstein L, Martin AD (2010) Untangling the causal effect of sex on judging. Am J of Pol Sci 54(2):389–411

Braun V, Clarke V (2013) Successful qualitative research: a practical guide for beginners. Sage, London

Brems E, Timmer A (ed) (2016) Introduction. In: Brems E, Timmer A (ed) Stereotypes and human rights law. Intersentia Ltd. https://backoffice.biblio.ugent.be/download/7225334/7226257

Cavaghan R (2013) Gender mainstreaming in the DGR as a knowledge process: epistemic barriers to eradicating gender bias. Crit Policy Stud 7(4):407–421

Childs S (2004) New labour's women MPs: women representing women. Routledge, New York

Cusack S (2014) Eliminating judicial stereotyping. Equal access to justice for women in gender-based violence cases. Office of the High Commissioner for Human Rights

Dawuni J (2018) African women judges on international courts: symbolic or substantive gains? U Balt Law Rev 47(2):199–246

Epure G, Brodeală E (2023) Gender (Im)balance and the making of the ECtHR bench: a critical discussion of Romania's selection process for its Strasbourg judge. The Strasbourg Observers Blog, 30 June 2023. https://strasbourgobservers.com/2023/06/30/gender-imbalance-and-the-making-of-the-ecthr-bench-a-critical-discussion-ofromanias-selection-process-for-its-strasbourg-judge/

Galligan Y, Haupfleisch R, Irvine L, Korolkova K, Natter M, Schultz U, Wheeler S (2017) Mapping the representation of women and men in legal professions across the EU. Policy department for citizen's rights and constitutional affairs. JURI Committee of the European Parliament

Halilović M, Huhtanen H (2014) Gender and the judiciary—selected findings and recommendations on the implications of gender within the judiciary of Bosnia Hertzegovina. Geneva Centre for Security Sector Governance and Atlantic Initiative

Holzleithner E (2018) Subversion from within—opposition to gender equality in the court of justice of the EU. In: Verloo M (ed) Varieties of opposition to gender equality in Europe. Gender and comparative politics. Routledge, London

Hunter R (2015) More than just a different face? Judicial diversity and decision-making. Current Legal Problems 68(1):119–141

Ioan, G–C (2024) Infracţiunile de viol săvârşit asupra unui minor şi agresiune sexuală săvârşită asupra unui minor – comentarii „necritice". Încadrarea juridică a faptelor şi stabilirea sancţiunilor penale. Forum Juridic nr. 1/2024. https://www.doi.org/10.31178/AUBD-FJ.2024.1.17

International Development Law Organization (2018) Women Delivering Justice: contributions, Barriers, and Pathway. https://www.idlo.int/sites/default/files/pdfs/publications/IDLO%20-%20Women%20Delivering%20Justice%20-%202018.pdf

Jelić I (2023) Feminist justice and the European Court of Human Rights. In: Krstić I, Evola M, Moreno MIR (eds) Legal issues of international law from a gender perspective. Springer, pp 35–55

Lorber J (1994) Paradoxes of Gender. Yale University Press, London

Montoya C (2013) From global to grassroots: the European Union, transnational advocacy, and combating violence against women. Oxford University Press, New York

Nemeş C, Crişan G (2017) Violenţa domestică. Paradigme şi practică judiciară. Universul Juridic, Bucharest

Peroni L, Timmer A (2016) Gender stereotyping in domestic violence cases. An analysis of the European Court of Human Rights' jurisprudence. In: Brems E, Timmer A (ed) Stereotypes and human rights law. Intersentia Ltd. https://backoffice.biblio.ugent.be/download/7225334/7226257
Reznik O, Borko A, Inshyn M, Kobzieva T, Kislitsyna I (2020) Professionalism of judges as the basis of the staffing in the courts. J Leg Ethical Regul Issues 23(1S):1–7
Roulston K (2018) Analysing interviews In: Flick U (ed) The Sage handbook of qualitative data collection, Sage, London
Scott JW (1986) Gender: a useful category of historical analysis. Am Hist Rev 91(5):1053–1075
The Judicial Inspection Report - Mixed Theme No. 20-2770/20-2771 on the 'Practice of Courts and Prosecutors' Offices in the Investigation and Resolution of Cases Related to Sexual Offenses with Minor Victims'

Oana Băluţă is Associate Professor at the Faculty of Political Science, National University of Political Studies and Public Administration, Romania. Her research interests are: anti-gender mobilization; political representation; contemporary feminist politics and movement; gender-based violence; media, gender and politics. She has also worked as a short-term gender consultant for United Nations Development Fund, and the World Bank. Her analysis focused on gender in public administration and politics, and critical aspects of domestic gender policies. Alongside her academic work, she is an active feminist advocate to end gender-based violence and build forms of resistance in anti-gender campaigns attacking LGBTQI rights and gender studies. She has published in European Journal of Politics and Gender, Perspectives on Politics, Feminist Review, Feminist Media Studies, Aspasia. International Yearbook of Central, Eastern, and Southeastern European Women's and Gender History. Recent articles include: Băluţă, O., & Băluţă, I. (2025). Where to? Gender studies, epistemic injustice and the politics of de-democratization in Romania. European Journal of Politics and Gender, (published online ahead of print 2025). https://doi.org/10.1332/25151088Y2025D000000081 and Băluţă O. (2023). What is in a name? Alternative gender knowledge and the retrogressive worlding of radical right digital media. Feminist Media Studies, 24(5), 1078–1094, https://doi.org/10.1080/14680777.2023.2274280.

Part IV
Doctrine

Gender Competent Legal Education of Criminal Justice Professionals—Case of Intimate Partner Violence

Natalija Lukić

Abstract The dominance of men in the creation and application of law is a fact that feminist writers have rightly drawn attention to. Although criminal law, that is based on the principle of legality and *lex certa* as its segment, should be gender neutral, its norms still leave room for different interpretation. This is a consequence of vague definitions of criminal offenses and the discretionary power that the court must have in determining the type and amount of the criminal sanction. This paper consists of three parts. The first part focuses on the analysis of gender competent legal knowledge of public prosecutors and judges who deal with domestic violence in practice and importance of specialized domestic violence courts. The second part of the paper is devoted to analysis of domestic violence legislation in Serbia and the empirical analysis of 81 judicial verdicts of seven basic courts in Serbia. The aim of the qualitative analysis is to determine how judges apply criminal law in relation to intimate partner violence, whether dominant prejudices regarding partner violence are present and whether crucial etiological factors that lead to violence are recognized. In the third part, author points to the importance of gender competent legal knowledge in international legal documents.

1 Introduction

Male dominance in law, and criminal law as well, is a fact very thoroughly explained in literature. Male orientation in law, legal theory and legal knowledge is not only a characteristic feature from the past, but is present in modern period

N. Lukić (✉)
University of Belgrade, Belgrade, Serbia
e-mail: natalija.lukic@ius.bg.ac.rs

© The Author(s), under exclusive license to Springer Nature Switzerland AG 2025
S. Baer et al. (eds.), *The Gender and the Judiciary*, Gender Perspectives in Law 7,
https://doi.org/10.1007/978-3-032-06885-9_11

as well.[1] Although legal norms are formulated as gender neutral, the truth is that formal equality does not mean equality in practice. Liberal feminists assert that legal norms are formulated so to correspond to male differences in respect to women, whereas feminists who advocate dominance approach emphasize that men use law as a tool for achieving dominance and subjection of females.[2] Male dominance and power relations are embedded in law and in the same way in its interpretation and implementation. Regarding domestic violence, and intimate partner violence as one of its forms, it took a long time before behaviour that has been approved not just within societies to greater or lesser extent, but in law as well, has become prohibited and defined as a crime. Comparative history examples indicate that even at the beginning of the twentieth century courts regarded domestic violence as a private matter that does not deserve to be officially proceeded and punished[3] unless the violence was "severe enough".

From the beginning of the twentieth century until 1970s, women tried to solve the problem of abuse in intimate relationships through personal strategies of resistance, help of relatives, friends and neighbors and through the intervention of child welfare agencies.[4] Starting from the 1960s and early 1970s the second feminist movement has brought more important changes.[5] Although from that period domestic violence gradually started to be recognized as a social problem that deserves legal reaction, the criminal justice professionals (police, public prosecutors and judges) were still reluctant to accept changes and treat domestic violence in the same manner as other types of violence that occur in the public or semi-public spaces.[6] Some feminists assert that states generally are reluctant to make changes in capitalist systems that are founded on male expected characteristics of dominance, rationality and assertiveness. On the other hand, states are more ready to accept these changes in respect to domestic violence problem than for example in relation to women and employment.[7] Social changes are slow, especially if they are spontaneous and not encouraged. Adoption of new laws in the field of combating domestic violence is therefore only the first step. In order to ensure effectiveness of all new solutions, their proper application and education of all professionals who act in those cases is necessary. Prejudices about the causes of domestic violence, about the "typical" behaviour of the victim, and the consequences that these acts exemplify prevent the achievement of the objective of the new legal solution, and lead to further negative consequences, such as discouraging the victims from reporting violence and testifying in criminal proceedings or the secondary victimization. Therefore, gender competent legal

---

[1] Vujadinović et al. (2023), pp. 1–2.

[2] Baer (1999), pp. 39–41.

[3] Schneider (2000), pp. 14–17.

[4] Schneider (2000), pp. 19–20.

[5] Epstein (1999), p. 11.

[6] McQuigg (2017), pp. 11–12.

[7] Mirchandani (2006), p. 785.

knowledge represents one of the mechanisms to achieve not just gender equality but more gender sensitivity in law creation and its implementation.

This article is structured into three levels. The first part is dedicated to exploring the theory and positive examples of gender competent legal knowledge in respect to intimate partner violence and similar crimes. Secondly, results of the empirical study conducted on a research sample of 81 final judicial verdicts in cases of intimate partner violence in Serbia are presented. The aim of the study is to analyse the implementation of criminal law through gender lens and to determine whether gender competent legal education of judges would be more beneficial not just for victims but for offenders as well. The third part analyses international legal framework that regulates legal education of criminal justice professionals in gender issues.

2 Gender Competent Legal Knowledge in Intimate Partner Violence Cases

Public prosecutors, defence counsels and judges all have an important role in effectively responding to domestic violence cases. All of them encounter certain difficulties in dealing with domestic violence actors and to some extent these cases do not fit into the general framework of criminal proceedings for other crimes. One of these hurdles of special importance is the ability to recognize domestic violence, especially in situations when victim reports it for the first time and when violence had no serious injuries as a consequence. Also, the literature points to a problem in criminal proceedings when victims decide not to testify against the offender since this leads to a large number of case attrition and further reluctance of victims to seek help. Finally, in order to be able to help victims, professionals should have specialized knowledge on domestic violence factors, consequences for the victim, cycles of violence and secondary victimization of victims. The second-wave feminist movement led to various legal and institutional novelties from the late 1970s. These include mandatory arrest laws, no-drop policies, domestic violence courts, restrictive orders.[8] The following text elaborates on some of these issues.

No-drop policies are very well documented in the literature and they allow public prosecutors to pursue charges irrespective of victims' approval. This approach is argued to be controversial since it can be questionable whether it is always in victim's interest to continue with the criminal proceedings.[9] On the other side, victims' withdrawal from the proceedings explains to a great extent the enormous case attrition.[10] Victim's refusal to testify against the perpetrator can then reinforce frustration and cynicism among employees in the public prosecutor's office and lead to case charges being dropped. If the victim decides to

---

[8] Cissner et al. (2015), p. 1103.

[9] Gover et al. (2021), p. 372; Škulić (2012), p. 138.

[10] Buzawa et al. (2017), p. 506.

withdraw, the public prosecutor considers numerous factors in deciding whether to continue proceedings: seriousness of the crime, injuries of the victim, the effect on children in the household, the used weapon, history of the relationship and previous violence, etc.[11] However, in many cases withdrawal of the victim is sufficient enough for the prosecutor to drop charges. This can be due to unwillingness of prosecutors to continue, lack of resources and staff or lack of training and understanding of victim's behaviour.[12] The lack of empathy of the professionals in conjunction with the lack of gender competent training leads to reliance on stereotypical attitudes such as that domestic violence is not serious enough or that it is a private matter. Without training, professionals rely on their own cognitive abilities and past experience.[13] Battered women often hesitate when they need to tell what happened to them, they tend to suppress the violent event, they are torn between their emotions towards the abuser and the desire to change his behaviour, they are insecure, tend to at least partially blame themselves for the victimization, etc. And when all that affects their testimony, which does not have to correspond to the pre-trial proceedings, it is likely they no one will believe them.[14] Without proper education is very difficult for public prosecutors to know that the motives of the victims to report violence differ between those who want to punish the offender and protect themselves and their children, those who want to use criminal justice system as a mechanism to influence the offender's behaviour and to change him while staying in the relationship, those who initiate criminal proceedings because of fear and threats, those who want to get legitimacy as a victim for later divorce or custody hearings, etc.[15] Some studies point to significance of the relationship between the offender and the victim with results showing that public prosecutors are more hesitant to continue proceedings if the victim is in a marriage or cohabitates with the perpetrator.[16] However, the withdrawal should not be immediately interpreted as reconciliation and in many cases there is no family to be protected by dropping charges.[17] Namely, public prosecutors prosecute cases that have a high probability of ending in a conviction. Therefore, they will be guided by this in their discretionary assessment of whether to continue the criminal proceedings or not.[18] In many cases that does not include considering the wellbeing of the victim and how to help her. Also, especially with the introduction of mandatory arrest laws for domestic violence cases, public prosecutors according to some research reject cases in almost 80% in order to avoid enormous burden and save resources. In cases of misdemeanour domestic violence offenders were charged

[11] Burton (2008), p. 99.

[12] Buzawa et al. (2017), p. 506.

[13] Craig-Taylor (2008), p. 44.

[14] Schneider (2000), p. 106.

[15] Buzawa et al., p. 500.

[16] Buzawa et al., p. 508.

[17] Burton (2008) p. 101.

[18] Pinchevsky (2017), pp. 750–751.

only when the victim came to a charging conference the day after arrest and this was policy not specified by statute.[19] However, that should not lead to the approach that is in accordance with victim's wishes but contrary to its interest and public interest as well.[20] If public prosecutors decide to drop charges every time a victim refuses to testify against the offender, then the perpetrator knows that if he makes a threat to the victim or in other way forces a victim to withdraw, he will get the control over the result in criminal proceedings.

Apart from the decision whether to prosecute or not, public prosecutors have to decide on other procedural issues. For example, the custody decision is for many victims of domestic violence important especially if they are afraid for their personal safety and in that case a detention order would provide protection. The other relevant issue is plea bargain and whether it is appropriate in cases of violent crimes generally, and not just domestic violence, to make an agreement with the offender in exchange for a more lenient penalty or for a dismissal of charges.

Similar to prosecutors, judges often lack knowledge regarding the phenomenon of domestic violence. Domestic violence is viewed superficially by the courts as the result of personal traits, family disorganization, broken relationships or jealousy. Economic, social and cultural aspects of the problem are neglected.[21] They misinterpret victims' behaviour and believe that they do not want to leave abusive partners even though they can. This indicates the need for their education, that needs to be objective so that it does not happen that they always have an attitude against the perpetrator.[22] Furthermore, the intersectional nature of gender, race and culture is ignored.[23] For example, it is not uncommon for African-American women to have to choose between gender and race, and because of political oppression they give priority to race. Asian women are brought up in the spirit of collective values, where the family and its preservation are more important than the individual, etc.[24]

2.1 Specialized Domestic Violence Courts

Specialized domestic violence courts have been established in countries such as the USA, United Kingdom and Canada,[25] with the aim of achieving more efficient legal response to domestic violence. Although these courts differ and do not follow a unique model, the idea is to take a problem-solving approach that will be

[19] Buzawa et al., p. 514.

[20] Burton, p. 102.

[21] Craig-Taylor (2008), pp. 43–44.

[22] Epstein (1999), p. 6.

[23] Cruz et al. (2023), p. 492.

[24] Craig-Taylor (2008), p. 52.

[25] Cissner et al. (2015), p. 1102.

oriented toward understanding of each case brought before the court and the underlying causes. These courts, similarly as other problem-oriented courts such as drug courts or juvenile courts, apply theory of therapeutic jurisprudence with the aim of improvement of psychological, emotional or physical health of the person.[26] On one hand, domestic violence courts are oriented toward deterrence and accentuate responsibility of the offender, while on the other hand they strive to assist victims, to help them in getting needed services. Further, they monitor compliance of treatment programmes for offenders which are usually mandatory. The courts include judges specialized in domestic violence issues, trained personnel and victim services.[27]

Efficiency of domestic violence courts is evaluated on the basis of recidivism rates but some authors assert that this should not be the only indicator. Instead, they posit that expedited and more efficient case processing are the two most important benefits of these courts.[28] Regarding the recidivism rate, the results of the studies are mixed, but this can be explained considering that authors apply different methodology, definition of recidivism (new arrest or new conviction) and period for evaluation. Comparisons with traditional courts show that there are no important differences between factors related to recidivism. In most cases, no matter whether the offender is re-arrested for domestic violence or other crime, male and young defendants, with more extensive prior criminal history, with previous records for domestic violence and for non-adherence to court orders were significantly more likely to be re-arrested.[29] However, some studies indicate that male offenders have higher probability to receive imprisonment and longer terms of imprisonment when sentenced before domestic violence courts. The reason for this situation is that judges specialized in domestic violence cases better understand the phenomenon and manipulative tactics that perpetrators use.[30] Also, these judges do not always follow the usual criteria that criminal law implies. For example, although the perpetrator did not use weapon while committing domestic violence, the court decides to impose prison sentence.[31] Of course, deterrence should not be an imperative and primary aim of penal sanctions and domestic violence courts are generally oriented toward policy of reintegration of offenders. Empirical studies confirm that treatment programmes do have a positive effect and, in the long run, this is in victim's interest as well.[32]

Apart from statistical evaluation of domestic violence courts' effectiveness, the evaluation of court's culture and beliefs and ideologies is equally important. In the empirical study of domestic violence court in Salt Lake City, Rekha Mirchandani

[26] Gover et al. (2021), p. 368.

[27] Shaffer (2004), p. 988.

[28] Gover et al. (2021), p. 373.

[29] Cissner et al. (2015), p. 1112; Collins et al. (2021), p. NP6897.

[30] Cissner et al. (2015), p. 1116.

[31] Pinchevsky (2017), p. 762.

[32] Shaffer (2004), p. 995.

explores this problem and argues that this court is an example of a "feminist regime devoted to individual and social change".[33] This study yielded some very important qualitative results and we will present some of them: the courts, that is, the judges, did not invite the abuser and the victim to reconcile, to kiss as if nothing had happened; they insisted on the defendant's responsibility; the judges taught the victim that she/he is not to blame for the behaviour of the defendant, that no one has the right to physically attack her/him, etc. At the same time, they addressed the defendants in such a way as to emphasize that their behaviour is unacceptable: "I don't know if you are used to watching scenes of violence in your house when you were little and if it is normal for you, but you have no right to solve the problem by using physical force". The next important conclusion is the acceptance of views by court personnel that violence is the result of patriarchal patterns and the desire for dominance and control, and the constant need to criticize it.[34]

3 Intimate Partner Violence in Serbia

Serbia began implementing concrete legal and institutional reforms regarding domestic violence at the beginning of the millennium. Namely, in 2002, the criminal offense of domestic violence was introduced into the Criminal Code.[35] The Criminal Code prescribes basic and aggravated forms of domestic violence. The basic form is formulated as endangerment of a family member's tranquillity, physical integrity or mental condition by use of violence, threat of attack against life and body, insolent or ruthless behaviour. The range of prescribed penalty of prison is from three months to three years. Aggravated forms exist if the offender uses weapons, dangerous implements or other means suitable to inflict serious injury to body or seriously impair health (imprisonment of six months to five years), if the offence results in serious bodily harm or serious health impairment, if committed against a minor (imprisonment of two to ten years) or if results in death of a family member (imprisonment of five to fifteen years) and if that family member is a minor at least 10 years of imprisonment shall be imposed. The special form of this crime is prescribed if the offender violates a measure against domestic violence that was imposed by the court in accordance with the law regulating family relations.

However, at the beginning, the implementation of the newly introduced criminal offence was slow and gradual. For example, in 2011 according to data of the Statistical Office of the Republic of Serbia[36] the total of 1.115 persons were

[33] Mirchandani (2006), p. 787.

[34] Mirchandani (2006), pp. 788–793.

[35] Official gazette of the Republic of Serbia 85/2005, 88/2005–107/2005–72/2009, 111/2009, 121/2012, 104/2013, 108/2014, 94/2016, 35/2019.

[36] https://www.stat.gov.rs/en-US/oblasti/pravosudje.

convicted for domestic violence[37] whereas in 2022 the number of convicted persons doubled[38] (rate of approx. 30 per 100.000 citizens). Courts initially had certain doubts in the application of that criminal act. For example, it was disputed whether it is enough that there is only one act of violence or more, bearing in mind that the law prescribes that the basic form of a criminal offense exists if the tranquillity, physical or mental integrity of the victim is endangered (permanent verb). The position was that even one action is enough. On the other hand, this also means that if there were several acts of a criminal offence in a period of time, the perpetrator is responsible for one criminal offence.[39] In the first decade of the implementation of the new criminal offence of domestic violence, the courts most often (in two thirds of cases) pronounced a suspended sentence.[40] This sanction is the most frequently imposed in relation to all committed criminal acts in the country. One of the explanations is the significantly more frequent number of reported offenders for the basic form of the criminal act of domestic violence in practice, for which a more lenient penalty is prescribed than for more severe forms.[41] However, the bigger problem was the fact that in cases where the perpetrator was already convicted of domestic violence, the courts again imposed a suspended sentence,[42] and there was no implementation of protective supervision for the perpetrators who had a problem with alcohol abuse.[43] Furthermore, the problem is in the application of the safety measure of the restraining order and order of prohibited communication with the injured party, the violation of which did not lead to consequences, but only to the possibility of initiating criminal proceedings for the criminal offence of violating the ban established by the safety measure.[44]

Issues were observed on the procedural side in cases of the victim's refusal to testify and the protection of especially vulnerable witnesses. Case attrition is high and amounts to over 60%, i.e. that is the percentage of rejected criminal charges. In this sense, Serbia is facing similar problems that have been discussed, and one of

[37] Rate of 15,4 per 100.000 citizens.

[38] Rate of approx. 29,6 per 100.000 citizens.

[39] Ćorović, Milić (2016), pp. 434–435.

[40] This trend is still present. For example, in 2022 in 33% of all convictions for domestic violence, a prison sentence was imposed (increase from 2021 when this share was 25%), while in 75% of all prison sentences its duration did not exceed one year. It should be noted that the share of persons sentenced to house arrest is about 10%, which increases the percentage of the prison sentence. Considering that for the basic, and at the same time, the least serious form of domestic violence in terms of defined penalties, Article 194 of the Criminal Code prescribes an imprisonment ranging from three months to three years, it is obvious that judges choose punishments closer to the minimum. In 55% of cases in 2022, a suspended sentence was imposed, while other alternative penal sanctions, similarly to general practice of the courts for all crimes, are negligible.

[41] Petrušić, Žunić, Vilić (2018), p. 30.

[42] Kolarić (2021), p. 183.

[43] Kolarić (2021), p. 183.

[44] Ćorović, Milić (2016), pp. 440–441.

the most common reasons for this situation is the refusal of the victim to testify against the offender. However, the Supreme Court of Cassation has taken a stand that it is in accordance with the criminal law procedure to use other evidence in cases when victims choose not to testify against the offender. For example, testimony of a witness who has gained relevant information regarding crime from the victim.[45] Problems can also be seen in terms of rejecting criminal charges when the public prosecutor assesses that it is an isolated incident and not a case of repeated violence, when the injuries are not severe enough, and one of the reasons for the long duration of the proceedings is excessive work, meaning that a public prosecutor is in charge of approximately 260 investigations.[46] In respect to especially vulnerable victims, the Criminal Procedure Code sets forth the possibility for the authority conducting the proceedings to designate as an especially vulnerable witness a witness who is especially vulnerable in view of his/her age, life experience, lifestyle, gender, state of health, nature, the manner or the consequences of the criminal offence committed, or other circumstances, but in practise this has been rarely applied.[47]

Research also pointed to the often inadequate and untimely reaction to cases of domestic violence, weak coordination of competent authorities, sexist attitudes of professionals who are involved in those cases, which is partly a reflection of adopted cultural values that must be changed by strengthening the position of women and eliminating gender inequality.[48]

Due to ratification of the Convention on Preventing and Combating Violence Against Women and Domestic Violence and weaknesses in the application of criminal offence of domestic violence, the Law on Prevention of Domestic Violence[49] (hereinafter: the LPDV) was introduced. The term of violence according to this law is more broadly defined in relation to the Criminal Code and for the first time, the category of economic violence is introduced. Also, the term family member is more broadly defined and includes not only current or former spouses or common-law partners, but also other partners (Article 3, para 3). According to that law, the police received new powers to assess the risk of violence and, accordingly, to impose an emergency measure of temporary removal of the perpetrator from the premises where he/she lives and a temporary ban on the perpetrator from contacting and approaching the victim of violence (Article 17). Application of this Law led to a striking increase in reports of violence. This does not mean that all of these cases in which the police officer determined the risk and ordered restrictive measure[50] would lead to a conviction in criminal proceedings. This Law was

[45] Sinanović (2017), p. 97.

[46] Lacmanović (2022), p. 47.

[47] Sinanović (2017), p. 98.

[48] Petrušić, Žunić, Vilić (2018), pp.12–13.

[49] Official gazette of the Republic of Serbia 94/2016, 10/2023.

[50] Approximately between 25 and 30 thousand restrictive measures per year.

introduced to stop violence immediately and thus sets forth that these measures can be imposed against "possible offenders" (Article 3).

Beside criminal law provisions, measures for protection against domestic violence were introduced in the Family Law in 2005. Article 197 of the Law defines domestic violence and provides examples. Unlike the Criminal Code, domestic violence stipulated by this law includes sexual violence as well. Further, the list of family members is broader in comparison to the Criminal Code and includes current and ex emotional and sexual partners. The Law also prescribes protection measures that can last up to one year which is much longer than measures stipulated by the Law on Prevention of Domestic Violence (police order lasts up to 48 hours and the court has the right to extend these measures up to 30 days). However, protection measures have been rarely applied in practice. The majority of procedures have been initiated by victims although public prosecutors and centres for social welfare are able to do that.[51]

Other actors that deal with domestic violence, such as centres for social welfare, the police and the public prosecutor's office also experience certain difficulties. In the report for Serbia, GREVIO warns of excessively long procedures, problems in risk assessment rules, supervision of the imposed restrictive measures and sanctioning of their violation.[52] Conclusion is that the state enacts laws that should improve the suppression of domestic violence, but without expanding the capacity, similar objections regarding work of professionals can be expected, while at the same time the pressure on the non-governmental sector, that provides support and assistance to victims to large extent, further increases.

4 Methodological Framework and Sample of the Study

The goal of the qualitative study is to analyse and present main findings on application of criminal law in intimate partner violence judicial cases in Serbia. We start from the idea that criminal law is in some respects created for men, and without consideration of women's experiences, such as for example law on self-defence,[53] and that criminal law, its application and even its understanding in the academia often reflects patriarchal values in the society and neglects other knowledges and experiences. For example, feminism has influenced law but only through its already existing mechanisms of rights or of welfare, but it faced obstacles in attempts to create its one terms.[54] The method used is discourse analysis that is a "generic term for all spoken or written texts" that construct social reality. That does not mean that this construction has to be deliberate and the person is just

[51] Kolarić (2021), p. 183.

[52] GREVIO (2020), pp. 50–56.

[53] Baer (1999), p. 19.

[54] Smart (1989), p. 20.

"doing something naturally" trying to make sense of a phenomenon.[55] Discourses can be understood as frameworks or ways of viewing issues with the following consequences: the way subjects and subjectivities are represented within discourses; limits of what can be said and "lived effects" or the realization that the way we think has its roots in socially constructed meanings.[56] Apart from the discourse analysis, critical discourse analysis has gained significance in the literature and it is focused on the use of discourse as a power mechanism.[57] Interpretation of legal texts often neglects cultural and social relations that are behind and help in understanding creation and application of legal norms. We start from these assumptions in interpretation of judicial verdicts and the ways violence between intimate partners, offenders and victims is constructed and hence the ways in which judges decide on sanctioning.

The study consists of 81 final judicial verdicts on crime of domestic violence prescribed in Article 194 of the Criminal Code of Serbia. The sample includes verdicts from seven different criminal courts[58] and only cases of intimate partner violence. The aim of the study was, firstly, to include analysis of court decisions from different parts of the country i.e. from four regions. Considering different levels of development in different regions of Serbia in terms of education, employment, salaries and economy,[59] we wanted to include nationwide verdicts. However, we do not assert that the sample is representative since we did not include all courts that decide on this crime in the first instance. Secondly, we opted for judicial practice of the first instance courts since they deal with the largest number of all domestic violence cases. The first instance courts in Serbia have jurisdiction in cases of criminal offences for which the maximum penalty of imprisonment of ten years is prescribed, unless differently regulated.[60] Considering that in many cases parties in criminal proceedings do not appeal, the verdicts are not being supervised by higher courts and that means that judges in the first instance decide finally on issues of domestic violence. Further, the verdicts as constructs of social reality represent values and attitudes regarding domestic violence and especially intimate partner violence of a specific region and of the local level to greater extent than for example the judicial practice of appellate courts that express opinions regarding specific substantial and procedural legal questions and influence judicial practice generally.

[55] Potter and Wetherell (1987), p. 34.

[56] Bacchi (1999), pp. 40–45.

[57] Burman (2010), p.177.

[58] The Third Basic Court in Belgrade, the Basic Court in Novi Sad, the Basic Court in Sremska Mitrovica, the Basic Court in Kragujevac, the Basic Court in Niš, the Basic Court in Velika Plana and the Basic Court in Vranje.

[59] According to Молнар and Јандрић (2019) these disparities between the regions in Serbia are among the greatest in Europe, p. 92.

[60] Article 24 of the Law on Organization of Courts, Official Gazette of the Republic of Serbia 10/2023.

5 Results

5.1 Types of Batterers and Court Decisions

In respect to offender-victim relationship in most cases violence in this sample is committed against spouse (39%), then extramarital partner (34%) and ex-partners (26,6%). Except in two verdicts, in all other cases victims were females, which is not representative of the general population of convicted persons for domestic violence in Serbia (females comprise approximately 10% of all convicted persons for this crime).[61] Offenders are mostly (72%) convicted of Article 194, paragraph 1 of the Criminal Code according to which "whoever by use of violence, threat of attacks against life or body, insolent or ruthless behaviour endangers the tranquillity, physical integrity or mental condition of a member of his family, shall be punished with imprisonment of three months to three years." These cases include numerous different acts against the victim in practise. In most situations these are death threats and offenders usually threat that they will slaughter victims. In three cases, offenders have threatened with publishing explicit materials of victims on social networks and in two cases batterers have threatened to rape victims together with other men. Further, physical attacks are very common and they include slapping, kicking, pushing, throwing things on the victim, etc.

Many verdicts confirm that domestic violence has its roots in gender inequalities. This can be concluded from statements of defendants such as "you have no right to decide", "I will tell you whether you can leave the house", "you will end up six feet under if you abandon me", "only whores go to seminar". In many cases offenders disparage victims with statements such as "you are horrible mother and spouse" and as many as 90% of all verdicts include insulting word "whore".

We notice that cases of mutual violence are exceptional. These situations would include female violence no matter who started first. It is possible that these cases were not included in our sample, but further analysis should be oriented toward decisions of public prosecutors and the problem of case attrition has already been discussed. On the other hand, literature points to differences in male and female violence in domestic setting. The consequences are, at least in respect to physical injuries, more severe for women even in the cases of mutual violence, and it is woman who will most often be seen in an emergency room or doctor's office after domestic violence incident.[62] In one case, the court has sentenced the defendant for causing injury (bleeding and wound) to female partner by seriously biting her lips. In the same event, they had been previously arguing and she slapped him. The court didn't take into account this as victim precipitation.

---

[61] In respect to all crimes women generally comprise 10% of the population of convicted persons in Serbia. See: Ignjatović and Lukić (2014), p. 341.

[62] Walker (2007), p. 65.

Analysis of verdicts allows us to conclude that the court practice in imposing sentences differs. Even within the same court, judges impose different sanctions in similar cases. For example, in one case, the court in Velika Plana sentenced the defendant to a suspended sentence for two criminal acts of domestic violence.[63] Among other things, he threw a hunting knife on his wife but missed because she slipped away, and on another occasion, under the influence of alcohol, he forced his wife to undress in front of his friends and threatened that they would all rape her. He committed another act of domestic violence against his mother. Since the defendant admitted the crime, the court did not need any other evidence, such as expert testimony or the report of social service. On the contrary, in one case, the court in Kragujevac sentenced the defendant to imprisonment for death threats to his spouse on three occasions. He had no previous criminal record but several months before these events the victim reported violence to the police and restrictive measures were imposed on the defendant. The verdict is upheld with numerous evidence.[64] Although courts in deciding what type of penalty to impose take into account criminal history, imposed restrictive measures and very often opinions of experts in mental health, it can be noticed that practice differs and judges have no uniform view of these circumstances.[65] Decisions in cases of domestic violence should be guided not only by general rules, such as that previous criminal history in most cases leads to heavier penalty, but by scientific knowledge on domestic violence typology, factors related to this crime and effects of different treatments for offenders. The literature, for example, points to batterer typology and it is possible to make distinction between: 1) family-only perpetrators who commit the least serious crimes against partners and outside home and who are characterized by no or little signs of psychopathology; 2) dysphoric/borderline batterers engage in modestly severe violence, primarily against the spouse but violence outside the home can also occur. In this group of offenders, characteristics of borderline personality disorder are often present (extreme emotional lability, intense, unstable interpersonal relationships, fear of rejection); 3) generally violent/antisocial offenders who are characterized as the most violent in and outside of home. They are most likely to be diagnosed with antisocial personality disorder.[66] This classification has its clinical significance considering that it gives some evidence on the success of treatment and types of appropriate treatments for different categories of offenders.

[63] The Basic Court in Velika Plana, K.n.448/19, 14.10.2021.

[64] The Basic Court in Kragujevac, 7 K-988/20, 1.9.2022.

[65] It should be mentioned that courts, in accordance with Article 66 of the Criminal Code, have to respect restrictions in respect to imposition of a probation. Article 66, para.3 stipulates that "A suspended sentence may not be imposed when more than five years have not elapsed from the time the prison sentence or probation imposed on a perpetrator for intentional criminal offence became final".

[66] Holtzworth-Munroe (2007), pp. 98–99.

5.2 *Aggravating/Mitigating Circumstances*

According to Article 54 of the Criminal Code the court shall determine a punishment for a criminal offender within the limits set forth by law for such criminal offence, with regard to the purpose of punishment and taking into account all circumstance that could have bearing on severity of the punishment (extenuating and aggravating circumstances), and particularly the following: degree of culpability, the motives for committing the offence, the degree of endangering or damaging protected goods, the circumstances under which the offence was committed, the past life of the offender, his personal situation, his behaviour after the commission of the criminal offence and particularly his attitude towards the victim of the criminal offence, and other circumstances related to the personality of the offender. In practice when deciding on severity of punishment courts almost always mention one or more mitigating circumstances. Regarding aggravating circumstances, previous criminal record is always treated in this way.

Alcohol affects human mind and according to the Criminal Code of Serbia it can lead to a state of substantially diminished ability to understand the significance of the criminal act or ability to control actions (Article 23). In that situation, perpetrator is not regarded insane but his/her penalty can be mitigated and the decision is left to the court. If the court decides not to mitigate the penalty due to diminished responsibility, it is possible to take it into account when deciding on the penalty (Article 54). For example, if the minimum prescribed penalty of prison is three months, Article 23 would allow court to mitigate penalty but not under thirty days. If only this state of the offender is taken into account when deciding on the penalty (Article 54), the court would impose more lenient penalty but not under three months. Alcohol abuse is often mentioned as a risk factor for domestic violence. In one study conducted in Serbia on a representative sample of 2.406 women, researchers have found that females from families with alcohol abuse (WAAF) have been twice as often (59,2% v.29,1%) victims of psychological violence in the last year in comparison to women who had no experience with alcohol abuse in their families. In respect to physical violence this ratio was 28,4% v. 8,7% at the expense of WAAF and 5,7% v. 0,7% for sexual violence.[67] The problem with alcohol abuse in domestic violence in Serbia can be understood better if we take into consideration that out of all imposed compulsory alcohol addiction treatment measures in criminal proceedings in 2022, 70% were imposed for crimes against family.[68] In this regard, it is questionable whether courts should treat alcohol abuse as a mitigating circumstance. For example, in one case the defendant, returning from the lawyer's office where he was with his wife due to the divorce process, suddenly started hitting her in the head, and when she lost consciousness and fell on the ground, he continued to kick her in the head and body area, breaking her nasal bone, nasal septum and caused fracture of the bones of the eye socket. Since

[67] Dragišić-Labaš (2019), p. 116.

[68] Statistical Office of the Republic of Serbia, Adult Offenders of Crimes in Serbia, 2021.

it was estimated that he was significantly impaired due to alcohol abuse, the court in Novi Sad reduced his sentence.[69] He had previous convictions. In this and less serious cases some courts decided, if not to mitigate, then to impose more lenient penalty due to alcohol abuse. Since they are, according to the law, not obliged to consider alcohol abuse in that way, the question is how does this lenient treatment of relation between alcohol abuse and domestic violence affect future behaviour of the defendant and other citizens? At least in situations when mental state of the defendant is not impaired due to alcohol abuse it is questionable whether courts should always treat alcohol abuse as a mitigating circumstance. Also, compulsive measure of alcohol addiction treatment is reserved only when experts confirm that the addiction has been developed, but in many cases, in which there is no addiction determined, offenders need treatment because they regularly abuse alcohol and this is related to domestic violence incidents. Further, biological and psychological explanations of aggression under the influence of alcohol are criticized in the literature and it is pointed to the importance of cultural and social factors. Abuse of alcohol is more widespread than violence and data show that countries with high prevalence of alcohol abuse do not necessary record higher rates of violent crimes. In many cases, people under the influence of alcohol behave in accordance with cultural, gender and social expectations.[70]

In many cases children were present in domestic violence incidents. The Criminal Code in Art. 194, paragraph 3 prescribes heavier penalty if the victim is a minor, that is, a person who has not reached the age of 18 and in this situation imprisonment is mandatory. In cases where a minor is present, and the violence is not committed directly against him/her, the court should value that fact as an aggravating circumstance, and not, as can be found in some court decisions, to value that being a father is a mitigating circumstance. For example, in one verdict, the expert expressed the opinion in criminal proceedings that the child is afraid of the father and of spending time with him due to violence against the child's mother. The court valued parenthood as a mitigating circumstance.[71] On the other hand, the Istanbul Convention prescribes in Article 46 that presence of a child should be treated as an aggravating circumstance.

It is further unacceptable that some judges treat the victim's non-insistence on criminal charges and non-submission of the restitution motion as a mitigating circumstance. Namely, non-insistence on criminal prosecution has no procedural legal effect since the public prosecutor represents the indictment. Only if the public prosecutor decides to dismiss charges, the injured party has the right to assume criminal proceedings. In some situations, however, the victim only wants the procedure to end, to be protected and is not interested in restitution motion for physical and mental pain caused. In one case, for example, the defendant took a screwdriver and held it to the victim's throat, telling her that he would kill her.

[69] The Basic Court in Novi Sad, K-1990/2019, 12.1.2021.

[70] Ignjatović and Lukić (2022), pp. 790–791.

[71] The verdict of the Third Basic Court in Belgrade, 21.4.2022.

He was previously convicted of domestic violence against the same victim. The judge treated victim's refusal to submit a motion for restitution as a mitigating circumstance.[72]

The courts should pay attention to further consequences of the criminal act which affect victim's wellbeing. For example, in one case, the defendant knew that his daughter has problems with breathing in stressful situations. When the child experienced breathing issues as a result of the violence against her and her mother, he ironically said "come on, mom will calm you down". At the trial, he said that she gets upset over the smallest things and has problems breathing. He received a prison sentence below the legal minimum even though he committed two criminal acts—paragraph 3 and paragraph 1 of Article 194.[73] The court accepted victim's statement that he is otherwise a good father and that his behaviour becomes problematic when he drinks. He was previously convicted. In this concrete case the defendant was aware what his violent behaviour would cause to his daughter and therefore intentionally made her suffer. Thus, there is no reason not to consider this as an aggravating circumstance.[74]

5.3 *Type of Penalty*

In most cases courts decide to impose suspended sentence of imprisonment or imprisonment. In the sample 62% of defendants received suspended sentence of imprisonment and in the rest of the cases prison penalty was imposed. Imprisonment is usually reserved for recidivists and more serious injuries and in most cases duration of the prison penalty does not go beyond six months. Release on parole is possible (the court decides) after two thirds of penalty was enforced. In respect to suspended sentence, it is not such a huge problem to opt for this penal sanction, since sometimes it is better than to send the defendant to prison, but it is not good that courts absolutely do not use option prescribed in Article 71 of the Criminal Code and this is suspended sentence with protective supervision. Protective supervision includes different options including, for example, treatment in a competent medical institution, visits to professional and counselling centres and institutions, refraining from drug and alcohol abuse, etc. These obligations would certainly tackle problems that are in relation to domestic violence (alcohol abuse and certain traits of personality) and highly likely produce positive results and reduce recidivism rates. Without solving factors that are related to domestic violence, a permanent solution that would be of interest for the defendant and the victim can't be achieved. This non-existence of suspended sentence with protective supervision in judicial practice is not a failure of the courts only, but of the whole system that is not coordinated and of the fact that

---

[72] The verdict of the Third Basic Court in Belgrade, 26.3.2021.

[73] The verdict of the Third Basic Court in Belgrade, 7.11.2022.

[74] Vuković (2021), p. 473.

many alternative sanctions are not being applied. This is the consequence of the lack of coordination, overburdening of probation officers with administrative work, improper classification of offenders for alternative sanctions, the lack of contracts with companies, organizations and institutions in which offenders could work or receive a treatment, etc. In rare verdicts in which judges have imposed protective supervision the obligation was to refrain from alcohol abuse and to regularly visit a doctor.

Similar problems are found in the enforcement of imprisonment. Namely, according to the report of the Council of Europe published in 2022, the capacity of penal institutions in Serbia is predicted to be around 11.500 places. Data indicate that in 2021, there were 10.160 persons in Serbian institutions for deprivation of liberty (including detention). Serbia is in the group of countries with high rate of persons deprived of liberty (rate of 155 vs. the European average of 117).[75] Many penal institutions lack staff responsible for the treatment of convicted persons and that will certainly affect rehabilitation of all, including prisoners sentenced for domestic violence. In many cases, due to short imposed prison penalty there is not enough time for the treatment to be completed. On the other hand, description of cases in judicial verdicts points to the importance of the treatment of offenders. It is therefore of the greatest importance for judges to be informed of types of treatment and time needed for their completion as well as possibilities and existence of special programmes in penal institutions. More repressive answer to domestic violence is constantly being required by the public and non-governmental organizations, but the question is what do we want to achieve with short prison sentences? If this is short, sharp shock, we should not forget negative influence of prisons. Considering that it is not easy for courts to decide whether to impose imprisonment or suspended sentence, and that often there is a fine line between the two, gender competent legal education would give judges more insights and make their decisions more adequate.

6 International Legal Framework And Gender Competent Legal Education In Domestic Violence Cases

As in many states worldwide, the international law has not recognized domestic violence as a legal and serious social problem until the end of 1980s. The UN activities in respect to domestic violence started in 1993 with the Declaration on the Elimination of Violence against Women.[76] The Declaration points to the importance of general education that should change existing social patterns that contribute to domestic violence.[77] Furthermore, the states are encouraged to take all appropriate measures so that professionals who are responsible for detection, prosecution and

[75] Aebi et al. (2022), p. 31.

[76] 815 Declaration on the Elimination of Violence against Women, GA 48/104 of 20 December 1993.

[77] Article 4 (j).

punishment of these offenders become more sensitive regarding women's needs.[78] Also, the recommendation that the states should take all necessary measures in order to prevent re-victimization of women due to laws insensitive to gender issues further accentuates the importance of education of professionals in gender sensitive legal cases. Similar solutions are incorporated into the "Convention of Belem do Para".[79] Suppression of all forms of discrimination against women is the main goal of the Convention on the Elimination of All Forms of Discrimination against Women (CEDAW), adopted in 1979 by the UN General Assembly. The progress of the implementation of this Convention is being monitored by the Committee on the Elimination of Discrimination against Women. In respect to all crimes against women as well as crimes committed by women the Committee requests state parties to apply gender perspective in order to prevent discrimination.[80]

The Council of Europe started to take steps in respect to domestic violence after almost 40 years since its establishment.[81] In 1985 the Committee of Ministers of the Council of Europe passed the Recommendation on Violence in the Family.[82] This document produced numerous recommendations for states, *inter alia,* the third recommendation emphasizes the importance of providing appropriate professional training for all those responsible for intervening in domestic violence cases. Also, following a domestic violence event, the states should "study the possibility of entrusting cases of violence in the family only to specialist members of prosecuting or investigating authorities or of trial courts".[83] However, this document explicitly holds a position that criminal law should be the last legal mechanism (*ultima ratio*) and the criminal proceedings depend on the approval of the victim to prosecute the offender or on the existence of a public interest. The Committee of Ministers adopted the Recommendation Rec (2002)5 on the protection of women against violence in 2002. This Recommendation also points to the importance of education of all professionals in the criminal justice system and differentiates between basic training programmes, specialized training programmes and programmes for judges in respect to domestic violence as well as other types of violence against women. This document encourages states to organize education programmes at university level that particularly deal with violence against women.[84] Adherence to this recommendation would allow students of law, for example, to start education in

[78] Article 4 (i).

[79] Inter-American Convention on the Prevention, Punishment and Eradication of Violence against Women, GA to the Organization of American States, 1994.

[80] See for example: Communication No. 153/2020, Sandra Luz Román Jaimes v. Mexico, Communication No.23/2009, Inga Abramova v. Belarus, Communication No. 5/2005, The Vienna Intervention Centre against Domestic Violence and the Association for Women's Access to Justice on behalf of Hakan Goekce, Handan Goekce, and Guelue Goekce (descendants of the deceased) v. Austria, Communication No. 47/2012, Angela González Carreño v. Spain.

[81] McQuigg (2017), p. 38.

[82] Recommendation No. R (85) 4 on Violence in the Family.

[83] Recommendation No. R (85) 4 on Violence in the Family.

[84] Appendix to Recommendation Rec (2002)5, No. 6–11.

gender sensitive issues before they have reached the positions within the criminal justice system. That would lead to more comprehensive and continuous education instead of temporary and fast courses and programmes.

The Council of Europe Convention on preventing and combating violence against women and domestic violence (Istanbul Convention)[85] builds on previous international and regional documents and formulates a broad framework of goals to be achieved. Violence against women is seen, as formulated in the Preamble, as a manifestation of historically unequal power relations between men and women, whereas the violence represents one of the mechanisms that men use to subordinate women. The Convention is oriented toward achieving protection, prevention, prosecution and integrated policies. The Istanbul Convention accepts gender perspective and uses terms such as gender-based violence, gender sensitive policies, non-stereotyped gender roles, gendered understanding and gender guidelines.[86] Accepting that criminal law is only one mechanism to fulfil defined goals, the Convention prescribes that the parties shall take different measures among which are awareness raising, education, training of professionals, preventive intervention and programmes, participation of private sector and media. These policies, aimed at prevention and suppression of violence against women, are to be performed by different actors: government agencies, the national, regional and local parliaments and authorities, national human rights institutions and civil society organizations (Article 7 (3)). The training of professionals is stipulated in Article 15 and it includes all professionals dealing with victims or perpetrators of violence against women. The second paragraph of Article 15 emphasizes the importance of mutual cooperation and coordination of agencies involved in these cases.

The Istanbul Convention invokes the European Convention on Human Rights in the first paragraph of its Preamble. The European Court of Human Rights has developed a substantial body of decisions in cases of violence against women.[87] In most cases these decisions are based on Article 2 (the right to life),[88] Article 3 (the right not to be subjected to torture, inhuman or degrading treatment)[89] and Article 8 (the right to private life).[90] The Court has defined positive state obligations in respect to these articles as: (1) the obligation to criminalize harmful conduct; (2) the procedural obligation to investigate allegations of criminal conduct; (3) the obligation to take protective operational measures; (4) the obligation to adopt effective regulatory frameworks for general prevention and (5) the obligation to offer remedies.[91] Although training of professionals is not among these positive

[85] Council of Europe Convention on preventing and combating violence against women and domestic violence, Istanbul, 2011.

[86] Gender equality and the Istanbul Convention: a decade of action, Berlin, 2021, 11–12.

[87] Niemi et al. (2020), p. 4.

[88] See for example: Kurt v. Austria, No. 62903/15, June 2021.

[89] See for example Volodina v. Russia, No. 41261/17, July 2019.

[90] See for example Ž.B. v. Croatia, No. 47666/13, July 2017.

[91] Stoyanova (2020), p. 104.

state obligations, this is implied in interpretation of certain obligations. For example, when deciding upon adequate measures in situations of real and immediate risks of harm against a specific individual, the Court shall decide whether the State had taken all necessary measures to protect the victim. The Court has adopted several standards as guidance in appraisal of applied measures: they should not represent an impossible or disproportionate burden for the authorities, they should be reasonably judged and with respect of the due process and other guarantees.[92] Therefore, in order for the state to fulfil its positive obligations related to the criminalization, investigation and protection of victims, it is of the utmost importance that professionals in the field of criminal justice who deal with the crime of domestic violence should not only have the necessary knowledge regarding domestic violence, the consequences that it has for the victim, risks for violence and adequate treatment programs for offenders, but they must also be gender sensitive so that they understand that a legal norm, although apparently gender neutral, in practice does not necessarily mean equality. The passivity of state authorities, lack of interest and lack of understanding that domestic violence disproportionately affects women can only contribute to strengthening the culture of tolerance and to repeated violence. For example, in the case of *Opuz v. Turkey* the Court determined that the authorities' reactions to repeated violence of the husband were not appropriate, that judicial decisions had no noticeable preventive or deterrent effect and have even disclosed a degree of tolerance considering the short prison sentence that was imposed and a small fine for stabbing the victim seven times. This represented violation of Article 3 considering that despite applicant's request for help, authorities had failed to take protective measures. This case is one of the best known and regarded as the "most gender-conscious case of the Strasbourg Court"[93] considering that Articles 2 and 3 were interpreted in conjunction with principle of non-discrimination under Article 14.

6.1 Situation in Serbia

First step regarding education of professionals who work with offenders and victims in cases of domestic violence was the General Protocol for Action and Cooperation of Institutions, Bodies and Organizations in Situations of Domestic and Intimate Partner Violence against Women.[94] Subsequently, several other protocols were adopted—the Special Protocol on Conduct of Police Officers in Cases

---

[92] Stoyanova (2020), p. 122.

[93] Jelić (2023), p. 45.

[94] The General Protocol for Action and Cooperation of Institutions, Bodies and Organizations in Situations of Domestic and Intimate Partner Violence against Women adopted by the Government of the Republic of Serbia in November 2011.

of Domestic and Intimate Partner Violence against Women,[95] the Special Protocol for Action of Social Welfare Centres—Guardianship Authorities in Cases of Domestic and Intimate Partner Violence against Women,[96] the Special Protocol of the Ministry of Health for the Protection and Treatment of Women Victims of Violence[97] and the Special Protocol for Judicial Bodies in Cases of Domestic and Intimate Partner Violence against Women[98] In 2014, the office of the Ombudsman for protection of citizen's rights published a report[99] on implementation of these protocols. The report identified many obstacles and issues in that respect including, for example: non-recognition of domestic violence especially in cases when it occurred for the first time when it is characterized as an incident, lack of understanding of causes of domestic violence, the imbalance of power between the actors, of the history of previous violence and the consequences that violence has for the victim. The report especially emphasizes insufficient training for professionals, small number of courses, imbalance of education among institutions, the lack of knowledge in respect to training needs of employees etc. The Law on Prevention of Domestic Violence stipulates mandatory training organized by the Judicial Academy in Belgrade for public prosecutors and judges. These training are divided in two parts. The first part deals with international principles and European standards in combating domestic violence, cases of the European Court for Human Rights and with an overview at the LPDV. The second part is a joint training for police officers, public prosecutors and judges and it deals mainly with the LPDV. Every year several hundred trainees attend courses which certainly is an important step in education of professionals who deal with cases of domestic violence.[100] However, the emphasis is on the LPDV that is aimed at stopping violence by determining the risk of the future violence and ordering restrictive measures. Criminal proceedings and convictions do not have to be a result of these orders considering that the LPDV has a wider area of application and includes persons who are estimated by police officers as "potential offenders". In criminal proceedings verdict and penalty depends not primarily on the future risk for the victim, but on the committed crime of domestic violence, guilt and personal circumstances of

[95] The Special Protocol on Conduct of Police Officers in Cases of Domestic and Intimate Partner Violence against Women adopted by the Ministry of Interior in February 2013.

[96] The Special Protocol for Action of Social Welfare Centers—Guardianship Authorities in Cases of Domestic and Intimate Partner Violence against Women adopted by the Ministry of Labor, Employment and Social Policy in March 2013.

[97] The Special Protocol of the Ministry of Health for the Protection and Treatment of Women Victims of Violence adopted by the Ministry of Health in June 2010.

[98] The Special Protocol for Judicial Bodies in Cases of Domestic and Intimate Partner Violence against Women adopted by the Ministry of Justice and Public Administration in January 2014.

[99] Special Report of the Protector of Citizens on the Implementation of the General and Special Protocols on Protection of Women Against Violence, Republic of Serbia Ombudsman for protection of citizen's rights, 22–21/14.

[100] For example, in 2022 the overall number of training events organized by the Judicial Academy was 21 attended by 452 professionals. Godišnji izveštaj Pravosudne akademije (2022), p. 16.

offenders. Notwithstanding the differences between the Criminal Code and the LPDV, there is a need for further training in according to the abovementioned hurdles determined by the Ombudsman for protection of citizen's rights. Recent research confirms this and emphasises the importance of further enhancement of knowledge in respect to factors related to domestic and intimate partner violence, behaviour of the victim that is not "typical" as expected by professionals leads to drop of charges, etc.[101]

Beside education of professionals, of great importance are educational programmes at university level. Students of law faculties should have possibility to attend programmes and courses that specifically deal with issues of domestic violence. Courses in Criminal Law are the first step but the knowledge on legal concepts and regulation should be complemented with Criminology, namely explanation of domestic violence, its trends, causes and consequences for the victim, typology of offenders etc. At all law faculties in Serbia students have possibility to choose Criminology but only at Law Faculty University of Niš this is an obligatory subject.[102] Therefore, those who have not passed exam in Criminology at undergraduate studies, are left with the option to enrol at postgraduate studies and choose Criminology or to attend training courses organized by Judicial Academy or for example non-governmental organizations.[103] Considering that the number of reports for domestic violence according to LPDV is approximately 20.000 cases per year, it is obvious that many lawyers deal with this criminal offence in practice and in order to do that properly education is a precondition.

7 Conclusion

In the last few decades, a lot of activities to combat domestic violence have been undertaken internationally. A similar trend is also noticeable in Serbia, which is characterized by the adoption of new legal solutions, the activity of the non-governmental sector and the increased attention of researchers to understanding the phenomenon of domestic violence. Although many training activities have been organized by the Judicial Academy in Belgrade and many professionals have completed that training, there is still room for improvement. First of all, law faculties should offer more learning opportunities to students, because it does not necessarily mean that those who learned more about domestic violence within the criminology course will later work in the criminal justice system. Second, the training of professionals can be additionally complemented by understanding the

[101] Ignjatović (2022), p. 42.

[102] Ignjatović and Lukić (2014), p. 330.

[103] For example, training for police officers, public prosecutors and judges organized by non-governmental organization "Women's support center". Information available at: https://www.cpz.rs/program-obuke-za-unapredjenje-multisektorske-saradnje-u-slucajevima-nasilja-nad-zenama/.

gender perspective in domestic violence cases. Finally, the research conducted should respond to specific problems faced by professionals in practice, and at the same time this would represent the basis for further education.

With the analysis of court verdicts for domestic violence between partners in Serbia, we wanted to determine how criminal law is being applied in these cases. Although numerous steps have been taken in terms of legislative and institutional reforms with respect to domestic violence, for the successful application of criminal law, it is of great importance that the subjects who apply it acquire knowledge of the phenomenon of domestic violence not only as a legal but a real category. In this sense, we can first conclude that judges often approach these cases like other criminal offences, focusing primarily on the legal elements. Such a technical approach ignores the cycles of violence, the consequences experienced by the victim and future risks. Although, on the one hand, it is clear that criminal law should not be used in cases that are to be defined as family conflicts, rather than violence, and that it should be taken into account that the object of protection of the criminal act of domestic violence is the family, on the other hand, more serious cases that include a serious risk for the victim, should be treated more harshly, considering that in these situations there is no longer a family that needs to be protected, but only the psychological and physical integrity of the victim.

The perpetrator of the criminal offense is unjustifiably privileged, so the courts consider as a mitigating circumstance for example that he is an elderly man, that he has health problems, that alcohol affected his ability to make decisions and that he is otherwise not like that, regardless of the fact that he is diagnosed with a long-term addiction, that he is a parent even though his actions cause stress to his children, that he is employed even though he spends that money on alcohol, that he is unemployed and therefore under stress, etc. On the other hand, it is not recognized that he violated the duties of respecting his partner as an equal human being and not the one who should be subordinated to him, that he is the one who did nothing to treat alcohol addiction, that in the majority of cases, although it is certainly allowed according to the rules of criminal procedure, he does not admit the crime, he does not apologize for everything he did and he does not express sincere remorse, that expert reports indicate serious psychological and health consequences suffered by the victim, etc.

Obviously, the criminal law cannot be the only instrument in solving the problem of domestic violence and it is necessary to work on prevention. Education at all levels is one of the preventive measures. Furthermore, the courts are only one link of the criminal justice system. Future research should focus on the qualitative analysis of dismissed criminal charges in prosecutor's offices, because in Serbia, similarly to other countries, there is a large case attrition. Additionally, the enforcement of penal sanctions is of great importance for achieving results, because the treatment officers in prisons and probation officers for alternative penal sanctions can play a key role in the resocialization of convicted persons and influence the reduction of recidivism. However, as recidivism is not dependent only upon the personality of the individual, it is necessary to change widespread gender patterns of behaviour and sanction them informally instead of relying only on criminal law.

References

Aebi M, et al (2022) Prison populations, SPACE I—2022. Strasbourg

Bacchi CL (1999) Women, policy and politics. The construction of policy problems. Sage Publications, London

Baer JA (1999) Our lives before the law, constructing feminist jurisprudence. Princeton University Press, New Jersey

Burman M (2010) The ability of criminal law to produce gender equality: judicial discourse in the Swedish criminal legal system. Violence Against Women 16(2):173–188

Burton M (2008) Legal response to domestic violence. Routledge, London

Buzawa ES, Buzawa CG, Star ED (2017) Responding to domestic violence, the integration of criminal justice and human services, 5th edn. Sage, Los Angeles

Вуковић И (2021) Кривично право – општи део. Београд

Синановић Б (2017) Заштита права жртава насиља у породици у кривичном поступку и поступку за спречавање насиља у породици. Билтен Врховног касационог суда 2:91–108

Cissner B, et al (2015) Domestic violence courts: a multisite test of whether and how they change offender outcomes. Violence Against Women 21(9):1102–1122

Collins M, et al (2021) Predicting recidivism among defendants in an expedited domestic violence court. J Interpers Violence 36(13–14):NP6890–NP6903

Ćorović E, Milić I (2016) Zaštita od nasilja u porodici u zakonodavstvu Republike Srbije sa posebnim osvrtom na krivičnopravnu legislative, in: krivičnopravni instrumenti suprotstavljanja terorizmu i drugim krivičnim djelima nasilničkog karaktera, Ministarstvo pravde Republike Srpske, Srpsko udruženje za krivičnopravnu teoriju i praksu, Internacionalna asocijacija kriminalista. Banja Luka, pp 419–451

Craig-Taylor P (2008) Lifting the Veil: the Intersectionality of Ethics, Culture and Gender Bias in Domestic Violence Cases. Rutgers L Rec 32:31–63

Cruz B, Lukić N, Strand S (2023) Gender perspective of victimization, crime and penal policy. In: Vujadinović D, Fröhlich M, Giegerich T (eds) Gender-competent legal education. Springer, Cham, pp 467–502

Dragišić LS (2019) Partnersko nasilje, tradicionalni stavovi i upotreba alkohola u Srbiji. Crimen 10(2):109–121

Epstein D (1999) Effective intervention in domestic violence cases: rethinking the roles of prosecutors, judges and the court system. Yale J Law Feminism 11(1):3–50

Gover R, et al. (2021) Courting justice: tracing the evolution and future of domestic violence courts. Feminist Criminol 16(3):366–381

GREVIO's (Baseline) evolution Report on legislative and other measures giving effect to the provisions of the council of Europe convention on preventing and combating violence against women and domestic violence (Istanbul convention) Serbia. (2020) Group of experts on action against violence against women and domestic violence. Strasbourg

Holtzworth-Munroe A (2007) Batterer typology. In: Jackson NA (ed) Encyclopedia of domestic violence. Routledge, New York, pp 98–103

Hon. Shaffer C (2004), Therapeutic Domestic Violence Courts: An Efficient Approach to Adjudication? *Seattle University Law Review,*27(4): 981–997.

Ignjatović Đ, Lukić N (2014) Criminology and crime in Serbia. In Getoš-Kalač, et al (ed) Mapping the criminological landscape of the Balkans. Duncker &Humbolt, Berlin, pp 329–352

Ignjatović Đ, Lukić N (2022) O povezanosti alkohola i ubistava u uzorku osuđenih u Beogradu. Anali Pravnog Fakultete 70(3):765–792

Jelić I (2023) Feminist justice and European court of human rights. In I K, et al (ed) Legal issues of international law from a gender perspective. Springer, Cham, pp 35–53

Kolarić D (2021) Jedan osvrt na primenu Zakona o sprečavanju nasilja u porodici u Republici Srbiji, Pravni fakultet Univerziteta u Beogradu, Beograd, pp 182–197

Lacmanović V (2022) Kad institucije zakažu ostaje tišina—analiza institucionalnog odgovora na prijave nasilja koje su prethodile femicidima (2017–2018). Autonomni ženski centar, Beograd

McQuigg RJA (2017) The Istanbul convention, domestic violence and human rights. Routledge, London
Mirchandani R (2006) Hitting is not manly, domestic violence court and the re-imagination of the patriarchal state. Gender Soc 20(6):781–804
Молнар Д, Јандрић М (2019) Унутаррегионалне неједнакости у Србији – тестирање клупске конвергенције. Зборник Матице српске за друштвене науке 169(1):91–108
Niemi J, et al. (2020) Introduction: the Istanbul convention as a response to violence against women in Europe. In: Niemi J et al (eds) International law and violence against women, Europe and Istanbul convention, Routledge, London, pp 1–21
Petrušić N, Žunić N, Vilić V (2018) Krivično delo nasilja u porodici u sudskoj praksi—nove tendencije i izazovi. OEBS, Beograd
Pinchevsky GM (2017) Understanding decision-making in specialized domestic violence courts: can contemporary theoretical frameworks help guide these decisions? Violence Against Women 23(6):749–771
Potter J, Wetherell M (1987) Discourse and social psychology, beyond attitudes and behaviour. Sage Publications, London
Schneider EM (2000) Battered women and feminist lawmaking. Yale University Press, New Heaven
Škulić M (2012) Nasilje u porodici. Nedovoljno kvalitetno zakonsko rešenje, nedosledna praksa i brojni problemi i dileme. Revija Za Kriminologiju I Krivicno Pravo 50(1-2):117–141
Smart C (1989) Feminism and the power of law. Routledge, London
Stoyanova V (2020) Due diligence versus positive obligations, critical reflections on the council of Europe convention on violence against women. In: Niemi J, et al (ed) International law and violence against women, Europe and istanbul convention. Routledge, London, pp 95–129
Vujadinović D, Fröhlich M, Giegerich T (2023) Introduction. In: Vujadinović D, Fröhlich M, Giegerich T (eds) Gender-competent legal education. Springer, Cham, pp 1–14
Walker E (2007) Battered woman syndrome. In: Jackson NA (ed) Encyclopedia of domestic violence. Routledge, New York, 63–70

Natalija Lukić is Associate Professor of Criminology at the University of Belgrade Faculty of Law where she teaches Criminology, Penal Sanctions Execution Law, Organized Crime and Politics of Crime Suppression. She holds a Ph.D. (2017) and Master's degree (2009) in Criminology from the Law Faculty in Belgrade. Her research field includes politics of crime suppression, gender and crime and corporate crime.

Reframing Evidentiary Reasoning through a Gender Perspective

Marianela Delgado Nieves

Abstract The concept of "gender perspective" has gained substantial recognition within the legal sphere. Nonetheless, diverse interpretations exist regarding the specific requirements associated with this perspective in the legal field. This diversity of perspectives is evident across all levels. Notably, within the realm of jurisdiction, there is no unanimous consensus on what employing a gender perspective in judicial proceedings truly entails. This lack of consensus engenders a degree of uncertainty concerning the specific measures that the judiciary must employ to be deemed to fulfil its obligations from a gender perspective. This uncertainty also hinders understanding how a gender perspective contributes to the administration of justice. With this in mind, the primary aim of this paper is to establish a conceptual framework of a gender perspective that can serve as an underlying assumption for exploring its implications in two specific phases of the evidentiary process: the collection of evidence and the admission of evidence. The emphasis on these two stages is motivated by the prevailing literature, which predominantly concentrates on the assessment of evidence, emphasising the influence of gender stereotypes on legal reasoning. Nevertheless, the gender

This work was conducted with the support of the project PID2020-114765GB-I00, funded by MCIN/AEI/10.13039/501100011033. Early versions of this work were presented at the 1st Michele Taruffo Girona Evidence Week at the University of Girona and the International Seminar of Evidence Reasoning at the National University of the South, Argentina. I am thankful for the insightful discussions and feedback received at these seminars. Additionally, I wish to express my gratitude to the legal philosophy research group at the University of Girona, particularly Jordi Ferrer, Diego Dei Vecchi, Edgar Aguilera, Carmen Vázquez, and Marco Segatti. I also appreciate the valuable comments provided by the anonymous reviewer.

M. Delgado Nieves (✉)
University of Girona, Girona, Spain
Department of Legal Theory, University of Zagreb, Zagreb, Croatia
e-mail: mdelgadonieves@pravo.hr

© The Author(s), under exclusive license to Springer Nature Switzerland AG 2025

S. Baer et al. (eds.), *The Gender and the Judiciary*, Gender Perspectives in Law 7,
https://doi.org/10.1007/978-3-032-06885-9_12

perspective, construed as a concept encompassing aspects beyond the mere identification of gender stereotypes, may be equally pivotal in these earlier stages as it is in the subsequent assessment of evidence.

1 Introduction

The scrutiny of the judiciary's function in maintaining and reproducing gender inequality and the overarching patriarchal system is a matter that has pervaded various feminist legal theories to a greater or lesser degree. Despite the substantial differences among these theories, a common thread emerges as they collectively cast doubt on the operational dynamics of the judiciary. In particular, they question the interpretation and enforcement of the law,[1] the detrimental influence of gender stereotypes on legal reasoning,[2] the neglect of contextual considerations surrounding the pertinent facts, and the inability to recognize instances of intersectional discrimination,[3] to mention just a few examples.

The legal considerations developed around the judiciary's role have not merely defined the problem, its different manifestations, and consequences but have also sought to lay the foundations for questioning and rethinking how justice is administered. This has brought two fundamental ideas to the forefront of the debate. On the one hand, it has brought to light the importance of incorporating a gender perspective into the work of the judiciary.[4] On the other hand, it has consolidated

[1] This objection could be said to underly all the different approaches within feminist legal theories, be it questioning, for example, the critical application of standards underpinned by false neutrality, objectivity and rationality, asserting that standards are interpreted and applied on the basis of androcentric assumptions and standards, or considering that the problem does not lie in or with the law—barring some discriminatory standards—but rather in the androcentric bias of those who enforce and interpret it. For a general review of these theories, *Cf.* Alvez del Cuvillo et al. (2023), Bartlett and Kennedy (2018), Facio (1999), Smart (1992).

[2] Feminist perspectives within the legal domain have transcended the mere identification of gender stereotypes inherent in legal norms. Instead, especially in recent decades, these approaches have predominantly focused on the repercussions of these stereotypes within the realm of justice administration. This includes both their influence on individual cases and their broader implications. For instance, these perspectives emphasize how gender stereotypes can lend credibility to and normalize biased gender perspectives, bolster an environment of impunity, and erode the legitimacy and impartiality of the legal system, among other concerns.

[3] Crenshaw (1989) initially addressed the issue of intersectionality through an examination of three cases associated with Title VII of the Civil Rights Act of 1964 (*Graffenreid v General Motors*, *Moore v Hughes Helicopter* and *Payne v Travenol*). In these cases, the respective courts concluded that black women were deemed a "compound class" not covered by Title VII's protective provisions. Furthermore, the courts held that any discrimination experienced by black women could only be attributed to their gender or race, but not both simultaneously.

[4] One of the most illustrative projects of the contributions of the gender perspective in legal reasoning is the Feminist Judgements Project, which has set out to rewrite rulings issued in paradigmatic cases using feminist methods and perspectives. For an overview, *Cf.* Berger et. al. (2016), Evola et al. (2023), Hunter (2012).

the notion that the judiciary holds substantial potential to instigate transformative change, particularly through its decisions.[5]

This perspective, to wit, that the judiciary can bring an influence to bear on maintaining and reproducing gender inequality but, at the same time, operate as an essential factor of change, has been reflected in the different international and regional instruments that define the specific framework of protection of women's rights.[6] The allusion to the judiciary as one of the key institutions in eradicating all forms and manifestations of discrimination and violence has been expressly present ever since the adoption of the Convention on the Elimination of All Forms of Discrimination against Women (CEDAW) and has been replicated in the different subsequent conventions,[7] not to mention the different recommendations issued by the committees created to monitor them.[8]

However, these international instruments, beyond underscoring the importance of the judiciary in the accomplishment of the objectives pursued by the specific framework of protection, also share another aspect: they acknowledge that for this effect to be attained, it is indispensable that the work of the judiciary be executed by gender-aware court officials, or in other words by courts that are capable of implementing their functions based on a gender perspective.

At first sight, the preceding prescription is clear and comprehensive. The term "gender perspective" seems to enjoy sufficient consolidation in the legal domain to generate confusion. Nevertheless, on further thought, it transpires that a certain degree of uncertainty continues to persist regarding what specific actions the judiciary needs to deploy for it to be effectively considered that it performs its functions from a gender perspective.

[5] For example, UN Women (2011) documented 13 groundbreaking legal cases that have increased women´s access to justice by confirming that women's human rights under international law are enforceable at the national level, clarifying laws already on record, challenging laws that should be repealed, and creating new laws.

[6] The aforementioned framework of protection is taken as a point of departure not because the gender studies and the discussions that such studies have prompted are synonymous with "studies about women" but rather because it is the domain in which the gender perspective was profiled as a pivotal tool for the fulfilment of the obligations incumbent upon the States that signed the different constituent conventions.

[7] CEDAW Article 2 (c), (d); Inter-American Convention on the Prevention, Punishment and Eradication of Violence Against Women (Convention of Belém do Pará) Articles 7, 8 (c); Convention on Preventing and Combating Violence Against Women and Domestic Violence (Istanbul Convention) Articles 5, 18 (2), 49; Protocol to the African Charter on Human and Peoples' Rights on the Rights of Women in Africa (Protocol of Maputo) Articles 8, 25 (b).

[8] Committee on the Elimination of Discrimination against Women (CEDAW Committee) General Recommendation 19, para. 24(b); General Recommendation 23, paras. 5, 15; General Recommendation 24, paras. 13, 17; General Recommendation 27, para. 33; General Recommendation 28, paras. 17, 25, 33, 36, 37(d); General Recommendation 30, paras. 38(c), 74–76; General Recommendation 33; General Recommendation 35, paras. 22, 26(c), 30(e), 32(a).

Providing an immediate answer to this question is a challenging task. There is no single and extensively shared opinion on what judging from a gender perspective involves. On the contrary, there are myriad ways of understanding what demands such a perspective imposes in the legal domain. However, beyond being a simple theoretical disagreement, this mirrors the diversity of the feminist theories that have set out to develop methods that make it possible to include questions or issues hitherto omitted by traditional methods into the legal analysis, thus providing numerous tools that can be applied to the analysis of a phenomenon which, by dint of its complexity and contingency, would appear to be unapproachable from one standpoint alone.[9]

The foregoing does not mean that it is impossible to construct a notion of what the gender perspective involves in the domain of the courts. Instead, the challenge lies in positing a notion that: (1) is compatible or consistent with the idea that different feminist approaches exist, and (2) is helpful for the analysis of the contributions made in judging from a gender perspective—which has a practical, rather than a theoretical, objective.

Given this premise and the main objective of this paper, which is to explore the contributions of the gender perspective at two specific moments of the evidentiary activity, the first section will be dedicated to stipulating a notion of gender perspective that can operate as an analytical presupposition. What I will call "minimal notion" is intended to highlight three elements that may be regarded as minimum and indispensable and which would purport to be applicable, whether or not they converge with a specific feminist position.

In the following section, I shall highlight the contributions made by the gender perspective in evidence reasoning before and during the initial stage of legal proceedings, that is, in the evidence-gathering stage and during the admission of evidence.[10] The analysis is focused on these two moments because the literature that conjugates the topics of evidence and gender perspective has tended to focus upon the assessment of evidence, thereby almost exclusively underlining the impact of gender stereotypes in or on legal reasoning. Nevertheless, and as I shall seek to demonstrate further below, the gender perspective—understood as a notion that involves other aspects besides the mere identification of gender stereotypes—may be just as crucial at these two stages as in the actual appraisal of the evidence.

---

[9] For an overview of the different feminist legal methods, *Cf.* Battlet (2018 [1990]), Hernádez-Truyol (2016), Hunter (2012).

[10] Evidentiary activity in the judicial process is not limited to these stages. However, covering all of them would be beyond the scope of this paper. For a general analysis of the different stages, see Ferrer (2007, 2022), ch. II.

2 The Gender Perspective in the Judicial Domain: Minimum Elements for Its Implementation

The point of departure for analysing the extent to which gender perspective contributes to the administration of justice and, more particularly, to the questions related to the evidence of the facts calls for the development of some notion about what this perspective involves in the judicial domain. The notion proposed as a working concept is constructed around three elements that underlie a large part of the different feminist theories and which are regarded as the minimum aspects that must be observed by those tasked with resolving a legal controversy—although, and as we shall see later, they are also relevant to the other legal actors involved in the process.[11] These aspects are: (a) gender awareness, (b) contextualisation, and (c) the identification of the influence of gender stereotypes.

As may be noted, the first element refers to the type of competency or skill held by the different actors (police, litigants, expert witnesses, judges, etc.) who are party to the process. While this might appear to be self-evident, it is actually the requirement on which not only the effectiveness of the other elements hinges but also the possibility of administering justice taking the gender perspective into account. The lack of (or blatant opposition to) a minimum degree of gender sensitivity is one of the most patent shortcomings in justice systems.[12] If the parties to legal proceedings lack even an elemental level of gender-competent knowledge, it will be challenging for them to realise how and to what extent gender impacts the facts at issue, the rules applicable to the case, or the work carried out both individually and by the other legal actors.

The preceding does not mean that the parties involved in the process, particularly those tasked with resolving the legal controversy, must subscribe to a feminist ideology. It simply means they should have the necessary theoretical grounding—or at least a working knowledge—to perform their functions from a gender perspective. This circumstance, i.e., having a certain degree of training in gender matters and, ideally, acting accordingly, is not only a necessary assumption but rather, given the specific framework of protection of women's rights, is an obligation incumbent upon the judiciary and, on a more general level, upon all state authorities.[13]

---

[11] The emphasis on the fact that they are simply *minimum* aspects is because it is perfectly understandable that, depending on each society's reality, it would be relevant to highlight one particular aspect or add other items or elements.

[12] *Cf.* General Recommendation 33, paras. 6, 13, 14(d), 15(c), 22, 25(a), (b).

[13] *Cf.* Article 2 (c) of the CEDAW, Articles 7 and 8 (c) of the Convention of Belém do Pará, Article 49 of the Istanbul Convention and Article 8 of the Maputo Protocol. Similarly, the CEDAW Committee has been emphatic in this regard through its General Recommendation 28, paras. 17, 25, 33, 35, 36, 37 (d); General Recommendation 29, para. 24 (b); General Recommendation 33, paras. 6, 22, 28, 38, 39(a), 41, 51(c), (g); General Recommendation 35, paras. 22, 26(c), 31(a)(i), (b), 32(a). Moreover, and according to the UN Human Rights Council's special rapporteur on violence against women (2006), paras. 32 and 92, awareness-raising in the criminal justice system in gender issues is part of the obligations contained in the due diligence standard.

The second element, on the other hand, pertains to the need to bring context into the analysis of legal controversies. I mean context in both the objective sense (the general circumstances surrounding the facts of the case) and the subjective sense (the specific circumstances of those involved in the legal process).[14]

Considering context has significant repercussions at all levels. First of all, it extends the scope of the appraisal, making it possible to acknowledge or recognise aspects of the controversy that would otherwise seem irrelevant.[15] Secondly, it provides specific information that renders it possible to identify, for example, the presence of asymmetric power relationships between the parties or in society in general,[16] the disproportionate impact caused by specific norms, policies, or court rulings on particular social groups,[17] the presence of gender stereotypes implicit in the law, the facts of the case or on how state authorities operate,[18] as well as the presence of gender-based violence contexts. Thirdly, it makes it possible to identify cases that require an intersectional analysis given the specificities of the actors involved in the litigation.[19] These considerations enable introducing a series of questions into the legal dispute, which, in numerous instances, may significantly impact the verdict. Furthermore, this framework ensures effective access to justice for women, making it possible to integrate their particular circumstances, needs, and expectations into the legal discourse, ultimately counterbalancing the prevailing male-centred perspective.[20]

Lastly, the third element emphasises the need to recognise the impact of gender stereotypes. There are numerous ways of conceptualising and classifying stereotypes. In this paper, I will avail myself of the distinction between descriptive and normative stereotypes proposed by Arena.[21] According to this author, descriptive stereotypes attribute a property or a characteristic to the members of a social group merely because they belong to it. On the other hand, normative stereotypes do not seek to describe the characteristics of a group or its members but rather to establish the roles or behaviours that they should adopt. Similarly, I will assume that what leads a stereotype to be regarded as a *gender* stereotype is determined by some of the following traits: (a) that sex or gender is what distinguishes the social group in question (the group of women, men, trans* persons, non-binary or intersexual) or (b) that it refers to questions associated with the cultural construct of sexual difference.

Gender stereotypes, as such, can influence legal matters in diverse ways. They might: (a) prominently contribute to the circumstances under consideration, for

[14] Hereinafter, any reference to context will have both meanings unless otherwise specified.

[15] Bartlett (2018 [1990]), pp. 377–381; Stanchi et. al. (2016), p. 11, footnote 11.

[16] Hernádez-Truyol (2016), 50.

[17] Bartlett (2018 [1990]), pp. 373–74; Rhode (2018 [1990]), p. 336.

[18] Cook and Cusack (2010), pp. 230–31; Stanchi et. al. (2016), p. 16; Timmer (2011), p. 719.

[19] Bartlett (2018 [1990]), p. 376; Hernádez-Truyol (2016), pp. 24, 49.

[20] Hunter (2010), p. 35; Evola et al. (2023), p. 174; Minow (2018 [1988]), pp. 357–58.

[21] *Cf.* Arena (2016, 2019).

instance, serving as the basis for perpetrating discriminatory acts, (b) be inherent in legal norms, or (c) shape the conduct of involved parties in legal proceedings, even extending to the investigative phase in criminal cases. Regardless of their manifestation, it is crucial for the judiciary to identify and acknowledge these stereotypes, examining whether they instigate any detrimental effects, and subsequently combat or lay the groundwork for addressing them.[22] Yet, this responsibility goes further: judges must also ensure that they do not introduce gender stereotypes into the matter, whether implicitly or explicitly, in their reasoning at any stage of the judicial process.

The abovementioned question about combating stereotypes in the courts is a matter of debate. There are different positions on the so-called "anti-stereotyping principle" scope.[23] The myriad approaches in this regard, to a certain extent, run parallel to the evolution of the concept of stereotype in the domain of the cognitive sciences.[24] Once the idea that stereotypes are by necessity incorrect generalisations is abandoned, and it is accepted that there are cases in which they may prove to be accurate and can therefore provide a certain cognitive input, there begins a stage of conceptual clarification which leads to talk about stereotypes with and without a statistical basis and which are intended to distinguish between descriptive and prescriptive or normative stereotypes.[25] This conceptual richness has led, among other things, to rethink combating all stereotypes without exception.[26] Nevertheless, and while the cognitivist conception has garnered a certain degree of acceptance in the legal domain, significant criticism has been levelled at the way it is applied, as well as its incapacity to pick up on certain types of damage caused by stereotypes, such as failing to realise that they do not constitute neutral cognitive mechanisms but are rather mechanisms that justify, naturalise and mask the oppression brought to bear upon certain social groups.[27]

[22] *Cf.* Cook and Cusack (2010), chs. 6 and 8. Timmer (2011), pp. 718–26, on the one hand, synthesises the aforementioned functions into two stages: naming, which involves determining the actual role of gender stereotypes in a particular case, and contesting, which entails how to proceed against gender stereotypes in legal reasoning. Arena (2022), pp. 240–43, on the other hand, underscores the need to name the stereotype, ascertain whether it enjoys statistical support (in the case of descriptive stereotypes), and finally assess its relevance to the specific circumstances of the individual case.

[23] With regard to this principle, see Franklin (2010).

[24] Initially, the expression "stereotype" was employed to denote cognitive representations concerning social groups that seemingly exhibited an undesirable rigidity, permanence, and lack of variability. They were viewed as inaccurate generalizations characterized by oversimplification and partiality. With the passage of time, these objections waned, and stereotypes came to be recognized as possessing significant functions, not always deleterious, both at an individual and collective level. *Cf.* Ashmore and Del Boca (2017), pp. 1–9; Stroebe and Insko (1989), pp. 4–5.

[25] With regard to the so-called "cognitivist conception", see Arena (2022), Brown (2010), Campbell (1967), Schauer (2003), Tajfel (1969).

[26] See, for example, Arena (2019), Timmer (2015), Puddifoot (2021).

[27] In a similar vein, Ghidoni and Morondo (2022), Ghidoni (2022), ch. VIII.

Regardless of the stance adopted, there is a consensus within the legal sphere that the judiciary has a duty to combat all stereotypes that result in harmful effects. Where disagreement arises is in determining what defines or might constitute a "harmful effect." Beyond the scope of this discussion, it is crucial to underline that the detrimental impact of a stereotype must be assessed on a case-by-case basis. To this end, judges have several criteria at their disposal, including but not limited to: the nature of the stereotype (whether normative or descriptive), the specific social group targeted, the historical discrimination or subordinate status of the affected group, the actual or potential influence of the stereotype on the exercise of rights by the individual and the group at large, the societal repercussions of the stereotype, its potential intersectional characteristics, whether a (descriptive) stereotype is statistically supported, the rationale behind its statistical support, and whether, despite such support, it generates a harmful effect, and so forth.[28]

Such an analysis will only be possible if the judge possesses some gender-competent knowledge. Furthermore, attaching any meaning to the gender stereotype, acknowledging its impact, and laying the foundations for combating it also call for an analysis of the context. This means the three elements previously referred to as minimum aspects feed off each other. Nevertheless, the fact that the three elements are not present in the same case is by no means an assertion that the work of the judiciary lacks a gender perspective. In any event, what matters most is that the judiciary and the other actors involved in the process recognise these guidelines and apply them in their everyday work whenever they are relevant.

3 Contributions of a Gender Perspective in Evidence Reasoning

Before addressing the quid of the matter, it is important to note that the analysis pursued in this section takes for granted three theses derived from the so-called "rationalist conception of evidence".[29] In the first place, I will assume that finding out the truth is one of the objectives of the legal process.[30] In this regard, I will subscribe to the position according to which the concept of truth is best adapted to the procedural context is that of the truth understood as correspondence.[31]

[28] For some of these criteria, see Arena (2019, 2022), ch. 4; Cook and Cusack (2010), ch. 2; Morondo (2022), Timmer (2015), Timmer and Sosa (2022).

[29] For a comprehensive exploration of the theses that underpin this perspective, widely embraced in both Anglo-American and continental contexts, see Accatino (2019). For an elucidation within the common law tradition, see Anderson et al. (2015), ch. 3.

[30] The debate regarding the role of truth within the legal process remains open. For an exhaustive account of the different positions, see Ferrer (2007), Taruffo (2002b), ch. 1.

[31] On the relevance of the correspondence theory of truth in the legal setting, see Gascón (2010a), pp. 50–67; Taruffo (2002a), pp. 39–41; Tuzet (2021), pp. 75–96. According to this conception,

Secondly, I will assume that the fundamental objective of the evidentiary activity is the ascertainment of the truth about the factual statements of the case.[32] Finally, I shall depart from the idea that while finding the truth is the fundamental objective of the evidentiary activity in the legal process, it is not the only one. In this process, different values and purposes that share legal protection interact with the objective of finding the truth; values which, in some cases, are regarded as legally relevant to the extent that such an objective is sacrificed, even if only partially.[33]

On this basis, I will divide my analysis into two main stages: evidence-gathering and evidence-admission. These stages deserve to be addressed separately, although each of them involves very different acts concerning the evidence, meaning that the gender perspective potential varies depending on the type of activity involved.

3.1 Evidence-gathering

This phase encompasses the comprehensive array of procedures undertaken to collect all pertinent evidence intended for presentation to support the case's factual underpinnings. To elucidate the influence of a gender perspective on this stage, it is imperative to distinguish between criminal cases and those encompassing alternative domains such as civil, labor, or administrative litigation. The rationale behind this distinction is straightforward: within the sphere of criminal proceedings, it is mandated that investigating authorities incorporate a gender perspective into their investigative processes, whereas in the context of other categories of cases, the involved parties retain the discretion to opt for or against the inclusion of such a perspective during the evidence-gathering phase.

The absence of a mandatory obligation in other disputes for the involved parties does not diminish the significance of the gender perspective. Quite the contrary, if the legal representative handling the case possesses a degree of gender awareness, they are more likely to recognize the presence of gender-related questions or issues warranting adjudication, which necessitate evidentiary support. As previously mentioned, there may exist imbalances in power dynamics between the parties that, if substantiated, would necessitate re-evaluating how the case is assessed. Alternatively, it may be pertinent to establish that a specific action, norm, or policy

affirming that a statement or assertion is true implies that the content articulated by such a statement corresponds to reality. This distinction between fact and factual statement contains an additional implicit assumption: what is proven in the legal process are not facts, but rather statements or propositions about the facts. *Cf.* Andersen et. al. (2015), p. 94; Dei Vecchi (2020), p. 50; Ferrer (2005), p. 49; Gascón (2010a), pp. 69–77; González Lagier (2022b); p. 20, Taruffo (2002b), pp. 117–119.

[32] For a discussion about the relationship between evidence and truth, see Ferrer (2005), ch. II.

[33] Damaška (1997), p. 12.

disproportionately impacts the group represented by the attorney,[34] or that the pertinent facts reveal the presence of stereotypical gender perceptions with detrimental consequences,[35] and so forth.

Due to their very nature, those factual assumptions unquestionably require substantiation through evidence highlighting contextual elements that render them meaningful. In other words, these are not facts that can be comprehended in isolation but necessitate a broader framework for their substantiation. For example, in *I.V. v. Bolivia*, about the sterilisation of a woman without informed consent, the Inter-American Court of Human Rights (IACtHR) underscored the existence of an imbalanced power dynamic between the patient and the medical professionals, further compounded by prevalent gender stereotypes that influenced the proceedings. This asymmetry was among the primary reasons for the IACtHR's conclusion that the unauthorized sterilization of Ms. I. V. amounted to an infringement upon her autonomy and reproductive rights, constituting an arbitrary and abusive intrusion into her private life.[36]

In an ideal scenario, the aspects outlined above should be rendered explicit when the specific items of evidence are offered, e.g., describing why the evidence is submitted, why it is relevant to the substantiation of a given fact, and why the substantiation of this fact is relevant to the issue. A robust argumentation in this regard is imperative, as it is frequently the case that these circumstances do not inherently embody the contested action but instead represent facets that encompass it, contributing significantly to a more profound comprehension of the intricacies within the dispute. Despite this, such nuances may elude the court's attention, underscoring the necessity of clearly articulating the reasons for submitting such evidence, thereby pre-empting its potential dismissal on the grounds of perceived irrelevance.

In the context of criminal cases, the scenario diverges significantly. This disparity primarily arises from the obligations mandated by the due diligence standard.[37] This standard, which has a long-standing history in international law

---

[34] For example, in the cases *Artavia Murillo et al. v. Costa Rica*, 29 November 2012, *Cuscul Pivaral et al. v. Guatemala*, 23 August 2018, and *Gonzales Lluy et al. v. Ecuador*, 1 September 2015, the IACtHR identified the disproportionate impact of an apparently neutral measure on the group of women, as well as the distinct impact of the rendering of healthcare or educational services in and on pregnant women or women who suffered from some health condition, such as HIV.

[35] For example, in *Konstantin Markin v. Russia*, App. No. 30078/06, 22 March 2012, the European Court of Human Rights (ECtHR) concluded that the refusal to consider equal paternity or maternity leave for military personnel was the outcome of the prevalence of the gender stereotype about the roles of men and women in the family (male breadwinner/female caretaker stereotype).

[36] *Cf. I.V. v. Bolivia*, 13 November 2016, paras. 160, 235.

[37] Concerning violence against women, the aforementioned standard entails the obligation of the States to act with due diligence to prevent, respond to, protect against and provide remedies for acts of violence against women whether such acts are committed by State or non-State actors. By imposing such obligations, the standard serves not only as a guideline, but also as a benchmark for assessing the fulfilment of the duties imposed on the States. *Cf.* Report E/CN.4/2006/61 of the Special Rapporteur on violence against women (2006), para. 30; UN Women (2014), para. 52.

and was explicitly adopted within the specific framework of protection of women's rights,[38] imposes, among other things, the duty to conduct a gender-aware criminal investigation.[39]

This obligation exerts a considerable influence on evidentiary matters. Initially, comprehensive gender-competence training for investigating authorities has a discernible impact on several aspects, including broadening the scope of potential lines of investigation,[40] raising awareness about the imperative nature of collecting specific evidence,[41] enriching the inventory of evidence that must be gathered and delineating the intended purposes for its procurement,[42] and facilitating the implementation of measures to prevent re-victimization through the acquisition of particular pieces of evidence,[43] among other effects.

Secondly, acquiring evidence that considers the broader context within which a criminal act occurs is crucial in pursuing truth. This is particularly salient in instances of violence against women, which necessitate examination as behaviours emanating from a specific cultural and structural milieu rather than as isolated incidents detached from their surroundings. Furthermore, the scrutiny of

---

[38] *Cf.* Report of the Special Rapporteur on violence against women (2006), paras. 19–29.

[39] *Cf.* Report of the Special Rapporteur on violence against women (2006), paras. 90, 92, which specifies that the due diligence standard involves providing police with training to deal with cases of violence against women in a gender-sensitive manner. In the regional domain, the IACtHR paved the way for conducting investigations with a gender perspective in *Gonalzéz et. al. ("Cotton Field") v. Mexico*, 16 November 2009.

[40] For example, bearing in mind that the vast majority of cases of violent deaths of woman or of sexual abuse are perpetrated by people known to or by the victim could be a good point of departure for beginning the investigation or for gathering evidence.

[41] Expediency is intended to avert the loss and deterioration of evidence and the failure to gather information that could cease to be available due to the passing of time. In many cases, the absence of a gender perspective renders it impossible to realise the urgency of collecting evidence, for example, about the circumstances that occurred before or during the actual offense or crime. *Cf. Gonalzéz et. al. ("Cotton Field") v. Mexico*; *Velásquez Paiz et. al. v. Guatemala*, 19 November 2015; UN Women (2014), paras. 171–75.

[42] One of the recurring deficiencies in investigations of cases of violence against women is the police's excessive emphasis on the testimony and the failure to order indispensable expert evidence such as anthropological findings, social workers' reports, the taking of physical evidence for comparison, physical inspection of the person assumed to be responsible, to mention a few. *Cf.* Di Corleto (2017), p. 419; UN High Commissioner of Human Rights (UN High Commissioner of Human Rights and Fiscalía General de la República del Salvador 2012), chs. 2–3; UN Women (2014), chs. III–V.

[43] An illustration of such measures includes the recommendations aimed at preventing the re-victimization of individuals testifying in cases involving violence against women. These guidelines encompass ensuring that evidence is gathered in a suitable and secure environment, conducted by trained professionals, and facilitated by interpreters when essential. Additionally, it emphasizes the importance of gathering comprehensive information to avoid unnecessary repetitions. See, for example, *Espinoza González v. Peru,* 20 November 2014; *Fernández Ortega et. al. v. Mexico*, 30 August 2010; General Recommendation 33, CEDAW Committee.

the context proves pivotal not only in cases where the victim is a woman but also in situations where women are accused. An illustrative case pertains to scenarios involving women who, having endured prolonged domestic abuse, eventually murdered their assailants. In these instances, in-depth comprehension of the context can significantly influence the determination of culpability levels and even the acknowledgement of potential excuses.

Thirdly, the adverse implications of gender stereotypes in the context of evidence collection during investigations manifest on various levels. As noted by Di Corleto, these stereotypes tend to revolve around the categories of "honest woman," "deceitful woman," "instrumental woman," "co-responsible woman," and "fabricator woman".[44] Such stereotypical perceptions of women can lead to various deleterious outcomes within investigations. These may include instances of complete or partial investigative inaction,[45] the minimisation or rationalisation of acts of violence,[46] the gathering of evidence for the purpose of shifting the blame on the victim,[47] the undermining of a witness's credibility,[48] and the propagation of the notion that gender-based crimes are challenging to substantiate, even though the principal issue may, in fact, lie in the deficiencies of the investigative process itself.[49]

While the responsibilities outlined above are primarily directed at investigating authorities, the judiciary must possess a comprehensive understanding of the extent of these obligations to counteract any instances of non-compliance, particularly when institutional frameworks incorporate mechanisms for overseeing investigations (for instance, when victims have legal remedies to challenge any irregular police conduct). The comprehensive applicability of the due diligence standard across all state authorities underscores that each entity is responsible for undertaking actions within the purview of their respective powers to meet or enforce the fulfilment of the constituent criteria.

[44] Di Corleto (2017), pp. 414–15.

[45] See, for example, *González et al. v. Mexico*, paras. 400–01; *J. v. Peru*, 27 November 2013, para. 352; *M. and Others v. Italy and Bulgaria*, App. No. 40020/03, 31 July 2012, paras. 104–08 (in this case, the ECtHR failed to name the stereotype but linked the inaction and the deficiencies involved in the investigation to certain conceptions about Romany traditions).

[46] See, for example, *Opuz v. Turkey,* App. No. 33401/13, 20 October 2020, para. 147; *A. T. v. Hungry*, Communication No. 2/2023, 26 January 2005, para. 9.3; *Fatma Yildiri v. Austria*, Communication No. 6/2006, 10 August 2007, para. 12.1.5; *Ángela González Carreño v. Spain*, Communication No. 47/2012, 18 July 2014, para. 9.4.

[47] See, for example, *Véliz Franco et al. v. Guatemala*, 19 May 2014, paras. 209–13; *López Soto et al. v. Venezuela*, 26 September 2018, paras. 238–39; *Velázquez Paiz et al. v. Guatemala*, paras. 183; *L.N.P. v. Argenitna*, Communication No. 1619/2007, 18 July 2008, paras. 13.7.

[48] See, for example, *Victims of Sexual Torture in Atenco v. Mexico*, 28 November 2018, para. 216–20; *J. v. Peru*, para. 352.

[49] See, for example, *Veliz Franco et al. v. Guatemala*, para. 187; *Velásquez Paiz et al. v. Guatemala*, para. 146; Ramírez (2020).

3.2 *Admission of Evidence*

The admission of evidence is one of the crucial activities in the legal process. Its significance arises from the distinct nature of the judicial domain, where, unlike other areas of knowledge where rational decision-making entails considering all available and relevant information, in the judicial process, the decision-maker is bound to consider exclusively the evidence that has been formally submitted, accepted, and presented during the course of the legal proceedings.[50] Any supplementary information, whether privately obtained by the decision-maker or explicitly excluded, must be omitted from their deliberation, even if it bears potential relevance.[51]

The decision as to which evidence should be included in the proceedings falls to the exclusive power of the judiciary: the judge must analyse each piece of evidence offered by the parties and determine whether or not it satisfies the criteria required for it to be heard in trial and ultimately taken into account in the decision on the proven facts.

In a broad sense, the criteria governing the admission, rejection, and exclusion of evidence can be categorized into epistemic and non-epistemic. Epistemic criteria contribute to the objective of establishing the truth, while non-epistemic criteria protect values other than this objective.[52] The preeminent epistemic criterion is that of relevance.[53] According to this criterion, evidence is deemed relevant if, either on its own or in conjunction with other evidence, it enables the construction of a conclusion regarding the truth of the factual assertion to be established,[54] or in other words, if it can alter the justification status of the proposition in question.[55] Furthermore, evidence may be classified as either directly or indirectly relevant, contingent upon its connection with legally relevant facts.[56]

---

[50] The comparison with other areas of knowledge stems from the extensive debate on the relevance of studying legal evidence through the general notion of evidence specific to general epistemic analogy. On this debate, see Taruffo (2002b), pp. 343–46; Twining (1990), 188 *et seq.*

[51] Ferrer (2007), 42 and their references.

[52] *Cf.* Dei Vecchi (2020), pp. 58–76; Ferrer (2007), pp. 68 *et seq*; Gascón (2010a), pp. 113–14, 116–20; Tuzet (2021), pp. 99–100; Wróblewski (2013), pp. 245–46. Such criteria are normally reflected in the different rules on the admissibility and exclusion of evidence that govern the different legal systems.

[53] The paramount significance of the relevance criterion rests upon a core principle: the greater the amount of relevant information available to the decision-maker, the higher the probability of reaching a correct decision. In legal proceedings, this translates to a greater likelihood that the established facts align with what actually transpired. Underlying this premise is an additional principle: any piece of evidence that can contribute relevant information regarding the pertinent facts should be admissible. However, it is important to note that this principle generally accommodates exceptions, which are linked to both epistemic and non-epistemic considerations. *Cf.* Ferrer (2007), p. 68; Gascón (2010a), p. 116.

[54] Taruffo (2008), p. 38.

[55] Dei Vecchi (2020), p. 57.

[56] Andersen et. al. (2015), pp. 97–98; Taruffo (2002b), p. 365. The circumstance whereby evidence is not always directly related to the legally relevant facts often imposes the need to

An important aspect regarding the assessment of relevance is the influence of the judge's background on this deliberation. It is the judge's particular worldview or system of beliefs that enables them to discern whether an item of evidence (the information it contains or may provide) can impact the justification status of a factual statement.[57] How the judge's set of beliefs is articulated within the reasoning process is contingent upon the generalizations employed to establish a connection between a given piece of evidence and the factual statement in question, thus determining its relevance or, in this context, its potential relevance.[58] The array of generalizations used in this context, as articulated by Anderson et al., "is a continuum that ranges from uncontested scientific truths, through 'knowledge' based on more or less established forms of expertise, to largely uncontested general knowledge, to less established 'common sense' generalisations, to beliefs that are based on limited experience, faith, speculation, myth or prejudices".[59]

This simplified formulation outlined above readily allows an intuitive understanding of the need to incorporate a gender perspective in evidence reasoning.[60] While the most apparent aspect often associated with this is the impact of gender stereotypes, it is essential to acknowledge that the other two elements of the minimum notion being employed, namely gender awareness and contextualization, independently assume a significant role in the admission of evidence.

What might be the potential implications if the judge responsible for the admission of evidence had some training in gender-related matters? Certainly, a critical issue: a judge who has undergone training in gender matters could substantially modify their criteria for assessing the relevance of evidence and the underlying rationale for such determinations. An individual possessing a comprehensive understanding of gender considerations at both the individual and societal levels is more likely to comprehend the profound influence that the substantiation of specific circumstances may have on the interpretation and resolution of disputes and even on the possibility of equitable access to justice.

As previously delineated, the existence of asymmetrical power dynamics and instances of violence, among other pertinent factors, often coexist alongside the core issue at hand. This coexistence can sometimes challenge recognizing the necessity of incorporating such evidence to substantiate these additional aspects.

---

take a holistic approach that will afford an overview and understand, for example, how the different items of evidence submitted by the parties affect each other.

[57] On this point—albeit oriented towards the justification of beliefs in general terms—, Haack (2009), p. 132, maintains the following: "What *evidence appears to A to be* relevant depends on various background beliefs, which may be true or may be false". What evidence *is* relevant, however, coincides with what evidence appears to A to be relevant only if A's background beliefs are *true*. "(emphasis in the original)".

[58] It is important to remember that when a judge rules on admissibility, the relevance judgement is purely hypothetical since the evidence in question has yet to be heard in court.

[59] Andersen et. al. (2015), p. 329.

[60] While I shall focus mainly on the relevance criterion, the considerations made below can readily be extrapolated to the analysis of other criteria.

However, what frequently eludes notice is that validating these seemingly unrelated circumstances to the legal dispute can potentially exert a profound influence on the final verdict. For example, in *Isatou Jallow v. Bulgaria*, the CEDAW Committee was emphatic in stating how the fact that the Bulgarian judicial authorities failed to realise that the plaintiff was a migrant and illiterate woman who was submitted by her partner for different reasons and who, together with her daughter, had been the object of physical, psychological and sexual abuse by the former, resulting in a divorce with conditions that were unfavourable to the plaintiff, compounded by an emergency protection order that separated her from her daughter for a considerable period.[61]

Furthermore, in addition to the aforementioned considerations, the presence of judges with an awareness of gender issues can also influence the application of certain rules governing the admissibility of evidence.[62] Drawing from Di Corleto's observations and focusing on the moment of admissibility, a judge who is sensible of the intricacies of violence against women is more likely to recognize that individuals who may have witnessed the abuse inflicted upon the victim, albeit without detailed knowledge of the specific facts of the case, often maintain some form of relationship with the victim (such as relatives, friends, colleagues, or healthcare professionals). These witnesses, who in other circumstances might be rejected for being regarded as "partial" or "hearsay," may, in these instances, possess relevance in corroborating the victim's testimony. For, as it is widely acknowledged, or should be, violence against women extends beyond isolated incidents of physical harm, verbal abuse, or specific sexual aggressions; rather, it typically manifests as a protracted continuum that evolves over time, assuming various forms, particularly within the domestic sphere or in the context of intimate partnerships.[63]

The discussion presented thus far inherently underscores the importance of integrating evidence into the legal proceedings to establish the context, constituting the second element. However, it is pertinent to offer two further clarifications. Firstly, while a profound comprehension of contextual aspects is of utmost importance, it is essential to recognize that not every detail necessarily holds relevance. The determination of which specific aspects of the context bear significance is contingent upon the arguments presented by the involved parties when offering their respective evidence, as well as the judge's training in gender awareness. This aspect assumes particular importance in light of the imperative to prevent the body of evidence from becoming overly inclusive and subsequently overwhelming for the adjudicator tasked with rendering a verdict.[64]

[61] Communication No. 32/2011, 28 August 2012, para. 8.1 *et seq.*

[62] The CEDAW Committee explicitly addressed this matter in its General Recommendation 33, paras. 15(g) and 25(a)(iii), about the need for the party States to review the standards regarding the burden of evidence to guarantee equality between parties in all areas in which power relationships deprive women of the chance to secure fair treatment from the judiciary.

[63] *Cf.* Di Corleto (2017), pp. 418–19. Regarding the continuum of violence, Kelly (1988), chs. 4 and 5.

[64] For the so-called "danger of unmanageable or overwhelming evidence", Ferrer (2007), pp. 74–76.

Secondly, the court must exercise particular caution to preclude the admission of context-related evidence intended solely for the purpose of stigmatizing any of the involved parties or attributing responsibility to the victim for the incidents based on factors such as their clothing, social activities, occupation, sexual orientation, or similar considerations.[65]

The aforementioned consideration is directly pertinent to the third element concerning the impact of gender stereotypes. One of the two dimensions in which the imperative to eliminate gender stereotypes during this phase of the proceedings must be comprehended is precisely as elucidated earlier: the judge, during the stage of evidence admission, assumes the role of a "gatekeeper" entrusted with the responsibility of ensuring the exclusion of evidence that might introduce biases in the interpretation of the facts underpinning the dispute. Within this framework, at least two plausible scenarios can be identified. The first scenario occurs when a gender stereotype causes a piece of evidence that lacks any genuine direct or indirect relevance to the facts of the case to appear as pertinent erroneously.[66] For example, in *L.N.P. v. Argentina*, a case concerning the collective sexual assault of an underage indigenous female, evidentiary materials were introduced to substantiate consent. These materials included a medical assessment, which concluded that the victim was not of virgin status, and various pieces of evidence related to her sexual history, "moral character," and alleged involvement in prostitution. In this regard, the Human Rights Committee concluded, among other things, that the persistent inquiry into the plaintiff's sexual history and moral conduct constituted an arbitrary encroachment upon her private life and an unlawful affront to her honour and reputation. This was particularly emphasized due to its lack of relevance to the investigation of the rape case, coupled with the fact that the victim was a minor.[67]

Conversely, the second scenario pertains to situations in which the evidence, while potentially relevant, is excluded due to a significant likelihood that its introduction could bias the fact-finding process. For instance, a noteworthy critique directed at psychological autopsies conducted on femicide victims is their potential to shift blame onto the victim, consequently discrediting and stigmatizing them. This has engendered the argument that it is preferable to refrain from including this category of evidence in legal proceedings, as it is frequently wielded to "justify" the act of murder or to bolster the hypothesis of suicide, thus disregarding evidence that contradicts such assertions.[68]

---

[65] *Cf. González et al. v. Mexico*, paras. 388–401; *Véliz Franco et al. v. Peru*, paras. 209–13, *L.N. P. v. Argentina*, paras. 13.3, 13.7.

[66] I adopt the concept of the judge serving as a gatekeeper, which stems from the ongoing debate concerning the admissibility of scientific evidence. For a general notion about this discussion, see Gascón (2010b), 3.1; Haack (2015), Vázquez (2015), ch. 2.

[67] *L.N.P. v. Argentina*, para. 13.7.

[68] *Cf.* Observatorio Ciudadano Nacional del Feminicidio (2018), pp. 33, footnote 130, 220–21. Given the number of documented cases, it would appear to be a frequent phenomenon in certain countries where public prosecutors refuse to investigate violent deaths of women as femicides and choose to handle them as suicide or simple accidents.

On a second tier of analysis, the obligation to eliminate gender stereotypes at this level extends beyond considerations external to the judge and encompasses those intrinsic to their deliberative process. Gender stereotypes infiltrate the judgments on admissibility primarily by serving as the foundational generalisations upon which the judge assesses the potential relevance of a particular piece of evidence in substantiating a specific factual assertion. For example, if the judge believes that, as a rule, a rape victim's underwear provides information as to whether the sexual intercourse was consensual or not, then they are likely to regard any evidence that substantiates the type of underwear worn by the victim at the time of the events as relevant.[69]

In an ideal scenario, the judge should explicitly articulate any generalizations employed to derive the potential relevance of a given item of evidence. This stipulation serves a dual purpose: firstly, it enhances the rationale underpinning the particular determination, thereby facilitating potential subsequent scrutiny; and secondly, it enables the judge to assess both the validity and plausibility of the inference made, including the identification of potential fallacies.[70] One of the criteria for epistemic rationality, which contributes to endorse the solidity of an evidentiary inference, pertains directly to the level of foundation underlying the generalization employed. According to this criterion, the greater the degree of foundation of the generalisation, the greater the degree of confirmation of the hypothesis.[71] In this regard, what the judge must analyse is the cognitive foundations of the generalisation on which their reasoning is based, i.e., whether it has a solid base or whether, on the contrary, it is a hasty or immediately spurious generalisation. This exercise will allow the judge to acknowledge whether they have used a gender stereotype and whether it is accurate or false.[72]

Nevertheless, the aforementioned undertaking is not without its challenges. Stereotypes tend to be deeply ingrained to such an extent that their identification within the reasoning process is often complex. Furthermore, they frequently exhibit resistance to contradictory evidence, thereby inducing a confirmation bias when individuals scrutinize their cognitive foundations. However, despite the complexity introduced by these factors, the requirement for judges to internally assess the extent to which the generalisations they rely upon are well-founded reduces the

---

[69] This example is taken from the proceedings 002822–2019-90-1401-JR-PE-03, 8 October 2020, in which a Peruvian court, based on the type of underwear worn by the victim on the day of the events (a red lace thong), inferred that she had prepared herself to or was willing to have sexual intercourse with the defendant, who was charged with rape.

[70] *Cf.* Andersen et. al. (2015), p. 140.

[71] *Cf.* González Lagier (2022a), ch. II.

[72] This consideration would apply only to descriptive stereotypes, which take the form of a generalisation and may therefore be regarded as either having a statistical base or lacking one. On the other hand, normative stereotypes have no truth value. This type of stereotypes often gives rise to generalisations such as "as a rule, women are more suitable than men for rearing children", which could actually be compared to reality—although it should not go unnoticed that the reason why this may be a reality is precisely because there is a gender stereotype that prescribes that women *must* rear children.

likelihood of judicial reliance on gender stereotypes. At the same time, if the judge embraces the perspective that allows for incorporating particular stereotypes in legal reasoning, this helps them provide a substantiated justification for asserting the statistical support underlying the chosen stereotype.

The preceding discussion highlights the indispensability of the gender perspective throughout each stage of the process. As initially mentioned, this significance is underscored by the fact that decisions made at this stage can significantly influence the evaluation of the pertinent facts. This, in turn, may have a direct consequence on the final judgment and, in a broader context, on the assurance or violation of the right to access justice under conditions of equality.

4 Conclusions

The persistent efforts of feminist theorists, both from the past and in contemporary times, as well as advocates of human rights, international organizations, and international human rights courts, have collectively contributed to the commonplace integration of gender perspective into current discourse. The fact that we are no longer compelled to expend the entirety of our efforts on dismantling the enduring resistance to the inclusion of gender-related issues within legal deliberations imposes upon us the responsibility to further refine our comprehension and arguments regarding a tool that, despite its integration into various legislations, the jurisprudence of numerous courts and tribunals, litigation strategies, and theoretical deliberations, still appears to possess certain opacities concerning its potential and practical implementation.

In my perspective, two fundamental ideas are beyond discussion. Firstly, the gender perspective involves rethinking the way that justice is administered. Secondly, it is an invaluable tool and, particularly within the realm of legal activities, it is crucial to ensure that all individuals can exercise their rights under equal conditions. Where there is room for debate, however, lies in the extent of its application. This divergence of viewpoints is a positive development for a discourse still in its formative stages, yet it underscores the importance of consolidating shared assumptions. Accordingly, the main objective of this paper was to develop a concept of gender perspective that enables us to demonstrate specific contributions during the evidence-gathering and evidence-admission stages, which can be summarized as follows.

In the collection of evidence, possessing a degree of gender awareness enables one to identify the presence of gender-related questions or issues that require adjudication, which necessitates evidentiary support. In criminal cases, it also broadens the scope of potential lines of investigation and facilitates the implementation of measures to prevent re-victimization through the acquisition of particular pieces of evidence. At the same time, acquiring evidence that considers the broader context becomes indispensable in ascertaining the truth, especially when the dispute revolves around facts that cannot be comprehended in isolation but necessitate a broader framework for their substantiation. Ultimately, it also enables acknowledgement that among the detrimental consequences of gender stereotypes is the failure to recognize the necessity of collecting certain types of evidence. Particularly within the domain of criminal investigation, this also entails the downplaying or justification of violent acts, the inaction of the investigative authorities, and the collection of evidence aimed at shifting culpability onto the victim, among other manifestations.

In the evidence-admission stage, on the other hand, gender perspective becomes crucial in determining which pieces of evidence meet the necessary criteria for being heard in trial and ultimately be taken into account in the decision on the proven facts. Having some training in gender-related matters, for example, could substantially modify the criteria applied by the judge for assessing the relevance of evidence and the underlying rationale for such determinations. It can also influence the application of certain rules governing the admissibility of evidence and become important for determining which specific aspects of the context bear significance and, at the same time, for precluding the admission of context-related evidence intended solely for the purpose of stigmatizing any of the involved parties. Concerning the influence of gender stereotypes, the gender perspective enables the adjudicator to discern at least two plausible scenarios: one in which a gender stereotype leads to the erroneous perception of a piece of evidence lacking genuine direct or indirect relevance to the case's facts as being pertinent; and another in which the evidence, although potentially relevant, must be excluded due to a substantial likelihood that its introduction could bias the process of fact-finding. Furthermore, it underscores the imperative for judges to exercise caution in employing gender stereotypes as the foundational generalizations upon which they evaluate the potential relevance of a particular piece of evidence in corroborating a specific factual assertion.

The aforementioned discussion exemplifies the importance of incorporating a gender perspective in the administration of justice. Simultaneously, it emphasizes the need to convert theoretical discourse into practical tools that enable the gender perspective to emerge as an efficacious instrument in the pursuit of broader objectives, including the eradication of structural discrimination, dismantling oppressive frameworks that underpin patriarchal structures, and addressing all forms and manifestations of violence directed towards women.

References

Accatino D (2019) Teoría de la prueba: ¿somos todos "racionalistas" ahora? Revus 39:85–102

Alvez del Cuvillo A, Macioce F, Strid S (2023) Feminist political and legal theories. In: Vujadinović D, Fröhlich M, Giegerich T (eds) Gender competent legal education, Springer Textbooks in Law, pp 58–90

Anderson T, Schum D, Twining W (2015) Análisis de la prueba. Marcial Pons, Madrid

Arena F (2016) Los estereotipos normativos en la decisión judicial. Una exploración conceptual. Revista de Derecho XXIX(1):51–75
Arena F (2019) Algunos criterios metodológicos para evaluar la relevancia jurídica de los estereotipos. In: Risso V, Pezzano S, Bouvier H, Arena F (dir) Derecho y Control, Ferreyra Editor, Córdoba, pp 11–44
Arena F (2022) Los estereotipos detrás de las normas. In: Barale L, Traballini M (dir) Toledo Ediciones, Córdoba
Ashmore R, Del Boca F (2017) Conceptual approaches to stereotypes and stereotyping. In: Hamilton D (ed) Cognitive processes in stereotyping and intergroup behaviour, Routledge, pp 1–35
Bartlett K (2018 [1990]) Feminist legal methods. In: Bartlett K, Kennedy R (eds) Feminist legal theory: readings in law and gender. Routledge, New York-London, pp 370–403
Bartlett K, Kennedy R (eds) (2018) Feminist legal theory: readings in law and gender, Routledge, New York-London
Berger L, Crawford B, Stanchi K (2016) Introduction to the U.S. feminist judgements project. In: Berger L, Crawford B, Stanchi K (eds) Feminist judgements. Rewritten opinions of the United States Supreme Court, Cambridge University Press, New York, pp 3–23
Brown R (2010) Prejudice: its social psychology. John Wiley & Sons, Incorporated, Hoboken
Campbell D (1967) Stereotypes and the perception of group differences. Am Psychol 22(10):817–829
Cook R, Cusack S (2010) Esterotipos de género. Perspectivas legales transnacionales. Profamilia
Crenshaw K (1989) Demarginalizing the intersection of race and sex: a black feminist critique of antidiscrimination doctrine, feminist theory and antiracist politics. Univ Chicago Leg Forum 1:139–167
Damaška M (1997) Evidence law adrift. Yale University Press
Dei Vecchi D (2020) Los confines pragmáticos del razonamiento probatorio CEJI-Grupo Editorial Zela, México-Perú
Di Corleto J (2017) Pautas para la recolección y valoración de la prueba con perspectiva de género. In: Hurtado J (dir) Género y Derecho penal: homenaje al Prof. Wolfgang Schöne, Instituto Pacífico, Lima, pp 409–433
Ertürk Y (2006) Report of the special rapporteur on violence against women, its causes and consequences: The due diligence standard as a tool for the elimination of violence against women [E/CN.4/2006/61], United Nations
Evola M, Krstic I, Fuensanta R (2023) Feminist judgements. In: Vujadinović D, Fröhlich M, Giegerich T (eds) Gender competent legal education, Springer Textbooks in Law, pp 144–177
Facio A (1999) Hacia una teoría crítica del Derecho. In: Fries L, Facio A (comp) Género y Derecho, comp. LOM Ediciones, Chile, pp 15–44
Ferrer J (2005) Prueba y verdad en el derecho, 2nd edn. Marcial Pons, Madrid
Ferrer J (2007) La valoración racional de la prueba. Marcial Pons, Madrid
Ferrer J (2022) Los momentos de la actividad probatoria en el proceso. In: Ferrer J (cord) Manual de razonamiento probatorio, Suprema Corte de Justicia de la Nación, México, pp 47–78
Franklin C (2010) The anti-stereotyping principle in constitutional sex discrimination law. N Y Univ Law Rev 85:83–173
Gascón M (2010a) Los hechos en el derecho. Bases argumentales de la prueba, 3rd edn. Marcial Pons, Madrid
Gascón M (2010b) Prueba científica: mitos y paradigmas. Anales de la Cátedra Francisco Suárez 44:81–103
Ghidoni E (2022) Aproximación a los estereotipos como elementos del razonamiento judicial a través de las presunciones. In Arena F (cord) Manual sobre los efectos de los estereotipos en la impartición de justicia, Suprema Corte de Justicia de la Nación, Mexico, pp 287–318
Ghidoni E, Morondo D (2022) El papel de los estereotipos en las formas de la desigualdad compleja: algunos apuntes desde la teoría feminista del derecho antidiscriminatorio. Discusiones 28(1):37–70

González Lagier D (2022a) Quaestio facti. Ensayos sobre la prueba, causalidad y acción, vol I. Palestra, Lima
González Lagier D (2022b) Inferencia probatoria y valoración conjunta de la prueba. In: Ferrer J (cord) Manual de razonamiento probatorio, Suprema Corte de Justicia de la Nación, Mexico, pp 353–395
Haack S (2009) Evidence and inquiry: a pragmatist reconstruction of epistemology, 2nd exp edn. Prometheus Books, New York
Haack S (2015) The expert witness: lessons from the U.S. experience. Humana Mente J Philos Stud 28:39–70
Hernández-Truyol B (2016) Talking back: from feminist history and theory to feminist legal methods and judgments. In: Berger L, Crawford B, Stanchi K (eds) Feminist Judgements. Rewritten opinions of the United States Supreme Court, Cambridge University Press, New York, pp 24–51
Hunter R (2010) An account of feminist judging. In: Hunter R, McGlynn C, Rackley E. Feminist judgments. From theory to practice, Hart Publishing, London, pp 30–43
Hunter R (2012) The power of feminist judgements? Fem Leg Stud 20:132–148
Kelly L (1988) Surviving sexual violence. Polity Press, Cambridge
Minow M (2018 [1988]) Feminist reason: getting it and losing it. In: Bartlett K, Kennedy R (eds) Feminist legal theory: readings in law and gender, Routledge, New York-London, pp 357–369
Morondo D (2022) Estereotipos, interseccionalidad y desigualdad estructural. In: Arena F cord Manual sobre los efectos de los estereotipos en la impartición de justicia, Suprema Corte de Justicia de la Nación, Mexico, pp 141–178
Observatorio Ciudadano Nacional del Feminicidio (2018) Informe implementación del tipo penal de feminicidio en México: desafíos para acreditar las razones de género 2014–2017
Puddifoot K (2021) How stereotypes deceive us. Oxford University Press
Ramírez JL (2020) El testimonio único de la víctima en el proceso penal desde la perspectiva de género. Quaestio Facti Revista Internacional Sobre Razonamiento Probatorio 1:201–246
Rhode D (2018 [1990]) Feminist critical theories. In: Bartlett K, Kennedy R (eds) Feminist legal theory: readings in law and gender, Routledge, New York-London, pp 333–350
Schauer F (2003) Profiles, probabilities and stereotypes. Harvard University Press, Cambridge
Smart C (1992) The woman of legal discourse. Social & Legal Studies 1(1):29–44
Stanchi K, Berger L, Crawford B (2016) Feminist judgements. Rewritten opinions of the United States Supreme Court, Cambridge University Press
Stroebe W, Insko C (1989) Stereotype, prejudice and discrimination: changing conceptions in theory and research. In: Bar-Tal D, Graumann C, Kruglanski A, Stroebe W (eds) Stereotyping and prejudice. Changing conceptions, Springer Science+Business, Media, LLC, Nueva York, pp 3–34
Tajfel H (1969) Cognitive aspects of prejudice. J Soc Issues 25(4):79–97
Taruffo M (2002a) Algunas discusiones sobre la relación entre prueba y verdad. Discusiones 3 (3):15–41
Taruffo M (2002b) La prueba de los hechos. Trotta, Madrid
Taruffo M (2008) La prueba. Marcial Pons, Madrid
Timmer A (2011) Toward an anti-stereotyping approach for the european court of human rights. Hum Rights Law Rev 11(4):707–738
Timmer A (2015) Judging stereotypes: what the European court of human rights can borrow from American and Canadian equal protection law. Am J Comp Law 63(1):239–284
Timmer A, Sosa L (2022) Los estereotipos en la jurisprudencia del Tribunal Europeo de Derechos Humanos. In: Arena F (cord) Manual sobre los efectos de los estereotipos en la impartición de justicia, Suprema Corte de Justicia de la Nación, Mexico, pp 49–110
Tuzet G (2021) Filosofía de la prueba jurídica. Marcial Pons, Madrid
Twining W (1990) Rethinking evidence. Exploratory essays, 2nd edn. Northwestern University Press, Illinois

UN High Commissioner of Human Rights and Fiscalía General de la República del Salvador (2012) Protocolo de actuación para la investigación del feminicidio. https://www.oacnudh.org/wp-content/uploads/2021/11/Protocolo-feminicidios-20042012-FINAL-2.pdf. Accessed 5 May 2024
UN Women (2011) 2011–2012 progress of the world's women. In Pursuit of justice. https://www.unwomen.org/sites/default/files/Headquarters/Attachments/Sections/Library/Publications/2011/ProgressOfTheWorldsWomen-2011-en.pdf. Accessed 5 May 2024
UN Women (2014) Modelo de protocolo latinoamericano de investigación de las muertes violentas de mujeres por razones de género (femicidio/feminicidio). https://www.unwomen.org/es/digital-library/publications/2014/8/modelo-de-protocolo-latinoamericano. Accessed 5 May 2024
Vázquez C (2015) De la prueba científica a la prueba pericial. Marcial Pons, Madrid
Wróblewski (2013) Sentido y hecho en el derecho, 2nd edn. Grijley, Perú

Marianela Delgado Nieves holds a PhD from the University of Girona, Spain. She has a Master's degree in Evidentiary Reasoning from the same university and the University of Genoa, Italy, and a Law degree from the National Autonomous University of Mexico. She clerked in the Supreme Court of Mexico from 2015 to 2018, became a Public Defense Attorney for Indigenous Communities from 2018 to 2019, and served as Deputy Director General of Human Rights of the Supreme Court from 2019 to 2020, where she was in charge of co-writing the Handbook for Judging from a Gender Perspective. Since then, she has been working on topics related to gender, evidence, femicide and hate crimes.

A Feminist Critique of Traditional Patriarchal Professional Stereotypes: The Example of the Czech Custody Justice System

Kateřina Šimáčková

Abstract The article examines the limitations of the Czech custody justice system, focusing on parental custody disputes and the impact of traditional patriarchal professional stereotypes. Drawing from in-depth interviews with legal professionals and experts, it elucidates the intersecting social, legal, and systemic factors contributing to the system's failure in seeking consensual solutions post-divorce or separation. The article starts by highlighting entrenched societal perceptions wherein divorce is deemed a failure, leading to a blame-driven environment and a preference for court intervention rather than dialogue between parents. The article highlights legal barriers, revealing how custody categorisation sparks debates and intensifies conflicts, often hindering the promotion of joint custody and complicating parental responsibilities. It emphasises the role of the Office for Social and Legal Protection of Children (OSPOD), advocating for a shift from its current extensive role to a focus on mediating parental disputes, urging a child-centric approach. Furthermore, the piece critiques inadequate involvement of the child in decision-making processes, advocating for a more inclusive mechanism that considers children's perspectives and needs as integral to custody decisions. The article emphasises the necessity for a multidisciplinary approach to challenge stereotypes, biases, and professional norms, stressing the importance of diverse expertise, collaboration, and parental and societal education regarding the significance of consensual resolutions in order to safeguard the child's best interest. In conclusion, the article calls for transcending traditional gender and professional roles, exposing biases inherent in the custody justice system, and advocates for a child-centric approach to transform the custody justice system towards more consensual and holistic approach.

K. Šimáčková (✉)
European Court of Human Rights, Strasbourg, France
e-mail: Katerina.Simackova@echr.coe.int

© The Author(s), under exclusive license to Springer Nature Switzerland AG 2025
S. Baer et al. (eds.), *The Gender and the Judiciary*, Gender Perspectives in Law 7,
https://doi.org/10.1007/978-3-032-06885-9_13

1 Introduction

In examining the causes of certain dysfunctions in the current Czech custody justice system, particularly in the area of parental custody disputes, I have employed a feminist perspective to critique traditional patriarchal professional stereotypes. While Czech legislation classifies these proceedings as aimed at finding solutions for the vulnerable person, the child, rather than litigation, Czech lawyers frequently use litigative methods that align with traditional perception of legal practice. I will present a feminist critique of the patriarchal traditional manner of practising law, under which court proceedings do not inherently seek to reach agreements beneficial to all parties, but rather aim at 'winning' or enforcing one's own solution to the dispute. I draw on my personal experience as both an attorney and judge, supplemented by discussions with experienced professionals from the legal community, academia, and the judiciary, to identify areas of contention.[1] I also draw on insights from children's focus groups, as published by the Czech Judicial Academy during its symposia, along with first-hand childhood experiences of parental divorce, which law students shared with me in my capacity as a teacher focusing on the child's best interests in my academic work. Ultimately, both Czech legislation and the Convention on the Rights of the Child stress the utmost importance of considering custody proceedings from the child's perspective.

Although the primary responsibilities of custody courts and state social services pertain to protecting children at risk, such as living without parental care or being exposed to violence or neglect, the predominant efforts of the legal professional involved, including judges and attorneys, revolve around resolving parental disputes regarding child custody of a child following the dissolution of parental relationships. Due to the traditional mind-set of the legal actors in such disputes, judges typically prioritise determining an outcome rather than assisting parents and children in finding the optimal setting for their future family life. Similarly, attorneys tend to advocate for procedural victories for their clients, whereas the focus of the proceedings should be on determining the child's best interests. In the Czech legal system, certain authorities, including the competent local authority for the social and legal protection of children (OSPOD), act as the child's conflict guardian in disputes between parents. However, this authority has, under the law, numerous other responsibilities and roles, leading it to either partially surrender or, like many courts, assume the responsibility of determining the best solution to the conflict rather than representing the child's best interests in the mediating between the parents. This body is then defined, even under legislation, as the body essentially responsible

[1] I would like to thank Martin Beneš, Klára Cásková, Martina Grochová, Radka Korbelová Dohnalová, Terezie Pemová, Vladimír Polák, Jana Provazníková, Kateřina Skřivánková, Renata Šínová, Petra Vidmuchová, Jana Zapletalová Koláčková, Daniela Zemanová for the time they devoted to our interviews and their enthusiasm for improving the Czech custody justice system.

for the welfare of all children in the relevant territory.[2] These authorities are burdened with so many responsibilities, thus preventing them from fulfilling their most critical role in judicial procedures concerning children—namely, serving as a robust institution that prioritises the voice of the child above all else. On the one hand, Czech custody courts make authoritative decisions on child custody without making sufficient efforts to bring parents to an agreement. On the other hand, a consensual resolution of disputes by agreement is sometimes inappropriately imposed even in cases of families in which domestic violence occurs.[3]

Despite the presence of excellent professionals in various roles within the Czech custody justice system, such as judges, attorneys, or public officials, social and professional stereotypes can sometimes hinder their effectiveness. Those who do not conform to these stereotypes may sometimes opt to leave their role altogether. For instance, I have encountered female attorneys who have found greater fulfilment working as mediators rather than continuing in their roles as attorneys.

---

[2] Their task is to look after the interests and wellbeing of the child, the protection of parenthood and the family and the mutual right of parents and children to parental upbringing and care. In doing so, they also take into account into consideration the child's wider social environment. The social and legal protection of children is to focus in particular on children whose parents (1) have died, (2) are not fulfilling the obligations arising from parental responsibility or (3) are not exercising or are abusing the rights arising from parental responsibility, and (4) on children who have been placed in the care of an individual other than their parents, where such individual fails to perform the duties resulting from the placement of the child in their care, (5) children who lead an idle or immoral life, consisting in particular of failure to attend classes, not working despite not having a sufficient source of livelihood, consumption of alcohol or addictive substances, being at risk of addiction, making a living in prostitution, having committed a crime, children (6) who repeatedly run away from their parents or other natural or legal persons responsible for the child's upbringing, (7) against whom a criminal offence has been committed, or is suspected to have been committed, which threatens life, health, liberty, human dignity, moral development or property, (8) who, on the request of their parents or other persons responsible for the child's upbringing, have repeatedly been placed in institutions providing continuous care for children or their placement in such institutions lasts longer than 6 months, (9) who are threatened by violence between parents or other persons responsible for the upbringing of the child, or by violence between other natural persons or (10) children who are applicants for international protection, and who are in the territory of the Czech Republic without the accompaniment of their parents or other persons responsible for their upbringing, where the above circumstances have existed for a period of time or in such intensity that they have an adverse impact on children's development or can result in children's negative development. They are to carry out counselling and preventive activities and to implement educational measures. In addition to all this, they are also the conflict guardian of children in proceedings in which parents are in dispute over the care of their children (see Sections 5 and 6 of Act No 359/1999 Coll., on the Social and Legal Protection of Children).

[3] See the general critique in UN Special Rapporteur on Violence Against Women and Girls, 'Gender bias in custody battles places women and children at risk' (30 June 2023) https://www.ohchr.org/en/stories/2023/06/gender-bias-custody-battles-places-women-and-children-risk about "alarming tendency of family courts to dismiss the history of domestic violence and abuse in custody cases, particularly when mothers and/or children present credible allegations of such abuse, including coercive control and physical or sexual violence. Such practices are widespread, unacceptable and require urgent action".

In the Czech custody justice system, we can encounter two lines of decision-making. The first, more complex, is based on proactive efforts to assist parents in agreeing on future family arrangements. The second approach relies on different types of routines that either do not help facilitating agreements or lead to agreements that are forced or unsustainable in the long term. Although feminist critiques of law associate the consensual approach to dispute resolution with the feminine principle and, conversely, stereotype litigation approaches with the masculine principle, the environment of the Czech custodial justice system often contradicts these assumptions. It reveals that some female judges may uphold patriarchal stereotypes and fulfil traditional professional roles, while progressive approaches in the Czech custodial justice system are often embraced by male judges.

Feminist theories of law and justice based on literary archetypes (Antigone, Portia) and psychological research reveal the traditional gendered conditioning of why a litigative (dispute-oriented) approach is preferred in law and justice rather than a search for a conciliatory (consensual) solution.

Reaching agreements is a means of prioritising the best interests of the child. Markéta Nováková, an advocate of the Cochem practice in the Czech Republic, eloquently illustrates this point—when parents refer to each other as a 'cow' and a 'fool', it is obvious that their child will internalise these negative perceptions.[4] Moreover, appropriate mediation in disputes leads to more enduring positive outcomes; well-negotiated agreements tend to be more stable in the long term. From the perspective of efficiency and reducing the burden on the judiciary, it is advantageous for a judge invest greater effort at the outset in establishing mutual negotiation between parents in relation to child custody, rather than continually referring the dispute to the court for resolution. Additionally, one cannot ignore the hard-to-quantify sense of satisfaction, or at least the absence of dissatisfaction, that arises from individuals who handle their separation amicably to minimise distress for themselves and their children. Such individuals are likely to experience less frustration, better health, and greater happiness. Ultimately, a well-managed divorce can serve as the foundation of a healthy family and a fulfilling life for all concerned.

This text will commence by delineating the reasons and arguments for the continued adherence of legal professionals to a litigious approach in custody proceedings, despite the preference for uncontested resolutions. Many professionals persist in their traditional professional roles, which may hinder the search for amicable solutions to post-divorce or post-break-up child custody disputes. In the Czech custodial justice system, female judges constitute the majority of decision-makers.[5] Frequently, female judges perpetuate gender stereotypes and conform to the prevailing operational paradigm of the justice system. From one

---

[4] Deseti tisícům dětí ročně se rozpadá rodina. Rozvod zvládnou, když ho zvládnete vy, říká Nováková—DVTV na Aktuálně.cz (aktualne.cz).https://video.aktualne.cz/dvtv/deseti-tisicum-deti-rocne-se-rozpada-rodina-rozvod-zvladnou/r~cd09ae2e746b11e882090cc47ab5f122/

[5] Havelkova et al. (2021).

perspective, they often cite a career in the judiciary as a personal decision that is naturally influenced by societal norms surrounding "women's fate".[6] This includes conforming to social expectations regarding female behaviour and the traditional division of roles within the family. Consequently, it is not surprising that women's adherence to professional expectations and traditional standards, or their strong loyalty to the patriarchal way of resolving court disputes, faces criticism within feminist literature.

Furthermore, the text will address possible factors contributing to the shortcomings of the Czech custody justice system in finding consensual solutions. These factors may include established traditionalist social norms, legal intricacies, administrative hurdles, and organisational inefficiencies, alongside the lack of understanding of the specific needs of children involved in these proceedings. In the conclusion, emphasis will be placed on advocating for a multidisciplinary, collaborative, holistic approach within the custody justice system, and for the dismissal of stereotypes, prejudices and myths that hinder finding the optimal outcomes.

Traditional patriarchal professional stereotypes can encumber the process of finding optimal solutions in custody disputes. To be sure, traditional patriarchal professional stereotypes are not tied to whether a man or a woman is acting in a particular professional role. Rather, they are a legacy of the patriarchal perception of judicial work as simply weighing rights and evaluating people, not as finding the best and most comprehensive solution to a conflict situation that is both acceptable to and respectful of all actors involved. While social gender biases can predetermine people's behaviour in their professional and family roles, traditional professional stereotypes associated with the role of attorneys—to win and maximize earnings—can also complicate custody proceedings. The challenge will be for legal professionals—including judges—to move beyond these stereotypes and view their role within the system in a way that allows them to overcome gendered social and patriarchal professional stereotypes.

2 A Feminist Perspective on the Traditional Setup of Professional Legal Roles

Feminist critiques of the inadequacies inherent in traditional legal paradigms tend to draw on two female literary figures who criticise the establishment of current norms, Antigone and Portia.

The narrative of Antigone is a tragic and familiar one. Antigone defied the order of her uncle, King Creon, refusing to leave the body of her brother Polyneices, unburied—who had been killed in battle, and declared an enemy of the State. For this reason, she was punished (burned alive), although she justified her actions by referring to the principle of divine law that all people must be properly buried.

[6] Urbanikova et al. (2023).

Feminist critique is directed particularly against Hegel's interpretation in *The Phenomenology of Mind*, which uses Antigone's dilemma to explore conflicting conceptions of ethical life. According to Hegel, the conflict is between the lower, less developed feminine rules associated with family and home, and the higher political rules protecting the coherence of political citizenship (protection of the State from traitors), thus offering a construction of masculinity and femininity as opposites. Moreover, he infers that complete ethical and political citizenship is incompatible with the protection of family values[7] or empathy. It is very reminiscent of situations where, in the context of judicial deliberations, a female judge tends to show compassion towards a party in the case, usually the more vulnerable or weaker one, is told that she is guided by emotion rather than reason. This echoes the prevalent idea among legal practitioners that adherence to rationality, not sentimentality, should guide our decisions. In other words, the law is expected to embody traiits of rationality, objectivity, abstraction, and adherence to principles—qualities traditionally associated with masculinity. Conservely, characteristics such as irrationality, subjectivity, contextualily, and personalised thinking are often associated with femininity.[8] Thus, laws are formulated to resolve disputes rather than facilitate consensual solutions—as if the two could not be reconciled to allow empathy and compassion as well as rationality into law and jurisprudence. That is, to create a legal environment that is both predictable and understandable -based on rules that take into account different human experiences- and flexible enough not to interfere inhumanely with communities and individuals' personal lives.

The story of Portia, the main female character in *The Merchant of Venice*, who, during a court hearing, disguised as a man, saves Antonio's life, or his pound of flesh, from the usurer Shylock. She is sometimes considered the standard metaphor for a female lawyer, and is the subject of great debate or interpretive dispute among feminist writers. In the original feminist literature, Portia's narrative is often construed as her ability in presenting legal arguments before the court capable "to bring into the masculine citadel of justice the feminine plea for mercy".[9] However, subsequent literature argues that there is a better way to interpret her story: that women should instead appropriate "masculine" justice. Indeed, it is necessary to recognise that our legal system currently fails to uphold its fundamental commitment of delivering equal justice, and there is reason to believe that previously excluded women, collectively marked by a history of oppression, could likely play a crucial role in achieving it.[10]

However, when interpreting Portia's narrative, we can certainly agree that female lawyers may still feel a strong pressure to conform to pre-existing patriarchal norms in the workplace and the need to minimise, rather than emphasise,

[7] Conaghan (2013), p. 100 and following pages.

[8] Menkel-Meadow (1985) p. 45.

[9] Gilligan (1982) p. 105.

[10] Cohen (2013).

their differences[11] or practices that might, in light of the above, be characterised as 'feminine', i.e., alien to the rational approach of the male world.

The abovementioned psychological studies (focusing on the ethical perceptions of adolescent children) reveal that girls and boys might be predisposed to approach moral or justice-related issues in slightly different ways. Carrol Gilligan[12] has written about a different moral perception than the traditionally male one—in this female conception, moral dilemmas arise from conflicting obligations rather than competing rights, necessitating a contextual and narrative-oriented approach for their resolution. Gilligan illustrates this through the different solutions to Heinz's problem by two eleven-year-old children (Amy and Jake). Heinz's wife is dying of cancer and requires medication priced beyond Heinz's means by the local pharmacist. The ethical question arises. Is Heinz morally justified in resorting to theft to obtain the medicine? Jake reasoning starts from the premise that life holds greater value than property, thus justifying stealing as a solution—a perspective framed as a balancing-of-rights. However, Amy, a girl of the same age, approaches the dilemma differently. She raises additional questions, such as whether Heinz and the pharmacist explored other options like obtaining a loan, or whether Heinz tried to explain to the pharmacist what is at stake—his wife's life. This story shows that while Jake explored Heinz's dilemma through the logic of justice, Amy used the ethics of care.

According to classical psychological assessment, such as *Kohlberg's Stages of Moral Development in Children*, Amy's score is lower because she perceives the problem as rooted in the individuals involved, while Jake is considered more developed for contemplating ethics in broader, universal terms. Amy's approach focused on involving and sensibilising the affected parties, asking about additional circumstances, such as who will look after Heinz's wife if he goes to prison. Her approach facilitates an agreement and communication among the parties involved. Amy considers Heinz, the pharmacist, and Heinz's wife, in her decision-making, therefore rooted in the context of bonds and relationships. Jake makes decisions in the abstract without considering specific individuals, and within the context of individual rights.[13] Moreover, Amy does not understand why she should be a neutral arbiter and make decisions based only on the information available to her. According to Gilligan, a greater emphasis on facts and a more contextual understanding of the dilemma helps the actor to realise the social conditioning embedded within the problem. For instance, if a patriarchal-minded judge emphasises justice, Judge Amy might prioritise mercy and seek a solution where no one is harmed.

Carrie Menkel Meadows generalises the aforementioned study, asserting that women perceive themselves through bonds and relationships with others, while men view themselves as self-identified individuals. She notes that adolescence represents a process of identification and connection for girls, contrasted with

[11] This is nicely described e.g., by Kanter (1993).

[12] Gilligan (1982) p. 19.

[13] Menkel-Meadow (1985) pp. 46, 47, 51.

a period of separation and individuation for boys. In conventional terms, Jake is considered to be a better lawyer because he evaluates individual rights against each other. However, Amy's approach is also legitimate and indicative of a different style of lawyering. Among other things, Amy shows a better understanding of the client's needs.[14] Meadows concludes by acknowledging the legitimacy of both seemingly opposing viewpoints, suggesting there may not be a single winner. Ultimately, both approaches are applicable in legal practice.

The basic model of traditional (patriarchal) judicial proceedings is that there are two attorneys who translate their cases to an impartial third party, who hears the evidence and arguments and declares one side the 'winner'. We are used to hierarchy and competition with a binary outcome.

The Czech experience confirms these conclusions. The author's interviews with experienced practitioners reveal a repeated critique of Czech custody judges: they are often perceived as too authoritative, preferring to impose solutions rather than soliciting input from the involved parties. This phenomenon persists despite the significant representation of female judges within the custody judicial system. Havelková, Urbánikova and Kosař's text[15] shows that Czech female judges had to adopt the traditionally set rules and norms, but at the same time retain their "women's fate"—therefore, they do not perceive their own experiences as evidence that acting differently within the system or effective change is feasible. In other words, female judges operate within a system in which there are not only professional stereotypes and pressures, but also social-gender stereotypes originating both within their own lives and communities and also in the broader society. In addition, they tend to view their participation within the system as an achievement and, thus, do not challenge the legitimacy of that system or its construction, but rather replicate its traditional patterns.

Simplistically speaking, a certain ambivalence in the Czech judiciary can be identified -but not demarcated along the lines of the gender or age of the judges-regarding whether its primarily concern lies in mediating human narratives or establishing norms and standards. However, the most adept judges demonstrate an ability to synthesise both aspects, therefore showing that a properly crafted persuasive judgment should rely on the human story, address it, while upholding a coherent legal system that provides sufficient rights, protections and legal certainty (i.e., essentially safety) for all parties involved.

Moreover, according to the interviewees, female judges often come from privilege backgrounds. Due to their status, professional position, and education, men are less inclined to mistreat them. Accordingly, female judges in positions of privilege and power may find it difficult to relate to, for example, someone who has been subjected to domestic violence. It seems that both male and female judges are somewhat detached from the realities experienced by the majority of people and are, consequently, unable to understand people in a situation they have not had the

---

[14] Menkel-Meadow (1985) pp. 43, 46, 47 and 51.

[15] Urbanikova et al. (2023).

opportunity to experience.[16] This observation is supported by critical academic texts pointing out that "the collision of judges' and litigants' lives is of particular consequence for a litigant: if the litigant's choices and preferences are dissimilar to the experiences of the judge, or counter to the dominant society's stock stories, the courtroom is a breeding ground for bias".[17] And that "fact finders, like all people, have subconscious tendencies to favour litigants and narratives that seem familiar".[18]

Using the example of the legal concept of the best interests of the child, the gender-based critique shows that the court's interpretive work, with this vague legal concept, exposes the gender biases of male and female judges: "Critics agree that the (best interest) standard is too vague. It invites each parent to engage in a full-scale attack on the other parent's worth as a parent and as a human being, a process that leaves scars of humiliation and rage on both combatants. An imprecise standard also means that judges are given wide latitude in deciding the best interests of a child in any particular case. This leaves courts vulnerable to accusations that gender bias and subjective value judgments influence their custody dispositions".[19] "Although courts rely on this "ultimate criterion" either by statute or by case law, there is no consensus of what is meant by a child's best interest. As a result, judges often have no legal framework for determining what is in a child's best interests, which gives trial judges broad discretion "to exercise their own views on what is best for children".[20] Exacerbating this problem is the fact that judges usually do not know enough about the family to make a valid assessment of what the child's best interest really is. As a result, custody decisions are often determined by what is "in the hearts of the trial judges," which may reflect their biases".[21]

3 The Czech Custody Justice System and Possible Reasons for Its Failure to Find Consensual Solutions

3.1 Social Background

Virtually all of the interviewees unanimously agreed that the pivotal factor in achieving consensual solutions lie in educating parents about the negative effects of conflict on the child and imparting skills to resolve to parental disputes. Furthermore, a shift in social perceptions towards acknowledging the vital of role of both parents in the child's life is deemed highly beneficial. Czech society perceives divorce as

[16] From the author's interview with attorney Radka Dohnalová Korbelová.

[17] Donahue (2020) p. 560.

[18] Donahue (2020) p. 575.

[19] Warshak (2005) p. 398.

[20] Jacobs (1997).

[21] Jacobs (1997).

a failure, leading partners to look for the culprit of that failure and assigning blame to each other rather than carry the blame individually. Consequently, they may discredit the other parent's suitability for spending time with their children. In court, they expect confirmation of their story, that they did not cause the breakdown of the relationship, and removing parental custody from the other parent can be used as a recourse to punishment for the breakdown of the family.

According to Judge Daniela Zemanová, the parties to the proceedings perceive the court as an authoritative environment. As a result, it is beneficial if parents are adequately prepared in advance by a experienced mediator to reach an amicable solution in court. However, she acknowledges that mediation services may not always be of sufficient quality or accessible to certain social groups due to financial constraints. In fact, there is generally limited awareness in Czech society about conflict management and seeking assistance from external professionals to resolve such issues. According to Judge Klára Cásková, parties perceive the court system as an authority that will resolve disputes for them. In her judicial practice, she encounters the socially established practice where, instead of engaging in direct communication to address post-divorce arrangements, parents seek to have their future resolved by the court. Consequenely, they are often surprised when the court encourages them to reach an agreement amongst themselves.

3.2 Legal Barriers and Types of Care

Czech law contains three distinct categories relating to post-divorce children's custody: joint custody, alternating custody, and sole custody (which is usually referred to as exclusive custody in commentaries).

In Czech public and legal debate, there is a fierce battle over alternating custody.[22] For some individuals, it represents a symbolic recognition of their parental role, while for others, it signifies a profound challenge for the child—moving between two homes with a backpack. Sole custody can also be problematic because the other parent may feel excluded. This is despite the fact that even after a child has been placed in the care of one parent, both parents usually retain parental responsibility, i.e., are entitled to share decision-making and all information about the child. However, some non-lawyers (e.g., a paediatrician or teacher) might not be aware of this and therefore only communicate information to the parent who has sole custody of the child. On the other hand, shared parental responsibility among disputing parents can lead to litigation over all aspects of the child's care, for example, which school or nursery the child should attend or whether the child should be vaccinated and against which diseases.

[22] The Czech Constitutional Court has actively entered this debate by supporting alternating custody as opposed to sole custody of one parent, which more fully realizes both the rights of both parents and the child's right to be with both parents.

The fact that public law sometimes neglects children from divorced families altogether, while other times strongly emphasises the custodial parent, can hinder the search for the best arrangement for both children and parents. This leaves some financial issues, such as child tax credit allocation, to parental agreement, while authoritative decisions are made, like who is seen as the carer for example for cases of paid time off to care for a sick child. Moreover, it is often administrative practice, rather than the law and its interpretation, that governs the matter. Judicial experience reveals instances where tax authorities disregard parental agreements on tax considerations, insisting instead on honoring judgments that designate sole custody of the child to one parent. This highlights a systematic stereotype within public law, assuming that custody courts typically assign sole custody to one parent, who consequently enjoys the benefits of parenthood. However, public law should be adapted to the needs of conflict resolution, so that parents can agree on who will benefit from which advantages, rather than imposing it in advance. Moreover, nonsensical and harmful rules are not found directly in the statute but are created by concrete administrative practices or interpretative guidelines.[23] All of this prevents parents and judges from leaning towards the so-called joint custody. Lastly, even if everything seems harmonious and it is clear that the parents are in agreement, one obstacle remains: the possibility of reaching a consensual decision in favour of joint custody is prevented by public law regulations or outdated commentary texts on the statute, claiming that it is necessary that all the parties involved share the same residential address.

Simultaneously, legal-administrative obstacles, or erroneous judicial interpretations often make it legally impracticable to respect the emotional decisions of the parents, thereby impeding the equitable recognition and consideration of both parent's roles in the child's life.

When a parental conflict arises, however, it is unreasonable to expect the State to conduct a pharmaceutical weighing on the scales of justice, determining which parent is more favourable or less harmful than the other. Instead, the state should play an active role towards the goal of de-escalating parental conflicts and educate them on the harmful effects of manipulative and antagosnistic behaviour on the child. In cases where both parents possess comparable parental competencies and the family does not present any pathological problem, such as domestic violence or serious addiction of either parent, recognising the importance of the other parent's role and the child's need for both of them should be prioritise as one of the most significant considerations.

To understand the dynamics of the relationship between parents, a classification of *de facto* childcare as joint, concurrent, or conflicting care, can be useful. Conflictual parenting is defined as competition or even open warfare between parents over the child. In such situations, one parent does not respect or ignores the importance of the other parent's role in the child's life—the parental conflict is thereby fully transferred to the child. Concurrent parenting without mutual

[23] From the author's interview with Judge Martin Beneš.

cooperation or harmony entails the child navigating between two completely impermeable worlds represented by the mother and father. In shared parenting, the ability to distinguish potential partner disagreements from the exercise of parenting stands out, actively involving children in resolving issues that affect them. Shared parenting does not imply that parents always share the same opinions, have identical parenting styles, ore are devoid of flaws and conflicts. Rather, shared parenting entails parents internalising values and principles such as mutual importance, respect, and esteem, which are manifested in their everyday actions. Shared parenting enables a child experiencing family breakdown to have the physical, psychological, and social presence of both parents as well as other close persons in their life (physical contact, indirect contact, whenever the child needs it, social presence, i.e., respect for the importance of the parental roles of both parents in the child's life). The types of real-life parenthood described, defined by the degree of recognition of the other parent's place in the child's life, are not contingent on the factual situation, such as whether the parents live together, or the legal arrangements post-dissolution of the parents' partnership. Even during the parents' partnership, conflictual care may occur, and alternating care often resembles concurrent care, where one parent cares for the child during their custody period without regard for the other parent's action.[24] The challenges of alternating care, having the nature of concurrent care, as mentioned before, were well demonstrated in the era of covid restrictions. In such cases of concurrent parenting, alternating care is only feasible if one can follow the prescribed schedule- until provisional measures interfere with that prescribed schedule.[25]

Most interviewees pointed out that it is the legal designation of types of care that can lead to an acceleration of conflict. The mother is stigmatised in her social environment if she agrees to a type of care other than sole maternal care; the father often seeks alternating care simply because he thinks he is entitled to it and that by fighting for it, he will express his commitment to be a good father. Property or maintenance issues may also be one reason, as the demand for alternating care (usually by the father's attorney) may be made simply to induce the mother to make concessions on property issues. Respondents therefore deduce the recommendation to simply determine the amount of time spent with the child by each parent without legally qualifying the type of custody as required by the current legislation. They believe that the frequent apple of discord would thus disappear.

Terezie Pemová affirms the significance of concepts for social actors, pointing out not only the stigmatisation of legally determined types of care but also the challenge of labelling a parent's new partner. Labels like 'stepmother' may be considered somewhat undignified. Recently, national and European case-law has tended towards the use of the term 'social parent' to recognise the important role of the parents' new partners in the child's life and their own.

[24] Ptáček et al. (2012).

[25] From the author's interview with social worker Terezie Pemová.

3.3 The Single Body Caring for Children in All Matters

The appropriate forum for bringing parents to an agreement should ideally not be the court or legal practicioners, but rather the competent State body, the social and legal protection authority for children (OSPOD). However, the OSPOD often faces an overwhelming workload due to its numerous responsibilities. Indeed, in addition to preventing disputes between parents, its role of OSPOD includes conflict guardianship, where they represent children in all legal proceedings involving them when the interests of the parents and the child conflict. Also, OSPOD is responsible for essentially all social and legal protection of children carried out by the State (i.e. prevention and supervision of problem families, protection of children at risk, mediation of adoption or foster care, filing petitions for court decisions in the case of minor children, and if necessary and appropriate, for example, petitions for removal of a child from unsuitable parental care).[26] The law thus imposes too many responsibilities on the OSPOD, which not only deprives its ability to address real cases of children at risk and but also prevents its capacity to fulfil these roles with the requisite degree of impartiality and attention.

The OSPOD defends the public interest, acting as the child's guardian in disputes between parents, or in situations where the child's interests clash with those of their parents. Simultaneously, it must also represent the child's exclusive interest, such as in quasi-criminal proceedings or cases involving deprivation of their liberty and placement in institutionalised care. However, these responsibilities place the OSPOD in an untenable position of conflict of interests. One one hand, it is in the public interest to separate a potentially harmful child from others; on the other hand, we have the experience and a number of statistics suggest that, where a child is in institutional care are at greater risk of criminal behaviour or maltreatment. For this reason, it may not be in the child's individual interest to be placed in such institutions. This conflict of several interests -public interest, child's individual interest, and the interests of other children in the family or at school- cannot be effectively resolved by a single authority which has the duty to defend all these interests and to represent a particular child in court proceedings, all at the same time.

The OSPOD faces a similar ambiguity in cases involving decisions on child custody, where it serves as both the child's representative and also the State body responsible for safeguarding the child's best interests. The only viable solution to this conflicting situation, without a change in the law, is to adopt the approach where, once the OSPOD assumes the role of the conflict guardian before the court, its function as an administrative body with some independent responsibility for finding a solution ceases. Instead, its primary duty becomes that of representing the child individually, advocating for the child's expectations and needs in the court proceedings. Even before that, it should play the role of a mediator of parental disputes, offering their professional expertise to facilitate the parents' search for agreement, rather than imposing a predetermined 'right' solution.

[26] Act No 359/1999 Coll., on the Social and Legal Protection of Children, as amended.

It is precisely in relation to the role of the OSPOD that Martina Grochová, an attorney and academic, expressed in our interview that amidst its multiple roles, the OSPOD fails in its primary mission in court proceedings—to be the voice of the child, which should be its first duty.

Judge Daniela Zemanová described the main problem as the justice system overly relying on the OSPOD and its opinion. The Czech Republic appears to pretend that children's rights are protected by entrusting everything in this area to the OSPOD, yet fails to provide it with enough well-trained and well-paid professionals. As a result, children caught in conflicts lack dedicated advocates—the OSPOD lacks time to adequately address their needs, and the courts "play the card" that the OSPOD is protecting them, by relying heavily on OSPOD's opinions.

Even Jana Zapletalová Koláčková, a lawyer working in the training of custody judges within the framework of the Judicial Academy, emphasises that—in the current situation, where the OSPOD is appointed as the child's guardian, it should first of all describe to the court why it has not been able to reach an amicable solution with the parents and formulate the child's position to the court. Its role should not be to provide the court with a solution, but rather to advocate for the child's best interests without prescribing a specific outcome. Attempting to have a decision-making role is counterproductive. Under the current legislation, the OSPOD should, on the contrary, have a greater role in the pre-trial phase, aiming to prevent a court decision to be resorted at all. It should not have the ambition to impose its idea of a solution to the family situation on the court, but rather to educate and guide parents from the outset towards an amicable solution.

Overall, however, it is necessary to consider a future conceptual solution to the situation. The considered representation of children by an attorney in custody proceedings would be extremely costly and would not bring the child's real voice to the proceedings anyway; in a case where the child's opinion needs to be ascertained and possibly their best interests identified, a qualified social worker could do better than a lawyer. The children's focus groups, on the other hand, highlighted the important role of the attorney in quasi-criminal proceedings (adjudicating cases involving children under the age of 15 who have committed an offence otherwise punishable), where the attorney is on the side of the child rather than any public interest.[27] This role needs to be strengthened because, as per a decision of the European Committee of Social Rights,[28] the Czech Republic does not provide sufficient procedural rights in such proceedings. It fails to provide them with a defence at the pre-trial stage of the proceedings or offer alternatives or diversions to formal court proceedings.

[27] The findings of the children's focus groups held by the Justice Academy as part of the Improving Access to Justice for Vulnerable Groups project showed that children who were involved in proceedings involving children under the age of 15 who had committed an offence otherwise punishable reported that they felt well informed about their situation and their rights and options as a result of being represented by an attorney.

[28] ICJ v. Czech Republic, No. 148/2017, 20. 10. 2020.

A noteworthy observation in this context is provided by Terezie Pemová, a court social worker, who higlights that during the training of social workers from the OSPOD, it is often emphasised by their superiors or representatives of the ministry, which guide them methodologically, to apply the law correctly, rather than on the necessity of effective and continuous communication with parents and children. Similarly, teachers are not provided with training regarding the Education Act, but rather on how to teach children better.

3.4 *Insufficient or Inappropriate Child Involvement or Child-Unfriendly Justice?*[29]

The traditional Czech legal and psychological environment is characterised by a paternalistic concern for the child, and the family associated with the communist era. Trying not to expose the child to unpleasant experiences and avoiding talking to the child about serious "adult" problems is characteristic of this approach. The guiding idea was to find a "good" solution for the child without engaging the child in conversations or explaining the situation. For this reason, I have always pointed out the discomfort children feel when they sense they are merely objects of care and interest, without any ability to influence their destiny or understand what is happening to them and why.[30] Moreover, lawyers often prefer precise rules that apply uniformly to all cases. However, in relation to decision-making about children, they must be aware that it is appropriate to be guided by the child's best interests in their particular life circumstances, rather than by abstract rules.[31]

Indeed, for many children (and especially adolescents between the ages of 15 and 18), the inability to adequately participate in a process that will result in a decision about their future lives is very painful. I recall the reflections of a law-enthusiastic high school student who was involved in the appeal of a case in which his future fate was being decided (a custody dispute between his parents. After being questioned, he asked the judge if he could remain in the courtroom because each parent had told him something different about the proceedings after the first instance hearing. The judge answered that he had to leave because he could be called as a witness later in the proceedings. Thus, he waited in the corridor for approximately two hours, only to receive a short verdict with minimal explanation given to him. The full text was not officially made available to him either. The child's participation must be seen as a conscious effort to be truly respectful and in no way harmful—the child is neither supposed to be a witness, nor is their participation to be reduced to a tick-box in the OSPOD and court files. However, we certainly should avoid transitioning from the

[29] With this title, the author paraphrases an important Council of Europe document on child-friendly justice.

[30] Šimáčková (2022) pp. 327–344.

[31] More on this in Šimáčková and Foukalová Molková (2015) pp. 76–89.

absolute objectification of the child to treating them as having equal status to the other adult participants in the proceedings.

The courts should prioritise understanding how the family functioned before the parents' separation, avoiding hasty recommendations or imposing plan. Instead, they should emphasise that the objective pursued by the custody proceedings is to find a course of action, rather than making a final decision on custody arrangements. In relation to children's participation in proceedings, Judge Daniela Zemanová has had an excellent experience with temporary custody arrangements before a final decision has been made, where the family experimented it and discovered what suits them best. These arrangements can be informally maintained during the proceedings for a period, or they can sometimes be formalised by a time-limited interim order. She herself has had good experience using this form in appeal proceedings.[32]

Court social worker Terezie Pemová emphasises that the child's participation in proceedings concerning them is an attitude or process, rather than on-time act. The child should always gain more information, explanations, and a sense of security from their participation, rather than merely serving as a source of facts for the judge or social worker. It is essential to avoid unintelligible legal terms when communicating with the child. For instance, Terezie Pemová advises against using, the word "wish" when seeking the child's opinion, as children often perceives wishes as something magical, hoping for their parents to reconcile. Instead, using the word "expectation" helps children grasp the reality of the situation and how they can best adapt to it.

Furthermore, the child has the right to the physical, emotional, and social presence of both parents, requiring each parent to acknowledge the role of the other. In this regard, it is recommended that after the parents separate, all reminders of the departed parent should be removed from the apartment within four months. Conversely, in the event of a parent's death, reminders of them (such as pictures or cherished items) should remain in the apartment, ensuring the child continues to perceive their emotional and social presence. In this aspect, a child whose parent has died might be left with a closer connection to that parent than a child who is in the care of only one parent with insufficient contact with the other.

4 The Path to a Solution as the Need to Expose Patriarchal Professional and Social Stereotypes

4.1 The Need for a Multidisciplinary and Holistic Approach

Returning to the way in which Amy handled the conflict between the pharmacist and Heinz, the resolution of the case from her perspective requires knowledge of all relevant circumstances. This holistic approach becomes necessary in cases involving decisions regarding a child's needs. Assessing the child's best interests in all

[32] Recommendations resulting from the author's interview with Judge Daniela Zemanová.

administrative and judicial proceedings necessitates an interdisciplinary approach. The child's best interests must be assessed with the help of all the professionals required, ensuring their protection and promotion for realisation. This holistic approach is often not possible when we impose this task on a single State body or social worker, who may lack the necessary expertise and finds themself in a conflict of interests which cannot be properly resolved. Judges also frequently require diverse support to assist them in making their decisions,[33] which must be tailored to the unique circumstances of each child.

However, to fulfil the State's positive obligations described above, a diverse range of expertise across various levels and domains is essential—it is necessary to work with social workers specialised in different fields, pedagogues, special pedagogues, psychologists, psychiatrists, addictionologists, etc., and to use qualified mediators. Indeed, Amy's approach involves working with others—a typical example would certainly be the use of case conferences, when appropriate, and, most importantly, respecting and thoroughly assessing theresults from the decision-making process.

It is precisely the multi-disciplinary and holistic approach that can assist in identifying situations of apparent domestic violence or parental pathology, as well as determining who is responsible for creating such a situation in a family in disrepair, thereby hindering agreement. Moreover, it is typically beyond a judge's professional competence to effectively address toxic manipulation without the assistance of experts.

4.2 Stereotypes, Prejudice, and Myths

As demonstrated in the preceding sections, the dominant professional mindset among the involved lawyers, wherein judges are perceived as the ultimate arbiters tasked with adjudicating ongoing disputes, and attorney are driven to secure victories against opposing parties for financial gain, often impedes parental agreement. This framework can make it difficult for legal professionals to go into the mode of searching for an agreement, which is the best solution to the dispute. As Judge Vladimir Polák stated during an interview with the author, "judges gather evidence instead of solving the problem of a particular family." Many respondents from the court environment sense an expectation among judges to provide solutions rather than merely mediate the parties' own solutions. The very perception of how the judicial process functions can hinder agreement—by the standard perception on the part of the parties to proceedings of how the court process is supposed to work—when the court invites parents to comment on the case, they often begin to denigrate the other parent, believing it to be the 'custom'. This aligns with the logic that divorce signifies failure, and that therefore, it is necessary to find the

[33] For example, specialist court social workers.

culprit and to place blame on the other parent. Moreover, both parents are often trying to convince the court that they are the 'better' parent, making the process a competition. In addition, one parent may perceive judicial bias in favour of the other parent, leading them to avoid further proceedings. Thus, the judge's approach can significantly influence whether they create an environment conducive to agreement or escalate conflict.

Another recurring obstacle to reaching agreements, echoed by nearly all respondents, lies in social prejudices and myths. The most widespread misconception is that if a woman agrees to a type of care other than her sole care, she is perceived as a bad mother.[34] Judge Vladimir Polák also commented on this, noted the tendency for human nature to conform to the views, norms and expectations of one's social group. In deciding some cases, he felt that it was not a "mere" conflict between the parents, but an unconscious value clash between various stakeholders, including the judge, the mother, the father, the child's representative, and possibly the professional service provider, as described by Susan Beth Jacobs. Instead of seeking the child's best interests, the personal value frameworks of all parties involved, often diverse and conflicting, influence the proceedings and decision-making. In many social groups, exists a prevailing expectation regarding the mother's role following the family breakdown. In such cases, conflict may arise from unconscious effort to conform to these social norms, which may result in hindering acknowledgement of the father's potential role in the child's life and, thus, reaching an agreement.

It is also necessary to educate parents regarding the fact that the first agreement to resolve the child's current situation is only the first step—parents do not realise that when they have once reached an agreement in court, it is not the end. Some parents feel that they have eliminated all conflicts by making an agreement in court, but suddenly see that from the next day onwards there are more agreements and micro-conflicts that need to be resolved altogether. This is also why it would be beneficial to educate parents and provide them with appropriate professional assistance (e.g., in the form of a mediator) in order for them to be supported in finding further agreements that respond to the changing situation (e.g., covid quarantine, changing needs and expectations of the child, new family constellation). For instances, the arrival of new partners or, conversely, the loneliness of one of the parents can constitute a major problem in finding an agreement. This can be compounded by the fact that from early childhood, children can be forced to mediate feelings and disputes between their parents, for instance, in having to balance one parent's loneliness and their other parent's new family. The services provided to the family and the child must be tailored to accommodate the role that the child may undergo.

---

[34] Tereza Pemová describes it as a mother telling her daughter, for example, that she will not help her with childcare if she agrees to alternating care. Moreover, there is a lot of demonisation of alternating care as poor homeless children running around with a backpack. This is why, among other reasons, she recommends that the parents or new partners of the child's parents be involved in education by the court or social workers.

5 Concluding Observations

Traditional patriarchal professional stereotypes may hinder the search for a joint solution to post-break-up or post-divorce conflicts over future childcare. These stereotypes are not tied to whether a man or a woman is acting in a particular professional role. They are a legacy of the patriarchal perception of judicial work as merely assessing rights and individuals, rather than striving for the most holistic and satisfactory solution to a conflict that all parties can accept. Social gender biases can also predetermine people's conduct in their professional and family roles, potentially preventing approaches respectful of children's autonomy. However, the persistence of these stereotypes also highlights the urgent need to integrate gender competence into judicial reasoning. Gender-sensitive judges are more likely to consider how power dynamics, societal expectations, and the lived experiences of mothers, fathers, and children intersect in custody cases. It is a great challenge for judges to move beyond the stereotypes and to view their role and the functioning of the system in a way that enables them to overcome these gendered social stereotypes and patriarchal professional stereotypes.

The State's idea that all issues relating to children's rights and care can be addressed solely by a single body—namely, the OSPOD—is not tenable. Quite on the contrary, parents and courts should leverage diverse professional assistance best suited to each family's unique circumstances.

To improve the unsatisfactory situation, it appears crucial to unveil and challenge the stereotypes and prejudices that prevail in the custody justice system, preventing them from obscuring potential solutions. Traditional gender and professional roles must be transcended, so that risks of certain aspects of social conformity can be confronted. Parents in conflict, along with society as a whole, require education and heightened awareness regarding the imperative to resolve disputes consensually for the sake of the child.

References

Cohen JM (2013) Feminism and Adaptive Heroinism: the Paradigm of Portia as a Means of Introduction. Tulsa Law J 25

Conaghan J (2013) Law and Gender. Oxford University Press

Donahue C (2020) The Unexamined Life: a Framework to Address Judicial Bias in Custody Determinations and Beyond. Geo J Gender & Law

DVTV (2018) Deseti tisícům dětí ročně se rozpadá rodina. Rozvod zvládnou, když ho zvládnete vy, říká Nováková. Aktuálně.cz. https://video.aktualne.cz/dvtv/deseti-tisicum-deti-rocne-se-rozpada-rodina-rozvod-zvladnou/r~cd09ae2e746b11e882090cc47ab5f122/

Gilligan C (1982) In a Different Voice: psychological Theory and Women's Development. Harvard University Press

Havelkova B, Kosar D, Urbanikova M (2021) The Family Friendliness That Wasn't: access, But Not Progress, for Women in the Czech Judiciary, Law Soc Inq. J Am Bar Found 47(4)

Jacobs SB (1997) The Hidden Gender Bias behind the Best Interest of the Child Standard in Custody Decisions. St U L 13:845
Kanter RM (1993) Men and Women in Corporations. New Edition Basic Books
Menkel-Meadow C (1985) Portia in a Different Voice: speculations on a Women's Lawyering Process. Berkeley Women's Law J. https://lawcat.berkeley.edu/record/1112304?ln=en
Ptáček P, et al. (2012) Sdílené rodičovství jako vztahový koncept. Grada
Šimáčková K (2022) Cesta od nahlížení na dítě jako na předmět ochrany k respektovanému aktérovi spolurozhodování o svém životě. In Вená KJ, Filip J, Šimíček V (eds) Pocta Janu Svatoňovik 70. narozeninám. Masarykovo univerzita, Brno
Šimáčková K, Foukalová Molková K (2015) Právo dítěte účastnit se soudního řízení jako jedno z participačních práv dětí pohledem judikatury Ústavního soudu. In:Cirbusová M, Kapitán Z eds. Tradiční jevy a nové tendence v oblasti ochrany práv dětí praxe participačních práv a kyberšikana, Tribun EU, Brno
The European Committee of Social Rights: International Commission of Jurists v. Czech Republic (2020), No. 148/2017
UN Special Rapporteur on Violence Against Women and Girls (2023) Gender bias in custody battles places women and children at risk. UN Human Rights Office. https://www.ohchr.org/en/stories/2023/06/gender-bias-custody-battles-places-women-and-children-risk
Urbanikova M, Havelkova B, Kosar D (2023) The Art of Waiting Humbly: women Judges Reflect on Vertical Gender Segregation. Fem Leg Stud 1
Warshak R (2005) Gender Bias in Child Custody Cases. Fam Court Rev 34(3)

Kateřina Šimáčková is a Judge of the European Court of Human Rights and President of the fifth section of the Court. Previously she served as a Judge of the Czech Constitutional Court and the Czech Supreme Administrative Court. She also worked as an attorney, a member of the Government Legislative Council of the Czech Republic, a member of the Committee on the selection of judges of the Civil Service Tribunal (CJEU) and a substitute member of the European Commission for Democracy through Law of the Council of Europe (Venice Commission). She is also an Assistant Professor (Department of Constitutional Law and Political Science, Faculty of Law, Masaryk University in Brno) and a Member of the Scientific Board of the Faculty of Law, Charles University in Prague and of the Academy Assembly of the Czech Academy of Sciences. She has published on human rights and co-authored several academic books, including *Mužské právo. Jsou právní pravidla neutrální? Lidská práva starších lidí, Budoucnost státu ?, Lidská práva: (ne) smysl české politiky ?, Dvacet let Evropské úmluvy v České republice a na Slovensku, Komunistické právo, Évolution des rapports entre les ordres juridiques de l'Union européenne, international et nationaux.* and book commentaries on the Law on the Illegality of the Communist Regime, the Charter of Fundamental Rights and Freedoms and the Civil Code.

Abortion in the U.S. After Dobbs v. Jackson Women's Health Organization. A Comparative Perspective

Rosalba Potenzano and Guido Smorto

Abstract The essay aims to provide a critical insight into the legal status of abortion and reproductive rights in the U.S. before and after Dobbs v. Jackson Women's Health Organization (2022). In this decision, the U.S. Supreme Court famously found that the U.S. constitution does not protect the right to choose to terminate pregnancy and affirmed that abortion is to be regulated by state legislators. In the face of the patchwork of laws governing abortion in the United States, the essay intends to explore the long-lasting impacts of Dobbs by conducting a comparative analysis. We argue that, contrary to the expectations of the Court, Dobbs has not distanced abortion from judicial power and that even lacking a constitutional right to abortion, the interplay between legislators and courts is critical in securing women's reproductive rights nationwide.

1 Introduction

Over the last fifty years, abortion has shifted its legal nature in the U.S. From being recognized as a fundamental right secured nationwide, it is but a profoundly moral issue now, not even implicitly grounded anymore in any federal constitutional provisions. The U.S. Supreme Court argued this in *Dobbs v. Jackson Women's*

The chapter is based on the original article published on Actualidad Jurídica Iberoamericana, 2023, N° 19-bis and updated to the end of 2023. Both authors share responsibility and accountability for the results of the present essay. G. Smorto authored Sects. 1, 2, and 4. R. Potenzano authored Sects. 3, 5, 6, and 7. Conclusions are written by both authors.

R. Potenzano (✉) · G. Smorto
University of Palermo, Palermo, Italy
e-mail: rosalba.potenzano@unipa.it
e-mail: guido.smorto@unipa.it

© The Author(s), under exclusive license to Springer Nature Switzerland AG 2025

S. Baer et al. (eds.), *The Gender and the Judiciary*, Gender Perspectives in Law 7,
https://doi.org/10.1007/978-3-032-06885-9_14

Health Organization,[1] returning to states the full power to protect, rule or outlaw abortion at any stage of pregnancy. As Justice Alito explained, in the past, "the Court usurped the power to address a question of profound moral and social importance that the Constitution unequivocally leaves for the people".[2] Such a power, the majority held, should be thus restored to the legitimate possessors, allowing each state legislator to meet its people's preferences on abortion.[3]

Nearly one year later, however, the abortion legal landscape is highly fragmented, and almost all U.S. Americans expressed dissatisfaction with their state abortion policies.[4] Several states have reinforced their reproductive healthcare services by adopting over-permissive legislation allowing abortion even post-viability.[5] Others have totally or nearly banned abortion or introduced severe gestational limits.[6] In the face of such a patchwork of laws, which is highly variable,[7] abortion requests have not ceased to exist, and women have continued seeking to terminate unwanted pregnancies by travelling out-of-state or completing abortion solely with pills in telehealth clinics.[8] The Biden presidency committed to uniformly protecting and expanding access to reproductive healthcare, including surgical and medication abortion.[9] Nevertheless, women reported having experienced severe disruptions in accessing such services, especially in low-income or marginalized communities.[10]

Against this backdrop, the essay aims to provide critical insight into the current legal status of abortion and reproductive rights in the U.S., reflecting on *Dobbs*' long-lasting impacts from a comparative perspective. The comparison will be internal, i.e., aimed at assessing the effects of the U.S. Supreme Court's decision in the federated states, and external, as it will examine how foreign law influenced the nine Justices either agreeing or dissenting on considering abortion a constitutional right.

---

[1] 142 S. Ct. 2228 (2022).

[2] 142 S. Ct. 2228 (2022), at 44.

[3] 142 S. Ct. 2228 (2022), at 44., at 31–35 (Opinion of the Court) and 3–5 (Justice Kavanaugh's concurring opinion).

[4] Gallup (2023) at https://news.gallup.com/poll/470279/dissatisfaction-abortion-policy-hits-high.aspx.

[5] See infra para. 7.

[6] See infra para. 7.

[7] Abortion laws are rapidly changing in almost all states after *Dobbs*. Nearly 700 abortion bills were introduced in the first semester of 2023, half expanding and half restricting access to abortion. See Guttmacher Institute, *The State Abortion Policy Landscape One Year Post-Roe* (June 1, 2023) at https://www.guttmacher.org/2023/06/state-abortion-policy-landscape-one-year-post-roe (accessed: 20.11.2023).

[8] Rosenberg (2022) at 34.

[9] White House, Executive Order on Protecting Access to Reproductive Healthcare Services (July 8, 2022) and Securing Access to Reproductive and Other Healthcare Services (August 3, 2022).

[10] Society of Family Planning, *#WeCount Report: April 2022 to March 2023* (June 2023) at https://societyfp.org/wp-content/uploads/2023/06/WeCountReport_6.12.23.pdf (accessed: 20.11.2023).

The essay unfolds as follows. Section two retraces the evolution of the right to abortion in the U.S. Supreme Court case law before *Dobbs* as a fundamental right grounded in the 'penumbras'[11] of the Bill of Rights or, progressively, in the Due Process Clause. Section three explores the implications flowing from such a legal status of abortion in terms of protecting women's reproductive rights, providing an outline of the existing state laws pre-*Dobbs*. Section four highlights the core of the Supreme Court's ruling in *Dobbs*, where the majority denies a constitutional foundation to the right to abortion. Section five focuses on the Court's use of foreign law in deciding such a national case as a practice embraced by the majority and the minority, both attempting to gain an advantage from foreign experience. In the last sections, the essay reflects upon the effects of the Supreme Court's landmark decision. Section six inquires how *Dobbs* may expand its impact beyond abortion, perhaps leading the Justices to overrule precedents protecting other reproductive rights. Section seven offers an insight into the post-*Dobbs* legal scenario, looking at legislators' and courts' interplay, both in the states and at the federal level, in shaping reproductive rights in the U.S. Finally, in section eight, the authors argue that contrary to the Court's expectations,[12] relying on judicial power to address abortion issues is still necessary and an option to allow women to control their reproductive lives.

2 Before Dobbs

The right to abortion as a fundamental right protected by the U.S. Constitution had its judicial origin in 1965, in a precedent that began to devise the close connection between the right to privacy and the most inner individual decisions related to whether to bear or beget a child.[13] This case is *Griswold v Connecticut*,[14] in which the Supreme Court invalidated an eighty-year-old Connecticut law prohibiting the use of "any drug, medical article or instrument for the purpose of preventing conception"[15] for violating the fundamental right to marital privacy.

[11] *Griswold v Connecticut*, 381 U.S. 479 (1965), at 484 (Justice Douglas).

[12] *Dobbs v. Jackson Women's Health*, cit., at 65 (Opinion of the Court): "The contending sides in this case make impassioned and conflicting arguments about the effects of the abortion right on the lives of women (. . .) This Court has neither the authority nor the expertise to adjudicate those disputes (. . .) Our decision (. . .) allows women on both sides of the abortion issue to seek to affect the legislative process by influencing public opinion, lobbying legislators, voting, and running for office. Women are not without electoral or political power".

[13] Gormley (1992), pp. 1391–1406.

[14] Cit.

[15] General Statute of Connecticut (1958 rev.), paras. 53–32.

Privacy, it was argued, has been silently lying within the 'penumbras' of the Bill of Rights. As Justice Douglas explained in authoring the opinion of the Court,[16] the right to privacy in marriage directly flows from the First, Third, Fourth, Fifth and Ninth Amendments as a whole. Their folds preserve the intimacy of the association made by husband and wife against governmental unnecessarily broad intrusions, such as blanket criminalization of birth control measures. The state legislator should thus have adopted less intrusive measures to discourage extra-marital and nonreproductive sex, regulating, for example, the manufacture or sale of contraceptives.[17]

However, the other six Justices concurring in the judgement split on the foundation of the marital privacy right. They argued it relied on the "liberty" protected by the Fourteenth Amendment, solely[18] or in conjunction[19] with the Ninth Amendment, thus the non-exhaustive character of enumerated fundamental rights. In doing so, they did not anchor privacy in the first Eight Amendments as Justice Douglas did but treated substantive Due Process as a source of new fundamental rights. Then, states can abridge these rights only by showing a compelling interest and a less intrusive mean to pursue it, under so-called strict scrutiny.[20]

In any case, what the Court introduced in *Griswold* was neither a fundamental right to personal autonomy in intimate reproductive choices nor to contraception.[21] By invoking the right to marital privacy, the judgment merely excluded the criminalization of the use of contraceptives for married couples[22] to protect the "sacred precincts of the marital bedroom".[23] Here, privacy emerging is still, so far, a relational and not an individual right, primarily intended to guarantee a physically identifiable domestic sphere free from governmental searches and seizures, in line with the Third, Fourth and Fifth Amendments.

[16] *Griswold v Connecticut,* cit., p. 484.

[17] *Griswold v Connecticut*, p. 485.

[18] See Justice Harlan and White's opinions, pp. 499–507.

[19] See Justice Goldberg's opinion, whom Justices Warren and Brennan joined, p. 486 ss.

[20] *Griswold v Connecticut*, cit., at 504. Justice Douglas refused to follow this approach since it echoed the highly criticized holding of *Lochner v New York* 198 U.S. 45 (1905), invalidating a law limiting the number of working hours in bakeries for infringing the individual liberty of contract under the Fourteenth Amendment Due Process Clause. As Justices Black and Stewart observed dissenting in *Griswold*, the unlashed recourse to such clause confers arbitrary supervisory power to the court and always appears highly suspicious, even beyond economic policy matters.

[21] Hart Ely (1973), pp. 929–30.

[22] In *Eisenstadt v Baird*, 405 U.S. 113 (1973), the Court extended under the Equal Protection Clause (XIV Am.) *Griswold* to the individual as such, married or single.

[23] *Griswold v Connecticut*, cit., p. 485.

The "leap"[24] to a right to privacy dealing with liberty of choice in childbearing was more decisively made by *Roe v Wade*[25] In 1973. In this case, the Supreme Court invalidated a Texas law that had been substantially unchanged since 1854, that prohibited procuring or attempting an abortion, except by medical advice for saving the mother's life.[26] Speaking for the Court, Justice Blackmun clarified that such legislation infringed the personal liberty embodied in the Due Process Clause of the Fourteenth Amendment. This provision, he argued, protects the unenumerated fundamental right to privacy, which "is broad enough to encompass a woman's decision whether or not to terminate her pregnancy".[27] However, he also stated, "the pregnant woman cannot be isolated in her privacy".[28] Indeed, other legitimate state interests, namely, in protecting the mother's health or the fetus's potential life, are also relevant in pregnancy and may even gradually prevail over a woman's choice to terminate it.[29]

In this regard, the Court defined some indications.[30] During the first trimester, women can freely seek abortion under their physician's advice. But once this initial term ends, the state interest in protecting maternal health, given the exceeding mortality rate in abortion over normal childbirth, is compelling and can justify regulation (but not a ban) of the pregnancy termination procedure, as far as it is narrowly tailored to pursue that interest. Later, the state interest in fetal life becomes compelling at viability, i.e. when the foetus is capable of life outside the mother's womb, which at the time was set between twenty-four and twenty-eight weeks. In this third trimester, the Court said, states can thus rule and even outlaw abortion, under the strict scrutiny standard. However, they may not prohibit therapeutic abortions necessary to protect maternal life or health.

Although clear at first glance, such a trimestral framework showed its blurred boundaries very soon. Advances in medical technology made abortion safer in the second trimester, potentially reducing the strong state interest in protecting the health of pregnant women. At the same time, new means to support fetal life outside the maternal body were introduced, forwarding the moment of viability and possibly strengthening the state interest in protecting fetal life.

Not surprisingly, almost twenty years later, the Supreme Court rejected the trimester approach, holding that it is unnecessary to prevent states from regulating abortion procedures in the first twelve weeks to protect the women's right to choose to terminate or continue a pregnancy freely.

---

[24] Hart Ely J (1973) at 929; Gormley K (1992), p. 1393.

[25] 410 U.S. 113 (1973).

[26] Texas Penal Code (1961), Art. 1191–1194 and 1196.

[27] *Roe v Wade*, cit., at 153.

[28] *Roe v Wade*, cit., at 159.

[29] *Roe v Wade*, cit., at 154.

[30] *Roe v Wade*, cit., p. 163.

In *Planned Parenthood v. Casey*,[31] although reaffirming *Roe*'s core, the Court argued that, to afford constitutional protection to abortion, state interests in safeguarding maternal health and the potential life of the foetus need not surrender in the earliest stages of the pregnancy. In the words of the plurality, abortion is guaranteed liberty under the Due Process Clause of the Fourteenth Amendment,[32] allowing women to make "choices central to personal dignity and autonomy",[33] such as about reproduction and childbearing, being free from governmental intrusions. It does not mean, however, that states cannot pursue pro-life legitimate interests and regulate abortion, even in the first trimester. The only limit was not outlawing it before viability and not imposing "an undue burden on a woman's ability to make this decision".[34] In other words, any restrictions on abortion need not be narrowly tailored anymore to serve a compelling interest but refrain from introducing a substantial obstacle in the path of the woman's choice.[35]

By relying on this new highly permissive standard, most of the challenged Pennsylvania Abortion Control Act of 1982 provisions passed judicial review smoothly.[36] The Court considered it to be constitutionally valid to impose the informed consent of the woman seeking an abortion or parental consent for a minor or a 24-hour waiting period before its performance, except in medical emergencies or requiring facilities to submit a report on every performed abortion. Indeed, such measures were deemed to pursue a legitimate interest, i.e., defending fetal life, by ensuring women make a thoughtful choice without impeding pregnancy termination. The spouse notification requirement was the only one struck down.[37] The Court considered it deterred pregnant women engaged in extra-marital affairs, victims of abuse by their husbands or whose children are seeking an abortion, introducing a sort of male veto over their personal choice.[38]

---

[31] 505 U.S. 833 (1992).

[32] 505 U.S. 833 (1992), p. 846 (Justice O'Connor, Kennedy and Souter's opinion): "The controlling word in the cases before us is 'liberty'." However, Justice Blackmun argued in its concurring opinion that "The Court today reaffirms the long-recognized rights of privacy and bodily integrity", p. 926.

[33] 505 U.S. 833 (1992), p. 851.

[34] 505 U.S. 833 (1992), p. 874.

[35] 505 U.S. 833 (1992), p. 877.

[36] *Planned Parenthood v. Casey*, cit., at 881–887, 899–901. However, in concurring with the judgment, Justice Blackmun kept applying strict scrutiny, considering all these provisions invalid. Justice Stevens concluded instead for their unconstitutionality (except for the informed consent and the parental one) under the new undue burden standard.

[37] *Planned Parenthood v. Casey*, cit., pp. 887–898.

[38] *Planned Parenthood v. Casey*, cit., p. 897.

3 Abortion Laws and Reproductive Rights: Status Quo Before Dobbs

Casey immediately overtly reassured state legislators about the validity of those struck-down restrictions under *Roe*,[39] which directly intended (or had the effect of) to persuade pregnant women not to terminate their pregnancies without formally and substantially impeding them from seeking abortion.[40] Indeed, from 1992 onward, several states copied the Pennsylvania Abortion Control Act by introducing mandatory waiting periods, state-prescribed counselling, parental consent, and reporting requirements.

Several restrictions aimed at protecting the unborn life also passed, including the medically unnecessary "targeted regulations of abortion providers" (so-called TRAP laws), which are still in force in nearly all the states.[41] For example, abortion clinics were required to meet standards for ambulatory surgical centres or negotiate written transfer agreements with the state every two years. Likewise, to provide pregnancy termination services, doctors were mandated to first perform and show pregnant women an ultrasound, determine whether the fetus has a detectable fetal heartbeat, or have admitting privileges at a hospital within thirty miles.[42] The federal courts did not consider any such laws an undue burden on the women seeking abortions, although they have led, over time, to the closure of many abortion facilities.[43]

To pursue the goal of overturning *Roe*, some states[44] went even further. They adopted total or nearly-total abortion bans designed to be effective only when terminating the pregnancy would no longer be a constitutional right (so-called "trigger laws"). Other states[45] decided not to repeal the old pre-*Roe* laws

---

[39] *Planned Parenthood v. Danforth*, 428 U.S. 52 (1976); *City of Akron v. Akron Center for Reproductive Health, Inc.*, 462 U.S. 416 (1983).

[40] On the misunderstanding of *Casey*'s undue burden standard, which could have been applied instead to meaningfully protecting the woman's dignity, see Wharton, Frietsche, Kolbert (2006).

[41] See https://www.guttmacher.org/state-policy/explore/targeted-regulation-abortion-providers (accessed: 20.11.2023).

[42] In 2013, for example, Texas passed a bill requiring physicians performing or inducing an abortion to have active admitting privileges at a hospital not further than 30 miles from the abortion facility and facility to meet minimum standards for ambulatory surgical centres. In 2016, in *Whole Woman's Health v. Hellerstedt* (579 U.S. 582 (2016), the Supreme Court invalidated the law, concluding that it did not cure a significant health-related problem or provide any health benefit outweighing its imposed burdens. The same conclusion was reached in 2020 in *June Medical Services v. Russo* [140 S. Ct. 2103 (2020)], declaring the substantially identical Louisiana Act 620 unconstitutional.

[43] Greenhouse, Siegel (2016).

[44] Arkansas, Idaho, Kentucky, Louisiana, Mississippi, Missouri, North Dakota, Oklahoma, South Dakota, Tennessee, Texas, Utah, and Wyoming (see Aceves (2022), p. 91).

[45] Alabama, Arizona, Arkansas, Michigan, Mississippi, Oklahoma, Texas, West Virginia, and Wisconsin (Id., p. 90).

criminalizing abortion so that they could be made effective again if *Roe* were overruled (so-called dormant or zombie laws), with the advantage of avoiding potential constitutional challenges.[46] However, in 2021, Texas showed states how to circumvent judicial review by adopting trigger laws that outlawed pre-viability abortion in breach of the standard that was still effective, based on *Roe*. Indeed, the Texas Heartbeat Act (S.B. 8) prohibited physicians from performing or inducing an abortion in case of fetal cardiac activity detection (usually in the sixth week), but relied exclusively on private citizens, and not on state officials, for enforcement, consequently making difficult bringing a constitutional challenge against the law.[47]

This restrictive widespread post-*Roe* legislative trend did not spare the federal legislator. In 2003, the Congress passed a law banning some medically approved abortion second-trimester procedures without exception, namely, the intact dilate and extraction technique, known as partial-birth abortion.[48] In *Gonzales v. Carhart*,[49] the Supreme Court upheld the Partial-Birth Abortion Ban Act, arguing that if access to that specific procedure were allowed, "some women might regret their choices".[50] Suddenly, it became clear that blanket pre-viability abortion bans were permitted and, as Professor Siegel noted,[51] that abortion restrictions not only protect fetal life and maternal health, but also serve women's autonomy and dignity, which offered new and powerful arguments to the anti-abortion movement.

In sum, by abandoning strict scrutiny in favor of an undue burden standard, the Supreme Court, contrary to what the Justices relied on in not overruling *Roe*[52] and what some scholars suggested,[53] did not settle the abortion controversies. Instead,

---

[46] See Berns (2009) (on the similarity between the two legislative instruments in manifesting state dissent to judicial decision and on the distance of zombie laws from trigger ones, enacted despite their patent unconstitutionality).

[47] S.B. 8, para. 171.207(a) ("the requirements of this subchapter shall be enforced exclusively through the private civil actions described in Section 171.208"). S.B. 8, §171.208 states that "Any person, other than an officer or employee of a state or local governmental entity in this state, may bring a civil action against any person who: (1) performs or induces an abortion in violation of this subchapter; (2) knowingly engages in conduct that aids or abets the performance or inducement of an abortion (...); or (3) intends to engage in the conduct described by Subdivision (1) or (2)". It also cleared that the court shall award the claimant injunctive relief, statutory damages in an amount of not less than $10,000 for each abortion that the defendant performed or induced, aided or abetted, costs and attorney's fees (S.B. 8, §171.208(b)).

[48] Partial-Birth Abortion Ban Act 2003.

[49] 550 U.S. 124, 127 S. Ct. 1610 (2007).

[50] *Gonzales v. Carhart*, cit., at 1634.

[51] Siegel (2008) (speaking of gender-paternalistic justifications for restricting abortion).

[52] *Planned Parenthood v. Casey*, cit., at 867: "Where, in the performance of its judicial duties, the Court decides a case in such a way as to resolve the sort of intensely divisive controversy reflected in *Roe* and those rare, comparable cases its decision (...) calls the contending sides of a national controversy to end their national division by accepting a common mandate rooted in the Constitution".

[53] Devins (2009), p. 1342.

Casey opened the floodgates to introducing restrictions that allowed the pro-life community to gain ground without pro-choice realized that. Indeed, the pro-life community managed to gradually erode women's reproductive rights by employing an incrementalist strategy,[54] far from relying on merely demanding to overrule *Roe v. Wade*. After all, regardless of the standard of judicial review adopted by the Supreme Court, there was a generous margin for weakening the right to abortion within the boundaries of constitutional law. Indeed, *Roe* and its progeny confined to primarily prevent states from criminalizing elective pre-viability and therapeutic post-viability abortion, to protect the women's negative right to privacy or the liberty to choose to terminate the pregnancy. They did not require, instead, that pregnant women could equally access and control their reproductive lives.[55]

On the one hand, anti-abortionists passed several constitutionally compliant TRAP laws, silently reducing the chance for women to freely decide to terminate their pregnancy, especially in low-income and minority communities. While the Court saw this to not as an undue burden for seeking an abortion, such laws enacted sex-based burdensome, expensive, inaccessible, and publicly unfunded pregnancy termination procedures,[56] forcing women to bear children and commit their bodies "to turn potential life into a person".[57] On the other hand, pro-lifers relied on such laws to silently prevent deconstructing the traditional legislative stereotype of women as mothers in society. As the majority of the Court recognized in *Casey*: "The ability of women to participate equally in the economic and social life of the Nation has been facilitated by their ability to control their reproductive lives".[58] Therefore, by limiting this ability, states reaffirmed the archaic but still embedded patriarchal concept that "the paramount destiny and mission of woman are to fulfil the noble and benign offices of wife and mother".[59]

Unveiling the sex-based discriminatory nature of abortion restrictions, some scholars have suggested grounding the right to abortion in the equal protection clause of the Fourteenth Amendment.[60] The right to equality, they have argued, forces states to remove any form of sex-based discrimination, and the Supreme Court would have to apply heightened scrutiny for abortion restrictions because they involve a gender-based classification. Then, states would have to offer an "exceedingly persuasive justification",[61] not relying on overbroad generalizations of assumed inherent differences in roles, talents and capacities between males and

[54] Siegel (2008), p. 1708 (also reporting the fight within the incrementalist and the purist wings of the anti-abortion movement about the best strategy).

[55] West (2009), p. 1403; Bader Ginsburg (1985), p. 384.

[56] See *Beal v. Doe*, 432 US 438 (1977); *Maher v. Roe*, 432 US 464 (1977); *Poelker v. Doe*, 432 US 519 (1977); *Harris v. McRea*, 448 US 297 (1980); *Webster v. Reproductive Health Services*, 492 US 490 (1989).

[57] Siegel RB (1992), p. 348.

[58] *Planned Parenthood v. Casey*, cit., p. 856.

[59] *Bradwell v. Illinois*, 83 U.S. (16 Wall.) 130, 141 (1872).

[60] See *ex multis* Law SA (1984); Bader Ginsburg R (1985); Siegel RS (2007).

[61] *United States v. Virginia*, 518 U.S. 515, pp. 533–34 (1996).

females, to show that such measures substantially further critical governmental objectives.[62] The Supreme Court, however, and still in *Dobbs*, has firmly refused to analyse abortion as an equality issue.[63]

Other scholars have suggested instead to de-constitutionalize abortion, adding it to the list of women's equality victories gained by ordinary political means rather than from the Supreme Court.[64] They have argued that relying on constitutional adjudication carries too many costs, eventually weakening women's reproductive rights. Yet now that *Dobbs* has accomplished this demand to de-constitutionalize abortion, it seems rather questionable whether that empowers women's reproductive rights.

4 Dobbs V. Jackson Women's Health

As anticipated, after nearly fifty years of considering abortion a constitutional right, the U.S. Supreme Court changed its mind in *Dobbs v. Jackson Women's Health.*[65] The law at stake was the Mississippi Gestational Age Act 2018, prohibiting abortion after fifteen weeks of pregnancy, except for medical emergencies or severe fetal abnormalities.[66] In a six-to-three decision, the Supreme Court found that the statute at odds with the viability line was constitutionally valid, as was any other pre-viability prohibition on elective abortions. In other words, the Court completely overturned *Roe* and *Casey*, which had secured women the right to choose to terminate their pregnancies before viability without unduly burdening state interference.

Justice Alito, joined by Justices Thomas, Gorsuch, Kavanaugh, and Barrett, framed the question of whether the pre-viability abortion ban complies with the constitutional text-. They considered first whether the Constitution, "properly understood",[67] confers a right to obtain an abortion, and if it does not, whether the doctrine of *stare decisis* requires the Court not to overturn *Roe* and *Casey,* regardless they were "egregiously wrong from the start".[68] In the majority's view, the constitution does neither expressly nor implicitly refer to abortion. Not only does the text not mention it, but it also does not protect it under the Fourteenth Amendment, since neither the Equal Protection Clause nor the Due Process Clause do guarantee the right to choose to terminate a pregnancy. As to the former, the

[62] *United States v. Virginia*, 518 U.S. 515, pp. 533.

[63] See Yoshino (2011).

[64] West (2009), p. 1403. See against Ziegler (2014).

[65] 142 S. Ct. 2228 (2022).

[66] Later, Mississippi passed even more restrictive abortion bans prohibiting pregnancy termination after six weeks, in line with the Texas Heartbeat Act 2021 (supra, para. 3).

[67] *Dobbs v. Jackson Women's Health*, cit., p. 8 (opinion of the Court).

[68] *Dobbs v. Jackson Women's Health*, cit., p. 6.

majority continued denying that abortion laws are sex-based classifications, in line with precedents.[69] As to the latter, departing from previous rulings, the majority argued that abortion does not flow from the concept of liberty, solely or incorporating, as in *Roe* ´s right to privacy, be it found in liberty itself or a combination of Amendments as in *Griswold.*

The Due Process Clause they stated protects only two types of substantive rights, namely, rights guaranteed by the first eight Amendments and what is deemed fundamental rights. "In deciding whether a right falls into either of these categories, the Court has long asked whether the right is 'deeply rooted in [our] history and tradition' and whether it is essential to our Nation's 'scheme of ordered liberty'".[70] After a lengthy historical analysis, they concluded that abortion is an unenumerated right that cannot be deemed fundamental. For centuries, the vast majority of states have criminalized performing abortion post-quickening (i.e., at the first felt movement of the fetus in the womb between the sixteenth and eighteenth week of pregnancy), and even pre-quickening, at the critical moment of ratification of the Fourteenth Amendment and until *Roe.*[71] Therefore, in their view, abortion has no deep roots in the national tradition.

Here, the majority relied on tradition as a mere historical practice rather than—as the dissenters in **Dobbs** suggested[72]—a "living thing"[73] or "inspirational principle",[74] guiding the court in balancing current individual needs and social demands over time. In other words, the majority did not consider that "what history teaches are the traditions from which [this country] developed as well as the traditions from which it broke".[75] That happened, for example, regarding the right to use contraceptives or to marry across racial lines, since decisions on both controversies broadened the established contours of liberty under the Due Process Clause. Subscribing to a historical practice approach instead, the majority focussed only on traditions that already existed when the Fourteenth Amendment was ratified, moving the contours of liberty backwards so much that abortion were to be excluded.[76] After **Dobbs**, abortion is no more a fundamental right but "just another interest to be resolved by political force".[77] As the majority of the Court clarified, it is an interest corresponding to "one of the many understandings of 'liberty', but it

[69] *Dobbs v. Jackson Women's Health*, cit., pp. 10–11.

[70] *Dobbs v. Jackson Women's Health*, cit., p. 12.

[71] *Dobbs v. Jackson Women's Health*, cit., p. 23.

[72] See Justices Breyer, Sotomayor and Kagan's dissenting joint opinion, p. 17.

[73] See Justice Harlan dissenting *Poe v. Ulmann* 367 U.S. 497, at 542 (1961).

[74] McClain, Fleming (2023).

[75] *Poe v. Ulmann*, cit., at 542 (Justice Harlan's dissenting opinion).

[76] As the dissenters pointed out, in strictly defining the Fourteenth Amendment, the Court followed Justice Rehnquist's approach in *Washington v. Glucksberg* (521 U.S. 702 (1997)) (see *Dobbs v. Jackson Women's Health.*, cit., at 17).

[77] Tribe (2022).

is certainly not ordered liberty"[78] essential to the whole Nation. On the contrary, the people of each state can decide how to regulate abortion and preference competing interests.

The second question was whether *stare decisis* should have refrained the Court from overturning *Roe* and *Casey*. Here, the majority answered negatively for five reasons. First, precedent was said to be based on an erroneous interpretation of the constitution, usurping from the people "the power to address a question of profound moral and social importance".[79] Second, precedent was characterized as founded on weak reasoning, lacking any constitutional grounding and persuasive justification for the rules, i.e., the trimestral framework, the viability line and the undue burden test.[80] Third, the difficulty to coherently applying the undue burden standard showed that these precedents did not introduce workable rules.[81] Fourth, they led, the majority said, to the distortion of several unrelated legal doctrines.[82] Fifth, their overruling would not compromise any specifically protected interest of reliance since "getting an abortion is generally unplanned activity",[83] and it seemed hard "to assess, namely, the effect of the abortion right on society and in particular on the lives of women".[84]

As the dissenters noted,[85] the majority exactly contravenes *Casey*, where the plurality considered it unwise to overrule *Roe* "under fire in the absence of the most compelling reason",[86] "at the cost of both profound and unnecessary damage to the Court's legitimacy, and to the Nation's commitment to the rule of law".[87] It was only Chief Justice Roberts who suggested to refrain from overruling *Roe* and *Casey,* and limit *Dobbs* to abandoning the line of viability they, he said, arbitrarily created.[88] The majority in *Dobbs* rejected any such concerns. It replied to the concurrence that it would be impossible to discard the viability line under *stare decisis*, being inextricably entangled with *Roe* and *Casey,*[89] which means they must be overruled, to return the authority to settle the abortion issue to the people and their elective representatives.[90]

---

[78] *Dobbs v. Jackson Women's Health*, cit., p. 31.

[79] *Dobbs v. Jackson Women's Health*, cit., p. 44.

[80] *Dobbs v. Jackson Women's Health*, cit., pp. 45–56.

[81] *Dobbs v. Jackson Women's Health*, cit., pp. 56–62.

[82] *Dobbs v. Jackson Women's Health*, cit., pp. 62–63.

[83] *Dobbs v. Jackson Women's Health*, cit., p. 64.

[84] *Dobbs v. Jackson Women's Health*, cit., p. 65.

[85] *Dobbs v. Jackson Women's Health*, cit., p. 56 (Justices Breyer, Sotomayor and Kagan's dissenting joint opinion).

[86] *Planned Parenthood v. Casey*, cit., p. 867.

[87] *Planned Parenthood v. Casey*, cit., p. 869.

[88] *Dobbs v. Jackson Women's Health*, cit., p. 7 (J. Robert's opinion).

[89] *Dobbs v. Jackson Women's Health*, cit., p. 73.

[90] *Dobbs v. Jackson Women's Health*, cit., p. 69 (opinion of the Court).

What follows from this is that states may regulate and even outlaw abortion entirely at any stage of the pregnancy, by enforcing laws that now enjoy a strong presumption of validity. Indeed, by devoid of constitutional protection for abortion, the Court discarded strict scrutiny and the undue burden standard, to be replaced with a highly permissive rational-basis test instead.[91] Now, citizens must prove that state laws do not pursue any legitimate government interest by means rationally related to it. Under this test, the Mississippi law banning abortion after fifteen weeks of pregnancy, except in a case of medical emergency or severe fetal abnormity, smoothly passed judicial review. Indeed, it was said to further legitimate interests, namely protecting the life of unborn human beings and avoiding barbaric procedures commonly used to terminate pregnancies from the second trimester onwards.[92]

5 The Use of Foreign Law in Dobbs

In Dobbs, one of the most debated arguments the court relied on to overturn *Roe* and *Casey* was that other countries nearly uniformly converged in eschewing the viability line and allowed elective abortions only at earlier stages of pregnancy.[93] As the concurrence underscored, "only a handful of countries, among them China and North Korea, permit elective abortion after twenty weeks".[94] The subtext was clear: The U.S., until *Dobbs*, had aligned with nations far from being models of democracy with a firm commitment to human rights protection.

Somewhat ironically, the dissenters also stressed the worldwide convergence in abortion laws. They also argued it to be a relevant fact for deciding whether to keep constitutional protection of the right of the woman to choose to terminate a pregnancy until viability or not. Contrary to the majority, they however pointed out that, for the past twenty-five years, the global trend had been to liberalize abortion laws, help women to access it, and even cover its costs.[95] The implication was equally clear: Overturning *Roe* and *Casey*, therefore, would make the U.S. an international outlier among Western democracies, including New Zealand, the Netherlands and Iceland, which permit on-demand abortion until the twentieth week of gestation and beyond, as mentioned by Justices Breyer, Sotomayor and Kagan.[96]

---

[91] *Dobbs v. Jackson Women's Health*, cit., p. 77.

[92] *Dobbs v. Jackson Women's Health*, cit., p. 78.

[93] *Dobbs v. Jackson Women's Health*, cit., p. 53.

[94] *Dobbs v. Jackson Women's Health*, cit., p. 5 (J. Robert's concurring opinion).

[95] *Dobbs v. Jackson Women's Health*, cit., p. 43 (Justices Breyer, Sotomayor and Kagan's dissenting joint opinion).

[96] *Dobbs v. Jackson Women's Health*, cit., p. 42.

Neither the majority nor the minority offered a legal justification for using foreign law to decide a domestic constitutional case. All the Justices in *Dobbs* limited themselves to substantially assert that a given policy or principle concerning a controversial matter like abortion, still lacking an American consensus, is generally widespread abroad.[97] Undoubtedly, the controversy lies on another level. The implicit theory behind the voluntary use of foreign law could be that this improves judicial reasoning by offering new insights for solving common legal problems, as Justice Breyer suggested in the past, in contrast to Justice Scalia, then the lead Justice for the Conservatives on the bench.[98] However, as some scholars pointed out,[99] this explanation would not be exhaustive as long as it fails to address some basic questions, such as the authority of foreign sources, the areas of law in which it is correct to cite them or which foreign legal system to select. Yet, it could be objected that behind these reservations merely lie the public's concern that judges may "smuggle" foreign values into the U.S. Constitution.[100]

Moreover, in *Dobbs*, neither the majority nor the minority explained foreign judicial legal reasoning underlying abortion laws outside the U.S. Quite the opposite, it seems that all the Justices, far from embarking on in-depth legal comparison, used foreign law only superficially. They concentrated on longer or shorter gestational time limits adopted in selected legal systems very similar or different from the U.S. to make them look in line or not with a trend of liberal democratic countries. Such a trend, however, as international and comparative scholars who authored an amicus brief suggested,[101] should not have focused on gestational time limits of foreign state laws; instead, the court should have investigated how, in liberal democratic countries, those laws are interpreted and applied within their respective legal systems, also considering their interaction with other domestic and international rules. In Europe, for example, the situation is highly

[97] On the use of foreign law for "consensus identification", i.e., to support the application of a rule for which there was not already an American consensus, by merely referring to a particular policy or principle prevalent in other countries generally see Simon (2013), pp. 290–291.

[98] See Justice Breyer in *Printz v. The United States* (521 U.S. 989 (1997) at 977 (arguing that foreign experience "may nonetheless cast an empirical light on the consequences of different solutions to a common legal problem"). See also Breyer (2003).

[99] On the insufficiency of justifications that avoid looking for a theoretical foundation of the practice, see Waldron (2005); Calabresi, Silverman (2015); Smorto (2011).

[100] Breyer (2008), p. 162. The author pointed out that "if the argument's heat reflects a concern about values, however, then an approach to constitutional interpretation that relies upon purpose and consequences may reduce the temperature": it involves the "examination of consequences (in light of the provision's underlying values)" for solving a practical problem, so implying "learning from foreign experience, not accepting foreign values" (Breyer (2008), p. 162). Moreover, selecting similar systems, e.g., democracies protecting basic human rights, could temper the risk of adopting values foreign to the US system (Breyer (2008), p. 164).

[101] Brief of International and Comparative Legal Scholars as Amicus Curiae in Support of Respondents, Dobbs v. Jackson Women's Health Organization, 142 S. Ct. (2022) (No. 19–1392), p. 5.

fragmented, which—unlike the minority implied—offers not only permissive[102] but also restrictive[103] examples of abortion laws. Against this backdrop, it could have been helpful to explore how other supranational courts have dealt with such diversity in abortion state laws,[104] when it is argued that there is no transnational women's right to terminate their pregnancies.[105] Indeed, the experience of abortion federalism in Europe could have cast light on the opportunity for the U.S. Supreme Court to strike a balance between state interest in protecting unborn lives and interests of women to seek abortion.[106] This may inform arguments to at least ensure that an abortion ban, or near—ban, does not turn into inhuman or degrading treatment,[107] and that it preserves free speech[108] and free movement rights.[109] In other words, by focussing on the legal reasoning of courts such as the ECtHR and the ECJ, the Court in *Dobbs* could have noted that, even allowing states to enjoy

---

[102] For example, in 2018, Ireland adopted the Health Regulation of Termination of Pregnancy Act, overturning its restrictive abortion law. It permitted elective abortion until the twelfth week of pregnancy and after only in case of risk to women's health and life or fatal foetal abnormality.

[103] In 2020, Poland *de facto* nearly totally banned the right to abortion. Indeed, the Polish Constitutional Tribunal declared unconstitutional an exception in the Family Planning Act of 1993 allowing abortion in case of "severe and irreversible foetal defect or incurable illness that threatens the foetus's life".

[104] See Fabbrini (2023) (noting that European supranational courts' case-law, so far avoiding establishing a transnational right to abortion, could offer a possible path to overcome *Dobbs*' ruling).

[105] As the ECtHR observed, "the margin of appreciation accorded to a State's protection of the unborn necessarily translates into a margin of appreciation for that State as to how it balances the conflicting rights of the mother [to respect her private life]", even allowing it to prohibit abortion (*A, B and C v. Ireland*, No. 25579/05, 16 December 2010, §237). However, many authors have criticized such position, promoting an evolutive interpretation of the Convention, from which inferring a right to abortion as an autonomous fundamental human right, see, e.g., Tucak, Blagojević (2020).

[106] ECtHR, *A, B and C v. Ireland*, No. 25579/05, 16 December 2010 (stating that while the right to respect women's private life under Art. 8 of the Convention cannot be interpreted as conferring a right to abortion, the State has a positive obligation to coherently shape effective and accessible procedures which allow women to establish whether they are eligible under domestic law to a lawful abortion on the ground of a relevant risk to a woman's life).

[107] ECtHR, *R.R. v. Poland and P & S v. Poland*, No. 27617/04, 26 May 2011 (affirming that the failure to provide adequate procedures for accessing prenatal genetic testing, being a prerequisite for legal abortion on the ground of fetal abnormality under statal law, amounts to a breach of private life and inhuman or degrading treatment under Articles 8 and 3 of the Convention).

[108] ECtHR, Open Door and Dublin Well Woman v. Ireland, no. 14234/88; 14235/88, 29 October 1992 (finding that the restraint from receiving or imparting information concerning the identity and location of abortion clinics outside the jurisdiction of the state forbidding abortion constituted an unjustified interference with the right to freedom of expression in breach of Article 10 of the Convention).

[109] ECJ, Case C-159/90, *Soc'y for the Prot. of Unborn Children Ir. Ltd. v. Grogan*, 4 October 1991 (considering medical termination of pregnancy constitutes a service within the meaning of Article 60 of the Treaty although allowing a Member State forbidding abortion to prohibit distributing information about the identity and location of abortion clinics in another Member State).

a wide margin of appreciation when regulate abortion, judges are still to set checks and balances to prevent restrictive state regulations that violate women's fundamental rights. This would be the case regardless of whether abortion lacks constitutional protection under the substantive Due Process Clause or not. However, as already mentioned, the Justices in *Dobbs* did not focus on that. Instead, they merely leveraged some selective information about abortion laws abroad to convey "a sort of consensus among judges, jurists, and lawmakers around the world".[110]

However, overseas information did help the Justices to support their judgment in one way or another.[111] The minority relied on foreign law to preserve the post-*Roe* legal landscape on abortion in the U.S., and the majority used foreign law to innovate and eschew the right to abortion from any constitutional protection. As some scholars noted,[112] this is surprising *per se*, since conservative Supreme Court Justices were always highly critical of using foreign law. Justice Thomas, for example, joining Justice Alito's opinion in *Dobbs*, returned to his own past words in *Foster v. Florida*,[113] in which he said to allow only Congress, as the legislature, and not the Supreme Court to "wish to consider the actions of other nations on any issue it likes".[114] He also appeared to distance himself from Justice Scalia's opinion in *Roper v. Simmons*,[115] which argued that "the basic premise of the Court's argument—that American law should conform to the laws of the rest of the world—ought to be rejected out of hand".[116] But upon closer inspection, the recourse to foreign law by the majority is not at all surprising. Rather, it perfectly aligns with the ambivalence of American lawyers towards such a controversial issue as the opportunity of voluntarily using external sources in the courtroom. As Markesinis and Fedtke noted, "occasionally, even an 'anti-foreign law' judge may himself have recourse to the 'condemned' practice",[117] and, after all, even Justice Scalia sometimes did.[118]

In our view, what is genuinely striking in *Dobbs* is that conservative justices used external sources in "one main area of American constitutional law—judicial review".[119] In doing so, *Dobbs* rebutted the thesis that hostility toward foreign law was "consistent with the view that restricting the sources of legal ideas and the ultimate authority of constitutional interpretation is essential to the maintenance of

[110] Waldron (2005), p. 132.

[111] On using foreign law to help judges to make moral judgments, see Waldron (2005) and Tripkovic (2019).

[112] Kalantry (2022).

[113] 537 U.S. 990 (2002).

[114] 537 U.S. 990 (2002).

[115] 543 U.S. 551(2005) (sentencing juveniles under eighteen to death violates the Eight Amendment).

[116] 543 U.S. 551(2005).

[117] Markesinis, Fedtke (2005), p. 24.

[118] Markesinis, Fedtke (2005), p. 24 (mentioning Scalia's dissenting opinion in *Mcintyre v Ohio Elections Commission,* 514 U.S. 334,371 (1995), pp. 381–382.

[119] Markesinis, Fedtke (2005), p. 152.

a coherent body of law".[120] Indeed, in mentioning foreign law to corroborate their constitutional interpretation excluding the right to abortion from the Fourteenth Amendment, the *Dobbs*' majority was prone to enrich its structural constraint reasoning, grounded on the original understanding of the U.S. Constitution,[121] with foreign sources. In doing so, the Supreme Court did not expand rights; it reduced them:[122] This marks a break from cases like *Atkin v. Virginia,*[123] *Lawrence v. Texas,*[124] and *Roper v. Simmons.*[125] In these cases, by underscoring a global consensus, the Supreme Court had appealed to the aspiration of the U.S. to ensure, on an international scale, a high level of protection of human rights. In *Dobbs*, instead, foreign law was invoked by the majority to narrow constitutional interpretation, renouncing, in the end, a leading American position in the field of women's reproductive rights.

6 The Future of Reproductive Rights in the U.S.

Abortion is just one aspect of reproductive autonomy. In U.S. terms, such autonomy includes several substantive Due Process rights involving intimate and personal reproductive choices other than deciding to terminate a pregnancy, namely, the right not to have a child, the right to have one, and to parent as desired.[126] Over time, the Supreme Court afforded constitutional protection to all such reproductive choices, in line with emerging societal needs to free people from reproductive oppression that existed at the Nation's founding.[127] In other words, *Roe* and *Casey* did not emerge in a vacuum. On the contrary, they cap a long series of judicial efforts to recognize privacy-derived rights equally to all men and women.[128] *Meyer v. Nebraska,*[129] for example, in 1923, guaranteed the right to parent, thus decide how to raise and educate children free from any state interferences. The right to

[120] Markesinis, Fedtke (2005), p. 153.

[121] On the originalist approach of the majority in *Dobbs*, see SiegeL (2023) (arguing that Dobbs' originalism does not employ the methods of academic originalists since it accepts substantive Due Process Clause, so being living constitutionalism. Dobbs' originalism is instead a goal-oriented political practice making constitutional order less democratic).

[122] Kalantry S (2022), p. 37.

[123] 536 U.S. 304 (2002) (sentencing a mentally disabled individual to death violates the Eighth Amendment).

[124] 539 U.S. 558 (2003) (criminalizing same-sex intimate acts violates the liberty protected by the Fourteenth Amendment's Due Process Clause).

[125] Cit.

[126] Ross, Solinger (2017), p. 9.

[127] Soohoo (2021).

[128] Sanger (2023), p. 121.

[129] 262 U.S. 390 (1923).

procreate was recognized in 1942 in *Skinner v. Oklahoma*,[130] which prohibited forced sterilisation to secure the choice to have a child. In 1965, *Griswold v. Connecticut*[131] protected the opposite right, i.e., not to have children, by guaranteeing the marital right to use contraceptives (then extended to any individual).[132] Shortly thereafter, *Loving v. Virginia*[133] continued defending sexual intimacy by declaring unconstitutional state interracial marriage bans. This culminated in the recognition of a right to abortion in *Roe* and *Casey*, allowing for the future expansion of reproductive rights. Relying on such precedents, the Supreme Court also opened constitutional protection to same-sex couples, based on rights to sexual intimacy and marriage, respectively, in 2003 with *Lawrence v. Texas*[134] and in 2015 with *Obergefell v Hodges.*[135]

After *Dobbs*, all these intertwined reproductive rights seem at risk. Indeed, by overruling *Roe* and *Casey*, the Supreme Court did not merely exclude abortion from constitutional protection. It also dangerously lighted a path to overturn several other rights, which—like abortion—the text neither explicitly mentions nor implicitly considers among the deeply-rooted national historical liberties protected under the Due Process Clause at the time the constitution was drafted. In overtly addressing the issue, the majority argued that "nothing in this opinion should be understood to cast doubt on precedents that do not concern abortion,"[136] since "what sharply distinguishes the abortion right from the rights recognized in the cases on which *Roe* and *Casey* rely is something that both those decisions acknowledged: abortion destroys what those decisions call 'potential life'".[137] It follows that overruling *Roe* and *Casey* would not imperil other not deeply-rooted-in-national-history rights to sexual intimacy, familial relationships, and procreation.

From their perspective, the dissenters objected. To look at all these rights as "hermetically sealed containers"[138] that differ from abortion is, they argued, of little reassurance since "they are all part of the same constitutional fabric, protecting autonomous decision-making over the most personal of life decisions".[139] This fabric is best preserved when courts employ gender-sensitive legal reasoning, which ensures that judicial interpretations reflect the actual experiences and inequalities women face in exercising reproductive autonomy. Therefore, if the majority's legal reasoning is correct, they are all close to being overruled. After all,

---

[130] 316 U.S. 535 (1942).

[131] Cit.

[132] *Supra*, para. 2.

[133] 388 U.S. 1 (1967).

[134] Cit. (right to engage in private, consensual sexual acts).

[135] 576 U.S. 644 (2015) (right to marry same-sex person).

[136] *Dobbs v. Jackson Women's Health*, cit., p. 66.

[137] *Dobbs v. Jackson Women's Health*, cit., p. 32.

[138] *Dobbs v. Jackson Women's Health*, cit., at 23 (Justices Breyer, Sotomayor and Kagan's dissenting joint opinion).

[139] *Dobbs v. Jackson Women's Health*, cit., p. 5.

Justice Thomas expressly admitted such an intention in his concurring opinion, saying that "in future cases, we should reconsider all of this Court's substantive due process precedents, including *Griswold*, *Lawrence*, and *Obergefell*".[140]

However, *Dobbs* itself can already significantly restrict women's reproductive rights, not only by obstructing their choice not to have a child by abortion but also by using contraceptives. Ironically, as we will see, it can also affect the right to choose to have a child. *Dobbs*' first immediate effect is allowing states to strictly regulate and even outlaw, at any pregnancy stage, abortion, now excluded from federal constitutional protection. Overruling *Roe* and *Casey* does not formally mean that women can no longer choose to terminate their pregnancies in the U.S. They still can—as Justice Kavanaugh pointed out[141]—either if their states consider abortion legal or by travelling to states that do. However, such a view seems fairly narrow and neglects several issues that hinder, in practice, women's choice to terminate a pregnancy.

Firstly, not all women can afford to travel to states that do not ban abortion. Some pre-viability restrictions and abortion bans are thus highly disproportionate for women living in poverty or with disabilities. The state will force them to continue unwanted pregnancies, compelling women to "make" a new generation of citizens and workers and enriching society without compensation for their sacrifices.[142]

Secondly, women may travel out of state to seek a therapeutic abortion, but risk their health or life. Indeed, after *Dobbs*, states may ban abortion entirely without exceptions[143] or press physicians to perform legal abortion only in a state of emergency, due to the fear of being prosecuted.[144]

Thirdly, some states could seek to impose abortion restrictions beyond their borders, exposing providers that help non-resident women, and sanction the women themselves.[145] The rise of telehealth, allowing women to terminate pregnancies at home with pills, cannot solve these problems but only temper them. In 2021, the Food and Drug Administration (FDA) modified the mifepristone's Risk Evaluation and Mitigation System (REMS), removing the requirement that the abortive pill for intrauterine-within-ten-weeks pregnancy was dispensed in person, so allowing its remote prescription and by mailed delivery by certified providers. In 2023, certified pharmacies were also allowed to sell abortion medication under the

[140] *Dobbs v. Jackson Women's Health*, cit., p. 3 (Justice Thomas's concurring opinion).

[141] *Dobbs v. Jackson Women's Health*, cit., p. 11 (J. Kavanaugh's concurring opinion).

[142] Suk (2022) (affirming that conscripting women to carry their pregnancies to term unwillingly is unjust enrichment of the state, giving rise to a duty of restitution).

[143] Gilles (2023) (arguing that even after *Dobbs*, a mother's life-preserving abortion is secured, being a deeply-rooted-in history fundamental right. Mother's health-preserving abortion has been abolished instead).

[144] Petersen (2023), p. 344.

[145] On the interstate implications of *Dobbs*, see Appleton (2023); Cohen et al. (2023).

prescription of accredited prescribers.[146] Such liberalization appeared particularly advantageous for low-income populations, people of colour and individuals with disabilities who cannot, physically or financially, afford to travel to clinics. However, all of these groups are still required to do just that if the pregnancy is already past the tenth week or ectopic and requires a surgical abortion,[147] as well as if they live in states prohibiting telemedicine.[148] Moreover, such women may not have access to the internet or electronic payment or be unfamiliar with the digital market and resort to black market pills.[149] Finally, they may be more easily prosecuted if they need post-abortive care, when suspicious doctors report them.[150]

A further effect of *Dobbs*, beyond restricting women's access to abortion care, is limiting their right to contraception. As the majority stressed, overturning *Roe* and *Casey* would allow states to protect "potential life" even by deciding when life begins.[151] As some scholars have noted,[152] none of the Justices considered that this could raise serious concerns about the distinction between abortion and contraception, especially regarding emergency contraceptives, like the Plan B pill or intrauterine devices (IUDs). The reason is twofold. It may be traced not only to a religious-based equating of emergency contraceptives with abortion-inducing drugs but also to a vast misunderstanding about their deemed capacity to prevent

[146] US FDA, *Information about Mifepristone for Medical Termination of Pregnancy Through Ten Weeks Gestation* (March 2023) at https://www.fda.gov/drugs/postmarket-drug-safety-information-patients-and-providers/information-about-mifepristone-medical-termination-pregnancy-through-ten-weeks-gestation (accessed: 20.11.2023).

[147] The Emergency Medical Treatment and Labor Act 1986 (EMTALA) consider emergency medical conditions "ectopic pregnancy, complications of pregnancy loss, or emergent hypertensive disorders, such as preeclampsia with severe features (. . .) Stabilizing treatment could include medical and/or surgical interventions (e.g., dilation and curettage (D&C), removal of one or both fallopian tubes, anti-hypertensive therapy, etc.)" (see, Department of Health & Human Services—Centers for Medicare & Medicaid Services, *Memorandum on Reinforcement of EMTALA Obligations specific to Patients who are pregnant or are Experiencing Pregnancy Loss* (Sept. 17, 2021—revised Oct. 3, 2022), at https://www.cms.gov/files/document/qso-21-22-hospital.pdf) (accessed: 20.11.2023).

[148] Indiana, for example, bans telehealth and requires an in-person visit for abortion (Guttmacher Institute, Medication Abortion (June 1, 2023) at https://www.guttmacher.org/state-policy/explore/medication-abortion.

[149] Upadhyay, Cartwright, Grossman (2022) (showing that most common methods used to attempt self-managing abortion are: herbs, supplements, or vitamins (52%); emergency contraception or many contraceptive pills (19%); mifepristone and/or misoprostol (18%); and abdominal or other physical trauma (18%)).

[150] Petersen (2023), pp. 341–342: "One thing is certain: the people who will be targeted for this type of investigation will be women living at or near the poverty line, and women of color. (. . .) The National Advocates for Pregnant Women has tracked 1,600 such cases since 1973 and found that the victims of this abuse were "overwhelmingly low income, and disproportionately Black and Brown".

[151] *Dobbs v. Jackson Women's Health*, cit., pp. 38–39 (opinion of the Court).

[152] Minow (2024).

the implantation of a fertilized egg.[153] In Kansas, for example, the health system temporarily stopped providing emergency contraception after *Dobbs* until a governmental clarification of the ambiguous Missouri trigger law, which bans abortion 'from the moment of conception'.[154]

By allowing states to restrict abortion to prevent the destruction of potential life without limits, *Dobbs* has also affected the right to procreate for patients seeking in vitro fertilization (IVF). Indeed, laws banning abortion from conception or fertilization could not only prohibit abortion. They could also apply to any practice affecting potential human lives, including embryos outside a woman's body. Then, any selection, freezing or destruction of in-vitro-fertilized human eggs within medically assisted reproduction treatments would be illegal.[155] In other words, *Dobbs* paved the way for states to criminalize IVF,[156] beyond Louisiana, which prohibits the intentional destruction of a viable in-vitro-fertilized human ovum considered a legal person.[157] This is far from hypothetical. States like Indiana have already banned abortions, explicitly underscoring that in vitro fertilization will be exempted.[158]

Furthermore, some IVF practices are performed on in-vitro-fertilized embryos inside the uterus. An example is reducing multiple fetuses in one pregnancy, leaving others to complete gestation to prevent the mother and offspring from suffering life and health risks. Now, multifetal reduction could violate abortion laws in states like Texas, which prohibits any act intended "to cause the death of an unborn child of a woman known to be pregnant",[159] regardless of whether the pregnancy is terminated.[160]

7 Post-Dobbs Scenario

The future of women's abortion rights in the U.S. depends on how states react to *Dobbs* and implement their abortion policies. The power to regulate the women's interest in pregnancy termination has been returned to state legislators, who will be able to decide whether to continue to guarantee the right to pre-viability abortion

153 Frank (2019).

154 Whelan (2023), p. 168.

155 Macintosh (2023).

156 Greely (2022) (arguing that such a scenario is unlikely). See also the Author's updated view at https://law.stanford.edu/2023/02/27/slss-hank-greely-discusses-in-vitro-fertilization-post-dobbs/.

157 LA Rev Stat § 9:129 (2022).

158 IN Code § 16–34-1-0.5 (2022).

159 TX Health & Safety Code § 170A.001, § 245.002 (2022).

160 Ward (2022) at https://www.politico.com/newsletters/politico-nightly/2022/05/23/how-abortion-bans-might-affect-ivf-00034409.

or, on the contrary, restrict or forbid it. That has resulted in a fragmented legislative landscape across the country.

Half of U.S. states still considers abortion legal, although not uniformly. While the significant part protects abortion until viability throughout the second trimester, or even beyond, others allow abortion up to the first trimester or some weeks later.[161] However, the line between states with or without shorter or longer gestational limitations blurs when considering the web of policies concerning, for example, health insurance plans, public funding for abortion, or provider requirements.[162] As under *Roe*, several restrictions to access abortion services still exist, even in states that allow women to seek elective abortions pre-viability.[163]

Abortion-supportive states have nevertheless devoted significant efforts to reinforce protection afforded to women seeking to terminate their pregnancies, especially in the face of the expected increase of bans and restrictions in the aftermath of *Dobbs*. Several means were adopted to secure the right to abortion, from enshrining it explicitly in the state constitutions,[164] as in California,[165] Michigan[166] and Vermont,[167] to overtly committing to broaden access to all women in the U.S. even by a joint interstate program. To achieve this, the West Coast Governors launched the "Multi-State Commitment to Reproductive Freedom" to collaborate in expanding access to abortion procedures, to counter out-of-state restrictive measures.[168] The initiative has recently extended, reaching twenty states.[169] In the same vein, other states, headed by Connecticut,[170]

[161] McCann et al. (2023) at https://www.nytimes.com/interactive/2022/us/abortion-laws-roe-v-wade.html (accessed: 20.11.2023).

[162] Guttmacher Institute, *Interactive Map: US Abortion Policies and Access After Roe*, June 26, 2023, https://states.guttmacher.org/policies/montana/abortion-policies.

[163] In Michigan, for example, patients are forced to wait 24 hours after counselling to obtain an abortion; parental content is required; only physicians, not other qualified health care professionals, can perform it; and state Medicaid coverage or private health insurance for abortion is nearly-total banned.

[164] On November 8, 2022, in all three states, a proposal to amend Constitution to add the right to reproductive freedom was on the ballot and passed by 66.88% (California), 56.66% (Michigan), and 76.77% (Vermont) of the voters.

[165] California Constitution, Article I, Section 1.1.

[166] Michigan Constitution, Article I, Section 28.

[167] Vermont Constitution, Chapter I, Article 22.

[168] On June 24, 2022, California, Oregon and Washington signed the document available at https://www.gov.ca.gov/wp-content/uploads/2022/06/Multi-State-Commitment-to-Reproductive-Freedom_Final-1.pdf.

[169] Roubein (2023) at https://www.washingtonpost.com/politics/2023/02/21/twenty-governors-are-forming-new-coalition-support-abortion-rights/.

[170] Stracqualursi, LeBlanC (2022) at https://edition.cnn.com/2022/05/05/politics/connecticut-abortion-protection-law-out-of-state-lawsuits/index.html.

adopted so-called "shield laws" to protect providers helping non-resident women against sanctions imposed abroad by states criminalizing abortion.[171]

The other half of states in the U.S. consider pregnancy termination illegal, prohibiting abortion entirely or after six weeks of pregnancy.[172] After *Dobbs*, some states have enforced their trigger laws, like the Heartbeat Act 2021 in Texas.[173] Others, like Indiana[174] and West Virginia,[175] have adopted new legislation. At the midpoint of 2023, such abortion laws have been fully enforced in only fourteen states, mainly in the South, since a significant number of these bans has been temporarily halted, pending a review of their constitutional validity by state high courts. In South Carolina, for example, a six-week abortion ban signed into law in May 2023 was paused, making abortion legal up to twenty-two weeks of pregnancy under pre-*Dobbs* law. This suspended state law reflected the title and the content of the Fetal Heartbeat and Protection from Abortion Act 2021 that the Supreme Court of South Carolina had struck down in *Planned Parenthood South Atlantic v. State of South Carolina et al.* a few months prior.[176] The majority of the Court held that the Act violated Article I, Section 10 of the state constitution protecting the right to privacy, which, unlike in the federal constitution, is explicitly mentioned in the text, and understood to cover abortion. Applying the strict scrutiny standard, the Court argued, by a three-to-two vote, that the law banning pregnancy termination at the fetus's detectable cardiac activity unreasonably invaded a woman's fundamental privacy right. First, it pursued fetal interests at a too-early stage, at which a fetus cannot be considered a legal entity under state law reflecting the viability line. Second, it furthered the interest in maternal health, allowing women to make informed choices by knowing the likelihood of the fetus

[171] Shield laws can, for example, forbid medical boards and malpractice insurance companies from negatively considering out-of-state lawsuits and complaints for providers helping non-resident women seeking abortions; or prevent interstate investigation and discovery into care provided to non-resident patients. However, no such laws "would protect the patients and helpers who stay in, or return to, an antiabortion state if a law targets their conduct" (see Cohen et al. (2023), pp. 44–45).

[172] McCann et al. (June 26, 2023).

[173] *Supra*, para. 3.

[174] In the aftermath of *Dobbs*, the Indiana General Assembly passed Senate Bill 1 in September 2022, making the state the first to adopt an abortion ban after *Roe* and *Casey*'s overruling. Ind. Code § 16–34-2-1(a) states that "Abortion shall in all instances be a criminal act", except when abortion is necessary to prevent any serious health risk to the pregnant woman or to save the pregnant woman's life; when there is a lethal fetal anomaly; or when pregnancy results from rape or incest.

[175] WV Code § 16–2 R-3 (2022): "(a) An abortion may not be performed or induced or be attempted to be performed or induced unless in the reasonable medical judgment of a licensed medical professional: (1) The embryo or fetus is nonviable; (2) The pregnancy is ectopic; or (3) A medical emergency exists". The prohibition shall not apply in case of abortion within eight weeks (fourteen for minors and incompetent or incapacitated adults) in case of sexual assault or incest, as far as reported to the authorities at least 48 hours before the abortion is performed.

[176] *Planned Parenthood South Atlantic v. State of South Carolina et al.*, 438 S.C. 188, 882 S.E.2d 770 (2023).

surviving, based on its heartbeat. However, by forbidding abortion at six weeks, when women are unaware of the pregnancy, the law rendered their informed choice merely illusionary.[177]

In August 2023, the South Carolina Supreme Court did not follow that precedent, departing from the leading opinion then authored by (the only female judge of the all-male court and now retired) Justice Kaye Hearn.[178] Indeed, the majority considered the new Act banning abortion at the fetal heartbeat "materially different"[179] from the 2021 one declared unconstitutional because the legislature has now carefully clarified to have taken into consideration, in supporting its policy judgment, "the interests of the pregnant woman and balanced them against the legitimate interest of the State to protect the life of the unborn".[180] As noted Justice Kittredge, "Specifically, the legislature explained it had placed weight on the fact that a woman could learn of her pregnancy within seven to fourteen days of conception and would have several weeks after that to make her decision and have an abortion if she so chose".[181] It follows that the new Act, although infringing on a woman's right to privacy and bodily autonomy, does not that unreasonably, and thus it does not violate Article I, section 10 of the constitution, which—as to the current majority—does not include any fundamental right to abortion.

Other states high courts had already adopted similar views. For example, on the very same day that a nearly-total abortion ban was declared unconstitutional in South Carolina, the Supreme Court of Idaho upheld a state law as equally restrictive,[182] arguing that protecting privacy does not imply safeguarding the right to abortion: "Regardless of whether the overarching rights to 'privacy', 'bodily autonomy' and 'intimate familial decisions' exist—there is nothing to indicate that the particular 'right of abortion' is part of any of those rights"[183] under a state constitution lacking to mention it. In sum, the future of many state abortion bans largely depends on the changeable opinion of the respective courts interpreting state constitutions.

To counter such uncertainty, however, some antiabortionist states have passed constitutional amendments excluding protection for abortion. While in Tennessee,[184]

---

[177] *Planned Parenthood South Atlantic v. State of South Carolina et al.*, at para. V(D).

[178] *Planned Parenthood S. Atl. v. State of South Carolina et al.*, 440 S.C. 465, 892 S.E.2d 121 (2023).

[179] *Planned Parenthood South Atlantic v. State of South Carolina et al.*, para. IV (Justice Kittredge's opinion).

[180] *Planned Parenthood South Atlantic v. State of South Carolina et al.*, para. II (Justice Kittredge's opinion).

[181] *Planned Parenthood South Atlantic v. State of South Carolina et al.*, para. IV.

[182] Idaho Code sections 18–622(2) ("Total Abortion Ban"), 18–8804 and – 8805 ("6—Week Ban"), and 18–8807(1) ("Civil Liability Law").

[183] *Planned Parenthood Great Northwest at al. v. State of Idaho,* no. 49615, 49817, 49899, January 5, 2023, at 25.

[184] In 2014, 56.60% of voters endorsed providing that "Nothing in this Constitution secures or protects a right to abortion or requires the funding of an abortion." (See Tennessee Constitution, Article I, Section 36).

West Virginia,[185] Alabama,[186] and Louisiana,[187] voters have supported such proposals, it came as a surprise that, after *Dobbs*, in Kentucky,[188] voters have not, rejecting an amendment saying that no right to abortion exists, even though total abortion-ban legislation has been in force in the Republican-led state since the day after *Dobbs.*[189]

This is perhaps emblematic of a trend. In general, support for abortion has been growing among Americans after *Roe* and *Casey*'s overruling. As results of midterm elections[190] and polls[191] have shown, U.S. citizens, for the most part, regardless of their being pro-life or pro-choice, do not embrace super-restrictive abortion policies without exceptions. Such policies, however, are, in practice, very common, beyond the law on the books. Indeed, although no absolute prohibitions have been formally adopted by states considering abortion illegal, their laws very often act as if they were blanket bans due to the ambiguity of the rules allowing pregnancy termination in cases of fatal congenital disabilities, rape or incest, or for saving the mother's health and life. Doctors are likely not to perform an abortion even when women are entitled to legally interrupt their pregnancies, encouraging them to travel out-of-state instead to avoid any possible charge.[192] As we have seen above,[193] that suggestion is not a solution for vulnerable, poor women living in marginalized communities. Moreover, it does not prevent either patients or providers from being sanctioned respectively for accessing or performing abortion care

[185] In 2018, 51.73% of the voters supported the proposal to specify that "nothing in this Constitution secures or protects a right to abortion or requires the funding of abortion". See West Virginia Constitution, Article VI, Section 58.

[186] In 2018, 59.01% of the voters passed the proposal to amend the Constitution to recognize and support the sanctity of unborn life, protect the rights of unborn children and exclude any protection as a right or funding for abortion. See Alabama Constitution, Article I, Section 36.06.

[187] In 2020, 62.06% of voters supported denying constitutional protection to the right to abortion. See Louisiana Constitution, Article I, Section 20.1: "To protect human life, nothing in this constitution shall be construed to secure or protect a right to abortion or require the funding of abortion".

[188] In 2022, 52.35% of the voters rejected the proposal to add the Constitution that nothing in the state constitution creates a right to abortion or requires government funding for abortion.

[189] KY Rev Stat § 311.772 (2022) (adopted on June 27, 2019).

[190] Schneider, Otterbein (2022) at https://www.politico.com/news/2022/12/19/dobbs-2022-election-abortion-00074426.

[191] Gallup (2023) at https://news.gallup.com/poll/470,279/dissatisfaction-abortion-policy-hits-high.aspx; Pew Research Center (2023) at https://www.pewresearch.org/politics/2023/04/26/nearly-a-year-after-roes-demise-americans-views-of-abortion-access-increasingly-vary-by-where-they-live/. See also Zernike (2023) at https://www.nytimes.com/2023/06/23/us/roe-v-wade-abortion-views.html.

[192] Schoenfeld, Walker (2023) at https://www.nytimes.com/interactive/2023/01/21/us/abortion-ban-exceptions.html.

[193] *Supra*, para. 6.

services out-of-state.[194] This risk exists even if such services are provided remotely from another state by doctors prescribing abortive pills via telemedicine or online providers selling such drugs delivered to women's homes.[195] Indeed, antiabortionist legislators have tried to hinder women from seeking abortion abroad, even by adopting restrictions on abortive pills conflicting with the FDA's regulation on mifepristone. Some states require that only physicians provide abortion medication (prohibiting other certified health care providers from prescribing or certified pharmacies from dispensing it); some only after an in-person visit or until an earlier gestational stage than the tenth week of pregnancy.[196] Others, like Arizona, ban mailing pills to patients[197] or, like Wyoming, forbid abortive drugs *per se*, explicitly and separately from general abortion bans.[198]

Whether states can hinder or prohibit abortion medication contrary to federal prescriptions is paramount. Indeed, the actual breadth of abortion bans depends on its positive or negative answer, significantly affecting women's reproductive lives in pro-life states. The issue is on the table in federal courts. An abortion pill manufacturer has filed a lawsuit in the U.S. District Court for the Southern District of West Virginia, arguing that federal rules on mifepristone, as adopted by the FDA under a legislative mandate by Congress, preempt conflicting state regulations.[199] Likewise, a physician has challenged North Carolina laws on the

[194] In Missouri, two amendments to abortion law expressly intended to sanction who helps, assists or induces abortion regardless of the place of performance were introduced in 2022. On the issue, Appleton (2023) and Cohen et al. (2023).

[195] Delivering abortive pills in states banning abortion is not illegal. The Assistant Attorney General in charge of the Office of Legal Counsel at the U.S. Department of Justice released a written opinion saying the mere mailing by the U.S. Postal Service ("USPS") or other senders of drugs that can be used to perform abortions to recipients in jurisdictions banning abortion does not violate the Comstock Act (i.e., section 1461, title 18, U.S.C., forbidding mailing of every article or thing, including drugs and medicines, designed, adapted, or intended for producing abortion or advertised or described in a manner calculated to lead another to use or apply them for producing abortion), lacking the sender the intent that the recipient of legally-multiple-use drugs will use them unlawfully (see *Application of the Comstock Act to the Mailing of Prescription Drugs That Can Be Used for Abortions*, December 23, 2022, at https://www.justice.gov/olc/opinion/application-comstock-act-mailing-prescription-drugs-can-be-used-abortions.

[196] Alaska, Arizona, Florida, Georgia, Indiana, Iowa, Kansas, Michigan, Minnesota, Nebraska, Nevada, North Carolina, Ohio, Pennsylvania, South Carolina, Utah (see Guttmacher Institute, *Medication Abortion* (June 1, 2023) at https://www.guttmacher.org/state-policy/explore/medication-abortion).

[197] AZ Rev Stat § 36–2160 (2022): "A manufacturer, supplier or physician or any other person is prohibited from providing an abortion-inducing drug via courier, delivery or mail service".

[198] The Wyoming law is currently suspended by the court, pending a lawsuit challenging its legality (see Belluck (2023) at https://www.nytimes.com/2023/06/22/health/wyoming-abortion-pill-ban.html.

[199] *Genbiopro, Inc., V. Mark A. Sorsaia et al.* (N.D.W. Va. 2023), No. 3:23-cv-00058, Complaint (January 25, 2023) at https://storage.courtlistener.com/recap/gov.uscourts.wvsd.235957/gov.uscourts.wvsd.235957.1.0.pdf.

same ground.[200] These cases have not been decided yet, but according to some scholars, the preemption argument could be successful,[201] since the congressional purpose of requiring the FDA to impose additional control on certain approved drugs is to uniformly balance the public interests in drug safety and drug access nationwide using the least restrictive means.[202] If correct, states can neither ban FDA-approved drugs nor more strictly regulate their providers' conduct, thus securing medical abortion availability nationwide.

So far, however, federal courts have shown some ambivalence in defining the FDA's authority to regulate abortive drugs. While the U.S. District Court for the Eastern District of Washington ordered the FDA not to restrict mifepristone distribution unduly,[203] the District Court of the Northern District of Texas stayed the FDA's approval of mifepristone. It argued that, since its first authorization in 2000, there was insufficient information to evaluate its safety and effectiveness.[204] Thus, mifepristone would have been excluded from the U.S. market altogether. However, the Court of Appeal for the Fifth Circuit partially stayed that order pending appeal on the merit, restoring the mifepristone regimen at the time of approval, from 2000 until 2016, to be used in the first seven weeks of pregnancy and in-presence providing.[205] A few days later, the Supreme Court stayed the order of the Texas District Court entirely,[206] allowing again sales of medication abortion under the latest mild REMS conditions.[207]

Although this was the most significant abortion case to reach the Court since *Dobbs*, the reasons for the stay order have not been disclosed. Only Justice Alito argued in dissent that the applicants, the FDA, and the first U.S. manufacturer of mifepristone failed to show that they were likely to suffer irreparable harm since the drug would be anyway on the market (although under stricter conditions), and the appeal on the merit was already scheduled soon.[208] What was really at stake in the case, however, was something else, namely, that women living in states banning abortion would have been definitively prevented from accessing out-of-

[200] *Amy Bryant, Md, v. Joshua H. Stein et al.* (M.D.N.C. 2023), No. 1:23-cv-77, Complaint (January 25, 2023) at https://storage.courtlistener.com/recap/gov.uscourts.ncmd.94539/gov.uscourts.ncmd.94539.1.0.pdf.

[201] Cohen et al. (2023), p. 53 ss; Zettler et al. (2023).

[202] Cohen et al. (2023), p. 57; Zettler (2017), p. 875.

[203] *State of Washington et al. v. FDA et al.* (E.D. Wash. 2023), No. 1:2023cv03026, Document 80 (April 7, 2023).

[204] *Alliance for Hippocratic Medicine et al. v. FDA et al.* (N.D. Tex. 2023), No. 2:2022cv00223, Document 137 (April 7, 2023).

[205] *Alliance for Hippocratic Medicine et al. v. FDA et al.* (5th Cir. 2023), No. 23–10362 (April 12, 2023).

[206] *Danco Laboratories, Llc. v. Alliance for Hippocratic Medicine et al.*, April 21, 2023, 598 U.S. (2023).

[207] Supra, para. 6.

[208] Supra, para. 4.

state abortive pills, even via telemedicine, if the order were not stayed. Lacking any evidence, we can only hope that the Court's majority also relied on such consideration in deciding the case.

8 Conclusions

As illustrated in these pages,[209] by overruling *Roe* and *Casey*, the U.S. Supreme Court established a distance between judicial power and the abortion issue, arguing that its regulation "must be returned to the people and their elected representatives".[210] However, the post-*Dobbs* intricated legal landscape clearly shows that such an issue, while not protected under the U.S. Constitution according to a majority of the Court, still needs settlement by courts, both at the state and federal level. Far from removing abortion from judicial interventions, *Dobbs* has opened new grounds for courts to protect women living in pro-life states, totally or nearly banning pregnancy termination. Indeed, many laws forbidding abortion have been challenged under state constitutions or for attempting to supersede federal rules concerning mifepristone pills to prevent pregnancy termination either in or out of antiabortionist states.[211] Consequently, after *Dobbs*, the right to access to abortion health services nationwide depends precisely on judicial intervention. Lacking it, the future of women's reproductive rights in the U.S. is seriously imperilled.

The *Dobbs* majority firmly denied the Supreme Court a safeguard role for women beyond the states' authority. Neither the use of foreign law by the Justices helped them debunk such a belief, despite, in this regard, comparative law could have offered valuable teaching. Especially, it could have indicated that affording state legislators broad discretion on moral issues like abortion, not protected by interstate law, does not automatically exempt courts, whether national or supranational, from playing a relevant role. A transnational dialogue with the European Courts, the ECJ and the ECtHR, could have been indeed helpful to realize that the U.S. Supreme Court could have ensured that states weigh all interests involved in the abortion issue without jeopardising fundamental rights.[212] Such an interplay between legislators and courts could hopefully provide protection of women's reproductive rights in the United States, even after *Dobbs*.

---

[209] Supra, para. 4.

[210] *Dobbs v. Jackson Women's Health,* cit., at 64 (Opinion of the Court).

[211] Supra, para. 7.

[212] Supra, para. 5.

References

Aceves WJ (2022) The problem with Dobbs and the rule of legality. Geo Law J Online 111:75–105
Appleton SF (2023) Out of bounds? Abortion, choice of law, and modest role for congress. J Am Acad Matrim Law 35:461–504
Bader Ginsburg R (1985) Some thoughts on autonomy and equality in relation to Roe v. Wade. N C Law Rev 63:375–386
Belluck P (2023) Wyoming Judge temporarily blocks state's ban on abortion pills, The New York Times at https://www.nytimes.com/2023/06/22/health/wyoming-abortion-pill-ban.html. Accessed 22 June 2023
Berns M (2009) Trigger laws. Geo Law J 97:1639–1688
Breyer S (2003) Keynote address. Am Soc'y Int Law Proc 97:265–268
Breyer S (2008) Active liberty. Interpreting a democratic constitution, Oxford
Calabresi SG, Silverman BG (2015) Hayek and the citation of foreign law: a response to Professor Jeremy Waldron. Mich St Law Rev 1:1–181
Cohen D, Donley G, Rebouché R (2023) The new abortion battleground. Columb Law Rev 123:1–100
Devins N (2009) How planned Parenthood v. Casey (Pretty Much) settled the abortion wars. Yale Law J 118(7):1318–1354
Fabbrini F (2023) The 'European' Future of American Abortion law: Dobbs, federalism and constitutional equality. Vanderbilt J Trans Law. https://ssrn.com/abstract=4384264
Frank R (2019) Miss-conceptions: abortifacients, regulatory failure, and political opportunity. Yale Law J 129:208–250
Gallup (2023) Dissatisfaction With U.S. Abortion Policy Hits Another High. Feb 2023 at https://news.gallup.com/poll/470279/dissatisfaction-abortion-policy-hits-high.aspx
Gilles SG (2023) What does Dobbs mean for the constitutional right to a life-or-health-preserving abortion? Miss Law J 92:271–328
Gormley K (1992) One hundred years of privacy. Wis Law Rev 1992:1335–1442
Greely HT (2022) The death of Roe and the future of ex vivo embryos. J Law Biosci 9(2):1–26
Greenhouse L, Siegel RB (2016) Casey and the clinic closings: when protecting health obstructs choice. Yale Law J 125:1428–1480
Hart Ely J (1973) The Wages of crying Wolf: a comment on Roe v. Wade. Yale Law J 82:920–949
Kalantry S (2022) Foreign law in Dobbs: the need for a principled framework. Con Law Now 14:37–43
Law SA (1984) Rethinking sex and the constitution. U PA Law Rev 132:955–1040
Macintosh KL (2023) Dobbs, abortion laws, and in vitro fertilization. J Health Care Law Pol'y 26:1–48
Markesinis B, Fedtke J (2005) The judge as comparatist. Tulane Law Rev 80(1):11–168
McCann A et al. (2023) Tracking the states where abortion is now banned, The New York Times at https://www.nytimes.com/interactive/2022/us/abortion-laws-roe-v-wade.html. Accessed 26 June 2023
McClain LC, Fleming JE (2023) Ordered liberty after dobbs. J Am Acad Matrimonial Law 35:623–645
Minow M (forthcoming 2024) The unraveling: what Dobbs May mean for contraception, liberty, and constitutionalism. In: Bollinger L, Stone GR (eds.) Roe v. Dobbs: the past, present and future of a constitutional right to abortion, Oxford University Press, Oxford. Forthcoming. Available at https://ssrn.com/abstract=4343952 or http://dx.doi.org/10.2139/ssrn.4343952
Petersen CJ (2023) Women's right to equality and reproductive autonomy: the impact of Dobbs v. Jackson Women's Health Organization. U Haw Law Rev 45:305–345
Pew Research Center (2023) Nearly a year after Roe's demise, Americans' views of abortion access increasingly vary by where they live Apr 2023 at https://www.pewresearch.org/politics/2023/04/26/nearly-a-year-after-roes-demise-americans-viewsof-abortion-access-increasingly-vary-by-where-theylive/#:~:text=The%20new%20survey%20by%20Pew%20Research%20Center%2C%20conducted,changed%20in%20states%20where%20abortion%20is%20still%20legal
Rosenberg G (2022) Abortion after Dobbs. Law Courts Newsletter 32(2):18–41

Ross LJ, Solinger R (2017) Reproductive justice: an introduction. University of California Press, Oakland
Roubein R (2023) Twenty governors are forming a new coalition to support abortion rights. The Washington Post at https://www.washingtonpost.com/politics/2023/02/21/twenty-governors-are-forming-new-coalitionsupport-abortion-rights/. Accessed 21 Feb 2023
Sanger C (2023) The rise and fall of a reproductive right: Dobbs v. Jackson Women's Health Organization. Family Law Quart 56:117–160
Schneider E, Otterbein H (2022) 'THE central issue': how the fall of Roe v. Wade shook the 2022 election, POLITICO at https://www.politico.com/news/2022/12/19/dobbs-2022-election-abortion-00074426. Accessed 19 Dec 2022
Schoenfeld Walker A (2023) Most abortion bans include exceptions. In Practice, few are granted, The New York Times at https://www.nytimes.com/interactive/2023/01/21/us/abortion-ban-exceptions.html. Accessed 21 Jan 2023
Siegel RB (1992) Reasoning from the body: a historical perspective on abortion regulation and questions of equal protection. Stanford Law Rev 44:261–381
Siegel SR (2007) Sex equality arguments for reproductive rights: their critical basis and evolving constitutional expression. Emory Law J 56:815–842
Siegel RB (2008) Dignity and the politics of protection: abortion restrictions under casey/carhart. Yale Law J 117:1694–1801
Siegel RB (2023) Memory games: Dobbs's originalism as anti-democratic living constitutionalism—and some pathways for resistance. Texas Law Rev 101(5):1127–1204
Simon SA (2013) The supreme court's use of foreign law in constitutional rights cases. J Law Cts 1(2):279–302
Smorto G (2011) Il Giudice e il diritto straniero. In: Vacca L (ed) Scienza giuridica e prassi, Napoli, 291–308
Soohoo C (2021) Reproductive justice and transformative constitutionalism. Cardozo Law Rev 42 (3):819–876
Suk JC (2022) A World without Roe: the constitutional future of unwanted pregnancy. William & Mary Law Rev 32:443–524
Tribe LH (2022) Deconstructing Dobbs, N.Y. Review (Online), 22 Sept 2022
Tripkovic B (2019) The morality of foreign law. Int J Const L 17(3):732–755
Tucak I, Blagojević A (2020). Abortion in Europe, EU and comparative law issues and challenges series (ECLIC) 4:1135–1174
Upadhyay UD, Cartwright AF, Grossman D (2022) Barriers to abortion care and incidence of attempted self-managed abortion among individuals searching Google for abortion care: a national prospective study. Contraception 106:49–56
Waldron J (2005) Foreign law and the modern ius gentium. Harv Law Rev 119(1):129–147
Ward M (2022) How abortion bans might affect IVF, POLITICO at https://www.politico.com/newsletters/politico-nightly/2022/05/23/how-abortion-bans-might-affect-ivf-00034409. Accessed 23 May 2022
Whelan AM (2023) Aggravating inequalities: state regulation of abortion and contraception. Harv J Law Gender 46:131–204
West R (2009) From choice to reproductive justice: de-constitutionalizing abortion rights. Yale Law J 118:1394–1432
Wharton LJ, Frietsche S, Kolbert K (2006) Preserving the core of roe: reflections on planned parenthood v. Casey. Yale J Law and Fem 18(2):317–388
Yoshino K (2011) The New Equal Protection. Harv Law Rev 124:747–803
Zernike K (2023) How a year without roe shifted American views on abortion, The New York Times at https://www.nytimes.com/2023/06/23/us/roe-v-wade-abortion-views.html. Accessed 23 June 2023
Ziegler M (2014) The price of privacy, 1973 to the present. Harv J Law Gend 37(2):285–329
Zettler PJ (2017) Pharmaceutical federalism. Indiana Law J 92: 845–900
Zettler PJ, Adashi EY, Cohen G (2023) Alliance for Hippocratic Medicine v. FDA—Dobbs's collateral consequences for pharmaceutical regulation. N Engl J Med 388:e29(1)–e29(3)

Rosalba Potenzano is an Assistant Professor of Comparative Law at the University of Palermo, where she teaches Comparative Law and Digital Markets Law. She has held visiting scholar positions in the USA (University of Pennsylvania) and Taiwan (National Yang Ming Chiao Tung University). She earned her JD (2016) and Ph.D. in Legal System Dynamics (2021) from the University of Palermo, and is qualified for the Italian Bar.

Guido Smorto is a Full Professor of Comparative Law at University of Palermo, where he holds the EU Jean Monnet Chair in Comparative and European Digital Law. He has held research and visiting professor positions in several academic institutions in Europe, as well as in the US, Japan, and Latin America. He is also Vice President of Società Italiana per la Ricerca nel Diritto Comparato (SIRD).

Part V
Conflicts of Rights

Discrimination of Women Under Sharia Law and the *Molla Sali* Judgment of the ECHR

Ioannis Ktistakis

Abstract When the Molla Sali judgment of the European Court of Human Rights (Grand Chamber) was published, it did not end the application of Sharia law in Greece, nor did it end the operation of Sharia courts. What was stopped was the application of Sharia law by ordinary Greek civil courts. Therefore, discrimination against (Muslim) women has not ceased, since Sharia law, at least as applied in Greece, does not incorporate gender equality.

1 Muslim Divorce in Greece

The marriage of Kemal, a Greek national, and Angela, a Ukrainian national, was dissolved by decision no. 80/1995 of the Sharia Court of Xanthi on the basis of a joint application. Only thirty-five days earlier, Angela had changed her religion from Orthodox Christian to Muslim and had been given the name "Aiten" by decision (no. 66/1995) of the same Sharia Court.

Five years later, Kemal asked the Civil Court of First Instance of Xanthi to declare decision no. 80/1995 enforceable.[1] Within four days of the filing of the application, the Civil Court issued its decision and accepted it (no. 284/2000).

[1] This special judicial review by the civil courts was first introduced by article 5 of Law no. 1920/ 1991. The current Law no. 4964/2022 (article 146(9)) provides the followings: "Decisions issued by the Mufti in cases of contested jurisdiction may not be enforced or constitute a precedent, unless they are declared enforceable by the single-member district court of the district where the Mufti's seat is located, in accordance with the procedure of voluntary jurisdiction. The [civil] court shall only investigate whether the judgment was rendered within the limits of the Mufti's

I. Ktistakis (✉)
European Court of Human Rights, Strasbourg, France
e-mail: Ioannis.Ktistakis@echr.coe.int

© The Author(s), under exclusive license to Springer Nature Switzerland AG 2025

S. Baer et al. (eds.), *The Gender and the Judiciary*, Gender Perspectives in Law 7,
https://doi.org/10.1007/978-3-032-06885-9_15

At the beginning of 2004, the Sharia Court of Xanthi issued a new decision (no. 7/2004) on the divorce of Kemal and Angela (no longer referred to as "Aiten"), following a unilateral this time application by Kemal. Angela was not present, nor was she summoned to the trial.

Following another application by Kemal, the Civil Court of First Instance of Xanthi again declared the Sharia Court's decision enforceable, ruling that it was not contrary to the Constitution (no. 83/2004). Angela was not present, nor was she summoned to the trial.

However, this was just one of the similar 3633 cases adjudicated by the three Sharia Courts of Thrace (northeastern Greece)[2] at the time (2014) when Molla Sali decided to file her application to the European Court of Human Rights.[3]

Until then, in the Greek legal order, Sharia law was applied in personal matters (family and inheritance disputes) of all Greek Muslims, no matter if these disputes had been adjudicated either by the special Sharia Courts or by the ordinary civil courts of the country.[4] A Greek Muslim woman could not claim the application of the Greek Civil Code.[5] In other words, whether they went to the special Sharia courts or to the ordinary civil courts, the law that would apply in both cases was Sharia law. They could not therefore claim the application of Greek civil law, which alone guarantees equality between spouses.

The first part of this article examines the application of Sharia law by special Greek Sharia courts in light of gender equality. This application is still in force.

The second part examines the application of Sharia law by Greek civil courts in light of gender equality. This ended after the adoption of the Grand Chamber judgment of the European Court of Human Rights in the case of *Molla Sali v. Greece*. In other

jurisdiction and whether the provisions applied are contrary to the Constitution, in particular para. 2 of Article 4 and the European Convention on Human Rights. The decision of the single-member court of first instance may be appealed against before the relevant multi-member court of first instance, which shall hear the case in the same procedure. No appeal, whether ordinary or extraordinary, may be brought against the judgment of the Multipartite Court of First Instance".

[2] Ktistakis (2013), p. 141.

[3] *Molla Sali v. Greece* (merits and just satisfaction).

[4] See section 4 of Law no. 147/1914 of 5 January 1914 (enacted pursuant to the Treaty of Athens, 14.11.1913, concluded between the Ottoman Empire and the Kingdom of Greece): "All matters relating to the marriage of persons belonging to the Muslim or Jewish religion, that is to say all matters relating to the lawful contracting and dissolution of marriage and personal relations between spouses during their marital life, as well as kinship, shall be governed by religious law and adjudicated in conformity with such law. As regards Muslims, the special conditions applicable to them as provided in the latest treaty between Greece and Turkey are also in force". According to the relevant explanatory report, "as an exception [to the rule of the Greek civil law] we should accept the law on marriage and divorce of Jews and Muslims. These relations, according to all oriental people, who are close linked to their own Holy law, must remain governed under their own legal system". When the Greek Civil Code was adopted in 1946, section 6 of the Introductory Law to the Code repealed section 4 of Law no. 147/1914 in respect of Greek nationals of Jewish faith only.

[5] Court of Cassation, judgments nos. 231/1932, 105/1937, 14/1938, 322/1960, 738/1967, 1723/1980, 1041/2000, 1097/2007 and 1862/2013. See, also, Roucounas (1981), p. 150.

words, while those who have recourse to the civil courts now enjoy the substantive guarantees of gender equality in family relations (because the civil code applies exclusively), the problem of inequality persists for those who have recourse to the Sharia courts (which the Molla Sali decision did not examine), because the latter apply Sharia law exclusively.

2 Greek Sharia Courts and Sharia Law

The organisation of Greek Sharia Courts is regulated, today, by Law no. 4964/2022.[6] These special courts that still exist in the Greek legal order, are composed of one member, which is one of the three Muslim religious ministers of Thrace ("Mufti"). The Mufti is not a jurist, but a "profound scholar of the Qur'an, Muslim tradition and Sharia Law".[7] As such, the Mufti is not chosen in a competition by the School of Judges, like Greek judges. Instead, he is chosen by the Minister of Education and Religious Affairs,[8] after consultation with a committee of members of the Muslim minority of Thrace,[9] on the basis of "their ethics, their theological training, preferably in the knowledge and interpretation of the Qur'an or the Muslim tradition or sacred Muslim law, and their religious activity in general".[10] The Mufti has no personal or functional independence: He is a "civil servant equivalent to a director-general"[11] and "he is appointed for a renewable term of five years".[12] Finally, the Mufti can be dismissed by the Minister of Education and Religious Affairs, sometimes following the opinion of medical or other non-judicial committees, and in three of the six grounds for dismissal without any other opinion.[13]

[6] Law no. 2345/1920 provided that Mouftis, in addition to their religious duties, had the power to adjudicate family and inheritance disputes among Muslims to the extent that such disputes were governed by Islamic law. Under the Decree-Law of 24 December 1990 (subsequently Law no. 1920/1991), the duties and qualifications of mouftis remained largely unchanged. However, they were now to be appointed by presidential decree, based on the proposal from the Minister of Education, who, in turn, must consult a committee composed of the local prefect and various Muslim officials chosen by the State. The current legal status is determined by the Law no. 4964/2022 (articles 137–158).

[7] Articles 143(2) & 146(8) of Law no. 4964/2022. According to articles 87–91 of the Greek Constitution, Greek judges shall (i) be jurists; (ii) have passed the relevant competition for the recruitment of judges; (iii) enjoy functional and personal independence; (iv) be impartial and subject only to the Constitution and the laws; and (v) be integrated into the judicial structure and subject only to disciplinary control by other judges.

[8] Article 154 of Law no. 4964/2022.

[9] Articles 155–156 of Law no. 4964/2022.

[10] Article 148 of Law no. 4964/2022.

[11] Article 143(3) of Law no. 4964/2022.

[12] Article 147(1) of Law no. 4964/2022.

[13] Article 157 of Law no. 4964/2022.

What are the Sharia rules in the Greek legal order that still regulate divorce of Greek Muslim couples, such as Angela and Kemal, before a special Greek Sharia court?

The Sharia court dissolves the marriage upon the husband's sole request. At the same time, it decides the issue of the "contractual Mahr (dowry) amount" (a donation due to dissolution of marriage),[14] and of the minimum three months' alimony to the wife (nafaqah). Based on a relevant opinion of the Mufti of Komotini[15] and the jurisprudence of the Sharia Courts, there are three reasons for a dissolution of marriage: mutual consent of the spouses; serious reasons (fault); and a unilateral declaration of the husband. The issue of alimony is also relevant in the sense that, depending on the grounds for divorce, alimony was (or was not) awarded.

a) Dissolution by mutual consent (hul)

Dissolution of marriage by mutual consent (hul) is very common. The two spouses appear in person, or inform the Sharia Court (through a lawyer, representative or by telephone) that they jointly wish to dissolve their marriage. The Court registers their joint will and dissolves the marriage; it orders the ex-spouses to refrain from marital relations. Research on all Muslim divorces by mutual consent between 1991 and 2013 confirms that a divorce by mutual consent requires the wife's explicit renunciation (tefrik) of her rights to Mahr/Dowry and of the three months' alimony.[16] The wife's renunciation of her rights is also found in cases of divorce by mutual consent in which the religious court—incidentally—holds her responsible for the husband's violent behaviour.[17]

In addition, there are (rare) cases in which the wife renounces the right to custody of her children, as such quite surprising.[18] In one case, the wife eventually

---

[14] The Holy Quran, *Women*, D', verse 24.

[15] Opinion of the Mufti of Komotini (protocol no. 173/00/F.56/10.5.2000, attached to Civil First Instance Court of Xanthi, dec. no. 344/2000). According to article 146(6) of Law no. 4964/2022, besides his judicial responsibilities, the Mufti has the responsibility to give his opinion on issues related to the Holy Muslim Law (i.e. the fetwa).

[16] Sharia Court of Komotini, dec. nos. 48/1990, 4/1992, 52/1993, 33/1994, 59/1994, 89/1994, 15/1995, 38/1995, 43/1996, 74/1997, 12/1998, 35/1998, 25/1999, 69/1999, 7/2000, 21/2000, 50/2000, 3/2001, 4/2001, 8/2001, 12/2001, 15/2001, 24/2001, 51/2002, 63/2002, 88/2002, 8/2003, 30/2003, 32/2003, 257/2003, 4/2004, 48/2004, 52/2004 and 57/2004. Sharia Court of Xanthi, dec. nos. 26/1992, 17/1995, 78/1995, 100/1997, 29/1999, 88/1999, 129/1999, 37/2000, 92/2002, 150/2003, 6/2004, 39/2004 and 41/2004. Sharia Court of Didymoteicho, dec. nos. 28/1996, 15/2000, 17/2003 and 23/2003. All the above decisions were declared enforceable by the competent Civil Court of First Instance.

[17] Sharia Court of Xanthi, dec. no. 53/1995; Sharia Court of Xanthi, dec. no. 72/1997; and Sharia Court of Xanthi dec. no. 72/2001. All the above decisions were declared enforceable by the competent Civil Court of First Instance.

[18] Sharia Court of Komotini, dec. no. 70/1979; Sharia Court of Komotini, dec. no. 35/1993; Sharia Court of Xanthi, dec. no. 65/1978. All the above decisions were declared enforceable by the competent Civil Court of First Instance.

declared that she was giving up her rights so that the marriage could finally be dissolved, after her successive applications for divorce had been rejected by the Sharia Court.[19]

In other words, by divorcing by mutual consent, Greek Muslim women effectively "buy" their freedom from the constraints of marriage.

b) Dissolution on serious reasons (fault)

At the request of one of the spouses, the Sharia Court may also dissolve the marriage if, after a brief investigation, it finds that there is a serious reason (fault) relating to the other spouse. It has been said that such serious reasons, regardless of whether they burden the man or the woman, are the abandonment of the marital home,[20] extramarital affairs,[21] inharmonious marital partnership,[22] absence of carnal contact[23] and change of religion, as by conversion to Christianity.[24] It is important to note that even then, the Sharia Court generally does not order the husband to pay the wife's Mahr/Dowry and the three months' alimony.[25] In this respect, decision no. 25/2003 of the Court is typical: Although the husband was described as having "disappeared" (in a state of oblivion?) for at least five years, the wife was forced to relinquish the custody of her minor children, which she had

[19] Sharia Court of Xanthi, dec. no. 12/1999. The decision was declared enforceable by the competent Civil Court of First Instance.

[20] Sharia Court of Komotini, dec. nos. 19/1989, 10/1991, 16/1994, 71/1994, 81/1994, 70/1996, 11/1999, 42/1999, 12/2001, 25/2003 and 38/2004. Sharia Court of Xanthi, dec. nos. 26/1991, 47/1991, 67/1994, 29/1997, 83/1997, 87/1997, 89/1997, 124/1999, 60/2000, 142/2000, 165/2003 and 34/2004. All the above decisions were declared enforceable by the competent Civil First Instance Court.

[21] Sharia Court of Komotini, dec. no. 7/1992; Sharia Court of Komotini, dec. no. 18/1996; Sharia Court of Komotini, dec. no. 31/2002; Sharia Court of Komotini 47/2002; Sharia Court of Komotini, dec. no. 53/2003; Sharia Court of Xanthi, dec. no. 68/1997. Sharia Court of Xanthi, dec. no. 48/1978; Sharia Court of Xanthi, dec. no. 115/1995; Sharia Court of Xanthi, dec. no. 48/1998; Sharia Court of Xanthi, dec. no. 48/2002. All the above decisions were declared enforceable by the competent Civil Court of First Instance.

[22] Sharia Court of Xanthi, dec. no. 47/1966; Sharia Court of Xanthi, dec. no. 56/2000; Sharia Court of Xanthi, dec. no. 231/2003; Sharia Court of Xanthi, dec. no. 12/2004; and Sharia Court of Xanthi, dec. no. 41/2004. Also, Sharia Court of Komotini, dec. no. 48/1990. All the above decisions were declared enforceable by the competent Civil Court of First Instance.

[23] Sharia Court of Xanthi, dec. no. 68/1982; Sharia Court of Xanthi, dec. no. 14/1988; Sharia Court of Xanthi, dec. no. 32/1988; Sharia Court of Xanthi, dec. no. 42/1998; and Sharia Court of Xanthi, dec. no. 49/1998. Also, Sharia Court of Komotini, dec. no. 48/1990. All the above decisions were declared enforceable by the competent Civil Court of First Instance.

[24] Sharia Court of Komotini, dec. no. 65/1985; Sharia Court of Komotini, dec. no. 4/2001 (Fetwas, unpublished). All the above decisions were declared enforceable by the competent Civil Court of First Instance.

[25] Sharia Court of Xanthi, dec. no. 95/1996; Sharia Court of Xanthi, dec. no. 68/1997; Sharia Court of Xanthi, dec. no. 69/1997. All the above decisions were declared enforceable by the competent Civil Court of First Instance.

exercised until then, in order for her divorce petition to be admitted by the Court. Eventually, custody was awarded to the paternal grandmother.[26]

c) Dissolution by unilateral declaration of the husband (talāq)

Dissolution of marriage by unilateral declaration of the husband (talāq) is found in a limited number of divorce decrees issued by a Greek Sharia Court.[27] In these cases, the husband gives some reason, but the dissolution of the marriage is essentially based on his unilateral will to end the marriage, even if the wife objects.[28] Moreover, in these cases, the Sharia Court does not verify the seriousness of the grounds for divorce, nor does he verify their accuracy, with witnesses or in any other way. In fact, the Court usually does not even summon the separated wife to appear before him and oppose the divorce petition.[29] However, if the wife is summoned and does not appear, the mufti punishes her by depriving her of the Mahr/Dowry and her alimony.[30] If the wife objects, the Court dissolves the marriage without examining her objection, but orders the husband to pay both her Mahr/Dowry and her alimony.[31]

d) Alimony

Along with the dissolution of the marriage, the Sharia Court also resolves the issue of the payment of the Mahr/Dowry and of the minimum three months' alimony ("nafaqa") to the wife. According to Sharia law, the amount and nature of the Mahr/Dowry is explicitly written down in the marriage license—i.e. it was predetermined at another time. It is usually expressed in Ottoman gold lira; in most cases, the Sharia Court orders the payment of a sum of money of the same value.[32]

At first sight, their practical importance is not insignificant, since they limit the ease with which a Muslim marriage can be dissolved, while at the same time improving the financial situation of the divorced Muslim woman. This is indeed

[26] Sharia Court of Komotini, dec. no. 25/2003. See, also, Sharia Court of Xanthi, dec. no. 69/1992. All the above decisions were declared enforceable by the competent Civil Court of First Instance.

[27] Sharia Court of Xanthi, dec. no. 104/1981 and Sharia Court of Xanthi, dec. no. 78/1990. Although they avoid using the term "ouster", the following decisions of the Sharia Court of Komotini are based on the same way of dissolution of marriage: nos. 23/1987, 70/1987, 10/1997, 70/1998. All the above decisions were declared enforceable by the competent Civil Court of First Instance.

[28] Sharia Court of Komotini, dec. no. 50/2002. The above decision was declared enforceable by the competent Civil Court of First Instance.

[29] Sharia Court of Xanthi, dec. no. 96/1986. The above decision was declared enforceable by the competent Civil Court of First Instance.

[30] Sharia Court of Xanthi, dec. no. 10/1994. The above decision was declared enforceable by the competent Civil Court of First Instance.

[31] Sharia Court of Komotini, dec. no. 55/2002. The above decision was declared enforceable by the competent Civil Court of First Instance.

[32] Sharia Court of Xanthi, dec. no. 115/1995; Sharia Court of Xanthi, dec. no. 48/1998; Sharia Court of Komotini, dec. no. 50/2002. The above decisions were declared enforceable by the competent Civil Court of First Instance.

true in the few cases of dissolution by unilateral declaration by the husband or of dissolution on the grounds of the husband's liability. However, in cases of divorce by consent, which are by far the majority, the wife renounces ("tefrik") not only the Mahr/Dowry and alimony, but often also custody of the children.

However, it is not clear whether the payment of Mahr/Dowry is a condition of divorce, or whether it is a transaction (independent of marriage) to compensate the wife for her loyalty to her husband, as allegedly provided for in the Qur'an.[33]

In the event that the husband is responsible for the dissolution of the marriage, the Sharia Court orders the payment of alimony (nafaqa) to the wife until the end of the "insurance" period. According to the Sharia,[34] the "insurance" period lasts for three months, which is essentially the time of what is understood as the woman's three periods of purity, i.e. periods during which she does not menstruate.[35] During the "insurance" period, the divorced woman also cannot remarry,[36] meant to ensure the paternity of the children based on their conception during the marriage.

The Sharia, as interpreted and applied by Greek Sharia courts, may be seen as the most anachronistic part of Islam. Even if one overcomes the essential conflict between the legal order of the Sharia and that of liberal Western constitutions and international conventions on the protection of human rights,[37] one cannot help but come to a standstill. Namely, the rules applied in Greece contain elements of conservatism, remaining officially unchanged since the beginning of the twentieth century, with no authority to modify them (in Islamic states, modification is slow, but possible, through the amendment of legislation, e.g. the Civil Code, which incorporates them). Also, the rules contain elements of arbitrariness, as no one but the local Mufti may verify the interpretation of the Sharia, because there is no provision for a Sharia court of second instance. Also, the special judicial review by civil courts provided for by Laws Nos 1920/1991 and 4964/2022[38] is not an effective remedy.[39]

---

[33] The Holy Quran, *Women*, D', verse 38; The Holy Quran, Women, D', verse 28.

[34] The Holy Quran, *The Cow*, B', verse 228.

[35] The only exception was Sharia Court of Xanthi, dec. no. 220/2003 (declared enforceable by Civil First Instance Court of Xanthi): the Sharia Court granted alimony to the woman for five years, without elaborating on the reasons why it moved away from the three months period, while also limiting itself to five years.

[36] See, for instance, Sharia Court of Xanthi, dec. no. 14/1988; and Sharia Court of Xanthi, dec. no. 47/1966. The above decisions were declared enforceable by the competent Civil Court of First Instance.

[37] See PACE, Resolution 2253 (2019), «Sharia, the Cairo Declaration and the European Court of Human Rights», 22 January 2019. PACE, Resolution 1704 (2010). "Freedom of religion and other human rights for non-Muslim minorities in Turkey and for the Muslim minority in Thrace (eastern Greece)," 27 January 2010. *Refah Partisi (The Welfare Party) and others v. Turkey*.

[38] See footnote 1.

[39] See *Molla Sali v. Greece*, §48: "Studying the case-law of the courts of first instance on this subject, legal commentators have noted that those courts do not in fact perform a proper review of constitutionality, but in most cases formally ratify the mufti's decision. Between 2007 and 2014, for example, the Xanthi and Rodopi courts declared enforceable 390 decisions by the Mufti of

3 Greek Civil Courts and Sharia Law

Two days before the hearing of the *Molla Sali* case at the Grand Chamber of the ECHR (4.12.2017), the Greek government introduced a bill in the Parliament to abolish the special regulations imposing recourse to Sharia law before Greek civil courts for the settlement of family-law and inheritance-law cases within the Muslim minority.[40] The draft law was adopted and its relevant provisions came into force on 11 October 2018.[41] According to them, recourse to Sharia Law (in matters of marriage, divorce, or inheritance) is now only possible (a) before the Sharia Courts and (b) with the agreement of all those concerned.[42] Therefore, from 2018 onwards, in order for Sharia Law to be applied, all parties must make an application to the Sharia courts. If one party disagrees, the Greek civil courts are automatically competent.

Xanthi and 476 decisions by the Mufti of Komotini respectively, and refused to do so in 34 and 17 cases respectively". For complete statistics, see Ktistakis, p. 141.

See also the report issued on 21 April 2009 by the Committee on Legal Affairs and Human Rights of the Parliamentary Assembly of Council of Europe, entitled "Freedom of religion and other human rights of non-Muslim minorities in Turkey and of the Muslim minority in Thrace (eastern Greece)", noted the following (§55): "The implementation of Sharia Law can also raise problems, and the rapporteur is particularly concerned about information from one of the Committee's experts to the effect that 99% of the muftis' decisions are ratified by the Greek courts, even where they infringe women's and children's rights as laid down in the constitution or the ECHR".

[40] The explanatory report pointed out that case-law and legal opinion had dealt with various aspects of the application of Sharia law and the issue of the hierarchy of certain provisions and their ranking in the domestic legal order, as well as their conformity with the Constitution and European human rights standards. The report acknowledged that the Greek State had not acted on this matter for ninety-seven years, during which time conceptions, practices and traditions had evolved at both international and national levels. The report pointed out that the State should not be a mere onlooker during a legal debate and should no longer leave it to the judiciary to resolve important issues that affected Greek citizens.

[41] Although Article 162 of Law No. 4964/2022, introduced on 30.07.2022, repealed the above-mentioned Law No. 4511/2018 (See footnote 6), Article 146 of the said Law (No. 4964/2022) enshrines the same provisions, reiterating that Greek nationals of Muslim faith, concerning their personal matters, may choose to adopt either civil or Islamic religious law.

[42] The relevant provisions of Law no. 4511/2018, read as follows: "1. … (a) The cases mentioned in subsection 2 above shall be governed by the provisions of ordinary law, and shall only exceptionally come under the jurisdiction of the mufti, that is to say where both parties jointly request that he settle a dispute in accordance with Islamic holy law … If one of the parties does not wish to submit the case to the mufti, that party may apply to the civil courts …, which are deemed to have jurisdiction in all cases […] (c) Inheritance matters relating to members of the Thrace Muslim minority shall be governed by the provisions of the Civil Code, unless the testator makes a notarised declaration of his or her last wishes … explicitly stating his or her wish to make the succession subject to the rules of Islamic holy law.' 2. Any wills drawn up before the entry into force of this Law in respect of which the property has not yet been transferred shall normally take legal effect at the time they are opened … .".

Obviously, this law was influenced by the *Molla Sali* case. There, the applicant's husband was a member of the Muslim community in Thrace. On his death, the applicant inherited all of his property under a notarised will drawn up in accordance with the Civil Code. A first instance court approved the will, the applicant accepted the estate and registered the property transferred to her. But the deceased's two sisters challenged the will. They were unsuccessful before the courts of first and second instance, but the Court of Cassation found that, pursuant to the Treaty of Athens,[43] matters of inheritance in the Muslim minority were to be settled according to Sharia law, according to which notarised wills drawn up by Greek nationals of Muslim faith were devoid of legal effect (Sharia law only recognises intestate succession and Islamic wills). As a result, the applicant lost three-quarters of the property her husband had bequeathed to her. The Chamber relinquished the case to the Grand Chamber. The latter examined her complaints under Article 14 of the ECHR ("Prohibition of discrimination") in conjunction with Article 1 of Protocol No. 1 to the ECHR ("Protection of property"), focusing on the refusal to apply the Civil Code given the Muslim faith of the testator. In its ruling, the Grand Chamber found a violation of these provisions.[44]

This is the first time that the ECtHR has considered the application of Sharia law by a national court against the wishes of the applicant. It did so through the prism of Article 14, focusing on the difference in treatment between the beneficiaries of a will made under the Civil Code by a Muslim testator, on the one hand, and a non-Muslim testator, on the other. While the ECtHR accepted that Greece may have wished to take into account its international obligations and the situation of the Thracian minority, it considered that the reasons for the difference in treatment at issue, derived in particular from international obligations, were not convincing. The ECtHR concluded that there was no objective and reasonable justification for the discriminatory treatment complained of.

The ECtHR also held that it could not be assumed that a testator of Muslim faith, having drawn up a will in accordance with the Civil Code, had automatically waived his right, or that of his beneficiaries (i.e. Molla Sali), not to be discriminated against on grounds of religion. The State could not assume the role of a guarantor of the minority identity of a particular group in its population to the detriment of the members of that group, who would be forced to choose not to belong to it or not to follow its practices and rules. The Grand Chamber stated:

> Refusing members of a religious minority the right to voluntarily opt for and benefit from ordinary law amounts not only to discriminatory treatment but also to a breach of a right of cardinal importance in the field of protection of minorities, that is to say the right to free self-identification. The negative aspect of this right, namely the right to choose not to be treated as a member of a minority, is not limited in the same way as the positive aspect of that right … . The choice in question is completely free, provided it is informed. It must be respected both by the other members of the minority and by the State itself. That is supported by Article 3 §1 of the Council of Europe Framework Convention for the

---

[43] See footnote 4.

[44] See footnote 3.

> Protection of National Minorities which provides as follows: "no disadvantage shall result from this choice or from the exercise of the rights which are connected to that choice". The right to free self-identification is not a right specific to the Framework Convention. It is the "cornerstone" of international law on the protection of minorities in general. This applies especially to the negative aspect of the right: no bilateral or multilateral treaty or other instrument requires anyone to submit against his or her wishes to a special regime in terms of protection of minorities".[45]

For the ECtHR, the comparative position was very clear. Outside private international law (and the possibility of applying Sharia law as a source of foreign law in the event of a conflict of laws, subject to the requirements of public policy), only France had officially applied some provisions of Sharia law, to citizens of one of its overseas territories (Mayotte), and this limited application of Sharia law had ended in 2011.[46] In the United Kingdom, the application of Sharia law by Sharia Councils is accepted only in so far as recourse to it remains voluntary.[47] This left Greece, at the time of the judgment, the only country in Europe to allow for the application of Sharia law, both before Greek Sharia Courts and Greek Civil Courts, to some of its citizens against their will.

According to a recent study carried out by the Greek National Commission for Human Rights,[48] thus after the application of Sharia law was limited to special Sharia courts, the number of cases before they received dropped by more than 40%. In other words, when Greek Muslims were allowed by law to have access to civil law before the Civil Courts, the overwhelming majority chose that.

4 Conclusion

As such, the ECtHR's *Molla Sali* judgment changed the lives of many Greek Muslim women. Before the judgment, Sharia Courts had compulsory jurisdiction over all their personal matters. Moreover, the Civil Courts either refused to apply

---

[45] See *Molla Sali v. Greece*, §157. See also the report issued on 21 April 2009 by the Committee on Legal Affairs and Human Rights of the Parliamentary Assembly of Council of Europe, entitled "Freedom of religion and other human rights of non-Muslim minorities in Turkey and of the Muslim minority in Thrace (eastern Greece)", noted the following (§55): "The implementation of Sharia Law can also raise problems, and the rapporteur is particularly concerned about information from one of the Committee's experts to the effect that 99% of the muftis' decisions are ratified by the Greek courts, even where they infringe women's and children's rights as laid down in the constitution or the ECHR.

[46] Guillaumont (2003), p. 43–57.

[47] Torrance (2019).

[48] In cooperation with the Law School of the Democritus University of Thrace, the official conclusions were published on 13 March 2020: "The attitude of the Thracian courts of first instance towards the decisions of the Thracian courts of appeal [2013 to 2019]". The research was conducted by the author of this article with the assistance of postgraduate students, within the framework of the protocol of cooperation between the Faculty and the Greek National Commission for Human Rights. See National Report (2020).

civil law and declared themselves incompetent to deal with Muslim women's personal matters, referring them to the Sharia Courts. Or, as in the case of *Molla Sali*, the Cicil Courts adjudicated personal matters cases based on Sharia law themselves, rather than apply the Civil Code. Given the Sharia rules described in the first part of this article, discrimination against women was obvious. **This underscores the necessity of applying a gender perspective in judicial analysis—not merely in the sense of safeguarding women's rights in individual cases, but by ensuring that legal systems and judicial reasoning incorporate gender sensitivity as a foundational interpretive approach. Such a perspective reveals how formal rules, neutral on their face, may perpetuate substantive inequality unless critically examined through the lens of lived gendered experiences.**

Even before the *Molla Sali* case was heard, the modernisation of the relevant legislation had been initiated; it became mandatory under Article 46 of the Convention after the *Molla Sali* judgment was published. Today, the situation is insofar compatible with rule of law principles. But the question of the jurisdiction of the Sharia Courts remains. In light of the European Convention of Human Rights and all relevant international treaties, is there room for a valid waiver by Greek Muslim women of their procedural and substantive rights, as provided for in the law currently in force,[49] to be adjudicated by Sharia courts based on their interpretation of the Sharia? **Any future assessment of such waivers must also incorporate a gender-sensitive legal analysis—one that examines the structural pressures that may influence a woman's 'choice' to forego equal rights protections and the broader implications of legitimizing parallel systems that operate without gender equality guarantees.** In the future, this may be question courts have to answer as well, based on the equality standard guaranteed by the Convention, as interpreted by the ECtHR.

[49] Paragraph 10 of Article 146 of Law No. 4964/2022 read as follows: "a) The cases referred to in para. 8 [personal matters disputes] shall be governed by the ordinary rules [Civil Code] and shall only exceptionally come under the jurisdiction of the Mufti if both parties to the dispute request him to settle the dispute in accordance with the sacred Muslim law. The submission of the case to the jurisdiction of the Mufti is irrevocable and excludes the jurisdiction of the ordinary courts over the dispute in question. If one of the parties does not wish to submit his case to the jurisdiction of the Mufti, he may appeal to the civil courts in accordance with the ordinary substantive and procedural rules, which shall in any case have a presumption of jurisdiction. (b) The succession of members of the Muslim minority in Thrace shall be governed by the provisions of the Civil Code, unless the testator draws up before a notary a testamentary disposition in the form of a public will, the sole content of which is his express wish to have his succession governed by Muslim law. This declaration is freely revocable, either by a subsequent declaration to the contrary before a notary or by the drawing up of a subsequent will, in accordance with the provisions of the Civil Code. It is forbidden to apply both the Civil Code and the Islamic Shari'a simultaneously to the inherited property or to a percentage or to certain elements of it".

References

Literature

Guillaumont O (2003) La Constitution et le statut civil de droit local applicable à Mayotte: état de réformes entreprises et des questions en suspens après la loi du 11 juillet 2001 relative à Mayotte. Civitas Europa 11(1):43-57

Ktistakis Y (2013) Charia, Tribunaux Religieux et Droit Grec. Istos, Istanbul

Roucounas E (1981) Compétence du Moufti pour connaître des matières qui relèvent du statut personnel des ressortissants grecs de religion musulmane. Revue hellénique de droit international 34(1):151-157

Torrance D (2019) Sharia Law Courts in the UK. House of Commons, at https://researchbriefings.files.parliament.uk/documents/CDP-2019-0102/CDP-2019-0102.pdf

Online Database

The HUDOC database of the European Court of Human Rights case-law, https://hudoc.echr.coe.int

Ktistakis I (2020) Research. Law School of the Democritus University of Thrace and Greek National Commission for Human Rights. National Report 2020, https://www.nchr.gr/images/pdf/aithsies_ektheseis/2020/2020_final_compressed.pdf (republished: https://www.constitutionalism.gr/2020-ktistakis-ierodikeia/)

Case Law

ECtHR, *Molla Sali v. Greece* [GC], No. 20452/14, Judgment 19 December 2018 (merits)

ECtHR, *Molla Sali v. Greece* [GC], No. 20452/14, Judgment 18 June 2020 (just satisfaction)

ECtHR, *Refah Partisi (The Welfare Party) and others v. Turkey*, Nos. 41340/98, 41342/98, 42343/98 and 41344/98, Judgment 13 February 2003

Ioannis Ktistakis is a judge of the European Court of Human Rights. Prior to that, he was an associate Professor of Public International Law at the Faculty of Law, Democritus University of Thrace [Komotini-Greece], assistant Professor at the Faculty of Political Science and International Relations, Boğaziçi University [Istanbul-Turkey] and visiting Professor at Faculty of Law, George Washington University [Washington DC—USA]. Former memberships included the Executive Board of European Union Monitoring Centre on Racism and Xenophobia, the Greek Equal Treatment Committee and the Greek National Commission for Human Rights. He has over 57 publications on issues related to public international law, European human rights law, immigration law, environmental law and religious freedom.

Part VI
Histories

Roman Woman on Trial: Limited Access to Justice

Mirjana Miškić

Abstract In the ancient Roman world, justice was not accessible to everyone. Due to prejudices rooted in the law regarding natural inferiority *(imbecillitas mentis)*, sexual weakness *(infirmitas sexus)*, and lightness of the spirit *(levitatem animi)*, it was almost impossible and utterly disgraceful for a woman to speak in public. A woman could bring a request *(postulare)* on her behalf only in civil cases. If she was under the *tutela mulierum*, she would need authorisation from her tutor. She was not generally allowed to represent others in court. Classical jurists associated this with the general ban on women interceding for another, outlined in the first century S. C. Velleanum. Also, she was denied the right to access litigation as a witness. Women were also restricted from bringing accusations in criminal procedures *(iudicium publicum)*, such as murder or adultery, unless they or a close relative were victims. Another exclusion of women's access to court is the impossibility of women to report to the fiscal court the persons who have not paid inheritance tax. As we can see, women´s right to initiate legal proceedings was restricted, as well as the right of representation and testimony. However, in Roman history, there were examples of women who overcame legal obstacles and managed to make a mark in Roman litigation. While trying to overcome the patriarchal Roman justice system, they faced condemnations in the form of infamy and calumnia. This paper sheds light on these pioneering women, but also emphasizes the enduring legacy of their exclusion and highlights the importance of developing gender-sensitive judicial reasoning today.

M. Miškić (✉)
Faculty of Law, University of Banja Luka, Banja Luka, Bosnia and Herzegovina
e-mail: mirjana.miskic@pf.unibl.org

© The Author(s), under exclusive license to Springer Nature Switzerland AG 2025

S. Baer et al. (eds.), *The Gender and the Judiciary*, Gender Perspectives in Law 7,
https://doi.org/10.1007/978-3-032-06885-9_16

1 Introduction

According to the ancient legal standards, adult Roman women enjoyed certain aspects of freedom in social and economic affairs. Those rights were not granted to women in early periods when they were placed under the *patria potestas* of the father or *manus* of the husband. Constrained by the power of the *paterfamilias*, or the *manus* of the husband, they could not obtain any property rights.[1] As women lacked the ability to own property, they were also unable to assert any legal claims. They could not serve as witnesses to formal legal acts or represent others in court. If they could not assert any legal claims in court or be considered a legal party, they were also ineligible as witnesses in court. According to the old civil law, a *testamentum* could only be made in one of two ways: by an oral declaration on the eve of battle, when the legion was drawn up in line *(in procinctu),* or by publication in an assembly called *comitia calata*, whose assent was necessary to the validity of the will. Both ways of making the will were only available to men, considering that women could not act as soldiers in Roman legions or participate in assemblies. Thus, based on the above, we can conclude that the right of property was reserved exclusively for men. On the other hand, women were not restricted from inheritance rights, although they were subject to strict patriarchal conditions. Roman women could make a will *per aes et libram* too, but there were some limitations: they had to have the consent of their tutor to make a will and beforehand, they needed to undergo *capitis deminutio*. This was a change of status that severed the agnatic ties.[2]

As per the Code of the Twelve Tables, a woman could inherit only if she was married with the *manus,* and a daughter could inherit only if she was under paternal power (person *alieni iuris*).[3] Consequently, upon entering the groom's household, the daughter would forfeit her inheritance rights within her own family. These provisions are viewed within the context of their time and are not typically regarded as discriminatory. The Code treated the son who would leave the family authority equally. However, over time, the heir's son, as a potential *pater familias,* becomes a more desirable successor.

In contrast to the preference for the *filli familias* as successors, with time, some women in Rome became very wealthy and influential. Despite facing legal restrictions on inheritance rights, their wealth tipically originated from inheritance. For

[1] Gaius, II, p. 96. Finally, it is to be observed that persons under power, in hand, or in mancipium, cannot acquire by surrender before a magistrate, for, as nothing can belong to such persons, it follows that they cannot vindicate anything as their own before a magistrate.

[2] Watson (1971), pp. 22–23, based on Cicero Topica 4.28 and Gaius, Institutiones 1.115a. Women who had been in manus had already undergone capitis deminutio when they had come into manus and did not have to do so again to make a will. Watson suggests that in earlier times only widows from a manus marriage were allowed to make a will, because their heirs in the case of intestacy were often not their natural relatives. By using capitis deminutio as a symbolic way to cut the agnatic ties, this rule was extended to women not married with manus.

[3] Raković, Miškić (2022), pp. 459–470.

instance, a wealthy widow from Oea in the second century B.C., Aemilia Pudentellia, possessed almost 4 million, a significant sum at the time.[4] Interestingly, her future husband, the philosopher Apuleio, was accused of being a fortune hunter and using magic to influence a rich widow into marriage. In court, he defended himself by pointing out that Aemilia Pudentillia was a well-educated woman,[5] making the case that she was an exception to the prevailing lack of education among women at that time.[6]

2 Roman Woman as a Defendant

The role of the woman in Roman trials was generally limited to three areas: serving as witnesses, being provided legal defence, or appearing as defendants. Female judges were not recognised in Roman society. For instance, in *D.5.1.12.2. Paulus, On the Edict, Book XVII,* women and slaves were customarily excluded from civil or public employments, not because of any deficiency in judgment but due to established norms. Despite being Roman citizens, women were denied the right to vote or hold political offices.[7]

Additionally, this exclusion extended to judicial duties, magisterial roles, litigation, suretyship, and legal representation:

> D.50.17.2. Ulpianus, On Sabinus, Book I. Women are excluded from all civil or public employments; therefore they cannot be judges, or perform the duties of magistrates, or bring suits in court, or become sureties for others, or act as attorneys.[8]

As they were not allowed to engage in the public interest of the Roman State, they typically did not receive legal education. Basic literacy and numeracy skills were generally considered sufficient for women. Some of them, from high society, were exceptions, such as Hortensia. Hortensia was the daughter of Quintus Hortensius Ortal, a famous lawyer and rival of Cicero who became consul in 69 BC and had allowed her daughter to get a higher education, the one the Romans reserved only for male children. Hortensia was the first known female jurist and practitioner of law. She is most famous for her brilliant speech delivered

[4] McClintock (2022), p. 113.

[5] Apuleius. Apulei Platonici Madaurensis, Pro se de magia liber (Apologia). Rudolf Helm. Lipsiae: B.G. Teubneri. 1912.

[6] Hemelrijk (1999).

[7] D.5.1.12.2. Paulus libro 17 ad edictum Non autem omnes iudices dari possunt ab his qui iudicis dandi ius habent: quidam enim lege impediuntur ne iudices sint, quidam natura, quidam moribus. Natura, ut surdus mutus: et perpetuo furiosus et impubes, quia iudicio carent. Lege impeditur, qui senatu motus est. Moribus feminae et servi, non quia non habent iudicium, sed quia receptum est, ut civilibus officiis non fungantur.

[8] D.50.17.2. Ulpianus libro primo ad Sabinus pr. Feminae ab omnibus officiis civilibus vel publicis remotae sunt et ideo nec iudices esse possunt nec magistratum gerere nec postulare nec pro alio intervenire nec procuratores existere.

at the beginning of the Second Triumvirate in 42. B.C. The second Triumvirate decided to levy strict taxes on 1400 wealthy Roman matrons to finance the impending civil war. The triumvirate's intention stemmed from a twofold rationale. The first and most well-known reason was to secure treasury revenues. The second, equally important reason, was to return to old customs and limit women's luxury and wealth. Influential and wealthy Roman women did not want to comply with this punishment and delegated Hortensia to advocate for their property rights. Hortensia demonstrated rhetorical skills and legal knowledge, which culminated in her famous speech before the triumvirate:

> Appian, Roman History, 4.32. You have already deprived us of our fathers, our sons, our husbands, and our brothers, whom you accused of having wronged you; if you take away our property also, you reduce us to a condition unbecoming our birth, our manners, our sex. If we have done you wrong, as you say our husbands have, proscribe us as you do them. But if we women have not voted any of you public enemies, have not torn down your houses, destroyed your army, or led another one against you; if we have not hindered you in obtaining offices and honors,—why do we share the penalty when we did not share the guilt?[9]

> Appian, Roman History 4.33. "Why should we pay taxes wnen we have no part in the honors, the commands, the state-craft, for which you contend against each other with such harmful results? 'Because this is a time of war," do you say? When have there not been wars, and when have taxes ever been imposed on women, who are exempted by their sex among all mankind? Our mothers did once rise superior to their sex and made contributions when you were in danger of losing the whole empire and the city itself through the conflict with the Carthaginians. But then they contributed voluntarily, not from their landed property, their fields, their dowries, or their houses, without which life is not possible to free women, but only from their own jewellery, and even these not according to the fixed valuation, not under fear of informers or accusers, not by force and violence, but what they themselves were willing to give. What alarm is there now for the empire or the country? Let war with the Gauls or the Parthians come, and we shall not be inferior to our mothers in zeal for the common safety; but for civil wars may we never contribute, nor ever assist you against each other! We did not contribute to Caesar or to Pompey. Neither Marius nor Cinna imposed taxes upon us. Nor did Sulla, who held despotic power in the state, do so, whereas you say that you are re-establishing the commonwealth."[10]

Although we cannot consider this historical speech as a genuine representation in court -since it occurred in the forum due to women's exclusion from court-, this precedent left a significant impact on Roman history. Hortensia presented two important arguments. She utilised Roman law and employed *argumentum a contrario* to present her first point. Roman women were excluded from public offices; hence they were not obliged to pay taxes to fund those offices. Another crucial argument and rejection of women's participation in the civil war stemmed from the imposition of taxes against the will of the Roman matrons. Hortensia clearly stated that Roman matrons were willing to support their husbands and brothers in war, as they always had, but only against foreign enemies (such as Carthaginians, Gauls, or Parthians). With this sentence, she clearly condemned the civil war and the mutual

[9] Appian's Roman History (translated by Horace White), Massachusetts 1961.
[10] Appian's Roman History (translated by Horace White), Massachusetts 1961.

struggle for male supremacy. Women clearly positioned themselves as neutral in a senseless, costly and exhausting civil war. Although said in defence of the Roman matrons, this can be interpreted as an open criticism of the Roman patriarchal government, which permitted the fratricidal war and all its negative societal consequences (such as proscriptions). Hortensia, as a very skilled spokeswoman, successfully defended the property rights of the majority of women, with a successful outcome of only 400 out of 1400 women being taxed. This was a great success for Roman matrons and a notable improvement in Roman litigation.[11] Women were given the opportunity to be heard in court and allowed to defend the interests of others (women). In this particular case, the woman served both as a defendant and as legal defence. It is worth mentioning the opinion of Valerius Maximus, who described women who successfully defended themselves in court, including Maesia Sentia, as Androgyne, meaning imbued with the masculine spirit *(quia sub specie feminae uirilem animum gerebat, Androgynen appellabant.).*[12]

Regarding the case of Maesia Sentia,[13] there is limited information about its nature, specifically the crime with which she was charge. It appears to have been a serious offense, as none of the men were willing to defend her, and the praetor himself, L. Titio, sat among the judges. Valerius Maximus speaks with great sympathy of Maesiae Sentiae, admiring her courage and ability to defend herself *(non solum diligenter, sed etiam fortiter executa)*, without condemnation. However, he describes her as Androgynen *("quia sub specie feminae uirilem animum gerebat*"), suggesting that she possessed a masculine spirit in a woman's body, and asserting that rhetorical talent and rational argumentation belong to the male domain. The violation of legal and social conventions, leading to women intruding into the male domain, is considered so serious that Valerius Maximus must explain it in a patriarchal context. Although he welcomes her ability to defend herself, he clearly emphasises that such a precedent was possible only because women possessed male talents of argumentation.

Another intriguing case is the one of Manilia, a prostitute brought to court by Aedilus curulis Hostilius Mancinus. He accused her of hitting him with a stone when he approached her home at night.[14] Manilia defended herself in court *(tribune plebis),*

[11] Valerius Maximus, Dicta et facta memorabilia, 8.3.3. Hortensia uero Q. Hortensi filia, cum ordo matronarum graui tributo a triumuiris esset oneratus nec quisquam uirorum patrocinium eis accommodare auderet, causam feminarum apud triumuiros et constanter et feliciter egit: repraesentata enim patris facundia impetrauit ut maior pars imperatae pecuniae his remitteretur. reuixit tum muliebri stirpe Q. Hortensius uerbisque filiae aspirauit, cuius si uirilis sexus posteri uim sequi uoluissent, Hortensianae eloquentiae tanta hereditas una feminae actione abscissa non esset.

[12] Valerius Maximus, Dicta et facta memorabilia, 8.3.1. Maesia Sentinas rea causam suam L. Titio praetore iudicium cogente maximo populi concursu egit modosque omnes ac numeros defensionis non solum diligenter, sed etiam fortiter executa, et prima actione et paene cunctis sententiis liberata est. quam, quia sub specie feminae uirilem animum gerebat, Androgynen appellabant.

[13] Marshall (1990), pp. 46–59.

[14] Aulus Gellius, Noctes Atticae, 4. 14. IV Narratur historia de Hostilio Mancino aedilium et Manilia meretrice; verbaque decreti tribunorum, ad quos a Manilia provocatum est. 1 Cum librum IX Atei Capitonis coniectaneorum legeremus, qui inscriptus est de iudiciis publicis, decretum tribunorum visum est gravitatis antiquae plenum. 2 Propterea id meminimus, idque ob hanc

pointing out the inappropriate behaviour of the *aedile curule*, who approached her house at night, likely drunk, and violently knocked on the door. In addition, it should be emphasised that the *aedile curule* was not injured, and that the charges against Manilia were dismissed. Although we consider this case a successful defence for a female defendant, the truth is that case against Manilia was not based on legal arguments. Aedilus curulis Hostilius Mancinus did not suffer physical injury from the thrown stone, thus there was no harm. The stone was thrown in self-defence, so illegality was excluded. Ultimately, *actio popularis* could not be invoked, as the stone-throwing was a provoked reaction to persistent calling and i knocking on the door late at night. Eventually, Hostilius Macinus was prepared to break down the door, and she was compelled to deter him by throwing stones in his direction. As we can see, Manilia was accused as an underprivileged woman, and Hostilius Macinus, expected as a prominent Roman magistrate, considered his word enough to accuse a prostitute. Unexpectedly, Manilia gave a well-grounded answer to the accusation and was acquitted of all allegations against her. Her main argument was that she dared to speak in public and tell the truth, which ultimately led to her acquittal. From the available sources, we do not learn whether Manilia accused Horatius Macinius of trespassing or whether the judges reacted to such an accusation. This would still be a contemporary interpretation of the situation rather than a possible epilogue at that time.

There is a wide range of cases involving women as defendants. As we can see, they could act in their own behalf *(pro se)* or on behalf of another *(pro alias)*. An exception to the general rule that women could be defendants in court involved very young girls under paternal authority.

> D.2.4.22. (Gaius) 2.4.22 Gaius libro primo ad legem duodecim tabularum pr. Neque impuberes puellas, quae alieno iuri subiectae essent, in ius vocare permissum est.

The most common female crimes were poisoning, adultery and premarital sex *(stuprum)*. Another crime that was exclusively applicable to women was drinking wine.[15] In the Annals, Tacitus recounts the trials of nine aristocratic women accused of practicing magic, often in conjunction with sexual misconduct or

---

causam et in hanc sententiam scriptum est: Aulus Hostilius Mancinus aedilis curulis fuit. 3 Is Maniliae meretrici diem ad populum dixit, quod e tabulato eius noctu lapide ictus esset, vulnusque ex eo lapide ostendebat. 4 Manilia ad tribunos plebi provocavit. 5 Apud eos dixit comessatorem Mancinum ad aedes suas venisse; eum sibi recipere non fuisse e re sua, sed cum vi inrumperet, lapidibus depulsum. 6 Tribuni decreverunt aedilem ex eo loco iure deiectum, quo eum venire cum corollario non decuisset; propterea, ne cum populo aedilis ageret, intercesserunt.

[15] Ius osculi or the right to a kiss was allowed to a husband or the closest male relative (father, father in law, brother). This practice was used to check that they had not drunk wine. In the case woman tests positive, husband is allowed to make severe punishment, even to kill his wife. This ancient practice is mentioned by Horace, in Carmina 3.12.3. as patruae verbera linguae ("the lashing of an uncle's tongue."). In Quaestiones Romanae 6, Plutarch addresses the custom of the so-called ius osculi, as well as Valerius Maximus in his Facta Memorabilia 6.3.9. and Pliny in HN 14.90.

treason, during the reigns of Tiberius, Claudius, and Nero.[16] Accusations of magic against women of these families served as attacks against the families themselves and played a role in the negotiation of authority and legitimacy during this period of political change.

Lenocinium is another crime in which woman, especially female slaves and wives, were involved. It was *lenocinium*, if husband allowed his wife to commit adultery in order to share a gain. The *Lex Iulia de adulteris* prohibited *lenocinium. (D. 48.5.2.2. Lenocinii quidem crimen lege Iulia de adulteris praescriptum est, cum sit in eum maritum poena statuta, qui de adulterio uxoris suae quid ceperit, item in eum, qui in adulterio deprehensam retinuerit.)*

3 Roman Woman as an Attorney in Court

When Hortensia successfully represented the collective protest of women (42 BC), it raised the question of wheater women could act as representatives in court. Some authors mention that following this, after Hortensia advocated for the property rights of 1400 Roman matrons, as well as Gaia Arfania,[17] a praetorian edict was promulgated prohibiting women from representing others in court (postulate *Pro aliis*). This effectively marked the end of the phenomenon of women's advocacy in the history of Roman law. This explanation is highlighted by several distinguished authors, including Benke.[18] However, there is no definitive evidence in Roman sources for the existence of such a praetorian edict. Benke argues that prior to the enactment of such an act, women enjoyed the same rights to litigation as men. This opinion aligns with the general consensus that the status of Roman women at the time of the adoption of the Law of the Twelve Tables was relatively equal to that of men.[19,20] Furthermore, the comparison between the rights of Roman women during the classical period and those of American and European women from the early twentieth century is well-known and often cited. It is believed that Roman women had more rights than their female counterpearts in Europe two thousand years later.[21]

However, even after Hortensia's and Gaia Cafrania's pioneering legal performances, women continued to be absent from court proceedings, except as parties, plaintiffs, or defendants. In addition, wives were not allowed to defend their husbands in court.

---

[16] Pollard (2014).

[17] In Digest it was preserved her full name Carfania. although the shortened form of the name is more often used.

[18] Benke (1996), p. 204.

[19] Stanojević (2004), pp. 191–193; Jovanović (1984).

[20] On the discrepancy between the legal and factual position of women in Rome, see Mirjana Bogunović (Miškić), Woman in Roman Law—subject or object of the law?, Proceedings of the Faculty of Law, Novi Sad—012, vol. 46, No. 2, pp. 539–550.

[21] Evans Grubbs (2002).

D. 47.10.2. Paulus libro 50 ad edictum

Quod si viro iniuria facta sit, uxor non agit, quia defendi uxores a viris, non viros ab uxoribus aequum est.

This represented yet another restriction on woman's legal capacity, alongside Lex Voconia,[22] SC Velleanum,[23] and Lex Oppia.[24]

However, despite this prevailing attitude, Gaia Cafrania emerged as an important female figure in Roman litigation.

D.3.1.1.5. Ulpianus, libro sexto ad edictim, Secundo loco edictum proponitur in eos, qui pro aliis ne postulent: in quo edicto excepit praetor sexum et casum, item notavit personas in turpitudine notabiles. Sexum: dum feminas prohibet pro aliis postulare. Et ratio quidem prohibendi, ne contra pudicitiam sexui congruentem alienis causis se immisceant, ne virilibus officiis fungantur mulieres: origo vero introducta est a Carfania improbissima femina, quae inverecunde postulans et magistratum inquietans causam dedit edicto. Casum: dum caecum utrisque luminibus orbatum praetor repellit: videlicet quod insignia magistratus videre et revereri non possit. Refert etiam Labeo publilium caecum asprenatis noni patrem aversa sella a Bruto destitutum, cum vellet postulare. Quamvis autem caecus pro alio postulare non possit, tamen et senatorium ordinem retinet et iudicandi officio fungitur. Numquid ergo et magistratus gerere possit? Sed de hoc deliberabimus. Exstat quidem exemplum eius, qui gessit: Appius denique Claudius Caecus consiliis publicis intererat et in senatu severissimam dixit sententiam de Pyrrhi captivis. Sed melius "milius" est, ut dicamus retinere quidem iam coeptum magistratum posse, adspirare autem ad novum penitus prohiberi: idque multis comprobatur exemplis.

Ulpian's text dates back to the III century A.D., around 210. A.D., and discusses the case of Gaia Cafrania, which may have occurred around 60 B.C. Ulpian uses it as an introductory argument to illustrate how a woman's gender presents an obstacle in advocating for the rights of others. It is interesting to mention that Tony Honorè describes Ulpian as potentially the first lawyer who, given the scale and influence of his work, could be considered a pioneer of the human rights movement.[25] Unfortunately, as evident from Ulpian's text, woman's rights were not included in the concept of human rights. Considering the time gap between the occurence of the case and Ulpian's writing about it, it is challenging to assess

---

[22] Lex Voconia was a law established in 169. B.C. Introduced by tribune plebis Q.Voconius Saxa and with support of the Cato the Elder, this law prohibited those who owned property valued at 1,00,000 asses to appoint woman as heir.

[23] The Senatus consultum Vellaeanum, dating from the first century AD, barred women from any kind of intercessio for another's debt, whether by way of suretyship, assumption of debt, co-debtorship for security purposes or granting real security. The idea was presumably to protect women, not versed in commercial transactions, from the dangers of taking on burdens which were of no personal benefit to them. There were numerous exceptions (eg if the woman was acting in her own interests, or if the creditor did not know that it was an intercession), which were even extended under post-classical law. However, in 556 AD, Justinian forbade any intercession by wives for their husbands' debts unless the loan was used for the benefit of the wife.

[24] The Lex Oppia was enacted during the Second Punic War to curb the display of luxury by Roman women. Its enactment was followed with great debate in the Forum Romanum.

[25] Honorè (2002), p. 76.

Ulpian's personal attitude toward the case based solely on the accepted positions of his predecessors. In his text, Ulpian unequivocally states that public offices are reserved exclusively for men *(ne virilibus officiis fungantur mulieres).* Apart from this indisputable fact and her belonging to the senatorial rank, little is known about Gaia Carfania. The reason behind her behaviour being perceived as shameless remains unclear.

In fact, the wife of the Senator Licinius Bucco, C. Afrania, was always ready to litigate on her own behalf before the praetor. She did so not because she lacked advocates, but because of her confident assertiveness. Her persistent and audacious conduct in the courts, uncommon for women of her time, made her the most notorious example of female vexatious litigation, to the extent that the name C. Afrania became used as a label for the offense [made up] by women's disapproved habits. She lived until the consulships of C. Caesar -his second- and P. Servilius [48 B.C.]: "certainly it must be recorded when such a monster died rather than when it was born".[26]

Valerius Maximus portrays this woman, identified as (C) Arfania, Senator Licinius Bucco's wife, as a respectable and affluent woman who leveraged her social status to wield influence over the court and judges. As we can conclude from this source, Gaia Afrania was a brave, daring and educated Roman matron who did not care much about social conventions. From a contemporary perspective, we may regard her as a woman ahead of her time, but Valerio Maximus views her as a dishonorable woman who disrupts litigation and confuses the judiciary. Contrary to the reception of Hortensia's political speech before the triumvirate, Varius Maximus condemns Gaius Afranius's behaviour as improper *(quod inpudentia abundabat).* One could not help but ponder the reason behind such a stark contrast between these two cases. One of the possible explanations is that Hortensia represented herself in court once, in order to prevent the taxation of women, while Gaia Afrania continuously appeared in court, acting not only for herself but also for others. Hortensia's isolated act was hailed as heroic, whereas her repeated attempts would not have been regarded in the same light. Another possible explanation is that Hortensia conducted herself more modestly, signaling to the Roman triumvirate that she respected the boundaries of acceptable female behaviour as per the Roman customs.[27]

Acting as an independent woman was walking a thin line.[28] The rare woman who dared to venture beyond patriarchal limits could only go as far as society

---

[26] Valerius Maximus. 8.3.2 C. Afrania vero, Licinii Bucconis senatoris uxor prompta ad lites contrahendas pro se semper apud praetorem verba fecit, non quod advocatis deficebatur, sed quod inpudentia abundabat. Itaque inusitatisfuro latratibus adsidue tribunalia exercendo muliebris calumniae notissimum exemplum evasit, adeo ut pro crimine inprobis feminarum moribus C. Afraniae nomen obiciatur. Prorogavit autem spiritum suum ad C. Caesarem iterum P. Servilium consules: tale enim monstrum magis quo tempore extinctum quam quo sit ortum memorae tradendum est.

[27] van Galen (2016), p. 21.

[28] van Galen (2016), p. 183.

permited. Also, every woman was judged through the lens of feminine virtues, with society expecting her interests to b exclusively confined to the domestic sphere. Limiting a woman's influence to childcare and the domestic sphere perpetuated the type of isolation[29] that the Roman patriarchal community institutionalised. Any Roman woman seeking to stand out in society had to exemplify Roman virtues such as honesty and morality.[30] Chastity *(castitas)* served as the moral standard that every Roman matron was expected to uphold, as *auctoritas* was inherent to the *paterfamilias*. Chastity, innocence, fidelity, and obedience were the ideals every Roman woman was supposed to embody.

We learn from another Ulpian fragment that good behaviour was expected from distinguished Roman matrons.

D. 50.16.46 Ulpianus libro 59 ad edictum

"Matrem familias" accipere debemus eam, quae non inhoneste vixit: matrem enim familias a ceteris feminis mores discernunt atque separant. Proinde nihil intererit, nupta sit an vidua, ingenua sit an libertina: nam neque nuptiae neque natales faciunt matrem familias, sed boni mores.

The modest life *(puditicia)* of a Roman matron implied her primary dedication to childbirth (according to the *ius liberorum* preferably three or four children) and child-rearing. Any intrusion into the male sphere *"contra pudicitiam sexui congruentem"* would result in a harsh condemnation by those who transgressed social norms. As we can gather from sources, Gaia Carfania conducted her legal affairs independently before the magistrate, which proved deeply unsettling for the Roman legal system, particularly for its male representatives. The conservative Roman patriarchy framed Gaia Carfania's case within gender stereotypes.

4 Roman Woman as a Witness

The term 'witness' originates from the Latin word 'testis', which literally means 'male testicles'. This etymology suggests that only men were considered as witnesses. The testimony was conducted by witnesses swearing an oath to testify truthfully, often by placing their right hand on their testicle. This act was symbolic, signifying their commitment to truthfulness, witnessed by their descendants. According to the third title in Book 22 De testibus, women are not explicitly

---

[29] In ancient times, her isolation could be understood literally, because the Roman matron was not allowed to leave the house without an escort, nor could she be approached on the street. In addition, it was usual that roman matron during her daily visit to the market or some other appropriate place, veil her head. Another possible and frequently practiced way of public appearance is in the curtained litters carried by slaves, both to avoid the filth in the streets and to stay concealed and unseen in public.

[30] Burns (2007), p. 5.

allowed to be witnesses, but they are not prohibited to be either. They are prohibited in one particular case: if they are convicted under the Lex de Adulteria.

> D.22.5.18. Paulus libro secundo de adulteriis Ex eo, quod prohibet lex Iulia de adulteriis testimonium dicere condemnatam mulierem, colligitur etiam mulieres testimonii in iudicio dicendi ius habere.

Considering the above, it can be concluded that women who have not been convicted of adultery, and thus are not subject to the Augustan law on adultery, were eligible to testify in court.

In the earliest period of Roman Law, women were not allowed to testify in court.[31] Under archaic procedures, testifying was considered a male duty because the testator had to vouch for a claim. Subsequently, as the role oftestimony evolved from collective vouching to simply providing evidence, women were eventually allowed to testify in court. This change occured because testimony was no longer exclusively a virile officium.[32]

As deduced from the sources, women rarely appear in court as witnesses. Several assumptions can be made about this phenomenon. Firstly, it is plausible that women, although allowed, were less frequently involved in legal matters, reducing their likelihood of being present to witness contracts or their execution. Consequently, their appearances in court, either as parties or as witnesses, where less common. Even when women did appear in court, they were often represented by men, except in cases where they lacked male relatives to represent them. Another possible speculation could be that women were considered as less credible witnesses than men, although there is no explicit evidence for this asssertion in the sources. However, it can be inferred from the general societal attitude towards women. As highlighted earlier, the most famous Roman jurists characterised the legal status of women as less favorable compared to men.[33] The possible reasons for such discrimination include notions of natural inferiority *(imbecillitas mentis)*, sexual weakness *(infirmitas sexus)*, and lightness of spirit *(levitatem animi)*. This common belief in the weakness of women, both in body and mind, conveniently justified their legal incapacities.

Following the Roman era, lack of legal capacity was associated with increasing female dependance. As a concequence of indissoluble marriage, legal unity of spouses was dominated by husband. He was a legal representive of his wife. Concerning feudal inheritance rights, first born son was prioritised, over the other siblings. In contrast to the Roman tradition, relatively modest dowries were typically supplied, rather than equal inheritance rights.[34] The patriarchal matrix formed in Roman law remained preserved until the twentieth century, when the formal recognition of women's rights began.

---

[31] Thomas (2002), p. 137.

[32] Feldner (2000), p. 381.

[33] D. 1.5.9. Papinianus, libro trigenisimo primo questionum
In multis iuris nostri articulis deterior est condicio feminarum quam masculorum.

[34] Angela M. Lucas, Woman in the Middle Ages. Religion, Marriage and Letter, Harvester Press 1983.

5 Conclusion

Considering the cases above regarding women in the litigation process, the first thing we notice is the legal inferiority of women. In the most ancient times, women were not allowed to appear in court as either plaintiffs or defendants, witnesses, or legal representatives. Over time and changing circumstances, women were allowed to defend themselves in court and to act on behalf of others. Several conclusions can be drawn about women acting in court. Firstly, it was unusual for a woman to appear in court, and only a few cases were recorded. It can be assumed that these exceptional circumstances were notable and therefore inevitably mentioned by Roman jurists. In addition, it is necessary to note that most of the mentioned women (excluding the case of the prostitute) were from the upper class. Another important point is that women from the upper class received some education, especially families with legal backgrounds. It can be reasonably presumed (with the exception mentioned) that appearing in court was not available to women of modest origins and low education. Secondly, in all recorded cases, women were successful in defending their rights or those of others. The third and most important inference is about public perception of women appearing in court. Although Roman jurists generally permitted women's participation in litigation, sympathy waned when a woman repeatedly appeared in court. According to Roman jurists, it was acceptable for a woman to defend herself when accused, initiate litigation when her rights were violated, and even give a witness statement. However, when one woman repeatedly appeared in court, either in her own name or on behalf of another, pointing out failures of State authorities and thus carving out a career in that way, Roman jurists viewed such endeavors as scandalous. It was regarded as interference in *officium*, which was reserved only for men. This reveals the embedded patriarchal assumptions in Roman legal thinking that continue to shape implicit biases in modern legal systems. As a result, it can be firmly concluded that the participation of women in Roman litigation was accepted only as an exception rather than a norm. In light of this historical exclusion, the paper underscores the modern-day need for gender competence in judicial reasoning. Understanding how legal exclusion was constructed through assumptions of inferiority, irrationality, or sexual impropriety should inform current efforts to train judges and legal actors to identify and challenge gendered bias in legal interpretation and decision-making.

References

Apuleius (1912) Apulei Platonici Madaurensis, Pro se de magia liber (Apologia). Helm R. B. G. Teubneri, Lipsiae

Benke N (1996) Woman in the courts: an old thorn in men's side. Michigan J Gen Law

Bogunović (Miškić) M Woman in Roman Law—subject or Object of the Law? Proc Fac Law Novi Sad 46(2):539–550

Burns J (2007) Great women of Imperial Rome: mothers and wives of Caesars. Routledge, New York
Evans Grubbs J (2002) Women and law in Roman Empire: a sourcebook on marriage, divorce and widowhood. Routledge, London
Feldner B (2000) Zum Auschluss der Frau vom Römischen Officium. Revue Internationale Des Droits de L'antiquité 62
Hemelrijk E (1999) Matrona docta: educated women in the Roman Elite from Cornelia to Julia Domna. Routledge, London
Honorè T (2002) Ulpian, pioneer of human rights. Oxford University Press, New York
Marshall AJ (1990) Roman ladies on trial: the case of Maesia of Sentinum. "Phoenix". 44. Toronto
Jovanović M (1984) Position of woman in the ancient Roman Law (master thesis). Faculty of Law University of Belgrade
Lucas AM (1983) Woman in the middle ages. Religion, marriage and letter. Harvester Press
McClintock A (2022) La ricchiezza femminile e la „Lex Voconia". Jovene
Pollard EA (2014) Magic accusations against women in Tacitus's Annals, in Daughters of Hecate: woman and magic. In: Stratton KB, Kelleres DS (eds) Ancient world, Oxford University Press, New York
Raković Đ, Miškić M (2022) Historical development of woman's inheritance rights, International Scientific Conference "Challenges and perspectives of the development of legal systems in the XXI century". Conference Proceedings, Banja Luka
Stanojević O (2004) Roman Law. Službeni list SFRJ
Thomas Y (2002) The Division of Sexes in Roman Law. In: Duby G, Perrot M (eds) A history of woman in the West, Harvard University Press, Massachusetts
van Galen CW (2016) Women and citizenship in the late Roman Republic and the early Empire (doctoral dissertation). Radbound University Nijmigen
Watson A (1971) The law of succession in the later Roman Republic. Oxford University Press
White H (1961) Appian's Roman History (trans: White H). Massachusetts

Mirjana Miškić is an Associate Professor at the Faculty of Law at the University of Banja Luka, where she teaches Roman Law and Legal Rhetoric. She obtained her LL.M degree (2010) and LL. D degree (2019) at Faculty of Law, University of Belgrade. She trained at reputable scientific institutions in Austria and Italy. Participated in a large number of international scientific conferences, scientific projects, both regional and European. So far, she has written and published more than twenty scientific papers. She primarily research issues of Roman law and Legal History, but also writes about contemporary issues in the field of reproductive law and gender studies. She speaks English and uses German and Italian.

Gender and the Judiciary in Medieval Serbia

Nina Kršljanin

Abstract This article aims to analyse gender roles and the position of women in the judiciary in medieval Serbia, focusing on sex and gender in all the key roles in the judiciary: witnesses and jurors, parties and judges. The sources present a somewhat conflicting picture. While only men could occupy official positions appointed by the State, feudal lords possessed the right to judge the tenants of their lands, and thus widowed noblewomen might have acted as judges in such a role. Regarding women as parties in court, the Law Code of Emperor Dušan (1349) proclaims that a poor widow who could not stand trial on her own has the right to appoint her representative. Does this mean that a woman was not allowed to appear as a party in court without a man representing her—or is it merely a beneficial socially motivated norm aimed at only those women who would have practical problems with presenting their case in court? A norm transplanted from Byzantine law in the fourteenth century limits the testimony of women exclusively to feminine matters. However, there is evidence of a woman witness in a late twelfth century heresy case—and before the Sabor (Parliament), no less—and women also appear as witnesses in documents from the late fourteenth century. Were the rights of women as witnesses subsequently limited, making the preserved early case a political exception, or was the transplanted limitation ignored in practice? Finally, a norm from the same Code clearly shows that both men and women could be jurors—but this sex-specific formulation is not consistently present in all manuscripts. I shall attempt to address all these complexities -and some other dilemmas- and present a nuanced picture of the gender (im)balance before the courts of medieval Serbia.

N. Kršljanin (✉)
Faculty of Law, University of Belgrade, Belgrade, Serbia
e-mail: nina.krsljanin@ius.bg.ac.rs

© The Author(s), under exclusive license to Springer Nature Switzerland AG 2025
S. Baer et al. (eds.), *The Gender and the Judiciary*, Gender Perspectives in Law 7,
https://doi.org/10.1007/978-3-032-06885-9_17

1 Introduction

The Middle Ages—if not all premodern periods of human history—are often perceived as a period characterised by predominant masculinity in most areas, and law is hardly an exception. The logical and grammatical subjects of most legal norms were male, and it is the delicate task of historian to discern whether women were implicitly excluded or, on the contrary, if lawmakers intended for the rules to apply to both sexes equally. Context usually plays a crucial role in making such interpretations. On the other hand, while less obvious in the normative sources, women often had a quite active role in a country's legal (and social, and economic) life.[1]

An additional problem that presents itself when researching the subject in medieval Serbia is that sources from practice for the period are very few in number. Due to the Ottoman conquest in the mid-fifteenth century, most of the sources from practice (contracts, verdicts etc.) were destroyed, and the surviving ones can literally be counted on the fingers. Our main sources are normative texts, mostly legal codes and ecclesiastical charters (charters issued to noble families and cities are also preserved more by way of exception), as well as narrative, hagiographical and historiographical sources, which can provide valuable glimpses of medieval life. However, these sources mostly concern monarchs, saints and other important personages, rather than the common men and women.

While the analysis here will be limited to procedural law, knowledge of substantive law can also help at least outline some points of procedure. Thus, it is worth underlining that both in Serbian law, as well as in Rhomaian (Byzantine)[2] law, which was the main source of legal transplants[3] in Serbia, women had full legal capacity. While the society of the time was undoubtedly patriarchal, and the dominance of men in the role of husbands and fathers particularly visible in marriage and family

---

[1] See an overview of the often overlooked, but economically significant working women in medieval cities in Rubin (2020), pp. 72–80, 84–86; for the activities of women in the Rhomaian Empire (more on term in next footnote), see Neville (2019), pp. 59–78.

[2] While the term "Byzantine" is dominant in modern scholarly literature, I feel that it does not reflect the reality of the Greek-speaking Empire that still viewed itself as Roman, even though it lost control over Rome itself and other Western territories; in addition, it has acquired a pejorative meaning. Thus, I prefer the term "Rhomaian", the Greek word for "Roman", the one that "Byzantines" most often used to describe themselves. Some authors prefer referring to the Empire and its denizens as "Eastern Roman" or even "Medieval Roman", terms I likewise find valid. *Cf.* Neville (2019), pp. 2–4; more detail in Kaldellis (2019).

[3] I use the term in the sense elaborated and popularized by Alan Watson, implying not just the very fact of the reception of foreign law, but also all the factors involved in the choice of the law to be transplanted and the success of implementation, including personal and political ones. (See Watson 1993; Kršljanin 2023) For example, the choice of Matthew Blastares' Syntagma (see below) instead of Constantine Harmenopoulos' Hexabiblos as a source of transplantation of Rhomaian law was mostly determined by political and ecclesiastical factors of the time, and not their legal contents. See Šarkić (1990).

law,[4] there is still no doubt that women could own property separate from that of their husbands and engage in legal transactions regarding that property.[5]

Keeping the aforementioned factors in mind, let us then begin this foray into the possibility of women playing various roles in a judicial process in medieval Serbia. We shall begin with female witnesses, as the source material is richest there, continuing to women as jurors and as parties. Ultimately, we shall inquire whether it was possible for a woman to appear in the role of a judge.[6]

2 Women as Witnesses

Many premodern countries limited the capacity of women as witnesses, or at least viewed them as less trustworthy and reliable. For example, Shariah law explicitly prescribed that the testimony of two female witnesses had the same value as that of one man.[7] In many Western European countries a woman's testimony had lower value in practice,[8] while in systems based on Roman law, the acceptance of female witnesses was often limited to criminal procedure. This was the case with many Mediterranean communes, including the city of Budva (which was under Serbian sovereignty, but had autonomy similar to those of other maritime communes). Its Statute proclaimed that a woman could be trusted only regarding matters of working in a mill (which was a mostly female occupation), the age of children and a girl's virginity.[9] On paper, it would seem that the situation in Serbia was no different: however, some of the rare preserved sources from practice significantly alter that view.[10]

[4] For example, canonical grounds for divorce favoured men (with only a woman's adultery being sufficient grounds). The second Žiča charter of 1220 shows that, while neither husband nor wife was allowed to divorce when none of these grounds existed under threat of a hefty fine (depending on their estate), a woman who was unable to pay the fine due to not having (sufficient) property of her own could be beaten and even sold (in a form of debt bondage?) for arbitrarily attempting to leave her husband. No provision of the kind existed for men. (Still, these norms are part of the proof that married women *could* own property of their own.) Kršljanin (2019).

[5] As a curiosity, it might be mentioned that only two private contracts of sale were preserved from the entire period of medieval Serbia—but it happens that in both the sellers are women, and other women are mentioned as well. Mirković (2017), pp. 47, 52 and Kršljanin (2024a), pp. 244–250, 270–272. More on one of these contracts below.

[6] This matter was also analyzed, based on the draft version of this article, but with a slightly different layout, in Kršljanin (2024a), pp. 373–386.

[7] Fadel (1997), Stanimirović (2020), p. 128 and Divac (2023), p. 28.

[8] Van Houts (1999) and Kane (2018).

[9] Kršljanin (2015), pp. 288–290 and Bujuklić and Baljević (2023), p. 77, 215. On the other hand, Solovjev saw this not as testimony, but as a form of jury duty. Solovjev (1939), pp. 405–407. Female jurors will be discussed in the next section.

[10] This section of the paper is mostly based on the research in Kršljanin (2022b), pp. 444–446, 450–454.

The only normative source regarding female testimony can be found in the Abbreviated Syntagma of Matthew Blastares, a Rhomaian legal compilation translated and adapted for the use of Serbian courts as part of Stefan Dušan's Codification in 1349.[11] Its chapter D-7 (D-10 in the Complete Syntagma) mostly contained rules from the Procheiron and Basilica already known to Serbian law,[12] but also the novels of Justinian and Leo VI, the latter introducing severe limitations on the testimony of women (similar to those present in Western Romanised laws):

Жени не проходить моужьскыи сань, ни же вь завештани свѣ'дѣтелѥствоуѥть, развѣ вь нихь же моужїе не призивають се; нь ни же сьглаголавати симь попоштен'но ѥсть народнѣ, себѣ же тькмо сьглаголоуѥть и жена, и слѣп'ц; сь же и соудити можеть.

Четиридесете же и осма Новаа цара Лава вьз'бранѥть женамь о прикосифонѣхь свѣдѣтел'ствовати и сь замѣнѥн'ныхь брачнїихь. О рожденїахь же и о ихьже ѥдинѣ жен'сцѣи очи зрѣти проштен'нѣ соуть, повелѣваѥмѣ соуть свѣдѣтел'ствовати.

Women should not engage in men's duties, not bear testimony to wills, unless in matters where men are not called; it is not allowed to them to represent someone in public; a woman and a blind man can represent only themselves; the latter can also judge.

The forty-eighth Novel of Emperor Leo forbids women to testify of contracts and marriage arrangements. Yet they are commanded to testify of births and of what only female eyes are allowed to see.

This presents a limitation similar to those in other medieval legal systems. An elaboration present in the original text of the Novel (not present here) explained that it was inappropriate for women to mix with men in official occasions, and that men might be offended if women were to take over their duties.[13] It is clear that only testimony in civil matters was restricted to specifically feminine matters. Therefore, there might also have persisted a notion that legal issues were too complex for women to understand, either due to their natural ineptitude or simply their lack of knowledge and experience in such matters. Yet nothing in the norm implies that the testimony of a female eyewitness to a crime would be unacceptable or valued less than a man's.

Was this restriction applied in practice in Serbian law? There are solid grounds to doubt this. Before Dušan's Codification, the testimony of a woman before the Sabor (the estate assembly of medieval Serbia[14]) is documented in the Life of

[11] Original edition of the Full Syntagma in Novaković (1907), translation to modern Serbian in Vlastar (2013); Abbreviated Syntagma in Флоринскій (1888), pp. 95–203. More on the Syntagma and its place in the codification in Solovjev (1928), pp. 49–58.

[12] Many Rhomaian norms on testimony were also transplanted in the Nomocanon of St. Sava (*Zakonopravilo*) in 1219, which contained the entire Procheiron; however, those weren't concerned with the witnesses' sex, but mostly with their social standing, occupation, age and family relations to the parties. Kršljanin (2022b), pp. 446–450.

[13] Saradi-Mendelovici (1990), pp. 78–79.

[14] More on the Sabor in English in Kršljanin (2017) and Šarkić (2023), pp.178–184. In Serbian, see also Taranovski (1996), pp. 225–262, Radojčić (1940) and Blagojević (2008).

St. Simeon, i.e. Grand Župan Stefan Nemanja, in the late twelfth century. As the monarch and the Sabor were avidly discussing the danger stemming from a discovered group of heretics, a young noblewoman stepped forth. She was the daughter of one of Nemanja's orthodox noblemen, yet was married to one of the heretics, and came to testify first-hand of their abhorrent practices and to plead the monarch to defeat them—which indeed was the decision afterwards, and a decisive action was launched against the heretics, leading to their defeat, some banishments and executions.[15] Naturally, this situation differs from the subject of our analysis in several respects. Firstly, it seems that the Sabor was not acting in its judicial capacity[16] but debating a political matter of whether or not to act against the heretics and how. Secondly, even if the matter is interpreted as a trial of the heretics *in absentia*, it was obviously a criminal one, and the young noblewoman an eyewitness of the illegal practices. Thus, her testimony would have been acceptable even according to the previously mentioned Rhomaian rules. Finally, one could question the authenticity or even historicity of this episode, as no names are provided, and it conforms to many important medieval *topoi* (women appearing as defenders of the faith, heretics being shown as threatening the family).[17] Thus, it could have been either orchestrated to influence the nobility and clergy in the Sabor, or even invented later to properly present the danger the heretics posed to the readers of the Life.

However, despite these caveats, the episode remains significant to our research. Beyond the familial ties to the other relevant actors, the text does not place special emphasis on the witness being a woman. There is nothing to indicate that a woman's appearance before the Sabor was an unusual matter, nor that her testimony was treated as less credible due to her sex, whether legally or unofficially. There is no mention that she needed special permission or accompaniment by a man in order to testify before the Sabor. All that the text says is: "Си же глаголющоу светомоу семоу. и распри велицѣ быв'ши. прииде дьщи ѥдиного вельможь ѥго правовѣр'ныхь. ѡброучена бы'вши за моужь. ѡть кривовѣр'ныхь тѣхь'" ("As this holy one spoke, and there having been a great dispute, came the daughter of one of his noblemen of true faith, who had been betrothed to a husband of those ill-believers ...).[18] While she did then fall on her knees before Nemanja, this can be interpreted as obeisance before one's monarch, since a soldier who testified previously did the same. Thus, we can conclude that there was nothing unusual or inappropriate in a woman (at least one of high birth) testifying before the highest organ of medieval Serbia in the late twelfth century: with that in mind, it is hard to imagine that courts would spurn female testimony. It seems that Serbian customary law, then, did not

[15] Stefan Prvovenčani (2017), pp. 33–37.

[16] On medieval parliaments acting as courts or aiding monarchs in performing their judicial functions, see Boucoyannis (2021).

[17] See more in Radojčić (1940), p. 67 and Blagojević (2008), p. 8.

[18] Stefan Prvovenčani (2017), p. 34–35.

restrict the testimony of women: the Rhomaian restrictions would have, at least, fallen on infertile ground.[19]

But did they nevertheless manage to take root? Fortunately, we also have an actual voice from everyday practice from the period of the Serbian Empire: a private contract in which a widow named Dobroslava, accompanied by her three adult children, sold her house in the city of Prizren.[20] In addition to the seller and her daughter, a number of female names are also listed in the contract: three women are signed in the list of neighbours in the beginning,[21] and one of those (plus another unusual name that *could* be female) is found in the list of witnesses at the end. As the contract was written by a nomic (notary), it is hardly likely that the parties were simply ignorant of the legal restrictions: a professional would not have allowed them to call as witnesses individuals whose testimony would not be acceptable before a court in case of a dispute. Thus, it seems safe to assume that the rule from the Syntagma did not take root, and that female testimony was acceptable before courts.[22]

3 Women as Jurors

Firstly, a few words on the jury (*porota*) of medieval Serbia: it appears in the sources since the fourteenth century and is considered to have been a form of evidence, and not a trial jury (unlike e.g. the Common Law jury).[23] Having evolved from the institution of compurgators (as witnessed by the root "*rota*", oath), it represented a step towards objectivity, being composed of people from the social milieus of both parties, instead of just one (as compurgation was usually used by the defendant), and requiring a majority of votes instead of the traditional medieval unanimity.[24] This was perhaps a mixture of Slavic tradition and Rhomaian influence.[25]

---

[19] Kršljanin (2022b), p. 446.

[20] The contract is not dated, but mention of the Emperor places it in the timeframe of 1346–1371: thus it may not be certain, but is highly likely that the Codification predates it. Best editions of the text are Solovjev (1926), pp. 148–149 and Bubalo (2004), 250–252. The most up-to-date overview is in Bubalo (2004), pp. 143–152.

[21] In both Rhomaian and Serbian law, neighbours had the right of pre-emption (first refusal). Mirković (2017), p. 52.

[22] Kršljanin (2022a, 2022b), pp. 453–454 and Kršljanin (2024a), pp. 378–383.

[23] On such origins of the jury globally, including the Common Law one, see Brunner (1871), Forsyth (1878), Anand (2005).

[24] See Marković (1908), pp. 58–68, Jovanović (1959) and Taranovski (1996), pp. 760–764, 771–782. The old theory of the jury being a judging one was supported by Avakumović (1894) and Polićević (1923).

[25] Solovjev (1928), p. 219.

Stefan Dušan's Code regulates the jury in some detail, devoting four articles (151–154) to it. The first three regulate the composition and working of the jury, stating that a jury must be summoned for every case, with the number of jurors being 6, 12 or 24. They gave an oath before a priest and pledged their trust to one party or the other; the vote of the majority was taken into account. In case of parties coming from different social milieus, one half of jurors had to belong to the same group as each party, be that commoners and nobles or Serbian men and foreigners (or members of another faith, mostly implying Catholics). Relatives or enemies of either party could not be jurors. None of these rules mention sex; linguistically, they all refer to jurors as men. Finally, art. 154 prescribes sanctions for jurors who abuse their duty—and there, at least according to four manuscripts of the Code (the Struga, Studenica, Prizren and Rakovac manuscripts), a gendered norm can be found[26]:

Кои се поротници кльноу и оправѣ онога-зи по законоу, и ако се по тоо-зи оправѣ поличіе обрѣте истин'но оу онога-зи опрравʼчіе кога-но ѥ оправила порота; да оузме царство ми на тех'-зіи поротницѣхь по тысоуштоу перперь; а векѥ по томь да несоу ты-зіи поротници вѣрованіи; ни да се кто оть нихь ни моужи ни женіи.

When jurors acquit on oath according to the law, and after such an acquittal a true proof of guilt be found with him whom they have acquitted, I shall fine those jurors one thousand perpers each and in future those jurors shall not be believed and they may not take either husband or wife.

The phrasing of the prohibition of marriage clearly shows that women could be jurors, even though the idea seemed preposterous enough to some earlier researchers that they could not understand what the legislator meant by "taking a husband".[27] Such a sanction, however, seems very severe, much more so than the loss of public trust, a fairly logical sanction for such a crime. In a medieval setting, where every extramarital liaison was condemned as fornication, prohibition of marriage essentially meant condemnation to a life without family and children.[28] It must be noted that the fine of 1000 perpers (hyperpyra) is also an

[26] A long-time standard reference edition, Novaković (1898) was based on the Prizren manuscript, with text from other manuscripts provided as variants, and thus this was for a long time dominantly considered to be the dominant rendition; however, with the appearance of the new reference edition by Bubalo (2010) based on the Athos manuscript, this may change. English translations in the paper are given according to Burr (1949–1950), unless a change is stated. In this case, Burr has "... after acquittal guilt be proven against him ..."; I have modified the translation to clarify the type of proof of guilt: the Serbian phrase usually referred to the finding of the *corpus delicti*.

[27] Novaković (1898), p. 239. On the other hand, Зигель (1872) p. 130, Taranovski (1996) p. 423–424 and particularly Solovjev (1939) immediately accepted that it meant that women could be jurors.

[28] Due to a lack of sources from practice, we cannot know what would have happened if a convicted juror was already married: would this part of the sanction be ignored, or would they have had to divorce?.

immensely high one: such a fine appears only once more in the Code, for the murder of a commoner by a nobleman (art. 94)[29]: no other goes over 500. This proves that there is no mistake: the legislator obviously wanted to impose extremely high penalties on those who abuse their duty as jurors.

The remaining five manuscripts in which this article is preserved, however,[30] contain a different sanction instead of the prohibition of marriage: „И ако се изнагє ере соу знаюкє крыво ѡправили, или ѡтдали, или нѣкаа мита оузимали, платив'ше вышереченноѣ, и да се заточе оу иноу землю незнаємоу." („And should it be found that they have knowingly falsely justified, or given, or taken some bribe, after having paid the aforementioned, let them also be imprisoned in a foreign unknown land.") It seems most likely that the crime has been nuanced and the sanction made milder in the revision of the Code, perhaps also due to the problems of its application to married jurors.[31] But this does not change the fact that the provision originally existed, and thus indirectly showed that women could serve as jurors.

There is also the question of whether women could serve as jurors only in specifically feminine matters (as was at least the letter of the law for female witnesses), maybe only as jurors for a female party—or if they could be called upon as jurors regardless of the details of the case. Comparative examples of such restrictions exist in nearby Slavic lands,[32] yet nothing in the provisions of the Code shows a restriction. From the letter of the law, we see that one's estate position, nationality and faith were factors that influenced the composition of the jury: it would seem strange for sex not to be mentioned if it was likewise a mandatory factor. It seems to have gone without saying that women, too, could be jurors, and this was only explicitly mentioned due to the fact that different terms were used for men and women marrying. It seems safe to assume, then, that there was no legal restriction regarding the type of cases where women could be jurors, but that, due to social realities of the time, it was more likely in practice that they would be called if one of the parties was female as well.

The closest thing to evidence of this in practice can be found in a charter of the time of Ivan Crnojević (r. 1465–1490) in Zeta (modern day Montenegro), soon after the fall of Serbian lands to the Ottomans. In a local border dispute, the case was decided by the oath of 24 denizens of Bjeloševići *with their wives*,

[29] In the opposite case, the commoner who had killed a nobleman would pay only 300 hyperpyra—still a fine sufficiently high to cost him all his property—and would also have both arms cut off. Still, the death penalty was reserved only for the most gruesome forms of murder—those of a priest or close family member—or for the rape of a noblewoman by a commoner. See more on the social (estate) stratification in the punishment of these crimes in Kršljanin (2012, 2022a).

[30] Those are the Athos, Baranja, Bistrica, Hodoš and Šišatovac manuscripts.

[31] Solovjev (1980), pp. 299–301 and Bubalo (2010), p. 208.

[32] For example, in the Statute of Vinodol and some sources from practice in the city of Zagreb, Croatia, a woman's jurors/compurgators had to be female as well. Solovjev (1939) pp. 405–407.

supported by the oaths of 24 of Crnojević's noblemen.[33] Some authors consider this to be the same kind of jury as the one in Dušan's Code.[34] Still, while its composition was similar, including being appointed by both parties, the body of people consulted in country border disputes (art. 80) was closer to expert witnesses—people knowledgeable in local matters who could be trusted to know where the border ran.[35] They could be considered a middle line between classic witnesses and the advanced form of jurors. Still, the mention of women in this position (even though they seem to be following their husbands in a secondary role) can be taken as a further positive indication of at least relative gender equality when it came to the supporting roles in a judicial process—witnesses and jurors.

4 Women as Parties

Having seen that women could appear before courts as both witnesses and jurors, it stands to reason all the more that they could appear as parties in a case. The rules of the Syntagma, mentioned in the section on witnesses, also clearly state that while a woman could not represent another before a court, she *could* act on her own behalf. Another rule in the Syntagma (taken from the *Basilica*), regarding the postponement of court summons in the case of a death in the family, proclaimed that nobody was allowed to summon the deceased's "родителѥ или женоу или наслѣдникы или испороучникы" ("parents or wife or heirs or representatives") until nine days of mourning have passed.[36] It is clearly stated that in this period they cannot be sued either for the deceased's debts or their own, and no difference is made between how male and female family members are mentioned, showing a woman's full procedural capacity.

Still, we have also seen that the part regarding restrictions on female testimony does not seem to have been applied in practice. Thus, it could be that despite this Rhomaian norm, Serbian customary law might have required a female party to be represented by a man in court. While there are no clear provisions to support or

[33] Šekularac (1987), p. 211. The detail was first mentioned by Ровинскій (1888), p. 458. See also Božanić (2014) pp. 68–69.

[34] E.g., Burr (1949–1950), p. 529.

[35] "А за мегѥ сел'ске да дадоу ѡбои кои иштоу свѣдоке, онь половиноу, а ѡнь половиноу по закѡноу. Да коудѣ рекоу свѣдоци тоговази да ѥсть." ("Touching village boundaries, let both claimants bring witnesses, one a half and the other a half, according to the law. And whom the witnesses shall name, his shall it be.") Burr remarks here: "Such an appeal to the knowledge of 'good men of the vicinage' is common throughout early mediaeval Europe; it contains in itself the germs of the universal 'jury' system. A juror is merely a sworn witness." Burr (1949–1950), p. 213. See also Solovjev (1928), pp. 214–215, Solovjev (1980), pp. 241–242; Taranovski 760–761.

[36] In the Complete Syntagma, this rule was in the chapter D-9; the Abbreviated separated it into a standalone small chapter, D-5. See Solovjev (1928), 211.

reject this in the sources, some norms of Dušan's Code do provide at least circumstantial evidence.[37]

Several articles of the Code (art. 52, 66, 70–71) speak of the possibility of the collective liability of members of one family (living in the same house), or their possibility to represent each other, using only male nouns: "brothers", "father and son", (male) "relatives". With the standard of the time being living in large households with joint property (at least when it came to land),[38] the overall regime is perfectly logical: yet the nouns it uses should not be taken as proof that only men could appear in court. The old legislator commonly uses only male-gendered language unless there is an explicit need to mention a woman. However, that does not mean that women are ruled out, but only that they are tacitly there in the background. Men are presumed to have the primary role in social life, be it in its legal or illegal aspects. Thus, most buyers and sellers, criminals and victims are expected to be male. Similarly, it is expected that mostly men will engage in activities that would require them to go to court, and thus the norms speak of men.[39]

Two articles of the Code, nevertheless, mention women. One of them is art. 73: "Сирота коя нѣсть яка прети или ѡтпирати да даѥ пьр'ца кои се кѥ за ню прети." While there has been some confusion regarding the interpretation of the word "сирота" (*sirota*),[40] it is now widely accepted that it was used to refer to a widow living alone,[41] and thus the translation would be: "Let a poor woman who isn't strong enough to bring an action or defend one have a litigator to act for her."[42] One could interpret this provision in two different ways. It could mean that any woman living alone needed to appoint someone to represent her at court—and, thus,

[37] In addition to this, the Nomocanon of Saint Sava contains a provision from the Novels of Justinian, saying that nuns should not leave their nunneries to go to court, but rather send their representatives. (Petrović 2004, pp. 662–663.) However, even if this norm was consistently applied in practice, it obviously cannot be seen as representative for lay women, as it was obviously meant to protect the cloistered position of nuns, an intersection of their gender and their religious calling.

[38] This was also one of the reasons why fines were very high for most crimes, as they were expected to be paid not from one's own pocket, but from family property. See Krkljuš (2000) and Kršljanin (2011).

[39] In the same vein, we might ask why the aforementioned rule from the Syntagma concerning procedural postponement for persons in mourning spoke only of the deceased's wife, and not also husband. Surely, that was not because a man would not have been allowed a postponement if his wife had died, but merely because the male legislator, when speaking of a hypothetical deceased person, likewise had a man in mind.

[40] Zigel had interpreted the word with the meaning that it has in Russian, 'orphan', and thought the provision concerned minors without legal guardians. Зигель (1872). p. 134–135.

[41] *Cf.* Solovjev (1980), p. 236 and Bubalo (2010), p.175. On social norms protecting these women, see also Filipović (1953).

[42] Burr's translation is as follows: "A poor person who cannot bring an action nor defend one, let him have an advocate to act for him." (Burr 1949–1950, p. 212.) Beyond clarifying the person's gender, I've also added the notion of her being "strong enough" to litigate, omitted by Burr, and changed the reference to an "advocate", to avoid potential confusion of it being a hired attorney, while they did not exist in medieval Serbia.

that women had no procedural capacity. However, in the context of the legal system, a literal interpretation seems more likely: *if* a woman living alone was unable to go to court in person, then she was allowed to appoint a representative, *despite* the fact that she lived alone, and normally only members of the same household could represent each other.[43] The reason for this inability could be her being very old or ill—but we must also consider social factors: she could have lacked confidence in her ability to argue in court. In this context, the law allowed her leeway that would not have been granted to a man.

The contract from Prizren also contains a provision in this regard: namely, it was stipulated that in case the buyer had any complaints, the one to "answer" i.e. appear in court would be not the seller herself, but her son Prvoslav.[44] This, too, gives us no final answer. A man might have been necessary as a party, or it might just have been more convenient to the aged woman to delegate this unpleasant duty to her son. Still, the argument of Rhomaian law is strong here: as Solovjev remarks, the contract has been made fully in the Rhomaian form despite the fact that, at that time, Prizren had been firmly in Serbian hands for some 130 years.[45] While again not irrefutable proof, this is also a solid argument of the Rhomaian rules being likewise valid in the procedural sense—i.e. of there being no legal obstacle to a woman arguing at court.

Finally, art. 104 spoke of a specific situation—a court official (*pristav*)[46] coming with official summons to a married woman while her husband was away:

И да се не наведе приставь на женоу кьди нѣсть моужа дома, ни да се позива жена без моужа, нь да си дасть жена моужоу глас, да греде на соудь. Оу том'зи моужь да нѣсть кривь, докле моу не даде глас.

The officer of the court shall not call upon a wife when the husband is not at home, nor shall a wife be summoned to court without her husband, but a wife shall give her husband notice regarding going to court.[47] And in that matter a husband is guiltless, until she gives him notice.

This article has also elicited different interpretations, as it could refer either to the wife not being allowed to represent herself in court, but having to send her

[43] As Stepić points out, it seems that the widow had to find a representative herself (instead of, say, one being provided by the state), but that the court had to accept whomever she appointed. Stepić (2020), p. 21.

[44] This was noted by Taranovski (1996), p. 747 and Solovjev (1980), p. 236.

[45] "... весь этот договоръ о продажѣ городской недвижимости написанъ съ начала до конца по византiйскому формуляру, хотя городъ Призрѣнъ уже лѣтъ сто тридцать находился въ сербскихъ рукахъ." Soloviev (1931), p. 2.

[46] More on the pristav, who had a range of important functions regarding the public faith and judiciary, in Kostrenčić (1930), pp. 5–70 and Taranovski (1996), pp. 727–732.

[47] Burr's translation here is "... give her husband notice when she goes to court." (Burr 1949–1950, p. 516.) The Serbian phrase "да греде на соудь" can be translated either in that sense, as "that he/she is going to court", or in the sense of giving instruction, "that he/she *should* go to court". The verb is in the third person singular, but as a pronoun isn't grammatically needed here, the gender cannot be ascertained. I have thus replaced this translation with the vague "regarding going to court" to maintain the possibility of both interpretations.

husband instead,[48] or to the wife just not being allowed to accept the summons meant for her husband, let alone go to court in her husband's stead.[49] The latter seems more likely, particularly given the last sentence: it would be hard to speak of the husband's *guilt* if his role in the trial in question was only to speak in his wife's stead. Consequently, a wife was not allowed to take any actions regarding her husband's court case, or, maybe more so, the judicial system was forbidden to consider a summons served if the defendant was not at home to receive it, but his wife was. Burr comments: "This article shows a regard for the sanctity of the home which is quite in keeping with the Serbian tradition."[50] It does indeed fit not only Serbian, but generally medieval patriarchal standards. Given the fact that women were mostly engaged in keeping house and taking care of children, while men could far more often be out and about with their work, whatever their estate and trade, it must have been frequent in practice for a *pristav* to come and find the defendant away from home, but his wife present. It clearly would have been easier for the official to finish his business with the wife and consider his job done—but detrimental to the defendant. It is particularly important to keep in mind that only the highest layer of nobility (*velika vlastela*, 'great noblemen') and the higher ranks of the ecclesiastical hierarchy had the privilege of being granted a *written* summons: all others were merely orally informed by the *pristav*, who would prove he was there on official business by showing the judicial seal.[51] Thus, unless he was a great nobleman, the absent husband would have had only second-hand oral information from his wife regarding the time and cause of the trial; the situation obviously had great potential for miscommunication. The article was designed to prevent this.

One cannot help but wonder whether the opposite was tacitly implied: if the defendant was a married woman, was her husband allowed to accept the summons in her stead? Both options are possible. On the one hand, it would have been in accordance with the patriarchal family dynamics if the husband, as the head of the family, could receive a court summons for his wife. On the other hand, practical considerations outlined above might dictate that everyone should receive (thus, hear) the summons directly from the *pristav* to ensure accuracy and clarity of the information. Regardless of the answer, one thing is certain: it must have been much more common in practice for a wife to be at home while her husband was away

[48] Thus e.g. Зигель (1872), p. 140 and Dinić-Knežević (2005), p. 61, 63.

[49] Solovjev (1980), p. 262 and Bubalo (2010), p. 187. Taranovski seems to waver between these two options. Taranovski (1996), p. 739. Stepić even stipulates that the Code concerns both issues: that a married woman may not be summoned without her husband's knowledge (though he is not required to represent her) and that she cannot take summons meant for her husband in his stead. Stepić (2020), pp. 19–20.

[50] Burr (1949–1950), p. 516.

[51] Taranovski (1996) pp. 738–739 and Kršljanin (2014), pp. 388–390. The reason for this was likely twofold—both granting a privilege of having the details conveniently available in writing to the highest strata of society, and keeping things practical, as they were probably the only ones guaranteed to be literate, and thus a written summons would have been wasted on many others.

than the other way around. Thus, the legislator deemed it necessary to intervene only by regulating the frequent, usual case, leaving potential exceptions for practical resolution when they arose.

5 Women as Judges?

The notion of a woman as a judge—or in any appointed official capacity—in a medieval society may strike us as laughable, or sadly impossible, and would likely have been considered absurd by people of that era as well. Official positions appointed by the State or monarch were traditionally reserved for men, largely due to their historical association with military service. After all, even the Novel of Leo VI in the Syntagma, referenced here several times, explicitly stated that while a blind man could serve as a judge, a woman could not. Thus, there is no doubt the emperor's judges appointed by the State would have been exclusively male.[52] Historical sources reveal that judges often relied on their private servants for secondary duties, such as executing verdicts,[53] and those have to be presumed to have been male as well.

However, it was common practice in the Middle Ages to delegate local state power (*immunitas*), including judicial immunity, to private hands, allowing landowners—noble families and monasteries—to administer justice to peasants living and working on their lands. Naturally, heads of noble households (like all other households) were typically men, and most monasteries in medieval Serbia were men's monasteries, thus making such positions, predominantly male-oriented. Nevertheless, exceptions could occur: a widowed noblewoman could become the head of her household, and female monasteries did exist, although less is known of them.[54] Therefore, it is conceivable that a noblewoman or an abbess could have tried the disputes of her (or the monastery's) tenants in a patrimonial court.

However, due to the lack of data from practice, it remains uncertain whether these women in positions of power would personally pass judgement or appoint a man to do so on their behalf. Nonetheless, the documentation of noblewomen adjudicating disputes among their tenants in other countries[55] suggests that such

[52] On these judges see Mirković (2005) and Šarkić (2023) pp. 500–511.

[53] Taranovski (1996), pp. 726–727.

[54] Two are known from Stefan Nemanja's time (late twelfth century), one of which was certainly his endowment, and another in which his wife, Ana, took monastic vows at the same time as her husband did when he renounced the throne. Marković (2019), pp. 114, 121–122. Also, both the Zakonopravilo and Dušan's codification contain rules explicitly concerning nuns. A famous later example is Ljubostinja, the endowment of Princess Milica. Šuica (2004), pp. 145–150.

[55] This seems to have been relatively frequent in medieval Iberia, with many noblewomen documented in the role of the judge, a particularly prominent figure being Ermessenda, Countess of Barcelona, Girona, and Osona, who has been documented as presiding in many judicial assemblies. See Bowman (2014). In the Irish Calendar of Ormond Deeds, we find a case 1545

a scenario is at least plausible. Furthermore, numerous women from ruling families had held great power in Serbia. For instance, Queen Helen of Anjou/Angel possessed her own lands as a queen dowager following Stefan Uroš's death, and historical records indicate that she held her own assemblies there—marking the earliest mentions of a local Sabor in Serbian sources.[56] Empress Helen, Stefan Dušan's wife, actively participated in her husband's councils on political and even military matters.[57] Princess Milica, widow of Prince Lazar, effectively assumed power as regent of her son after Lazar's death at the Battle of Kosovo. During this time, she presided over a Sabor, making very challenging and sensitive political decisions, such as accepting vassalage to the man responsible for her husband's death and arranging her youngest daughter's marriage to him.[58]

Milica's daughters, too, were great ladies in their own right, and so on. Although there are no records of these powerful and influential women acting as judges, it is conceivable given their authority and position. If a widowed queen could convene assemblies of nobility and clergy on her own lands, it is plausible that a widowed noblewoman could adjudicate the affairs of her tenants.

We can conclude that the medieval norm, as anticipated, reserved the role of judge primarily for men. However, compelling evidence suggests that there could have been exceptions, such as noblewomen exercising patrimonial jurisdiction on their lands.

6 Conclusion

Overall, the legal status of women in medieval Serbia was, of course, inferior to that of men, but fairly good by medieval standards. The same appears to have applied to procedural law as well. It seems that a woman could appear before court as a party without being represented by a man (male family member), although she could have had such representation if she faced difficulties with appearing in court personally. Furthermore, women could also serve as witnesses and jurors without apparent legal restrictions in that regard. Although a Rhomaian norm restricted female testimony to feminine matters in the Abbreviated Syntagma, customary law permitting female witnesses appears to have held more weight, given some scarce evidence from practice. It is of particular importance that women could sit on juries, given how the significance of the jury was growing with time.

where one of the judges was a certain dame Eleanor Fitz John in her capacity as lady of the manor. (Despite her presence, the judges were signed as "we the aforesaid indifferent men and judges": nobody would have seen fit to change such a formulation because one of the 'men' was a woman.) Curtis (1937), pp. 282–283. My thanks to Dr Coleman Dennehy for bringing this to my attention, first in Dennehy (2021).

[56] Radojčić (1940), pp. 97–98, Popović (2010) and Kršljanin (2024b).

[57] Radojčić (1940), pp. 12–13, Purković (1975) and Sajlović (2015).

[58] Šuica (2019), pp. 91–116 and Kršljanin (2021).

Naturally, one cannot ignore that courts, as organs of the State or local lords and communities, belonged to a public sphere of power that was predominantly male-dominated. Parties, witnesses, and jurors were likely predominantly male due to social norms rather than legal ones. However, the extreme scarcity of practice-based sources hinders precise conclusions, let alone numbers. For the same reason, we cannot know what the attitude of the men in courts (judges, officials, opposing parties, and jurors etc.) was when a woman appeared before them. Was she subjected to more scrutiny and suspicion due to her gender, seen as treading in a domain that did not quite belong to her? Or was she, perhaps, treated with more sympathy and respect due to an image of gentle femininity and ideas of chivalry present in the society at the time? We can only speculate until perhaps a new source is discovered to shed more light on the matter.

The same can be said for the possibility of women appearing as judges in patrimonial courts. Given other outlines of the system (a fairly good legal and procedural position of women otherwise, known examples of politically powerful women), as well as comparative examples, it is possible that such cases could have occurred: but no real claims can be made in the absence of solid evidence. One thing is certain: even if such cases did exist, they would have been exceptions to the norm.

As distant as some of the tenets of medieval status and procedural law, naturally, are to twenty-first century norms, some similarities may give one cause for reflection. Despite the fact that women in the courtroom, whatever their role may be, are much more common today, male still seems to be the default in procedural law in many cases—as, no doubt, other texts in this volume will show in more detail. When pondering how to address the issues of gender stereotypes among judges or other participants in the judicial process it might help to bear in mind how similar challenges were—or were *not*—solved in earlier eras. This historical consciousness will render one more open to context and finesse regarding issues of gender equality.

References

Avakumović JĐ (1894) Stara srpska porota poređena sa engleskom porotom: pristupna beseda. Glas Srpske Kraljevske Akademije XLIV:3–36

Anand S (2005) The origins, early history and evolution of the English criminal trial jury. Alta Law Rev 43:407–432

Bowman JA (2014) Countesses in court: elite women, creativity, and power in northern Iberia, 900–1200. J Mediev Iber Stud 6(1):54–70

Blagojević M (2008) Srpski sabori i sabori otačastva Nemanjića i Lazarevića. Glas Srpske akademije nauka i umetnosti. Odeljenje Istorijskih Nauka 14(CDX):1–40

Boucoyannis D (2021) Kings as judges: power, justice, and the origins of parliaments. Cambridge University Press, Cambridge

Božanić S (2014) "Ratničke družine" sa prostora Zete i oblasti Crnojevića u imovinsko-pravnim sporovima oko zemljišta (1445–1492): paralele sa srednjovekovnom Srbijom. Istraživanja: J Hist Res 25:55–71

Brunner H (1871) Die Entstehung der Schwurgerichte. Weidnnsche Buchhandlung, Berlin

Bubalo Đ (2004) Srpski nomici. SANU, Beograd

Bubalo Đ (ed) (2010) Dušanov zakonik. Zavod za udžbenike, Beograd

Burr M (1949–1950) The Code of Stephan Dušan, Tsar and Autocrat of the Serbs and Greeks. Slavon East Eur Rev 70(28):198–217. 71 (28): 516–539

Bujuklić Ž, Baljević M (eds) (2023) Srednjovjekovni statut grada Budve sa propratnim dokumentima iz mletačkog perioda. JU Narodna biblioteka Budve/Turistička organizacija opštine Budva, Budva

Curtis E (1937) Calendar of Ormond Deeds vol. IV. 1509–1547 A.D. Irish Manuscripts Commission, Dublin 2

Dennehy C (2021) Ireland, the law, and a long history of the English colony in Ireland. Lecture held at the "Forvm Romanvm" club of the University of Belgrade Faculty of Law, May 7, 2021, https://youtu.be/qGKM0DowgA0

Dinić-Knežević D (2005) Žene u ogledalu Dušanovog zakonika. In Ćirković S, Čavoški K (eds) Zakonik cara Stefana Dušana: zbornik radova sa naučnog skupa održanog 3. oktobra 2000, povodom 650 godina od proglašenja. SANU, Beograd, pp 57–65

Divac U (2023) Gender issues in comparative legal history. In Vujadinović D, Fröhlich M, Giegerich T, et al. (eds) Gender-competent legal education. Springer, Cham, pp 15–56

Fadel M (1997) Two women, one man: knowledge, power, and gender in medieval sunni legal thought. Int J Middle East Stud 29(2):185–204

Filipović M (1953) Sirota kudeljnica: prilog objašnjenju čl. 64 Dušanova zakonika. Zbornik Matice Srpske Za Društvene Nauke 5:40–47

Forsyth W (1878) History of trial by Jury. Cockcroft/Company, New York

Jovanović M (1959) Porota srednjevekovne Srbije. Savez udruženja pravnika Jugoslavije, Beograd

Kaldellis A (2019) Romanland: ethnicity and empire in Byzantium. Harvard University Press, Cambridge, MA; London

Kane BC (2018) Defamation, gender and hierarchy in late medieval Yorkshire. Soc Hist 43(3):356–374

Kostrenčić M (1930) Fides publica (javna vera) u pravnoj istoriji Srba i Hrvata do kraja XV veka. Srpska kraljevska akademija, Beograd

Krkljuš L (2000) Kolektivna odgovornost u Dušanovom zakoniku. In Kuzmanović R, Leovac S (eds) Dušanov zakonik—650 godina od njegovog donošenja. Akademija nauka i umjetnosti Republike Srpske, Banja Luka, pp 143–151

Kršljanin N (2011) Kolektivna odgovornost u Dušanovom zakoniku. Pravni Život 10:413–428

Kršljanin N (2012) Staleška nejednakost u kaznenom pravu Dušanovog zakonika. Strani Pravni Život 3:41–68

Kršljanin NV (2014) Srpske srednjovekovne povelje kao izvor Dušanovog zakonika. PhD dissertation defended at the University of Belgrade Faculty of Law

Kršljanin N (2015) Ostvarivanje prava po Splitskom statute. Radić Ž, et al (ed) Splitski statut iz 1312. godine: povijest i pravo. Književni krug Split/Odsjek za povijest Filozofskoga fakulteta Sveučilišta u Splitu/Pravni fakultet Sveučilišta u Splitu. Split, 273–314

Kršljanin N (2017) Interrupted evolution: the Serbian medieval assembly (*Sabor*). Parliam Estates Represent 37(1):1–16

Kršljanin N (2019) Kralj kao zaštitnik crkve: pravna analiza Žičkih povelja Stefana Prvovenčanog. In Maksimović L, Pirivatrić S (eds) Kraljevstvo i arhiepiskopija u srpskim i pomorskim zemljama Nemanjića. SANU/Srpski komitet za vizantologiju, Beograd, pp 413–439

Kršljanin N (2021) The State Assembly after the Battle of Kosovo in 1389: serbia at the Crossroads. *Вестник Московского университета им. С. Ю. Витте. Серия „Юридические науки"* 2:11–15

Kršljanin N (2022a) Legal regulation of sex crimes in medieval Serbia and the Mediterranean communes under its rule. In Zanetti Domingues LL, Caravaggi L, Paoletti GM (eds) Women and Violence in the Late Medieval Mediterranean, ca. 1100–1500. Routledge, London, pp 101–120

Kršljanin N (2022b) Ko je mogao biti svedok u srednjovekovnom srpskom pravu? In Milinković I, Vlaški B (eds) Međunarodni naučni skup „Izazovi i perspektive razvoja pravnih sistema u XXI vijeku": zbornik radova. Univerzitet u Banjoj Luci—Pravni fakultet, Banja Luka, pp 443–458
Kršljanin N (2023) Legal transplants. In Sellers M, Kirste S (eds) Encyclopedia of the philosophy of law and social philosophy. Springer, Dordrecht, pp 2085–2092. Available online at https://link.springer.com/referenceworkentry/10.1007/978-94-007-6730-0_1120-1
Kršljanin N (2024a) Pravni položaj žene u srednjovekovnoj Srbiji. Univerzitet u Beogradu—Pravni fakultet, Beograd
Kršljanin N (2024b) Death of St. Helen of Anjou/Angel and the Sabor. Studia Slavica Et Balcanica Petropolitana 1:175–192
Marković BV (1908) O dokazima u krivičnom postupku. Policijski glasnik, Beograd
Marković V (2019) Pravoslavno monaštvo i manastiri u srednjovekovnoj Srbiji. Talija izdavaštvo, Niš
Mirković Z (2005) Sudije "carstva mi" Dušanovog zakonika. In Ćirković S, Čavoški K (eds) Zakonik cara Stefana Dušana: zbornik radova sa naučnog skupa održanog 3. oktobra 2000, povodom 650 godina od proglašenja. SANU, Beograd, pp 21–36
Mirković ZS (2017) Srpska pravna istorija. Univerzitet u Beogradu—Pravni fakultet, Beograd
Neville L (2019) Byzantine Gender. Arc Humanities Press, Leeds
Novaković S (ed) (1898) Zakonik Stefana Dušana, cara srpskog, 1349 i 1354. Zadužbina Ilije M. Kolarca, Beograd
Novaković S (ed) (1907) Matije Vlastara Sintagmat. Srpska kraljevska akademija, Beograd
Ровинскій П (1888) Черногорія въ ея прошломъ и настоящемъ, томъ I. Императорская академія наукъ, Санктпетербургъ
Polićević M (1923) Ustrojstvo pravosuđa u staroj srpskoj državi u XIII i XIV veku. Arhiv Za Pravne I Društvene Nauke 6(23):1–16, 88–93, 193–209, 262–280, 330–354
Purković MA (1975) Jelena, žena cara Dušana. Srpska pravoslavna eparhija za zapadnu Evropu, Diseldorf
Petrović MM (ed) (2004) Zakonopravilo Svetoga Save na srpskoslovenskom i srpskom jeziku, knjiga 1. Eparhija žička/manastir Žiča/Miodrag M. Petrović, Manastir Žiča
Popović M (2010) Srpska kraljica Jelena između rimokatoličanstva i pravoslavlja. Univerzitet u Beogradu—Pravoslavni bogoslovski fakultet, Institut za teološka istraživanja, Beograd
Radojčić N (1940) Srpski državni sabori u srednjem veku, pristupna akademska beseda podnesena Srpskoj kraljevskoj akademiji 7. marta 1938. Srpska kraljevska akademija, Beograd
Rubin M (2020) Cities of strangers: making lives in Medieval Europe. Cambridge University Press, Cambridge
Sajlović M (2015) Susret cara Dušana i Grigorija Palame na Atosu. Godišnjak 14:96–109
Saradi-Mendelovici H (1990) A contribution to the study of the Byzantine notarial formulas: the *infirmitas sexus* of women and the SC. Velleianum. Byzantinische Zeitschrift 83(1):72–90
Šarkić S (1990) Zašto Sintagma a ne Heksabiblos. Zbornik Pravnog Fakulteta U Zagrebu 40(1):73–77
Šarkić S (2023) A history of Serbian Mediaeval law. Brill, Leiden—Boston
Šekularac BB (1987) Dukljansko—zetske povelje. Istorijski institut SR Crne Gore, Titograd
Soloviev A (1931) Особенность договора продажи недвижимостей въ славянскомъ правѣ. Przewodnik Historyczno-prawny II(1):1–22
Solovjev AV (1926) Odabrani spomenici srpskog prava (od XII do kraja XV veka). Geca Kon, Beograd
Solovjev AV (1928) Zakonodavstvo Stefana Dušana, cara Srba i Grka. Skopsko naučno društvo, Skoplje
Solovjev AV (1939) Žene kao porotnici u Dušanovom zakoniku. Arhiv Za Pravne I Društvene Nauke XXXVIII(LV):403–407
Solovjev AV (1980) Zakonik cara Stefana Dušana. SANU, Beograd
Stanimirović V (2020) Položaj žene u Starom zavetu i u Kur'anu. Arhiv Za Pravne I Društvene Nauke 4:101–143

Stefan Prvovenčani (2017) Sabrana dela. In: Lj. Juhas Georgievska J, Jovanović T (eds) SKZ —Narodna biblioteka „Stefan Prvovenčani“, Beograd—Kraljevo
Stepić Đ (2020) Pravni položaj žene u Dušanovom zakoniku sa posebnim osvrtom na vlastelinke. Vesnik Pravne istorije/Herald of Legal History 2(I):9–37
Šuica M (2019) Milica—kneginja nemirnog doba. Evoluta, Beograd
Taranovski T (1996) Istorija srpskog prava u Nemanjićkoj državi. Službeni list SRJ, Beograd
Van Houts E (1999) Gender and authority of oral witnesses in Europe (800–1300). Trans R Hist Soc 9:201–220
Vlastar M (2013) Sintagma (translated into modern Serbian by T. Subotin-Golubović). SANU, Beograd
Watson A (1993) Legal transplants: an approach to comparative law. The University of Georgia Press, Athens, GE and London
Зигель Θ (1872) Законникъ Стефана Душана. Типографія товарищества «Общественная польза», Санктпетербургъ
Флоринскій Т (1888) Памятники законодательной дѣятельности Душана, Царя Сербовъ и Грековъ. Типографія Императорскаго Университета Св. Владиміра, Кіевъ

Nina Kršljanin is Associate Professor at the University of Belgrade Faculty of Law, Department of Legal History, where she teaches the courses Serbian Legal History and Serbia in International Relations, and assists with the teaching of Comparative Legal Traditions. She has a PhD in medieval Serbian law ('Serbian medieval charters as the source of Dušan's Code'). Her other research areas include constitutional and parliamentary history, customary law and the influence of personal factors (such as class, gender and religion) on an individual's legal status throughout history, and she has recently started researching the issues of views of law and legal institutions in art and popular culture. She is the editor-in-chief of the *Herald of Legal History*, a student journal publishing young researchers' work in the field of legal history.

MIX
Papier aus verantwortungsvollen Quellen
Paper from responsible sources
FSC® C105338

If you have any concerns about our products,
you can contact us on
ProductSafety@springernature.com

In case Publisher is established outside the EU,
the EU authorized representative is:
Springer Nature Customer Service Center GmbH
Europaplatz 3, 69115 Heidelberg, Germany

Printed by Libri Plureos GmbH
in Hamburg, Germany